重庆2012统计年鉴

CHONGQING STATISTICAL YEARBOOK 2012

重庆市统计局　国家统计局重庆调查总队 编
CHONGQING MUNICIPAL BUREAU OF STATISTICS
NBS SURVEY OFFICE IN CHONGQING

(京)新登字041号

图书在版编目（C I P）数据

重庆统计年鉴. 2012 : 汉英对照 / 重庆市统计局, 国家统计局重庆调查总队编. -- 北京 : 中国统计出版社, 2012.8
ISBN 978-7-5037-6581-0/C.2663

Ⅰ. ①重… Ⅱ. ①重… ②国… Ⅲ. ①统计资料－重庆市－2011－年鉴－汉、英 Ⅳ. ①C832.719-54

中国版本图书馆CIP数据核字(2012)第155481号

重庆统计年鉴-2012

作　　者/ 重庆市统计局 国家统计局重庆调查总队
责任编辑/ 佘竞雄 王立群
责任校对/ 何相莹
封面设计/ 王波 杨雄
版面制作/ 重庆海耐特广告有限公司
出版发行/ 中国统计出版社
通信地址/ 北京市西城区月坛南街57号
邮　　编/ 100826
办公地址/ 北京市丰台区西三环南路甲6号
电　　话/ (010)63376907
E-mail: yearbook@gj.stats.cn
印　　刷/ 重庆市开源印务有限公司
经　　销/ 新华书店
开　　本/ 880×1230毫米 1/16
字　　数/ 170万字
印　　张/ 37
版　　别/ 2012年7月第1版
版　　次/ 2012年7月第1次印刷
书　　号/ ISBN 978-7-5037-6581-0/C.2663
定　　价/ 350.00元

《重庆统计年鉴2012》
编辑委员会

CHONGQING STATISTICAL YEARBOOK 2012
EDITORIAL BOARD

编者说明
EDITOR'S NOTE

一、《重庆统计年鉴—2012》是由重庆市统计局和国家统计局重庆调查总队编纂、中国统计出版社公开出版发行的一部全面记录重庆市经济建设和社会发展情况的大型资料性年刊。本书收录了重庆市历史重要年份和2011年经济和社会各方面的统计数据，以及各区县（自治县）主要统计资料。

二、全书共二十二章，包括1.综合;2.国民经济核算;3.人口与就业;4.固定资产投资;5.能源消费;6.财政;7.人民生活与物价;8.城镇建设;9.资源和环境;10.要素市场;11.农业和农村经济;12.工业;13.建筑业;14.运输和邮电;15.国内贸易;16.对外经济贸易和旅游业;17.金融业;18.教育、科技和文化业;19.卫生、体育和其他社会活动;20.区县;21.三峡工程重庆库区移民;22.基本单位名录库。同时附录一个篇章：全国及各省（自治区、直辖市）主要统计资料。每章前设《简要说明》，介绍本章节的主要内容和资料来源，章末附有《主要统计指标解释》。

三、本年鉴统计资料：大部分来自统计年报，部分来自抽样调查。

四、本年鉴所使用的度量衡单位均采用国际统一标准计量单位；各种分类标准均采用国家统一分类标准。

五、本年鉴部分数据的合计数或相对数，由于计量单位取舍不同而产生的计算误差未作机械调整。

六、本年鉴各表的部分指标注解位于该表下方或最后一张续表的下方。

七、符号使用说明：年鉴各表中的“空格”表示该项统计指标数据不足本表最小单位数、数据不详或无该项数据；“＃”表示其中的主要项。

八、本年鉴在编辑、翻译过程中得到诸多单位和同志的大力支持，在此深表谢意。限于我们的水平，加之时间仓促，各界人士在使用资料时如发现错误和不足，恳请提出批评指正。

编者说明
EDITOR'S NOTE

Ⅰ. Chongqing Statistical Yearbook 2011 is a large statistical yearbook compiled by Chongqing Municipal Bureau of Statistics and NBS Survey Office in Chongqing and published by China Statistics Press, which records the economic construction and social development of Chongqing in an all-round way. The yearbook covers the comprehensive data on Chongqing's social and economic development in 2010 and some major years in the history, as well as the major statistics on all the districts and counties (autonomous counties).

Ⅱ. The yearbook contains 22 chapters, namely 1. Comprehensive Statistics;2. National Economic Accounting;3. Population and Employment;4. Investment in Fixed Assets;5. Energy Consumption;6. Government Finance;7. People's Livelihood and Prices;8. Urban Construction;9. Resources and Environment;10. Markets of Key Factors;11. Agriculture and Rural Economy;12. Industry;13. Construction;14. Transport, Postal and Telecommunication Services;15. Domestic Trade;16. Foreign Economic Relations, Trade and Tourism;17. Financial Intermediation;18. Education, Science & Technology and Culture;19. Public Health, Sports and Other Social Activities;20. Districts;21. Resettlement of Chongqing Reservoir Area of Three Gorges Project and 22. Statistics on Basic Units. There is also an Appendix which covers the main data of the whole nation and other provinces, autonomous regions and municipalities. There is a Brief Introduction at the beginning of each chapter, which introduces the main contents of the chapter and the sources of data. The Explanatory Notes on Main Statistical Indicators is provided at the end of each chapter.

Ⅲ. Most of the data in this publication are obtained from the annual statistical reports, while some others are obtained from sample surveys.

Ⅳ. The units of measurement used in this yearbook are international standard measurement units; and the basis of classification of this book complies with the national uniform standard.

Ⅴ. The statistical discrepancies of the total values or relative values due to rounding are not adjusted in this yearbook.

Ⅵ. The notes concerning individual indicators are placed at the lower part of the table or the lower part of the last page.

Ⅶ. Notations used in this yearbook: (blank space) indicates that the figure is not large enough to be measured with the smallest unit in the table, or data are unknown, or are not available; "#" indicates a major breakdown of the total.

Ⅷ. We'd like to send our sincere acknowledgement various units and comrades for their vigorous assistances during the edition and translation of this yearbook. Due to our limited ability and the hasty time, faults and shortage are unavoidable. Any criticism or suggestion is appreciated.

目录 CONTENTS

第一章 CHAPTER 1 综合 COMPREHENSIVE STATISTICS

第二章 CHAPTER 2 国民经济核算 NATIONAL ECONOMIC ACCOUNTING

目 录

CONTENTS

目 录 CONTENTS

第四章 CHAPTER 4 固定资产投资 INVESTMENT IN FIXED ASSETS

第五章 CHAPTER 5 能源消费 ENERGY CONSUMPTION

目 录
CONTENTS

第六章 CHAPTER 6 财 政 GOVERNMENT FINANCE

第七章 CHAPTER 7 人民生活与物价 PEOPLE'S LIVING CONDITIONS AND PRICE OF GOODS

第八章 CHAPTER 8 城镇建设 URBAN CONSTRUCTION

第九章 CHAPTER 9 资源和环境 RESOURCES AND ENVIRONMENT

目录 CONTENTS

第十章 CHAPTER 10 要素市场 MARKETS OF KEY FACTORS

第十一章 CHAPTER 11 农业和农村经济 AGRICULTURE AND RURAL ECONOMY

C 目录 ONTENTS

第十二章 CHAPTER 12 工 业 INDUSTRY

第十三章 CHAPTER 13 建筑业 CONSTRUCTION

第十四章 CHAPTER 14 运输和邮电 TRANSPORT, POSTAL AND TELECOMMUNICATION SERVICES

第十五章 CHAPTER 15 国内贸易 DOMESTIC TRADE

第十六章 CHAPTER 16 对外经济贸易和旅游业 FOREIGN ECONOMIC RELATIONS, TRADE AND TOURISM

第十七章 CHAPTER 17 金融业 FINANCIAL INTERMEDIATION

第十八章 CHAPTER 18 教育、科技和文化业 EDUCATION, SCIENCE, TECHNOLOGY AND CULTURE

目 录

CONTENTS

第十九章 CHAPTER 19 卫生、体育和其他社会活动 PUBLIC HEALTH, SPORTS AND OTHER SOCIAL ACTIVITIES

目录 CONTENTS

第二十章 CHAPTER 20 区 县 DISTRICTS, COUNTIES

附 录 APPENDIX

第1章

综 合

COMPREHENSIVE STATISTICS

简要说明

BRIEF INTRODUCTION

本章主要包括重庆市行政区划、国民经济和社会发展综合资料，由市统计局综合处根据有关部门资料进行整理和编辑。

行政区划资料由市民政局提供。

This chapter mainly covers the data of Chongqing's administrative divisions and national economic and social development. The data of this chapter are sorted and compiled by Division of Comprehensive Statistics, Chongqing Municipal Bureau of Statistics on the basis of the information provided by the relevant departments.

The data of administrative divisions are provided by Chongqing Civil Affairs Bureau.

表1.1 行政区划（2011年）
ADMINISTRATIVE DIVISIONS(2011)

单位：个(unit)

地 区	Region	乡 Townships	镇 Towns	街道办事处 Urban Sub--district Offices	居委会 Neighborhood Committees	村委会 Village Committees
全市总计	**Total**	**225**	**598**	**189**	**2370**	**8575**
万州区	Wanzhou District	12	29	11	187	448
涪陵区	Fuling District	6	12	8	83	334
渝中区	Yuzhong District			12	76	
大渡口区	Dadukou District		3	5	44	32
江北区	Jiangbei District		3	9	82	48
沙坪坝区	Shapingba District		8	18	124	86
九龙坡区	Jiulongpo District		11	7	98	107
南岸区	Nan'an District		7	7	85	62
北碚区	Beibei District		12	5	58	118
綦江区	Oijiang District		25	5	88	365
大足区	Dazu District		24	3	92	220
渝北区	Yubei District		11	15	128	218
巴南区	Ba'nan District		14	8	81	198
黔江区	Qianjiang District	12	12	6	77	141
长寿区	Changshou District		14	4	27	223
江津区	Jiangjin District		23	5	81	184
合川区	Hechuan District		23	7	60	327
永川区	Yongchuan District		16	7	51	208
南川区	Nanchuan District	16	15	3	58	185
潼南县	Tongnan County		20	2	21	281
铜梁县	Tongliang County		25	3	57	269
荣昌县	Rongchang County		15	6	75	92
璧山县	Bishan County		9	6	37	150
梁平县	Liangping County	7	24	2	28	313
城口县	Chengkou County	17	6	2	22	184
丰都县	Fengdu County	7	21	2	53	277
垫江县	Dianjiang County	4	21		57	243
武隆县	Wulong County	14	12		24	186
忠 县	Zhongxian County	6	22		46	319
开 县	Kaixian County	7	26	7	72	437
云阳县	Yunyang County	12	26	4	83	396
奉节县	Fengjie County	11	19		54	332
巫山县	Wushan County	13	11	2	30	307
巫溪县	Wuxi County	15	15	2	38	292
石柱土家族自治县	Shizhu County	15	17		27	214
秀山土家族苗族自治县	Xiushan County	6	18	3	32	235
酉阳土家族苗族自治县	Youyang County	23	15		8	270
彭水苗族土家族自治县	Pengshui County	22	14	3	26	274

表1.2 国民经济和社会发展总量与速度指标
PRINCIPAL AGGREGATE AND GROWTH RATE INDICATORS OF NATIONAL ECONOMIC AND SOCIAL DEVELOPMENT

指　标	Item	总量指标 Aggregate Indicators	
		1996	2000
人口与就业	**Population and Employment**		
人　口（万人）	**Population (10 000 persons)**		
年末常住人口	Year-end Resident Population	2875.30	2848.82
#城镇	Urban	848.21	1013.88
乡村	Rural	2027.09	1834.94
#男性	Male	1465.99	1388.25
女性	Female	1409.31	1460.57
就　业（万人）	**Employment (10 000 persons)**		
从业人员数	Employed Persons	1719.43	1661.16
#职工人数	Staff and Workers	294.63	208.87
城镇登记失业人数	Regitered Unemployment in Urban Areas	10.95	10.15
宏观经济	**Macroeconomic Indicators**		
国民经济核算（亿元）	**National Economic Accounting (100 million yuan)**		
本市生产总值	Gross Domestic Product	1315.12	1791.00
第一产业	Primary Industry	287.56	284.87
第二产业	Secondary Industry	568.99	760.03
#工　业	Industry	502.06	633.98
第三产业	Tertiary Industry	458.57	746.10
固定资产投资（亿元）	**Investment in Fixed Assets (100 million yuan)**		
全社会固定资产投资总额	Total Investment in Fixed Assets	320.73	655.81
城　镇	Urban	228.60	531.38
建设项目	Construction Projects	172.98	391.75
房地产开发	Real Estate Development	55.62	139.63
农　村	Rural	92.13	124.43
农村非农户	Non-Rural Households	40.06	59.52
农　户	Rural Households	52.07	64.91
财　政（亿元）	**Government Finance (100 million yuan)**		
地方财政收入	Revenue of Local Government	54.94	104.46
地方财政支出	Expenditure of Local Government	79.42	202.46
物价指数（上年=100）	**Price Indices (preceding year=100)**		
居民消费价格指数	Consumer Price Index	109.7	96.7
工业生产者出厂价格指数	Producer Price Indices for Manufactured Goods	104.1	98.6
工业生产者购进价格指数	Purchasing Price Indices of Raw Material, Fuel and Power	106.3	105.6
商品零售价格指数	Retail Price Index	106.1	95.5
产　业	**Industry**		
农　业	**Agriculture**		
乡村从业人员（万人）	Rural Employment (10 000 persons)	1330.44	1352.60
农林牧渔业总产值（亿元）	Gross Output Value of Farming, Forestry, Animal Husbandry and Fishery (100 million yuan)	424.99	412.63
#农　业	Farming	271.38	244.74
林　业	Forestry	11.55	10.82
牧　业	Animal Husbandry	131.17	141.99
渔　业	Fishery	10.89	15.08
主要农产品产量（万吨）	Output of Major Farm Products (10 000 tons)		
粮　食	Grain	1172.14	1131.21
油　料	Oil-bearing Crops	23.60	31.06
烟　叶	Tobacco	13.24	10.41

注：本表数据本市生产总值、工业增加值速度指标按可比价计算，其余指标均为自然增长。

总量指标 Aggregate Indicators			速度指标（%） Growth Rate						
			指　数（2011为以下各年） Index (2011 as percentage of the following years)				平均增长速度 Average Annual Growth Rate		
2005	2010	2011	1996	2000	2005	2010	2001-2005	2006-2010	1997-2011
2798.00	2884.62	2919.00	101.5	102.5	104.3	101.2	-0.4	0.6	0.1
1265.95	1529.55	1605.96	189.3	158.4	126.9	105.0	4.5	3.9	4.3
1532.05	1355.07	1313.04	64.8	71.6	85.7	96.9	-3.5	-2.4	-2.9
1409.83	1460.89	1476.81	100.7	106.4	104.8	101.1	0.3	0.7	
1388.17	1423.73	1442.19	102.3	98.7	103.9	101.3	-1.0	0.5	0.2
1456.30	1539.95	1585.16	92.2	95.4	108.8	102.9	-2.6	1.1	-0.5
209.66	250.22	292.10	99.1	139.8	139.3	116.7	0.1	3.6	-0.1
16.89	13.02	12.96	118.4	127.7	76.7	99.5	10.7	-5.1	1.1
3467.72	7925.58	10011.37	559.4	395.3	233.6	116.4	11.1	14.9	12.2
463.40	685.38	844.52	169.8	158.3	130.0	105.1	4.0	4.3	3.6
1564.00	4359.12	5543.04	863.0	584.0	294.9	121.8	14.6	19.3	15.5
1293.81	3697.83	4690.46	886.1	612.6	305.9	122.2	14.9	20.1	15.7
1440.32	2881.08	3623.81	489.4	320.5	201.3	110.8	9.8	12.7	11.2
2006.32	6934.80	7685.87				131.0	25.1	28.2	
1838.42	6342.98	7099.02				128.7	28.2	28.1	
1320.69	4722.73	5083.93				130.5	27.5	29.0	
517.73	1620.26	2015.09				124.4	30.0	25.6	
167.90	591.81	586.85				166.9	6.2	28.7	
96.09	497.17	480.43				186.9	10.1	38.9	
58.29	94.64	106.42				112.5	2.0	10.2	
394.96	1990.59	2908.91							
625.35	2746.79	3959.87							
100.8	103.2	105.3							
103.0	103.1	103.8							
108.2	106.9	105.7							
98.7	101.7	104.7							
1366.91	1379.35	1369.98	103.0	101.3	100.2	99.3	0.2	0.2	0.2
662.19	1021.13	1265.33	297.7	306.7	191.1	123.9	3.8	9.0	7.5
358.30	623.33	751.22	276.8	306.9	209.7	120.5	2.6	11.7	7.0
19.97	30.40	38.09	329.8	352.0	190.7	125.3	8.0	8.8	8.3
249.50	326.55	425.33	324.3	299.5	170.5	130.2	5.0	5.5	8.2
23.80	27.21	34.94	320.9	231.7	146.8	128.4	5.7	2.7	8.1
1168.19	1156.13	1126.9	96.1	99.6	96.5	97.5	0.6	-0.2	-0.3
42.71	44.45	46.51	197.1	149.7	108.9	104.6	6.6	0.8	4.6
9.02	8.10	9.36	70.7	89.9	103.8	115.6	-2.8	-2.1	-2.3

Note: The growth rate of GDP and value added of industry is calculated on the basis of comparable price, while the other indices are natural growth rate.

表1.2 续表1 continued1

指标	Item	总量指标 Aggregate Indicators 1996	2000
茶叶	Tea	1.55	1.45
水果	Fruit	56.62	81.68
肉类	Meat	133.22	143.91
#猪肉	Pork	114.18	122.45
水产品	Aquatic Products	14.07	20.03
工业（规模以上）	**Industry (above Desingated Size)**		
工业总产值（亿元）	Gross Output Value of Industry (100 million yuan)	730.41	962.32
主营业务收入（亿元）	Revenue from Principal Business (100 million yuan)	711.34	959.36
利税总额（亿元）	Total Pre-tax Profits (100 million yuan)	48.04	85.57
经济效益综合指数（%）	Comprehensive Index of Economic Benefit (%)	63.8	87.1
产品销售率（%）	Sales as Percentage of Output (%)	96.5	99.1
全员劳动生产率（元/人年）	Overall Labor Productivity (yuan/person-year)	13546	31081
主要工业产品产量	Output of Major Industrial Products		
原煤（万吨）	Coal (10 000 tons)	1498.72	1149.90
天然气（亿立方米）	Natural Gas (100 million cu.m)	26.10	38.98
发电量（亿千瓦时）	Electricity (100 million kwh)	128.73	167.90
钢材（万吨）	Steel Products (10 000 tons)	117.55	156.98
铝材（万吨）	Aluminum Products (10 000 tons)	7.36	13.98
微型计算机设备（万台）	Micro-computers (10 000units)		
水泥（万吨）	Cement (10 000 tons)	648.76	1402.78
汽车（万辆）	Motor Vehicles (10 000 vehicles)	12.41	24.59
#轿车（万辆）	Cars (10 000 vehicles)	1.34	4.82
摩托车（万辆）	Motorcycles (10 000 vehicles)	177.36	191.07
啤酒（万千升）	Beer (10 000 kiloliters)	28.54	50.42
卷烟（亿支）	Cigarettes (100 million units)	453.91	343.50
建筑业	**Construction**		
建筑业总产值（亿元）	Gross Output Value of Construction (100 million yuan)	205.30	348.66
房屋施工面积（万平方米）	Floor Space Under Construction (10 000 sq.m)	4065	6088
房屋竣工面积（万平方米）	Floor Space Completed (10 000 sq.m)	2277	3084
交通运输业	**Transportation**		
客运量（万人）	Passenger Traffic (10 000 persons)	42370	56969
铁路	Railway	972	1442
公路	Highway	37410	53170
水运	Waterway	3900	2240
民航	Civil Aviation	88	117
货运量（万吨）	Freight Traffic (10 000 tons)	24339	26852
铁路	Railway	1633	1812
公路	Highway	20214	23646
水运	Waterway	2491	1392
民航	Civil Aviation	1.20	2.40
港口货物吞吐量（万吨）	Cargo Throughput of Ports (10 000 tons)	1076	2448

注：1）工业总产值的绝对值和指数按现价计算；工业增加值的绝对值按现价计算，指数按可比价计算。
2）建筑业2003年起的所有数据均不包括劳务分包企业；其增加值2003年前按工程结算利润计算，从2003年起按营业利润计算（以下各表同）。
3）从2000年起民航货运量按新制度统计，旅客行李不再计入货运。
4）1996年起铁路数据按重庆现地域进行了调整（以下各表同）。
5）2008年公路、水路数据按部门专项调查作了调整，速度按可比价计算。

总量指标 Aggregate Indicators			速度指标（%） Growth Rate						
			指　数（2011为以下各年） Index (2011 as percentage of the following years)				平均增长速度 Average Annual Growth Rate		
2005	2010	2011	1996	2000	2005	2010	2001-2005	2006-2010	1997-2011
1.65	2.52	2.79	180.0	192.4	169.1	110.7	2.6	8.8	4.0
154.63	238.47	261.16	461.3	319.7	168.9	109.5	13.6	9.1	10.7
178.39	192.46	196.28	147.3	136.4	110.0	102.0	4.4	1.5	2.2
144.46	147.56	148.55	130.1	121.3	102.8	100.7	3.4	0.4	1.5
25.06	22.43	27.56	195.9	137.6	110.0	122.9	4.6	-2.2	4.6
2525.87	9143.55	11847.06				128.2	21.3	29.3	20.4
2515.17	9039.03	11382.34	1600.1	1186.5	452.5	125.9	21.3	29.2	20.3
256.48	1011.88	1164.30	2423.6	1360.6	454.0	115.1	24.6	31.6	23.7
139.4	226.0	244.1							
98.8	98.1	97.4							
77511	183033	213463.0	1575.8	686.8	275.4	116.6	20.1	18.7	20.2
1957.79	4547.03	4464.61	297.9	388.3	228.0	98.2	11.2	18.4	7.5
57.09	67.48	62.94	241.1	161.5	110.2	93.3	7.9	3.4	6.0
234.03	456.71	529.57	411.4	315.4	226.3	116.0	6.9	14.3	9.9
294.70	699.92	948.17	806.6	604.0	321.7	135.5	13.4	18.9	14.9
39.36	102.79	134.45	1826.8	961.7	341.6	130.8	23.0	21.2	21.4
	189.19	2547.82				1203.9			
2100.69	4598.04	4935.15	760.7	351.8	234.9	107.3	8.4	17.0	14.5
42.15	161.58	172.20	1387.6	700.3	408.5	106.6	11.4	30.8	19.2
15.33	85.17	93.67	6990.3	1943.4	611.0	110.0	26.0	40.9	32.7
420.84	849.23	879.59	495.9	460.3	209.0	103.6	17.1	15.1	11.3
53.87	75.19	77.31	270.9	153.3	143.5	102.8	1.3	6.9	6.9
396.08	501.00	516.00	113.7	150.2	130.3	103.0	2.9	4.8	0.9
783.57	2534.32	3328.83	1621.4	954.7	424.8	131.4	17.6	26.5	20.4
10723	19489	21976	540.6	360.9	204.9	112.8	12.0	12.7	11.9
5155	8292	8989.56	397.9	293.8	175.8	109.3	10.8	10.0	9.6
60436	126804	141204	272.3	202.5	190.9	111.4	1.2	11.4	6.9
1224	2663	2933	301.8	203.4	239.6	110.1	-3.2	16.8	7.6
57600	122125	136142	295.0	207.6	191.6	111.5	1.6	11.4	7.5
1388	1277	1322	30.0	52.3	84.4	103.5	-9.1	-4.0	-7.7
224	739	807	916.9	689.6	360.2	109.2	13.9	27.0	15.9
39200	81385	96779	352.4	319.4	218.8	118.9	7.9	13.0	8.8
1923	2280	2190.81	134.2	120.9	113.9	96.1	1.2	3.5	2.0
33378	69438	82818.00	355.4	303.8	215.2	119.3	7.1	12.5	8.8
3896	9660	11762	471.5	843.8	301.5	121.8	22.8	19.9	10.9
2.88	7.49	7.66	638.3	319.2	266.0	102.3	3.7	21.1	13.2
5251	9668	11606	1078.6	474.1	221.0	120.0	16.5	13.0	17.2

Note: a) The value and index of gross output value of industry are calculated at current price; the value-added of industry is calculated at current price while the index is calculated at constant price.
b) All the data of construction has not included labor subcontractors since 2003. The value-added is calculated upon the settled profit before 2003 and upon the operation profit since 2003 (the same for the tables below).
c) Since 2000, the cargo turnover of civil aviation has been calculated by the new statistic system, and the luggage of passengers is no longer accounted in.
d) The data of railway has been modified based on the present administrative division of Chongqing since 1996 (the same for the tables below).
e) The data of highway and waterway has been modified according to the specialized survey by the related departments since 2008.and the growth rate is calculated on the basis of comparable price.

表1.2 续表2 continued2

指　标	Item	总量指标 Aggregate Indicators 1996	2000
邮电通信业	**Postal and Telecommunication Services**		
邮电业务总量（亿元）	Business Volume (100 million yuan)	15.99	85.82
本地电话用户（万户）	Local Telephone Subscribers (10 000 subscribers)	66.50	268.43
移动电话用户（万户）	Mobile Telephone Subscribers (10 000 subscribers)	9.00	160.00
固定互联网络用户（万户）	Internet Subscribers (10 000 subscribers)	0.03	10.00
国内贸易（亿元）	**Domestic Trade(100 million yuan)**		
社会消费品零售总额	Retail Sales of Consumer Goods	498.63	719.95
#批发零售贸易业	Wholesale and Retail Trade	438.07	627.36
住宿餐饮业	Catering Trade	54.45	84.16
对外贸易（亿美元）	**Foreign Trade(USD 100 million)**		
进出口总值	Total Imports and Exports	15.85	17.85
进口总值	Imports	9.92	7.90
出口总值	Exports	5.93	9.95
利用内外资	**Utilization of Domestic and Foreign Capital**		
实际利用外资额（亿美元）	Foreign Capital Actually Utilized (USD 100 million)	4.42	3.45
#外商直接投资额	Foreign Direct Investment	2.19	2.44
实际利用内资额（亿元）	Domestic Capital Actually Utilized (100 million yuan)	34.11	43.04
国际旅游	**International Tourism**		
国际旅游人数（万人次）	International Tourists (10 000 person-time)	16.18	26.61
旅游外汇收入（万美元）	Foreign Exchange Earnings from International Tourism (USD 10 000)	7090	13837
金融保险业（亿元）	**Finance and Insurance (100 million yuan)**		
金融机构人民币存款年末余额	Deposit Balance of RMB of Financial Institutions	846.43	1904.71
#个人存款	Saving Deposits of Residents	500.71	1085.36
金融机构人民币贷款年末余额	Loan Balance of RMB of Financial Institutions	913.93	1881.29
股票筹资额（亿元）	Raised Capital of Shares (100 million yuan)	10.41	22.63
保险公司保费收入	Insurance Premium of Insurance Companies	12.82	27.71
保险公司赔款及给付	Indemnity Expenditure and Payment of Insurance Companies	6.48	8.27
教育、科技、文化	**Education, Science & Technology and Culture**		
教　育	**Education**		
专任教师（万人）	Full-time Teachers (10000 person)		
#普通高等学校	Regular Institutions of Higher Education	0. 94	1.04
普通中学	Regular Secondary Schools	6. 95	8.18
小　学	Primary Schools	11. 77	11.9
在校学生数（万人）	Student Enrollment (10 000 persons)		
#普通高等学校	Regular Institutions of Higher Education	7.99	13.25
普通中学	Regular Secondary Schools	101.27	147.79
小　学	Primary Schools	273.71	276.13
教育经费支出（亿元）	Expenditure on Education (100 million yuan)		
科　技	**Science and Technology**		
技术市场成交额（亿元）	Transaction Value of Technology Market (100 million yuan)	3. 43	29.66

注：1）邮电业务总量2001年前为1990年不变价，2001年及以后为2000年不变价口径（以下各表同）。
2）普通高等学校数据含研究生。
3）实际利用外资2004年起均不包括对外借款；2010年及2011年"外商直接投资"数据口径为"外商投资"。
4）因全国银行业统计制度调整，报表项目归属发生变化，2011年银行业部分指标与去年同期不具可比性，无法计算同比增长率。
5）因国家保险核算制度改变，2011年保费收入指标同期不可比，保险公司赔款及给付同比增长率按新口径调整计算所得。

总量指标 Aggregate Indicators			速度指标（%） Growth Rate						
			指 数（2011为以下各年） Index (2011 as percentage of the following years)				平均增长速度 Average Annual Growth Rate		
2005	2010	2011	1996	2000	2005	2010	2001-2005	2006-2010	1997-2011
210.15	199.74	242.64	6114.5	1139. 0	350. 3	121. 5	26.6	23.6	31. 5
688.91	582.70	571.25	859.0	212. 8	82. 9	98. 0	20.7	-3.3	15. 4
943.40	1664.40	1801.19	20013.2	1125. 7	190. 9	108. 2	42.6	12.0	42. 4
128.66	263.10	326.78	1089266.7	3267. 8	254. 0	124. 2	66.7	15.4	85. 8
1227.80	2938.60	3487.81	699.5	484.5	284.1	118.7	11.3	19.1	13.8
1052.92	2430.75	2894.16	660.7	461.3	274.9	119.1	10.9	18.2	13.4
163.57	447.29	521.73	958.2	619.9	319.0	116.6	14.2	22.3	16.3
42.93	124.26	292.18	1843.4	1636.9	680.6	235.1	19.2	23.7	21.4
17.72	49.37	93.80	945.6	1187.3	529.3	189.9	17.5	22.7	16.2
25.21	74.89	198.38	3345.4	1993.8	786.9	264.9	20.4	24.3	26.4
5.21	63.70	105.79	2393.4	3066.4	2030.5	166.1	15.3	65.0	23.6
5.16	63.44	105.29	4807.8	4315.2	2040.5	166.0	16.2	65.2	29.5
205.90	2638.29	4919.84	14423.5	11430.9	2389.4	186.5	36.8	66.5	39.3
52.39	137.02	186.40	1152.0	700.5	355.8	136.0	14.5	21.2	17.7
26436	70320	96806	1365.4	699.6	366.2	137.7	13.8	21.6	19.0
4727.72	13454.98	15832.81	1870.5	831.2	334.9	117.7	19.9	23.3	21.6
2545.85	5839.66	7045.99					18.6	18.1	
3719.52	10888.15	13001.39	1422.6	691.1	349.5	119.4	14.6	24.0	19.4
	149.00	158.02	1518.0	698.3		106.1			19.9
73.10	321.08	311.81					21.4	34.4	
17.59	62.10	73.98	1141.7	894.6	420.6	121.4	16.3	28.7	17.8
2.02	3.11	3.31	352.2	316.9	164.0	106.6	14.2	9.0	8.8
9.40	10.93	11.10	159.6	135.7	118.0	101.5	2.8	3.1	3.2
11.43	11.61	11.53	98.0	96.9	100.9	99.4	-0.8	0.3	-0.1
35.79	56.59	61.30	767.2	462.6	171.3	108.3	22.0	9.6	14.5
173.52	190.82	183.89	181.6	124.4	106.0	96.4	3.3	1.9	4.1
260.98	199.94	195.48	71.4	70.8	74.9	97.8	-1.1	-5.2	-2.2
	390.21	497.14				127.4			
35.71	147.53	101.08	2943.0	340.8	283.1	68.5	3.8	32.8	25.3

Note: a) The business volumes of postal and telecommunication services before 2001 are calculated at the constant price of 1990,while the data after 2000 are calculated at the constant price of 2001 (the same for the tables below).
b) The data of regular institutions of higher education include the postgraduates.
c) Since 2004, foreign loans have been excluded from actual utilized foreign capital. In 2010 and in 2011 ,the statistic scope of "Foreign Direct Investment" equals to "Foreign Investment".
d) Due to the adjustment of national statistic system for banking, the scope of indices has been changed. Therefore, some indices of banking in 2011 are incomparablewith the previous year and the growth rate YOY cannot be calculated.
e) Due to the change of national insurance accounting system, the insurance premium in 2011 is incomparable with the previous year, and the growth rate of indemnity expenditure and payment of insurance companies is calculated according to the new statistic scope.

表1.2 续表3 continued3

指　标	Item	总量指标 Aggregate Indicators 1996	2000
文　化	**Culture**		
图书出版数量（万册、万张）	Books Published (10 000 copies)	13023	11198
杂志出版数量（万册）	Magazines Published (10 000 copies)		3480
报纸出版数量（万份）	Newspaper Published (10 000 copies)		48674
电视人口覆盖率（%）	Television Coverage of Population (%)	78.90	93.70
广播人口覆盖率（%）	Radio Coverage of Population (%)	86.30	89.90
家庭、生活	**Family and Living Standards**		
家　庭	**Family**		
城镇居民平均每户家庭人口（人）	Population per Urban Household (person)		
农村居民平均每户家庭人口（人）	Population per Rural Household(person)	3.85	3.70
婚　姻	**Marital Statistics**		
内地居民登记结婚对数（万对）	Marriages of Inland Residents (10 000 couples)	26.44	19.02
内地居民登记离婚对数（万对）	Divorces of Inland Residents (10 000 couples)	1.68	2.07
居　住	**Residence**		
城镇居民人均房屋建筑面积（平方米）	Per Capita Residential Space of Urban Residents (sq.m)		
农村居民人均住房面积（平方米）	Per Capita Residential Space of Rural Residents (sq.m)	24.44	29.58
工资和收入	**Wages and Income**		
城镇非私营单位职工工资总额（亿元）	Total Wages of Staff and Workers of Urban Nonprivate Units (100 million yuan)	145.49	173.23
城镇非私营单位在岗职工平均工资（元）	Average Annual Wages of Staff and Workers of Urban Non-private Units(yuan)	5010	8020
城镇居民人均可支配收入（元）	Per Capita Disposable Income of Urban Residents (yuan)		
农村居民人均纯收入（元）	Per Capita Net Income of Rural Residents (yuan)	1479	1892
城乡居民人均人民币储蓄存款余额（元）	Per Capita Saving Deposits of Urban and Rural Resident (yuan)	1656	3511
卫　生	**Public Health**		
医院、卫生院（个）	Hospitals and Health Centers (unit)	2567	2250
卫生技术人员（人）	Medical Technical Personnel (person)	87542	88619
#执业（助理）医师	Licensed (Assistant) Doctors	30733	44940
卫生机构床位数（张）	Number of Beds in Health Care Institutions (bed)	66339	65666
市政建设	**Municipal Construction**		
供水总量（万立方米）	Water Supply (10 000 cu.m)	84548	70722
天然气供气总量（万立方米）	Natural Gas Supply (10 000 cu.m)	111980	75257
排水管道长度（公里）	Length of Draining Pipelines (km)	1857	2806
道路长度（公里）	Length of Urban Roads (km)	2652	3299
公共绿地面积（公顷）	Public Green Areas (hectare)	1104	1588
环　境	**Environment**		
化学需氧量排放量（万吨）	Discharged Volume of COD (10 000 tons)		
二氧化硫排放量（万吨）	Discharged Volume of SO_2 (10 000 tons)		

注：2002年起卫生统计指标名称变更，统计口径变化，不可与往年同比；2002年起卫生技术人员和床位不包括医学院校、卫生学校和计生站；执业（助理）医师2002年以前统计口径为“医生”（以下各表同）。2010年指标卫生技术人员、执业（助理）医师为调整数，均含村卫生室。

总量指标 Aggregate Indicators			速度指标（%） Growth Rate						
			指 数（2011为以下各年） Index (2011 as percentage of the following years)				平均增长速度 Average Annual Growth Rate		
2005	2010	2011	1996	2000	2005	2010	2001-2005	2006-2010	1997-2011
11320	15694	15597	119.8	139.3	137.8	99.4	0.2	6.8	1.2
4082	5409	5183		148.9	127.0	95.8	3.2	5.8	
54731	76484	66057		135.7	120.7	86.4	2.4	6.9	
95.96	97.39	98.56	124.9	105.2	102.7	101.2	0.5	0.3	1.5
92.49	95.71	98.02	113.6	109.0	106.0	102.4	0.6	0.7	0.9
	2.91	2.88					98.6		
3.71	3.63	3.82	99.2	103.2	103.0	105.2	0.1	-0.4	-0.1
18.32	31.25	60.78	229.9	319.6	331.8	194.5	-0.7	11.3	5.7
5.65	9.49	10.54	627.4	509.2	186.5	111.1	22.2	10.9	13.0
	31.69	31.77					100.3		
32.91	37.56	40.18	164.4	135.8	122.1	107.0	2.2	2.7	3.6
345.82	862.95	1156.53	794.9	667.6	334.4	134.0	14.8	20.1	14.8
16630	35326	40042	799.2	499.3	240.8	113.3	15.7	16.3	14.9
	17532.43	20249.70				115.5			
2809	5277	6480	438.1	342.4	230.7	122.8	8.2	13.4	10.1
8033	17677	20993	1267.7	597.9	261.3	118.8	18.0	17.1	66.2
1463	1449	1407	54.8	62.5	96.2	97.1			
78780	111079	120169	137.3	135.6	152.5	108.2			
37321	47969	49585	161.3	110.3	132.9	103.4			
64674	103624	115657	174.3	176.1	178.8	111.6			
82751	103949	107571	127.2	152.1	130.0	103.5	2.6	4.7	4.9
204679	309480	314354	280.7	417.7	153.6	101.6	22.8	8.6	22.9
7095	9663	11212	603.8	399.6	158.0	116.0	14.8	6.4	43.3
5547	6733	7158	269.9	217.0	129.0	106.3	6.9	4.0	22.0
7977	17762	23755	2151.7	1495.9	297.8	133.7	26.8	17.4	84.7
	23.45	41.68				177.7			
	71.94	58.69				81.6			

Note: Due to the change of names and statistic scopes of the indicators of public health in 2002, the indicators are not comparable with the data in previous years: since 2002, the medical technical personnel and the number of beds have no longer included the data of medical universities, health schools and family plan service stations; the indicator of licensed (assistant) doctor was formerly "doctor" before 2002 (the same for the tables below). The data of medical technical personnel and licensed (assistant) doctors are adjusted data, with village health stations included.

表1.3 国民经济和社会发展结构指标
STRUCTURAL INDICATORS OF NATINAL ECONOMIC AND SOCIAL DEVELOPMENT

单位：% (%)

指　标	Item	1995	1996	2000	2009	2010	2011
人口与就业	**Population and Employment**						
人　口	**Population**						
城镇乡村人口结构	By Urban and Rural Areas		100.0	100.0	100.0	100.0	100.0
城　镇	Urban		29.5	35.6	51.6	53.0	55.0
乡　村	Rural		70.5	64.4	48.4	47.0	45.0
性别结构	By Sex		100.0	100.0	100.0	100.0	100.0
男	Male		51.0	51.3	50.6	50.6	50.6
女	Female		49.0	48.7	49.4	49.4	49.4
就　业	**Employment**						
产业结构	By Industry	100.0	100.0	100.0	100.0	100.0	100.0
第一产业	Primary Industry	59.6	58.3	55.4	42.2	40.3	38.1
第二产业	Secondary Industry	18.2	18.6	17.5	21.5	22.9	24.7
第三产业	Tertiary Industry	22.2	23.1	27.1	36.3	36.8	37.2
登记注册类型结构	By Status of Registration		100.0	100.0	100.0	100.0	100.0
国有经济	State-owned		11.5	9.0	7.9	8.1	8.3
集体经济	Collective-owned		71.5	66.8	48.1	45.5	40.9
私营和个体	Private and Individuals		16.3	22.0	36.1	37.9	39.6
其他经济	Others		0.7	2.2	7.9	8.5	11.2
宏观经济	**Macroeconomic Indicators**						
国民经济核算	**National Economic Accounting**						
本市生产总值结构	GDP by Industry	100.0	100.0	100.0	100.0	100.0	100.0
第一产业	Primary Industry	23.5	21.9	15.9	9.3	8.6	8.4
第二产业	Secondary Industry	43.9	43.3	42.4	52.8	55.0	55.4
#工　业	Industry	38.8	38.2	35.4	44.7	46.7	46.9
第三产业	Tertiary Industry	32.6	34.8	41.7	37.9	36.4	36.2
固定资产投资	**Investment in Fixed Assets**						
城乡结构	By Urban and Rural Areas		100.0	100.0	100.0	100.0	100.0
城　镇	Urban		71.3	81.0	93.2	91.5	92.4
建设项目	Construction Projects		53.9	59.7	69.9	68.1	66.1
房地产开发	Real Estate Development		17.4	21.3	23.3	23.4	26.2
农　村	Rural		28.7	19.0	6.8	8.5	7.6
农村非农户	Non-Rural Households		12.5	9.1	5.1	7.1	6.3
农　户	Rural Households		16.2	9.9	1.7	1.4	1.4
产业结构	By Industry	100.0	100.0	100.0	100.0	100.0	100.0
第一产业	Primary Industry	0.6	0.7	1.4	3.7	3.8	3.6
第二产业	Secondary Industry	39.4	36.1	21.7	35.6	35.0	36.5
第三产业	Tertiary Industry	60.0	63.2	76.9	60.7	61.2	59.9

表1.3 续表1 continued1

单位：% (%)

指　标	Item	1995	1996	2000	2009	2010	2011
财　政	**Government Finance**						
财政收入结构	By Level of Government	100.0	100.0	100.0	100.0	100.0	100.0
中　央	Central	45.1	41.7	36.0	24.1	20.6	17.4
地　方	Local	54.9	58.3	64.0	75.9	79.4	82.6
产　业	**Industry**						
农　业	**Agriculture**						
农林牧渔业产值结构	Gross Output Value of Farming, Forestry, Animal Husbandry and Fishery	100.0	100.0	100.0	100.0	100.0	100.0
农　业	Farming	60.3	63.9	59.3	57.3	61.0	59.4
林　业	Forestry	2.8	2.7	2.6	3.7	3.0	3.0
牧　业	Animal Husbandry	34.5	30.9	34.4	35.0	32.0	33.6
渔　业	Fishery	2.4	2.5	3.7	2.7	2.7	2.8
农林牧渔服务业	Agricultural Services				1.4	1.3	1.2
工　业	**Industry**						
规模以上工业增加值结构	Value-added of Industrial Enterprises above Designated Size		100.0	100.0	100.0	100.0	100.0
轻工业	Light Industry		28.9	36.1	31.0	30.1	27.0
重工业	Heavy Industry		71.1	63.9	69.0	69.9	73.0
运输业	**Transportation**						
货运量结构	Freight Traffic	100.0	100.0	100.0	100.0	100.0	100.0
#铁　路	Railway	13.0	6.7	6.7	3.2	2.8	2.3
公　路	Highway	80.1	83.1	88.1	85.5	85.3	85.6
水　运	Waterway	6.9	10.2	5.2	11.3	11.9	12.2
国内商业	**Domestic Trade**						
社会消费品零售总额结构	Retail Sales of Consumer Goods	100.0	100.0	100.0	100.0	100.0	100.0
市	City	58.6	58.9	57.0	61.4		
县	County	12.9	12.3	13.2	13.4		
县以下	Below County Level	28.5	28.8	29.8	25.2		
#城　镇	Urban					94.5	95.1
乡　村	Village					5.5	4.9
对外经济贸易	**Foreign Economic Relations and Trade**						
实际利用外资结构	Actual Utilization of Foreign Capital	100.0	100.0	100.0	100.0	100.0	100.0
对外借款	Foreign Loans	33.2	47.0	28.8			
外商直接投资	Foreign Direct Investment	61.6	49.6	70.8	99.3	99.6	99.5
外商其他投资	Other Foreign Investment	5.2	3.4	0.4	0.7	0.4	0.5
进出口总值结构	Imports and Exports	100.0	100.0	100.0	100.0	100.0	100.0
进　口	Imports	40.3	62.6	44.3	44.5	39.7	32.1
出　口	Exports	59.7	37.4	55.7	55.5	60.3	67.9
旅　游	**Tourism**						
国际旅游人数结构	International Tourists	100.0	100.0	100.0	100.0	100.0	100.0
#外国人	Foreigners	65.5	66.9	72.5	80.9	75.9	71.1
港澳台同胞	Compatriots from Hongkong, Macao and Taiwan	34.3	32.9	27.5	19.1	24.1	28.9

注：2004年及以后年份实际利用外资不再包括对外借款；2010年及2011年“外商直接投资”的数据口径为“外商投资”。
Note: The data of foreign capital actually utilized no longer includes foreign loans since 2004; the index of "foreign direct investment"in 2010 and 2011 refers to “foreign investment”.

表1.3 续表2 continued2

单位：% (%)

指　标	Item	1995	1996	2000	2009	2010	2011
生活、环境	**Living Standards and Environment**						
生　活	**Living Standards**						
城市居民消费结构	Consumption of Urban Households	100.0	100.0	100.0	100.0	100.0	100.0
#服务性消费支出	Expenditure for Services				26.3	25.9	25.0
#食　品	Food	48.7	49.0	40.4	37.2	37.6	39.1
衣　着	Clothing	14.0	14.5	10.1	12.5	12.7	13.7
居　住	Residence	5.5	5.5	9.0	8.7	9.6	8.1
农村居民生活消费结构	Consumption for Living of Rural Households	100.0	100.0	100.0	100.0	100.0	100.0
#食　品	Food	64.7	63.2	53.6	49.1	48.3	46.8
衣　着	Clothing	5.3	5.5	4.4	6.3	6.2	6.9
居　住	Residence	12.7	13.2	14.3	12.9	15.1	12.3
卫　生	**Public Health**						
卫生技术人员结构	Medical Technical Personnel	100.0	100.0	100.0	100.0	100.0	100.0
#执业（助理）医师	Licensed (Assisstant) Doctors	36.2	35.1	50.7	43.2	43.2	41.3
注册护士	Registered Nurses	21.7	22.0	23.4	56.8	33.9	35.6
卫生机构床位结构	Beds in Health Care Institutions			100.0	100.0	100.0	100.0
#医　院	Hospitals			59.0	63.0	62.6	64.7
环　境	**Environment**						
治理工业污染资金使用结构	Uses of Fund in Industrial Pollution Control			100.0	100.0	100.0	100.0
治理废水	Waste Water Control			48.1	40.7	48.7	50.0
治理废气	Waste Gas Control			41.9	53.0	35.3	27. 4
治理固体废物	Solid Waste Control			3.8	0.8	4.1	19. 6
治理噪声	Noise Control			0.8	1.0	0.6	0.5
其　他	Others			5.4	4.4	11.2	2. 5

表1.4 人均主要社会经济活动水平
PER CAPITA MAIN SOCIAL AND ECONOMIC ACTIVITIES

单位：元(yuan)

指　标	Item	1995	1996	2000	2009	2010	2011
国民经济核算	**National Economic Accounting**						
本市生产总值	Gross Domestic Product	3931	4574	6274	22920	27596	34500
主要农产品产量（公斤）	**Output of Major Farm Products (kg)**						
粮　食	Grain	385	389	367	347	350	338
油　料	Oil-bearing Crops	8	11	10	12	13	14
肉　类	Meat	42	44	47	57	58	59
#猪　肉	Pork	38	38	40	45	45	45
水产品	Aquatic Products	4	5	6	6	7	8
水　果	Fruit	20	19	27	65	72	78
主要工业产品产量（规模以上工业）	**Output of Major Industrial Products (Industrial Enterprises over Designated Size)**						
原　煤（公斤）	Coal (kg)		498	373	1310	1376	1341
天然气（立方米）	Natural Gas (cu.m)		87	126	231	204	189
发电量（千瓦时）	Electricity (kwh)		427	545	1307	1383	1590
钢　材（公斤）	Steel Products (kg)		39	51	146	212	285
铝　材（公斤）	Aluminum Products (kg)		2	5	23	31	40
水　泥（公斤）	Cement (kg)		215	455	1102	1392	1482
啤　酒（升）	Beer (liter)		9	16	22	23	23
卷　烟（支）	Cigarettes (unit)		1507	1115	1453	1517	1550
国内商业	**Domestic Trade**						
社会消费品零售总额	Retail Sales of Consumer Goods	1386	1734	2522	8701	10233	12019
财政、金融	**Government Finance and Financial Intermediation**						
地方财政收入	Revenue of Local Government	153	182	339	3559	6026	8736
城乡居民储蓄存款余额	Saving Deposits of Urban and Rural Residents	1337	1656	3511	14986	17677	20993
职工工资、居民收入	**Wages and Income**						
城镇非私营单位职工平均工资	Average Non-private Wages of Staff and Workers Of Urban Economic Units	4508	5010	8020	30965	35326	40042
城镇居民人均可支配收入	Per Capita Disposable Income of Urban Households				15749	17532	20250
农村居民人均纯收入	Per Capita Net Income of Rural Residents	1270	1479	1892	4478	5277	6480

注：本市人均生产总值、人均社会消费品零售总额按常住人口计算，城市、农村居民收入为抽样调查数，其他人均指标均按户籍人口计算。
Note: The Per capita GDP and the per capita ris calculated by permanent population; the per capita income of urban and rural residents is the data of sample survey, and other per capita indicators in this talbe are based on registered population.

表1.5 平均每天主要社会经济活动
AVERAGE DAILY SOCIAL AND ECONOMIC ACTIVITIES

指　标	Item	1995	1996	2000	2009	2010	2011
每天创造的财富	**Daily Production**						
本市生产总值（万元）	Gross Domestic Product (10 000 yuan)	30769	36031	49068	178904	217139	274284
第一产业	Primary Industry	7238	7878	7805	16625	18778	23138
第二产业	Secondary Industry	13498	15589	20823	94487	119428	151864
#工　业	Industry	11951	13755	17369	79929	101310	128506
第三产业	Tertiary Industry	10033	12564	20441	67793	78934	99282
地方财政收入（万元）	Revenue of Local Government (10 000 yuan)	1254	1500	2862	31937	54537	79696
粮　食（吨）	Grain (ton)	31608	32113	30992	31156	31675	30874
油　料（吨）	Oil-bearing Crops (ton)	688	647	851	1111	1218	1274
肉　类（吨）	Meat (ton)	3485	3560	3943	4014	5273	5378
#猪　肉	Pork	3076	3128	3355	5143	4042	4070
水产品（吨）	Aquatic Products (ton)	332	385	549	559	615	755
原　煤（吨）	Coal (ton)		41061	31504	117556	124576	122318
天然气（万立方米）	Natural Gas (10 000 cu.m)		715	1068	2074	1849	1724
发电量（万千瓦小时）	Electricity (10 000 kwh)		3527	4600	11733	12513	14509
钢　材（吨）	Steel Products (ton)		3221	4301	13081	19176	25977
水　泥（吨）	Cement (ton)		17774	38432	98931	125974	135210
汽　车（辆）	Motor Vehicles (unit)		340	674	3251	4427	4718
#轿　车	Cars		37	132	1734	2333	2566
摩托车（辆）	Motorcycles (unit)		4859	5235	20870	23267	24098
每天消费量	**Daily Consumption**						
最终消费（万元）	Final Consumption Expenditures(10 000 yuan)	16235	20421	27340	87242	104434	127168
居民消费	Household Consumption Expenditure	13375	16691	21157	64852	76502	94064
农　村	Rural Households	5529	6962	8159	12072	13708	16867
城　镇	Urban Households	7846	9729	12998	52780	62795	77197
政府消费	Government Consumption Expenditure	2860	3731	6183	22390	27932	33104
地方财政支出（万元）	Expenditure of Local Government (10 000 yuan)	1814	2176	5547	49481	75225	108490
社会消费品零售总额（万元）	Total Retail Sales of Consumer Goods (10 000 yuan)	11401	13661	19725	67918	80510	95556
每天其他经济活动	**Other Daily Economic Activities**						
资本形成总额（万元）	Gross Capital Formation (10 000 yuan)	9669.59	11478.90	19202.47			
固定资产形成	Fixed Assets Formation		8660.27	17205.75	99540.27		
存货增加	Changes in Inventory		2818.63	1996.71	5079.18	5405.21	6747.12
客运量（万人）	Passenger Traffic (10 000 persons)	108.85	116.08	156.08	313.97	347.41	386.86
货运量（万吨）	Freight Traffic (10 000 tons)	62.45	66.68	73.57	187.65	222.97	265.15
港口货物吞吐量（万吨）	Cargo Throughput of Ports (10 000 tons)	2.34	2.95	6.71	23.59	26.49	31.80
邮电业务总量（万元）	Business Volume of Postal and Tele-communication Services (10 000 yuan)	300	438	2351	13420	5472	6648
进出口总额（万美元）	Total Imports and Exports (USD 10 000)	388.65	434.36	489.17	2111.94	3404.48	8004.89
进口总额	Imports	156.51	271.72	216.51	939.32	1352.76	2569.79
出口总额	Exports	232.14	162.64	272.66	1172.62	2051.72	5435.10
实际利用外资（万美元）	Actual Utilization of Foreign Capital (USD 10 000)	168.64	120.96	94.61	1107.90	1745.08	2898.25
国际旅游人数（人）	International Tourists (person)	391	443	729	2872	3754	5107
居民新增储蓄额（万元）	Newly Increased Amount of Saving Deposits (10 000 yuan)	3179	2719	4829	25198	25506	31523

注：1)本表价值指标除邮电业务总量按不变价计算外，其余均按当年价计算。
2)2006年以前工业产品产量为国有及规模以上非国有工业企业数，2007年起为规模以上工业企业数（下表同）。

Note: a) All the value indicators in this table are calculated at current prices except the total business volume of postal and telecommunication services, which is calculated at constant prices.
b) The output of industrial products before 2006 is based on the state-owned industrial enterprises and non-state-owned industrial enterprises above designated size; while it is based on the industrial enterprises above designated size since 2007(the same below).

表1.6 各部门机构数（2010－2011年）
GRASSROOTS UNITS IN VARIOUS SECTORS (2010-2011)

单位：个(unit)

部　门	Sector	2010	2011
农村基层单位	**Rural Grassroots Units**		
乡政府	Township Governments	252	225
镇政府	Town Governments	587	598
村民委员会	Village Committees	8605	8575
工　业（规模以上）	**Industry (above Designated Size)**	**7130**	**4778**
#国有及国有控股	State-owned and State-holding	547	458
建筑业	**Construction Enterprises**	**2467**	**2530**
邮政局所	**Postal Offices**	**1775**	**1678**
批发零售业和餐饮业（限额以上）	**Wholesale & Retail and Catering Trade (above Designated Size)**		
批发业企业	Wholesale Enterprises	1341	1623
零售业企业	Retail Enterprises	1244	1807
餐饮业企业	Catering Enterprises	554	762
教育事业	**Education**		
普通高等学校	Regular Institutions of Higher Education	53	59
普通中学	Regular Secondary Schools	1273	1259
小　学	Primary Schools	5544	5248
幼儿园	Kindergartens	4105	4114
特殊教育	Special Education	36	36
文化机构数	**Cultural Institutions**		
#艺术业	Art Institutions	427	329
文物事业	Cultural Relic Institutins	89	92
图书馆事业	Public Libraries	43	43
群众文化事业	Mass Cultural Institutions	1041	1037
出版、发行事业	**Publishing and Distribution Establishments**		
出版社	Publishing Houses	3	3
书刊印刷厂	Printing Houses	41	86
国有书店	State-owned Book Stores	271	271
卫生事业	**Health Care**	**17495**	**17660**
#医院、卫生院	Hospitals 、Health Centers	1449	1407
社会福利	**Social Welfare**	**3398**	**3503**
#收养性单位	Residential Institutions	2196	2241
社会福利企业单位	Social Welfare Enterprises	748	758

重/庆/统/计/年/鉴

主要统计指标解释

行政区划

指国家对行政区域的划分。根据宪法规定，我国的行政区划分如下：（1）全国分为省、自治区、直辖市；（2）省、自治区分为自治州、县、自治县、市；（3）自治州分为县、自治县、市；（4）县、自治县分为乡、民族乡、镇；（5）直辖市和较大的市分为区、县；（6）国家在必要时设立的特别行政区。

可比价格

指计算各种总量指标所采用的扣除了价格变动因素的价格，可进行不同时期总量指标的对比。按可比价格计算总量指标有两种方法：一种是直接用产品产量乘某一年的不变价格计算；另一种是用价格指数进行缩减。

不变价格

指以同类产品某年的平均价格作为固定价格，用于计算各年的产品价值。按不变价格计算的产品价值消除了价格变动因素，不同时期对比可以反映生产的发展速度。新中国成立后，随着工农业产品价格水平的变化，国家统计局先后五次制定了全国统一的工业产品不变价格和农业产品不变价格。从1952年到1957年使用1952年工（农）业产品不变价格，从1957年到1970年使用1957年不变价格，从1971年到1980年使用1970年不变价格，从1981年到1990年使用1980年不变价格，从1991年开始使用1990年不变价格。

平均增长速度

平均增长速度表明社会经济现象在一个较长的时期内逐期平均增长变化的程度，它不能根据各个环比增长速度直接求得，但与平均发展速度之间存在着一定的数量关系：平均增长速度＝平均发展速度－1。

平均发展速度是一种根据环比发展速度计算的序时平均数，由于各时期对比的基础不同，所以计算平均发展速度不能采用一般的序时平均数的计算方法，计算方法分为水平法和累计法。水平法，又称几何平均法，即将环比发展速度按连乘法用几何平均数公式计算。累计法，也称方程法，根据一段时期内各年发展水平总和与基期水平的关系，列出方程式计算平均发展速度。水平法着重考虑最后一年所达到的发展水平；累计法着重考虑整个时期累计发展水平的总量。

本《年鉴》内所列的平均增长速度，除固定资产投资用“累计法”计算外，其余均用“水平法”计算。从某年到某年平均增长速度的年份，均不包括基期年在内。如建国四十三年以来的平均增长速度是以1949年为基期计算的，则写为1950-1992年平均增长速度，其余类推。

国民经济行业分类

自2003年定期报表开始使用新的《国民经济行业分类》（GB/T4754-2002）该分类是由国家统计局组织修订，经国家质量监督检验检疫总局批准，于2002年5月10日发布实施。这次修订是在1994年分类标准的基础上，参照联合国《全部经济活动的国际标准产业分类》（ISIC/Rev.3）进行的。修订后的《国民经济行业分类》（GB/T4754-2002）共有门类20个，大类95个，中类396个，小类913个。新增门类4个，大类增加3个，中类增加28个，小类增加67个。

企业（单位）登记注册类型

是以在工商行政管理机关登记注册的各类企业为划分对象，以工商行政管理部门对企业登记注册的类型为依据，将企业登记注册类型分为内资企业、港澳台商投资企业和外商投资企业三大类。内资企业包括国有企业、集体企业、股份合作企业、联营企业、有限责任公司、股份有限公司、私营公司和其他企业，港澳台商投资企业和外商投资企业分别包括合资经营企业、合作经营企业、独资经营企业和股份有限公司。对不在工商行政管理部门进行登记注册的行政机关、事业单位和社会团体，主要按其经费来源和管理方式进行划分。

国有企业

指企业全部资产归国家所有，并按《中华人民共和国企业法人登记管理条例》规定登记注册的非公司制的经济组织。不包括有限责任公司中的国有独资公司。

主要统计指标解释

■ 集体企业

指企业资产归集体所有，并按《中华人民共和国企业法人登记管理条例》规定登记注册的经济组织。

■ 股份合作企业

指以合作制为基础，由企业职工共同出资入股，吸收一定比例的社会资产投资组建，实行自主经营，自负盈亏，共同劳动，民主管理，按劳分配与按股份红相结合的一种集体经济组织。

■ 联营企业

指两个及两个以上相同或不同所有制性质的企业法人或事业单位法人，按自愿、平等、互利的原则，共同投资组成的经济组织。联营企业包括国有联营企业、集体联营企业、国有与集体联营企业和其他联营企业。

■ 有限责任公司

指根据《中华人民共和国公司登记管理条例》规定登记注册，由两个以上、五十个以下的股东共同出资，每个股东以其所认缴的出资额对公司承担有限责任，公司以其全部资产对其债务承担责任的经济组织。有限责任公司包括国有独资公司以及其他有限责任公司。

■ 股份有限公司

指根据《中华人民共和国公司登记管理条例》规定登记注册，其全部注册资本由等额股份构成并通过发行股票筹集资本，股东以其认购的股份对公司承担有限责任，公司以其全部资产对其债务承担责任的经济组织。

■ 私营企业

指由自然人投资设立或由自然人控股，以雇用劳动为基础的营利性经济组织。包括按照《公司法》、《合伙企业法》、《私营企业暂行条例》规定登记注册的私营有限责任公司、私营股份有限公司、私营合伙企业和私营独资企业。

■ 其他企业

指上述企业之外的其他内资经济组织。

■ 与港澳台商合资经营企业

指港澳台地区投资者与内地企业依照《中华人民共和国中外合资经营企业法》及有关法律的规定，按合同规定的比例投资设立、分享利润和分担风险的企业。

■ 与港澳台商合作经营企业

指港澳台地区投资者与内地企业依照《中华人民共和国中外合作经营企业法》及有关法律的规定，依照合作合同的约定进行投资或提供条件设立、分配利润和分担风险的企业。

■ 港澳台商独资经营企业

指依照《中华人民共和国外资企业法》及有关法律的规定，在内地由港澳台地区投资者全额投资设立的企业。

■ 港澳台商投资股份有限公司

指根据国家有关规定，经外经贸部依法批准设立，其中港、澳、台商的股本占公司注册资本的比例达25%以上的股份有限公司。凡其中港、澳、台商的股本占公司注册资本的比例小于25%的，属于内资企业中的股份有限公司。

■ 中外合资经营企业

指外国企业或外国人与中国内地企业依照《中华人民共和国中外合资经营企业法》及有关法律的规定，按合同规定的比例投资设立、分配利润和分担风险的企业。

■ 中外合作经营企业

指外国企业或外国人与中国内地企业依照《中华人民共和国中外合作经营企业法》及有关法律的规定，依照合作合同的约定进行投资或提供条件设立、分配利润和分担风险的企业。

■ 外资企业

指依照《中华人民共和国外资企业法》及有关法律的规定，在中国内地由外国投资者全额投资设立的企业。

主要统计指标解释

■ 外商投资股份有限公司

指根据国家有关规定，经外经贸部依法批准设立，其中外资的股本占公司注册资本的比例达25%以上的股份有限公司。凡其中外资股本占公司注册资本的比例小于25%的，属于内资企业中的股份有限公司。

■ 行政机关、事业单位和社会团体

参照企业登记注册类型，主要按其经费来源和管理方式划分。具体规定如下：

（1）行政机关：包括国家机关和政党机关，原则上均列为“国有”。但有特殊规定的，如供销社等，列为“集体”。

（2）事业单位：包括经国家机构编制部门和有关业务主管部门批准成立的各类事业单位，不包括实行企业化管理的事业单位。事业单位的划分办法如下：

① 由国家财政预算拨款或列入财政预算外资金管理以及经费主要来源于国有主管部门或国有上级单位的事业单位，列为“国有”。

② 经费主要来源于集体单位的事业单位，列为“集体”。

③ 公民个人（或个人合伙）开办的事业单位，列为“私营”。

④ 上述以外的其他事业单位，如果其经费来源不明确，按管理方式进行归类。

（3）社会团体：包括经民政部门批准成立以及未纳入社会团体管理条例范围的工会、妇联等各类社会团体。社会团体的划分办法如下：

① 未纳入民政部社会团体管理条例范围的工会、妇联、共青团、青联、工商联、科协、侨联等社会团体，国家拨款设立的基金会或基金管理组织以及经费主要来源于国有业务主管部门或国有上级单位的社会团体，列为“国有”。

② 经费主要来源于集体单位的社会团体，列为“集体”。

③ 公民个人（或个人合伙）开办的社会团体，划为“私营”。

④ 上述以外的其他社会团体，如果其经费来源不明确，改按管理方式进行归类。

Explanatory Notes on Main Statistical Indicators

□ Division of Administrative Areas

Refers to the division of administrative areas by the state. The relative laws stipulate that; (Ⅰ) the whole country is divided into provinces, autonomous regions and municipalities directly under the Central Government; (Ⅱ) provinces and autonomous regions are further divided into autonomous prefectures, counties, autonomous counties and cities; (Ⅲ) autonomous prefectures are divided into counties, autonomous counties and cities; (Ⅳ) counties and autonomous counties are further divided into townships, ethnic townships and towns; (Ⅴ) municipalities and large cities are divided into districts and counties; (Ⅵ) the state shall, when necessary, establish special administrative regions.

□ Comparable Prices

Refer to prices that are used to remove the factors of price change in calculating economic aggregates, so as to facilitate comparison of aggregates over time. Two methods are used for calculating economic aggregates at comparable prices: (a) Multiplying the output of products by their constant prices of certain year. (b) Deflation of data at current prices by relevant price index.

□ Constant Price

Refers to the average price of a given product in certain year, which is used for comparison of output value over time. As the output value at constant prices removers the factor of price changes, it reflects the trend of production development over time. Since 1949,with the changes in general price level, the State Statistical Bureau has issued nationally unified constant prices five times: the 1952 constant prices for 1949-1957;the 1957 constant prices for 1957-1971;the 1970 constant prices for 1971-1981;the 1980 constant prices for 1981-1990; and the 1990 constant prices have been used since 1991.

□ Average Annual Growth Rate

Shows the average growth rate of social and economic development during a longer period. It can not be directly calculated by chain based growth rate. The relation is:

Average Annual Growth Rate = Average Speed of Development – 1

Average speed of development is the time series average of speed which calculated by chain based. Because the reference bases during the different periods are not same, average speed of development can not be calculated by the general method. Level approach and accumulative approach for calculating average speed of development rate are applied. The “level approach”, or the method of calculating the geometric average, is derived by the formula of geometric average of the chain-based speeds of development, or comparing the level of the last year of the interval with that of the beginning year; the other is called the “accumulative approach” or the “algebraic average”, “equation” method, which is derived by the summation of the actual figure of each year in the interval divided by the figure in the base year. The level approach focuses on the level of the last year, while the accumulative approach emphasizes the aggregate development in the duration.

The average annual growth rates listed in the Yearbook are calculated by the level approach except for the growth rate of investment in fixed assets. The base year is not listed in the duration for which average annual growth rates are computed. For instance, the average annual growth rate of the 43 years since 1949 is shown as the average annual growth rate of 1950-1992 without showing the base year 1949.

□ Industrial Classification of the National Economy

The new Industrial Classification of the National Economy (GB/T 4754-2002) is introduced starting from the compilation of 2003 annual statistics. The revision of the 1994 classification was organized by the National Bureau of Statistics taking into consideration of the International Standards of the Industrial Classification of All Economic Activities (ISIC/Rev.3) of the United Nations, and the new Classification was promulgated by the National Administration of Quality Supervision, Inspection and Quarantine on May 10, 2002. The revised version of the Industrial Classification of the National Economy (GB/T 4754-2002) is composed of 20 major divisions, 95 divisions, 396 major groups and 913 groups, including 4 new major divisions, 3 new divisions, 28 major groups and 67 groups.

EXPLANATORY NOTES TO MAJOR STATISTICAL INDICATORS

☐ Registration Status of Enterprises

Is classified into 3 categories, namely domestic-funded enterprises, enterprises with foreign investment, in the light of the registration status of an enterprise in industrial and commercial administration agencies. Domestic-funded enterprises include state-owned enterprises, collective-owned enterprises, cooperative enterprises, joint ownership enterprises, limited liability corporations, share-holding corporations Ltd., private enterprises and other enterprises. Included in the enterprises with investment from Hong Kong, Macao and Taiwan and enterprises with foreign investment are joint-venture enterprises, cooperative enterprises, sole investment enterprises and share-holding corporations Ltd. For government agencies, institutions and social organizations that are not requested to register in industrial and commercial administration agencies, they are classified mainly by their sources of funds and way of management.

☐ State-owned Enterprises

Refer to non-corporation economic units where the entire assets are owned by the state and which have registered in accordance with the Regulation of the People's Republic of China on the Management of Registration of Corporate Enterprises. Excluded from this category are sole state-funded corporations in the limited liability corporations.

☐ Collective-owned Enterprises

Refer to economic units where the assets are owned collectively and which have registered in accordance with the Regulation of the People's Republic of China on the Management of Registration of Corporate Enterprises.

☐ Cooperative Enterprises

Refer to a form of collective economic units (enterprises) where capitals come mainly from employees as their shares, with certain proportion of capital from the outside, where production is organized on the basis of independent operation, independent accounting for profits and losses, joint work, democratic management, and a distribution system that integrates remuneration according to work with dividend according to capital share.

☐ Joint Ownership Enterprises

Refer to economic units established by two or more corporate enterprises or corporate institutions of the same or different ownership, through joint investment on the basis of equality, voluntary participation and mutual benefits. They include state joint ownership enterprises, collective joint ownership enterprises, joint state-collective enterprises, other joint ownership enterprises.

☐ Limited Liability Corporations

Refer to economic units established with investment from 2-50 investors and registered in accordance with the Regulation of the People's Republic of China on the Management of Registration of Corporations, each investor bearing limited liability to the corporation depending on its share of investment, and the corporation bearing liability to its debt to the maximum of its total assets. Limited liability corporations include exclusive state-funded limited liability corporations and other limited liability corporations.

☐ Share holding Corporations Ltd

Refer to economic units registered in accordance with the Regulation of the People's Republic of China on the Management of Registration of Corporations, with total registered capitals divided into equal shares and raised through issuing stocks. Each investor bears limited liability to the corporation depending on the holding of shares, and the corporation bears liability to its debt to the maximum of its total assets.

☐ Private Enterprises

Refer to profit-making economic units invested and established by natural persons, or controlled by natural persons using employed labor. Included in this category are private limited liability corporations, private share-holding corporations Ltd., private partnership enterprises and private-funded enterprises registered in accordance with the Corporation Law, Partnership Enterprises Law and Interim Regulations on Private Enterprise.

☐ Other Domestic-funded Enterprises

Refer to domestic-funded economic units other than those mentioned above.

☐ Joint-venture Enterprises with Funds from Hong Kong, Macao and Taiwan

Refer to enterprises jointly established by invertors from Hong Kong, Macao and Taiwan with enterprises in the mainland of China in accordance with the Law of the People's Republic of China on Sino-foreign Joint Venture Enterprises and other relevant laws, where the share of investment, profits and risks is stipulated in the contract.

EXPLANATORY NOTES TO MAJOR STATISTICAL INDICATORS

□ Cooperative Enterprises with Funds from Hong Kong Macau and Taiwan

Established by investors from Hong Kong, Macau and Taiwan with enterprises in the mainland of China in accordance with the Law of the People's Republic of China on Sino-foreign Cooperative Enterprises and other relevant laws, where the investment or provision of facilities, and the share of profits and risks is stipulated in the cooperative contract.

□ Enterprises with Sole (exclusive) Investment from Hong Kong, Macau and Taiwan

Refer to enterprises established in the mainland of China with exclusive investment from investors from Hong Kong, Macau and Taiwan in accordance with the Law of the People's Republic of China on Foreign-Funded Enterprises and other relevant laws.

□ Share-holding Corporations Ltd. with Investment from Hong Kong, Macau and Taiwan

Refer to share-holding corporations Ltd. established with the approval from the former Ministry of Foreign Trade and Economic Relations in line with relevant state regulations, where the share of investment from Hong Kong, Macau or Taiwan businessmen exceeds 25% of the total registered capital of the corporation. In case the share of investment from Hong Kong, Macau or Taiwan is less than 25% of the total registered capital, the enterprise is to be classified as domestic-funded share-holding corporation Ltd.

□ Joint-venture Enterprises with Foreign Investment

Refer to enterprises jointly established by foreign enterprises or foreigners with enterprises in the mainland of China in accordance with the Law of the People's Republic of China on Sino-foreign Joint Venture Enterprises and other relevant laws, where the share of investment, profits and risks is stipulated in the contract.

□ Cooperation Enterprises with Foreign Investment

Refer to enterprises jointly established by foreign enterprises or foreigners with enterprises in the mainland of China in accordance with the Law of the People's Republic of China on Sino-foreign Cooperative Enterprises and other relevant laws, where the investment or provision of facilities, and the share of profits and risks is stipulated in the cooperative contract.

□ Enterprises with Sole (exclusive) Foreign Investment

Refer to enterprises established in the mainland of China with exclusive investment from foreign investors in accordance with the Law of the People's Republic of China on Foreign-Funded Enterprises and other relevant laws.

□ Share-holding Corporations Ltd. with Foreign Investment

Refer to share-holding corporations Ltd. established with the approval from the Ministry of Foreign Trade and Economic Relations in line with relevant state regulations, where the share of investment from foreign investors exceeds 25% of the total registered capital of the corporation. In case the share of foreign investment is less than 25% of the total registered capital, the enterprise is to be classified as domestic-funded share-holding corporation Ltd.

□ Government Agencies, Institutions and Social Organizations

Are classified into following categories by source of funds and way of management taking reference of the registration status of enterprises:

(Ⅰ) Government agencies: include state and party agencies, classified in principle as "state-owned". There are exceptions, such as supply and marketing cooperatives, which are classified, as "collective".

(Ⅱ) Institutions: include institutions of various types established with the approval by organization and staffing departments of the government, but exclude institutions where enterprise management system is introduced. Institutions are further classified as follows:

(a) Institutions whose main budget is listed in the government budget appropriations or extra-budget funds, or allocated from the budget of their competent government agencies. Such institutions are classified as "state-owned".

(b) Institutions whose budget mainly comes from collective units. Such institutions are classified as "collective".

(c) Institutions other than those mentioned above whose source of budget are not clear. Such institutions are classified by way of management.

(III) Social organizations: include social organizations established with the approval from the Ministry of Civil Affairs, and organizations that are not covered by social organization management regulations such as trade unions, women's federations etc. Social organizations are further classified as follows:

(a) Social organizations that are not covered by social organization management regulations of the Ministry of Civil Affairs such as trade unions, women's federations, communist youth leagues, youth associations, industrial and commerce associations, scientists associations, overseas Chinese associations, etc., foundations and fund management organizations established with founds from the state, and social organizations whose funds mainly come from the budget of their competent government agencies. Such institutions are classified as "state-owned".

(b) Social organizations whose budget mainly comes from collective units. Such institutions are classified as "collective".

(c) Social organizations established by individual or a group of citizens, which are classified as "private".

(d) Social organizations other than those mentioned above whose source of budget are not clear. Such organizations are classified by way of management.

第 2 章

国民经济核算

NATIONAL ECONOMIC ACCOUNTING

简要说明
BRIEF INTRODUCTION

本章本市生产总值资料包括各年度地区生产总值的绝对值、构成和指数，三次产业贡献率，三次产业拉动力，地区生产总值收入法构成项目结构、支出法地区生产总值以及重庆市“一圈两翼”及三大经济区生产总值的绝对值和指数。

经济普查后，为保持GDP数据的历史可比性，按照国际惯例，对2008年以前的年度GDP历史数据进行了修订。本章所有数据是根据全市第二次经济普查结果修订后的数据，与以往年份年鉴数据有出入，请以本年度年鉴数据为准。

本章资料由市统计局核算处提供。

The data of Gross Domestic Product (GDP) in this chapter includes the values, composition and indices of GDP in all the years, the share of the contributions of the growth of three strata of industry to the increase of the GDP, the contribution of the three strata of industry to GDP growth, the composition of GDP in income approach, the GDP by expenditure approach, and the value and indices of the GDP of the “one circle and two wings” and the three major economic zones of Chongqing.

After the economic census, to remain the comparability of GDP in all the years and according to the international practice, the GDPs of the years before 2008 are modified. All the data in this chapter have been modified according to the result of the Second Economic Census of Chongqing, and have some difference with the data in the year books of the previous years. The data in this year book shall prevail.

All the data in this chapter are provided by Division of National Economic Accounting, Chongqing Municipal Bureau of Statistics.

表2.1 地区生产总值（1949－1978年）
GROSS DOMESTIC PRODUCT (1949-1978)

单位：亿元(100 million yuan)

年 份 Year	本 市 生产总值 Gross Domestic Product	其 中 of which			
		第一产业 Primary Industry	第二产业 Secondary Industry	其 中 of which	
				工 业 Industry	建筑业 Construction
1949	13.89	9.74	2.71	2.50	0.21
1950	15.02	10.23	3.00	2.77	0.23
1951	15.97	10.72	3.37	3.11	0.26
1952	17.97	11.86	3.94	3.59	0.35
1953	21.26	13.57	5.63	4.96	0.67
1954	22.79	13.89	6.52	6.00	0.52
1955	23.32	13.86	7.04	6.61	0.43
1956	26.37	15.01	8.33	7.70	0.63
1957	26.56	13.12	10.03	9.45	0.58
1958	34.81	15.43	14.53	13.52	1.01
1959	38.03	12.02	20.40	18.90	1.50
1960	38.82	11.10	21.38	19.89	1.49
1961	28.96	10.35	12.52	11.90	0.62
1962	25.12	9.92	9.67	9.42	0.25
1963	27.92	12.08	10.30	9.91	0.39
1964	32.58	13.37	13.07	12.49	0.58
1965	38.29	16.21	15.79	14.74	1.05
1966	39.61	16.18	17.75	16.52	1.23
1967	34.70	15.21	13.76	12.96	0.80
1968	28.25	15.18	7.81	7.41	0.40
1969	32.79	14.75	11.96	11.23	0.73
1970	39.96	15.96	17.41	16.10	1.31
1971	45.97	16.71	22.18	20.81	1.37
1972	45.37	16.67	20.82	19.67	1.15
1973	46.32	18.14	19.66	18.24	1.42
1974	45.70	18.43	18.00	16.85	1.15
1975	53.37	18.81	24.00	22.49	1.51
1976	53.43	19.07	23.44	22.00	1.44
1977	60.22	21.74	26.99	24.98	2.01
1978	71.70	24.81	34.46	31.53	2.93

表2.1 续表 continued

单位：亿元(100 million yuan)

年 份 Year	第三产业 Tertiary Industry	交通运输、仓储及邮政业 Transport, Storage, Post	批发和零售业 Wholesale and Retail Trades	住宿和餐饮业 Hotels and Catering Services	金融业 Financial Intermediation	房地产业 Real Estate	其他服务业 Others	本市人均生产总值（元） Per Capita GDP (yuan)
1949	1.44	0.61	0.44	0.26	0.03	0.02	0.08	87
1950	1.79	0.70	0.50	0.28	0.06	0.05	0.20	91
1951	1.88	0.74	0.56	0.29	0.09	0.07	0.13	94
1952	2.17	0.83	0.64	0.31	0.06	0.08	0.25	103
1953	2.06	0.78	0.65	0.32	0.07	0.09	0.15	120
1954	2.38	0.87	0.70	0.34	0.10	0.11	0.26	124
1955	2.42	0.88	0.69	0.37	0.10	0.13	0.25	125
1956	3.03	1.08	0.81	0.44	0.13	0.14	0.43	135
1957	3.41	1.23	0.97	0.44	0.14	0.15	0.48	131
1958	4.85	1.75	1.53	0.46	0.21	0.14	0.76	170
1959	5.61	2.04	1.81	0.52	0.34	0.17	0.73	185
1960	6.34	2.04	1.82	0.53	0.57	0.16	1.22	193
1961	6.09	1.82	1.54	0.53	0.57	0.18	1.45	154
1962	5.53	1.61	1.23	0.66	0.46	0.18	1.39	139
1963	5.54	1.47	1.21	0.58	0.35	0.19	1.74	151
1964	6.14	1.70	1.52	0.52	0.58	0.18	1.64	169
1965	6.29	1.71	1.55	0.52	0.86	0.21	1.44	191
1966	5.68	1.41	1.33	0.50	0.35	0.22	1.87	191
1967	5.73	1.35	1.44	0.48	0.41	0.25	1.80	164
1968	5.26	1.22	1.18	0.46	0.56	0.30	1.54	131
1969	6.08	1.37	1.40	0.49	0.72	0.36	1.74	147
1970	6.59	1.41	1.52	0.50	0.85	0.40	1.91	172
1971	7.08	1.47	1.56	0.60	1.09	0.45	1.91	192
1972	7.88	1.61	1.72	0.66	0.96	0.52	2.41	185
1973	8.52	1.76	1.79	0.66	1.06	0.55	2.70	183
1974	9.27	1.83	1.81	0.64	1.23	0.62	3.14	177
1975	10.56	2.04	2.02	0.69	1.45	0.71	3.65	201
1976	10.92	1.94	2.04	0.67	1.59	0.78	3.90	199
1977	11.49	2.11	2.21	0.69	1.90	0.87	3.71	221
1978	12.43	2.38	2.34	0.78	2.00	0.88	4.05	287

注：第三产业下“其中 of which”包括交通运输至其他服务业各列；本表人均生产总值按户籍人口计算。

Note: The per capita GDP hereof is calculated by registered population.

表2.2 地区生产总值构成（1949－1978年）
COMPOSITION OF GROSS DOMESTIC PRODUCT (1949-1978)

单位：%（%）

年 份 Year	本 市 生产总值 Gross Domestic Product	其 中 of which			
		第一产业 Primary Industry	第二产业 Secondary Industry	其 中 of which	
				工 业 Industry	建筑业 Construction
1949	100.0	70.1	19.5	18.0	1.5
1950	100.0	68.1	20.0	18.4	1.6
1951	100.0	67.1	21.1	19.5	1.6
1952	100.0	66.0	21.9	20.0	1.9
1953	100.0	63.8	26.5	23.3	3.2
1954	100.0	60.9	28.6	26.3	2.3
1955	100.0	59.4	30.2	28.3	1.9
1956	100.0	56.9	31.6	29.2	2.4
1957	100.0	49.4	37.8	35.6	2.2
1958	100.0	44.3	41.7	38.8	2.9
1959	100.0	31.6	53.6	49.7	3.9
1960	100.0	28.6	55.1	51.2	3.9
1961	100.0	35.7	43.2	41.1	2.1
1962	100.0	39.5	38.5	37.5	1.0
1963	100.0	43.3	36.9	35.5	1.4
1964	100.0	41.0	40.1	38.3	1.8
1965	100.0	42.3	41.2	38.5	2.7
1966	100.0	40.8	44.8	41.7	3.1
1967	100.0	43.8	39.7	37.3	2.4
1968	100.0	53.7	27.6	26.2	1.4
1969	100.0	45.0	36.5	34.2	2.3
1970	100.0	39.9	43.6	40.3	3.3
1971	100.0	36.3	48.2	45.3	2.9
1972	100.0	36.7	45.9	43.4	2.5
1973	100.0	39.2	42.4	39.4	3.0
1974	100.0	40.3	39.4	36.9	2.5
1975	100.0	35.2	45.0	42.1	2.9
1976	100.0	35.7	43.9	41.2	2.7
1977	100.0	36.1	44.8	41.5	3.3
1978	100.0	34.6	48.1	44.0	4.1

表2.2 续表 continued

单位：% (%)

年 份 Year	其 中 of which						
	第三产业 Tertiary Industry	其 中 of which					
		交通运输、仓储及邮政业 Transport, Storage, Post	批发和零售业 Wholesale and Retail Trades	住宿和餐饮业 Hotels and Catering Services	金融业 Financial Intermediation	房地产业 Real Estate	其他服务业 Others
1949	10.4	4.4	3.2	1.9	0.2	0.1	0.6
1950	11.9	4.7	3.3	1.9	0.4	0.3	1.3
1951	11.8	4.6	3.5	1.8	0.6	0.4	0.9
1952	12.1	4.6	3.6	1.7	0.3	0.4	1.5
1953	9.7	3.7	3.1	1.5	0.3	0.4	0.7
1954	10.5	3.8	3.1	1.5	0.4	0.5	1.2
1955	10.4	3.8	3.0	1.6	0.4	0.6	1.0
1956	11.5	4.1	3.1	1.7	0.5	0.5	1.6
1957	12.8	4.6	3.7	1.7	0.5	0.6	1.7
1958	14.0	5.0	4.4	1.3	0.6	0.4	2.3
1959	14.8	5.4	4.8	1.4	0.9	0.4	1.9
1960	16.3	5.3	4.7	1.4	1.5	0.4	3.0
1961	21.1	6.3	5.3	1.8	2.0	0.6	5.1
1962	22.0	6.4	4.9	2.6	1.8	0.7	5.6
1963	19.8	5.3	4.3	2.1	1.3	0.7	6.1
1964	18.9	5.2	4.7	1.6	1.8	0.6	5.0
1965	16.5	4.5	4.0	1.4	2.2	0.5	3.9
1966	14.4	3.6	3.4	1.3	0.9	0.6	4.6
1967	16.5	3.9	4.1	1.4	1.2	0.7	5.2
1968	18.7	4.3	4.2	1.6	2.0	1.1	5.5
1969	18.5	4.2	4.3	1.5	2.2	1.1	5.2
1970	16.5	3.5	3.8	1.3	2.1	1.0	4.8
1971	15.5	3.2	3.4	1.3	2.4	1.0	4.2
1972	17.4	3.5	3.8	1.5	2.1	1.1	5.4
1973	18.4	3.8	3.9	1.4	2.3	1.2	5.8
1974	20.3	4.0	4.0	1.4	2.7	1.4	6.8
1975	19.8	3.8	3.8	1.3	2.7	1.3	6.9
1976	20.4	3.6	3.8	1.3	3.0	1.5	7.2
1977	19.1	3.5	3.7	1.1	3.2	1.4	6.2
1978	17.3	3.3	3.3	1.1	2.8	1.2	5.6

表2.3 地区生产总值指数（1949－1978年）（上年=100）
INDICES OF GROSS DOMESTIC PRODUCT (1949-1978) (PRECEDING YEAR =100)

年 份 Year	本市生产总值 Gross Domestic Product	其 中 of which			
		第一产业 Primary Industry	第二产业 Secondary Industry	其 中 of which	
				工 业 Industry	建筑业 Construction
1949	100.0	100.0	100.0	100.0	100.0
1950	105.7	103.0	112.5	112.0	118.2
1951	103.4	104.0	110.9	111.2	107.7
1952	109.3	107.0	115.4	113.7	135.7
1953	111.2	103.4	135.2	131.1	177.1
1954	110.6	106.0	120.1	125.1	82.3
1955	102.7	100.2	109.6	111.9	82.4
1956	113.5	105.1	127.4	125.5	157.1
1957	102.3	97.3	108.3	110.3	83.4
1958	118.9	100.7	137.4	135.7	165.6
1959	97.4	67.8	123.9	123.4	130.3
1960	111.0	74.7	133.6	134.2	127.0
1961	64.8	83.7	58.2	59.4	41.4
1962	100.0	135.4	83.3	85.4	44.7
1963	114.9	124.0	109.3	108.1	154.4
1964	115.0	106.1	124.0	123.3	144.0
1965	114.5	109.8	122.2	119.2	185.6
1966	105.9	101.9	113.3	113.0	118.1
1967	90.2	99.4	82.9	83.9	70.5
1968	84.4	106.4	66.3	66.9	57.4
1969	112.1	91.4	135.8	134.3	163.7
1970	120.7	102.6	138.9	136.8	170.1
1971	111.9	100.4	125.2	127.0	102.3
1972	100.1	101.6	95.4	96.0	85.0
1973	103.2	109.5	96.3	94.5	127.1
1974	101.6	101.6	98.8	99.6	87.4
1975	111.8	92.8	130.4	130.6	128.4
1976	95.1	98.5	89.1	89.3	86.7
1977	120.0	111.8	134.2	132.4	162.3
1978	117.1	109.9	125.8	124.6	141.3

注：本表按可比价格计算（下表同）。
Note: The indices hereof are calculated at constant prices (the same below).

表2.3 续表 continued

年 份 Year	其 中 of which							本市人均生产总值 Per Capita GDP
	第三产业 Tertiary Industry	其 中 of which						
		交通运输、仓储及邮政业 Transport, Storage, Post	批发和零售业 Wholesale and Retail Trades	住宿和餐饮业 Hotels and Catering Services	金融业 Financial Intermediation	房地产业 Real Estate	其他服务业 Others	
1949	100.0	100.0	100.0	100.0	100.0	100.0	100.0	100.0
1950	118.6	127.6	105.6	107.4	197.3	250.4	102.5	102.2
1951	94.9	93.2	98.7	103.4	148.0	140.2	9.0	100.5
1952	120.1	113.0	116.0	106.7	65.9	114.5	380.3	106.3
1953	111.4	110.3	125.3	103.1	113.5	115.1	164.5	109.5
1954	112.4	109.3	106.4	106.1	140.1	122.2	112.6	109.1
1955	98.7	94.7	99.1	105.7	99.1	120.9	95.1	100.7
1956	118.4	118.0	113.9	118.9	130.0	111.9	132.9	109.1
1957	105.6	112.4	104.6	100.0	107.7	111.2	115.1	98.3
1958	134.9	139.0	138.0	104.5	146.7	91.6	218.4	118.6
1959	103.2	107.3	103.7	110.9	161.1	115.2	115.4	98.1
1960	101.1	102.3	102.6	102.0	163.1	90.4	122.4	113.4
1961	70.8	69.4	61.7	100.0	86.3	111.3	44.1	68.2
1962	105.1	92.0	91.9	123.1	77.8	98.5	101.0	102.8
1963	112.6	103.5	113.2	89.1	79.7	107.9	149.5	112.7
1964	109.0	102.5	97.7	89.5	173.1	95.7	124.2	110.8
1965	100.5	102.5	110.3	100.0	153.1	117.7	69.6	111.2
1966	85.3	96.8	107.2	98.0	40.8	105.2	104.2	102.8
1967	102.9	96.7	102.7	96.0	117.4	114.3	76.2	87.6
1968	101.6	98.3	84.3	95.8	136.1	121.9	76.5	81.9
1969	105.7	117.4	115.5	106.5	130.9	121.7	98.7	109.3
1970	101.9	109.6	108.1	102.0	118.5	111.6	131.7	117.2
1971	104.7	104.1	105.0	118.0	129.6	111.6	84.5	108.2
1972	111.9	110.4	110.1	108.5	88.7	114.1	111.5	97.3
1973	108.8	104.7	102.2	100.0	107.8	106.0	141.5	100.6
1974	109.0	107.3	100.5	96.9	115.8	112.8	112.7	99.1
1975	110.0	108.4	109.9	106.5	118.2	113.3	172.7	109.0
1976	104.4	105.3	100.5	98.5	109.9	108.4	80.5	94.0
1977	103.8	107.3	107.1	103.1	117.8	110.8	41.8	118.9
1978	105.1	101.7	103.5	116.4	103.7	100.4	150.8	117.2

注：本表人均生产总值按户籍人口计算。
Note: The per capita GDP hereof is calculated by registered population.

表2.4 地区生产总值指数（1949－1978年）（1949年=100）
INDICES OF GROSS DOMESTIC PRODUCT (1949-1978) (1949=100)

年 份 Year	本 市 生产总值 Gross Domestic Product	其 中 of which			
		第一产业 Primary Industry	第二产业 Secondary Industry	其 中 of which	
				工 业 Industry	建筑业 Construction
1949	100.0	100.0	100.0	100.0	100.0
1950	105.7	103.0	112.5	112.0	118.2
1951	109.3	107.1	124.8	124.5	127.3
1952	119.5	114.6	144.0	141.6	172.7
1953	132.9	118.5	194.7	185.6	305.9
1954	147.0	125.6	233.8	232.2	251.8
1955	151.0	125.9	256.2	259.8	207.5
1956	171.4	132.3	326.4	326.0	326.0
1957	175.3	128.7	353.5	359.6	271.9
1958	208.4	129.6	485.7	488.0	450.3
1959	203.0	87.9	601.8	602.2	586.7
1960	225.3	65.7	804.0	808.2	745.1
1961	146.0	55.0	467.9	480.1	308.5
1962	146.0	74.5	389.8	410.0	137.9
1963	167.8	92.4	426.1	443.2	212.9
1964	193.0	98.0	528.4	546.5	306.6
1965	221.0	107.6	645.7	651.4	569.0
1966	234.0	109.6	731.6	736.1	672.0
1967	211.1	108.9	606.5	617.6	473.8
1968	178.2	115.9	402.1	413.2	272.0
1969	199.8	105.9	546.1	554.9	445.3
1970	241.2	108.7	758.5	759.1	757.5
1971	269.9	109.1	949.6	964.1	774.9
1972	270.2	110.8	905.9	925.5	658.7
1973	278.8	121.3	872.4	874.6	837.2
1974	283.3	123.2	861.9	871.1	731.7
1975	316.7	114.3	1123.9	1137.7	939.5
1976	301.2	112.6	1001.4	1016.0	814.5
1977	361.4	125.9	1343.9	1345.2	1321.9
1978	423.2	138.4	1690.6	1676.1	1867.8

注：本表按可比价格计算（下表同）。
Note: The indices hereof are calculated at constant prices (the same below).

表2.4 续表 continued

年 份 Year	其 中 of which							本市人均生产总值 Per Capita GDP
	第三产业 Tertiary Industry	其 中 of which						
		交通运输、仓储及邮政业 Transport, Storage, Post	批发和零售业 Wholesale and Retail Trades	住宿和餐饮业 Hotels and Catering Services	金融业 Financial Intermediation	房地产业 Real Estate	其他服务业 Others	
1949	100.0	100.0	100.0	100.0	100.0	100.0	100.0	100.0
1950	118.6	127.6	105.6	107.4	197.3	250.4	102.5	102.2
1951	112.6	118.9	104.2	111.1	292.0	351.1	9.2	102.7
1952	135.2	134.4	120.9	118.5	192.4	402.0	35.0	109.2
1953	150.6	148.2	151.5	122.2	218.4	462.7	57.6	119.6
1954	169.3	162.0	161.2	129.7	306.0	565.4	64.9	130.5
1955	167.1	153.4	159.7	137.1	303.2	683.6	61.7	131.4
1956	197.8	181.0	181.9	163.0	394.2	764.9	82.0	143.4
1957	208.9	203.4	190.3	163.0	424.6	850.6	94.4	141.0
1958	281.8	282.7	262.6	170.3	622.9	779.1	206.2	167.2
1959	290.8	303.3	272.3	188.9	1003.5	897.5	238.0	164.0
1960	294.0	310.3	279.4	192.7	1636.7	811.3	291.3	186.0
1961	208.2	215.3	172.4	192.7	1412.5	903.0	128.5	126.9
1962	218.8	198.1	158.4	237.2	1098.9	889.5	129.8	130.5
1963	246.4	205.0	179.3	211.3	875.8	959.8	194.1	147.1
1964	268.6	210.1	175.2	189.1	1516.0	918.5	241.1	163.0
1965	269.9	215.4	193.2	189.1	2321.0	1081.1	167.8	181.3
1966	230.2	208.5	207.1	185.3	947.0	1137.3	174.8	186.4
1967	236.9	201.6	212.7	177.9	1111.8	1299.9	133.2	163.3
1968	240.7	198.2	179.3	170.4	1513.2	1584.6	101.9	133.7
1969	254.4	232.7	207.1	181.5	1980.8	1928.5	100.6	146.1
1970	259.2	255.0	223.9	185.1	2347.2	2152.2	132.5	171.2
1971	271.4	265.5	235.1	218.4	3042.0	2401.9	112.0	185.2
1972	303.7	293.1	258.8	237.0	2698.3	2740.6	124.9	180.2
1973	330.4	306.9	264.5	237.0	2908.8	2905.0	176.7	181.3
1974	360.1	329.3	265.8	229.7	3368.4	3276.8	199.1	179.7
1975	396.1	357.0	292.1	244.6	3981.4	3712.6	343.8	195.9
1976	413.5	375.9	293.6	240.9	4375.6	4024.5	276.8	184.1
1977	429.2	403.3	314.4	248.4	5154.5	4459.1	115.7	218.9
1978	451.1	410.2	325.4	289.1	5345.2	4476.9	174.5	256.6

注：本表人均生产总值按户籍人口计算。
Note: The per capita GDP hereof is calculated by registered population.

表2.5 地区生产总值（1978－2011年）
GROSS DOMESTIC PRODUCT (1978-2011)

单位：亿元(100 million yuan)

年 份 Year	本 市 生产总值 Gross Domestic Product	其 中 of which				
		第一产业 Primary Industry	第二产业 Secondary Industry	其 中 of which		第三产业 Tertiary Industry
				工 业 Industry	建筑业 Construction	
1978	71.70	24.81	34.46	31.53	2.93	12.43
1979	80.98	28.79	38.21	35.00	3.21	13.98
1980	90.68	32.57	42.42	38.89	3.53	15.69
1981	97.20	36.32	43.69	40.07	3.62	17.19
1982	108.08	40.62	47.14	43.26	3.88	20.32
1983	120.01	45.44	50.56	46.20	4.36	24.01
1984	141.64	50.66	60.63	55.46	5.17	30.35
1985	164.32	53.73	73.49	66.16	7.33	37.10
1986	184.60	60.06	81.38	72.52	8.86	43.16
1987	206.73	62.69	90.77	79.66	11.11	53.27
1988	261.27	75.00	117.61	104.79	12.82	68.66
1989	303.75	81.99	135.84	123.86	11.98	85.92
1990	327.75	100.40	135.62	117.60	18.02	91.73
1991	374.18	109.49	154.00	135.14	18.86	110.69
1992	461.32	117.28	194.40	171.42	22.98	149.64
1993	608.53	141.99	272.17	241.15	31.02	194.37
1994	833.60	196.19	376.75	339.59	37.16	260.66
1995	1123.06	264.19	492.67	436.21	56.46	366.20
1996	1315.12	287.56	568.99	502.06	66.93	458.57
1997	1509.75	307.21	650.40	567.88	82.52	552.14
1998	1602.38	300.89	675.64	574.41	101.23	625.85
1999	1663.20	286.16	697.81	589.52	108.29	679.23
2000	1791.00	284.87	760.03	633.98	126.05	746.10
2001	1976.86	294.90	841.95	695.44	146.51	840.01
2002	2232.86	317.87	958.87	787.94	170.93	956.12
2003	2555.72	339.06	1135.31	933.75	201.56	1081.35
2004	3034.58	428.05	1376.91	1132.70	244.21	1229.62
2005	3467.72	463.40	1564.00	1293.81	270.19	1440.32
2006	3907.23	386.38	1871.65	1566.83	304.82	1649.20
2007	4676.13	482.39	2368.53	2004.51	364.02	1825.21
2008	5793.66	575.40	3057.78	2607.15	450.63	2160.48
2009	6530.01	606.80	3448.77	2917.40	531.37	2474.44
2010	7925.58	685.38	4359.12	3697.83	661.29	2881.08
2011	10011.37	844.52	5543.04	4690.46	852.58	3623.81

表2.5 续表 continued

单位：亿元(100 million yuan)

年 份 Year	其 中 of which						本市人均生产总值（元） Per Capita GDP (yuan)
	交通运输、仓储及邮政业 Transportation, Storage, Postal Services	批发和零售业 Wholesale and Retail Trade	住宿和餐饮业 Hotels and Catering Trade	金融业 Financial Intermediation	房地产业 Real Estate	其他服务业 Other Services	
1978	2.38	2.34	0.78	2.00	0.88	4.05	287
1979	2.69	2.59	0.92	2.21	0.99	4.58	321
1980	3.08	2.90	1.02	2.46	1.11	5.12	357
1981	3.39	3.22	1.07	2.73	1.12	5.66	379
1982	4.18	3.89	1.11	2.99	1.28	6.87	419
1983	5.94	4.49	1.24	3.83	1.44	7.07	461
1984	6.50	5.73	1.52	6.63	1.81	8.16	542
1985	6.97	8.90	1.80	7.40	2.09	9.94	624
1986	6.59	10.08	2.17	8.71	2.64	12.97	694
1987	6.82	12.30	2.71	14.91	3.59	12.94	766
1988	8.67	17.10	3.29	17.92	4.47	17.21	958
1989	12.18	21.61	3.89	24.78	4.95	18.51	1103
1990	11.93	17.19	5.41	26.21	5.73	25.26	1181
1991	12.34	20.33	6.35	31.65	7.23	32.79	1338
1992	21.59	33.03	7.23	40.30	7.30	40.19	1641
1993	22.68	49.63	9.37	52.91	9.12	50.66	2156
1994	27.43	64.66	12.78	74.91	11.03	69.85	2935
1995	47.22	85.53	19.00	97.77	17.43	99.25	3931
1996	63.40	110.22	23.46	103.84	25.22	132.43	4574
1997	81.14	130.86	30.91	116.53	32.60	160.10	5253
1998	87.08	142.99	31.68	126.66	45.00	192.44	5579
1999	94.39	151.89	33.62	120.18	50.69	228.46	5804
2000	101.25	163.38	35.93	118.53	65.45	261.56	6274
2001	128.26	178.39	38.46	125.90	76.38	292.62	6963
2002	151.54	195.64	42.36	134.52	90.48	341.58	7912
2003	167.22	216.35	47.11	147.04	113.69	389.94	9098
2004	190.62	246.52	57.67	162.38	129.12	443.31	10845
2005	218.97	277.68	66.56	185.18	143.88	548.05	12404
2006	259.59	314.33	77.24	213.70	158.20	626.14	13939
2007	265.74	366.19	91.85	247.46	196.06	657.91	16629
2008	309.59	449.32	111.63	303.01	191.21	795.72	20490
2009	347.98	524.36	132.88	389.97	229.09	850.16	22920
2010	389.55	624.33	142.11	496.56	266.38	962.15	27596
2011	456.25	747.30	166.31	704.66	396.28	1153.01	34500

注：本表人均生产总值按常住人口计算。
Note: The per capita GDP hereof is calculated by resident population.

表2.6 地区生产总值构成（1978－2011年）
COMPOSITION OF GROSS DOMESTIC PRODUCT (1978-2011)

单位：% (%)

年 份 Year	本 市 生产总值 Gross Domestic Product	其 中 of which				
		第一产业 Primary Industry	第二产业 Secondary Industry	其 中 of which		第三产业 Tertiary Industry
				工 业 Industry	建筑业 Construction	
1978	100.0	34.6	48.1	44.0	4.1	17.3
1979	100.0	35.6	47.2	43.2	4.0	17.2
1980	100.0	35.9	46.8	42.9	3.9	17.3
1981	100.0	37.4	44.9	41.2	3.7	17.7
1982	100.0	37.6	43.6	40.0	3.6	18.8
1983	100.0	37.9	42.1	38.5	3.6	20.0
1984	100.0	35.8	42.8	39.2	3.6	21.4
1985	100.0	32.7	44.7	40.3	4.4	22.6
1986	100.0	32.5	44.1	39.3	4.8	23.4
1987	100.0	30.3	43.9	38.5	5.4	25.8
1988	100.0	28.7	45.0	40.1	4.9	26.3
1989	100.0	27.0	44.7	40.8	3.9	28.3
1990	100.0	30.6	41.4	35.9	5.5	28.0
1991	100.0	29.3	41.2	36.1	5.1	29.5
1992	100.0	25.4	42.1	37.2	4.9	32.5
1993	100.0	23.3	44.7	39.6	5.1	32.0
1994	100.0	23.5	45.2	40.7	4.5	31.3
1995	100.0	23.5	43.9	38.8	5.1	32.6
1996	100.0	21.9	43.3	38.2	5.1	34.8
1997	100.0	20.3	43.1	37.6	5.5	36.6
1998	100.0	18.8	42.2	35.8	6.4	39.0
1999	100.0	17.2	42.0	35.4	6.6	40.8
2000	100.0	15.9	42.4	35.4	7.0	41.7
2001	100.0	14.9	42.6	35.2	7.4	42.5
2002	100.0	14.2	42.9	35.3	7.6	42.9
2003	100.0	13.3	44.4	36.5	7.9	42.3
2004	100.0	14.1	45.4	37.3	8.1	40.5
2005	100.0	13.4	45.1	37.3	7.8	41.5
2006	100.0	9.9	47.9	40.1	7.8	42.2
2007	100.0	10.3	50.7	42.9	7.8	39.0
2008	100.0	9.9	52.8	45.0	7.8	37.3
2009	100.0	9.3	52.8	44.7	8.1	37.9
2010	100.0	8.6	55.0	46.7	8.3	36.4
2011	100.0	8.4	55.4	46.9	8.5	36.2

表2.6 续表 continued

单位：% (%)

年 份 Year	其 中 of which					
	其 中 of which					
	交通运输、仓储及邮政业 Transportation, Storage, Postal Services	批发和零售业 Wholesale and Retail Trade	住宿和餐饮业 Hotels and Catering Trade	金融业 Financial Intermediation	房地产业 Real Estate	其他服务业 Other Services
1978	3.3	3.3	1.1	2.8	1.2	5.6
1979	3.3	3.2	1.1	2.7	1.2	5.7
1980	3.4	3.2	1.1	2.7	1.2	5.7
1981	3.5	3.3	1.1	2.8	1.2	5.8
1982	3.9	3.6	1.0	2.8	1.2	6.3
1983	4.9	3.7	1.0	3.2	1.2	6.0
1984	4.6	4.0	1.1	4.7	1.3	5.7
1985	4.2	5.4	1.1	4.5	1.3	6.1
1986	3.6	5.5	1.2	4.7	1.4	7.0
1987	3.3	5.9	1.3	7.2	1.7	6.4
1988	3.3	6.5	1.3	6.9	1.7	6.6
1989	4.0	7.1	1.3	8.2	1.6	6.1
1990	3.6	5.2	1.7	8.0	1.7	7.8
1991	3.3	5.4	1.7	8.5	1.9	8.7
1992	4.7	7.2	1.6	8.7	1.6	8.7
1993	3.7	8.2	1.5	8.7	1.5	8.4
1994	3.3	7.8	1.5	9.0	1.3	8.4
1995	4.2	7.6	1.7	8.7	1.6	8.8
1996	4.8	8.4	1.8	7.9	1.9	10.0
1997	5.4	8.7	2.0	7.7	2.2	10.6
1998	5.4	8.9	2.0	7.9	2.8	12.0
1999	5.7	9.1	2.0	7.2	3.0	13.8
2000	5.7	9.1	2.0	6.6	3.7	14.6
2001	6.5	9.0	1.9	6.4	3.9	14.8
2002	6.8	8.8	1.9	6.0	4.1	15.3
2003	6.5	8.5	1.8	5.8	4.4	15.3
2004	6.3	8.1	1.9	5.4	4.3	14.5
2005	6.3	8.0	1.9	5.3	4.1	15.9
2006	6.6	8.0	2.0	5.5	4.0	16.1
2007	5.7	7.8	2.0	5.3	4.2	14.0
2008	5.3	7.8	1.9	5.2	3.3	13.8
2009	5.3	8.0	2.0	6.0	3.5	13.1
2010	4.9	7.9	1.8	6.3	3.4	12.1
2011	4.6	7.5	1.7	7.0	4.0	11.4

表2.7 地区生产总值指数（1978－2011年）（上年=100）

INDICES OF GROSS DOMESTIC PRODUCT (1978-2011)(PRECEDING YEAR=100)

年　份 Year	本　市 生产总值 Gross Domestic Product	其　中　of which				
		第一产业 Primary Industry	第二产业 Secondary Industry	其　中　of which		第三产业 Tertiary Industry
				工　业 Industry	建筑业 Construction	
1978	117.1	109.9	125.8	124.6	141.3	105.1
1979	111.1	109.1	112.2	112.3	111.7	112.1
1980	107.7	104.4	109.1	109.0	110.0	109.9
1981	106.2	105.8	105.5	105.2	108.1	110.3
1982	108.9	107.5	107.6	107.7	107.1	115.8
1983	110.3	107.3	110.2	110.2	111.8	117.3
1984	115.9	106.5	121.0	121.1	119.8	121.4
1985	108.6	109.3	105.6	104.0	121.9	112.3
1986	108.6	110.3	106.5	105.4	115.9	110.4
1987	105.3	96.7	108.6	107.3	119.3	111.9
1988	109.5	103.5	113.3	114.2	106.2	109.9
1989	104.9	104.6	102.5	103.7	91.5	109.5
1990	107.0	107.8	108.0	104.0	144.2	104.8
1991	109.2	106.7	109.4	110.8	100.2	111.5
1992	116.5	101.8	121.9	122.3	118.7	124.2
1993	115.6	105.0	122.0	122.4	118.8	115.5
1994	113.5	102.9	116.4	117.7	105.8	117.6
1995	112.3	104.5	114.2	114.1	114.3	115.0
1996	111.4	104.8	112.2	112.3	111.3	114.5
1997	111.2	103.2	112.5	111.8	118.5	114.1
1998	108.6	102.1	107.2	105.2	122.8	114.0
1999	107.8	100.4	110.6	111.0	107.7	107.6
2000	108.7	101.4	110.8	110.8	110.7	109.1
2001	109.2	102.2	112.2	111.7	114.7	109.0
2002	110.5	104.2	114.3	114.2	114.7	108.9
2003	111.7	104.4	116.6	116.9	115.1	109.0
2004	112.4	104.8	116.9	117.3	114.9	109.8
2005	111.7	104.5	113.3	114.5	107.2	112.1
2006	112.4	94.5	117.1	118.2	111.9	113.2
2007	115.9	109.5	120.9	122.4	113.4	112.1
2008	114.5	106.8	118.2	119.9	109.2	112.2
2009	114.9	105.5	117.9	117.4	121.2	113.5
2010	117.1	106.1	122.7	122.9	121.4	112.4
2011	116.4	105.1	121.8	122.2	119.6	110.8

注：本表按可比价格计算（下表同）。
Note: The indices hereof are calculated at constant prices (the same below).

表2.7 续表 continued

年 份 Year	其 中 of which						本市人均生产总值 Per Capita GDP
	交通运输、仓储及邮政业 Transportation, Storage, Postal Services	批发和零售业 Wholesale and Retail Trade	住宿和餐饮业 Hotels and Catering Trade	其 中 of which			
				金融业 Financial Intermediation	房地产业 Real Estate	其他服务业 Other Services	
1978	101.7	103.5	116.4	103.7	100.4	150.8	117.2
1979	111.8	110.6	115.8	111.4	111.6	115.2	110.4
1980	105.9	106.3	113.6	107.4	106.8	122.4	107.1
1981	107.6	108.7	107.3	109.9	99.1	117.1	105.4
1982	115.5	115.3	107.0	108.3	111.4	120.9	108.0
1983	130.2	115.1	107.1	130.1	121.2	100.8	109.5
1984	108.1	124.0	124.2	171.5	122.6	112.7	115.5
1985	96.9	137.2	117.4	103.1	105.3	116.7	108.0
1986	99.7	106.6	117.4	111.9	118.5	117.5	107.5
1987	108.3	110.0	114.3	157.4	123.3	84.8	103.9
1988	105.9	122.8	119.1	104.0	105.9	112.5	108.2
1989	116.6	108.2	112.8	122.0	96.4	94.1	104.0
1990	100.7	83.5	133.5	108.6	116.8	134.7	106.1
1991	102.4	108.5	116.6	113.9	117.2	117.9	108.4
1992	133.5	142.3	116.4	120.4	96.4	123.3	115.8
1993	102.8	138.5	124.4	109.3	109.4	112.7	115.1
1994	109.1	104.1	133.3	115.3	102.8	139.8	112.8
1995	123.1	111.2	137.0	116.5	114.5	117.5	111.7
1996	115.6	115.9	120.3	104.0	131.5	121.3	110.7
1997	114.7	113.5	126.3	109.6	124.5	114.6	111.2
1998	104.1	115.0	104.4	110.4	122.4	120.8	108.7
1999	101.9	108.3	108.2	89.7	110.2	121.7	108.1
2000	104.0	112.2	108.1	101.8	111.6	114.5	109.1
2001	116.2	108.9	106.2	101.5	112.6	109.2	109.7
2002	105.2	110.1	109.5	107.9	113.8	110.8	111.1
2003	104.8	109.3	110.1	107.9	116.1	109.6	112.2
2004	114.6	110.8	118.0	105.9	103.7	111.2	112.8
2005	112.4	114.0	113.7	109.9	109.8	113.0	111.8
2006	120.3	111.4	115.2	112.4	107.7	112.6	112.2
2007	112.5	112.3	112.0	109.7	116.8	111.5	115.5
2008	113.7	116.9	113.0	112.9	89.1	114.8	113.9
2009	103.3	119.9	115.6	131.2	120.3	107.2	114.1
2010	113.8	117.5	101.4	119.8	107.3	108.4	116.2
2011	113.6	114.3	110.4	105.4	105.5	111.7	115.1

注：本表人均地区生产总值按常住人口计算。
Note: The per capita GDP hereof is calculated by resident population.

表2.8 地区生产总值指数（1978－2011年）（1978年=100）
INDICES OF GROSS DOMESTIC PRODUCT (1978-2011) (1978=100)

年份 Year	本市生产总值 Gross Domestic Product	其中 of which				
		第一产业 Primary Industry	第二产业 Secondary Industry	其中 of which		第三产业 Tertiary Industry
				工业 Industry	建筑业 Construction	
1978	100.0	100.0	100.0	100.0	100.0	100.0
1979	111.1	109.1	112.2	112.3	111.7	112.1
1980	119.7	113.9	122.4	122.4	122.9	123.2
1981	127.1	120.5	129.1	128.8	132.9	135.9
1982	138.4	129.5	138.9	138.7	142.3	157.4
1983	152.7	139.0	153.1	152.8	159.1	184.6
1984	177.0	148.0	185.3	185.0	190.6	224.1
1985	192.2	161.8	195.7	192.4	232.3	251.7
1986	208.7	178.5	208.4	202.8	269.2	277.9
1987	219.8	172.6	226.3	217.6	321.2	311.0
1988	240.7	178.6	256.4	248.5	341.1	341.8
1989	252.5	186.8	262.8	257.7	312.1	374.3
1990	270.2	201.4	283.8	268.0	450.0	392.3
1991	295.1	214.9	310.5	296.9	450.9	437.4
1992	343.8	218.8	378.5	363.1	535.2	543.3
1993	397.4	229.7	461.8	444.4	635.8	627.5
1994	451.0	236.4	537.5	523.1	672.7	737.9
1995	506.5	247.0	613.8	596.9	768.9	848.6
1996	564.2	258.9	688.7	670.3	855.8	971.6
1997	627.4	267.2	774.8	749.4	1014.1	1108.6
1998	681.4	272.8	830.6	788.4	1245.3	1263.8
1999	734.5	273.9	918.6	875.1	1341.2	1359.8
2000	798.4	277.7	1017.8	969.6	1484.7	1483.5
2001	871.9	283.8	1142.0	1083.0	1703.0	1617.0
2002	963.4	295.7	1305.3	1236.8	1953.3	1760.9
2003	1076.1	308.7	1522.0	1445.8	2248.2	1919.4
2004	1209.5	323.5	1779.2	1695.9	2583.2	2107.5
2005	1351.0	338.1	2015.8	1941.8	2769.2	2362.5
2006	1518.5	319.5	2360.5	2295.2	3098.7	2674.4
2007	1759.9	349.9	2853.8	2809.3	3513.9	2998.0
2008	2015.1	373.7	3373.2	3368.4	3837.2	3363.8
2009	2315.3	394.3	3977.0	3954.5	4650.7	3817.9
2010	2711.2	418.4	4879.8	4860.1	5645.9	4291.3
2011	3154.6	439.8	5943.6	5939.0	6750.5	4754.4

注：本表按可比价格计算（下表同）。
Note: The indices hereof are calculated at constant prices (the same below).

表2.8 续表 continued

年份 Year	其中 of which						本市人均生产总值 Per Capita GDP
	其中 of which						
	交通运输、仓储及邮政业 Transportation, Storage, Postal Services	批发和零售业 Wholesale and Retail Trade	住宿和餐饮业 Hotels and Catering Trade	金融业 Financial Intermediation	房地产业 Real Estate	其他服务业 Other Services	
1978	100.0	100.0	100.0	100.0	100.0	100.0	100.0
1979	111.8	110.6	115.8	111.4	111.6	115.2	110.4
1980	118.4	117.6	131.5	119.6	119.2	141.0	118.2
1981	127.4	127.8	141.1	131.4	118.1	165.1	124.6
1982	147.1	147.4	151.0	142.3	131.6	199.6	134.6
1983	191.5	169.7	161.7	185.1	159.5	201.2	147.4
1984	207.0	210.4	200.8	317.4	195.5	226.8	170.2
1985	200.6	288.7	235.7	327.2	205.9	264.7	183.8
1986	200.0	307.8	276.7	366.1	244.0	311.0	197.6
1987	216.6	338.6	316.3	576.2	300.9	263.7	205.3
1988	229.4	415.8	376.7	599.2	318.7	296.7	222.1
1989	267.5	449.9	424.9	731.0	307.2	279.2	231.0
1990	269.4	375.7	567.2	793.9	358.8	376.1	245.1
1991	275.9	407.6	661.4	904.3	420.5	443.4	265.7
1992	368.3	580.0	769.9	1088.8	405.4	546.7	307.7
1993	378.6	803.3	957.8	1190.1	443.5	616.1	354.2
1994	413.1	836.2	1276.7	1372.2	455.9	861.3	399.5
1995	508.5	929.9	1749.1	1598.6	522.0	1012.0	446.2
1996	587.8	1077.8	2104.2	1662.5	686.4	1227.6	493.9
1997	674.2	1223.3	2657.6	1822.1	854.6	1406.8	549.2
1998	701.8	1406.8	2774.5	2011.6	1046.0	1699.4	597.0
1999	715.1	1523.6	3002.0	1804.4	1152.7	2068.2	645.4
2000	743.7	1709.5	3245.2	1836.9	1286.4	2368.1	704.1
2001	864.2	1861.6	3446.4	1864.5	1448.5	2586.0	772.4
2002	909.1	2049.6	3773.8	2011.8	1648.4	2865.3	858.1
2003	952.7	2240.2	4155.0	2170.7	1913.8	3140.4	962.8
2004	1091.8	2482.1	4902.9	2298.8	1984.6	3492.1	1086.0
2005	1227.2	2829.6	5574.6	2526.4	2179.1	3946.1	1214.1
2006	1476.3	3152.2	6421.9	2839.7	2346.9	4443.3	1362.2
2007	1660.8	3539.9	7192.5	3115.2	2741.2	4954.3	1573.3
2008	1888.3	4138.1	8127.5	3517.1	2442.4	5687.5	1792.0
2009	1950.6	4961.6	9395.4	4614.4	2938.2	6097.0	2044.7
2010	2219.8	5829.9	9526.9	5528.1	3152.7	6609.1	2375.9
2011	2521.7	6665.0	10515.7	5826.5	3327.0	7319.8	2735.8

注：本表人均地区生产总值按常住人口计算。
Note: The per capita GDP hereof is calculated by resident population.

表2.9 三次产业贡献率（1990－2011年）

SHARE OF THE CONTRIBUTIONS OF THE GROWTH OF THREE STRATA OF INDUSTRY TO THE INCREASE OF THE GDP(1990-2011)

单位：%（%）

年 份 Year	本 市 生产总值 Gross Domestic Product	其 中 of which 第一产业 Primary Industry	第二产业 Secondary Industry	其 中 of which 工 业 Industry	第三产业 Tertiary Industry
1990	100.0	33.9	46.8	21.2	19.3
1991	100.0	22.5	42.2	42.1	35.3
1992	100.0	3.2	54.9	49.2	41.9
1993	100.0	8.5	61.2	55.0	30.3
1994	100.0	5.0	55.3	53.0	39.7
1995	100.0	7.8	53.8	48.1	38.4
1996	100.0	8.3	50.7	45.7	41.0
1997	100.0	5.3	53.2	45.0	41.5
1998	100.0	4.3	40.3	26.2	55.4
1999	100.0	0.8	64.4	58.5	34.8
2000	100.0	2.4	60.3	53.0	37.3
2001	100.0	3.7	55.9	44.7	40.4
2002	100.0	5.9	58.9	48.6	35.2
2003	100.0	5.2	63.5	53.7	31.3
2004	100.0	5.0	63.7	54.2	31.3
2005	100.0	4.6	55.1	50.2	40.3
2006	100.0	-6.0	62.1	54.6	43.9
2007	100.0	6.7	61.6	55.1	31.7
2008	100.0	4.9	61.3	56.5	33.8
2009	100.0	3.6	60.7	50.5	35.7
2010	100.0	3.2	68.6	59.1	28.2
2011	100.0	2.7	73.3	63.3	24.0

表2.10 三次产业拉动力（1990－2011年）
CONTRIBUTION OF THE THREE STRATA OF INDUSTRY TO GDP GROWTH (1990-2011)

单位：%（%）

年 份 Year	本 市 生产总值 Gross Domestic Product	其 中 of which			
		第一产业 Primary Industry	第二产业 Secondary Industry	其 中 of which 工 业 Industry	第三产业 Tertiary Industry
1990	7.0	2.4	3.3	1.5	1.3
1991	9.2	2.1	3.9	3.9	3.2
1992	16.5	0.5	9.1	8.1	6.9
1993	15.6	1.3	9.5	8.6	4.8
1994	13.5	0.7	7.5	7.2	5.3
1995	12.3	1.0	6.6	5.9	4.7
1996	11.4	0.9	5.8	5.2	4.7
1997	11.2	0.6	6.0	5.0	4.6
1998	8.6	0.4	3.5	2.3	4.7
1999	7.8	0.1	5.0	4.6	2.7
2000	8.7	0.2	5.2	4.6	3.3
2001	9.2	0.3	5.1	4.1	3.8
2002	10.5	0.6	6.2	5.1	3.7
2003	11.7	0.6	7.4	6.3	3.7
2004	12.4	0.6	7.9	6.7	3.9
2005	11.7	0.5	6.4	5.9	4.8
2006	12.4	-0.7	7.7	6.8	5.4
2007	15.9	1.1	9.8	8.8	5.0
2008	14.5	0.7	8.9	8.2	4.9
2009	14.9	0.5	9.0	7.5	5.4
2010	17.1	0.5	11.7	10.1	4.9
2011	16.4	0.4	12.0	10.4	4.0

表2.11 地区生产总值收入法构成项目结构（2011年）
COMPOSITION OF GROSS DOMESTIC PRODUCT IN INCOME APPROACH (2011)

单位：亿元(100 million yuan)

项目	Item	增加值 Value-added	其中 of which			
			劳动者报酬 Compensation of Employees	生产税净额 Net Product Tax	固定资产折旧 Depreciation of Fixed Assets	营业盈余 Earned Surplus
本市生产总值	**Gross Domestic Product**	**10011.37**	**4930.41**	**1486.41**	**1068.85**	**2525.70**
第一产业	Primary Industry	844.52	815.18	2.67	26.67	
第二产业	Secondary Industry	5543.04	2639.65	965.17	631.33	1306.89
工业	Industry	4690.46	2158.99	842.73	593.47	1095.27
建筑业	Construction	852.58	480.66	122.44	37.86	211.62
第三产业	Tertiary Industry	3623.81	1475.58	518.57	410.85	1218.81
交通运输、仓储和邮政业	Transport, Storage and Post	456.25	174.81	46.00	72.48	162.96
信息传输、计算机服务和软件业	Data Transmission, Computer Services and Software	173.34	35.20	19.13	57.70	61.31
批发和零售业	Wholesale and Retail Trades	747.30	214.88	195.25	37.09	300.08
住宿和餐饮业	Hotels and Catering Services	166.31	120.45	10.42	13.91	21.53
金融业	Financial Intermediation	704.66	179.14	108.02	19.54	397.96
房地产业	Real Estate	396.28	79.87	90.01	110.24	116.16
租赁与商务服务业	Leasing and Business Services	156.37	49.40	31.79	27.86	47.32
科学研究、技术服务与地质勘查业	Scientific Research, Technical Services and Geological Prospecting	90.22	43.72	5.75	6.71	34.04
水利、环境和公共设施管理业	Administration of Water Conservancy, Environment and Public Utilities	37.71	15.97	1.90	10.88	8.96
居民服务和其他服务业	Household Services and Other Services	86.85	71.33	4.82	3.62	7.08
教育	Education	210.78	170.52	1.24	22.29	16.73
卫生、社会保障和社会福利业	Public Health, Social Security and Social Welfare	120.57	86.78	0.83	9.93	23.03
文化、体育与娱乐业	Culture, Sports and Entertainment	48.68	24.47	3.05	3.21	17.95
公共管理与社会组织	Public Administration and Social Organizations	228.49	209.04	0.36	15.39	3.70

表2.12 支出法地区生产总值（2010－2011年）
GROSS DOMESTIC PRODUCT BY EXPENDITURE APPROACH (2010-2011)

单位：亿元(100 million yuan)

项　目	Item	2010	2011
本市生产总值	**Gross Domestic Product**	**7925.58**	**10011.37**
最终消费支出	Final Consumption Expenditures	3811.85	4641.64
居民消费支出	Household Consumption Expenditures	2792.34	3433.33
食品类支出	Foods	1022.39	1246.48
衣着类支出	Clothing	287.15	362.67
居住类支出	Residence	238.10	279.90
家庭设备、用品及服务类支出	Household Appliances, Articles and Services	216.78	262.81
医疗保健类支出	Medical and Health Care	211.05	262.77
交通和通信类支出	Traffic and Telecommunications	247.00	320.04
文教娱乐用品及服务类支出	Culture, Education and Entertainment Articles and Services	259.02	316.53
银行中介服务支出	Financial Intermediation Services	87.68	112.48
保险服务消费支出	Consumption of Insurance Services	39.94	47.92
自有住房服务虚拟支出	Imaginary Expenditure of Freeform Resident Services	68.40	79.38
实物消费支出	Reality Consumption	38.37	48.66
其他商品和服务类支出	Other Goods and Services	76.46	93.69
#农村居民支出	Rural Households Expenditure	500.34	615.65
食品类支出	Food	244.74	289.68
衣着类支出	Clothing	31.20	40.22
居住类支出	Residence	39.46	50.85
家庭设备、用品及服务类支出	Household Appliances, Articles and Services	35.72	44.47
医疗保健类支出	Medical and Health Care	37.63	48.06
交通和通信类支出	Traffic and Telecommunications	39.10	50.58
文教娱乐用品及服务类支出	Culture, Education and Entertainment Articles and Services	33.55	44.67
银行中介服务支出	Financial Intermediation Services	9.25	11.24
保险服务消费支出	Consumption of Insurance Services	11.08	13.23
自有住房服务虚拟支出	Imaginary Expenditure of Freeform Resident Services	11.66	13.72
其他商品和服务类支出	Other Goods and Services	6.95	8.93

表2.12 续表 continued

单位：亿元(100 million yuan)

项目	Item	2010	2011
#城镇居民支出	Urban Households Expenditure	2292.00	2817.68
食品类支出	Foods	777.65	956.80
衣着类支出	Clothing	255.95	322.45
居住类支出	Residence	198.64	229.05
家庭设备、用品及服务类支出	Household Appliances, Articles and Services	181.06	218.34
医疗保健类支出	Medical and Health Care	173.42	214.71
交通和通信类支出	Traffic and Telecommunications	207.90	269.46
文教娱乐用品及服务类支出	Culture, Education and Entertainment Articles and Services	225.47	271.86
银行中介服务支出	Financial Intermediation Services	78.43	101.24
保险服务消费支出	Consumption of Insurance Services	28.86	34.69
自有住房服务虚拟支出	Imaginary Expenditure of Freeform Resident Services	56.74	65.66
实物消费支出	Reality Consumption	38.37	48.66
其他商品和服务类支出	Other Goods and Services	69.51	84.76
政府消费支出	Government Consumption	1019.51	1208.31
资本形成总额	Gross Capital Formation	4576.55	5757.51
固定资本形成总额	Gross Fixed Capital Formation	4379.26	5511.24
住宅	Residential Buildings	841.29	1224.11
非住宅建筑物	Non-residential Buildings	2110.39	2829.26
机器和设备	Machinery and Equipment	513.94	639.63
土地改良支出	Land Improvement	6.46	3.29
矿藏勘探费	Mine Exploration	1.27	1.41
计算机软件	Computer Software	32.13	66.45
其他	Others	873.78	747.09
存货增加	Increase of Inventories	197.29	246.27
第一产业	Primary Industry	0.77	0.74
第二产业	Secondary Industry	119.03	152.32
第三产业	Tertiary Industry	77.49	93.21
货物和服务净流出	Net Exports of Goods and Services	-462.82	-387.78
流出	Exports (Outflow)	913.51	1075.69
流入	Imports (Inflow)	1376.33	1463.47

表2.13 分区域地区生产总值（2010－2011年）
GROSS DOMESTIC PRODUCT BY REGION (2010-2011)

单位：亿元(100 million yuan)

指　标	Item	2010	2011	指　数 上年=100 Index Preceding Year=100
本市生产总值	**Gross Domestic Product**	**7925.58**	**10011.37**	**116.4**
#一小时经济圈	One-Hour Economic Circle	6145.32	7762.88	116.1
渝东北翼	Northeast of Chongqing	1347.53	1710.51	117.6
渝东南翼	Southeast of Chongqing	432.73	537.98	116.0
#都市发达经济圈	Developed Metropolitan Economic Circle	3490.83	4368.49	115.2
渝西经济走廊	West Chongqing Economic Corridor	1984.65	2509.93	116.7
三峡库区生态经济区	Ecological Economic Zone in Three Gorges Reservoir Area	2450.10	3132.95	117.8
第一产业	**Primary Industry**	**685.38**	**844.52**	**105.1**
#一小时经济圈	One-Hour Economic Circle	403.17	493.13	104.7
渝东北翼	Northeast of Chongqing	209.27	260.53	105.7
渝东南翼	Southeast of Chongqing	72.94	90.86	105.4
#都市发达经济圈	Developed Metropolitan Economic Circle	75.19	89.76	102.3
渝西经济走廊	West Chongqing Economic Corridor	276.23	338.39	105.2
三峡库区生态经济区	Ecological Economic Zone in Three Gorges Reservoir Area	333.96	416.37	105.7
第二产业	**Secondary Industry**	**4359.12**	**5543.04**	**121.8**
#一小时经济圈	One-Hour Economic Circle	3450.40	4375.26	121.2
渝东北翼	Northeast of Chongqing	691.31	895.57	124.7
渝东南翼	Southeast of Chongqing	217.41	272.21	122.3
#都市发达经济圈	Developed Metropolitan Economic Circle	1870.61	2298.60	119.4
渝西经济走廊	West Chongqing Economic Corridor	1154.53	1494.00	122.9
三峡库区生态经济区	Ecological Economic Zone in Three Gorges Reservoir Area	1333.98	1750.44	124.4
第三产业	**Tertiary Industry**	**2881.08**	**3623.81**	**110.8**
#一小时经济圈	One-Hour Economic Circle	2291.75	2894.49	110.5
渝东北翼	Northeast of Chongqing	446.95	554.41	112.0
渝东南翼	Southeast of Chongqing	142.38	174.91	112.2
#都市发达经济圈	Developed Metropolitan Economic Circle	1545.03	1980.13	110.9
渝西经济走廊	West Chongqing Economic Corridor	553.89	677.54	109.3
三峡库区生态经济区	Ecological Economic Zone in Three Gorges Reservoir Area	782.16	966.14	111.7

表2.14 分经济类型地区生产总值（1996－2011年）
GROSS DOMESTIC PRODUCT BY STATUS OF REGISTRATION(1996-2011)

单位：亿元(100 million yuan)

年 份 Year	本市生产总值 Gross Domestic Product	公有制经济 Public-owned Economy	非公有制经济 Non-public-owned Economy	其 中 of which	
				个体私营经济 Individual and Private	外商港澳台经济 Funded by HK, Macao, Taiwan & Foreign
1996	1315.12	987.66	327.46	286.70	40.76
1997	1509.75	1111.18	398.57	341.20	57.37
1998	1602.38	1104.04	498.34	442.26	56.08
1999	1663.20	1111.02	552.18	487.32	64.86
2000	1791.00	1156.99	634.01	560.58	73.43
2001	1976.86	1209.84	767.02	682.02	85.00
2002	2232.86	1295.06	937.80	799.36	138.44
2003	2555.72	1385.20	1170.52	955.84	214.68
2004	3034.58	1574.95	1459.63	1271.49	188.14
2005	3467.72	1719.99	1747.73	1511.93	235.80
2006	3907.23	1836.40	2070.83	1734.81	336.02
2007	4676.13	2099.58	2576.55	2118.29	458.26
2008	5793.66	2386.99	3406.67	2827.31	579.36
2009	6530.01	2613.93	3916.08	3197.94	718.14
2010	7925.58	3079.02	4846.56	3851.89	994.67
2011	10011.37	3836.12	6175.25	4894.32	1280.93

表2.14 续表 continued

单位：% (%)

年　份 Year	生产总值构成 Compositon of Gross Domestic Product	公有制经济 Public-owned Economy	非公有制经济 Non-public-owned Economy	其　中 of which 个体私营经济 Individual and Private	外商港澳台经济 Funded by HK, Macao, Taiwan & Foreign
1996	100.0	75.1	24.9	21.8	3.1
1997	100.0	73.6	26.4	22.6	3.8
1998	100.0	68.9	31.1	27.6	3.5
1999	100.0	66.8	33.2	29.3	3.9
2000	100.0	64.6	35.4	31.3	4.1
2001	100.0	61.2	38.8	34.5	4.3
2002	100.0	58.0	42.0	35.8	6.2
2003	100.0	54.2	45.8	37.4	8.4
2004	100.0	51.9	48.1	41.9	6.2
2005	100.0	49.6	50.4	43.6	6.8
2006	100.0	47.0	53.0	44.4	8.6
2007	100.0	44.9	55.1	45.3	9.8
2008	100.0	41.2	58.8	48.8	10.0
2009	100.0	40.0	60.0	49.0	11.0
2010	100.0	38.8	61.2	48.6	12.6
2011	100.0	38.3	61.7	48.9	12.8

年　份 Year	生产总值指数（上年=100） Compositon of Gross Domestic Product (Preceding Year =100)	公有制经济 Public-owned Economy	非公有制经济 Non-public-owned Economy	其　中 of which 个体私营经济 Individual and Private	外商港澳台经济 Funded by HK, Macao, Taiwan & Foreign
1996	111.4	107.3	126.1	127.8	115.1
1997	111.2	109.0	117.9	115.3	136.3
1998	108.6	101.7	127.9	132.6	100.1
1999	107.8	104.5	115.1	114.4	120.1
2000	108.7	105.1	115.9	116.1	114.3
2001	109.2	103.5	119.7	120.4	114.5
2002	110.5	104.7	119.6	114.7	159.3
2003	111.7	104.4	121.8	116.7	151.3
2004	112.4	107.6	118.0	125.9	83.0
2005	111.7	106.7	117.0	116.2	122.5
2006	112.4	106.6	118.2	114.5	142.2
2007	115.9	110.8	120.5	118.3	132.1
2008	114.5	105.1	122.2	123.4	116.9
2009	114.9	111.6	117.3	115.4	126.4
2010	117.1	113.5	119.6	116.4	133.9
2011	116.4	111.8	119.3	118.3	123.0

主要统计指标解释

国内（地区）生产总值（GDP）

是按市场价格计算的一个国家（或地区）所有常住单位在一定时期内生产活动的最终成果。国内（地区）生产总值有三种表现形态，即价值形态、收入形态和产品形态。从价值形态看，它是所有常住单位在一定时期内所生产的全部货物和服务价值超过同期中间投入的全部非固定资产货物和服务价值的差额，即所有常住单位的增加值之和；从收入形态看，它是所有常住单位在一定时期内所创造并分配给常住单位和非常住单位的初次收入之和；从产品形态看，它是所有常住单位在一定时期内最终使用的货物和服务价值减去货物和服务进口价值。在实际核算中，国内（地区）生产总值的三种表现形态表现为三种计算方法，即生产法、收入法和支出法。三种方法分别从不同的方面反映国内（地区）生产总值及其构成。

三次产业

三次产业的划分是世界上较为常用的产业结构分类，但各国的划分不尽一致。我国的三次产业划分是：

第一产业是指农业、林业、畜牧业、渔业和农林牧渔服务业。

第二产业是指采矿业，制造业，电力、煤气及水的生产和供应业，建筑业。

第三产业是指除第一、二产业以外的其他行业。

收入法国内（地区）生产总值

是从常住单位从事生产活动形式收入的角度来反映一个国家（或地区）一定时期内生产活动最终成果的一种方法，包括劳动者报酬、生产税净额、固定资产折旧、营业盈余四部分。计算公式为：

收入法国内（地区）生产总值=劳动者报酬+生产税净额+固定资产折旧+营业盈余

（1）劳动者报酬：指劳动者因从事生产活动所获得的全部报酬。包括劳动者获得的各种形式的工资、奖金和津贴，既包括货币形式的，也包括实物形式的，还包括劳动者所享受的公费医疗和医药卫生费、上下班交通补贴和单位支付的社会保险费、住房公积金等。对于个体经济来说，其所有者所获得的劳动报酬和经营利润不易区分，这两部分统一作为劳动者报酬处理。

（2）生产税净额：指生产税减生产补贴后的差额。生产税指政府对生产单位生产、销售和从事经营活动以及因从事生产活动使用某些生产要素（如固定资产、土地、劳动力）所征收的各种税、附加费和规费。生产补贴与生产税相反，是政府对生产单位的单方面转移支出，因此视为负生产税，包括政策亏损补贴、价格补贴等。

（3）固定资产折旧：指一定时期内为弥补固定资产损耗按照规定的固定资产折旧率提取的固定资产折旧，或按国民经济核算统一规定的折旧率虚拟计算的固定资产折旧。它反映了固定资产在当期生产中的转移价值。各类企业和企业化管理的事业单位的固定资产折旧指实际计提的折旧费；不计提折旧的政府机关、非企业化管理的事业单位和居民住房的固定资产折旧是按照统一规定的折旧率和固定资产原值计算的虚拟折旧。原则上，固定资产折旧应按固定资产当期的重置价值计算，但是我国目前尚不具备对全社会固定资产进行重估价的基础，所以暂时只能采用上述方法。

（4）营业盈余：指常住单位创造的增加值扣除劳动者报酬、生产税净额和固定资产折旧后的余额。它相当于企业的营业利润加上生产补贴，但要扣除从利润中开支的工资和福利等。

支出法国内（地区）生产总值

是从最终使用的角度反映一个国家（或地区）一定时期内生产活动最终成果的一种方法，包括最终消费支出、资本形成总额及货物和服务净流出三部分。计算公式为：

支出法国内(地区)生产总值=最终消费支出+资本形成总额+货物和服务净流出

主要统计指标解释

最终消费支出

指常住单位为满足物质、文化和精神生活的需要，从本国经济领土和国外购买的货物和服务的支出。它不包括非常住单位在本国经济领土内的消费支出。最终消费支出分为居民消费支出和政府消费支出。

（1）居民消费支出：指常住住户在一定时期内对于货物和服务的全部最终消费支出。居民消费支出除了直接以货币形式购买的货物和服务的消费支出外，还包括以其他方式获得的货物和服务的消费支出，即所谓的虚拟消费支出。居民虚拟消费支出包括如下几种类型：单位以实物报酬及实物转移的形式提供给劳动者的货物和服务；住户生产并由本住户消费了的货物和服务，其中的服务仅指住户的自有住房服务；金融机构提供的金融媒介服务；保险公司提供的保险服务。

（2）政府消费支出：指政府部门为全社会提供的公共服务的消费支出和免费或以较低的价格向居民住户提供的货物和服务的净支出，前者等于政府服务的产出价值减去政府单位所获得的经营收入的价值，后者等于政府部门免费或以较低价格向居民住户提供的货物和服务的市场价值减去向住户收取的价值。

资本形成总额

指常住单位在一定时期内获得的减去处置的固定资产和存货的净额，包括固定资产形成总额和存货增加。

（1）固定资产形成总额：指常住单位在一定时期内获得的固定资产减处置的固定资产的价值总额。固定资产是通过生产活动生产出来的，且其使用年限在一年以上、单位价值在规定标准以上的资产，不包括自然资产。可分为有形固定资本形成总额和无形固定资本形成总额。有形固定资本形成总额包括一定时期内完成的建筑工程、安装工程和设备工器具购置(减处置)价值，以及土地改良、新增役、种、奶、毛、娱乐用牲畜和新增经济林木价值。无形固定资本形成总额包括矿藏的勘探、计算机软件等获得减处置。

（2）存货增加：指常住单位在一定时期内存货实物量变动的市场价值，即期末价值减期初价值的差额，再扣除当期由于价格变动而产生的持有收益。存货增加可以是正值，也可以是负值，正值表示存货上升，负值表示存货下降。存货包括生产单位购进的原材料、燃料和储备物资等存货，以及生产单位生产的产成品、在制品和半成品等存货。

货物和服务净流出

指货物和服务流出减货物和服务流入的差额。流出包括常住单位向非常住单位出售或无偿转让的各种货物和服务的价值；流入包括常住单位从非常住单位购买或无偿得到的各种货物和服务的价值。由于服务活动的提供与使用同时发生，一般把常住单位从本地区外得到的服务作为流入，非常住单位从本地区得到的服务作为流出。

产业部门贡献率

是各产业部门增加值可比价增量与国内生产总值可比价增量之比。

产业部门拉动力

拉动力是指总的经济增长率中带动的百分点数，产业部门拉动力是指在GDP增长中各产业部门拉动的百分点数。其计算公式为：

拉动力（%）=贡献率（%）×GDP增长率（%）

CHONGQING STATISTICAL YEARBOOK

Explanatory Notes on Main Statistical Indicators

☐ Gross Domestic Product (GDP)

Refers to the final products at market prices produced by all resident units in a country (or a region) during a certain period of time. Gross domestic product is expressed in three different perspectives value added, income, and products respectively. The form of value added refers to the total value of all products and services produced by all resident units during a certain period of time minus total value of intimidate input of materials and services of the nature of non-fixed assets or the summation of the value added of all resident units; the form of income includes all the income created by all resident units and distributed primarily to all resident and non-resident units; the form of products refers to all final goods and services of final use by all resident units plus the value of net exports of goods and services. In the practice of national accounting, gross domestic product is calculated with three approaches, i.e. product approach, income approach and expenditure approach, which reflect gross domestic product and its composition from different aspects.

☐ Three Strata of Industry

Classification of economic activities into three strata of industry is a common practice in the world, although the grouping varies to some extent form country to country. In China economic activities are categorized into the following three strata of industry:

Primary industry refers to agriculture, forestry, animal husbandry and fishery and services in support of these industries.

Secondary industry refers to mining and quarrying, manufacturing, production and supply of electricity, water and gas, and construction.

Tertiary industry refers to all other economic activities not included in the primary or secondary industries.

☐ GDP by Income Approach

Refers to the method of measuring the final results of production activities of a country (region) during a given period from the income items produced by all resident units. It includes laborers' remuneration, net taxes on production, depreciation of fixed assets and operating surplus, i.e.:

GDP by income approach =compensation of employee + net taxes on production + depreciation of fixed assets + operating surplus

(Ⅰ) Compensation of Employee refers to the total payment of various forms to employees for the productive activities they are engaged in. It includes wages, bonuses and allowances, which the employees earn in cash or in kind. It also includes the free medical services provided to the employees and the medicine expenses, transport subsidies and social insurance, and housing fund paid by the employers. As regards the individual economy, since compensation of employees is not easily distinguishable from the operating surplus, both parts are treated as compensation of employees.

(Ⅱ) Net Taxes on Production refers to the difference of the taxes on production minus the subsidies on production. The taxes on production refers to the various taxes, extra charges and fees levied on the production units on their production, sale and business activities as well as on some factors of production, such as fixed assets, land and labor force, used in the production activities they are engaged in. In contrast to the taxes on production, the subsidies on production is the unilateral transfer of part of the government's revenue to the production units and is therefore treated as the negative taxes on production, They include subsidies on the loss due to implementation of government policies, price subsidies, etc.

(Ⅲ) Depreciation of Fixed Assets refers to the depreciation of fixed assets drawn in accordance with the stipulated depreciation rate for the purpose of compensating the wear loss of the fixed assets or the depreciation of fixed assets calculated in a fictitious way in accordance with the stipulated unified depreciation rate in the national economic accounting system. It reflects the value of transfer of the fixed assets in the production of the current period. The depreciation of fixed assets in various enterprises and institutions managed as enterprises refers to the depreciation expenses actually drawn and calculated as part of the cost. In the units, which do not draw the depreciation expenses, such as government agencies, institutions not managed as enterprises as well as the houses of residents, the depreciation of fixed assets is the fictitious depreciation, which is calculated in accordance with the stipulated unified depreciation rate. In principle, the depreciation of fixed assets should be calculated on the basis of the re-purchased value of the fixed assets. However, there is no actual condition to re-evaluate all the fixed assets in China. Therefore, the above-mentioned methods are temporarily adopted at present.

(Ⅳ) Operating Surplus refers to the balance of the value added created by the resident units deducting the laborers' remuneration, net taxes on production ant the depreciation of fixed assets. It is equivalent to the business profit of the enterprises plus subsidies on production, but the wages and welfare expenses paid from the profits should be deducted.

□ GDP by Expenditure Approach

Refers to the method of measuring the final results of production activities of a country (region) during a given period from the perspective of final use. It includes final consumption expenditure, total capital formation and net export of goods and services, i.e.:

GDP by expenditure approach = final consumption expenditure + gross capital formation + net export of goods and services

□ Final Consumption Expenditure

Refers to the total expenditure of resident units on final consumption of goods and services from domestic economic territory and abroad to meet the requirements of material, cultural and spiritual life. It excludes the expenditure of non-resident units on consumption in the economic territory of the country. The final consumption expenditure is broken down into household consumption expenditure and government consumption expenditure.

(Ⅰ) Household consumption Expenditure refers to the total expenditure of resident households on the final consumption of goods and services. In addition to the consumption of goods and services bought by the households directly with money, the households consumption expenditure also includes expenditure on goods and services obtained by the households in other ways, i.e. the so-called fictitious consumption expenditure, which includes the following types: (a) the goods and services provided to the households by the employer in the form of payment in kind and transfer in kind; (b) the goods and services produced and consumed by the households themselves, in which the services refer only to the owner-occupied housing and domestic and individual services provided by the paid household workers; (c) financial intermediate services provided by the financial institutions; (d) the insurance services provided by insurance companies.

(Ⅱ) Government consumption Expenditure refers to the expenditure on the consumption of the public services provided by the government to the whole society and the net expenditure on the goods and services provided by the government to the households for free charge or at lower prices. The former equals to the output value of the government services minus the value of operating in come obtained by the government departments. The latter equals to the market value of the goods and services provided by the government to the households minus the value received by the government from the households.

□ Gross Capital Formation

Refers to the net amount of the fixed assets and stock acquired minus those disposed, including the gross fixed assets formation and changes in inventories.

(Ⅰ) Gross fixed capital formation refer to the value of fixed assets purchased, transferred in by the resident units and those produced and used by themselves deducting the value of fixed assets sold and transferred out. It can by classified into total tangible assets formation and total intangible assets formation. The total tangible assets formation include the value of the construction projects, installation projects completed and the equipment, apparatus and instruments purchased as well as the value of land improved, the value of draught animals, breeding stock, milk, wool and recreational animals and the newly increased economic forest in a certain period. The total intangible assets formation includes the prospecting of minerals, the acquisition of computer software, the originals of recreational works and works of literature and arts minus the disposal of them.

(Ⅱ) Changes in Inventories refers to the market value of the change in the physical volume of inventory of resident units during a given period, i.e. the difference between the values at the beginning and the end of the period minus the gains due to the change in prices. The changes in inventories can have a positive or a negative value. A positive value indicates an increase in inventory while a negative value indicates a decrease in inventory. The inventory includes raw materials, fuels and reserve materials purchased by the production units as well as the inventory of finished products, semi-finished products and work-in-progress.

EXPLANATORY NOTES TO MAJOR STATISTICAL INDICATORS

□ Net Export of Goods and Services

Refers to the difference of the exports of goods and services minus the imports of goods and services. The imports include the value of various goods and services sold or gratuitously transferred by the resident units to the non-resident units. The imports include the value of various goods and services purchased or gratuitously acquired by the resident units from the non-resident units. Because the provision of services and the use of them happen simultaneously, the import and export of services by the resident units from abroad is usually treated as import while the acquisition of services by non-resident units in this country is usually treated as export. The export and import of goods are calculated at FOB.

□ Share of the contributions of the industry

Refers to the proportion of the increment of the value-added of each industry to the increase of GDP.

□ Contribution of the industry

Contribution is the driven percentage points to GDP growth. Contribution of the industry is the driven percentage points of each industry to GDP growth. Its calculation formula is:

Contribution (%) = share of contribution (%) × GDP growth rate (%)

第3章

人口与就业

POPULATION AND EMPLOYMENT

简要说明
BRIEF INTRODUCTION

本章内容主要包括全市的户籍人口、常住人口、第五、六次人口普查的主要数据，以及计划生育、就业、工资等情况，由市统计局人口就业处整理编辑。

户籍统计人口资料由市公安局提供；计划生育资料由市人口计划生育委员会提供；失业资料由市人力资源和社会保障局提供；常住人口、人口普查主要数据、就业和工资资料由市统计局人口就业处提供。

The data in this chapter include the basic statistics on the registered population, resident population and the main indicators in the 5th and the 6th population censuses, as well as the statistics on family planning, employment and wages. All the data are prepared and compiled by Division of Population and Employment Statistics, Chongqing Municipal Bureau of Statistics.

The data on registered population are provided by Chongqing Municipal Public Security Bureau; the data on family planning are provided by Chongqing Population and Family Planning Commission; the data on unemployment are provided by Chongqing Municipal Human Resources and Social Security Bureau and the main indicators of resident population, population censuses, employment and wages are provided by Division of Population and Employment Statistics, Chongqing Municipal Bureau of Statistics.

表3.1 主要年份总户数、总人口（户籍统计）
TOTAL HOUSEHOLDS AND TOTAL POPULATION IN MAJOR YEARS (HOUSEHOLD REGISTRATION)

单位：万人 (10 000 persons)

年 份 Year	总户数 （万户） Total Households (10 000 households)	总人口 Total Population	按性别分 By Sex		按农业、非农业分 By Agriculture and Non-agriculture	
			男 Male	女 Female	农 业 Agriculture	非农业 Non-agriculture
1952	401.93	1776.52	927.91	848.61		
1957	434.66	2005.18	1040.82	964.36	1692.77	312.41
1962	442.01	1797.19	916.99	880.20	1528.95	268.24
1965	455.55	1974.89	1010.19	964.70	1685.08	289.81
1970	518.02	2289.64	1173.57	1116.07	1989.66	299.98
1975	579.36	2592.59	1332.89	1259.70	2280.39	312.20
1978	601.07	2635.56	1357.98	1277.58	2304.66	330.90
1980	610.19	2664.79	1376.22	1288.57	2291.51	373.28
1985	684.46	2768.26	1437.35	1330.91	2310.89	457.37
1986	716.53	2807.60	1458.75	1348.85	2343.23	464.37
1987	751.96	2845.14	1478.88	1366.26	2370.06	475.08
1988	784.83	2873.34	1494.20	1379.14	2390.36	482.98
1989	812.65	2897.01	1507.74	1389.27	2405.25	491.76
1990	833.78	2920.90	1520.83	1400.07	2427.92	492.98
1991	844.66	2938.99	1531.11	1407.88	2439.61	499.38
1992	849.77	2950.78	1538.46	1412.32	2438.94	511.84
1993	855.75	2964.92	1546.50	1418.42	2438.27	526.65
1994	870.20	2985.59	1558.05	1427.54	2440.41	545.18
1995	879.35	3001.77	1566.86	1434.91	2442.33	559.44
1996	888.56	3022.77	1577.97	1444.80	2445.65	577.12
1997	897.78	3042.92	1588.10	1454.82	2448.34	594.58
1998	907.17	3059.69	1596.88	1462.81	2445.66	614.03
1999	922.73	3072.34	1602.42	1469.92	2437.18	635.16
2000	938.87	3091.09	1611.68	1479.41	2430.20	660.89
2001	950.56	3097.91	1614.91	1483.00	2408.39	689.52
2002	961.69	3113.83	1623.13	1490.70	2392.38	721.45
2003	977.01	3130.10	1631.66	1498.44	2376.18	753.92
2004	988.59	3144.23	1637.18	1507.05	2358.40	785.83
2005	1010.41	3169.16	1649.26	1519.90	2351.88	817.28
2006	1030.66	3198.87	1662.77	1536.10	2353.44	845.43
2007	1056.97	3235.32	1681.10	1554.22	2358.35	876.97
2008	1080.15	3257.05	1690.56	1566.49	2349.67	907.38
2009	1110.70	3275.61	1697.69	1577.92	2326.92	948.69
2010	1154.83	3303.45	1709.03	1594.42	2196.45	1107.00
2011	1205.20	3329.81	1720.53	1609.28	2052.17	1277.64

表3.2 主要年份人口自然变动（户籍统计）
POPULATION NATURAL DYNAMICS IN MAJOR YEARS (HOUSEHOLD REGISTRATION)

单位：万人、‰ (10 000 persons，‰)

年 份 Year	出 生 Birth		死 亡 Death		自然增长 Natural Growth	
	人 口 Population	出生率 Birth Rate	人 口 Population	死亡率 Death Rate	人 口 Population	自然增长率 Natural Growth Rate
1957	54.20	27.32	21.78	10.98	32.42	16.34
1962	43.72	24.36	27.87	15.53	15.85	8.83
1965	74.01	38.03	21.43	11.01	52.58	27.02
1970	87.78	38.99	22.11	9.82	65.67	29.17
1975	72.03	28.06	21.33	8.31	50.70	19.75
1978	26.09	9.91	17.18	6.52	8.91	3.39
1980	29.68	11.16	17.19	6.46	12.49	4.70
1985	36.13	13.10	18.76	6.80	17.37	6.30
1986	54.47	19.54	18.36	6.59	36.11	12.95
1987	48.72	17.24	18.42	6.52	30.30	10.72
1988	38.58	13.49	19.43	6.79	19.15	6.70
1989	39.79	13.79	19.99	6.93	19.80	6.86
1990	42.53	14.62	19.59	6.73	22.94	7.89
1991	37.61	12.83	19.20	6.55	18.41	6.28
1992	35.62	12.09	20.89	7.09	14.73	5.00
1993	35.75	12.09	20.23	6.84	15.52	5.25
1994	40.05	13.46	19.95	6.70	20.10	6.76
1995	39.39	13.16	21.45	7.17	17.94	5.99
1996	41.06	13.63	21.62	7.18	19.44	6.45
1997	36.99	12.20	20.95	6.91	16.04	5.29
1998	35.51	11.64	21.64	7.09	13.87	4.55
1999	30.68	10.01	20.68	6.74	10.00	3.27
2000	35.22	11.43	24.59	7.98	10.63	3.45
2001	26.26	8.48	18.76	6.06	7.50	2.42
2002	28.65	9.20	18.07	5.80	10.58	3.40
2003	30.00	9.61	18.05	5.78	11.95	3.83
2004	33.72	10.74	23.44	7.47	10.28	3.27
2005	30.66	9.71	13.88	4.40	16.78	5.31
2006	36.57	11.49	14.89	4.68	21.68	6.81
2007	44.66	13.88	16.56	5.15	28.10	8.73
2008	43.26	13.33	24.56	7.57	18.70	5.76
2009	40.82	12.50	26.13	8.00	14.69	4.50
2010	62.83	19.10	38.97	11.85	23.86	7.25
2011	41.27	12.44	19.55	5.90	21.72	6.54

表3.3 常住人口及城镇化率（1996－2011年）
RESIDENT POPULATION AND URBANIZATION RATE (1996-2011)

单位：万人 (10 000 persons)

年 份 Year	常住人口 Resident Population	其 中 of which		城镇化率 (%) Urbanization Rate (%)
		城 镇 Urban	乡 村 Rural	
1996	2875.30	848.21	2027.09	29.5
1997	2873.36	890.74	1982.62	31.0
1998	2870.75	935.86	1934.89	32.6
1999	2860.37	981.11	1879.26	34.3
2000	2848.82	1013.88	1834.94	35.6
2001	2829.21	1058.12	1771.09	37.4
2002	2814.83	1123.12	1691.71	39.9
2003	2803.19	1174.55	1628.64	41.9
2004	2793.32	1215.42	1577.90	43.5
2005	2798.00	1265.95	1532.05	45.2
2006	2808.00	1311.29	1496.71	46.7
2007	2816.00	1361.35	1454.65	48.3
2008	2839.00	1419.09	1419.91	50.0
2009	2859.00	1474.92	1384.08	51.6
2010	2884.62	1529.55	1355.07	53.0
2011	2919.00	1605.96	1313.04	55.0

表3.4 1%人口抽样调查（2010－2011年）
1% SAMPLE SURVEY OF POPULATION (2010-2011)

单位：万人 (10 000 persons)

项　目	Item	2010	2011
常住人口	Resident Population	2884.62	2919.00
#城　镇	Urban	1529.55	1605.96
乡　村	Rural	1355.07	1313.04
#男　性	Male	1460.89	1476.81
女　性	Female	1423.73	1442.19
#0-14岁	Age 0-14	489.80	493.02
15-64岁	Age 15-64	2061.41	2088.25
65岁及以上	Age 65 and Over	333.41	337.73
外出人口	Population outside Residential Area	985.34	1004.52
#外出至市外	Outside Chongqing	522.54	528.57
市外外来人口	Population from Other Areas to Chongqing	104.20	121.00
城镇化率（%）	Urbanization Rate (%)	53.02	55.02
一小时经济圈	One-Hour Economic Sphere	64.36	66.24
渝东南翼	Northeast of Chongqing	29.96	31.58
渝东北翼	Southeast of Chongqing	36.94	38.63
出生人口	Birth Population	29.43	28.67
出生率（‰）	Birth Rate (‰)	10.25	9.88
死亡人口	Dead Population	18.55	19.47
死亡率（‰）	Death Rate (‰)	6.46	6.71
自然增长人口	Natural Growing Population	10.88	9.20
自然增长率（‰）	Natural Growth Rate (‰)	3.79	3.17

表3.5 第五次人口普查基本情况
BASIC STATISTICS ON POPULATION CENSUSES IN 2000

指　标	Item	2000
总人口（万人）	**Total Population (10 000 persons)**	**3051.28**
男	Male	1584.15
女	Female	1467.13
性别比（女=100）	Sex Ratio (female=100)	107.98
家庭户户数（万户）	**Family Households (10 000 households)**	**914.16**
家庭户规模（人/户）	**Average Family Size (person/household)**	**3.23**
各年龄组人口（万人）	**Population by Age Group (10 000 persons)**	
0-14岁	Age 0-14	666.29
15-64岁	Age 15-64	2140.45
65岁及以上	Age 65 and Over	244.54
预期寿命（岁）	**Life Expectancy (years old)**	71.9
城乡人口（万人）	**Population by Residence (10 000 persons)**	
城镇人口	Urban Population	1009.55
乡村人口	Rural Population	2041.73
民族人口（万人，%）	**Nationality Population (10 000 persons, %)**	
汉　族	Han Nationality	2853.92
占总人口比重	Percentage as Total Population	93.5
少数民族	Minority Nationalities	197.36
占总人口比重	Percentage as Total Population	6.5
每十万人拥有的各种受教育程度人口（人）	**Population with Various Education Attainment Per 100 000 Population (person)**	
大专及以上	Junior College and Above	2819
高中和中专	Senior Secondary/Secondary Technical School	8600
初　中	Junior Secondary School	29474
小　学	Primary School	43357
文盲人口及文盲率	**Illiterate Population and Illiterate Rate**	
文盲人口（万人）	Illiterate Population (10 000 persons)	212.24
文盲率（%）	Illiterate Rate (%)	8.9

注：此表是按照直接登记直接汇总的数据，不包括人口普查漏登人口（漏登率为1.31%）。
Note:The data in this table are the directly registered and directly summarized data, not including the underreported population in the population census (the underreporting rate is 1.31%).

表3.6 第五次人口普查基本情况
BASIC STATISTICS ON POPULATION CENSUSES IN 2000

指 标	Item	2000
总人口（万人）	**Total Population (10 000 persons)**	**2848.82**
男	Male	1460.57
女	Female	1388.25
性别比（女=100）	Sex Ratio (female=100)	105.21
家庭户户数（万户）	**Family Households (10 000 households)**	**923.4**
家庭户规模（人/户）	**Average Family Size (person/household)**	**3.02**
各年龄组人口（万人）	**Population by Age Group (10 000 persons)**	
0-14岁	Age 0-14	665.20
15-64岁	Age 15-64	1931.78
65岁及以上	Age 65 and Over	251.84
预期寿命（岁）	**Life Expectancy (years old)**	**71.9**
城乡人口（万人）	**Population by Residence (10 000 persons)**	
城镇人口	Urban Population	1013.88
乡村人口	Rural Population	1834.94
民族人口（万人，%）	**Nationality Population (10 000 persons, %)**	
汉 族	Han Nationality	2664.50
占总人口比重	Percentage as Total Population	93.5
少数民族	Minority Nationalities	184.32
占总人口比重	Percentage as Total Population	6.5
每十万人拥有的各种受教育程度人口（人）	**Population with Various Education Attainment Per 100 000 Population (person)**	
大专及以上	Junior College and Above	3154
高中和中专	Senior Secondary/Secondary Technical School	8815
初 中	Junior Secondary School	27190
小 学	Primary School	42863
文盲人口及文盲率	**Illiterate Population and Illiterate Rate**	
文盲人口（万人）	Illiterate Population (10 000 persons)	212.24
文盲率（%）	Illiterate Rate (%)	9.7

注：此表为常住人口推算数据。
Note:The data in the table above are calculated on the basis of resident population.

表3.7 第六次人口普查基本情况
BASIC STATISTICS ON POPULATION CENSUSES IN 2010

指　标	Item	2010
总人口（万人）	**Total Population (10 000 persons)**	**2884.62**
男	Male	1460.89
女	Female	1423.73
性别比（女=100）	Sex Ratio (female=100)	102.61
家庭户户数（万户）	**Family Households (10 000 households)**	**1000.10**
家庭户规模（人/户）	**Average Family Size (person/household)**	**2.70**
各年龄组人口（万人）	**Population by Age Group (10 000 persons)**	
0-14岁	Age 0-14	489.80
15-64岁	Age 15-64	2061.41
65岁及以上	Age 65 and Over	333.41
城乡人口（万人）	**Population by Residence (10 000 persons)**	
城镇人口	Urban Population	1529.55
乡村人口	Rural Population	1355.07
民族人口（万人，%）	**Nationality Population (10 000 persons, %)**	
汉　族	Han Nationality	2690.91
占总人口比重	Percentage as Total Population	93.3
少数民族	Minority Nationalities	193.71
占总人口比重	Percentage as Total Population	6.7
每十万人拥有的各种受教育程度人口（人）	**Population with Various Education Attainment Per 100 000 Population (person)**	
大专及以上	Junior College and Above	8478
高中和中专	Senior Secondary/Secondary Technical School	13223
初　中	Junior Secondary School	33441
小　学	Primary School	33653
文盲人口及文盲率	**Illiterate Population and Illiterate Rate**	
文盲人口（万人）	Illiterate Population (10 000 persons)	121.52
文盲率（%）	Illiterate Rate (%)	5.1

表3.8 六次人口普查主要指标
MAIN INDICATORS OF SIX POPULATION CENSUSES

单位：万人、% (10 000 persons，%)

普查时间	Census Time	总人口 Total Population 合 计 Total	男 Male	女 Female	性别比(女=100) Sex Ratio (female =100)	年平均增长率 Annual Average Growth Rate
第一次人口普查（1953年7月1日）	First Population Census (July 1, 1953)	1766.39	924.56	841.83	109.83	
第二次人口普查（1964年7月1日）	Second Population Census (July 1, 1964)	1889.17	969.02	920.15	105.31	0.61
第三次人口普查（1982年7月1日）	Third Population Census (July 1, 1982)	2705.89	1402.46	1303.43	107.60	2.02
第四次人口普查（1990年7月1日）	Fourth Population Census (July 1, 1990)	2886.62	1499.83	1386.79	108.15	0.81
第五次人口普查（2000年11月1日）	Fifth Population Census (November 1, 2000)	3090.45	1604.95	1485.50	108.04	0.66
第五次人口普查（2000年11月1日）（按常住人口推算）	Fifth Population Census (November 1, 2000)	2848.82	1460.57	1388.25	105.21	-0.13
第六次人口普查（2010年11月1日）	Sixth Population Census (November 1, 2010)	2884.62	1460.89	1423.73	102.61	0.12

表3.9 计划生育基本情况（1986－2011年）
BASIC STATISTICS ON FAMILY PLANNING (1986-2011)

单位：万人、% (10 000 persons，%)

年 份 Year	政策性生育率 Policy Fertility Rate	已婚育龄妇女人数 Married Women at Childbearing Age	领独生子女证人数 Women with Only-child Certificates	领证率 Coverage of Only-child Certificates	采取节育措施人数 Women under Contraception	避孕率 Contraception Rate
1986	90.88	481.28	109.56	68.74	424.89	88.28
1987	90.16	503.67	126.44	71.91	451.19	89.58
1988	93.83	523.17	141.28	72.14	480.27	91.80
1989	92.78	540.80	151.72	70.35	491.35	90.86
1990	94.15	560.09	166.56	70.53	512.38	91.48
1991	95.11	577.54	178.27	69.31	527.88	91.40
1992	95.83	589.35	188.00	68.34	538.37	91.35
1993	93.23	599.23	199.97		548.27	91.50
1994	86.58	611.48	206.76		559.62	91.52
1995	89.22	625.71	220.32		573.38	91.64
1996	88.73	637.31	227.59	65.45	587.93	92.25
1997	91.94	644.56	230.99	64.11	588.75	91.34
1998	85.06	644.68	219.05	59.69	589.28	91.40
1999	94.09	640.70	214.79	57.43	587.94	91.77
2000	91.26	639.20	217.43	57.11	589.95	92.29
2001	91.05	632.25	203.30	53.04	583.65	92.31
2002	92.19	620.38	180.36	47.65	571.18	92.07
2003	92.39	622.26	195.38	51.11	571.87	91.90
2004	92.95	615.20	200.49	52.42	564.60	91.77
2005	92.57	618.97	212.37	55.08	569.74	92.05
2006	90.93	626.73	203.23	52.07	572.73	91.38
2007	75.62	637.95	198.86	51.62	579.79	90.88
2008	85.05	501.74	131.84	43.54	454.63	90.61
2009	89.91	494.34	138.22	46.04	449.13	90.85
2010	89.06	500.02	133.28	43.93	454.08	90.81
2011	86.95	495.79	124.73	41.89	440.87	88.92

表3.10 从业人员基本情况（1985－2011年）
BASIC STATISTICS ON EMPLOYMENT (1985-2011)

单位：万人 (10 000 persons)

年 份 Year	从业人员总计 Total Employment	其 中 of which #城 镇 Urban	按经济类型分 By Ownership 国 有 State-owned	集 体 Collective-owned	私营和个体 Private and Individuals	其 他 Others
1985	1432.03	269.37				
1986	1469.13	275.35				
1987	1507.33	282.39				
1988	1512.49	288.70				
1989	1540.03	291.29				
1990	1569.34	296.92				
1991	1620.67	307.87				
1992	1662.58	313.51				
1993	1658.95	310.05				
1994	1729.55	326.75				
1995	1709.26	347.06				
1996	1719.43	463.98	198.16	1228.60	280.24	12.43
1997	1715.40	483.74	189.07	1201.03	307.29	18.01
1998	1710.97	505.22	175.52	1176.65	334.24	24.56
1999	1699.06	518.40	161.15	1151.98	354.15	31.78
2000	1661.16	528.97	149.28	1109.96	365.86	36.06
2001	1616.08	539.80	136.63	1058.10	379.86	41.49
2002	1551.77	549.17	130.66	975.92	395.96	49.23
2003	1499.99	560.28	125.88	903.90	412.41	57.80
2004	1471.34	573.97	124.72	854.48	425.18	66.96
2005	1456.30	589.27	123.50	822.48	437.72	72.60
2006	1454.77	602.99	123.90	789.42	457.52	83.93
2007	1468.87	631.65	115.79	765.19	484.88	103.01
2008	1492.43	665.74	119.83	746.54	514.89	111.17
2009	1513.00	696.82	119.79	727.99	546.66	118.56
2010	1539.95	733.70	125.29	701.34	583.02	130.30
2011	1585.16	790.70	131.00	647.82	628.15	178.19

表3.10 续表 continued

年 份 Year	按产业分 By Sector			分产业比重（%） Compositon By Sector		
	第一产业 Primary Industry	第二产业 Secondary Industry	第三产业 Tertiary Industry	第一产业 Primary Industry	第二产业 Secondary Industry	第三产业 Tertiary Industry
1985	1042.22	223.37	166.44	72.8	15.6	11.6
1986	1048.32	241.66	179.15	71.4	16.4	12.2
1987	1064.06	258.93	184.34	70.6	17.2	12.2
1988	1056.49	262.83	193.17	69.8	17.4	12.8
1989	1082.41	263.81	193.81	70.3	17.1	12.6
1990	1103.04	263.86	202.44	70.3	16.8	12.9
1991	1130.47	275.72	214.48	69.8	17.0	13.2
1992	1118.59	277.77	266.22	67.3	16.7	16.0
1993	1088.70	287.88	282.37	65.6	17.4	17.0
1994	1062.90	301.13	365.52	61.5	17.4	21.1
1995	1018.30	310.88	380.08	59.6	18.2	22.2
1996	1001.89	320.31	397.23	58.3	18.6	23.1
1997	989.07	313.77	412.56	57.6	18.3	24.1
1998	979.48	303.18	428.31	57.3	17.7	25.0
1999	959.71	296.12	443.23	56.5	17.4	26.1
2000	920.92	290.23	450.01	55.4	17.5	27.1
2001	870.52	287.31	458.25	53.9	17.8	28.3
2002	801.04	285.09	465.64	51.6	18.4	30.0
2003	742.90	280.83	476.26	49.5	18.7	31.8
2004	704.22	280.73	486.39	47.8	19.1	33.1
2005	678.32	283.08	494.90	46.6	19.4	34.0
2006	664.35	286.46	503.96	45.7	19.7	34.6
2007	658.52	294.43	515.92	44.8	20.1	35.1
2008	652.19	307.66	532.58	43.7	20.6	35.7
2009	638.08	326.04	548.88	42.2	21.5	36.3
2010	621.29	351.86	566.80	40.3	22.9	36.8
2011	604.38	390.80	589.98	38.1	24.7	37.2

表3.11 从业人员年末数（1999－2011年）
TOTAL EMPLOYMENT AT YEAR-END (1999-2011)

单位：万人 (10 000 persons)

指 标	Item	1999	2000	2001	2002	2003	2004
从业人员总计	**Total Employment**	**1699.06**	**1661.16**	**1616.08**	**1551.77**	**1499.99**	**1471.34**
城 镇	Urban	518.40	528.97	539.80	549.17	560.28	573.97
乡 村	Rural	1180.66	1132.19	1076.28	1002.60	939.71	897.37
按经济类型分	**By Ownership**						
国有经济	State-owned	161.15	149.28	136.63	130.66	125.88	124.72
集体经济	Collective-owned	1151.98	1109.96	1058.10	975.92	903.90	854.48
私 营	Private	66.43	74.92	84.44	95.22	105.95	112.91
个 体	Individual	287.72	290.94	295.42	300.74	306.46	312.27
其他经济	Others	31.78	36.06	41.49	49.23	57.80	66.96
#联 营	Joint Ownership	0.63	0.86	4.11	4.93	5.78	6.84
股份制	Shareholding	10.95	11.49	13.21	15.55	15.72	16.71
外商投资	Foreign-funded	2.42	2.74	2.86	2.91	3.23	4.16
港澳台投资	Funded by Hong Kong, Macao and Taiwan	2.50	2.44	2.66	2.25	2.55	2.33
按行业分	**By Sector**						
第一产业	Primary Industry	959.71	920.92	870.52	801.04	742.90	704. 22
第二产业	Secondary Industry	296.12	290.23	287.31	285.09	280.83	280.73
采矿业	Mining and Quarrying	17.89	16.59	15.72	15.14	14.00	14.14
制造业	Manufacturing	160.07	156.02	152.59	149.91	146.38	144.23
电力、燃气及水的生产和供应业	Electricity, Gas & Water Production and Supply	6.18	6.20	6.22	6.26	6.27	6.32
建筑业	Construction	111.98	111.42	112.78	113.78	114.18	116.04
第三产业	Tertiary Industry	443.23	450.01	458.25	465.64	476.26	486.39
交通运输、仓储及邮政业	Transportation, Storage, Posta Servicesl	40.02	40.23	40.93	41.02	42.11	43.25
信息传输、计算机服务和软件业	Data Transmission, Computer Service and Software	5.60	5.91	6.03	6.14	6.34	6.58
批发与零售业	Wholesale and Retail Trade	113.05	115.65	117.43	118.87	120.03	121.16
住宿和餐饮业	Hotels and Restaurants	70.18	70.52	71.14	72.03	73.36	74.27
金融业	Financing	6.38	6.41	6.46	6.53	6.61	6.65
房地产业	Real Estate	4.88	5.03	5.11	5.22	5.45	6.11
租赁与商务服务业	Renting and Business Activities	16.09	16.34	16.95	17.53	18.23	19.33
科学研究、技术服务与地质勘查业	Scientific Research, Technical Services and Geological Prospecting	7.58	7.71	7.96	8.15	8.25	8.35
水利、环境和公共设施管理业	Administration of Water Conservancy,Environment and Public Utilities	5.26	5.31	5.40	5.50	5.56	5.71
居民服务和其他服务业	Personal Services and Other Services	108.75	110.16	112.59	115.05	118.23	122.36
教 育	Education	29.79	30.59	31.69	32.09	33.33	33.68
卫生、社会保障和社会福利业	Public Health, Social Security and Social Welfare	12.98	13.00	13.08	13.18	13.41	13.50
文化、体育与娱乐业	Culture, Sports and Entertainment	2.73	2.74	2.79	2.84	2.88	2.94
公共管理与社会组织	Public Administration and Social Organizations	19.94	20.41	20.69	21.49	22.47	22.50

表3.11 续表 continued

单位：万人 (10 000 persons)

指　标	Item	2005	2006	2007	2008	2009	2010	2011
从业人员总计	**Total Employment**	**1456.30**	**1454.77**	**1468.87**	**1492.43**	**1513.00**	**1539.95**	**1585.16**
城　镇	Urban	589.27	602.99	631.65	665.74	696.82	733.70	790.70
乡　村	Rural	867.03	851.78	837.22	826.69	816.18	806.25	794.46
按经济类型分	**By Ownership**							
国有经济	State-owned	123.50	123.90	115.79	119.83	119.79	125.29	131.00
集体经济	Collective-owned	822.48	789.42	765.19	746.54	727.99	701.34	647.82
私　营	Private	118.48	130.28	151.49	175.00	203.50	235.10	271.87
个　体	Individual	319.24	327.24	333.39	339.89	343.16	347.92	356.28
其他经济	Others	72.60	83.93	103.01	111.17	118.56	130.30	178.19
#联　营	Joint Ownership	5.57	4.62	2.03	1.95	2.56	2.36	1.55
股份制	Share Holding	14.84	12.86	16.47	21.04	22.48	24.91	30.00
外商投资	Foreign-funded	4.86	5.01	7.06	7.33	8.47	9.43	13.14
港澳台投资	Funded by Hong Kong, Macao and Taiwan	2.32	2.33	2.80	2.40	3.89	5.20	14.55
按行业分	**By Sector**							
第一产业	Primary Industry	678.32	664.35	658.52	652.19	638.08	621.29	604.38
第二产业	Secondary Industry	283.08	286.46	294.43	307.66	326.04	351.86	390.80
采矿业	Mining and Quarrying	14.66	14.77	16.83	19.77	22.24	24.84	28.11
制造业	Manufacturing	144.46	145.72	148.33	152.11	159.37	168.67	190.51
电力、燃气及水的生产和供应业	Electricity, Gas & Water Production and Supply	6.52	6.85	7.14	7.43	7.91	8.20	8.54
建筑业	Construction	117.44	119.12	122.13	128.35	136.52	150.15	163.64
第三产业	Tertiary Industry	494.90	503.96	515.92	532.58	548.88	566.80	589.98
交通运输、仓储及邮政业	Transportation, Storage, Posta Servicesl	44.29	45.05	46.17	47.25	48.42	50.12	53.49
信息传输、计算机服务和软件业	Data Transmission, Computer Service and Software	7.03	7.39	8.09	8.58	8.85	9.43	10.57
批发与零售业	Wholesale and Retail Trade	122.88	125.63	127.29	131.46	134.72	138.22	142.25
住宿和餐饮业	Hotels and Restaurants	75.40	77.22	78.76	80.28	82.64	85.07	88.22
金融业	Financing	6.76	6.90	8.03	9.09	9.74	10.85	12.34
房地产业	Real Estate	6.83	7.74	8.81	10.24	12.02	14.66	16.83
租赁与商务服务业	Renting and Business Activities	19.97	19.97	21.41	22.50	23.41	24.63	26.31
科学研究、技术服务与地质勘查业	Scientific Research, Technical Services and Geological Prospecting	8.39	8.43	8.57	8.75	8.93	9.05	9.44
水利、环境和公共设施管理业	Administration of Water Conservancy,Environment and Public Utilities	5.76	5.94	6.19	6.44	6.78	7.03	7.45
居民服务和其他服务业	Personal Services and Other Services	124.75	126.15	126.62	129.21	131.76	132.97	133.83
教　育	Education	33.91	34.20	35.01	36.02	36.91	38.17	39.88
卫生、社会保障和社会福利业	Public Health, Social Security and Social Welfare	13.51	13.65	13.94	14.55	15.38	16.10	17.42
文化、体育与娱乐业	Culture, Sports and Entertainment	2.96	3.05	3.44	3.88	4.08	4.30	4.64
公共管理与社会组织	Public Administration and Social Organizations	22.46	22.64	23.59	24.33	25.24	26.29	27.31

表3.12 城镇从业人员年末数（2010－2011年）

TOTAL URBAN EMPLOYMENT AT YEAR-END (2010-2011)

单位：万人 (10 000 persons)

指　标	Item	2010	2011
从业人员总计	**Total Employment**	**733.70**	**790. 70**
按经济类型分	**By Ownership**		
国有经济	State-owned	125.29	131.00
集体经济	Collective-owned	86.97	44.33
私　营	Private	194.43	231.00
个　体	Individual	196.71	206.18
其他经济	Others	130.30	178.19
#联　营	Joint Ownership	2.36	1.55
股份制	Share Holding	24.91	30.00
外商投资	Foreign-funded	9.43	13.14
港澳台投资	Funded by Hong Kong, Macao and Taiwan	5.20	14.55
按行业分	**By Sector**		
第一产业	Primary Industry	46.52	41.79
第二产业	Secondary Industry	286.16	325.65
采矿业	Mining and Quarrying	18.77	21.88
制造业	Manufacturing	133.84	155.32
电力、燃气及水的生产和供应业	Electricity, Gas & Water Production and Supply	8.20	8.54
建筑业	Construction	125.35	139.91
第三产业	Tertiary Industry	401.02	423.26
交通运输、仓储及邮政业	Transportation, Storage, Postal Services	29.49	31.83
信息传输、计算机服务和软件业	Data Transmission, Computer Service and Software	8.66	10.02
批发与零售业	Wholesale and Retail Trade	93.88	97.73
住宿和餐饮业	Hotels and Restaurants	58.54	60.60
金融业	Financing	10.85	12.34
房地产业	Real Estate	14.66	16.83
租赁与商务服务业	Renting and Business Activities	16.42	18.05
科学研究、技术服务与地质勘查业	Scientific Research, Technical Services and Geological Prospecting	7.30	7.73
水利、环境和公共设施管理业	Administration of Water Conservancy, Environment and Public Utilities	4.78	5.29
居民服务和其他服务业	Personal Services and Other Services	79.57	81.50
教　育	Education	35.27	37.02
卫生、社会保障和社会福利业	Public Health, Social Security and Social Welfare	14.06	15.61
文化、体育与娱乐业	Culture, Sports and Entertainment	3.99	4.27
公共管理与社会组织	Public Administration and Social Organizations	23.55	24.44

表3.13 主要年份城镇非私营单位职工人数
NUMBER OF STAFF AND WORKERS OF URBAN NON-PRIVATE UNITS IN MAJOR YEARS

单位：万人 (10 000 persons)

年份 Year	合计 Total	按产业分 By Industry			按经济类型分 By Registration		
		第一产业 Primary Industry	第二产业 Secondary Industry	第三产业 Tertiary Industry	国有 State-owned	集体 Collective-owned	其他 Others
1949	5.34				5.34		
1952	47.62				47.62		
1957	71.19				71.19		
1962	80.79				80.79		
1965	91.96				91.96		
1970	109.98				109.98		
1975	127.99				127.99		
1978	154.44				154.44		
1980	220.06				162.97	57.09	
1985	257.63	4.80	144.90	107.93	186.74	70.81	0.08
1986	264.01	4.79	151.13	108.09	191.47	72.43	0.11
1987	270.46	5.39	153.80	111.27	196.79	73.36	0.31
1988	277.70	5.45	157.28	114.97	201.88	75.42	0.40
1989	280.69	5.66	158.65	116.38	205.98	74.01	0.70
1990	285.68	5.68	159.47	120.53	209.61	75.16	0.91
1991	293.59	5.68	163.94	123.97	215.78	76.58	1.23
1992	297.07	5.46	165.35	126.26	218.41	76.94	1.72
1993	290.02	4.16	164.74	121.12	215.05	70.79	4.18
1994	293.23	4.24	162.90	126.09	212.02	71.03	10.18
1995	294.25	4.35	160.58	129.32	212.34	69.85	12.06
1996	294.63	4.43	159.37	130.83	214.01	67.47	13.15
1997	289.29	4.13	153.73	131.43	211.13	61.64	16.52
1998	236.61	3.83	115.89	116.89	172.24	40.91	23.46
1999	222.34	3.58	106.07	112.69	158.64	35.54	28.16
2000	208.87	3.43	96.01	109.43	146.91	29.74	32.22
2001	201.23	2.94	91.73	106.56	134.79	23.77	42.67
2002	199.93	2.64	92.63	104.66	128.41	20.82	50.70
2003	204.99	2.46	97.56	104.97	121.27	18.94	64.78
2004	208.04	2.35	100.50	105.19	120.85	16.85	70.34
2005	209.66	2.14	101.00	106.52	120.09	13.66	75.91
2006	212.97	2.12	102.22	108.63	120.37	12.22	80.38
2007	220.84	1.80	104.87	114.17	112.55	10.63	97.66
2008	229.59	1.80	108.92	118.87	115.19	10.23	104.17
2009	234.90	1.68	111.88	121.34	114.32	9.88	110.70
2010	250.22	1.79	121.20	127.23	118.76	10.26	121.20
2011	292.10	1.51	149.34	141.25	116.47	9.88	165.75

注：“城镇非私营单位”与原“城镇经济单位”口径相同（以下各表同）。
Note: The scope of "urban economic units" is identical to the former "urban non-private units"(the same for the tables below).

表3.14 主要年份城镇非私营单位职工工资总额
TOTAL WAGES OF STAFF AND WORKERS OF Urban NON-PRIVATE ECONOMIC UNITS IN MAJOR YEARS

单位：万元 (10 000 yuan)

年 份 Year	合 计 Total Wages	按产业分 By Industry			按经济类型分 By Registration		
		第一产业 Primary Industry	第二产业 Secondary Industry	第三产业 Tertiary Industry	国 有 State-owned	集 体 Collective-owned	其 他 Others
1949	1368				1368		
1952	18577				18577		
1957	37710				37710		
1962	45532				45532		
1965	51159				51159		
1970	60866				60866		
1975	74645				74645		
1978	91615				91615		
1980	159426				125305	34121	
1985	259688	4528	149468	105692	195684	63939	65
1986	300882	4960	177126	118796	233311	67396	175
1987	349808	5802	206458	137548	271210	78190	408
1988	435140	6771	256248	172121	340494	94048	598
1989	497553	7713	294228	195612	392179	104065	1309
1990	573310	8232	335056	230022	454776	116718	1816
1991	637968	9313	373271	255384	501204	134105	2659
1992	728780	10757	415886	302137	577638	146315	4827
1993	831520	8623	489684	333213	664939	152705	13876
1994	1144546	12990	618503	513053	902585	190980	50981
1995	1309344	15878	715405	578061	1016056	222720	70568
1996	1454905	18116	782060	654729	1132834	237510	84561
1997	1580484	17286	828011	735187	1225441	244245	110798
1998	1588049	18478	815904	753667	1223697	201028	163324
1999	1606804	19304	760591	826909	1207329	184757	214718
2000	1732318	20606	777295	934417	1290215	176693	265410
2001	1941508	21510	833110	1086888	1381940	158228	401340
2002	2196175	21857	921105	1253213	1520518	159655	516002
2003	2535070	22059	1104724	1408287	1661336	160049	713685
2004	2939800	23358	1291498	1624944	1904154	164332	871314
2005	3458237	23019	1503886	1931332	2224886	157943	1075408
2006	4034057	26173	1757357	2250527	2542465	165315	1326277
2007	4998743	27226	2111205	2860312	2814125	160900	2023718
2008	6137760	30232	2592679	3514849	3390954	177772	2569034
2009	7161387	31720	2989883	4139784	3855720	198908	3106759
2010	8629547	37250	3690436	4901861	4435431	242086	3952030
2011	11565329	48201	5241459	6275669	5206171	274421	6084737

表3.15 主要年份城镇非私营单位职工平均工资
AVERAGE WAGES OF STAFF AND WORKERS OF URBAN NON-PRIVATE UNITS IN MAJOR YEARS

单位：元 (yuan)

年 份 Year	平均工资 Average Wages	按产业分 By Industry			按经济类型分 By Registration		
		第一产业 Primary Industry	第二产业 Secondary Industry	第三产业 Tertiary Industry	国 有 State-owned	集 体 Collective-owned	其 他 Others
1949	284				284		
1952	330				330		
1957	535				535		
1962	448				448		
1965	588				588		
1970	581				581		
1975	588				588		
1978	632				632		
1980	737				783	606	
1985	1038				1110	930	861
1986	1154	1034	1197	1100	1234	941	1842
1987	1309	1140	1354	1254	1397	1073	1943
1988	1588	1249	1647	1522	1708	1264	1685
1989	1782	1388	1863	1691	1923	1393	2380
1990	2025	1452	2106	1942	2189	1565	2256
1991	2203	1640	2308	2089	2356	1768	2485
1992	2468	1931	2526	2415	2661	1906	3273
1993	2833	1793	2967	2694	3068	2067	4704
1994	3925	3093	3776	4151	4227	2693	7100
1995	4508	3657	4423	4527	4789	3162	6346
1996	5010	4127	4889	5033	5352	3603	6607
1997	5502	4188	5412	5649	5828	4016	6845
1998	6433	4713	6529	6394	6732	4891	6907
1999	7182	5296	7184	7240	7541	5200	7641
2000	8020	5884	7704	8372	7431	4534	7450
2001	9523	6521	8925	10053	10035	6614	9503
2002	10960	7587	9905	11905	11745	7601	10339
2003	12440	8877	11425	13462	13616	8552	11316
2004	14357	9871	13125	15624	15847	9839	12831
2005	16630	10676	14962	18345	18614	11614	14373
2006	19215	12279	17434	21031	21402	13522	16805
2007	23098	14852	20703	25401	25365	15149	21336
2008	26985	16571	24134	29736	29761	17444	24864
2009	30965	18864	27445	34313	34023	20337	28723
2010	35326	20894	31555	39043	38075	24205	33552
2011	40042	31868	35592	45353	44585	28490	37543

表3.16 城镇非私营单位职工人数（2010－2011年）

NUMBER OF STAFF AND WORKERS IN NON-PRIVATE ECONOMIC UNITS (2010-2011)

单位：万人 (10 000 persons)

指 标	Item	合 计 Total		其中 of which #国 有 State-owned		#集 体 Collective-owned	
		2010	2011	2010	2011	2010	2011
总 计	**Total**	**250.22**	**292.10**	**118.76**	**116.47**	**10.26**	**9.88**
按企业、事业、机关分	**By Enterprise, Institution and Agency**						
企 业	Enterprises	171.83	209.05	43.24	37.84	8.56	8.22
事 业	Institutions	57.74	59.60	54.96	56.32	1.66	1.59
机 关	Agencies	20.65	23.45	20.56	22.31	0.04	0.07
按行业分	**By Sector**						
第一产业	Primary Industry	1.79	1.51	1.37	1.22	0.11	0.10
第二产业	Secondary Industry	121.20	149.34	24.70	18.49	6.81	6.64
采矿业	Mining and Quarrying	9.25	10.19	3.54	2.98	0.64	0.77
制造业	Manufacturing	59.62	71.69	12.96	8.21	2.37	1.91
电力、燃气及水的生产和供应业	Electricity, Gas & Water Production and Supply	6.46	6.66	2.08	2.12	0.13	0.12
建筑业	Construction	45.87	60.80	6.12	5.18	3.67	3.84
第三产业	Tertiary Industry	127.23	141.25	92.69	96.76	3.34	3.14
交通运输、仓储及邮政业	Transportation, Storage, Postal Services	13.28	14.50	8.96	9.58	0.29	0.33
信息传输、计算机服务和软件业	Data Transmission, Computer Service and Software	2.68	2.73	1.00	0.79	0.01	0.01
批发与零售业	Wholesale and Retail Trade	10.77	15.69	2.68	2.95	0.59	0.49
住宿和餐饮业	Hotels and Restaurants	4.19	6.89	0.79	0.75	0.19	0.22
金融业	Financing	6.35	6.77	2.31	2.16	0.32	0.21
房地产业	Real Estate	4.88	6.28	1.29	1.47	0.13	0.07
租赁与商务服务业	Renting and Business Activities	5.11	5.58	2.38	2.74	0.11	0.15
科学研究、技术服务与地质勘查业	Scientific Research, Technical Services & Geologic Prospecting	5.05	4.65	2.80	2.82	0.02	0.03
水利、环境和公共设施管理业	Administration of Water Conservancy, Environment and Public Utilities	3.38	3.70	2.68	2.86	0.26	0.28
居民服务和其他服务业	Personal Services and Other Services	0.89	0.86	0.16	0.15	0.05	0.06
教 育	Education	33.57	34.56	32.45	33.25	0.05	0.09
卫生、社会保障和社会福利业	Public Health, Social Security and Social Welfare	11.16	12.19	9.77	10.92	1.27	1.16
文化、体育与娱乐业	Culture, Sports and Entertainment	2.53	2.53	2.06	2.03	0.02	0.01
公共管理与社会组织	Public Administration and Social Organizations	23.39	24.32	23.36	24.29	0.03	0.03

表3.17 城镇非私营单位职工工资总额（2010－2011年）

TOTAL WAGES OF STAFF AND WORKERS OF NON-PRIVATE ECONOMIC UNITS (2010-2011)

单位：万元 (10 000 yuan)

指 标	Item	合 计 Total		其 中 of which #国 有 State-owned		#集 体 Collective-owned	
		2010	2011	2010	2011	2010	2011
总 计	**Total**	**8629547**	**11565329**	**4435431**	**5206171**	**242086**	**274421**
按企业、事业、机关分	**By Enterprise, Institution and Agency**						
企 业	Enterprises	5740106	7902969	1639238	1661954	195325	221917
事 业	Institutions	2104600	2597962	2014073	2501810	45043	49534
机 关	Agencies	784841	1064398	782120	1042407	1718	2970
按行业分	**By Sector**						
第一产业	Primary Industry	37250	48201	29737	41351	2387	2470
第二产业	Secondary Industry	3690436	5241459	862774	789310	149551	178072
采矿业	Mining and Quarrying	291609	390196	126960	133182	14713	23177
制造业	Manufacturing	1865017	2576483	472073	360231	48869	51670
电力、燃气及水的生产和供应业	Electricity, Gas & Water Production and Supply	330075	389923	93353	112278	2372	2884
建筑业	Construction	1203735	1884857	170388	183619	83597	100341
第三产业	Tertiary Industry	4901861	6275669	3542920	4375510	90148	93879
交通运输、仓储及邮政业	Transportation, Storage, Postal Services	450707	523461	314706	352403	5929	7961
信息传输、计算机服务和软件业	Data Transmission, Computer Service and Software	173876	200441	37160	36952	236	227
批发与零售业	Wholesale and Retail Trade	314399	533083	109473	142252	9427	8852
住宿和餐饮业	Hotels and Restaurants	89091	169557	16027	18992	2659	4204
金融业	Financing	475483	622767	147140	170957	19167	15967
房地产业	Real Estate	170553	269691	33003	47658	2286	942
租赁与商务服务业	Renting and Business Activities	127691	134525	54174	68719	2252	3406
科学研究、技术服务与地质勘查业	Scientific Research, Technical Services & Geologic Prospecting	284448	299421	144629	161079	557	814
水利、环境和公共设施管理业	Administration of Water Conservancy, Environment and Public Utilities	73240	97212	59272	78821	4139	5712
居民服务和其他服务业	Personal Services and Other Services	22402	23292	5778	6158	1029	1454
教 育	Education	1271465	1562197	1234289	1514324	949	2142
卫生、社会保障和社会福利业	Public Health, Social Security and Social WelfareSocial Welfare	490721	624914	447224	580441	40493	41345
文化、体育与娱乐业	Culture, Sports and Entertainment	86551	107753	69415	89985	508	267
公共管理与社会组织	Public Administration and Social Organizations	871234	1107355	870630	1106769	517	586

表3.18 城镇非私营单位职工平均工资（2010－2011年）

AVERAGE WAGES OF STAFF AND WORKERS OF URBAN NON-PRIVATE ECONOMIC UNITS (2010-2011)

单位：元 (yuan)

指 标	Item	合 计 Total		其 中 of which			
				#国 有 State-owned		#集 体 Collective-owned	
		2010	2011	2010	2011	2010	2011
总 计	**Total**	**35326**	**40042**	**38075**	**44585**	**24205**	**28490**
按企业、事业、机关分	**By Enterprise, Institution and Agency**						
企 业	Enterprises	34331	38386	38791	43752	23460	27721
事 业	Institutions	37014	44120	37224	44414	27637	32196
机 关	Agencies	38857	46591	38858	46627	38403	46380
按行业分	**By Sector**						
第一产业	Primary Industry	20894	31868	21617	33865	21719	25952
第二产业	Secondary Industry	31555	35592	36165	40019	22642	27642
采矿业	Mining and Quarrying	31769	37738	36113	43111	22583	30283
制造业	Manufacturing	31960	36654	36348	43502	20617	27215
电力、燃气及水的生产和供应业	Electricity, Gas & Water Production and Supply	51172	60061	45063	51871	18777	23675
建筑业	Construction	28014	32091	32261	34021	24183	27472
第三产业	Tertiary Industry	39043	45353	38822	45884	27428	30473
交通运输、仓储及邮政业	Transportation, Storage, Postal Services	34321	40403	35725	42181	20781	24286
信息传输、计算机服务和软件业	Data Transmission, Computer Service and Software	58290	63537	36218	40205	14686	16007
批发与零售业	Wholesale and Retail Trade	30054	35084	40057	48815	16447	18860
住宿和餐饮业	Hotels and Restaurants	21380	24526	20555	25791	14311	18646
金融业	Financing	78593	94149	65962	76898	60371	74862
房地产业	Real Estate	32674	40617	26530	33837	18493	13789
租赁与商务服务业	Renting and Business Activities	25547	28143	23141	25824	20439	22304
科学研究、技术服务与地质勘查业	Scientific Research, Technical Services & Geologic Prospecting	55793	66419	52838	58011	24017	31184
水利、环境和公共设施管理业	Administration of Water Conservancy, Environment and Public Utilities	22883	27445	23386	28582	16472	21267
居民服务和其他服务业	Personal Services and Other Services	26171	28385	35621	41436	21517	25824
教 育	Education	38251	45087	38431	45422	20592	24343
卫生、社会保障和社会福利业	Public Health, Social Security and Social Welfare	44828	52355	46757	54306	32212	36302
文化、体育与娱乐业	Culture, Sports and Entertainment	34544	44620	34074	44655	22762	20859
公共管理与社会组织	Public Administration and Social Organizations	37911	45402	37945	45433	17934	19784

表3.19 城镇非私营单位从业人员劳动报酬（2010－2011年）
EARNINGS OF EMPLOYMENT OF URBAN NON-PRIVATE UNITS (2010-2011)

单位：万元 (10 000 yuan)

指 标	Item	合 计 Total		其 中 of which #国 有 State-owned		#集 体 Collective-owned	
		2010	2011	2010	2011	2010	2011
总 计	**Total**	**8977192**	**12987743**	**4564096**	**5654343**	**249685**	**303142**
按企业、事业、机关分	**By Enterprise, Institution and Agency**						
企 业	Enterprises	6025022	9200999	1708300	1990036	201700	249380
事 业	Institutions	2151938	2675780	2058287	2576239	46267	50775
机 关	Agencies	800232	1110964	797509	1088068	1718	2987
按行业分	**By Sector**						
第一产业	Primary Industry	38133	49138	29957	41731	2423	2485
第二产业	Secondary Industry	3822277	6210689	900113	1020093	154894	202362
采矿业	Mining and Quarrying	294601	397168	127265	137501	14880	23248
制造业	Manufacturing	1949555	2797766	490435	377417	50470	54847
电力、燃气及水的生产和供应业	Electricity, Gas & Water Production and Supply	332857	405937	93834	118520	2383	2891
建筑业	Construction	1245264	2609818	188579	386655	87161	121376
第三产业	Tertiary Industry	5116782	6727916	3634026	4592519	92368	98295
交通运输、仓储及邮政业	Transportation, Storage, Postal Services	473705	596080	332872	409817	6031	8268
信息传输、计算机服务和软件业	Data Transmission, Computer Service and Software	179441	256893	37967	42356	243	234
批发与零售业	Wholesale and Retail Trade	320547	547886	111151	146640	9554	10630
住宿和餐饮业	Hotels and Restaurants	90322	175003	16616	20612	2664	4229
金融业	Financing	574129	752161	155124	190554	19811	16916
房地产业	Real Estate	174778	281047	33780	48351	2313	973
租赁与商务服务业	Renting and Business Activities	131909	154859	54869	71702	2395	3526
科学研究、技术服务与地质勘查业	Scientific Research, Technical Services & Geologic Prospecting	296798	326042	148912	177168	558	820
水利、环境和公共设施管理业	Administration of Water Conservancy, Environment and Public Utilities	76819	104793	62575	85810	4166	5780
居民服务和其他服务业	Personal Services and Other Services	22712	23712	5933	6445	1100	1504
教 育	Education	1295524	1596455	1256538	1546082	973	2174
卫生、社会保障和社会福利业	Public Health, Social Security and Social Welfare	503917	645119	459302	599492	41530	42375
文化、体育与娱乐业	Culture, Sports and Entertainment	87680	112851	70495	93072	508	268
公共管理与社会组织	Public Administration and Social Organizations	888501	1155015	887892	1154418	522	598

表3.20 城镇登记失业人数（1985－2011年）
NUMBER OF REGISTERED UNEMPLOYMENT IN URBAN AREAS (1985-2011)

单位:万人、% (10 000 persons, %)

年 份 Year	登记失业人数 Registered Unemployment	其 中 of which #女 性 Female	按失业时间分 By Unemployment Period 6个月以上 Over 6 Months	6个月以下 Less than 6 Months	登记失业率 Rate of Registered Unemployment
1985	6.46				2.3
1986	6.00				2.1
1987	6.29				2.2
1988	6.25				2.1
1989	8.43				2.8
1990	8.81				2.9
1991	9.42				3.0
1992	10.01				3.1
1993	10.23				3.2
1994	10.80				3.2
1995	10.47				2.9
1996	10.95				3.0
1997	10.85	6.18	6.92	3.93	3.5
1998	10.10	5.71	6.46	3.64	3.5
1999	10.08	5.48	6.15	3.93	3.5
2000	10.15	5.26	5.30	4.85	3.5
2001	13.72	7.24	7.72	6.00	3.9
2002	16.18	7.70	7.79	8.39	4.1
2003	16.16	8.20	8.62	7.54	4.1
2004	16.76	8.19	9.44	7.32	4.12
2005	16.89	8.27	9.67	7.22	4.12
2006	15.41	8.12	8.98	6.43	4.00
2007	14.13	7.60	8.01	6.12	3.98
2008	13.02	6.94	6.27	6.75	3.96
2009	13.44	6.55	6.02	7.42	3.96
2010	13.02	6.20	4.06	8.96	3.90
2011	12.96	7.01	3.34	9.62	3.50

主要统计指标解释

人口数

指一定时点、一定地区范围内的有生命的个人的总和。年度统计的年末人口数是指每年12月31日24时的人口数。

出生率（又称粗出生率）

指在一定时期内（通常为一年）一定地区内出生人数与同期内平均人数（或期中人数）之比，一般用千分率表示。本资料中的出生率指年出生率。计算公式为：

出生率=年出生人数/年平均人数×1000‰

式中：出生人数是指活产婴儿，即胎儿脱离母体时（不管怀孕月数）有过呼吸或其他生命现象。年平均人数是年初、年底人口数的平均数，也可用年中人口数代替。

死亡率（又称粗死亡率）

指在一定时期内（通常为一年）一定地区的死亡人数与同期平均人数（或期中人数）之比，一般用千分率表示。本资料中的死亡率指年死亡率。计算公式为：

死亡率=年死亡人数/年平均人数×1000‰

人口自然增长率

指在一定时期内（通常为一年）人口自然增加数（出生人数减死亡人数）与该时期内平均人数（或期中人数）之比，一般用千分率表示。计算公式为：

人口自然增长率=(本年出生人数-本年死亡人数)/年平均人数×1000‰=人口出生率-人口死亡率

常住人口

常住人口在人口调查中的定义为下列几款人：（1）居住本乡镇街道，户口在本乡镇街道或户口在本乡镇街道，但人离开本乡镇街道不满半年的人；（2）居住本乡镇街道，　离开户口登记地半年以上的人；（3）居住本乡镇街道，户口待定的人；（4）原住本乡镇街道，现在国外工作学习的人。

文盲人口

指15岁及以上不识字或识字很少的人口。

文盲率

指文盲人口占15岁及以上人口比重。

城镇人口和乡村人口

指居住在城区和镇区范围内的全部人口；乡村人口是除上述人口以外的全部人口。

历年城乡人口数据是按照当时国家《统计上划分城乡的规定》计算。

三次普查之间年份的城乡人口根据1990年和2000年人口普查数据进行了调整。

从业人员

指在16周岁及以上，从事一定社会劳动并取得劳动报酬或经营收入的人员。这一指标反映了一定时期内全部劳动力资源的实际利用情况，是研究我国基本国情国力的重要指标。

职工

指在国有、城镇集体、联营、股份制、外商和港、澳、台投资、其他单位（不包括私营单位和个体经营户）及其附属机构工作，并由其支付工资的各类人员。不包括离休、退休、退职人员；再就业的离、退休人员；在城镇单位中工作的外方及港、澳、台人员；其他按有关规定不列入职工统计范围的人员。（1998年及以后的数据均为在岗职工数据，其他相关指标如职工工资总额，职工平均工资等指标也从1998年按此口径进行了相应调整）。

国有单位

指资产归国家所有的经济组织。包括按《中华人民共和国企业法人登记管理条例》规定登记注册的非公司制的经济组织，以及中央、地方各级国家机关、事业单位和社会团体。

主要统计指标解释

集体单位

指生产资料归集体所有，并按《中华人民共和国企业法人登记管理条例》规定登记注册的经济组织。

职工工资总额

指各单位在一定时期内直接支付给本单位全部职工的劳动报酬总额。工资总额的计算原则应以直接支付给职工的全部劳动报酬为根据。各单位支付给职工的劳动报酬以及其他根据有关规定支付的工资，不论是计入成本的还是不计入成本的，不论是以货币形式支付的还是以实物形式支付的，均包括在工资总额内。

职工平均工资

指企业、事业、机关单位的职工在一定时期内平均每人所得的工资额。它表明一定时期职工工资收入的高低程度，是反映职工工资水平的主要指标，计算公式为：

职工平均工资=报告期实际支付的全部职工工资总额/报告期全部职工平均人数

就业人员劳动报酬

指各单位在一定时期内直接支付给本单位全部就业人员的劳动报酬总额。包括职工工资总额和其他就业人员劳动报酬总额。

城镇登记失业人员

指在劳动年龄（16周岁至退休年龄）内，有劳动能力，有就业要求，处于无业状态并在公共就业服务机构进行失业登记的城镇常住人员。其中，没有就业经历的城镇户籍人员，在户籍所在地登记；农村进城务工人员和其他非本地户籍人员在常住地稳定就业满6个月的，失业后可以在常住地登记。

城镇登记失业率

指报告期末，登记失业人数占期末城镇就业人员总数与期末实有城镇登记失业人数之和的比重。计算公式为：

城镇登记失业率=期末实有登记失业人数/（期末就业人员总数+期末实有登记失业人数）×100%

Explanatory Notes on Main Statistical Indicators

□ Total population

Refers to the total number of people alive at a certain point of time within a given area.The annual statistics on total population is taken at midnight, the 3lst of December.

□ Birth Rate (or Crude Birth Rate)

Refers to the ratio of the number of births to the average population during a certain period of time (usually a year), which is often expressed in ‰. Birth rate in the chapter refers to annual birth rate. The following formula is used:

Birth Rate = Number of Births / Average Number of Population × 1000‰

Number of Births refers to live births, i.e. the births when babies had showed any vital phenomena regardless of the length of pregnancy.

Annual Average Number of Population is the average of the number of population at the beginning of the year and that at the end of the year. Sometimes it is substituted for with the mid-year population.

□ Death Rate (or Crude Death Rate)

Refers to the ratio of the number of deaths to the average population (or mid-year population) during a certain period of time (usually a year), which is often expressed in ‰. Death rate in the chapter refers to annual death rate. The following formula is used:

Death Rate = Number of Deaths / Annual Average Number of Population × 1000‰

□ Natural Growth Rate of Population

Refers to the ratio of natural increase in population (number of births minus number of deaths) in a certain period of time (usually a year) to average population (or mid-year population) of the same period, which is often expressed in ‰. The following formulas are applied:

Natural Growth of Population = Number of Births - Number of Deaths / Average number of Population × 1000‰

Natural Growth Rate of Population = Birth Rate - Death Rate

□ Resident Population

According to survey of population, it includes the following main items: (I)population who reside in this township or town (sub-district) with residence registered in this area, or population who have residence registered in this township or town (sub-district) but have been away from this area for less than half a year; (II)population having actually resided in this township or town (sub-district) for over half a year with residence registered in other area; (III)population residing in this townships or towns (sub-district) with residence not registered; (IV)population with residence registered in this township or town (sub-district) who work or study abroad.

□ The Illerate Population

Refers to those over 15 years of age who have inability to read or write, or can read or write only a few words.

□ Illiteracy Rate

Refers to the percentage of the illiterate population in the total population above 15 years of age.

□ Urban Population and Rural Population

Urban population refers to all people residing in the urban and township areas, while rural population refers to population other than urban population.

Statistics on urban and rural population over the years are compiled in line with the regulations of statistical classification on urban and rural population stipulated by the government, which were in effect at different times.

Figures on urban/rural population for the years between the 3 censuses are adjusted in accordance with the 1990 and 2000 population census data.

□ Employees

Refer to the persons aged 16 and over who are engaged in social working and receive remuneration payment or earn business income. This indicator reflects the actual utilization of total labor force during a certain period of time and is often used for the research on China's economic affairs and national power.

EXPLANATORY NOTES TO MAJOR STATISTICAL INDICATORS

□ Staff and Workers

Refer to persons working in, and receive payment from units of state ownership, collective ownership, joint ownership, share holding ownership, foreign ownership, and ownership by entrepreneurs from Hong Kong, Macao, and Taiwan, and other types of ownership and their affiliated units(excluding private enterprises and owners of self-employed). They exclude: retirees; re-employed retirees; foreigners and persons from Hong Kong, Macao and Taiwan who work in urban units; 8) other persons not to be included by relevant regulations. (Data of 1998 and afterward refer to fully employed staff and workers. Other related statistics such as total wage bill and average wage are adjusted since 1998 accordingly).

□ State-owned Units

Refer to economic units whose assets are owned by the state. Included are non-corporation units registered according to Regulation of the People's Republic of China on the Registration of Enterprises and Corporations, state organs, institutions and social organizations at the central and local levels.

□ Collective Units

Refer to economic units registered according to Regulation of the People's Republic of China on the Registration of Enterprises and Corporations where the means of production are collectively owned.

□ Total Wages of Bill

Refers to total remuneration payment to staff and workers in various units during a certain period of time. The calculation of total wages is based on the total remuneration payment to the staff and workers. Therefore, all the wages and salaries and other payments to staff and workers are included in the total wage bill regardless of sources, reckoning the cost of production or not, category, listing as items of premium taxation or not, and forms, paying in cash or in kind.

□ Average Earning

Refers to average earning level in money terms per employee in the enterprise, institutions, and government agencies, which reflects the general level of wage income during a certain period of time and is calculated as follows:

Average Earning of Employees=Total Earning of Employees at Reference Period/Average Number of Employees at Reference Period

□ Earning

Refer to total remuneration payment to all employees in various units in urban areas(did not include urban private units and self-employed individuals) during a certain period of time, including staff and workers and other employee(i.e.,reemployed retirees or those who are from Hong Kong, Macao, Taiwan province or other countries).

□ Registered Unemployed Persons in Urban Areas

Refers to the unemployed urban resident population at the labor age (from 16 to the age of retirement), with labor capability and employment demand, who have been registered at the public employment service institutions. Among whom, the urban resident population without employment experience shall be registered at the place of household registration; the off-farm workers and other persons with the household registration at other places who have been employed for 6 consecutive months may be registered at the place of their usual residence.

□ Registered Unemployment Rate in Urban Areas

Refers to the ratio of the number of the registered unemployed persons at the end of the reference period to the sum of total employment and the number of the registered unemployed persons at the end of the reference period. The formula is as the follows:

Registered urban unemployment rate = number of registered urban unemployed persons at the end of reference period / (total employment+ number of registered urban unemployed persons at the end of reference period) × 100%

第4章

固定资产投资

INVESTMENT IN FIXED ASSETS

简要说明
BRIEF INTRODUCTION

本章内容主要包括全社会固定资产投资、城镇建设项目投资、房地产开发和商品房销售、重点项目完成情况，由市统计局固定资产投资处整理提供。

The data in this chapter cover the total investment in fixed assets, investment in urban construction, real estate development, sales of commercialized buildings and completed investment in key projects. All the data are prepared and provided by Division of Statistics of Investment in Fixed Assets, Chongqing Municipal Bureau of Statistics.

表4.1 主要年份全社会固定资产投资
TOTAL INVESTMENT IN FIXED ASSETS IN MAJOR YEARS

单位：万元(10 000 yuan)

年份 Year	固定资产投资额总计 Total Investment in Fixed Assets	新增固定资产 Newly Increased Fixed Assets	固定资产投资按构成分 Investment in Fixed Assets by Use of Funds		
			建筑安装工程 Construction and Installation	设备工具器具购置 Purchase of Equipment and Instruments	其他费用 Others
1949	39	37	39		
1952	9535	7107	7027	1751	757
1957	21330	20591	12563	6636	2131
1962	7769	7650	5853	1654	262
1965	37677	32844	24658	10280	2739
1970	62448	44331	26528	31658	4262
1975	64359	29973	26446	26539	11374
1978	59026	46834	37630	16958	4438
1980	102789	101499	71220	26265	5304
1985	364822	265993	238027	101461	25334
1986	420675	343008	265430	124895	30350
1987	482445	345528	329053	114844	38548
1988	558331	378150	374833	148913	34585
1989	547540	405769	370687	140033	36820
1990	693140	462056	450344	192115	50681
1991	851614	636525	548518	234255	68841
1992	1063852	871892	703962	261333	98557
1993	1550546	1036205	1008107	389367	153072
1994	2029178	1377025	1336181	509362	183635
1995	2709663	1886888	1707448	737819	264396
1996	3207278	2306996	2076949	733537	342156
1997	3709485	3143528	2418273	879477	411735
1998	4981452	3693019	3248271	1083808	649373
1999	5628679	3706704	3860379	1080062	688238
2000	6558116	4364464	4599909	1055220	902987
2001	8018228	4722181	5460064	1435621	1122543
2002	9956645	6868792	6961365	1482391	1512889
2003	12693544	7244753	8608006	1594910	2490628
2004	16219203	8377655	10155324	2512064	3551815
2005	20063180	15268045	12487360	2990736	4585084
2006	24518351	13817208	15250559	3530668	5737124
2007	31615147	18087476	20238311	4438013	6938823
2008	40452509	16147872	26504524	5793319	8154666
2009	53179185	28027347	35607657	6552634	11018894
2010	69347966	35223421	47667591	7271738	14408637
2011	76858699	46195551	55881173	7582702	13394824

表4.1 续表1 continued1

单位：万元(10 000 yuan)

年 份 Year	固定资产投资按城乡分 Investment in Fixed Assets by Urban and Rural Areas					
	城 镇 Urban	其 中 of which		农 村 Rural	其 中 of which	
		建设项目 Construction Projects	房地产开发 Real Estate Development		农 户 Rural Households	非农户 Non-Rural Households
1949						
1952						
1957						
1962						
1965						
1970						
1975						
1978						
1980						
1985						
1986						
1987						
1988						
1989						
1990						
1991						
1992						
1993						
1994						
1995						
1996	2286027	1729842	556185	921251	520639	400612
1997	2747402	2072380	675022	962083	518255	443828
1998	4012210	3039196	973014	969242	509535	459707
1999	4504619	3379484	1125135	1124060	589147	534913
2000	5313816	3917489	1396327	1244300	649150	595150
2001	6720308	4753624	1966684	1297920	707500	590420
2002	8568780	6109650	2459130	1387865	722554	665311
2003	11375600	8096719	3278881	1317944	666529	651415
2004	14771164	10720373	4050791	1448039	715951	732088
2005	18384226	13206935	5177291	1678954	718040	960914
2006	22914581	16618281	6296300	1603770	771833	831937
2007	29713639	21214673	8498966	1901508	740000	1161508
2008	37815574	27905604	9909970	2636935	824161	1812774
2009	49587435	37198310	12389125	3591750	902424	2689326
2010	63429833	47227262	16202571	5918133	946416	4971717
2011	70990170	50839287	20150883	5868529	1064245	4804284

表4.1 续表2 continued2

单位：万元(10 000 yuan)

年 份 Year	固定资产投资按登记注册类型分 Investment in Fixed Assets by Status of Registration						
	国 有 State - owned	集 体 Collective -owned	联 营 Joint- owned	股份制 Share- holding	港澳台及外商投资 Foreign- funded	私营个体 Individuals	其 他 Others
1949	39						
1952	9535						
1957	21330						
1962	7769						
1965	37662	15					
1970	62447	1					
1975	64355	4					
1978	56823	2203					
1980	91150	4718				3692	
1985	243927	66862				44712	9321
1986	301256	60497				48260	10662
1987	345509	58155				67033	11748
1988	410106	56588				78012	13625
1989	405239	46813				82058	13430
1990	528648	49525				92235	22732
1991	639554	69943				120515	21602
1992	739230	137945				165300	21377
1993	979597	276425	2798	32512	25320	206511	27383
1994	1364920	353815	2598	8013	13340	243119	43373
1995	1433244	424399	5834	101846	232079	370479	141782
1996	1597680	513195	6857	100805	278214	598918	111609
1997	1763147	550970	11428	354040	154602	669117	31148
1998	2598535	599304	7963	691371	402084	637275	44920
1999	2839011	664552	9951	612007	353199	1097082	52877
2000	3132534	730555	31555	877503	319730	1381098	85141
2001	3849113	821206	65544	1077977	432826	1715384	56178
2002	4603442	884409	45739	1678915	731767	1989250	23123
2003	5517224	845591	30177	3055216	648829	2514803	81704
2004	6625116	958051	30942	4199655	1174341	3114906	116192
2005	7978697	698801	75405	5902555	1176890	4063795	167037
2006	10219239	383345	62156	7208381	1420900	4939191	285139
2007	12551060	497937	92315	8796251	2293560	7036673	347351
2008	16091842	489458	158560	10398474	3026064	9663932	624179
2009	23241164	513318	149177	12949452	3052163	12497309	776602
2010	30610270	741840	203204	16450400	4120685	15949286	1272281
2011	32146574	761211	360273	18903732	5125101	18129197	1432611

表4.1 续表3 continued3

单位：万元、万平方米 (10 000 yuan, 10 000 sq.m)

年 份 Year	固定资产投资按三次产业分 Investment in Fixed Assets by Three Strata of Industry			本年房屋施工面积 Floor Space under Construction	其 中 of which	本年房屋竣工面积 Floor Space Completed	其 中 of which
	第一产业 Primary Industry	第二产业 Secondary Industry	第三产业 Tertiary Industry		#住 宅 Residential Buildings		#住 宅 Residential Buildings
1949						1	
1952	37	4616	4882			5	1
1957	203	15421	5706			153	84
1962	314	6080	1375			18	7
1965	5130	25482	7065			103	43
1970	1291	56173	4984			121	49
1975	2716	54692	6951			95	39
1978	3790	45516	9720			121	39
1980	2101	69188	31500			323	166
1985	4848	184918	175056	2536		1341	680
1986	3359	238569	178747	2596		2141	1445
1987	4794	282515	195136	2752		2169	1474
1988	5490	346847	205994	2632		1970	1478
1989	5919	314655	226966	2400		1851	706
1990	13220	413776	266144	2522		2057	1620
1991	19966	487813	343835	2753		2258	1756
1992	20329	558021	485502	3228		2473	1947
1993	14208	701890	834448	3619		2631	1994
1994	14449	839691	1175038	4045		2926	2119
1995	17117	1066810	1625736	4964		3306	2503
1996	23128	1156837	2027313	6026	4164	4209	3313
1997	33820	1309109	2366556	6145	4198	4302	3363
1998	44133	1418980	3518339	6587	4474	4285	3267
1999	65652	1217277	4345750	7170	4799	4660	3527
2000	89657	1423981	5044478	8494	5931	5337	4087
2001	108038	1462479	6447711	8812	6055	4939	3664
2002	191128	1956665	7808852	10643	7305	6403	4665
2003	264249	3033987	9395308	10962	7398	5959	4293
2004	360891	4301999	11556313	11797	7835	5560	3962
2005	441953	5860896	13760331	13300	8792	6385	4341
2006	519301	7553189	16445861	14993	9693	5979	4098
2007	597371	10850790	20166986	16278	10912	5523	3810
2008	890989	14370570	25190950	17629	12091	5456	3990
2009	1991057	18914538	32273590	20131	13816	4961	3208
2010	2647737	24231237	42468992	25068	17698	6559	4983
2011	2787694	27847512	46223493	32627	20571	7404	5870

表4.2 全社会固定资产投资（2010－2011年）
TOTAL INVESTMENT IN FIXED ASSETS (2010-2011)

指　标	Item	投资额 Investment		构　成（%） Composition(%)	
		2010	2011	2010	2011
投资总额（万元）	**Total Investment (10 000 yuan)**	**69347966**	**76858699**	**100.0**	**100.0**
按隶属关系分	**By Jurisdiction of Administration**				
中央项目	Central Investment	5259713	4945038	7.6	6.4
地方项目（包括无隶属关系的）	Local Investment (including non-governmental investment)	64088253	71913661	92.4	93.6
按登记注册类型分	**By Status of Registration**				
内　资	Domestic-funded	65227281	71733598	94.1	93.3
#国　有	State-owned	30610270	32146574	44.1	41.8
集　体	Collective-owned	741840	761211	1.1	1.0
联　营	Joint-owned	203204	360273	0.3	0.5
股份制	Share-holding	16450400	18903732	23.7	24.6
私营个体	Individual	15949286	18129197	23.0	23.6
其　他	Others	1272281	1432611	1.8	1.9
港澳台投资经济	Funded by Entrepreneurs from Hong Kong, Macao and Taiwan	2573832	3001173	3.7	3.9
外商投资经济	Foreign-funded	1546853	2123928	2.2	2.8
按城乡分	**By Rural and Urban Areas**				
城　镇	Urban	63429833	70990170	91.5	92.4
#房地产开发	Real Estate Development	16202571	20150883	23.4	26.2
农　村	Rural	5918133	5868529	8.5	7.6
#农　户	Rural Households	946416	1064245	1.4	1.4
按构成分	**By Use of Funds**				
建筑工程	Construction	43710073	51229955	63.0	66.6
安装工程	Installation	3957518	4651218	5.7	6.1
设备工具器具购置	Purchase of Equipment and Instruments	7271738	7582702	10.5	9.9
其他费用	Others	14408637	13394824	20.8	17.4
新增固定资产（万元）	**Newly Increased Fixed Assets (10 000 yuan)**	**35223421**	**46195551**		
固定资产交付使用率（%）	**Rate of Fixed Assets Put into Use (%)**	**51**	**61**		
房屋建筑面积（万平方米）	**Floor Space of Buildings (10 000 sq.m)**				
施工面积	Floor Space under Construction	23714	32627		
#住　宅	Residential Buildings	16353	20571		
竣工面积	Floor Space Completed	5170	7404		
#住　宅	Residential Buildings	3610	5870		

表4.3 按行业分的全社会固定资产投资（2010－2011年）
TOTAL INVESTMENT IN FIXED ASSETS BY SECTOR (2010-2011)

单位：万元(10 000 yuan)

行　业	Sector	2010	2011
总　计	**Total**	**69347966**	**76858699**
第一产业	Primary Industry	2647737	2787694
第二产业	Secondary Industry	24231237	27847512
工　业	Industry	22336924	25312080
采矿业	Mining	1763630	1841855
制造业	Manufacturing	17662897	20694684
电力、燃气及水的生产和供应业	Electricity, Gas & Water Production and Supply	2910397	2775541
建筑业	Construction	1894313	2535432
第三产业	Tertiary Industry	42468992	46223493
交通运输、仓储及邮政业	Transport, Storage, Post	7911280	8335061
信息传输、计算机服务和软件业	Information Transmission, Computer Services and Software	766908	625201
批发与零售业	Wholesale and Retail Trades	920755	799881
住宿和餐饮业	Hotels and Catering Services	368653	459208
金融业	Financial Intermediation	37258	25742
房地产业	Real Estate	19978425	24080892
租赁与商务服务业	Leasing and Business Services	607368	235491
科学研究、技术服务与地质勘查业	Scientific Research, Technical Services and Geological Prospecting	110342	149988
水利、环境和公共设施管理业	Administration of Water Conservancy, Environment and Public Facilities	7850011	7785800
居民服务和其他服务业	Household Services and Other Services	127677	331431
教　育	Education	1215463	922153
卫生、社会保障和社会福利业	Health, Social Security and Social Welfare	453625	454422
文化、体育与娱乐业	Culture, Sports and Entertainment	536903	589168
公共管理与社会组织	Public Administration and Social Organizations	1584324	1429055

表4.4 全社会固定资产投资资金来源（2010－2011年）
TOTAL INVESTMENT IN FIXED ASSETS BY SOURCE OF FUNDS (2010-2011)

单位：万元(10 000 yuan)

指　标	Item	总　计 Total		其　中 of which 农　村 Rural		其　中 of which #农　户 Rural Households	
		2010	2011	2010	2011	2010	2011
本年资金来源合计	**Total Investment from All Sources in This Year**	**92951031**	**107458534**	**6257299**	**6324078**	**946416**	**1064245**
上年末结余资金	Balance of the Previous Year	7371418	14213017	90417	197548		
本年资金来源小计	Subtotal of Funds Invested in This Year	85579613	93245517	6166882	6126530	946416	1064245
国家预算内资金	State Budgetary Appropriation	6511479	5769172	883299	674822		
国内贷款	Domestic Loans	17477058	16144094	377860	270145		
债　券	Bonds	332344	202017				
利用外资	Foreign Investment	1492287	1094087	15657	8424		
自筹资金	Self-raised Funds	38201511	46176053	3373694	4671072	946416	1064245
其他资金来源	Others	21564934	23860094	1516372	502067		

指　标	Item	其　中 of which 城　镇 Urban		其　中 of which 建设项目 Construction Investment		房地产开发 Real Estate Development	
		2010	2011	2010	2011	2010	2011
本年资金来源合计	**Total Investment from All Sources in This Year**	**86693732**	**101134456**	**52300060**	**56801656**	**34393672**	**44332807**
上年末结余资金	Balance of the Previous Year	7281001	14015469	1482593	2639569	5798408	11375893
本年资金来源小计	Subtotal of Funds Invested in This Year	79412731	87118987	50817467	54162087	28595264	32956914
国家预算内资金	State Budgetary Appropriation	5628180	5094350	5628180	5094350		
国内贷款	Domestic Loans	17099198	15873949	11252038	8923149	5847160	6950754
债　券	Bonds	332344	202017	332344	202017		
利用外资	Foreign Investment	1476630	1085663	637365	486463	839265	599183
自筹资金	Self-raised Funds	34827817	42045726	27977851	33508526	6849966	8537163
其他资金来源	Others	20048562	22817282	4989689	5947482	15058873	16869814

表4.5 按行业分建设项目投资和建设总规模（2011年）
INVESTMENT IN CONSTRUCTION PROJECTS AND TOTAL CONSTRUCTION INVESTMENT SIZE BY SECTOR (2011)

指　标	Item	建设总规模 Total Investment in Construction	在建总规模 Total Investment in In-process Projects
总　计	**Total**	**165347810**	**163565646**
第一产业	Primary Industry	5019710	4971470
第二产业	Secondary Industry	74973411	74777622
工　业	Industry	70466646	70241978
采矿业	Mining	3175855	3215306
制造业	Manufacturing	56723407	56486943
电力、燃气及水的生产和供应业	Electricity, Gas & Water Production and Supply	10567384	10539729
建筑业	Construction	4506765	4535644
第三产业	Tertiary Industry	85354689	83816554
交通运输、仓储及邮政业	Transport, Storage, Post	31966075	31591958
信息传输、计算机服务和软件业	Information Transmission, Computer Services and Software	1601841	1227681
批发与零售业	Wholesale and Retail Trades	2024068	2033788
住宿和餐饮业	Hotels and Catering Services	919795	919795
金融业	Financial Intermediation	133625	133625
房地产业	Real Estate	7217401	7207311
租赁与商务服务业	Leasing and Business Services	806720	607420
科学研究、技术服务与地质勘查业	Scientific Research, Technical Services and Geological Prospecting	333646	305993
水利、环境和公共设施管理业	Administration of Water Conservancy, Environment and Public Facilities	31449253	31078533
居民服务和其他服务业	Household Services and Other Services	512633	512633
教　育	Education	3216961	2982582
卫生、社会保障和社会福利业	Health, Social Security and Social Welfare	1095919	1096960
文化、体育与娱乐业	Culture, Sports and Entertainment	1771861	1766184
公共管理与社会组织	Public Administration and Social Organizations	2304891	2352091

单位：万元(10 000 yuan)

在建净规模 Net Investment in In-process Projects	投资额 Investment	其中 of which					
		#新 建 New Constuction	#扩 建 Expansion	#改 建 Reconstruction	建筑安装工程投资 Construction and Installation	设备工器具购置 Purchase of Equipment and Instruments	其他费用 Other Expenses
93833309	**50839287**	**36415327**	**5096708**	**7618539**	**36871139**	**6990748**	**6977400**
3040333	1653730	1298453	141283	202414	1154580	40118	459032
44598361	26353316	17656038	3274221	4301390	17227074	5856225	3270017
42478561	24221692	16254498	3032291	3895815	15418511	5811894	2991287
1660663	1652587	529956	427181	661575	1271931	295201	85455
37200877	19952974	13538535	2429253	2981496	12321074	5024280	2607620
3617021	2616131	2186007	175857	252744	1825506	492413	298212
2119800	2131624	1401540	241930	405575	1808563	44331	278730
46194615	22832241	17460836	1681204	3114735	18489485	1094405	3248351
13576376	7672867	6254566	482495	878129	6139283	537058	996526
393159	625201	75223	453094	96884	378273	241072	5856
1227479	783265	649416	29615	81737	553257	55091	174917
403040	419329	313273	48410	52946	341386	25590	52353
88822	25742	7375		18367	25242	500	
4585964	2329469	1771264	45707	436045	1870899	23679	434891
276045	222008	149728	5167	62674	176215	7366	38427
164771	139259	117108		17366	114496	6666	18097
20569834	7181591	5585808	372933	1178939	5995179	72898	1113514
332649	238804	140330	29207	56556	204225	2305	32274
1696048	901107	568066	107151	24074	746334	24684	130089
546148	427081	280977	58593	23442	353832	21068	52181
819692	559868	517923	13339	25537	455695	16450	87723
1514588	1306650	1029779	35493	162039	1135169	59978	111503

表4.6 按行业分城镇建设项目施工、投产项目个数（2011年）

NUMBER OF URBAN CONSTRUCTION PROJECTS IN PROCESS AND COMPLETED BY SECTOR (2011)

行　业	Sector	施工项目（个） Number of In-process Projects (unit)	其中 of which #新开工 Started This Year	全部建成投产项目（个） Number of Projects Completed & Put into Use (unit)	项目建成投产率（%） Rate of Projects Completed& Put into Use(%)
总　计	**Total**	**9947**	**6435**	**6225**	**62.6**
第一产业	Primary Industry	470	338	311	66.2
第二产业	Secondary Industry	5156	3365	3455	67.0
工　业	Industry	4600	2907	3124	67.9
采矿业	Mining	461	351	364	79.0
制造业	Manufacturing	3680	2293	2505	68.1
电力、燃气及水的生产和供应业	Electricity, Gas & Water Production and Supply	459	263	255	55.6
建筑业	Construction	556	458	331	59.5
第三产业	Tertiary Industry	4321	2732	2459	56.9
交通运输、仓储及邮政业	Transport, Storage, Post	773	512	469	60.7
信息传输、计算机服务和软件业	Information Transmission, Computer Services and Software	134	61	12	9.0
批发与零售业	Wholesale and Retail Trades	163	118	93	57.1
住宿和餐饮业	Hotels and Catering Services	116	68	64	55.2
金融业	Financial Intermediation	8	2	5	62.5
房地产业	Real Estate	518	347	355	68.5
租赁与商务服务业	Leasing and Business Services	51	34	27	52.9
科学研究、技术服务与地质勘查业	Scientific Research, Technical Services and Geological Prospecting	50	17	37	74.0
水利、环境和公共设施管理业	Administration of Water Conservancy, Environment and Public Facilities	1473	892	837	56.8
居民服务和其他服务业	Household Services and Other Services	69	55	31	44.9
教　育	Education	252	146	130	51.6
卫生、社会保障和社会福利业	Health, Social Security and Social Welfare	156	96	69	44.2
文化、体育与娱乐业	Culture, Sports and Entertainment	133	72	69	51.9
公共管理与社会组织	Public Administration and Social Organizations	425	312	261	61.4

表4.7 全社会房屋施工面积（2010－2011年）
TOTAL FLOOR SPACE OF BUILDINGS UNDER CONSTRUCTION (2010-2011)

单位：万平方米(10 000 sq.m)

指　标	Item	房屋施工面积 Floor Space of Buildings under Construction		其　中 of which #住　宅 Residential Buildings	
		2010	2011	2010	2011
总　计	**Total**	**25068**	**32627**	**17698**	**20571**
建设项目	Construction	5272	9808	1884	2498
房地产开发	Real Estate Development	17138	20397	13745	15924
农村非农户	Non-Rural Households	1303	899	724	636
农　户	Rural Households	1354	1523	1345	1513

表4.8 全社会房屋竣工面积（2010－2011年）
TOTAL FLOOR SPACE OF BUILDINGS COMPLETED (2010-2011)

单位：万平方米(10 000 sq.m)

指　标	Item	房屋竣工面积 Floor Space of Buildings Completed		其　中 of which #住　宅 Residential Buildings	
		2010	2011	2010	2011
总　计	**Total**	**6559**	**7404**	**4983**	**5870**
建设项目	Construction	1701	1951	941	1162
房地产开发	Real Estate Development	2627	3424	2180	2827
农村非农户	Non-Rural Households	842	465	490	336
农　户	Rural Households	1389	1563	1373	1545

表4.9 全社会房屋造价（2010－2011年）
COST OF COMPLETED BUILDINGS (2010-2011)

单位：元/平方米(yuan/sq.m)

指　标	Item	每平方米造价 Cost of Buildings Completed per Sq.m		其　中 of which #住　宅 Residential Buildings	
		2010	2011	2010	2011
建设项目	Construction	1174	1316	1018	762
房地产开发	Real Estate Development	2467	2698	2340	2662
农村非农户	Non-Rural Households	504	814	580	708

表4.10 城镇建设项目投资（2010－2011年）
INVESTMENT IN URBAN CONSTRUCTION (2010-2011)

指　标	Item	2010	2011
投资总额（万元）	**Total Investment (10 000 yuan)**	**47227262**	**50839287**
#住　宅	Residential Buildings	1543014	1448589
按隶属关系分	By Jurisdiction of Administration		
中央项目	Central Investment	4558783	4110246
地方项目	Local Investment	42668479	46729041
按构成分	By Use of Funds		
建筑工程	Construction	29559174	33702412
安装工程	Installation	2858412	3168727
设备、工具、器具购置	Purchase of Equipment and Instruments	6622985	6990748
其他费用	Others	8186691	6977400
按建设性质分	By Type of Construction		
#新　建	New Construction	31762634	36415327
扩　建	Expansion	6043963	5096708
改建和技术改造	Reconstruction and Technical Transformation	7284159	7618539
按国民经济行业分	By Sector		
第一产业	Primary Industry	1698835	1653730
第二产业	Secondary Industry	22285187	26353316
#工　业	Industry	20801172	24221692
第三产业	Tertiary Industry	23243240	22832241
新增固定资产（万元）	**Newly Increased Fixed Assets (10 000 yuan)**	**23904286**	**32141831**
建设项目（个）	**Construction Project (unit)**		
施工项目	Project under Construction	10206	9947
本年投产项目	Project Completed in This Year	6143	6225
房屋建筑面积（万平方米）	**Floor Space of Buildings (10 000 sq.m)**		
施工面积	Floor Space under Construction	5272	9807
#住　宅	Residential Buildings	1884	2498
竣工面积	Floor Space Completed	1701	1951
#住　宅	Residential Buildings	941	1162

表4.11 按行业分的城镇建设项目投资（2011年）
INVESTMENT IN URBAN CONSTRCTION PROJECTS BY SECTOR (2011)

单位：万元(10 000 yuan)

行业	Sector	施工项目个数（个） Number of In-process Project (unit)	计划总投资 Planned Total Investment	本年完成投资 Investment Completed in Current Year
总计	**Total**	9947	171641150	50839287
第一产业	Primary Industry	470	5081413	1653730
第二产业	Secondary Industry	5156	77747596	26353316
工业	Industry	4600	72298376	24221692
采矿业	Mining	461	3283437	1652587
#石油和天然气开采业	Extraction of Petroleum and Natural Gas	14	933630	541267
制造业	Manufacturing	3680	58429923	19952974
#化学原料及化学制品制造业	Manufacture of Raw Chemical Materials and Chemical Products	171	7780241	1787886
医药制造业	Manufacture of Medicines	94	1082067	544589
通用设备制造业	Manufacture of General Purpose Machinery	275	3611215	1495955
专用设备制造业	Manufacture of Special Purpose Machinery	172	1827262	712527
交通设备制造业	Manufacture of Transport Equipment	708	9913209	3541045
电力、燃气及水的生产和供应业	Production and Supply of Electricity, Gas and Water	459	10585016	2616131
电力、热力的生产和供应业	Production and Supply of Electric Power and Heat Power	189	8536463	1917514
燃气生产和供应业	Production and Supply of Gas	70	729614	199502
水的生产和供应业	Production and Supply of Water	200	1318939	499115
建筑业	Construction	556	5449220	2131624
第三产业	Tertiary Industry	4321	88812141	22832241
交通运输、仓储及邮政业	Transport, Storage and Post	773	32716045	7672867
#邮政业	Post	2	15550	4059
信息传输、计算机服务和软件业	Data Transmission, Computer Services and Software	134	1606646	625201
#电信和其他信息传输服务业	Telecommunications and Other Information Transmission Services	126	1536568	604014
批发与零售业	Wholesale and Retail Trades	163	2121788	783265
住宿和餐饮业	Hotels and Catering Services	116	1031495	419329
金融业	Financial Intermediation	8	133625	25742
房地产业	Real Estate	518	7642221	2329469
租赁与商务服务业	Leasing and Business Services	51	816420	222008
科学研究、技术服务与地质勘查业	Scientific Research, Technical Services and Geological Prospecting	50	351286	139259
水利、环境和公共设施管理业	Administration of Water Conservancy, Environment and Public Utilities	1473	33113473	7181591
居民服务和其他服务业	Household Services and Other Services	69	512633	238804
教育	Education	252	3257213	901107
卫生、社会保障和社会福利业	Public Health, Social Security and Social Welfare	156	1171624	427081
#卫生	Public Health	103	890223	303659
文化、体育与娱乐业	Culture, Sports and Entertainment	133	1947061	559868
公共管理与社会组织	Public Administration and Social Organizations	425	2390611	1306650

表4.12 城镇建设项目新增主要产品生产能力（2010－2011年）

NEWLY INCREASED PRODUCTION CAPACITY OF THE MAJOR PRODUCTS IN URBAN CONSTRUCTION (2010-2011)

能力名称	Item	2010	2011
铁合金（万吨/年）	Iron Alloy (10 000 tons/year)	3	11
原煤开采（万吨/年）	Coal Mining (10 000 tons/year)	330	776
发电机组容量（万千瓦）	Capacity of Power Generating Sets (10 000 kw/year)	260	516
火　电	Thermal Power	2	1
水　电	Hydropower	258	497
汽车制造（万辆/年）	Motor Vehicles (10 000 units/year)	11	1
水泥（万吨/年）	Cement (10 000 tons/year)	2121	920
机制纸及纸板（万吨/年）	Machine-made Paper and Paperboards (10 000 tons/year)	2	10
新（扩）建港口码头年吞吐量（万吨）	Annual Handling Capacity of Newly Built (Expanded) Ports (10 000 tons)		51
泊　位（个）	Berths (unit)	4	4
新建公路（公里）	Length of New Highways (km)	3489	5615
改建公路（公里）	Length of Reconstructed Highways (km)	3122	4049
各类院校：学生席位（个）	Students Capacity of Universities and Colleges (unit)		
医院病床床位（张）	Number of Hospital Beds (bed)		
城市自来水供水能力（万吨/日）	Tap Water Supply Capacity (10 000 tons/day)	34	59

表4.13 基础设施建设投资额（2010－2011年）
INVESTMENT IN INFRASTRUCTURE CONSTRUCTION (2010-2011)

单位：万元(10 000 yuan)

指　标	Item	2010	2011
合　计	**Total**	**19114457**	**19263031**
电力、燃气及水的生产和供应业	Production and Supply of Electricity, Gas and Water	2910397	2775541
#电力、热力的生产和供应业	Production and Supply of Electric Power and Heat Power	2060850	2005228
燃气生产和供应业	Production and Supply of Gas	368078	209232
水的生产和供应业	Production and Supply of Water	481469	561081
交通运输及邮政业	Transport, Storage and Post	7591366	8097676
#交通运输业	Transport	7587893	8093617
#城市公共交通业	City Public Transport	1228189	1798419
邮政业	Post	3473	4059
电信和其他信息传输服务业	Telecommunications and Other Information Transmission Services	762683	604014
水利、环境和公共设施管理业	Administration of Water Conservancy, Environment and Public Facilities	7850011	7785800
#水利管理业	Administration of Water Conservancy	1072883	890781
环境管理业	Administration of Environment	521877	672111
公共设施管理业	Administration of Public Facilities	6255251	6222908

表4.14 房地产开发基本情况（1990－2011年）
BASIC STATISTICS ON REAL ESTATE DEVELOPMENT (1990-2011)

年 份 Year	企业数（个） Number of Enterprises (unit)	从业人员（人） Number of Employees (person)	本年土地购置面积 Land Space Purchased in This Year	本年完成投资总额（万元） Investment Completed in This Year (10 000 yuan)	其 中 of which #住 宅 Residential Buildings	资金来源（万元） Sources of Funds (10 000 yuan)	房屋施工面 积 Floor Space under Construction	其 中 of which #住 宅 Residential Buildings
1990				17503	10600	17568	107.80	65.48
1991				19185	14040	18042	112.57	83.54
1992				33868	21239	33148	160.91	94.56
1993				123151	66833	107210	437.73	293.03
1994				279089	196411	377959	650.71	394.43
1995				468845	252085	612121	1267.96	810.36
1996	635	22512	588.65	556185	259881	836655	1424.35	855.64
1997	622	24911	259.49	675022	282592	1060761	1652.32	904.18
1998	991	50088	521.48	973014	440889	1391253	2058.35	1223.66
1999	1073	50526	624.53	1125135	523357	1504042	2103.76	1285.41
2000	1339	63925	619.21	1396327	728125	1784950	2833.42	1896.18
2001	1474	78961	870.34	1966684	1107126	2373982	3653.71	2508.30
2002	1559	76582	1320.26	2459130	1306998	3148171	4414.96	3081.57
2003	1597	54148	1637.19	3278881	1774341	4793499	5287.80	3747.34
2004	1828	70711	1137.61	4050791	2171303	6220133	6247.86	4544.54
2005	1862	70563	1385.40	5177291	3004026	8819371	7487.36	5514.75
2006	1936	70094	1467.69	6296300	3767847	9985438	8864.37	6655.00
2007	2039	87606	1737.74	8498966	5218209	15546697	10578.84	8179.29
2008	2280	86094	1164.41	9909970	6195250	15595559	11639.27	9166.21
2009	2359	87818	1227.79	12389125	7890183	22026661	13052.60	10338.12
2010	2391	86602	1354.93	16202571	10914854	34393672	17138.50	13744.78
2011	2453	94535	1664.55	20150883	14384457	44332807	20397.24	15923.84

单位：万平方米(10 000 sq.m)

年 份 Year	房屋新开工面积 Floor Space Started This Year	其 中 of which #住 宅 Residential Buildings	房屋竣工面 积 Floor Space Completed	其 中 of which #住 宅 Residential Buildings	商品房销售面积 Floor Spaces of Commercialized Buildings Sold	其 中 of which #住 宅 Residential Buildings	商品房销售额（万元） Sales of Commercialized Buildings (10 000 yuan)	其 中 of which #住 宅 Residential Buildings
1990			46.16	34.16	23.29		17648	
1991			37.33	28.61	27.48		20007	
1992			45.90	30.48	32.87		29583	
1993			81.05	66.01	37.39		42221	
1994			141.27	115.05	46.32		55336	
1995			258.25	208.70	114.61		116657	
1996	348.68	220.54	351.76	275.62	166.21	142.98	189856	145507
1997	470.34	299.69	459.92	358.36	260.78	215.33	313111	222376
1998	914.23	596.44	600.04	422.61	416.82	359.73	554786	417609
1999	847.51	608.43	619.56	438.56	429.98	364.56	591992	393569
2000	1290.05	969.26	849.42	622.08	579.96	491.09	783709	528698
2001	1661.19	1259.38	1020.63	738.41	746.05	635.04	1076534	719196
2002	1709.47	1277.55	1390.73	1033.60	1016.58	870.41	1581505	1111929
2003	2098.24	1580.04	1676.97	1231.75	1316.83	1132.95	2102260	1499915
2004	2191.00	1692.00	1585.98	1227.66	1329.32	1157.95	2327978	1817280
2005	2335.00	1825.00	2209.82	1713.55	2017.66	1792.41	4307679	3406768
2006	2709.28	2176.75	2224.84	1700.05	2228.46	2011.70	5056850	4186980
2007	3555.87	2903.82	2253.07	1769.19	3552.92	3310.13	9673125	8567327
2008	3508.62	2857.70	2367.94	1951.35	2872.19	2669.93	8000006	7048198
2009	3813.68	2989.72	2907.05	2384.51	4002.89	3771.22	13777615	12317053
2010	6312.64	5268.76	2626.59	2179.81	4314.39	3986.31	18469396	16106444
2011	6824.36	5214.42	3424.33	2826.78	4533.50	4063.42	21460860	18254119

表4.15 房地产开发主要指标（2010－2011年）
MAIN INDICATORS OF REAL ESTATE DEVELOPMENT (2010-2011)

指　标	Item	2010	2011
企业个数（个）	**Number of Enterprises (unit)**	**2391**	**2453**
内资企业	Domestic Funded	2275	2341
#国　有	State-owned	101	99
有限责任	Limited Liability	721	786
私　营	Private	1374	1352
港、澳、台投资企业	Enterprises with Funds from Hong Kong, Macao and Taiwan	77	70
外商投资企业	Foreign-Funded	39	42
从业人员（人）	**Number of Employees (person)**	**86602**	**94535**
内资企业	Domestic Funded	80748	88241
#国　有	State-owned	4573	5030
有限责任	Limited Liability	28741	34493
私　营	Private	44730	45591
港、澳、台投资企业	Enterprises with Funds from Hong Kong, Macao and Taiwan	4135	3546
外商投资企业	Foreign-Funded	1719	2748
土地开发及购置（万平方米）	**Land Development and Purchase (10 000 sq.m)**		
本年土地购置面积	Land Space Purchased in This Year	1354.93	1664.55
本年完成投资总额(万元)	**Investment Completed in This Year (10 000 yuan)**	**16202571**	**20150883**
按工程用途分	By Purpose of Projects		
住　宅	Residential Buildings	10914854	14384457
#别墅、高档公寓	Villas and High-Grade Flats	1044474	1199848
办公楼	Office Buildings	315305	526701
商业营业用房	Buildings for Commercial Use	1344039	2180277
其　他	Others	3628373	3059448
资金来源（万元）	**Total Funds by Source (10 000 yuan)**	**34393672**	**44332807**
#国内贷款	Domestic Loans	5847160	6950754
利用外资	Foreign Investment	839265	599183
自筹资金	Self-raised Fund	6849966	8537163
房屋建筑面积(万平方米)	**Floor Space of Buildings (10 000 sq.m)**		
施工面积	Floor Space under Construction	17138.50	20397.24
#住　宅	Residential Buildings	13744.78	15923.84
竣工面积	Floor Space Completed	2626.59	3424.33
#住　宅	Residential Buildings	2179.81	2826.78
本年新开工面积	Floor Space Started in This Year	6312.64	6824.36
#住　宅	Residential Buildings	5268.76	5214.42
商品房销售	**Sales of Commercialized Buildings**		
商品房销售面积（万平方米）	Floor Space of Sales (10 000 sq.m)	4314.39	4533.50
#住　宅	Residential Buildings	3986.31	4063.42
商品房销售额（万元）	Total Sales of Commercialized Buildings (10 000 yuan)	18469396	21460860
#住　宅	Residential Buildings	16106444	18254119
实收资本合计（万元）	**Total Capital Hold (10 000 yuan)**	**11120610**	**14933242**
资产负债率（%）	Ratio of Liabilities to Assets (%)	68.6	67.8
房地产开发经营情况（万元）	**Real Estate Development and Operation (10 000 yuan)**		
主营业务收入	Revenue from Major Business	14732183	16325869
#土地转让收入	Land Transferred	254129	552361

表4.16 商品房施工、竣工和销售面积情况（2010－2011年）

FLOOR SPACE OF COMMERCIALIZED BUILDINGS IN PROCESS, COMPLETED AND SOLD (2010-2011)

单位：万平方米(10 000 sq.m)

指　标	Item	2010	2011
商品房施工面积	**Floor Space of Commercialized Buildings in Process**	**17138.50**	**20397.24**
#主城九区	9 Central Urban Districts	10281.95	11995.73
#住　宅	Residential Buildings	13744.78	15923.84
#别墅、高档公寓	Villas and High-Grade Flats	834.36	877.66
办公楼	Office Buildings	247.56	386.84
商业营业用房	Buildings for Commercial Use	1549.77	1956.25
商品房竣工面积	**Floor Space of Commercialized Buildings Completed**	**2626.59**	**3424.33**
#主城九区	9 Central Urban Districts	1486.99	1764.56
#住　宅	Residential Buildings	2179.81	2826.78
#别墅、高档公寓	Villas and High-Grade Flats	93.64	121.05
办公楼	Office Buildings	30.03	44.77
商业营业用房	Buildings for Commercial Use	229.44	298.79
商品房销售面积	**Floor Space of Commercialized Buildings Sold**	**4314.39**	**4533.50**
#主城九区	9 Central Urban Districts	2014.96	2088.06
#住　宅	Residential Buildings	3986.31	4063.42
#别墅、高档公寓	Villas and High-Grade Flats	222.96	142.19
办公楼	Office Buildings	62.60	43.88
商业营业用房	Buildings for Commercial Use	194.25	266.32

表4.17 房地产开发企业资产负债情况（2010－2011年）
ASSET BALANCE OF ENTERPRISES FOR REAL ESTATE DEVELOPMENT (2010-2011)

单位：万元(10 000 yuan)

指　标	Item	2010	2011
实收资本合计	Total Paid-in Capital	11120610	14933242
资产总计	Total Assets	69379522	101264347
累计折旧	Accumulated Depreciation	527388	548221
#本年折旧	Depreciation in This Year	145033	125843
负债总计	Total Liabilities	47600719	68677757
所有者权益	Owners' Equity	21778803	32586590
资产负债率（%）	Asset-Liability Ratio (%)	68.6	67.8

表4.18 房地产开发企业经营情况（2010－2011年）
STATISTICS ON THE OPERATION OF THE ENTERPRISES OF REAL ESTATE DEVELOPMENT (2010-2011)

单位：万元(10 000 yuan)

指　标	Item	2010	2011
主营业务收入	Revenue from Major Business	14732183	16325869
土地转让收入	Land Transferred	254129	552361
商品房屋销售收入	Commercialized Buildings Sold	13792490	14989210
房屋出租收入	Houses Leased	250326	274870
其他收入	Others	435239	509428
主营业务税金及附加	Tax and Extra Charges on Major Business	967134	1329494
利润总额	Total Profits	1588098	1923773

表4.19 重点项目完成情况（2011年）
COMPLETED INVESTMENT IN KEY PROJECTS (2011)

单位：亿元（100 million yuan）

指　标	Item	计划总投资 Total Planned Investment	完成投资 Total Investment Completed	完成计划(%) Percentage of Completion(%)
重点项目完成情况	**Completed Investment in Key Projects**	2100	2167.0	103.2
交通运输	Transport	300	298.0	99.3
能　源	Energy	80	81.0	101.3
城市基础设施	Urban Infrastructure	300	294.6	98.2
园区基础设施	Industrial Park Infrastructure	130	195.0	150.0
节能减排及生态建设	Energy saving,Emission Reduction and Ecologic Construction	170	204.0	120.0
水利基础设施	Water Conservancy Infrastructure	30	28.5	95.0
社会民生	People's livelihood	280	343.4	122.6
科　技	Science and Technology	10	5.5	55.0
工　业	Industry	510	438.0	85.9
社会文化旅游	Society, Culture and Tourism	100	98.0	98.0
农业产业化	Agriculture	30	26.3	87.7
商贸流通	Commerce and Trade	80	72.7	90.9
房地产	Real Estate	80	82.0	102.5

重/庆/统/计/年/鉴

主要统计指标解释

■ 固定资产投资

以货币形式表现的在一定时期内建造和购置固定资产的工作量以及与此有关的费用的总称。该指标是反映固定资产投资规模、结构和发展速度的综合性指标,又是观察工程进度和考核投资效果的重要依据。

■ 城镇固定资产投资

包括建设项目投资和房地产开发投资。

■ 建设项目

指城镇各种登记注册类型的企业、事业、行政单位及个体户进行的计划总投资（或实际需要总投资）500万元及500万元以上的建设项目。（2010年及以前为50万元及50万元以上的建设项目，2011年开始为500万元及500万元以上的建设项目）

■ 房地产开发投资

指各种登记注册类型的房地产开发公司、商品房建设公司及其他房地产开发法人单位和附属于其他法人单位实际从事房地产开发或经营的活动单位统一开发的包括统代建、拆迁还建的住宅、厂房、仓库、饭店、宾馆、度假村、写字楼、办公楼等房屋建筑物和配套的服务设施，土地开发工程（如道路、给水、排水、供电、供热、通讯、平整场地等基础设施工程）的投资；不包括单纯的土地交易活动。

■ 农村投资

包括在农村区域范围内进行固定资产活动的企业、事业、行政单位及个人投资，包括农村非农户投资、农村农户投资。

■ 建设总规模

是指在报告期内所有施工项目的计划总投资。这个指标和施工项目相对应。

■ 在建总规模

是指在报告期末所有在建项目的计划总投资。

■ 在建净规模

是指报告期末所有在建项目建成投产尚需的投资总量。

在建净规模＝在建总规模－未投产项目（期末在建）累计完成投资。

■ 新增固定资产

指报告期内交付使用的固定资产价值。包括本年内建成投入生产或交付使用的工程投资和达到固定资产标准的设备、工具、器具的投资及有关应摊入的费用。该指标是反映固定资产投资成果的价值指标，也是反映建设进度，计算固定资产投资效果的重要指标。

■ 固定资产投资按构成分

固定资产投资活动按其工作内容和实现方式分为建筑安装工程，设备、工具、器具购置，其他费用三个部分。

（1）建筑安装工程（建筑工作量）：指各种房屋、建筑物的建造工程和各种设备、装置的安装工程。在安装工程中，不包括被安装设备本身的价值。

（2）设备、工具、器具购置：指把工业企业生产的产品转为固定资产的购置活动，包括建设单位或企业、事业单位购置或自制达到固定资产标准的设备、工具、器具的价值。新建单位及扩建单位的新建车间，按照设计或计划要求购置或自制的全部设备、工具、器具，不论是否达到固定资产标准均计入“设备、工具、器具购置”中。

（3）其他费用：指在固定资产建造和购置过程中发生的，除建筑安装工程和设备、工器具购置投资完成额以外的费用，不指经营中财务上的其他费用。

■ 固定资产投资按资金来源

根据固定资产投资的资金来源不同，分为国家预算内资金、国内贷款、利用外资、自筹资金和其他资金。

（1）本年资金来源合计：指固定资产投资单位在本年内收到的可用于固定资产建造和购置的各种资金，包括上年末结余资金、本年度内拨入或借入的资金以及各种方式筹集的资金。

（2）上年末结余资金：指上年资金来源中没有形成固定资产投资额而结余的资金。包括尚未用到工程上的材料价值、未开始安装的需要安装的设备价值及结存的现金和银行存款等。

（3）本年资金来源小计：指固定资产投资单位在报告期收到的，用于固定资产投资的各种货币资金。包括国家预算内资金、国内贷款、债券、利用外资、自筹资金和其他资金。

① 国家预算资金：自2011年起，按照全国人大和国务院的要求，各级财政的所有资金，包括税收和非税收入，均必须纳入预算管理，我国已不存在预算外资金的概念，因此各级政府用于固定资产投资的财政资金均为预算资金。包括中央预算资金和地方预算资金，旧的国家预算内资金的内容和现中央预算资金的内容基本一致。国家预算包括一般预算、政府性基金预算、国有资本经营预算和社保基金预算。各类预算中用于固定资产投资的资金全部作为国家预算资金填报，其中一般预算中用于固定资产投资的部分包括基建投资、车购税、灾后恢复重建基金和其他财政投资。各级政府债券也应归入国家预算资金。

② 国内贷款：指报告期固定资产投资单位向银行及非银行金融机构借入的用于固定资产投资的各种国内借款，包括：银行利用自有资金以及吸收的存款发放的贷款，上级主管部门拨入的国内贷款、国家专项贷款（包括煤代油贷款、劳改煤矿专项贷款等），地方财政专项资金安排的贷款、国内储备贷款、周转贷款等。

③ 债券：指企业（公司）或金融机构通过发行各种债券，筹集用于固定资产投资的资金。包括由银行代理国家专业投资公司发行的重点企业债券和基本建设债券。

④ 利用外资：指报告期收到的用于固定资产投资的境外资金（包括设备、材料、技术在内）。包括外商直接投资、对外借款（外国政府、国际金融组织贷款、出口信贷、外国银行商业贷款、对外发行债券和股票）以及外商其他投资（包括补偿贸易和加工装配由外商提供的设备价款、国际租赁）。

⑤ 自筹资金：指固定资产投资单位报告期收到的，由各地区、各部门及企事业单位筹集用于固定资产投资的预算外资金。

⑥ 其他资金来源：指在报告期收到的除以上各种资金以外其他用于固定资产投资的资金，包括社会集资，个人资金、无偿损赠的资金及其他单位拨入的资金等。

固定资产投资按建设性质分

（1）新建：一般是指从无到有、“平地起家”开始建设的企、事业和行政或独立的工程单位。有的单位原有的基础很小，经过建设后其新增加的固定资产价值超过原有固定资产价值（原值）三倍以上的也算新建。

（2）扩建：是指为扩大原有产品的生产能力、在厂内或其他地点增建主要生产车间（或主要工程）、独立的生产线或总厂之下的分厂的企业；事业单位和行政单位在原单位增建业务用房（如学校增建教学用房、医院增建门诊部或病床用房、行政机关增建办公楼等）也作为扩建。

（3）改建和技术改造：指现有企业、事业单位，对原有设施进行技术改造或更新（包括相应配套的辅助性生产、生活福利设施）的建设项目。现有企业、事业单位为适应市场变化的需要，而改变企业的主要产品种类（如军工企业转产民用品等）的建设项目，应作为改建。原有产品生产作业线由于各工序（车间）之间能力不平衡，为填平补齐充分发挥原有生产能力而增建不增加本企业主要产品设计能力的车间，也应作为改建。技术改造是指企业、事业单位在现有基础上，用先进的技术代替落后的技术，用先进的工艺和装备代替落后的工艺和装备，以改变企业落后的技术经济面貌，实现以内涵为主的扩大再生产，达到提高产品质量、促进产品更新换代、节约能源、降低消耗、扩大生产规模、全面提高社会经济效益的目的。技术改造具体包括以下内容：机器设备和工具的更新改造；生产工艺改革、节约能源和原材料的改造；厂房建筑和公共设施的改造；劳动条件和生产环境的改造等。

新增生产能力（或工程效益）

指在本年度内按照新增生产能力（或工程效益）的计算条件和标准，实际建成投入生产或交付使用的生产能力（或工程效益），即通过固定资产投资活动而增加的设计能力。

计算新增生产能力（或工程效益）是以能独立发挥生产能力（或工程效益）的工程为对象，如一座矿

主要统计指标解释

井、一座转炉、一套化工装置、一条铁路专用线等。当工程建成，经有关部门验收鉴定合格，正式移交投入生产，即应计算新增生产能力（或效益）。

新增生产能力的数量，原则上应按设计（计划）能力计算。设计能力指设计中规定的主体工程（或主体设备）及相应配套的辅助工程（或配套设备）在正常情况下能够达到的生产能力。在建设过程中需要调整设计能力时，必须经原有设计的管理机关批准后，才能按批准修改后的能力计算。如尚未批准，仍按原设计能力计算，并加以说明。无设计（或计划）能力的，可根据验收时鉴定能力计算。

建成投产的工程，各生产环节的设备已经配齐，符合计算新增生产能力条件的，应该按工程的全部设计能力计算。各生产环节的设备虽未按设计全部配套建成，但保证生产所需的主体设备、配套设备、主体工程、附属工程都已部分完成，形成生产作业线，经负荷试运转交付使用单位正式投入生产的，只计算设备配齐部分的能力。这部分建成投入生产的工程，填报新增生产能力时，需附有计算依据，并说明工程或主要设备配齐部分的情况，以及尚未建成的工程主要内容或尚缺的设备情况。

■ 施工项目个数

指报告期内所有施工的建设项目个数，包括本年新开工的项目和以前年度开工在本年继续施工的建设项目。

■ 本年投产项目个数

按设计文件规定的全部生产能力（或效益）在本年内全部建成投产，经验收合格交付使用的建设项目个数。

■ 本年房屋施工面积

指报告期内施工的全部房屋建筑面积。包括本期新开工的面积和上期开工跨入本期继续施工的房屋面积，以及上期已停建在本期复工的房屋面积。本期竣工和本期施工后又停缓建的房屋，其建筑面积仍计入本期施工房屋面积中。

■ 本年房屋竣工面积

指在报告期内房屋建筑按照设计要求已全部完工，达到住人和使用条件，经验收鉴定合格（或达到竣工验收标准），可正式移交使用的各栋房屋建筑面积的总和。

■ 本年竣工房屋价值

指在报告期内竣工房屋本身的建造价值。竣工房屋价值按房屋设计和预算规定的内容计算。竣工房屋本身的基础、结构、房屋、装修以及水、电、卫等附属工程的建造价值，也包括作为房屋建筑组成部分而列入房屋建筑工程预算内的设备（如电梯、通风设备等）的购置和安装费用。不包括厂房内的工艺设备、工艺管线的购置和安装，工艺设备基础的建造，室外的水、暖、电、卫、道路工程、挡土墙等环境工程的费用，办公及生活用家具的购置等费用，购置土地的费用，迁移补偿费和场地平整的费用等。

■ 固定资产交付使用率

指一定时期新增固定资产与同期完成投资额的比率。该指标是反映固定资产动用速度，衡量建设过程中宏观投资效果的综合指标。由于新增固定资产是较长时期内形成的结果，而投资额则是当年完成的，因此，该指标一般适宜于反映较长时期内固定资产的动用情况。

■ 别墅、高档公寓

指建筑造价和销售价格明显高于一般商品住宅的商品住宅。别墅一般指地处郊区，独立成栋的商品住宅；高档公寓一般指地处市内高尚社区，高层或多层的商品住宅。别墅、高档公寓的确定标准：一是经有房地产投资计划审批权的主管部门审批建设的别墅、高档公寓开发项目；二是销售价格高于当地同等地段商品住宅平均销售价格一倍以上的别墅、公寓开发项目。该指标可以分析房地产投资结构，反映高收入家庭商品住宅的供求平衡情况。

■ 商品房销售面积

指报告期内出售商品房屋的合同总面积(即双方签署的正式买卖合同中所确定的建筑面积)。由现房销售建筑面积和期房销售建筑面积两部分组成。

（1）现房销售面积：是指在报告期内正式签订买卖合同、已经竣工达到入住条件的商品房屋建筑面

主要统计指标解释

积。包括以一次性付款方式和分期付款方式销售的现房建筑面积。

（2）期房销售面积： 是指在报告期内正式签订买卖合同、正在建设尚未竣工交付使用的商品房屋建筑面积。包括以一次性付款方式和分期付款方式销售的商品房屋建筑面积。期房销售建筑面积竣工后不再结转为现房销售建筑面积。

■ 完成开发土地面积

指报告期内对土地进行开发并已完成七通一平等前期开发工程，具备进行房屋建筑物施工或达到出让条件的土地面积。

■ 本年购置土地面积

指在本年内通过各种方式获得土地使用权的土地面积。

CHONGQING STATISTICAL YEARBOOK

Explanatory Notes on Main Statistical Indicators

□ Total Investment in Fixed Assets

Refers to the volume of activities in construction and purchases of fixed assets and related fees, expressed in monetary terms. It is a comprehensive indicator which shows the size, structure and growth of the investment in fixed assets, providing basis for observing the progress of construction projects and evaluating results of investment.

□ Urban Investment in Fixed Assets

Refers to investment in construction and investment in real estate development.

□ Investment of Construction

Refers to construction projects involving a total planned(or required)investment of 500,000 yuan and over by enterprises of various types of ownership, institutions, administrative units and individuals in urban areas,investment in real estate development,and private investment.

□ Investment in Real Estate Development

Refers to investment by real estate development companies, commercialized buildings construction companies and other real estate development units of various types of ownership in the construction of buildings, such as residential buildings, factory buildings, warehouses, hotels, guesthouses, holiday villages, office buildings, and the complementary service facilities and land development projects, such as roads, water supply, water drainage, power supply, heating supply, telecommunications, land leveling and other infrastructural projects. It does not include activities in pure land transactions.

□ Investment in Rural Areas

Refers to investment in fixed assets by enterprises, institutions, administrative units and individuals in rural areas, including rural household and non-rural household in rural areas.

□ Total Size of Construction

Refers to the planned total investment for all construction projects during the reference period. This item should correspond with projects under work.

□ Total Size of Investment in Projects under Construction

Refers to the planned total investment of all projects under construction at the end of the reference period.

□ Net Size of Investment in Projects under Construction

Refers to the outstanding requirement of investment of all projects under construction at the end of the reference period.

Net size of investment in projects under construction= Total size of investment – Accumulated completed investment of projects under construction.

□ Newly Increased Fixed Assets

Refers to the newly increased value of fixed assets, constructed or purchased, that have been transferred to the investor and have been including equipment and instruments.This is an indicator that demnstrates the results of investment in fixed assets in monetary terms, and an important indicator to reflect the speed of construction and to calculate the efficiency of investment.

□ Investment in Fixed Assets by Structure

By their contents, investment activities are classified into 3 categories, i.e. construction and installation, purchase of equipment and instrument, and other expenses.

(Ⅰ)Construction and installation (work volume of construction): refers to the construction of various houses and buildings and installation of various kinds of equipment and instruments. The value of equipment installed is not included in the value of installation projects.

(Ⅱ)Purchase of equipment and instruments: refers to the

purchase converting products produced by industrial enterprises to the purchase of fixed assets, including the total value of equipment, tools, and vessels purchased or self - produced. Equipment, tools and vessels purchased or self - produced for new workshops by newly established or expanded units are categorized as "purchase of equipment and instruments" no matter whether they come up to the standards for fixed assets or not.

(III) Other expenses: refer to expenses occurring during the construction or purchase of fixed assets other than construction, installation or purchase of equipment and instruments, excluding other expenses in financial management.

□ Sources of Funds for Investment in Fixed Assets

Are categorized as funds from the State budget, domestic loans, foreign investment, self-raised funds, and others, depending on the sources of investment.

(I) Total of source of funds in this year: refers to the various funds received by investing enterprises in this year for the purpose of construction and purchase of investment in fixed assets. It includes balance of funds brought forward from the previous year, funds appropriated and brought in this year, and funds collected by various ways.

(II) Balance of funds brought forward from the previous year: refers to the surplus funds which didn't form the investment in fixed assets in the sources of funds in previous year. It includes material values that will be used in the projects, facilities values that must be and will be installed, and surplus cashes and deposits in bank.

(III) Subtotal of source of funds in this year: refers to the monetary funds received by investing enterprises during the reference period for the purpose of investment in fixed assets. It includes funds from state budgetary appropriation, domestic loans, bonds, foreign investment, self-raised funds, and others.

(a) State budgetary appropriation consists of budgetary appropriation and loans from state budget. More specifically, it includes, from the budget of the central government, capital construction fund (operation fund and non-operational fund), special expenses (e.g. expenses on substituting petroleum with coal), loans from repayment, discount fund, expenses on innovation and trial production of new products, expenses on urban construction, expenses on temporary construction by trade departments, development fund for less developed areas, as well as local budgetary fund transferred from the central budget.

(b) Domestic loans refer to loans of various forms borrowed by investing units from banks and non-bank financial institutions during the reference period, including loans issued by banks from their self-owned funds and deposit, loans appropriated by higher responsible authorities, special loans by government (including loan for substituting petroleum with coal, special loan for reform-through-labour coal mines), loans arranged by local government from special funds, domestic reserve loan, and working loan, etc.

(c) Bonds refer to the funds collected by enterprises or financial institutions by bonds issuance for the purpose of investment in fixed assets. It includes emphasis enterprises bonds issued by banks substituting special nation investment enterprises and capital construction bonds.

(d) Foreign Investment refers to foreign funds received during the reference period for investment in fixed assets (covering equipment, materials and technology), including foreign direct investment, foreign borrowings (loans from foreign governments and international financial institutions, export credit, commercial loans from foreign banks, issuance of bonds and stocks overseas), and other foreign investment (covering facilities' funds provided by foreign investment by compensation trade and processing & assembly, as well as international lease).

(e) Self-raised funds refer to extra-budgetary funds for investment in fixed assets received by investing units from central government ministries, local governments, enterprises and institutions during the reference period.

(f) Others refer to funds for investment in fixed assets received from the sources other than those listed above, including funds raised from social and individuals, through donations, and funds transferred from other units.

□ Investment in Fixed Assets by Type of Construction

(I) New construction in general: refers to newly constructed enterprises, institutions, administrative agencies or independent projects from scratch. In case the asset of the existing unit is quite small, and the value of newly added fixed assets exceeds the

EXPLANATORY NOTES TO MAJOR STATISTICAL INDICATORS

original value of assets by three times, the expansion will be considered as new construction.

(Ⅱ) Expansion: refers to construction of new major production workshop, branch factory or independent production line within a factory or in other locations, for the purpose of increasing the production capacity (or improving efficiency) of the original products. Newly constructed houses for the operation of institutions and administrative organizations (such as the newly constructed buildings for teaching in schools, buildings for clinics or wards in hospitals, buildings for administrative agencies, etc.) are also classified as expansion.

(Ⅲ) Reconstruction and Technical Transformation: refer to construction projects by existing enterprises or institutions in innovation or technical transformation of the old facilities (including auxiliary production equipment and welfare facilities). Also considered as reconstruction is the construction of new workshops by the existing enterprises or institutions to change the variety of products to meet the market demand (such as the production of civil products by defence industries), or to bring the designed production capacity into full play through a more balanced production process on production lines. Technical transformation refers to replacement of old technology or equipment by new technology or equipment, in order to expand the reproduction through improvement of technology contents in production, to improve product quality, to promote new products, to save energy and reduce consumption and to improve overall social-economic efficiency. Contents of technical transformation include: updating of machinery, equipment and tools; reforming production process by using energy or materials saving technology; construction of factory workshops and transformation of public facilities; improvement of working conditions and environment, etc.

□ Newly Increased Production Capacity (or Project Efficiency)

Refers to the production capacity put into produce or put into use actually according to calculation conditions and standards of newly increased production capacity (or project efficiency) in the reference period, that is increase of designed capacity (or project efficiency) through investment in fixed assets.

The target of calculation of newly increased production capacity (project efficiency) is project can produce production capacity (or project efficiency) independently, such as a mineral well, a turn kiln, a set of chemical appliance, a special rail line, etc. When the project completes and has been checked, accepted and formally put into production, it can be calculate as newly increased production capacity (or project efficiency).

Newly increased production capacity is calculated according to design capacity (or plan capacity). Design capacity refers to the production capacity of major projects (or major facilities) and subsidiary projects (or subsidiary facilities) which can be come true in normal situation. When there are some changes in construction process of design capacity, the new capacity can be calculated after the approval of management. If it didn't have the approval, it must be calculated by original design capacity and give a explanation. If it hasn't design capacity, it can be calculated by the capacity according to checkout and verification.

Newly increased production capacity of projects completed and put into produce, whose facilities are assorted in every part and correspond with conditions of calculation is calculated by total design capacity. If the total facilities aren't assorted while a part of major and subsidiary facilities and projects complete that can meet the need of production and put into produce, the newly increased production capacity is calculated by capacity of assorted part. When newly increased production capacity is infilled and reported the projects put into produce must have calculation warranty and give an explanation of situation of projects and major parts assorted, major content of projects uncompleted and missing facilities.

□ Number of Projects under Construction

Refers to the number of projects having construction in the reference period, including new projects in current year and projects started in the reference period and continued in current year.

□ Number of Projects Put into Produce

Refers to the number of projects completed and have been checked, accepted and formally put into use in this year according to total production capacity (or efficiency) prescribed in design document.

EXPLANATORY NOTES TO MAJOR STATISTICAL INDICATORS

□ Floor Space under Construction in this Year

Refers to total floor space of all buildings under construction during the reference period, including floor space of newly started buildings during the reference period, floor space of construction extended from the previous period to the current period, and floor space of construction suspended during the previous period and resumed in the current period. Floor space of construction completed in the current period, and floor space of construction started and then suspended in the current period are also included in the floor space under construction of the current year.

□ Floor Space of Buildings Completed in this Year

Refers to the floor space of all buildings completed in the reference period, which have been appraised and accepted (or come up to the designed standards) and have been transferred to the owners for use.

□ Value of Buildings Completed in this Year

Refers to the intrinsic construction value of buildings completed in the reference period. It is figured by the rules of buildings design and budget, which not only includes the construction value of foundations, structure, furnishings, subsidiary projects such as water, electricity, toilet, etc. but also includes purchase and installation expenditures of facilities (such as lift, ventilation, etc.) listed into buildings budget as component of building construction. It excludes the purchase and installation of technical facilities, leads and lines in factories, construction of technical facilities' basis, expenditures of environment projects such as water, eructate, electricity, toilet, road projects, wall fended to earth outside, purchase of furniture in office or house, purchase of lands, as well as expenditures of move compensation and land leveling etc.

□ Rate of Projects of Fixed Assets Completed and Put into Operation

Refers to the ratio of the newly increased fixed assets to the total investment made in the same period. This is a comprehensive indicator reflecting the speed of the employment of fixed assets and the investment efficiency at the macro-level. As the newly increase fixed assets is the result of a long period while the investment is completed in the current year, this indicator is expected to be used to reflect the employment of fixed assets over a long period of time.

□ Villas, High-Grade Apartments

Refer to commercial houses whose construction costs and marketing prices are significantly higher than ordinary housing. Villas are independent structures generally located in the suburbs; high-grade apartments are multi-story buildings located in elegant urban neighborhoods. Criteria for villas and high-grade apartments include: 1) projects for the construction of villas or high-grade apartments have to be approved by competent departments in charge of real estate development and investment plans, and 2) prices for projects on villas or high-grade apartments are higher by over 100% compared with the average prices of ordinary commercial housing projects in similar location. This indicator helps to analyze the investment structure of the real estate industry and the demand and supply of housing for high-income households.

□ Floor Space of Commercial Buildings Actually Sold

Refers to the total contracted floor space of commercial buildings actually sold in reporting period(the floor space provided in the formal contract),which consists of the floor space of the sold completed buildings and the floor space of the sold forward-delivery buildings.

(Ⅰ) Floor Space of Sold Completed Buildings refers to the floor space of the completed commercial buildings prepared for occupancy with the formally signed sales contract in the reporting period, including the floor space of the completed buildings purchased by one-off payment and by installment.

(Ⅱ) Floor Space of Sold Forward-Delivery Buildings refers to the floor space of the uncompleted commercial buildings still under construction with the formally signed sales contract in the reporting period, including the floor space of the commercial buildings purchased by one-off payment and by installment. The floor space of sold forward-delivery buildings,afer completion,will not be carried forward into the floor space of sold completed buildings.

EXPLANATORY NOTES TO MAJOR STATISTICAL INDICATORS

□ Developed Land Area Completed

Refers to the land area of land development and prophase development projects completed, which can carry out construction or remise.

□ Purchased Land Area in Current Year

Refers to the land area accessible by various means in current year.

第 5 章

能源消费

ENERGY CONSUMPTION

B 简要说明 BRIEF INTRODUCTION

本章主要内容包括能源消费及品种构成，能源消费弹性系数，平均每万元GDP能源消费量及日均能源消费量，综合能源平衡表，按工业行业分的能源消费量和工业产值综合能耗。本章资料由市统计局能源处根据有关资料和调查结果编制。

The data in this chapter mainly cover energy consumption and its composition, the elasticity ratio of energy consumption, average energy consumption per 10,000 yuan of GDP, average daily energy consumption, overall energy balance sheet, energy consumption by industrial sector and comprehensive energy consumption per unit output value. This chapter is compiled by Division of Industry and Transport Statistics, Chongqing Municipal Bureau of Statistics on the basis of the related materials and the results of surveys.

表5.1 主要年份能源消费总量
TOTAL CONSUMPTION OF ENERGY IN MAJOR YEARS

单位：万吨标准煤(10 000 tons of SCE)

年份 Year	能源消费总量 Total Consumption of Energy	其中 of which			
		煤炭 Coal	天然气 Natural Gas	油料 Oil	电力 Electricity
1949	91.71	88.97		2.06	0.68
1952	155.47	150.64		3.43	1.40
1957	263.73	247.95	3.41	7.00	5.37
1962	476.37	429.30	18.20	14.21	14.66
1965	342.88	295.00	19.65	9.85	18.38
1970	469.56	379.80	50.13	14.04	25.59
1975	651.21	514.03	78.58	21.99	36.61
1978	889.20	703.87	103.87	32.20	49.26
1980	985.59	752.60	129.08	40.53	63.38
1981	1004.30	766.33	137.82	33.83	66.32
1982	1050.33	794.01	138.62	48.30	69.40
1983	1110.05	838.14	148.22	51.06	72.63
1984	1160.49	872.47	151.97	60.05	76.00
1985	1241.40	938.21	160.83	62.83	79.53
1986	1271.14	938.66	173.38	75.61	83.49
1987	1395.65	1036.28	195.61	76.12	87.64
1988	1513.18	1157.08	183.73	80.37	92.00
1989	1565.46	1194.44	190.36	84.08	96.58
1990	1516.59	1130.76	196.44	88.00	101.39
1991	1558.56	1151.68	197.06	96.63	113.19
1992	1601.01	1172.98	198.32	103.34	126.37
1993	1644.85	1194.68	200.89	108.20	141.08
1994	1696.72	1216.78	216.74	105.70	157.50
1995	1776.91	1239.85	258.36	102.87	175.83
1996	1871.09	1317.32	260.86	97.39	195.52
1997	2030.13	1383.98	282.80	145.47	217.88
1998	2119.46	1393.43	291.30	183.62	251.11
1999	2278.42	1495.55	308.19	196.34	278.34
2000	2410.82	1599.80	312.20	202.17	296.65
2001	2573.68	1700.43	322.51	206.20	344.54
2002	2823.05	1928.90	331.87	213.84	348.44
2003	3137.90	2206.42	349.11	220.81	361.56
2004	3668.41	2505.08	403.52	379.97	379.84
2005	4464.58	3151.71	472.15	411.86	428.86
2006	4881.63	3381.87	532.67	469.11	497.98
2007	5512.44	3832.29	578.95	549.12	552.08
2008	5895.10	4048.95	648.38	600.57	597.20
2009	6431.63	4499.83	657.82	619.73	654.25
2010	7117.41	4857.64	750.39	741.20	768.18
2011	7951.12	5338.03	819.81	912.06	881.22

注：本表各年能源品种均已折合为按当量值计算的吨标准煤。
Note: All the data hereof has been adjusted according to the result of the 2nd National Economic Census, and each type of energy has been converted into tons of SCE calculated in equivalent value.

表5.2 规模以上工业按行业分能源消费量（2010－2011年）
ENERGY CONSUMPTION OF ENTERPRISES ABOVE DESIGNATED SIZE BY SECTOR (2010-2011)

行　业	Sector	原　煤（吨） Coal(ton)		焦　炭（吨） Coke(ton)	
		2010	2011	2010	2011
工业消费总量	**Total Industry Consumption**	**46534370**	**52618102**	**2434838**	**3024825**
采矿业	**Mining**	**21418719**	**22456405**	**2958**	**4059**
#煤炭开采和洗选业	Mining and Washing of Coal	20917241	21874768	2958	4059
石油和天然气开采业	Extraction of Petroleum and Natural Gas				
黑色金属矿采选业	Mining and Processing of Ferrous Metal Ores	44738	40585		
有色金属矿采选业	Mining and Processing of Non-Ferrous Metal Ores	10			
非金属矿采选业	Mining and Processing of Non-metal Ores	456730	541052		
制造业	**Manufacturing**	**11622264**	**14039634**	**2431800**	**3020766**
农副食品加工业	Processing of Food from Agricultural Products	98484	137002		
食品制造业	Manufacture of Foods	96402	199597	131	75
饮料制造业	Manufacture of Beverages	80618	76503	914	747
烟草制品业	Manufacture of Tobacco	11620	5897		
纺织业	Manufacture of Textile	237078	173743		
纺织服装、鞋、帽制造业	Manufacture of Textile Wearing Apparel, Footware and Caps	35	933		
皮革、毛皮、羽毛（绒）及其制品业	Manufacture of Leather, Fur, Feather and Related Products	6418	2423		
木材加工及木、竹、藤、棕、草制品业	Processing of Timber, Manufacture of Wood, Bamboo, Rattan, Palm, and Straw Products	20272	14955		
家具制造业	Manufacture of Furniture	968	1296		
造纸及纸制品业	Manufacture of Paper and Paper Products	998788	975158		
印刷业、记录媒介的复制	Printing, Reproduction of Recording Media	635			
文教体育用品制造业	Manufacture of Articles For Culture, Education and Sport Activities	12			
石油加工、炼焦及核燃料加工业	Processing of Petroleum, Coking, Processing of Nuclear Fuel	593587	1088211		

注：2010年数据因汇总单位由主营业务收入500万元以上调整为主营业务收入2000万元以上，与去年年鉴2010年数据不一致。

汽 油（吨） Gasoline(ton)		煤 油（吨） Kerosene(ton)		柴 油（吨） Diesel Oil(ton)		天然气（万立方米） Natural Gas(10 000 cu.m)		电 力（万千瓦时） Electricity(10 000 kw.h)	
2010	2011	2010	2011	2010	2011	2010	2011	2010	2011
85457	**85823**	**6476**	**6484**	**197807**	**228396**	**411948**	**427581**	**4161452**	**4824286**
4760	**5411**	**173**	**98**	**22010**	**27747**	**4586**	**3642**	**212267**	**220058**
3970	4843	173	98	10336	15620	205	218	157594	169067
153	66			29	32	4224	3289	5602	2611
192	122			1345	1379	138	128	4507	4094
59	21			92	6			1187	2097
386	359			10208	10710	19	7	43377	42189
74467	**74113**	**6278**	**6370**	**162033**	**190230**	**406765**	**423448**	**3229805**	**3717464**
1390	1924		1	1496	2449	1664	2794	34366	44296
1342	1298		9	6752	5300	2508	3326	14158	18794
3563	2448	4	1	1948	2411	2249	3163	25106	27052
294	279			1341	1093	699	667	6329	5665
1314	736	2	5	804	807	2180	2903	71763	64409
729	686			247	333	359	315	4354	6630
706	571			18	64	230	230	5021	6439
79	359		34	210	282	4	35	4612	7724
418	408		10	413	547	31	126	4787	5038
732	462			3988	4745	1323	1330	96899	97687
675	934	7	9	621	645	551	602	9065	10989
7	2			4	7			451	789
161	170	271	80	889	1554	216	160	6657	10305

Note: Because the statistic scope is changed from the units with the major business revenue of 5 million yuan and above to the units with the major business revenue of 20 million yuan and above, the data in 2010 in this table is different from that in the yearbook of last year.

表5.2 续表 continued

行 业	Sector	原 煤（吨） Coal(ton)		焦 炭（吨） Coke(ton)	
		2010	2011	2010	2011
化学原料及化学制品制造业	Manufacture of Raw Chemical Materials and Chemical Products	2990174	3359867	17603	23951
医药制造业	Manufacture of Medicines	239674	209271		155
化学纤维制造业	Manufacture of Chemical Fibres	1091	5035		
橡胶制品业	Manufacture of Rubber	153583	112811		
塑料制品业	Manufacture of Plastics	20819	13660	38	86
非金属矿物制品业	Manufacture of Non-metallic Mineral Products	4951525	6070183	3122	23
黑色金属冶炼及压延加工业	Smelting and Pressing of Ferrous Metals	742954	1097883	2293748	2896110
有色金属冶炼及压延加工业	Smelting and Pressing of Nonferrous Metals	206078	320885	22404	19632
金属制品业	Manufacture of Metal Products	23952	13891	1302	949
通用设备制造业	Manufacture of General Purpose Machinery	28361	24802	41475	36031
专用设备制造业	Manufacture of Special Purpose Machinery	2644	1736	2488	2044
交通运输设备制造业	Manufacture of Transport Equipment	100240	115816	47668	39792
电气机械及器材制造业	Manufacture of Electrical Machinery and Equipment	5752	4834	309	523
通信设备、计算机及其他电子设备制造业	Manufacture of Communication Equipment, Computers and Other Electronic Equipment	711	1906		
仪器仪表及文化、办公用机械制造业	Manufacture of Measuring Instruments and Machinery for Cultural Activity and Office Work	1975	1750	598	558
工艺品及其他制造业	Manufacture of Artwork and Other Manufacturing	7032	9066		90
废弃资源和废旧材料回收加工业	Recycling and Disposal of Waste	782	520		
电力、燃气及水的生产和供应业	**Electric Power, Gas and Water Production and Supply**	**13493387**	**16122063**	**80**	
电力、热力的生产和供应业	Production and Supply of Electric Power and Heat Power	13493387	16122063	80	
燃气生产和供应业	Production and Supply of Gas				
水的生产和供应业	Production and Supply of Water				

汽 油（吨） Gasoline(ton)		煤 油（吨） Kerosene(ton)		柴 油（吨） Diesel Oil(ton)		天然气（万立方米） Natural Gas(10 000 cu.m)		电 力（万千瓦时） Electricity(10 000 kw.h)	
2010	2011	2010	2011	2010	2011	2010	2011	2010	2011
11845	3499	431	673	5635	10988	236620	234677	614246	737529
1416	1586	85	54	1232	1150	4038	4427	33741	34349
42	3			46	16	300		1784	1424
1798	1772		6	488	499	856	1741	30244	39194
1127	1069	4	36	1603	1451	118	184	32152	43539
3661	2939	97	164	81057	102271	71662	78118	554996	671081
1452	2982	67	93	4434	4225	17845	10742	645502	719912
997	1030	1	1	1956	1886	12093	16785	337201	350989
2198	2278	93	88	1459	1887	5463	11736	33874	46108
4348	5065	1484	1110	8453	9619	8143	7933	115831	138663
2175	2170	97	48	2341	1420	1534	806	32215	28197
26453	32444	3539	3549	28794	29916	32327	36558	424115	471150
3009	3468	14	68	1350	1932	1611	2130	43032	54956
522	640	7	8	267	267	676	792	19503	49497
1790	1988	75	278	1054	1052	829	125	21185	11479
200	863		45	134	982	20	669	1820	12089
24	40			2999	432	616	374	4796	1491
6230	**6299**	**25**	**16**	**13764**	**10419**	**597**	**491**	**719380**	**886764**
5126	5066	25	15	13291	9906	405	250	660582	819838
735	864			283	308	191	240	6070	6311
369	369		1	190	205	1	1	52728	60615

表5.3 规模以上工业企业产值综合能耗（2010－2011年）
COMPREHENSIVE ENERGY CONSUMPTION OF INDUSTRIAL ENTERPRISES ABOVE DESIGNATED SIZE PER UNIT OUTPUT VALUE (2010-2011)

行 业	Sector	综合能源消费量（吨标准煤） Comprehensive Energy Consumption (ton of SCE)		产值能耗（吨标准煤/万元） Energy Consumption per Unit Output Value (ton of SCE/10 000 yuan)	
		2010	2011	2010	2011
工业消费总量	**Total Industry Consumption**	**30879192**	**35546429**	**0.35**	**0.30**
采矿业	**Mining**	**2958362**	**3139707**	**0.63**	**0.65**
#煤炭开采和洗选业	Mining and Washing of Coal	2637976	2771649	0.87	0.71
石油和天然气开采业	Extraction of Petroleum and Natural Gas	57243	43314	0.08	0.43
黑色金属矿采选业	Mining and Processing of Ferrous Metal Ores	46834	79611	0.30	0.81
有色金属矿采选业	Mining and Processing of Non-Ferrous Metal Ores	1676	2665	0.02	0.06
非金属矿采选业	Mining and Processing of Non-metal Ores	214633	242468	0.31	0.35
制造业	**Manufacturing**	**21394182**	**24568773**	**0.27**	**0.23**
农副食品加工业	Processing of Food from Agricultural Products	138372	193174	0.04	0.04
食品制造业	Manufacture of Foods	129394	181908	0.14	0.15
饮料制造业	Manufacture of Beverages	125460	137436	0.12	0.11
烟草制品业	Manufacture of Tobacco	25090	20239	0.02	0.02
纺织业	Manufacture of Textile	284174	238761	0.18	0.14
纺织服装、鞋、帽制造业	Manufacture of Textile Wearing Apparel, Footware and Caps	10055	13001	0.03	0.02
皮革、毛皮、羽毛（绒）及其制品业	Manufacture of Leather, Fur, Feather and RelatedProducts	13802	12917	0.03	0.02
木材加工及木、竹、藤、棕、草制品业	Processing of Timber,Manufacture of Wood, Bamboo, Rattan, Palm, and Straw Products	22669	35059	0.17	0.13
家具制造业	Manufacture of Furniture	7495	9238	0.02	0.02
造纸及纸制品业	Manufacture of Paper and Paper Products	737321	706576	0.57	0.41
印刷业、记录媒介的复制	Printing, Reproduction of Recording Media	19290	22181	0.04	0.03
文教体育用品制造业	Manufacture of Articles For Culture, Education and Sport Activities	559	982	0.04	0.05
石油加工、炼焦及核燃料加工业	Processing of Petroleum, Coking, Processing of Nuclear Fuel	278175	387463	0.70	0.69

注：2010年数据因汇总单位由主营业务收入500万元以上调整为主营业务收入2000万元以上，与去年年鉴2010年数据不一致。
Note: Because the statistic scope is changed from the units with the major business revenue of 5 million yuan and above to the units with the major business revenue of 20 million yuan and above, the data in 2010 in this table is different from that in the yearbook of last year.

表5.3 续表 continued

行　业	Sector	综合能源消费量（吨标准煤）Comprehensive Energy Consumption (ton of SCE)		产值能耗（吨标准煤/万元）Energy Consumption per Unit Output Value (ton of SCE/10 000 yuan)	
		2010	2011	2010	2011
化学原料及化学制品制造业	Manufacture of Raw Chemical Materials and Chemical Products	6022660	6453435	1.16	0.87
医药制造业	Manufacture of Medicines	251892	241761	0.14	0.11
化学纤维制造业	Manufacture of Chemical Fibres	9816	5357	0.14	0.08
橡胶制品业	Manufacture of Rubber	154310	165101	0.22	0.14
塑料制品业	Manufacture of Plastics	97214	86111	0.12	0.06
非金属矿物制品业	Manufacture of Non-metallic Mineral Products	6397263	7288867	1.51	1.18
黑色金属冶炼及压延加工业	Smelting and Pressing of Ferrous Metals	4145747	5385655	0.86	0.75
有色金属冶炼及压延加工业	Smelting and Pressing of Nonferrous Metals	727523	917718	0.18	0.19
金属制品业	Manufacture of Metal Products	132196	192923	0.09	0.09
通用设备制造业	Manufacture of General Purpose Machinery	313913	338456	0.07	0.06
专用设备制造业	Manufacture of Special Purpose Machinery	65111	48965	0.03	0.02
交通运输设备制造业	Manufacture of Transport Equipment	1084100	1231361	0.04	0.04
电气机械及器材制造业	Manufacture of Electrical Machinery and Equipment	82284	103921	0.02	0.01
通信设备、计算机及其他电子设备制造业	Manufacture of Communication Equipment,Computers and Other Electronic Equipment	32536	70862	0.01	0.01
仪器仪表及文化、办公用机械制造业	Manufacture of Measuring Instruments and Machinery for Cultural Activity and Office Work	42453	21449	0.04	0.02
工艺品及其他制造业	Manufacture of Artwork and Other Manufacturing	22390	48705	0.15	0.04
废弃资源和废旧材料回收加工业	Recycling and Disposal of Waste	20918	9191	0.03	0.01
电力、燃气及水的生产和供应业	**Electric Power, Gas and Water Production and Supply**	**6526648**	**7837949**	**1.24**	**1.23**
电力、热力的生产和供应业	Production and Supply of Electric Power and Heat Power	6450466	7750525	1.44	1.42
燃气生产和供应业	Production and Supply of Gas	10752	12306	0.02	0.02
水的生产和供应业	Production and Supply of Water	65430	75118	0.37	0.37

表5.4 能源消费弹性系数（1985－2011年）
ELASTICITY RATIO OF ENERGY CONSUMPTION (1985-2011)

年　份 Year	能源消费比上年增长% Growth Rate of Energy Consumption over Preceding Year (%)	本市生产总值比上年增长% Growth Rate of GDP over Preceding Year (%)	能源消费弹性系数 Elasticity Ratio of Energy Consumption
1985	7.0	8.6	0.81
1986	2.4	8.6	0.28
1987	9.8	5.3	1.85
1988	8.4	9.5	0.89
1989	3.5	4.9	0.71
1990	-3.1	7.0	-0.45
1991	2.8	9.2	0.30
1992	2.7	16.5	0.17
1993	2.7	15.6	0.18
1994	3.2	13.5	0.23
1995	4.7	12.3	0.38
1996	5.3	11.4	0.46
1997	8.5	11.2	0.76
1998	4.4	8.6	0.51
1999	7.5	7.8	0.96
2000	5.8	8.7	0.67
2001	6.8	9.2	0.73
2002	9.7	10.5	0.92
2003	11.2	11.7	0.95
2004	16.9	12.4	1.36
2005	21.7	11.7	1.85
2006	9.3	12.4	0.75
2007	12.9	15.9	0.81
2008	6.9	14.5	0.48
2009	9.1	14.9	0.61
2010	11.8	17.1	0.69
2011	11.9	16.4	0.73

注：本市能源消费增长速度按等价值计算；生产总值增长速度按可比价格计算。
Note:All the data hereof has been adjusted according to the result of the 2nd National Economic Census, and the growth rate of GDP is calculated at constant prices.

表5.5 平均每万元本市生产总值能源消费量（2010－2011年）
AVERAGE ENERGY CONSUMPTION PER 10 000 YUAN OF GDP (2010-2011)

品　种	Type	2010	2011
单位生产总值能源消费量（吨标煤/万元）	**Energy Consumption per Unit of GDP (ton of SCE/10 000 yuan)**	**0.991**	**0.953**
#煤　炭	Coal	0.50	0.47
天然气	Natural Gas	0.09	0.09
油　料	Oil	0.09	0.10
电　力	Electricity	0.30	0.29

注：本表GDP按2010年价计算；能源品种均已折合为按等价值计算的吨标准煤。
Note: The data of energy consumption and GDP in 2008 have been adjusted according to the result of the 2nd National Economic Census, and calculated at the prices of 2010; each type of energy has been converted into tons of SCE calculated in equivalent value.

表5.6 平均每天主要能源消费量（2010－2011年）
AVERAGE DAILY ENERGY CONSUMPTION (2010-2011)

品　种	Type	2010	2011
每天能源消费量	**Average Daily Energy Consumption**	**21.52**	**24.09**
#煤　炭	Coal	10.94	11.92
天然气	Natural Gas	2.06	2.25
油　料	Oil	2.03	2.50
电　力	Electricity	6.49	7.42

注：本表能源品种均已折合为按等价值计算的吨标准煤，2010年数据有调整。
Note: The data of energy consumption in 2008 has been adjusted according to the result of the 2nd National Economic Census, and calculated at the prices of 2005; each type of energy has been converted into tons of SCE calculated in equivalent value.

表5.7 主城九区主要能源消费量（2010–2011年）
MAIN ENERGY CONSUMPTION OF 9 CENTRAL URBAN DISTRICTS(2010-2011)

单位：万吨标准煤 (10 000 tons of SCE)

品　种	Type	2010	2011
规模以上工业企业能源消耗总量	Total Energy Consumption of Industrial Enterprises above Designated Size	888.46	1025.98
清洁能源使用量	Use of Clean Energy	2166.00	2384.77
终端能源消费总量	Total End-User Energy Consumption	2544.00	2778.05

注：2010年数据有调整。
Note: The data in 2010 has been adjusted.

表5.8 综合能源平衡表（2010－2011年）
OVERALL ENERGY BALANCE SHEET (2010-2011)

单位：万吨标准煤 (10 000 tons of SCE)

项　目	Item	2010		2011	
		按当量值计算 Equivalent Weight	按等价值计算 Equivalent Value	按当量值计算 Equivalent Weight	按等价值计算 Equivalent Value
可供消费的能源总量	**Total Energy Available for Consumption**	**7117.41**	**7855.52**	**7951.12**	**8791.97**
#一次能源生产量	Primary Energy Output	4576.57	4952.17	4224.44	4595.34
调进量	Imports	4466.43	5021.97	5225.59	5798.11
调出量（-）	Exports (-)	-1839.30	-2032.33	-1417.36	-1519.94
能源消费总量	**Total Energy Consumption**	**7117.41**	**7855.52**	**7951.12**	**8791.97**
终端消费	End-use Consumption	5861.23	7388.26	6524.66	8235.07
第一产业	Primary Industry	258.43	262.01	279.02	283.66
第二产业	Secondary Industry	4359.64	5413.18	4862.23	6050.90
第三产业	Tertiary Industry	800.39	1017.68	869.91	1083.20
生活消费	Household Consumption	442.77	695.39	513.49	817.30
城　镇	Urban	237.15	401.23	291.75	496.75
乡　村	Rural	205.62	294.16	221.74	320.55
加工转换投入（-）产出（+）量	Input (-) and Output (+) during the Process of Enery Conversion	-1215.78	-352.02	-1365.92	-380.25
损失量	Energy Losses	40.41	115.24	60.54	176.65

重/庆/统/计/年/鉴

主要统计指标解释

■ 能源消费总量

指一定时期内全国（地区）物质生产部门、非物质生产部门和生活消费的各种能源的总和，是观察能源消费水平、构成和增长速度的总量指标。能源消费总量包括：煤和原油及其制品、天然气、电力。不包括：低热值燃料、生物质能和太阳能等的利用。能源消费总量分为终端能源消费量、能源加工转换损失量和损失量三部分。

（1）终端能源消费量：指一定时期内全国（地区）生产和生活消费的各种能源在扣除了用于加工转换二次能源消费量和损失量以后的数量。

（2）能源加工转换损失量：指一定时期内全国（地区）投入加工转换的各种能源数量之和与产出各种能源产品之和的差额，是观察能源在加工转换过程中损失量变化的指标。

（3）能源损失量：指一定时期内能源在输送、分配、储存过程中发生的损失和由客观原因造成的各种损失量。不包括各种气体能源放空、放散量。

■ 能源消费弹性系数

是反映能源消费增长速度与国民经济增长速度之间比例关系的指标。计算公式为：

能源消费弹性系数=能源消费量平均增长速度/国民经济年平均增长速度

Explanatory Notes on Main Statistical Indicators

□ Total Energy Consumption

Refers to the total consumption of energy of various kinds by material production sectors, non-material production sectors and households in the country (region) in a given period of time. It is a comprehensive indicator to show the scale, composition and development of energy consumption. The total energy consumption includes that of coal, crude oil and their products, natural gas and electricity. However, it excludes the consumption of fuel of low calorific value, bio-energy and solar energy. Total domestic energy consumption can be divided into three parts:

(Ⅰ)Final energy consumption: refers to the total energy consumption by material production sectors, non-material production sectors and households in the country (region) in a given period of time, but excludes the consumption in conversion of the primary energy into the secondary energy and the loss in the process of energy conversion.

(Ⅱ)Loss during the process of energy conversion: refers to the total input of various kinds of energy for conversion, minus the total output of various kinds of energy in the country in a given period of time. It is an indicator to show the loss that occurs during the process of energy conversion.

(Ⅲ)Loss: refers to the total of the loss of energy during the course of energy transport, distribution and storage and the loss caused by any objective reason in a given period of time. The loss of various kinds of gas due to gas discharges and stocktaking is excluded.

□ Elasticity Ratio of Energy Consumption

Is an indicator to show the relationship between the growth rate of energy consumption and the growth rate of the national economy. The formula is:

Elasticity Ratio of Energy Consumption=Average annual Growth Rate of Energy Consumption/ Average Annual Growth Rate of National Economy.

第 6 章

财　政

GOVERNMENT FINANCE

简要说明 BRIEF INTRODUCTION

本章资料包括全市财政收入和支出情况、国税和地税税收收入情况，由市统计局综合处分别根据市财政局、市国税局和市地税局的有关资料整理编辑。

The data in this chapter include the revenue and expenditure of the municipal government, and the revenue from national taxation and local taxation. The data is sorted and compiled by Division of Comprehensive Statistics of Chongqing Municipal Bureau of Statistics on the basis of the materials from Chongqing Municipal Bureau of Finance, Chongqing Municipal Office of SAT and Chongqing Local Taxation Bureau.

表6.1 财政收入及支出（1994－2011年）
GOVERNMENT REVENUE AND EXPENDITURE (1994-2011)

单位：万元(10 000 yuan)

年 份 Year	财政收入 Government Revenue	其中 of which: #地方财政收入 Revenue of Local Government	其中 of which: #一般预算收入 General Budgetary Revenue	#中央两税（四税）收入 Revenue from the 2 (4) Taxes of Central Government	地方财政支出 Expenditure of Local Government	其中 of which: #一般预算支出 General Budgetary Expenditure
1994	716172	366325	366325	349847	560818	560818
1995	837748	460052	460052	377696	662235	662235
1996	942682	549412	549412	393270	794216	794216
1997	1180555	745296	593060	435259	1151627	1010110
1998	1338867	858046	711287	480821	1359474	1257608
1999	1402935	898912	767341	504023	1623685	1502365
2000	1632353	1044570	872442	587783	2024606	1876433
2001	1961761	1264090	1061243	697671	2555530	2375486
2002	2694610	1578651	1260674	991425	3450674	3058591
2003	3412781	2069315	1615618	1205457	3913564	3415775
2004	4629591	3024439	2006241	1435206	4851221	3957233
2005	5811921	3949624	2568072	1656599	6253516	4873543
2006	7421702	5294579	3177165	1944772	8201936	5942543
2007	10572948	7885604	4427000	2491920	11023545	7683886
2008	12901828	9633392	5775738	3023634	14485581	10160112
2009	15353975	11657132	6818189	3403122	18060672	13180913
2010	29751187	19905882	10182938	4687841	27467891	17691065
2011	35236522	29089103	14883336	5607771	39598745	25702404

注：财政收入2002年前为地方财政收入与中央两税（增值税和消费税）之和，2002年起为地方财政收入、中央四税收入和其他中央收入之和。其中其他中央收入不含关税，自2003年起包含车辆购置税(以下各表同）。

Note: Government revenue before 2002 is the sum of revenue of local government and revenue from the 2 taxes of Central Government (value-added tax and consumption tax), whereas since 2002 it is the sum of revenue of local government, revenue from the 4 taxes of Central Government and other revenue of Central Government. Other revenue of Central Government does not include tariff, while since 2003 vehicle purchasing tax is included (the same applies to the following tables).

表6.2 财政收入占地区生产总值的比重（1994－2011年）
PERCENTAGE OF GOVERNMENT REVENUE TO GROSS DOMESTIC PRODUCT (1994-2011)

年 份 Year	财政收入（亿元） Government Revenue (100 million yuan)	地区生产总值（亿元） Gross Domestic Product (100 million yuan)	财政收入占本市生产总值的比重（%） Percentage of Government Revenue to GDP (%)
1994	71.62	833.60	8.59
1995	83.77	1123.06	7.46
1996	94.27	1315.12	7.17
1997	118.06	1509.75	7.82
1998	133.89	1602.38	8.36
1999	140.29	1663.20	8.43
2000	163.24	1791.00	9.11
2001	196.18	1976.86	9.92
2002	269.46	2232.86	12.07
2003	341.28	2555.72	13.35
2004	462.96	3034.58	15.26
2005	581.19	3467.72	16.76
2006	742.17	3907.23	18.99
2007	1057.29	4676.13	22.61
2008	1290.18	5793.66	22.27
2009	1535.40	6530.01	23.51
2010	2975.12	7894.24	37.69
2011	3523.65	10011.37	35.20

表6.3 财政收入（2010－2011年）
GOVERNMENT REVENUE (2010-2011)

单位：万元(10 000 yuan)

项　目	Item	2010	2011	指数 上年同口径数=100 Index The Same-Scope Index of Previous Year=100
财政收入	**Government Revenue**	**25063346**	**35236522**	**140.6**
一、地方财政收入	**Revenue of Local Government**	**19905882**	**29089103**	**146.1**
#市　级	Municipal Level	9647322	15081414	156.3
一般预算收入	**General Budgetary Revenue**	**10182938**	**14883336**	**146.2**
#市　级	Municipal Level	4316008	6189970	143.4
工商各税	Industrial and Commercial Taxes	5342718	7577137	141.8
#增值税	Value-added Tax	777167	817765	105.2
营业税	Business Tax	2424493	3439155	141.9
企业所得税	Corporate Income Tax	742484	1151108	155.0
个人所得税	Individual Income Tax	262412	348983	133.0
资源税	Resource Tax	50244	80078	159.4
城市维护建设税	City Maintenance and Construction Tax	349435	504888	144.5
房产税	House Property Tax	140200	208943	149.0
印花税	Stamp Tax	96268	127803	132.8
农业四税	4 Taxes on Agriculture	872846	1233571	141.3
#农业税	Agricultural Tax			
契　税	Deed Tax	546488	763239	139.7
非税收入	Non-tax Revenue	3967374	6072628	153.1
#国有资产经营收入	Operating Revenue of State-owned Assets	662057	900178	136.0
国有资源（资产）有偿使用收入	Revenue from the Compensable Use of State-owned Resources (Assets)	425284	875254	205.8
行政性收费收入	Charge of Administrative and Institutional Units	2140124	3087804	144.3
罚没收入	Penalty Receipts	214145	226278	105.7
专项收入	Special Program Receipts	384998	663602	172.4
基金预算收入	**Budgetary Revenue of Funds**	**9722944**	**14205767**	**146.1**
#养路费	Road Toll			
国有土地使用权出让金	Transferring Fees of the Right to Use the State-owned Land	8893982	13092889	147.2
新增建设用地土地有偿使用费	Revenue from the Paid Use of the Increased Land for Construction Use	221791	247922	111.8
二、中央四税收入	**Revenue from 4 Taxes of Central Government**	**4687841**	**5607771**	**119.6**
增值税收入	Revenue from VAT	2331757	2453436	105.2
消费税收入	Revenue from Consumption Tax	854895	887237	103.8
企业所得税收入	Revenue from Corporate Income Tax	1107565	1743618	157.4
个人所得税收入	Revenue from Individual Income Tax	393624	523480	133.0
三、其他中央收入	**Other Revenue of Central Government**	**469623**	**539648**	**114.9**
#车辆购置税	Vehicle Purchase Tax	308848	390468	126.4

注：其他中央收入不含关税。
Note: Other revenue of Central Government excludes tariff.

表6.4 财政支出（2010－2011年）
GOVERNMENT EXPENDITURE (2010-2011)

单位：万元(10 000 yuan)

项　目	Item	2010	2011	指数 上年同口径数=100 Index The Same-Scope Index of Previous Year=100
地方财政支出	**Expenditure of Local Government**	**27467891**	**39598745**	**144.2**
#市　级	Municipal Level	10333428	16414291	158.8
一般预算支出	**General Budgetary Expenditure**	**17691065**	**25702404**	**145.3**
#市　级	Municipal Level	5344193	9154917	171.3
一般公共服务	Expenditure for General Public Services	1684896	2245806	133.3
公共安全	Expenditure for Public Security	980176	1338047	136.5
教　育	Expenditure for Education	2404608	3187008	132.5
科学技术	Expenditure for Science and Technology	178968	250383	139.9
文化体育与传媒	Expenditure for Culture,Sport and Media	240367	311598	129.6
社会保障和就业	Expenditure for Social Security and Employment Effort	2369806	3387635	142.9
医疗卫生	Expenditure for Medical and Health Care	948682	1436962	151.5
环境保护	Expenditure for Environment Protection	690101	1008122	146.1
城乡社区事务	Expenditure for Urban and Rural Community Affairs	2512632	3944586	157.0
农林水事务	Expenditure for Agriculture, Forestry and Water Conservancy	1610349	1989065	123.5
交通运输	Expenditure for Transportation	855835	1862307	217.6
工业商业金融等事务	Expenditure for Industry, Commerce and Banking	1829616	2562683	140.1
地震灾后恢复重建支出	Expenditure for the Reconstruction after Earthquake	67817	126	0.2
国土资源气象等事务	Expenditure for land Resources and Meteokology	319918	440236	137.6
住房保障支出	Expenditure for Housing Security	799099	1574711	197.1
其他支出	Other Expenditure	198195	163129	82.3
基金预算支出	**Budgetary Expenditure of Fund**	**9776826**	**13896341**	**142.1**
#文体与传媒	Expenditure for Culture, Sport and Media	10826	12119	111.9
社会保障和就业	Expenditure for Social Security and Employment Effort	65416	73666	112.6
城乡社区事务	Expenditure for Urban and Rural Community Affairs	9149202	13297825	145.3
农林水事务	Expenditure for Agriculture, Forestry and Water Conservancy	86578	80368	92.8
交通运输	Expenditure for Transportation	206637	228577	110.6
工业商业等事务	Expenditure for Industry, Commerce and Banking	195139	8155	4.2
其他基金	Other Funds	62966	195514	310.5

表6.5 国税和地税税收收入（1996－2011年）
REVENUE FROM NATIONAL AND LOCAL TAXATION (1996-2011)

单位：万元(10 000 yuan)

年 份 Year	国税税收收入 Revenue from National Taxation	其 中 of which		地税税收收入 Revenue from Local Taxation	其 中 of which		
		#增值税 Value-added Tax	#消费税 Consumption Tax		#营业税 Business Tax	#企业所得税 Corporate Income Tax	#个人所得税 Individual Income Tax
1996	611211	455912	92966	266489	130952	33616	17748
1997	645914	489770	108411	324758	155607	47121	29468
1998	715077	529607	123846	382948	195747	41808	42562
1999	881410	692354	120696	436999	218101	52873	54910
2000	929759	680489	144660	500530	243476	68614	72133
2001	1128638	795789	164879	602387	278516	97553	105450
2002	1295409	915425	193646	732964	367458	91953	120326
2003	1559085	1112204	217868	894415	466393	100102	148386
2004	1900477	1366125	257385	1115549	585415	125572	168282
2005	2139060	1525267	278540	1356424	702018	152846	203950
2006	2559190	1803377	346133	1660513	858693	181691	224558
2007	3261800	2240634	424683	2245537	1171243	233743	308283
2008	3922674	2658088	489991	2861162	1450449	319964	386364
2009	4411106	2892068	610367	3461226	1855471	334508	504270
2010	6084441	3612557	855149	5586777	2424494	531854	649130
2011	7244401	3929354	888068	8197820	3439157	834238	869476

注：国税收入对外公布数据从2001年起均包含车辆购置税，故对以前年度数据进行了调整。
Note: The released data of national taxation has included vehicle purchasing tax since 2001, so the data of the previous years is adjusted.

表6.6 国税税收收入（2010－2011年）
REVENUE FROM NATIONAL TAXATION (2010-2011)

单位：万元(10 000 yuan)

项 目	Item	2010	2011
税收收入合计	**Total Revenue from Taxation**	**6084441**	**7244401**
按税种分	**By Tax Category**		
增值税收入	Value-added Tax	3612557	3929354
#一般纳税人	General Taxpayer	3052319	3157353
消费税收入	Consumption Tax	855149	888068
企业所得税	Corporate Income Tax	1299784	2034727
内 资	Domestic Enterprise	736931	1176317
外 资	Foreign-Funded Enterprise	562853	858410
个人所得税	Individual Income Tax	6903	2984
城市维护建设税	City Maintenance and Construction Tax	1200	-1200
车辆购置税	Vehicle Purchasing Tax	308848	390468
按行业分	**By Sector**		
第一产业	Primary Industry	3454	5489
第二产业	Secondary Industry	4101544	4530410
工 业	Industry	4076854	4503320
建筑业	Construction	24690	27090
第三产业	Tertiary Industry	1979443	2708502
交通运输仓储及邮政业	Transport, Storage and Post	43018	54499
批发和零售业	Wholesale and Retail Trades	1089614	1310515
金融业	Financial Intermediation	249641	345453
信息传输、计算机服务和软件业	nformation Transmission, Computer Services and Software	69439	88334
住宿和餐饮业	Hotel and Catering Services	6927	9179
文化、体育和娱乐业	Culture, Sports and Entertainment	1842	1195
租赁和商务服务业	Leasing and Business Services	24860	56861
房地产业	Real Estate	213395	483768
其他行业	Other Trades	280707	358698

表6.7 按企业类型分的国税税收收入（2011年）
REVENUE FROM NATIONAL TAXATION BY STATUS OF REGISTRATION (2011)

单位：万元(10 000 yuan)

项 目	Item	合 计 Total	内资企业 Domestic-funded				
			国有企业 State-owned	集体企业 Collective-owned	股份合作企业 Cooperative	联营企业 Joint Ownership	股份公司 Share-holding corporations
总 计	**Total**	**7244401**	**988879**	**33755**	**19406**	**19322**	**2886133**
增值税收入	Value-added Tax	3929354	652660	28362	9721	2139	1507405
消费税收入	Consumption Tax	888068	233612	26	171		433748
营业税	Business Tax						
企业所得税	Corporate Income Tax	2034727	86167	325	807	540	919597
个人所得税	Individual Income Tax	2984					
资源税	Resource Tax						
固定资产投资方向调节税	Fixed Asset Investment Regulation Tax						
城市维护建设税	City Maintenance and Construction Tax	-1200					-1200
车辆购置税	Vehicle Purchasing Tax	390468	16440	5042	8707	16643	26583

项 目	Item	内资企业 Domestic-funded		港澳台投资企业 Funded By Hong Kong, Macao&Taiwan	外商投资企业 Foreign-funded	个体经营 Individuals	附：乡镇企业 Township Enterprises
		私营企业 Private	其他企业 Others				
总 计	**Total**	**786376**	**17955**	**251292**	**1846361**	**394922**	**183815**
增值税收入	Value-added Tax	605821	3447	102545	919573	97681	156682
消费税收入	Consumption Tax	3283		4376	212287	565	4199
营业税	Business Tax						
企业所得税	Corporate Income Tax	166210	2671	144155	714255		22934
个人所得税	Individual Income Tax					2984	
资源税	Resource Tax						
固定资产投资方向调节税	Fixed Asset Investment Regulation Tax						
城市维护建设税	City Maintenance and Construction Tax						
车辆购置税	Vehicle Purchasing Tax	11062	11837	216	246	293692	

表6.8 地税税收收入（2010－2011年）
REVENUE FROM LOCAL TAXATION (2010-2011)

单位：万元(10 000 yuan)

项　目	Item	2010	2011
税收收入合计	**Total**	**5586777**	**8197820**
#中央级	Central Government	708594	1022231
重庆市级	Chongqing Municipal Government	1781057	2562622
区县级	Distirct and County Governments	3097126	4612967
按税种分	**By Tax Category**		
营业税	Business Tax	2424494	3439157
企业所得税	Corporate Income Tax	531854	834238
个人所得税	Individual Income Tax	649130	869476
资源税	Resource Tax	50244	80078
固定资产投资方向调节税	Fixed Asset Investment Regulation Tax		
城市维护建设税	City Maintenance and Construction Tax	348083	506141
房产和城市房地产税	House Property and Urban Real Estate Tax	140200	208946
印花税	Stamp Tax	96267	127801
城镇土地使用税	Urban Land Use Tax	185005	252130
土地增值税	Land Appreciation Tax	297957	614669
车船税	Tax on Vehicles and Boat Operation	17054	31614
屠宰税	Slaughter Tax		
烟叶税	Tobacco Leaf Tax	23239	26688
耕地占用税	Farm Land Occupation Tax	302903	443643
契　税	Deed Tax	520347	763239
按行业分	**By Sector**		
第一产业	Primary Industry	4464	7878
第二产业	Secondary Industry	1604572	2332481
工　业	Industry	751905	1000179
建筑业	Construction	852667	1332302
第三产业	Tertiary Industry	3977741	5857461
交通运输仓储及邮政业	Transport, Storage and Post	204380	269479
批发和零售业	Wholesale and Retail Trades	235957	308060
金融业	Financial Intermediation	501658	708282
信息传输、计算机服务和软件业	Information Transmission, Computer Services and Software	75327	96532
住宿和餐饮业	Hotel and Catering Services	102551	130855
文化、体育和娱乐业	Culture, Sports and Entertainment	29013	38800
租赁和商务服务业	Leasing and Business Services	201631	369727
房地产业	Real Estate	1783149	2931742
其他行业	Other Trades	844075	1003984

表6.9 按企业类型分的地税税收收入（2011年）
REVENUE FROM LOCAL TAXATION BY STATUS OF REGISTRATION (2011)

单位：万元(10 000 yuan)

项 目	Item	合 计 Total	内资企业 Domestic-funded				
			国有企业 State-owned	集体企业 Collective-owned	股份合作企业 Cooperative	联营企业 Joint Ownership	股份公司 Share-holding corporations
总 计	**Total**	**8197820**	**750713**	**70743**	**49519**	**16438**	**4465687**
营业税	Business Tax	3439157	317336	26241	23577	7874	1956369
企业所得税	Corporate Income Tax	834238	33385	12834	4687	1849	579342
个人所得税	Individual Income Tax	869476	107308	5533	6919	1257	425499
资源税	Resource Tax	80078	23930	1834	342	60	32545
固定资产投资方向调节税	Fixed Asset Investment Regulation Tax						
城市维护建设税	City Maintenance and Construction Tax	506141	89887	3660	2836	942	245590
房产和城市房地产税	House Property and Urban Real Estate Tax	208946	22483	2176	1387	1119	106231
印花税	Stamp Tax	127801	11613	545	795	358	60761
城镇土地使用税	Urban Land Use Tax	252130	19577	1342	1403	652	160734
土地增值税	Land Appreciation Tax	614669	15554	2690	2719	1441	342002
车船税	Tax on Vehicles and Boat Operation	31614	719	2403	13	19	5418
屠宰税	Slaughter Tax						
烟叶税	Tobacco Leaf Tax	26688	26688				
耕地占用税	Farm Land Occupation Tax	443643	58121	8	2	86	254533
契 税	Deed Tax	763239	24112	11477	4839	781	296663

项 目	Item	内资企业 Domestic-funded		港澳台投资企业 Funded By Hong Kong, Macao&Taiwan	外商投资企业 Foreign-funded	个体经营 Individuals	附：乡镇企业 Township Enterprises
		私营企业 Private	其他企业 Others				
总 计	**Total**	**1160802**	**417518**	**335966**	**442648**	**487786**	**6058**
营业税	Business Tax	511184	79348	124400	224269	168559	2186
企业所得税	Corporate Income Tax	176336	25805				926
个人所得税	Individual Income Tax	85747	78231	21609	49563	87810	930
资源税	Resource Tax	10299	2023	1109	1344	6592	999
固定资产投资方向调节税	Fixed Asset Investment Regulation Tax						
城市维护建设税	City Maintenance and Construction Tax	69301	6335	15549	58439	13602	646
房产和城市房地产税	House Property and Urban Real Estate Tax	20762	11387	16968	14365	12068	37
印花税	Stamp Tax	17068	6635	5017	23013	1996	105
城镇土地使用税	Urban Land Use Tax	33016	3495	14314	16730	867	27
土地增值税	Land Appreciation Tax	116186	32435	43690	25037	32915	126
车船税	Tax on Vehicles and Boat Operation	3013	10821	101	60	9047	74
屠宰税	Slaughter Tax						
烟叶税	Tobacco Leaf Tax						
耕地占用税	Farm Land Occupation Tax	4986	118766	26	42	7073	2
契 税	Deed Tax	112904	42237	93183	29786	147257	

主要统计指标解释

财政收入

指国家财政参与社会产品分配所取得的收入，是实现国家职能的财力保证。主要包括：

（1）各项税收：包括国内增值税、国内消费税、进口货物增值税和消费税、出口货物退增值税和消费税、营业税、企业所得税、个人所得税、资源税、城市维护建设税、房产税、印花税、城镇土地使用税、土地增值税、车船税、船舶吨税、车辆购置税、关税、耕地占用税、契税、烟叶税等。

（2）非税收入：包括专项收入、行政事业性收费、罚没收入和其他收入。

财政支出

指国家财政将筹集起来的资金进行分配使用，以满足经济建设和各项事业的需要。主要包括：

（1）一般公共服务：指政府提供基本公共管理与服务的支出，包括人大事务、政协事务、政府办公厅（室）及相关机构事务、发展与改革事务、统计信息事务、财政事务、税收事务、审计事务、海关事务、人力资源事务、纪检监察事务、人口与计划生育事务、商贸事务、知识产权事务、工商行政管理事务、国土资源事务、海洋管理事务、测绘事务、地震事务、气象事务、民族事务、宗教事务、港澳台侨事务、档案事务、共产党事务、民主党派事务及工商联事务、群众团体事务、彩票事务等。

（2）外交：指政府外交事务支出，包括外交行政管理、驻外机构、对外援助、国际组织、对外合作与交流、边界勘界联检等方面的支出。

（3）国防：指政府用于国防方面的支出，包括用于现役部队、预备役部队、民兵、国防科研事业、专项工程、国防动员等方面的支出。

（4）公共安全：指政府维护社会公共安全方面的支出，包括武装警察、公安、国家安全、检察、法院、司法行政、监狱、劳教、国家保密、缉私警察等。

（5）教育：指政府教育事务支出，包括教育行政管理、学前教育、小学教育、初中教育、普通高中教育、普通高等教育、初等职业教育、中专教育、技校教育、职业高中教育、高等职业教育、广播电视教育、留学生教育、特殊教育、干部继续教育、教育机关服务等。

（6）科学技术：指用于科学技术方面的支出，包括科学技术管理事务、基础研究、应用研究、技术研究与开发、科技条件与服务、社会科学、科学技术普及、科技交流与合作等。

（7）文化教育与传媒：指政府在文化、文物、体育、广播影视、新闻出版等方面的支出。

（8）社会保障和就业：指政府在社会保障与就业方面的支出，包括社会保障和就业管理事务、民政管理事务、财政对社会保险基金的补助、补充全国社会保障基金、行政事业单位离退休、企业改革补助、就业补助、抚恤、退役安置、社会福利、残疾人事业、城市居民最低生活保障、其他城镇社会救济、农村社会救济、自然灾害生活救助、红十字事务等。

（9）医疗卫生：指政府医疗卫生方面的支出，包括医疗卫生管理事务支出、医疗服务支出、医疗保障支出、疾病预防控制支出、卫生监督支出、妇幼保健支出、农村卫生支出等。

（10）环境保护：指政府环境保护支出，包括环境保护管理事务支出、环境监测与监察支出、污染治理支出、自然生态保护支出、天然林保护工程支出、退耕还林支出、风沙荒漠治理支出、退牧还草支出、已垦草原退耕还草、能源节约利用、污染减排、可再生能源和资源综合利用等支出。

（11）城乡社区事务：指政府城乡社区事务支出，包括城乡社区管理事务支出、城乡社区规划与管理支出、城乡社区公共设施支出、城乡社区住宅支出、城乡社区环境卫生支出、建设市场管理与监督支出等。

（12）农林水事务：指政府农林水事务支出，包括农业支出、林业支出、水利支出、扶贫支出、农业综合开发支出等。

（13）交通运输：指政府交通运输和邮政业方面的支出，包括公路运输支出、水路运输支出、铁路运

主要统计指标解释

输支出、民用航空运输支出、邮政业支出等。

（14）工业商业金融等事务：指政府对工业、商业及金融等方面的支出，包括采掘业支出、制造业支出、建筑业支出、工业和信息产业监管支出、国有资产监管支出、商业流通事务支出、金融业监管支出、旅游业管理与服务支出等。

■ 中央财政收入和地方财政收入

指按现行分税制财政体制划分的中央本级收入和地方本级收入。属于中央财政的收入包括关税，进口货物增值税和消费税，出口货物退增值税和消费税，消费税，铁道部门、各银行总行、各保险公司总公司等集中交纳的营业税和城市维护建设税，增值税75%部分，纳入共享范围的企业所得税60%部分，未纳入共享范围的中央企业所得税、中央企业上交的利润，个人所得税60%部分，车辆购置税，船舶吨税，证券交易印花税97%部分，海洋石油资源税，中央非税收入等。属于地方财政的收入包括营业税（不含铁道部门、各银行总行、各保险公司总公司集中交纳的营业税），地方企业上交利润，城市维护建设税（不含铁道部门、各银行总行、各保险公司总公司集中交纳的部分），房产税，城镇土地使用税，土地增值税，车船税，耕地占用税，契税，烟叶税，印花税，增值税25%部分，纳入共享范围的企业所得税40%部分，个人所得税40%部分，证券交易印花税3%部分，海洋石油资源税以外的其他资源税，地方非税收入等。

■ 中央财政支出和地方财政支出

指根据政府在经济和社会活动中的不同职责，划分中央和地方政府的责权，按照政府的责权划分确定的支出。中央财政支出包括一般公共服务，外交支出，国防支出，公共安全支出，以及中央政府调整国民经济结构、协调地区发展、实施宏观调控的支出等。地方财政支出包括一般公共服务，公共安全支出，地方统筹的各项社会事业支出等。

Explanatory Notes on Main Statistical Indicators

Government Revenue

Refers to income for the government finance through participating in the distribution of social products. It is the financial guarantee to ensure government functioning. The contents of government revenue include the following main items:

(Ⅰ) Various tax revenues, including domestic value added tax (VAT), domestic consumption tax, VAT and consumption tax from imports, VAT and consumption tax rebate for exports, business tax, corporate income tax, individual income tax, resource tax, city maintenance and construct tax, house property tax, stamp tax, urban land use tax, land appreciation tax, tax on vehicles and boat operation, ship tonnage tax, vehicle purchase tax, tariffs, farm land occupation tax, deed tax, and tobacco leaf tax, etc.

(Ⅱ) Non-tax revenue, including special program receipts, charge of administrative and institutional units, penalty receipts and others non-tax receipts.

Government Expenditure

Refers to the distribution and use of the funds which the government finance has raised, so as to meet the needs of economic construction and various causes. It includes the following main items:

(Ⅰ) Expenditure for general public services: It refers to the spending on the basic public management and services which provided by governments, including the expense on affairs of People's Congress, affairs of People's Political Consultative Conference, affairs of government general office and relative institutions, affairs of development and reform, affairs of statistics, affairs of finance, affairs of taxation, affairs of audit, affairs of customs, affairs of human resources and social security, affairs of discipline inspection and supervision, affairs of population and family planning, affairs of commerce and trade, affairs of intellectual property, affairs of administration for industry and commerce, affairs of land and resources, affairs of oceanic administration, affairs of surveying and mapping, affairs of earthquake, ethnic affairs, religious affairs, affairs of Hong Kong, Macao, Taiwan, and Overseas Chinese, affairs of archives administration, affairs of Chinese Communist Party, affairs of democratic parties and federation of industry and commerce, affairs of mass organization, and affairs of lottery, etc.

(Ⅱ) Expenditure for foreign affairs: It refers to the spending of government on foreign affairs, including the expense on administration of foreign affairs, missions overseas, external assistance, international organizations, foreign cooperation and communication, surveying and joint inspection on borderline, etc.

(Ⅲ) Expenditure for national defence: It refers to the spending of government on national defence, including the expense on active force, reserve force, militia, scientific research on national defence, special projects, mobilization of national defence, etc.

(Ⅳ) Expenditure for public security: It refers to the spending of government on maintaining social and public security, including the expense on armed police force, public security, state security, prosecution, courts, justice, prison, labour education and rehabilitation, protection of state secrecy, anti-smuggling police, etc.

(Ⅴ) Expenditure for education: It refers to the spending of government on education, including the expense on the administration of education, pre-primary education, primary education, secondary education, high school education, regular higher education, primary vocational education, secondary vocational education, technical school education, vocational high school education and higher vocational education, radio and television education, student abroad education, special education, on the job training of cadres, education authorities services, etc.

(Ⅵ) Expenditure for science and technology: It refers to the spending of government on science and technology (S&T), including the expense on the administration of S&T, basic research, applied research, research and development, conditions and services of S&T, popularization of social science, science and technology, exchanges and cooperation of S&T, etc.

(Ⅶ) Expenditure for culture, sport and media: It refers to the spending of government on culture, cultural heritage, sports, radio, film, television, press and publication, etc.

(Ⅷ) Expenditure for social safety net and employment effort: It refers to the spending of government on social safety net and employment, including the expense on administration of social safety net and employment, civil affairs, budgetary subsidy on the

EXPLANATORY NOTES TO MAJOR STATISTICAL INDICATORS

social insurance funds, subsidy on National Social Security Fund, retirees of administrative units and institutions, subsidy on enterprise reform, subsidy on employment effort, pension, placement of ex-serviceman, social welfare, the handicapped undertakings, the system of cost of living allowances for urban residents, other urban social relief, rural social relief, living relief of natural disasters, affairs of Red Cross Society, etc.

(Ⅸ) Expenditure for medical and health care: It refers to the spending of government on medical and health care, including the expense on administration of medical and health care, medical services, health care, disease prevention and control, health inspection and supervision, women and children's health, rural health care, etc.

(Ⅹ) Expenditure for environment protection: It refers to the spending of government on environment protection, including the expense on administration of environment protection, environment monitoring and supervision, pollution control, natural ecology protection, project of virgin forests protection, reforesting farmland, controlling the sources of dust storms, returning pastureland to grassland, returning pastureland to grassland, returning cultivated land to grassland, energy conservation, emissions reduction, comprehensive utilization of renewable energy and resources, etc.

(Ⅺ) Expenditure for urban and rural community affairs: It refers to the spending of government on urban and rural community affairs, including the expense on administration of urban and rural community, planning and management of urban and rural community, public facilities of urban and rural community, housing of urban and rural community, sanitation of urban and rural community, management and supervision on the construction market, etc.

(Ⅻ) Expenditure for agriculture, forestry and water conservancy: It refers to the spending of government on agriculture, forestry and water conservancy, including the expense on agriculture, forestry, water conservancy, poverty alleviation, comprehensive agricultural development, etc.

(ⅩⅢ) Expenditure for transportation: It refers to the spending of government on transportation and postal services, including the expense on road transportation, waterway transportation, railway transportation, civil aviation transportation, and postal services.

(ⅩⅣ) Expenditure for industry, commerce and banking: It refers to the spending of government on industry, commerce and banking, including the expense on mining, manufacturing, construction, industry and information technology supervision and administration, State-owned assets supervision and administration, commerce and circulation affairs, financial intermediation supervision and administration, tourism administration and service, etc.

□ Revenue of the Central Government and Revenue of the Local Governments

Refers to the revenue collected by the Central Government and that by the local governments as defined by the decentralized taxation system. In accordance with this system, the revenue of the Central Government includes tariff, VAT and consumption tax from imports, VAT and consumption tax rebate for exports, consumption tax, business tax and city maintenance and construct tax from the Ministry of Railways, head offices of banks, head offices of insurance company, which are handed over to the government in a centralized way, 75% of the value added tax, 60% the share part of the corporate income tax, unshared part of corporate income tax of the central enterprises, profit handed in by the central enterprises, 60% of individual income tax, vehicle purchase tax, ship tonnage tax, 97% of stamp tax on securities transactions, resource tax on the offshore petroleum resources. The revenue of the local governments includes business tax (excluding the part of the Ministry of Railways, head offices of banks, head offices of insurance company, which are handed over to the government in a centralized way), profit handed in by the local enterprises, city maintenance and construct tax (excluding the part of the Ministry of Railways, head offices of banks, head offices of insurance company, which are handed over to the government in a centralized way), house property tax, urban land use tax, land appreciation tax, tax on vehicles and boat operation, farm land occupation tax, deed tax, and tobacco leaf tax, stamp tax, 25% of the value added tax, 40% the share part of the corporate income tax, 40% of individual income tax, 3% of stamp tax on securities transactions, resource tax other than the tax on offshore petroleum resources, local non-tax revenue, etc.

□ Expenditure of the Central Government and Expenditure of the Local Governments

According to the different functions of the Central Government and local governments in economic and social activities, the rights of affairs administration are demarcated between those of the Central Government and those of local governments; and the classification of the expenditure between the

Central Government and local governments are made on the basis of the classification of the rights of affairs administration between them. The expenditure of the Central Government includes the expenditure for general public services, expenditure for foreign affairs, expenditure for public security, and the expenditure of the Central Government for adjusting the national economic structure; coordinating the development among different regions; and exercising macroeconomic regulation. The expenditure of the local governments includes mainly the expenditure for general public services, expenditure for public security, and expenditures for social development which are planned by local governments, etc.

第 7 章

人民生活与物价

PEOPLE'S LIVING CONDITIONS AND PRICE OF GOODS

简要说明
BRIEF INTRODUCTION

本章资料反映全市城乡居民生活状况，主要内容包括城乡居民家庭基本情况、恩格尔系数、居民储蓄、年收入支出及其构成、主要商品购买数量、耐用消费品的拥有量，以及居民消费价格指数、商品零售价格指数、工业生产者价格指数、固定资产投资价格指数、住宅销售价格指数等。居民住户调查资料是抽样调查汇总的结果，价格调查是一种非全面调查，采用重点调查和典型调查相结合的方法。

城镇居民和农村居民生活状况和价格调查的数据来源于国家统计局重庆调查总队。城乡居民物质生活情况和居民储蓄由市统计局综合处整理编辑。

The data in this chapter present the living conditions of the urban and rural households in Chongqing, including basic conditions of urban and rural households, Engle's coefficient, saving deposits, annual income & expenditure and their compositions, purchases of major commodities, possession of durable consumer goods, as well as consumer price indices, retail price indices, purchasing price index, price indices of investment in fixed assets and price index of residential real estate sales, etc. The data of urban and rural households are the results of sample survey, while price survey is an incomplete survey, where the main unit survey and typical survey are combined.

The data about the living conditions of urban and rural residents and price survey are provided by NBS Survey Office in Chongqing. The data of material & cultural life and saving deposits of urban & rural residents are sorted and compiled by Division of Comprehensive Statistics, Chongqing Municipal Bureau of Statistics.

表7.1 城乡居民物质文化生活情况（2010－2011年）
MATERIAL AND CULTURAL LIFE OF URBAN & RURAL RESIDENTS (2010-2011)

指　标	Item	2010	2011
就　业	**Employment**		
每一城市就业者负担人数（人）	Number of Dependents per Metropolitan Employee (person)	1.88	1.99
每一城镇就业者负担人数（人）	Number of Dependents per Urban Employee (person)	1.88	1.99
每一农村劳动力负担人数（人）	Number of Dependents per Rural Laborer (person)	1.28	1.40
城镇登记失业率（%）	Registered Urban Unemployment Rate (%)	3.96	3.50
收入和支出	**Income and Expenditure**		
城镇非私营在岗职工平均工资（元）	Annual Average Wages of Staff and Workers of Urban Non -private Units (yuan)	35326	40042
城市居民人均可支配收入（元）	Annual per Capita Disposable Income of Metropolitan Households (yuan)	19099.73	21954.97
城镇居民人均可支配收入（元）	Annual per Capita Disposable Income of Urban Households (yuan)	17532.43	20249.70
农民人均纯收入（元）	Annual per Capita Net Income of Rural Households (yuan)	5276.66	6480.41
城市居民人均消费性支出（元）	Annual per Capita Consumption Expenditure of Metropolitan Households (yuan)	14754.74	16747.40
城镇居民人均消费性支出（元）	Annual per Capita Consumption Expenditure of Urban Households (yuan)	13335.02	14974.49
农村居民人均生活消费支出（元）	Annual per Capita Living Expenditure of Rural Households (yuan)	3624.62	4502.06
城市居民家庭恩格尔系数（%）	Engle's Coefficient of Metropolitan Households (%)	37.5	38.5
城镇居民家庭恩格尔系数（%）	Engle's Coefficient of Urban Households (%)	37.6	39.1
农村居民家庭恩格尔系数（%）	Engle's Coefficient of Rural Households (%)	48.3	46.8
人均储蓄存款余额（元）	Per Capita Balance of Saving Deposit (yuan)	17677	20993
住　房	**Housing**		
城市人均房屋建筑面积（平方米）	Per Capita Residential Floor Space in Metropolitan Areas (sq.m)	27.55	28.35
城镇人均房屋建筑面积（平方米）	Per Capita Residential Floor Space in Urban Residents (sq.m)	31.69	31.77
农村人均住房面积（平方米）	Per Capita Living Space in Rural Areas (sq.m)	37.56	40.18
交通邮电	**Traffic, Postal and Telecommunication Services**		
人均道路面积（平方米）	Per Capita Area of Paved Roads (sq.m)	9.09	9.97
每万人拥有电话(含移动)（部）	Number of Telephones per 10 000 Population(including mobile phones) (unit)	7790	2128
每人平均交寄函件（件）	Number of Letters Mailed per Capita (unit)	1.71	2.11
城市公用事业	**City Public Utilities**		
用水普及率（%）	Percentage of Population with Access to Tap Water (%)	91.5	91.7
燃气普及率（%）	Percentage of Population with Access to Gas (%)	90.0	91.3
人均公共绿地面积（平方米）	Per Capita Public Green Area (sq.m)	12.72	17.01
教　育	**Education**		
学龄儿童入学率（%）	Enrollment Ratio of School-Aged Children (%)	99.94	99.96
每万人口中在校大学生（人）	Number of Undergraduates per 10 000 Population (person)	171	184
文　化	**Culture**		
每百户城市家庭拥有彩色电视机（台）	Number of Color TV Sets per 100 Metropolitan Households (unit)	151.27	153.64
每百户城镇家庭拥有彩色电视机（台）	Number of Color TV Sets per 100 Urban Households (unit)	147.33	149.12
每百户农村家庭拥有彩色电视机（台）	Number of Color TV Sets per 100 Rural Households (unit)	97.72	106.50
广播人口覆盖率（%）	Rate of Radio Broadcast Coverage of the Population (%)	95.71	98.02
电视人口覆盖率（%）	Rate of TV Coverage of the Population (%)	97.39	98.56
卫　生	**Public Health**		
每万人拥有医院、卫生院病床（张）	Number of Beds of Hospitals and Health Centers per 10 000 Population (bed)	29.16	32.18
每万人拥有执业（助理）医师（人）	Number of Licensed (Assistant) Doctors per 10 000 Population (person)	13.57	14.89

表7.2 个人存款年末余额（1980－2011年）
YEAR-END SAVINGS DEPOSIT OF RMB OF HOUSEHOLDS (1980-2011)

年 份 Year	个人存款年末余额（亿元） Year-end Savings Deposit of RMB of Households (100 million yuan)	其 中 of which 定 期 Time Deposits	 活 期 Demand Deposits	人均个人存款余额（元） Per Capita Balance of Savings Deposit of RMB (yuan)
1980	6.22			23
1981	8.35			31
1982	10.56			39
1983	13.34			49
1984	18.39			67
1985	25.41			92
1986	34.79			124
1987	44.46			156
1988	50.50	40.65	9.85	176
1989	68.17	55.75	12.42	235
1990	92.17	77.63	14.54	316
1991	121.95	103.36	18.59	415
1992	154.45	128.64	25.81	523
1993	198.05	160.51	37.54	668
1994	285.40	231.23	54.17	956
1995	401.45	331.09	70.36	1337
1996	500.71	403.84	96.87	1656
1997	580.67	454.04	126.63	1908
1998	724.54	552.72	171.82	2368
1999	909.10	672.96	236.14	2959
2000	1085.36	774.38	310.98	3511
2001	1317.17	929.37	387.80	4252
2002	1595.01	1082.90	512.11	5122
2003	1896.56	1265.52	631.04	6059
2004	2189.73	1469.99	719.74	6964
2005	2545.85	1740.13	805.72	8033
2006	2949.05	1999.88	949.17	9219
2007	3228.15	2099.55	1128.60	9978
2008	3988.96	2640.70	1348.26	12247
2009	4908.68	3060.01	1848.67	14986
2010	5839.66	3475.19	2364.47	17677
2011	6990.25	4106.17	2708.61	20993

表7.3 城乡居民家庭人均收入及恩格尔系数（1978－2011年）
PER CAPITA ANNUAL INCOME AND ENGLE'S COEFFICIENT OF URBAN AND RURAL HOUSEHOLDS (1978-2011)

年份 Year	城市居民家庭人均可支配收入 Per Capital Annual Disposable Income of Metropolitan Households		城镇居民家庭人均可支配收入 Per Capital Annual Disposable Income of Urban Households		农村居民家庭人均纯收入 Per Capital Annual Net Income of Rural Households		城市居民家庭恩格尔系数（%） Engle's Coefficient of Metropolitan Households (%)	城镇居民家庭恩格尔系数（%） Engle's Coefficient of Urban Households (%)	农村居民家庭恩格尔系数（%） Engle's Coefficient of Rural Households (%)
	绝对数（元） Value (yuan)	指数（1979=100） Index（1979=100）	绝对数（元） Value (yuan)	指数（2007=100） Index（2007=100）	绝对数（元） Value (yuan)	指数（1978=100） Index（1978=100）			
1978					126.01	100.0			74.0
1979	354.54	100.0			150.18	119.2	61.9		72.9
1980	411.47	116.1			163.33	129.6	52.8		68.1
1985	812.40	229.1			325.24	258.1	51.8		63.9
1986	983.99	277.5			358.86	284.8	53.1		63.4
1987	1108.71	312.7			385.82	306.2	52.4		62.2
1988	1277.89	360.4			457.54	363.1	51.6		60.5
1989	1448.98	408.7			510.09	404.8	57.4		61.7
1990	1691.13	477.0			586.73	465.6	54.6		63.6
1991	1891.90	533.6			628.89	499.1	52.9		63.8
1992	2195.33	619.2			677.46	537.6	54.3		62.8
1993	2780.62	784.3			748.08	593.7	52.9		61.3
1994	3634.33	1025.1			1018.24	808.1	53.7		63.5
1995	4375.43	1234.1			1270.41	1008.2	50.6		64.7
1996	5022.96	1416.8			1479.05	1173.8	50.2		63.2
1997	5302.05	1495.5			1692.36	1343.0	46.7		65.8
1998	5442.84	1535.2			1801.17	1429.4	45.6		61.3
1999	5828.43	1643.9			1835.54	1456.7	42.8		60.7
2000	6176.30	1742.1			1892.44	1501.8	42.2		53.6
2001	6572.30	1853.8			1971.18	1564.3	40.8		54.1
2002	7238.07	2041.5			2097.58	1664.6	38.0		55.8
2003	8093.67	2282.9			2214.55	1757.4	38.0		52.5
2004	9220.96	2600.2			2510.41	1992.2	37.8		56.0
2005	10243.99	2889.4			2809.32	2229.4	36.4		52.8
2006	11569.74	3263.3			2873.83	2280.6	36.3		52.2
2007	13715.25	3868.5	12590.78	100.0	3509.29	2784.9	37.0	37.2	54.5
2008	15708.74	4430.7	14367.55	114.1	4126.21	3274.5	39.1	39.6	53.3
2009	17191.10	4848.8	15748.67	125.1	4478.35	3554.0	37.2	37.7	49.1
2010	19099.73	5387.2	17532.43	139.2	5276.66	4187.5	37.5	37.6	48.3
2011	21954.97	6192.5	20249.70	160.8	6480.41	5142.8	38.5	39.1	46.8

表7.4 城镇居民家庭基本情况（2010－2011年）
BASIC CONDITIONS OF URBAN HOUSEHOLDS (2010-2011)

项　目	Item	2010	2011
平均每户家庭人口（人）	**Average Household Size (person)**	**2.91**	**2.88**
平均每户就业人数（人）	**Average Number of Employed Persons per Household (person)**	**1.55**	**1.45**
#国有经济单位	State-owned Unit	0.61	0.40
城镇集体经济单位	Urban Collective-owned Unit	0.06	0.07
城镇个体私营经济	Urban Individual and Private Unit	0.56	0.65
平均每人全年总收入（元）	**Per Capita Annual Income (yuan)**	**18990.54**	**21794.27**
#可支配收入	Disposable Income	17532.43	20249.70
工薪收入	Income from Wages and Salaries	12738.20	13827.72
#工资及补贴收入	Salaries and Subsidies	12444.75	13438.34
经营净收入	Net Business Income	1263.20	1779.43
财产性收入	Income from Properties	312.64	433.71
转移性收入	Income from Transfer	4676.51	5753.42
平均每人全年消费支出（元）	**Per Capita Annual Consumption Expenditure (yuan)**	**13335.02**	**14974.49**
#服务性消费支出	Consumption Expenditure of Services	3454.92	3741.05
食　品	Food	5012.56	5847.90
#粮　食	Grain	311.81	364.42
衣　着	Clothing	1697.55	2056.79
#服　装	Garments	1249.02	1516.13
家庭设备用品及服务	Household Facilities, Articles and Services	1072.38	1079.27
医疗保健	Health Care and Medical Services	1021.48	1050.62
交通和通讯	Transport and Communication	1384.28	1718.73
教育娱乐文化服务	Educational, Recreational and Cultural Services	1408.02	1474.88
#教　育	Education	472.43	460.09
居　住	Residence	1275.96	1205.66
#住　房	Housing	460.67	336.25
杂项商品与服务	Miscellaneous Goods and Services	462.79	540.63

表7.5 按可支配收入分组的城镇居民家庭情况（2011年）
Conditions of Urban Households by Disposable Income (2011)

项　目	Item	合　计 Total	按平均每人每月可支配收入分组 By per Capita Monthly Disposable Income		
			200元以下 Below 200 yuan	200-400元 200-400 yuan	400-600元 400-600 yuan
比　重（%）	Percentage (%)	100.00	0.28	0.96	3.19
平均每户家庭人口数（人）	Average Household Size (person)	2.88	3.03	3.19	3.23
平均每户就业人口数（人）	Average Number of Employed Persons per Household (person)	1.45	1.06	0.97	1.29
平均每户就业面（%）	Percentage of Employment per Household (%)	50.70	34.98	30.41	39.94
平均每一就业者负担人数（人）	Number of Dependants per Employee (person)	1.97	2.86	2.29	2.50
平均每人每月总收入（元）	Per Capita Monthly Income (yuan)	1816.19	754.18	449.95	611.62
#可支配收入	Disposable Income	1687.48	-344.63	320.63	512.57
平均每人每月消费性支出（元）	Per Capita Monthly Consumption Expenditure (yuan)	1247.87	788.84	638.21	678.26
#服务性消费支出	Consumption Expenditure of Services	311.75	204.24	163.31	149.52

项　目	Item	按平均每人每月可支配收入分组 By per Capita Monthly Disposable Income			
		600-800元 600-800 yuan	800-1000元 800-1000 yuan	1000-1500元 1000-1500 yuan	1500元以上 Over 1500 yuan
比　重（%）	Percentage (%)	6.76	9.94	28.70	50.17
平均每户家庭人口数（人）	Average Household Size (person)	3.34	3.05	3.01	2.69
平均每户就业人口数（人）	Average Number of Employed Persons per Household (person)	1.32	1.47	1.47	1.47
平均每户就业面（%）	Percentage of Employment per Household (%)	39.52	48.20	48.84	54.65
平均每一就业者负担人数（人）	Number of Dependants per Employee (person)	2.53	2.07	2.05	1.83
平均每人每月总收入（元）	Per Capita Monthly Income (yuan)	792.68	1000.76	1359.73	2552.52
#可支配收入	Disposable Income	704.34	904.29	1246.53	2404.92
平均每人每月消费性支出（元）	Per Capita Monthly Consumption Expenditure (yuan)	724.83	801.67	993.91	1637.68
#服务性消费支出	Consumption Expenditure of Services	172.12	181.22	232.06	426.05

表7.6 城镇居民家庭平均每人全年收入及构成（2011年）

PER CAPITA ANNUAL INCOME OF URBAN HOUSEHOLDS AND ITS COMPOSITION (2011)

项　目	Item	总平均 Overall Average	最低收入户（10%） Lowest Income Households (10%)	其中 of which #困难户（5%） Poor Households (5%)	低收入户（10%） Low Income Households (10%)	中等偏下户（20%） Lower Middle Income Households (20%)
全年总收入（元）	**Annual Total Income (yuan)**	**21794.27**	**9898.02**	**8500.87**	**13463.83**	**16700.97**
#可支配收入	Disposable Income	20249.70	9008.04	7710.30	12276.36	15285.08
工薪收入	Income from Wages and Salaries	13827.72	5778.85	4807.55	8520.83	9646.30
#工资及补贴收入	Salaries and Subsidies	13438.34	5435.30	4433.50	8347.44	9286.14
经营净收入	Net Business Income	1779.43	1036.78	713.98	1514.90	2114.36
财产性收入	Income from Properties	433.71	204.26	232.68	319.07	300.89
转移性收入	Income from Transfer	5753.42	2878.12	2746.66	3109.03	4639.42
全年总收入构成（%）	**Composition of Annual Income (%)**	**100.0**	**100.0**	**100.0**	**100.0**	**100.0**
工薪收入	Income from Wages and Salaries	92.9	91.0	90.7	91.2	91.5
#工资及补贴收入	Salaries and Subsidies	63.4	58.4	56.6	63.3	57.8
非工薪收入	Non-Salary Income	7.1	9.0	9.3	8.8	8.5

项　目	Item	中等收入户（20%） Middle Income Households (20%)	中等偏上户（20%） Upper Middle Income Households (20%)	高收入户（10%） High Income Households (10%)	最高收入户（10%） Highest Income Households (10%)
全年总收入（元）	**Annual Total Income (yuan)**	**20185.13**	**25079.59**	**31670.83**	**48265.16**
#可支配收入	Disposable Income	18896.00	23249.40	29691.00	45517.62
工薪收入	Income from Wages and Salaries	11937.00	15713.76	20972.05	35844.99
#工资及补贴收入	Salaries and Subsidies	11648.97	15384.49	20649.54	34530.77
经营净收入	Net Business Income	1771.96	1688.23	1476.12	2741.96
财产性收入	Income from Properties	216.97	409.77	611.13	1707.24
转移性收入	Income from Transfer	6259.19	7267.82	8611.52	7970.96
全年总收入构成（%）	**Composition of Annual Income (%)**	**100.0**	**100.0**	**100.0**	**100.0**
工薪收入	Income from Wages and Salaries	93.6	92.7	93.7	94.3
#工资及补贴收入	Salaries and Subsidies	59.1	62.7	66.2	74.3
非工薪收入	Non-Salary Income	6.4	7.3	6.3	5.7

表7.7 城镇居民家庭平均每人全年消费支出及构成（2011年）
PER CAPITA ANNUAL LIVING EXPENDITURE OF URBAN HOUSEHOLDS AND ITS COMPOSITION (2011)

项 目	Item	总平均 Overall Average	最低收入户（10%） Lowest Income Households (10%)	其中 of which #困难户（5%） Poor Households (5%)	低收入户（10%） Low Income Households (10%)	中等偏下户（20%） Lower Middle Income Households (20%)
消费支出（元）	**Total Consumption Expenditure (yuan)**	**14974.49**	**7511.51**	**6855.39**	**9591.49**	**11578.76**
#服务性消费支出	Consumption Expenditure of Services	3741.05	1645.18	1555.39	2192.00	2684.39
食 品	Food	5847.90	3439.10	3209.15	4230.30	5002.70
#粮油类	Grain and Oils	709.92	565.48	560.13	620.68	687.29
#粮 食	Grain	364.42	305.13	305.10	320.10	357.55
肉禽蛋水产品类	Meat, Poultry, Eggs and Aquatic Products	1744.83	1168.02	1078.35	1355.20	1655.73
#肉 类	Meat	1053.09	781.76	738.85	863.31	1028.75
蔬菜类	Vegetable	624.99	477.53	445.63	539.79	606.38
糖烟酒饮料类	Candy, Cigarette, Alcohol and Beverage	533.94	225.07	238.16	333.21	378.69
糕点、奶及奶制品	Cake, Milk and Dairy Products	338.21	178.20	148.73	204.62	313.20
衣 着	Clothing	2056.79	692.02	637.57	1108.64	1584.36
#服 装	Garments	1516.13	492.08	448.50	799.21	1158.10
家庭设备用品及服务	Household Facilities, Articles and Services	1079.27	467.53	450.21	684.96	716.58
医疗保健	Health Care and Medical Services	1050.62	699.40	592.65	706.80	899.60
交通和通讯	Transport and Communications	1718.73	688.06	524.52	823.07	994.94
教育娱乐文化服务	Education, Recreation and Cultural Services	1474.88	617.20	602.03	851.20	1051.02
#教 育	Education	460.09	318.84	345.00	423.58	392.76
居 住	Residence	1205.66	753.61	718.56	867.20	1001.62
#住 房	Housing	336.25	220.83	226.05	219.12	244.45
杂项商品与服务	Miscellaneous Goods and Services	540.63	154.57	120.70	319.33	327.93
消费支出构成（%）	**Composition of Living Expenditure (%)**	**100.0**	**100.0**	**100.0**	**100.0**	**100.0**
#服务性消费支出	Consumption Expenditure of Services	25.0	21.9	22.7	22.9	23.2
食 品	Food	39.1	45.8	46.8	44.1	43.2
衣 着	Clothing	13.7	9.2	9.3	11.6	13.7
家庭设备用品及服务	Household Facilities, Articles and Services	7.2	6.2	6.6	7.1	6.2
医疗保健	Health Care and Medical Services	7.0	9.3	8.6	7.4	7.8
交通和通讯	Transport and Communications	11.5	9.2	7.7	8.6	8.6
教育娱乐文化服务	Education, Recreation and Cultural Services	9.8	8.2	8.8	8.9	9.1
居 住	Residence	8.1	10.0	10.5	9.0	8.7
杂项商品与服务	Miscellaneous Goods and Services	3.6	2.1	1.8	3.3	2.8

表7.7 续表 continued

项　目	Item	中等收入户（20%）Middle Income Households (20%)	中等偏上户（20%）Upper Middle Income Households (20%)	高收入户（10%）High Income Households (10%)	最高收入户（10%）Highest Income Households (10%)
消费支出（元）	**Total Consumption Expenditure (yuan)**	**13786.64**	**17196.49**	**22284.79**	**31195.20**
#服务性消费支出	Consumption Expenditure of Services	3217.34	4237.01	6050.72	9174.18
食　品	Food	5792.38	6712.28	7682.97	9559.51
#粮油类	Grain and Oils	731.38	779.28	779.97	777.95
#粮　食	Grain	372.76	390.15	396.32	400.18
肉禽蛋水产品类	Meat, Poultry, Eggs and Aquatic Products	1798.63	2009.74	2019.12	2178.15
#肉　类	Meat	1068.51	1189.50	1171.12	1225.64
蔬菜类	Vegetable	651.42	692.61	681.48	686.24
糖烟酒饮料类	Candy, Cigarette, Alcohol and Beverage	482.38	613.84	835.98	1254.22
糕点、奶及奶制品	Cake, Milk and Dairy Products	340.91	398.84	447.42	520.30
衣　着	Clothing	1852.30	2337.16	3174.60	5072.02
#服　装	Garments	1329.25	1715.53	2376.75	3887.97
家庭设备用品及服务	Household Facilities, Articles and Services	952.42	1290.72	1774.47	2485.95
医疗保健	Health Care and Medical Services	858.58	1233.94	1720.49	1716.76
交通和通讯	Transport and Communications	1521.90	2100.17	2801.10	4709.96
教育娱乐文化服务	Education, Recreation and Cultural Services	1265.24	1706.01	2285.29	3729.94
#教　育	Education	417.13	402.88	536.51	1055.82
居　住	Residence	1096.87	1240.10	1955.26	2199.86
#住　房	Housing	245.31	244.89	841.55	806.34
杂项商品与服务	Miscellaneous Goods and Services	446.95	576.11	890.62	1721.21
消费支出构成（%）	**Composition of Living Expenditure (%)**	**100.0**	**100.0**	**100.0**	**100.0**
#服务性消费支出	Consumption Expenditure of Services	23.3	24.6	27.2	29.4
食　品	Food	42.0	39.0	34.5	30.6
衣　着	Clothing	13.4	13.6	14.2	16.3
家庭设备用品及服务	Household Facilities, Articles and Services	6.9	7.5	8.0	8.0
医疗保健	Health Care and Medical Services	6.2	7.2	7.7	5.5
交通和通讯	Transport and Communications	11.0	12.2	12.6	15.1
教育娱乐文化服务	Education, Recreation and Cultural Services	9.2	9.9	10.3	12.0
居　住	Residence	8.0	7.2	8.8	7.1
杂项商品与服务	Miscellaneous Goods and Services	3.2	3.4	4.0	5.5

表7.8 城镇居民家庭平均每人全年购买的主要商品数量（2010－2011年）
PER CAPITA ANNUAL PURCHASES OF MAJOR COMMODITIES OF URBAN HOUSEHOLDS (2010-2011)

指　标	Item	2010	2011
粮　食（千克）	Grain (kg)	69.26	69.09
鲜　菜（千克）	Fresh Vegetables (kg)	133.91	131.1
食用植物油（千克）	Edible Vegetable Oil (kg)	13.26	13.76
猪　肉（千克）	Pork (kg)	31.64	32.35
牛羊肉（千克）	Beef and Mutton (kg)	3.45	3.67
家　禽（千克）	Poultry (kg)	14.42	14.26
鲜　蛋（千克）	Fresh Eggs (kg)	9.26	8.73
鱼　虾（千克）	Aquatic Products (kg)	9.98	10.09
鲜乳品（千克）	Fresh Dairy Products (kg)	17.83	16.14
酒　类（千克）	Liquor (kg)	6.78	6.44
茶　叶（千克）	Tea (kg)	0.33	0.29
鲜瓜果（千克）	Fresh Melons and Fruits (kg)	40.62	38.28
服　装（件）	Clothing (piece)	8.25	7.32
鞋　类（双）	Shoes (pair)	2.93	3.12

表7.9 城镇居民家庭平均每百户年末耐用消费品拥有量（2010－2011年）
OWNERSHIP OF MAJOR DURABLE CONSUMER GOODS PER 100 URBAN HOUSEHOLDS AT YEAR-END (2010-2011)

指　标	Item	2010	2011
摩托车（辆）	Motorcycle (unit)	12.49	10.76
家用汽车（辆）	Automobile (unit)	6.60	10.44
电冰箱（台）	Refrigerator (unit)	101.17	101.86
洗衣机（台）	Washing Machine (unit)	97.23	97.83
彩色电视机（台）	Color TV Set (unit)	147.33	149.12
组合音响（套）	Hi-Fi Stereo Component System (set)	34.05	22.80
摄像机（架）	Video Camera (unit)	7.02	7.18
照相机（架）	Camera (unit)	33.94	34.24
钢　琴（架）	Piano (unit)	1.68	1.28
中高档乐器（件）	Medium and High-Grade Musical Instrument (piece)	2.55	2.35
微波炉（台）	Microwave Oven (unit)	70.34	68.96
空调器（台）	Air Conditioner (unit)	158.35	164.31
淋浴热水器（台）	Water Heater for Shower (unit)	100.30	100.51
健身器材（套）	Health Equipment (set)	4.34	2.32
家用电脑（台）	Computer (unit)	69.03	76.07
普通电话（部）	Telephone (unit)	83.20	65.86
移动电话（部）	Mobile Telephone (unit)	190.48	207.11

表7.10 农村居民家庭基本情况（1985－2011年）
BASIC CONDITIONS OF RURAL HOUSEHOLDS (1985-2011)

年　份 Year	平均每户常住人口（人） Average Permanent Population per Household (person)	平均每户整半劳动力（人） Average Numberof Full/Semi Laborers per Household(person)	平均每个劳动力负担人口（人） Average Number of Dependants per Laborer (person)	平均每人纯收入（元） Per Capita Annual Net Income (yuan)	平均每人生活消费支出（元） Per Capita Annual Living Expenditure (yuan)	平均每人住房面积（平方米） Per Capita Residential Floor Space (sq.m)
1985	4.63	2.81	1.65	325.24	275.81	18.04
1986	4.58	2.85	1.61	358.86	312.34	18.06
1987	4.51	2.87	1.57	385.82	346.40	18.23
1988	4.40	2.89	1.53	457.54	427.19	19.03
1989	4.31	2.92	1.47	510.09	463.47	19.29
1990	4.21	2.93	1.44	586.73	519.26	19.37
1991	4.20	2.88	1.46	628.89	558.44	21.52
1992	4.12	2.88	1.43	677.46	573.65	21.94
1993	4.05	2.90	1.39	748.08	694.60	22.01
1994	3.98	2.88	1.38	1018.24	879.26	22.55
1995	3.90	2.83	1.38	1270.41	1097.52	23.50
1996	3.85	2.70	1.43	1479.05	1328.18	24.44
1997	3.82	2.69	1.42	1692.36	1389.99	24.74
1998	3.71	2.61	1.42	1801.17	1417.08	26.50
1999	3.68	2.59	1.42	1835.54	1388.64	26.67
2000	3.70	2.63	1.41	1892.44	1395.53	29.58
2001	3.66	2.56	1.43	1971.18	1475.16	31.00
2002	3.65	2.62	1.39	2097.58	1497.72	31.02
2003	3.65	2.69	1.36	2214.55	1583.31	31.45
2004	3.67	2.72	1.35	2510.41	1853.94	32.49
2005	3.71	2.80	1.32	2809.32	2142.12	32.91
2006	3.68	2.80	1.31	2873.83	2205.21	34.30
2007	3.67	2.80	1.31	3509.29	2526.70	34.56
2008	3.70	2.80	1.30	4126.21	2884.92	35.03
2009	3.61	2.78	1.31	4478.35	3142.14	35.73
2010	3.63	2.83	1.28	5276.66	3624.62	37.56
2011	3.82	2.81	1.40	6480.41	4502.06	40.18

表7.11 农村居民家庭基本情况（2010－2011年）
BASIC CONDITIONS OF RURAL HOUSEHOLDS (2010-2011)

指　标	Item	2010	2011
调查户数（户）	**Number of Households Surveyed (household)**	**1800.0**	**1800.0**
调查户常住人口（人）	Number of Permanent Residents (person)	6541.0	6872.0
整半劳动力	Full/Semi Labor Force	5093.0	5049.0
平均每户常住人口	Average Number of Permanent Residents per Household	3.63	3.82
平均每户整半劳力	Average Number of Full/Semi Laborers per Household	2.83	2.81
平均每个劳动力负担人口（含本人）	Average Number of Dependents per Laborer (including the laborer himself or herself)	1.28	1.40
平均每人年收入（元）	**Per Capita Annual Income (yuan)**		
总收入	Total Income	6726.70	8421.52
纯收入	Net Income	5276.66	6480.41
现金收入	Cash Income	5312.93	6963.29
农村居民纯收入按五等分分组（元）	**Per Capita Net Income of Rural Households by Quintile (yuan)**		
低收入户	Low Income Households	2161.77	2846.04
中下收入户	Lower Middle Income Households	3761.72	4624.65
中等收入户	Middle Income Households	5024.54	6054.48
中上收入户	Upper Middle Income Households	6586.06	7913.61
高收入户	High Income Households	10346.02	13117.82
平均每人年支出（元）	**Per Capita Annual Expenditure (yuan)**		
总支出	Total Expenditure	5495.62	7035.79
现金支出	Cash Expenditure	4313.91	5909.95
平均每人经营耕地面积（亩）	**Per Capita Cultivated Area (mu)**	**1.19**	**1.27**
平均每人生产性固定资产原值（元）	**Per Capita Original Value of Productive Fixed Assets (yuan)**	**1537.35**	**2982.79**
第一产业	Primary Industry	1241.83	2019.94
#役畜、产品畜	Draught Animals and Commodity Animals	206.67	313.57
大中型铁木农具	Large and Medium Wood and Iron Farm Tools	71.57	66.56
农林牧渔机械	Machinery of Farming, Forestry, Animal Husbandry and Fishery	82.99	128.82
第二产业	Secondary Industry	19.89	371.79
第三产业	Tertiary Industry	275.63	663.39

表7.12 农村居民家庭平均每人收入情况（2010－2011年）
PER CAPITA ANNUAL INCOME OF RURAL HOUSEHOLDS (2010-2011)

单位：元 (yuan)

指 标	Item	2010	2011
总收入	**Total Income**	**6726.70**	**8421.52**
工资性收入	Income from Wages and Salaries	2335.23	2894.53
#在本地劳动得到收入	From Local Enterprises	756.92	1089.98
外出从业得到收入	From Enterprises in Other Areas	1435.86	1641.59
家庭经营收入	Income from Household Business Operation	3646.62	4526.48
第一产业	Primary Industry	3161.91	3780.18
#农 业	Farming	1747.37	1950.03
牧 业	Animal Husbandry	1284.60	1707.41
第二产业	Secondary Industry	66.32	98.22
第三产业	Tertiary Industry	418.39	648.08
#交通运输、邮电业	Transportation, Postal and Telecommunication Services	134.36	206.60
批零贸易、餐饮业	Wholesale & Retail Trade and Catering Service	199.56	323.95
财产性收入	Income from Properties	90.50	139.67
转移性收入	Income from Transfer	654.35	860.84
纯收入	**Net Income**	**5276.66**	**6480.41**
工资性收入	Income from Wages and Salaries	2335.23	2894.53
#在本地劳动得到收入	From Local Enterprises	756.92	1089.98
外出从业得到收入	From Enterprises in Other Areas	1435.86	1641.59
家庭经营收入	Income from Household Business Operation	2323.51	2748.25
第一产业	Primary Industry	2003.03	2332.37
#农 业	Farming	1333.35	1427.58
牧 业	Animal Husbandry	586.19	843.54
第二产业	Secondary Industry	33.13	29.51
第三产业	Tertiary Industry	287.36	386.36
#交通运输、邮电业	Transportation, Postal and Telecommunication Services	84.94	106.66
批零贸易、餐饮业	Wholesale & Retail Trade and Catering Service	127.09	196.62
财产性收入	Income from Properties	90.50	139.67
转移性收入	Income from Transfer	527.41	697.96
现金收入	**Cash Income**	**5312.93**	**6963.29**
工资性收入	Income from Wages and Salaries	2334.82	2889.02
#在本地劳动得到收入	From Local Enterprises	756.75	1088.50
外出从业得到收入	From Enterprises in Other Areas	1435.68	1637.56
家庭经营收入	Income from Household Business Operation	2244.52	3095.48
第一产业	Primary Industry	1760.72	2349.22
#农 业	Farming	679.96	849.07
牧 业	Animal Husbandry	964.19	1380.54
第二产业	Secondary Industry	66.32	98.22
第三产业	Tertiary Industry	417.48	648.03
#交通运输、邮电业	Transportation, Postal and Telecommunication Services	134.36	206.60
批零贸易、餐饮业	Wholesale & Retail Trade and Catering Service	199.56	323.95
财产性收入	Income from Properties	81.32	121.16
转移性收入	Income from Transfer	652.27	857.64

表7.13 农村居民家庭平均每人支出情况（2010－2011年）
PER CAPITA ANNUAL EXPENDITURE OF RURAL HOUSEHOLDS (2010-2011)

单位：元 (yuan)

指 标	Item	2010	2011
总支出	**Total Expenditure**	**5495.62**	**7035.79**
家庭经营费用支出	Expenditure of Household Business Operation	1217.85	1571.89
第一产业	Primary Industry	1073.46	1309.73
第二产业	Secondary Industry	31.86	48.57
第三产业	Tertiary Industry	112.53	213.59
购置生产性固定资产支出	Expenditure of Purchasing Productive Fixed Assets	73.68	74.75
税费支出	Taxes and Fees	2.77	7.49
生活消费支出	Living Expenditure	3624.62	4502.06
食 品	Food	1750.01	2108.61
衣 着	Clothing	224.13	309.00
居 住	Residence	548.00	555.81
家庭设备、用品及服务	Household Facilities, Articles and Services	260.71	348.31
交通和通讯	Transport and Communications	270.31	401.65
文教娱乐用品及服务	Culture, Education, Recreation and Services	281.73	334.84
医疗保健	Health Care and Medical Services	239.03	375.26
其他商品和服务	Miscellaneous Goods and Services	50.70	68.57
财产性支出	Property Expenditure	0.68	1.69
转移性支出	Transfer Expenditure	564.37	873.69
现金支出	**Cash Expenditure**	**4313.91**	**5909.95**
家庭经营费用支出	Expenditure of Household Business Operation	823.82	1214.56
第一产业	Primary Industry	679.46	952.82
第二产业	Secondary Industry	31.86	48.57
第三产业	Tertiary Industry	112.50	213.17
购置生产性固定资产支出	Expenditure of Purchasing Productive Fixed Assets	73.68	74.75
税费支出	Taxes and Fees	2.75	7.47
生活消费支出	Living Expenditure	2837.12	3734.59
食 品	Food	994.70	1360.35
衣 着	Clothing	224.12	308.95
居 住	Residence	518.09	536.73
家庭设备、用品及服务	Household Facilities, Articles and Services	258.43	348.24
交通和通讯	Transport and Communications	281.73	401.65
文教娱乐用品及服务	Culture, Education, Recreation and Services	239.03	334.84
医疗保健	Health Care and Medical Services	270.31	375.26
其他商品和服务	Miscellaneous Goods and Services	50.70	68.57
财产性支出	Property Expenditure	0.68	1.69
转移性支出	Transfer Expenditure	564.21	872.68

表7.14 不同收入组农村居民家庭收入支出情况（2011年）
PER CAPITA ANNUAL INCOME AND EXPENDITURES OF RURAL HOUSEHOLDS BY INCOME QUINTILE (2011)

单位：元 (yuan)

指　标	Item	总平均 Total Average	低收入户（20%） Low Income Households (20%)	中低收入户（20%） Lower Middle Income Households（20%）
平均每人总收入	**Per Capita Total Income**	**8421.52**	**4457.73**	**6157.99**
#现金收入	Cash Income	6963.29	3460.07	4929.16
平均每人纯收入	**Per Capita Net Income**	**6480.41**	**2846.04**	**4624.65**
工资性收入	Income from Wages and Salaries	2894.53	1443.98	2225.39
家庭经营纯收入	Income from Family Business Operation	2748.25	924.82	1792.36
财产性收入	Income from Property	139.67	65.84	97.67
转移性收入	Income from Transfer	697.96	411.39	509.24
平均每人总支出	**Per Capita Total Expenditure**	**7035.79**	**5480.11**	**6105.52**
#现金支出	Cash Expenditure	5909.95	4568.43	5055.45
生活消费总支出	**Per Capita Living Expenditures**	**4502.06**	**3474.95**	**4045.59**
食　品	Food	2108.61	1700.44	1880.60
衣　着	Clothing	309.00	220.84	242.83
居　住	Residence	555.81	464.97	575.11
家庭设备用品及服务	Household Facilities, Articles and Services	348.31	223.59	316.64
交通通讯	Transport and Communications	401.65	260.02	314.00
文教娱乐用品及服务	Culture, Education, Recreation and Services	334.84	268.01	307.01
医疗保健	Health Care and Medical Services	375.26	286.53	346.38
其他商品及服务	Miscellaneous Goods and Services	68.57	50.56	63.03

指　标	Item	中等收入户（20%） Middle Income Households (20%)	中高收入户（20%） Upper Middle Income Households (20%)	高收入户（20%） High Income Households (20%)
平均每人总收入	**Per Capita Total Income**	**7731.50**	**9883.45**	**16379.29**
#现金收入	Cash Income	6220.68	8282.66	14174.81
平均每人纯收入	**Per Capita Net Income**	**6054.48**	**7913.61**	**13117.82**
工资性收入	Income from Wages and Salaries	2873.90	3867.88	4794.35
家庭经营纯收入	Income from Family Business Operation	2378.63	3082.91	6753.71
财产性收入	Income from Property	123.07	156.38	304.60
转移性收入	Income from Transfer	678.88	806.45	1265.15
平均每人总支出	**Per Capita Total Expenditure**	**6596.97**	**7465.36**	**10592.23**
#现金支出	Cash Expenditure	5462.90	6252.85	9164.23
生活消费总支出	**Per Capita Living Expenditures**	**4361.32**	**4790.41**	**6448.42**
食　品	Food	2083.44	2289.15	2829.17
衣　着	Clothing	289.12	375.63	473.00
居　住	Residence	458.13	474.57	878.87
家庭设备用品及服务	Household Facilities, Articles and Services	362.72	385.00	511.73
交通通讯	Transport and Communications	391.08	429.36	706.08
文教娱乐用品及服务	Culture, Education, Recreation and Services	320.41	318.95	505.96
医疗保健	Health Care and Medical Services	377.93	440.70	463.61
其他商品及服务	Miscellaneous Goods and Services	78.50	77.06	80.00

表7.15 农村居民家庭平均每人主要消费品消费量（2010－2011年）
PER CAPITA CONSUMPTION OF MAJOR FOODS OF RURAL HOUSEHOLDS (2010-2011)

指 标	Item	2010	2011
粮 食（原粮）（千克）	Grain (unprocessed) (kg)	186.47	171.15
蔬 菜（千克）	Fresh Vegetables (kg)	126.44	137.65
食用植物油（千克）	Edible Vegetable Oil (kg)	5.62	7.23
肉 类（千克）	Meat (kg)	35.58	29.68
#猪 肉	Pork	28.53	23.54
牛羊肉	Beef and Mutton	0.32	0.29
家 禽（千克）	Poultry (kg)	4.71	4.09
鲜 蛋（千克）	Eggs (kg)	7.12	5.48
鱼 虾（千克）	Aquatic Products (kg)	3.46	3.65
鲜 奶（千克）	Fresh Milk (kg)	1.73	3.62
酒 类（千克）	Liquor (kg)	13.96	13.75

表7.16 农村居民家庭平均每百户年末耐用消费品拥有量（2010－2011年）
NUMBER OF DURABLE CONSUMER GOODS OWNED
PER 100 RURAL HOUSEHOLDS AT YEAR-END (2010-2011)

指 标	Item	2010	2011
洗衣机（台）	Washing Machine (unit)	48.56	60.50
电冰箱（台）	Refrigerator (unit)	58.00	73.17
空调机（台）	Air Conditioner (unit)	14.56	21.67
抽油烟机（台）	Exhaust Fan (unit)	2.44	4.28
微波炉（台）	Microwave Oven (unit)	7.22	11.94
热水器（台）	Water Heater for Shower (unit)	20.61	34.33
摩托车（辆）	Motorcycle (unit)	27.06	36.28
家用计算机（台）	Computer (unit)	4.06	11.94
移动电话（部）	Mobile Telephone (unit)	132.00	175.78
彩色电视机（台）	Color TV Set (unit)	97.72	106.50
轿 车（台）	Automobile (unit)	0.67	2.56

表7.17 主要年份居民消费价格指数和商品零售价格指数
CONSUMER PRICE INDICES AND GENERAL RETAIL PRICE INDICES IN MAJOR YEARS

年 份 Year	以1950年为100 1950=100		以1978年为100 1978=100		以上年为100 Preceding Year=100	
	居民消费价格指数 Consumer Price Index	商品零售价格指数 Retail Price Index	居民消费价格指数 Consumer Price Index	商品零售价格指数 Retail Price Index	居民消费价格指数 Consumer Price Index	商品零售价格指数 Retail Price Index
1951						
1952	106.1	108.7			97.3	97.2
1957	114.0	116.5			104.6	103.9
1962	145.8	158.1			95.2	95.0
1965	125.1	133.1			98.0	98.2
1970	129.2	137.9			99.6	99.5
1975	131.2	140.2			100.3	100.3
1978	135.4	145.1	100.0	100.0	102.9	103.2
1980	148.3	160.1	109.5	110.3	107.9	108.6
1985	179.4	191.7	132.4	132.0	109.9	110.0
1986	186.9	199.8	138.0	137.5	104.2	104.2
1987	205.2	220.8	151.5	151.9	109.8	110.5
1988	251.8	272.2	185.9	187.3	122.7	123.3
1989	294.9	317.1	217.7	218.2	117.1	116.5
1990	299.0	317.4	220.7	218.4	101.4	100.1
1991	319.9	336.8	236.1	231.7	107.0	106.1
1992	355.7	369.8	262.5	254.4	111.2	109.8
1993	422.2	430.1	311.6	295.9	118.7	116.3
1994	547.6	544.1	404.1	374.3	129.7	126.5
1995	653.8	632.8	482.5	435.3	119.4	116.3
1996	717.2	671.4	529.3	461.9	109.7	106.1
1997	741.2	682.6	546.8	470.4	103.3	101.7
1998	714.5	645.1	527.1	444.5	96.4	94.5
1999	709.5	622.5	523.4	428.9	99.3	96.5
2000	686.1	594.5	506.1	409.6	96.7	95.5
2001	697.8	588.6	514.7	405.5	101.7	99.0
2002	695.0	582.1	512.6	401.0	99.6	98.9
2003	699.2	579.2	515.7	399.0	100.6	99.5
2004	725.1	587.3	534.8	404.6	103.7	101.4
2005	730.9	579.7	539.1	399.3	100.8	98.7
2006	748.4	589.0	552.0	405.7	102.4	101.6
2007	783.6	610.8	577.9	420.7	104.7	103.7
2008	827.5	641.3	610.3	441.7	105.6	105.0
2009	814.3	624.0	600.5	429.8	98.4	97.3
2010	840.3	634.6	619.8	437.1	103.2	101.7
2011	884.9	664.2	652.6	457.4	105.3	104.7

表7.18 居民消费价格分类指数（2010－2011年）
CONSUMER PRICE INDICES BY CATEGORY (2010-2011)

上年＝100 (preceding year=100)

项　目	Item	2010	2011
居民消费价格指数	**Consumer Price Index**	**103.2**	**105.3**
食　品	Food	106.5	114.1
#粮　食	Grain	113.1	115.4
油　脂	Oil and Fat	105.2	116.0
肉禽及其制品	Meat, Poultry and Processed Products	104.7	130.1
蛋	Eggs	106.4	120.2
水产品	Aquatic Products	106.0	107.2
菜	Vegetables	109.3	103.5
#鲜　菜	Fresh Vegetables	108.7	103.8
茶及饮料	Tea and Beverages	104.4	108.2
干鲜瓜果	Dried and Fresh Melons and Fruits	114.9	116.4
#鲜　果	Fresh Fruits	119.4	116.2
液体乳及乳制品	Milk and Its Products	103.3	107.5
在外用膳食品	Dinning Out	104.2	107.1
其它食品	Other Foods	96.7	106.8
烟酒及用品	Tobacco, Liquor and Articles	104.3	103.7
#烟　草	Tobacco	101.4	99.8
酒	Liquor	112.7	112.7
衣　着	Clothing	98.4	101.3
#服　装	Garments	99.6	101.6
家庭设备用品及维修服务	Household Facilities, Articles and Service	100.2	102.2
#耐用消费品	Durable Consumer Goods	96.0	97.3
家庭服务及加工维修服务	Household Services and Maintenance and Renovation	107.4	110.6
医疗保健和个人用品	Health Care and Personnal Articles	102.5	102.0
#医疗保健	Health Care	103.4	101.5
个人用品及服务	Personal Articles and Services	101.0	102.7
交通和通信	Transportation and Communications	99.5	99.1
#交　通	Transportation	103.6	103.2
通　信	Telecommunication	96.4	95.5
娱乐教育文化用品及服务	Recreational, Educational and Cultural Articles and Services	102.7	98.9
#教　育	Education	105.9	101.8
居　住	Residence	105.4	103.7

注：根据2011年国家统计局城市司流通消费价格调查制度规定，2011年起原“烟草及用品”指标改为“烟酒”。
Note: According to the regulation about the survey of circulating consumption price by the Urban Survey Department of NBS in 2011, the index of "tobacco and articles" is replaced by "tobacco and liquor" since 2011.".

表7.19 商品零售价格分类指数（2010－2011年）
RETAIL PRICE INDICES BY CATEGORY (2010-2011)

上年＝100 (preceding year=100)

项　目	Item	2010	2011
商品零售价格指数	**General Retail Price Index**	**101.7**	**104.7**
食　品	Food	106.5	113.6
饮料、烟酒	Beverages, Tobacco and Liquor	104.5	105.6
服装、鞋帽	Garments, Shoes and Hats	98.4	101.4
纺织品	Textiles	100.6	111.9
家用电器及音像器材	Household Appliances and Video Materials	88.4	90.5
文化办公用品	Cultural and Office Appliances	95.0	93.2
日用品	Articles for Daily Use	99.5	104.5
体育娱乐用品	Sports and Recreation Articles	96.8	96.9
交通、通信用品	Transportation and Communication Articles	92.3	93.2
家　具	Furniture	101.0	99.8
化妆品	Cosmetics	100.1	102.0
金银珠宝	Gold, Silver and Jewelry	119.2	113.3
中西药品及医疗保健用品	Traditional Chinese & Western Medicines and Health Care Articles	104.3	102.4
书报杂志及电子出版物	Books, Newspaper, Magazines and Electronic Publications	100.6	101.0
燃　料	Fuels	109.2	111.3
建筑材料及五金电料	Building Materials and Hardware	103.1	105.1

表7.20 农产品生产价格指数(2004—2011年)
PRODUCERS' PRICE INDICES FOR AGRICULTURAL PRODUCTS (2004－2011)

上年＝100 (preceding year=100)

指　标	Item	2004	2005	2006	2007	2008	2009	2010	2011
合　计	**Total**	**125.5**	**100.0**	**93.6**	**121.8**	**120.4**	**89.0**	**103.2**	**120.2**
农业产品	**Farm Products**	**120.3**	**102.2**	**100.4**	**108.6**	**108.9**	**104.2**	**109.1**	**113.8**
#谷　物	Cereal	139.6	101.3	97.3	108.2	108.5	100.4	108.4	114.4
#小　麦	Wheat	131.6	102.7	95.1	103.9	106.4	103.5	104.3	110.6
稻　谷	Rice	141.5	101.2	97.8	108.2	109.2	100.8	106.8	116.2
玉　米	Corn	130.4	101.7	94.9	109.0	106.2	97.9	113.4	111.4
大　豆	Beans	122.1	97.4	100.0	107.9	115.4	98.9	106.6	111.5
油　料	Oil-bearing Crops	123.2	93.1	102.8	120.1	118.9	80.3	108.8	109.0
蔬　菜	Vegetables	106.0	103.8	102.5	109.8	106.6	110.5	107.9	111.1
水果及坚果	Fruits and Nuts	103.0	103.4	101.3	104.5	109.2	107.0	111.2	119.5
饲养动物及其产品	**Animal Husbandry Products**	**128.8**	**98.8**	**89.8**	**128.8**	**126.1**	**80.8**	**98.4**	**126.6**
#活　猪	Pig	131.2	97.5	86.9	132.2	127.2	77.1	94.4	134.5
牛	Cattle and Buffaloes	101.7	103.9	101.6	120.6	116.0	104.2	103.4	107.6
羊	Sheep and Goats	111.1	102.8	101.2	108.0	128.9	100.7	100.0	116.6
活家禽	Poultry	117.2	104.3	100.2	116.2	111.7	102.8	105.6	111.8
禽　蛋	Eggs	111.9	103.9	98.9	110.1	112.1	101.9	104.2	105.6
渔业产品	**Fishery Products**	**107.8**	**105.7**	**101.7**	**105.9**	**110.3**	**104.7**	**102.2**	**108.2**
养殖淡水鱼	Bred Freshwater Fish								108.6
捕捞淡水鱼	Fished Freshwater Fish								110.5

注：根据新《农业产值和价格综合统计报表制度》，原“肉禽（毛重）”指标替换为“活家禽”，原“淡水鱼”指标替换为“养殖淡水鱼”和“捕捞淡水鱼”。2011年采用新指标指数，2010年及以前采用旧指标指数。

Note: In accordance with the "Comprehensive Statistic Reporting Rules for Agriculture Output and Price", the former "poultry (gross weight)" is replaced by "poultry", while the former "freshwater fish" is replaced by "bred freshwater fish" and "fished freshwater fish". The new indices are used since 2011 while the old indices are used for the data before 2010.

表7.21 工业生产者购进价格指数（2010－2011年）
PURCHASING PRICE INDICES OF RAW MATERIALS, FUELS AND POWER (2010-2011)

上年＝100 (preceding year=100)

指　标	Item	2010	2011
工业生产者购进价格指数	**Purchasing Price Indices of Raw Material, Fuel and Power**	**106.9**	**105.7**
燃料、动力类	Fuel and Power	108.7	107.2
黑色金属材料类	Ferrous Metals	107.1	107.3
有色金属材料及电线类	Nonferrous Metals and Wires	116.4	107.0
化工原料类	Raw Chemical Materials	108.6	108.0
木材及纸浆类	Timber and Paper Pulp	107.3	104.0
建筑材料及非金属类	Building Materials and Non-metal Minerals	103.5	105.6
其他工业原材料及半成品类	Other Industrial Raw Materials and Semi-products	103.0	103.2
农副产品类	Agricultural Products	112.4	110.4
纺织原料类	Textile Materials	113.5	123.3

表7.22 工业生产者出厂价格指数（2010－2011年）
PPI BY CATEGORY (2010-2011)

上年＝100 (preceding year=100)

指　标	Item	2010	2011
工业生产者出厂价格指数	**Producer Price Index for Industrial Products**	**103.1**	**103.8**
生产资料	Means of Production	103.9	104.2
采掘工业	Minming and Quarrying Industry	112.2	110.8
原料工业	Raw Materials Industry	108.2	105.7
加工工业	Processing Industry	102.4	103.4
生活资料	Consumer Goods	100.5	102.5
食　品	Food	102.5	107.2
衣　着	Clothing	103.2	104.7
一般日用品	Articles for Daily Use	100.4	101.4
耐用消费品	Durable Consumer Goods	99.1	100.1

表7.23 按工业行业分工业生产者出厂价格指数（2010－2011年）
PPI BY SECTOR (2010-2011)

上年＝100 (preceding year=100)

行 业	Sector	2010	2011
工业生产者出厂价格指数	**Producer Price Index for Industrial Products**	**103.1**	**103.8**
煤炭开采和洗选业	Mining and Washing of Coal	118.3	115.8
石油和天然气开采业	Extraction of Petroleum and Natural Gas	101.0	100.9
黑色金属矿采选业	Mining and Processing of Ferrous Metal Ores	101.8	105.3
有色金属矿采选业	Mining and Processing of Non-Ferrous Metal Ores	104.8	101.2
非金属矿采选业	Mining and Processing of Nonmetal Ores	104.7	104.8
农副食品加工业	Processing of Food from Agricultural Products	111.5	109.4
食品制造业	Processing of Foodstuff	104.7	106.9
饮料制造业	Manufacture of Beverages	100.5	103.9
烟草制品业	Manufacture of Tobacco	102.3	102.1
纺织业	Manufacture of Textile	133.1	109.5
纺织服装、鞋、帽制造业	Manufacture of Textile Wearing Apparel, Footware, and Caps	100.1	102.0
皮革、毛皮、羽毛(绒)及其制品业	Manufacture of Leather, Fur, Feather and Related Products	118.2	106.1
木材加工及木、竹、藤、棕、草制品业	Processing of Timber, Manufacture of Wood, Bamboo, Rattan, Palm and Straw Products	102.1	106.1
家具制造业	Manufacture of Furniture	102.7	102.5
造纸及纸制品业	Manufacture of Paper and Paper Products	106.7	105.7
印刷业和记录媒介的复制	Printing, Reproduction of Recording Media	101.8	101.0
文教体育用品制造业	Manufacture of Articles for Culture, Education and Sport Activities	110.0	105.8
石油加工、炼焦及核燃料加工业	Processing of Petroleum, Coking, Processing of Nuclear Fuel	109.8	113.4
化学原料及化学制品制造业	Manufacture of Raw Chemical Materials and Chemical Products	117.0	105.7
医药制造业	Manufacture of Medicines	102.8	105.1
化学纤维制造业	Manufacture of Chemical Fibers	121.0	98.5
橡胶制品业	Manufacture of Rubber	118.5	107.4
塑料制品业	Manufacture of Plastics	101.6	105.8
非金属矿物制品业	Manufacture of Non-metallic Mineral Products	104.3	106.2
黑色金属冶炼及压延加工业	Smelting and Pressing of Ferrous Metals	107.5	105.4
有色金属冶炼及压延加工业	Smelting and Pressing of Non-ferrous Metals	108.7	104.2
金属制品业	Manufacture of Metal Products	103.9	106.1
通用设备制造业	Manufacture of General Purpose Machinery	103.5	103.0
专用设备制造业	Manufacture of Special Purpose Machinery	101.5	101.9
交通运输设备制造业	Manufacture of Transport Equipment	99.3	99.5
电气机械及器材制造业	Manufacture of Electrical Machinery and Equipment	104.7	106.2
通信设备、计算机及其他电子设备制造业	Manufacture of Communication Equipment, Computers and Other Electronic Equipment	101.0	103.5
仪器仪表及文化、办公用机械制造业	Manufacture of Measuring Instruments and Machinery for Cultural Activity and Office Work	100.3	104.1
工艺品及其他制造业	Manufacture of Artwork and Other Manufacturing	107.2	106.8
废弃资源和废旧材料回收加工业	Recycling and Disposal of Waste		99.3
电力、热力的生产和供应业	Production and Supply of Electric Power and Heat Power	102.1	101.2
燃气生产和供应业	Production and Supply of Gas	121.2	110.3
水的生产和供应业	Production and Supply of Water	113.5	107.0

表7.24 固定资产投资价格指数（1994－2011年）

PRICE INDICES OF INVESTMENT IN FIXED ASSETS (1994-2011)

上年＝100 (preceding year=100)

年 份 Year	固定资产投资 Investment in Fixed Assets	其 中 of which		
		建筑安装工程 Construction and Installation	设备工、器具 Purchase of Equipment and Instruments	其他费用 Others
1994	108.9	109.4	107.4	109.8
1995	104.2	101.2	107.8	114.0
1996	108.1	108.5	100.4	129.1
1997	101.7	103.2	97.6	103.4
1998	98.7	100.0	94.9	99.5
1999	100.5	100.7	97.7	104.4
2000	102.5	103.1	97.0	108.7
2001	100.8	101.4	96.8	103.3
2002	100.7	101.9	96.2	100.4
2003	102.9	104.7	96.7	101.3
2004	105.1	107.0	98.8	102.7
2005	102.3	102.2	99.7	104.6
2006	101.7	101.1	100.7	104.3
2007	105.5	106.0	100.2	107.8
2008	110.2	113.7	100.6	106.6
2009	97.8	97.0	97.7	100.2
2010	102.1	102.7	99.6	101.9
2011	105.9	107.8	101.1	102.5

表7.25 住宅销售价格指数（1998－2011年）
SALES PRICE INDICES OF HOUSES (1998-2011)

上年＝100 (preceding year=100)

年 份 Year	新建住宅 New Buildings	二手住宅 Second-hand House
1998	105.6	
1999	102.8	
2000	102.5	
2001	102.5	
2002	102.9	
2003	108.5	
2004	114.7	
2005	107.0	106.1
2006	103.2	101.9
2007	108.0	104.5
2008	107.2	103.8
2009	101.3	103.7
2010	110.8	107.4
2011	104.1	100.6

重/庆/统/计/年/鉴

主要统计指标解释

■ 城乡居民储蓄存款余额

指某一时点城乡居民存入银行及农村信用社的储蓄金额，包括城镇居民储蓄存款和农民个人储蓄存款，不包括居民的手存现金和工矿企业、部队、机关、团体等单位存款。

■ 城镇居民家庭就业人口

指城市（城镇）居民从事社会劳动并取得劳动报酬或经营收入的人口。就业人口包括国有经济单位职工、城镇集体经济单位职工、其他各种经济类型单位职工、城镇个体或私营企业主、个体或私营被雇者、离退休再就业人员、其他就业人口。本指标可以反映城市居民的就业情况，是计算就业面，负担系数的重要资料。

■ 城镇居民家庭总收入

指调查户中生活在一起的所有家庭成员在调查期得到的工资性收入、经营净收入、财产性收入、转移性收入之和，不包括出售财物收入和借贷收入。

■ 城市（城镇）居民家庭可支配收入

指调查户可用于最终消费支出和其他非义务性支出以及储蓄的总和，即居民家庭可以用来自由支配的收入。它是家庭总收入扣除交纳的个人所得税、个人交纳的社会保障支出以及调查户的记账补贴后的收入。计算公式为：

可支配收入=家庭总收入-交纳个人所得税-个人交纳的社会保障支出-记账补贴

■ 城镇居民家庭总支出

指家庭除借贷支出以外的全部实际支出。包括消费性支出、财产性支出、转移性支出、社会保障支出、购房与建房支出。

■ 城镇居民家庭消费性支出

指调查户用于本家庭日常生活的支出，包括食品、衣着、居住、家庭设备用品及服务、医疗保健、交通和通信、教育文化娱乐服务、其他商品和服务八大类等。

■ 城镇居民家庭人均服务性消费支出

指调查户用于本家庭支付社会提供的各种文化和生活方面的非商品性服务费用。包括为别人付款的服务。服务消费与商品消费不同，其特点在于其劳动过程和消费过程在时间与空间上的统一。这一指标是派生的，根据其他粮食及制品、食品加工服务费用、在外饮食、衣着加工服务费、家庭服务、医疗费、交通工具服务支出、交通费、通信服务、教育文化娱乐服务费、教育费用、房租、住房装潢支出、居住服务费和其他服务费中的服务性消费支出的比重生成。

■ 城镇居民家庭收入分组方法

将所有调查户依户人均可支配收入由低到高排队，按10%，10%，20%，20%，20%，10%，10%的比例依次分成：最低收入户、低收入户、中等偏下收入户、中等收入户、中等偏上收入户、高收入户、最高收入户等七组。总体中最低5%的户为困难户。

■ 恩格尔系数

指食物支出金额在消费性总支出金额中所占的比例。计算公式为：

恩格尔系数 = 食物支出总额 / 消费性总支出总额×100%

■ 农村居民家庭整半劳动力

整劳动力指男子18周岁到50周岁，女子18周岁到45周岁；半劳动力指男子16周岁到17周岁，51周岁到60周岁；女子16周岁到17周岁，46周岁到55周岁，同时具有劳动能力的人。虽然在劳动年龄之内，但已丧失劳动能力的人，不应算为劳动力；超过劳动年龄，但能经常参加劳动，计入半劳动力数内。常住人口中的职工，若这些职工为劳动力，就包括在本户的整半劳动力中。

主要统计指标解释

农村居民家庭总收入

指调查期内农村住户和住户成员从各种来源渠道得到的收入总和。按收入的性质划分为工资性收入、家庭经营收入、财产性收入和转移性收入。

农村居民家庭现金收入

指农村住户和住户成员在调查期内得到以现金形态表现的收入。按来源分成工资性收入、家庭经营现金收入、财产性收入、转移性收入。

农村居民家庭纯收入

指农村住户当年从各个来源得到的总收入相应地扣除所发生的费用后的收入总和。计算方法：

纯收入= 总收入-家庭经营费用支出-税费支出-生产性固定资产折旧-调查补贴-赠送农村内部亲友支出

纯收入主要用于再生产投入和当年生活消费支出，也可用于储蓄和各种非义务性支出。“农民人均纯收入”按人口平均的纯收入水平，反映的是一个地区或一个农户农村居民的平均收入水平。

农村居民家庭总支出

指农村住户用于生产、生活和再分配的全部支出。家庭经营费用支出、购置生产性固定资产支出、生产性固定资产折旧、税费支出、生活消费支出、财产性支出和转移性支出。

农村居民家庭生活消费支出

指农村住户用于物质生活和精神生活方面的支出。生活消费支出包括食品、衣着、居住、家庭设备用品及服务、医疗保健、交通和通讯、文化教育娱乐用品及服务、其他商品和服务等消费。

农村居民家庭现金支出

指农村住户用于生产、生活和再分配所支付的现金。包括家庭经营费用支出、缴纳的税费、购买生产性固定资产、生活消费、财产性和转移性支出。

居民消费价格指数

居民消费价格指数是度量一组代表性消费商品及服务项目价格水平随着时间而变动的相对数，反映居民家庭购买的消费品及服务价格水平的变动情况。它是宏观经济分析和决策、价格总水平监测和调控以及国民经济核算的重要指标。其按年度计算的变动率通常被用来作为反映通货膨胀（或紧缩）程度的指标。

商品零售价格指数

商品的零售价格是商品在流通过程中最后一个环节的价格，是工业、商业、餐饮业和其他零售企业向城乡居民、机关团体出售生活消费品和办公用品的价格。通过系统地调查、搜集和整理市场商品零售价格资料，编制商品零售价格指数，以此反映市场商品零售价格的变动趋势和变动程度。其目的在于掌握商品价格的变动趋势，为国家宏观调控和国民经济核算提供参考依据。

农产品生产价格指数

是反映一定时期内，农产品生产者出售农产品价格水平变动趋势及幅度的相对数。该指数可以客观反映全国农产品生产价格水平和结构变动情况，满足农业与国民经济核算需求。其中某代表品生产价格指数是通过对全部有出售该产品行为的调查单位的个体指数进行几何平均求得的，类价格指数是通过对其所属的类（或代表品）的价格指数进行加权平均求得的。季度累计价格指数的计算方法与分季指数的计算方法相同。

工业生产者价格指数

即原来的工业品价格指数。它是反映工业产品价格变化趋势和变动幅度的统计指标，是工业企业的产品价格在不同时间和空间条件下平均变动的相对数。工业生产者价格包括工业品第一次出售时的出厂价格和企业作为中间投入的原材料、燃料、动力购进价格，简称为工业生产者出厂价格和工业生产者购进价格。工业生产者价格指数是进行国民经济核算和经济管理的重要依据。

固定资产投资价格指数

是反映全社会及各类工程固定资产投资中涉及的各类投资品和取费项目价格的变动趋势和变动幅度的相对数。编制固定资产投资价格指数可以消除按现价计算的固定资产投资指标中的价格变动因素。

住宅销售价格指数

是综合反映住宅商品价格水平总体变化趋势和变化幅度的相对数。中国住宅销售价格指数由70个大中城市的新建住宅销售价格指数和二手住宅销售价格指数组成。

Explanatory Notes on Main Statistical Indicators

□ Saving Deposits of Urban and Rural Residents

Refer to the total value of savings deposits of urban and rural households in banks and rural credit cooperatives at a given point of time, including the saving deposits of urban residents and the saving deposits of rural residents. The cash in hand by residents and the deposits of organizations such as enterprises, military units, government agencies, institutions, etc. are not included.

□ Employed Population in Urban (Town) Households

Refers to urban (town) residents engaged in certain work and receiving payment for their labor or income from their business operation, including those who work in state-owned or collective units and other various economic units; the owners and employees of urban private enterprises, reemployed retirees and other employed persons. This index indicates the employment condition of the urban residents, which is the key indicator for calculating employment rate and dependency ratio.

□ Total Income of Urban (Town) Households

Refers to the sum of wage and salary, net business income, income from properties, and income from transfers of members of the households under survey who live together during the period of survey, excluding income from selling of properties and income from borrowings.

□ Disposable Income of Urban (Town) Households

Refers to the actual income at the disposal of members of the surveyed households which can be used for final consumption, other non-compulsory expenditure and savings. This equals to total income minus income tax, personal contribution to social security and sample household subsidy for keeping dairies. Following formula is used:

Disposable income = total household income - individual income tax - personal contribution to social security – sample household subsidy for keeping dairies

□ Total expenditure of Urban (Town) Households

Refers to total actual expenditure of households apart from the loan expenditure, including consuming expenditure, property expenditure, transferred expenditure, social security expenditure and housing expenditure.

□ Consumption Expenditure of Urban (Town) Households

Refers to total expenditure of the sample households for consumption in daily life, including expenditure on eight categories such as food, clothing, household appliances and services, health care and medical services, transport and communications, recreation, education and cultural services, housing, miscellaneous goods and services.

□ Expenditure of Urban (Town) Households on Consumption of Services

Refers to expenditure of households on non-commodity services of various kinds provided by the society, including the payment service for other people. Service consumption is different from commodity consumption. Services are offered and consumed at the same time and place. This is a derivative indicator, which is derived from the percentage of the service consumption expenditure in other expenditures such as grain and products, food processing service, dining out, clothing processing service, household service, medical service, transporting vehicle service, transit, telecommunication service, education, cultural and entertainment service, tuition fees, housing rent, interior decoration, residential service and other services.

□ Urban (Town) Households by Income Group

All households in the sample are grouped, by per capita disposable income of the household, into groups of lowest income, low income, lower middle income, middle income, upper middle income, high income and highest income, each group consisting of 10%, 10%, 20%, 20%, 20%, 10% and 10% of all households respectively. The lowest 5% of households are also referred to as poor households.

EXPLANATORY NOTES TO MAJOR STATISTICAL INDICATORS

Engel Coefficient

Refers to the percentage of expenditure on food in the total consumption expenditure, using the following formula:

Engel Coefficient = (expenditure on food / total consumption expenditure) x 100%

Full/Semi Labor Force

Full labor force refers to persons capable of work, aged 18-50 for males and 18-45 for females. Semi labor force refers to persons capable of work, aged 16-17 and 51-60 for males and 16-17 and 46-55 for females. Persons at their working ages but not capable of work are not to be included as labor force. Persons not at working ages but participating regularly in work are included in semi labor force. For staff and workers as resident population of the household, they are included as full or semi labor force of the household if they are in the labor force.

Total Income of Rural Households

Refers to the sum of income earned from various sources by the rural households and their members during the reference period, and is classified as income from wages and salaries, income from household operations, income from properties and income from transfers.

Cash Income of Rural Households

Refers to income received by rural households and their members in the form of cash during the reference period. It is classified, by source of income, into income from wages and salaries, cash income from household operations, income from properties and income from transfers.

Net Income of Rural Households

Refers to the total income of rural households from all sources minus all corresponding expenses. The formula for calculation is as follows:

Net income = total income –household operation expenses – taxes and fees paid – depreciation of fixed assets for production – subsidy for participating in household survey – gifts to rural relatives

Net income is mainly used as input for reproduction and as consumption expenditure of the year, and also used for savings and non-compulsory expenses of various forms. "Per capita net income of farmers" is the level of net income averaged by population which reflects the average income level of rural households in a given area.

Total Expenditure of Rural Households

Refers to total expenses of rural households on production, consumption and redistribution, including expenditure on household operations, on purchase of productive fixed assets, depreciation of productive fixed assets, taxes and fees, expenses on household consumption, expenses on properties and expenses on transfers.

Expenditure on Household Consumption of Rural Households

Refers to expenditure by rural households on their material and cultural life, including expenditure on food; clothing; housing; household appliances, articles and services; health and medical service; transportation and communications; articles and services on culture, education and recreation; and other goods and services.

Cash Expenditure of Rural Households

Refers to cash expenditure by rural households for production, consumption and redistribution during the reference period, including cash expenses on household operations, taxes and fees, purchase of productive fixed assets, household consumption, and expenses on properties and transfers.

Consumer Price Index

Reflects the relative change in prices of consumer goods and services in a certain period of time, Formation of consumer price index aims to study the impact of consumer price changes on the actual living cost of urban and rural residents and to provide scientific basis for central government and relevant departments in drawing up consumer up consumer policy, price policy, wage policy and monetary policy and in accounting the nation economy. It is also a key index reflecting the fluctuation of inflation.

Retail Price Index

Refers to the prices at which industrial, commercial, catering and other retail enterprises sell daily consumer goods and products for office use to urban and rural residents and institutions and social organizations. It reflects the general change in prices of retail commodities in a certain period of time. Formation of retail price index aims to keep abreast of price fluctuation of retail commodities and provide the reference basis for the central government in working out economic policies.

EXPLANATORY NOTES TO MAJOR STATISTICAL INDICATORS

□ Producer Price Indices for Farm Products

Reflect the trend and degree of changes in producers' prices received by farmers when they sell farm products during a given period. These indices depict the change in the level and struture of producer prices for farm products of the country and meet the needs of agricultural statistics and national accounts statistics. The producer price index for a given product is calculated as the geometrical mean of individual indices for all surveyed units which sell such product, and the indices for a product category is obtained as the weighted mean of price indices for all products in the category. Method for calculating accumulative quarterly indices is the same as for calculating the individual quarterly indices.

□ Producer Price Index

Formerly Industrial Product Price Index, is a statistic indicator reflecting the fluctuating tendency and extent of the price of manufactured goods. It is a relative ratio of the average price fluctuation of manufactured goods in different times and places. The price of manufactured goods includes the factory price of the manufactured goods at the first sale and the price of the raw materials, fuel and power purchased by the enterprises as intermediate input, which is an important basis for national economic accounting and economic administration.

□ Price Indices of Investment in Fixed Assets

Is a relative ratio reflecting the trend and degree of changes in prices of investment goods and charging projects in fixed assets of various engineering projects during a given period. This indicator is used to remove the factor of price change in the aggregates of investment at current prices.

□ Price Index of Residential Real Estate Sales is a relative ratio reflecting

The general trend and variation degrees of the sales price of the residential real estate. This index of China is composed of the sales price of residential real estate and the sales price of second-hand residential real estate in 70 medium-large cities.

第 8 章

城镇建设

URBAN CONSTRUCTION

简要说明
BRIEF INTRODUCTION

本章资料反映全市城镇建设的基本情况。

城镇建设资料主要包括城镇建设用地、基础设施水平、市政设施、园林绿化、供水供气、公共交通、基础设施建设投资、房屋等，由市统计局固定资产投资处根据市建设委员会、市国土资源和房屋管理局资料整理提供。

The data in this chapter show the basic conditions of urban construction in Chongqing.

The statistics on urban construction mainly include the data of land for urban construction, urban infrastructure, municipal infrastructure, parks and green areas, tap water and gas supply, public traffic, investment in infrastructure construction and buildings and housing. The data concerned are provided by Chongqing Construction Commission and Chongqing Administration of Land, Resources and Housing, and sorted and compiled by Division of Statistics of Investment in Fixed Assets, Chongqing Municipal Bureau of Statistics.

表8.1 城镇建设用地（2010－2011年）
LAND FOR URBAN CONSTRUCTION (2010-2011)

单位：平方公里(sq.km)

项 目	Item	全 市 Total		其 中 of which #区合计 Total of Districts	
		2010	2011	2010	2011
建成区面积	**Built-up Area**	**1136.53**	**1325.44**	**870.23**	**1034.92**
建设用地面积	**Land for Urban Construction**	**1091.67**	**1209.78**	**855.67**	**945.48**
居住用地	Land for Residence	362.87	392.45	282.15	302.37
公共设施用地	Land for Public Utilities	117.78	127.31	88.63	98.48
工业用地	Land for Industry	240.03	266.32	200.94	221.01
仓储用地	Land for Storage	21.91	22.58	16.87	17.69
对外交通用地	Land for External Transport	38.75	50.84	27.43	39.60
道路广场用地	Land for Roads and Squares	161.68	177.55	131.55	141.94
市政公用设施用地	Land for Municipal Utilities	34.64	36.65	23.85	27.80
绿 地	Green Land	97.41	118.13	71.50	82.39
特殊用地	Land for Special Purpose	16.60	17.95	12.75	14.20

注："区合计"数为19个市辖区合计（下表同）。
Note: "Total of Districts" refers to the total data of 19 municipale districts (the same below).

表8.2 城镇基础设施水平（2010－2011年）
STATISTICS ON URBAN INFRASTRUCTURE (2010-2011)

项 目	Item	全 市 Total		其 中 of which #区合计 Total of Districts	
		2010	2011	2010	2011
人均日生活用水量（升）	Per Capita Daily Consumption of Domestic Water (liter)	130.15	135.47	136.75	145.43
用水普及率（%）	Percentage of Population with Access to Tap Water (%)	91.47	91.68	94.05	93.41
燃气普及率（%）	Percentage of Population with Access to Gas (%)	90.03	91.26	92.02	93.03
人均道路面积（平方米）	Per Capita Area of Paved Roads (sq.m)	9.09	9.97	9.37	10.43
污水处理厂集中处理率（%）	Rate of Intensive Treatment by Wastewater Treatment Plant (%)	88.86	92.21	90.79	93.15
人均公共绿地面积（平方米）	Per Capita Area of Public Green Land (sq.m)	12.72	17.01	13.24	17.87
建成区绿地率（%）	Green Land as Percentage of Built-up Area (%)	36.19	37.25	37.59	37.44
建成区绿化覆盖率（%）	Green Covered Area as Percentage of Built-up Area (%)	39.48	40.28	40.57	40.18

注：人均数为户籍人口口径。
Note: The data of average population refer to registration statistics.

表8.3 城镇市政设施（2010－2011年）
MUNICIPAL INFRASTRUCTURE (2010-2011)

项　目	Item	全　市 Total		其　中 of which #区合计 Total of Districts	
		2010	2011	2010	2011
道路长度（公里）	Length of Paved Roads (km)	6733	7158	5130	5435
道路面积（万平方米）	Area of Paved Roads (10 000 sq.m)	12694	13934	9931	10870
#人行道	Sidewalk	3834	4117	2956	3164
桥梁数（座）	Number of Bridges (unit)	1444	1522	1136	1211
#立交桥	Overpass	173	228	164	180
路灯盏数（盏）	Number of Street Lights (unit)	350593	389850	243524	267599
排水管道长度（公里）	Length of Drainpipes (km)	9663	11212	7073	8163
#污水管道	Sewage Pipe	4384	5401	3089	3878
污水年排放量（万立方米）	Annual Discharged Volume of Wastewater (10 000 cu.m)	78498	83733	64622	69142
污水处理厂处理总量（万立方米）	Total Volume of Wastewater Treated by Wastewater Treatment Plant (10 000 cu.m)	69753	77208	58673	64405
防洪堤长度（公里）	Length of Flood Protecting Embankment (km)	384	387	243	222

表8.4 城镇园林绿化（2010－2011年）
PARKS AND GREEN AREAS IN URBAN AREA (2010-2011)

指　标	Item	全　市 Total		其　中 of which #区合计 Total of Districts	
		2010	2011	2010	2011
绿化覆盖面积（公顷）	Green Covered Area (hectare)	51895	60895	41244	47637
#建成区	Built-up Area	44865	53385	35304	41580
园林绿地面积（公顷）	Area of Parks and Green Area (hectare)	47200	55929	37695	43883
#建成区	Built-up Area	41134	49374	32715	38752
公共绿地面积（公顷）	Area of Public Green Area (hectare)	17762	23755	14032	18626
动物园、公园个数（个）	Number of Parks and Zoos (unit)	273	386	175	248
动物园、公园面积（公顷）	Area of Parks and Zoos (hectare)	6767	11210	5532	8895

表8.5 城镇供水及供气情况（2010－2011年）
STATISTICS ON TAP WATER AND GAS SUPPLY IN URBAN AREA (2010-2011)

指 标	Item	全 市 Total		其 中 of which #区合计 Total of Districts	
		2010	2011	2010	2011
城镇供水	**Tap Water Supply in Urban Area**				
年末供水综合生产能力（万立方米/日）	Production Capacity of Tap Water Supply at Year-end (10 000 cu.m/day)	507.09	531.54	412.30	429.27
年末供水管道长度（公里）	Length of Water Supply Pipelines at Year-end (km)	12574	12388	9190	8914
供水总量（万立方米）	Total Volume of Water Supply (10 000 cu.m)	103949	107571	86926	89756
#生产运营用水	For Production Use	25849	25037	22603	22150
公共服务用水	For Public Services	10364	10956	8840	9185
居民家庭用水	For Residential Use	50177	52138	40835	42329
消防及其他用水	For Fire Fighting and Other Purposes	3543	4410	2808	3748
用水户数（户）	Households with Access to Tap Water (household)	3002601	3179561	2263592	2342039
#家庭用户	Residential Households	2736494	2865638	2069411	2111450
用水人口（万人）	Number of Residents with Access to Tap Water (10 000 persons)	1276.97	1280.67	996.55	973.78
城镇供气	**Gas Supply in Urban Area**				
天然气供气总量（万立方米）	Total Volume of Natural Gas Supply (10 000 cu.m)	309480	314354	254021	268790
#家庭用量	For Residential Use	114173	106279	81412	84894
天然气用气户数（户）	Households with Access to Natural Gas (household)	3938380	4031718	3282711	3328185
#家庭用户	Residential Households	3583151	3830244	2951653	3153308
天然气用气人口（万人）	Population with Access to Natural Gas (10 000 persons)	1062.53	1089.98	861	862
天然气汽车加气站（个）	Number of CNG Stations for Motor Vehicles (unit)	63	75	47	59
液化石油气供气总量（吨）	Total Volume of Liquefied Petroleum Gas Supply (ton)	124774	123848	92807	92861
#家庭用量	For Residentia Use	59031	51884	35393	29849
液化石油气用气户数（户）	Households with Access to Liquefied Petroleum Gas (household)	562435	504306	311435	266811
#家庭用户	Residential Households	446120	386092	243572	201352
液化石油气用气人口（万人）	Population with Access to Liquefied Petroleum Gas (10 000 persons)	194.29	184.78	114.41	107.50

表8.6 城镇公共交通情况（2011年）
PUBLIC TRAFFIC IN URBAN AREA (2011)

指标	Item	全市 Total	其中 of which #区合计 Total of Districts
营运客车	**Public Vehicles**		
年末营运线路网长度（公里）	Year-end Length of Public Transport Network (km)	8880	8880
运营车数（辆）	Number of Public Vehicles (unit)	7822	7822
#天然气燃料车	CNG Vehicles	7629	7629
客运量（万人次）	Passenger Volume (10 000 person-times)	174930	174930
轻　轨	**Light Rail Transits**		
通车里程（公里）	Length of Light Rail Transits in Operation	70	70
车辆数（辆）	Number of Vehicles (unit)	296	296
客运量（万人次）	Passengers Traffic (10 000 person-times)	8332	8332
轮　渡	**Ferries**		
年末实有轮渡总数（艘）	Year-end Total Ferries (unit)	44	16
出租汽车	**Taxis**		
车辆数（辆）	Number of Vehicles (unit)	11457	3547

表8.7 公用事业和市政建设投资额（2010－2011年）
INVESTMENT IN PUBLIC UTILITIES AND MUNICIPAL CONSTRUCTION (2010-2011)

单位：万元 (10 000 yuan)

指标	Item	2010	2011
公用事业	**Public Utilities**		
供　水	Tap Water Supply	118017	111448
燃　气	Gas Supply	104911	81191
轨道交通	Rail Transit	1169406	1671356
市政建设	**Municipal Construction**		
园林绿化	Parks and Green Areas	1320129	1803091
环境卫生	Environmental Sanitation	32194	39358

表8.8 城镇房屋及居住情况（2010－2011年）
STATISTICS ON BUILDINGS AND HOUSING IN URBAN AREA (2010-2011)

指　标	Item	全　市 Total		其　中 of which #区合计 Total of Districts	
		2010	2011	2010	2011
房屋状况（万平方米）	**Conditions of Buildings (10 000 sq.m)**				
年末实有房屋建筑面积	Total Floor Space of Buildings at Year-end	56062.98	61769.11	42178.03	48306.37
#住　宅	Residential Buildings	36872.50	41681.51	27111.76	32180.96
#自有（私有）住宅	Self-owned (private)	32510.96	36481.12	23686.63	28022.84
年末实有住宅套数（套）	Total Number of Residential Units at Year-end (set)	3683385	4394092	2773542	3561685
年末成套住宅建筑面积	Total Floor Space of Residential Buildings at Year-end	32938.30	38902.51	24689.26	30618.26
年末危险房屋建筑面积	Total Floor Space of Dilapidated Buildings at Year-end				
#住　宅	Residential Buildings				
居住状况	**Conditions of Housing**				
居住户数（万户）	Households of Housing (10 000 households)	372.52	462.43	256.94	314.96
人均住宅建筑面积（平方米/人）	Per Capita Floor Space of Residential Buildings (sq.m/person)	34.77	32.62	36.66	36.98
户均住宅套数（套/户）	Average Number of Apartments Per Household (set/household)	0.99	0.95	1.08	1.13

注：2011年10月，经国务院同意，重庆撤销万盛区、綦江县，设立綦江区；撤销双桥区、大足县，设立大足区，故2011年区合计中包含原綦江县，大足县的数据。表中人均住宅建筑面积计算的人口数据，来源于户籍人口统计数。

Note: In Oct. 2011, approved by the State Council, the former Wansheng District and Qijiang County were combined as Qijiang District; and the former Shuangqiao District and Dazu County were combined as Dazu District. Therefore, the data of districts in 2011 include the data of former Qijiang County and Dazu County. The data of population related to the per capita residential floor space in the table is the population of household registration.

重/庆/统/计/年/鉴

主要统计指标解释

■ 供水综合生产能力

指按供水设施取水、净化、送水、出厂输水干管等环节设计能力计算的综合生产能力。包括在原设计能力基础上，经挖、革、改增加的生产能力。计算时，以四个环节中最薄弱的环节为主确定能力。

■ 供水管道长度

指从送水泵到用户水表之间所有管道的长度。不包括新安装尚未使用的管道。

■ 供水总量

指报告期供水企业（单位）供出的全部水量。包括有效供水量和漏损水量。

■ 生活用水量

包括公共服务用水和居民家庭用水。公共服务用水指为城市社会公共生活服务的用水。包括行政事业单位、部队营区和公共设施服务、社会服务业、批发零售贸易业、旅馆饮食业及其他公共服务业等单位用水。居民家庭用水指城市范围内所有居民家庭的日常生活用水。包括城市居民、农民家庭、公共供水站用水。

■ 城市人口用水普及率

指城市用水人口数与城市人口总数之比。计算公式为：

用水普及率=（城市用水人口数/城市人口数）×100%

■ 全年供气总量

指全年燃气企业（单位）向用户供应的燃气数量，包括销售量和损失量。

■ 城市用气普及率

指报告期末使用燃气的城市人口数与城市人口总数的比率。计算公式为：

用气普及率=城市用气人口数/城市人口总数×100%

■ 道路长度

指年末道路长度和与道路相通的广场、桥梁、隧道的长度，按车行道中心线计算。在统计时只统计路面宽度在3.5米（含3.5米）以上的各种铺装道路，包括开放型工业区和住宅区道路在内。

■ 道路面积

为车行道与人行道面积之和。

■ 城市桥梁

指为跨越天然或人工障碍物而修建的构筑物。包括跨河桥、立交桥、人行天桥以及人行地下通道等。包括永久性桥和半永久性桥。

■ 城市排水管道长度

指所有排水总管、干管、支管、检查井及连接井进出口等长度之和。

■ 年末运营车数

指年末公交企业（单位）用于运营业务的全部车辆数。以企业（单位）固定资产台帐中已投入运营的车辆数为准。

■ 城市园林绿地面积

指报告期末用作园林和绿化的各种绿地面积。包括公共绿地、居住区绿地、单位附属绿地、防护绿地、生产绿地、道路绿地和风景林地面积。不包括：

（1）屋顶绿化、垂直绿化、阳台绿化和室内绿化。

（2）以物质生产为主的林地、耕地、牧草地、果园和竹园等。

（3）城市总体规划中不列入绿地的水域。

■ 公共绿地

指向公众开放的市级、区级、居住区级各类公园、街旁游园，包括其范围内的水域。其中居住区级公园应不小于1万平方米，街旁游园的宽度不小于8米，面积不小于400平方米。

Explanatory Notes on Main Statistical Indicators

□ Production Capacity of Water Supply

Refers to the designed comprehensive production capacity of water facilities, covering the 4 links of water collection, purification, conveyance, and outflow through trunk pipelines. Increase capacity through transformation and innovation projects is included as well. The capacity is determined mainly on the weakest of the above-mentioned 4 links.

□ Length of Water Supply Pipelines at the Year-end

Refers to the total length of all the pipelines between the water pumps and the user's water meters, excluding pipelines newly installed but not used yet.

□ Annual Volume of Water Supply

Refers to the total volume of water supplied by water-works (units) during the reference period, including both the effective water supply and loss during the water supply.

□ Consumption of Water for Residential Use

Refers to the water consumption of households for daily life and the water consumption of public service facilities. The latter refers to water consumption for urban public services, including the consumption of government agencies and public institutions, military barracks, public facilities, wholesale and retail outlets, restaurants, hotels, and other units providing public services. Household water consumption refers to consumption of water for daily life of all households in the boundary of cities, including households of urban residents and farmers, and public water supply stations.

□ Percentage of Urban Population with Access to Tap Water

Refers to the ratio of the urban population with access to tap water to the total urban population. The formula is:

Percentage of Population with access to Tap Water = Urban Population with Access to Tap Water / Urban Population ×100%

□ Volume of Gas Supply

Refers to the total volume of gas provided to users by gas-producing enterprises (units) in a year, including the volume sold and the volume lost.

□ Percentage of Urban Population with Access to Gas

Refers to the ratio of the urban population with access to gas to the total urban population at the end of the reference period. The formula is:

Percentage of population with access to gas = (Urban population with access to gas / Urban population) ×100%

□ Length of Roads

Refers to the length of roads with paved surface including squares bridges and tunnels connected with roads by the end of the year. Length of the roads is measured by the central lines for vehicles for paved roads with a width of 3.5 meters and over, including roads in open-ended factory compounds and residential quarters.

□ Area of Roads

Is the summed of carriageway and sidewalk.

□ Urban Bridges

Refer to bridges built to cross over natural or man-made barriers, including bridges over rivers, overpasses for traffic and for pedestrian, underpasses for pedestrian, etc. Both permanent and semi-permanent bridges are included.

□ Length of Urban Sewage Pipes

Refers to the total length of general drainage, trunks, branch and inspection wells, connection wells, inlets and outlets, etc.

□ Number of Vehicles under Operation at the Year-end

Refers to the total number of vehicles under operation by public transport enterprises (units) at year-end, based on the records of operational vehicles by the enterprises (units).

EXPLANATORY NOTES TO MAJOR STATISTICAL INDICATORS

□ Area of Urban Gardens and Green Areas

Refers to the total area occupied for green projects at the end of the reference period, including public green land, green land in residential quarters, green land attached to institutions, protection green land, production green land, roadside green land and forest in scenic spots. It does not include the following:

(I) Greenery and plants on roofs, balconies, indoors and vertical green areas;

(II) Forest, cultivated land, grassland, orchards and bamboo grooves that are for production purpose;

(III) Water areas that are not included in urban master plan as green land.

□ Public Green Area

Refers to green areas open to the public such as municipal, community and neighborhood parks and roadside parks, including waters within parks. Neighborhood parks should occupy an area larger than 10,000 square meters, and the width of roadside parks should occupy an area larger than 400 square meters, with a width of more that 8 meters.

第9章

资源和环境

RESOURCES AND ENVIRONMENT

简要说明
BRIEF INTRODUCTION

资源主要内容包括自然资源、自然地理、气象状况。自然资源中土地、矿产资源数据由市国土资源和房屋管理局提供，林木资源数据由市林业局提供，水资源数据由市水利局提供。气象状况由市气象局提供。

自然地理、气象综合资料，由市统计局综合处根据有关部门资料进行整理和编辑。环境主要内容包括工业废水、废气、固体废物的排放处理和利用，工业污染治理投资，生活污染物排放等，由市统计局社会科技处根据市环境保护局、市水利局、市林业局等部门的资料整理提供。

The scope of resources mainly covers natural resources, natural geography and climate. The data of land and mineral resources in natural resources are provided by Chongqing Municipal Bureau of Land & Resources and House Administration; the data of forest resources are provided by Chongqing Forestry Administration; the data of water resources are provided by Chongqing Water Resources Bureau; and the data of climate are provided by Chongqing Meteorological Bureau.

The data of natural environment and climate are provided by the departments concerned and sorted and compiled by Division of Comprehensive Statistics of Municipal Bureau of Statistics. The statistics of environment mainly includes the discharge, treatment and utilization of industrial waste water, waste gas and solid wastes, the investment in industrial pollution treatment and the discharge of domestic pollutants, which are provided by Chongqing Environmental Protection Bureau, Chongqing Water Resources Bureau and Chongqing Forestry Administration, and sorted and compiled by Division of Social and Technology Statistics, Municipal Bureau of Statistics.

表9.1 自然资源（2010－2011年）
NATURAL RESOURCES (2010-2011)

项　目	Item	2010	2011
林木资源	**Forest Resources**		
活立木总蓄积量（万立方米）	Total Standing Forest Stock (10 000 cu.m)	13019	13574
森林面积（万公顷）	Forest Area (10 000 hectares)	304.9	321.4
森林蓄积量（万立方米）	Stock Volume of Forest (10 000 cu.m)	12121	12638
森林覆盖率（%）	Forest Coverage Rate (%)	37.0	39.0
水资源（当年量）	**Water Resources (current quantity)**		
降水深（毫米）	Precipitation (mm)	1058.30	1091.8
地表径流量（亿立方米）	Surface Runoff (100 million cu.m)	464.30	514.58
地下水量（亿立方米）	Groundwater Resources (100 million cu.m)	96.26	98.31
水力资源蕴藏量（万千瓦）	Hydropower Resources (10 000 kw)	2296.43	2296.43
#技术可开发量	Technical Developable Resources	980.84	980.84
主要矿产资源（保有基础储量）	**Major Mineral Resources (retained Basic Reserves)**		
天然气（亿立方米）	Natural Gas (100 million cu.m)	1921.02	
煤（万吨）	Coal (10 000 tons)	224932.54	202865.02
铁（矿石万吨）	Iron Ore (ore, 10 000 tons)	112.00	29625.69
锰（矿石万吨）	Manganese Ore (ore, 10 000 tons)	2252.62	2754.81
锌（金属万吨）	Zinc Ore (metal, 10 000 tons)	14.80	12.56
铝　土（矿石万吨）	Aluminum Ore (ore, 10 000 tons)	3639.00	4103.06
汞（吨）	Mercury (ton)	1917.00	12397.00
锶（天青石万吨）	Strontium Ore (ore, 10 000 tons)	31.15	155.54
熔剂用灰岩（矿石万吨）	Limestone for Flux (ore, 10 000 tons)	10287.10	1221.00
冶金用白云岩（矿石万吨）	Dolomite for Metallurgy (ore, 10 000 tons)	4546.10	3751.10
冶金用石英砂岩（矿石万吨）	Quartzite for Metallurgy (ore, 10 000 tons)		193.80
陶瓷用砂岩（矿石万吨）	Sandstone for Ceramics (ore, 10 000 tons)	495.20	1091.00
耐火粘土（矿石万吨）	Refractory Clay (ore, 10 000 tons)	169.00	12135.29
重晶石（矿石万吨）	Barytes (ore, 10 000 tons)	185.00	432.61
毒重石（矿石万吨）	Witherite (ore, 10 000 tons)	487.30	1533.96
盐　矿（矿石万吨）	Salt Mine (ore, 10 000 tons)	100296.20	465259.30

注：1）林木资源数据为2002年森林资源二类调查补充数，该调查一般五年一次。
2）天然气数据为剩余技术可采储量。
Note: a) The data of forest resources were surveried and readjusted according to Class II survey in 2002, which is carried out every 5 years ordinarily.
b) The data of natural gas are technical recoverable reserves.

9.2 自然地理（2011年）
NATURAL ENVIRONMENT (2011)

位置：重庆位于北纬28度10分-32度13分，东经105度11分-110度11分之间，地处较为发达的东部地区和资源丰富的西部地区的结合部，东邻湖北、湖南，南靠贵州，西接四川，北连陕西，是长江上游最大的经济中心、西南工商业重镇和水陆交通枢纽。1997年3月14日，第八届全国人民代表大会第五次会议通过了设立重庆直辖市的决议，与北京、天津、上海同为四大直辖市。

面积：重庆幅员面积8.24万平方公里，南北长450公里，东西宽470公里。2011年全市共辖19个区：万州区、涪陵区、渝中区、大渡口区、江北区、沙坪坝区、九龙坡区、南岸区、北碚区、渝北区、巴南区、黔江区、长寿区、江津区、合川区、永川区、南川区、綦江区、大足区；19个县（自治县）：潼南县、铜梁县、荣昌县、璧山县、开县、忠县、梁平县、云阳县、奉节县、巫山县、巫溪县、城口县、垫江县、武隆县、丰都县、石柱县土家族自治县、彭水苗族土家族县、酉阳土家族苗族县、秀山土家族苗族县。

地势：重庆地势由南北向长江河谷逐级降低，西北部和中部以丘陵、低山为主，东南部靠大巴山和武陵山两座大山脉。

河流：主要河流有长江、嘉陵江、乌江、涪江、綦江、大宁河等。

气候：重庆属中亚热带湿润季风气候区，具有夏热冬暖，光热同季，无霜期长，雨量充沛，湿润多阴等特点。2011年平均气温17.7 ℃，年总降雨量992.8毫米。

Location:

Chongqing is located at 28° 10' ～ 32° 13' north latitude and 105° 11' ～ 110° 11' east longitude. As a joint between the eastern areas with developed economy and the western areas with rich resources, with Hubei and Hunan on its east, Guizhou on its south, Sichuan on its west and Shaanxi on its north, Chongqing is the largest economic center in the upper reaches of the Yangtze River, an important industrial and commercial city in the southwest and a hub of land and water communications. On March 14, 1997, the resolution to establish Chongqing Municipality was passed on the 5th Session of the 8th National People's Congress, and Chongqing became the fourth municipality directly under the Central Government after Beijing, Tianjin and Shanghai.

Area:

Chongqing covers an area of 82,400 square kilometers, stretching 450 kilometers from north to south and 470 kilometers from east to west. In 2011, Chongqing has 19 districts, namely Wanzhou, Fuling, Yuzhong, Dadukou, Jiangbei, Shapingba, Jiulongpo, Nan'an, Beibei, Yubei, Banan, Qianjiang, Changshou, Jiangjin, Hechuan, Yongchuan and Nanchuan, Qijiang , Dazu and 19 counties, namely Tongnan, Tongliang, Rongchang, Bishan, Kaixian, Zhongxian, Liangping, Yunyang, Fengjie, Wushan, Wuxi, Chengkou, Dianjiang, Wulong, Fengdu, Shizhu Tujia Autonomous County, Pengshui Miao Autonomous County, Youyang Tujia Autonomous County and Xiushan Tujia Autonomous County.

Topography:

The altitude of Chongqing declines gradually from the north and the south to the valley of the Yangtze River. There are mainly hills and low mountains in the northwest and central areas of Chongqing, while the two large mountains of Daba and Wuling are in the southeast of Chongqing.

River:

The rivers stretching through Chongqing mainly include Yangtze River, Jialing River, Wujiang River, Fujiang River, Qijiang River and Daning River.

Climate:

Chongqing has a humid subtropical monsoon climate, hot in summer and warm in winter with the rainy season coinciding with the hot season. It has the characteristics of long frost-free period, plenty of rainfall and a lot of humid and cloudy days. The annual average temperature of 2011 is 17.7℃, with the annual precipitation of 992.8mm.

表9.3 气象基本情况（1951－2011年）
BASIC STATISTICS ON CLIMATE (1951-2011)

年 份 Year	降水量（毫米） Precipitation (mm)	平均气温（℃） Average Temperature (℃)	日照时数（时） Sunshine Hours (hour)	平均相对湿度（%） Average Relative Humidity (%)	平均风速（米/秒） Average Wind Speed (m/s)	平均气压（百帕） Average Air Pressure (100 pa)
1951	1043.4	18.4		81	1.0	
1952	1227.9	18.5	1198.6	81	1.0	
1953	852.1	18.8	1245.6	80	0.9	
1954	1112.8	17.9	1061.2	81	0.9	981.2
1955	927.4	18.2	1388.6	77	0.8	982.0
1956	1497.4	18.2	1433.2	76	1.4	982.8
1957	1171.9	17.9	1094.2	80	1.3	983.3
1958	740.7	18.6	1260.7	77	1.4	983.3
1959	915.7	18.7	1378.3	76	1.4	983.0
1960	1026.0	18.4	1102.0	78	1.4	983.5
1961	787.7	18.7	1338.8	77	1.5	982.8
1962	1210.4	18.0	1323.9	80	1.4	983.3
1963	1072.8	18.9	1370.4	77	1.4	982.4
1964	1031.6	18.2	1170.4	80	1.5	982.9
1965	1318.9	18.1	1009.5	81	1.4	983.4
1966	958.9	18.6	1278.9	78	1.4	982.7
1967	1046.0	18.1	1216.3	79	1.4	983.4
1968	1384.5	17.7	1054.6	82	1.2	983.5
1969	1080.5	18.6	1357.1	76	1.2	982.8
1970	1097.5	18.1	1197.9	79	1.1	983.5
1971	854.3	18.6	1370.6	76	1.3	983.4
1972	1171.8	18.4	1284.1	78	1.3	982.9
1973	1092.3	18.9	1349.4	78	1.3	983.2
1974	1258.0	17.8	1068.3	79	1.3	983.0
1975	1025.4	18.5	1202.5	78	1.2	982.9
1976	1044.9	17.7	1129.2	79	1.1	983.5
1977	1151.2	18.1	1234.8	79	1.1	984.0
1978	1057.2	18.8	1495.7	77	1.2	983.5

注：此表为重庆市区资料。
Note: The table above shows the data of the downtown area of Chongqing.

表9.3 续表 continued

年 份 Year	降水量（毫米） Precipitation (mm)	平均气温（℃） Average Temperature (℃)	日照时数（时） Sunshine Hours (hour)	平均相对湿度（%） Average Relative Humidity (%)	平均风速（米/秒） Average Wind Speed (m/s)	平均气压（百帕） Average Air Pressure (100 pa)
1979	1160.0	18.4	1222.2	80	1.1	983.4
1980	1062.6	18.2	1071.8	79	1.4	983.6
1981	1157.9	18.1	1188.0	79	1.4	983.5
1982	1185.2	17.7	992.3	81	1.1	983.6
1983	1138.1	18.1	954.4	80	0.9	983.9
1984	1035.1	17.8	1028.7	79	1.1	983.1
1985	1004.0	17.9	997.1	79	1.3	983.3
1986	1141.4	17.8	946.1	80	1.3	984.2
1987	910.2	18.6	946.3	78	1.2	983.4
1988	1254.0	18.0	840.6	80	1.1	983.6
1989	1137.4	17.7	855.0	81	1.0	983.8
1990	956.7	18.7	1083.7	79	1.2	983.2
1991	1180.6	18.2	874.8	81	1.1	983.5
1992	987.4	18.1	975.0	78	1.6	984.0
1993	1164.3	17.8	894.6	81	1.5	984.0
1994	982.5	18.7	1063.8	80	1.4	983.2
1995	923.5	18.3	993.6	79	1.3	983.7
1996	1398.3	17.7	899.4	81	1.3	983.6
1997	898.8	18.5	943.0	79	1.4	983.8
1998	1508.0	19.2	941.9	79	1.5	983.0
1999	1305.6	18.5	833.6	81	1.5	983.2
2000	1010.9	18.2	961.1	80	1.4	983.0
2001	814.8	18.8	1050.4	78	1.6	983.3
2002	1430.6	18.8	1117.1	80	1.6	983.3
2003	1025.0	18.9	875.7	80	1.6	983.2
2004	1182.1	18.4	974.7	78	1.3	984.0
2005	1019.8	18.6	903.9	77	1.4	982.5
2006	839.6	19.2	1114.3	75	1.4	982.9
2007	1439.2	19.0	856.2	81	1.3	983.3
2008	985.3	18.6	703.8	82	1.3	983.9
2009	1198.9	19.0	943.9	79.8	1.4	982.8
2010	1044.7	18.7	910.6	77.6	1.3	983.0
2011	992.8	17.7	1270.2	74	1.2	971.1

表9.4 全年气象情况（2011年）
STATISTICS ON THE CLIMATE OF THE CURRENT YEAR (2011)

月 份 Month	降水量（毫米） Precipitation (mm)	平均气温（℃） Average Temperature (℃)	日照时数（时） Sunshine Hours (hour)	平均相对湿度（%） Average Relative Humidity (%)	平均风速（米/秒） Average Wind Speed (m/s)	平均气压（百帕） Average Air Pressure (100 pa)	大风日数（天） Days of Strong Wind (day)	雨日数（天） Days of Rain (day)
全 年 Total	992.8	17.7	1270.2	74.0	1.2	971.1	39	137
1	14.6	3.9	15.6	75.0	1.1	982.3		11.5
2	12.3	9.3	56.9	73.8	1.1	973.4	1	5.2
3	50.6	11.3	86.9	69.6	1.2	977.6	4	10.9
4	69.3	18.3	120.9	72.9	1.1	970.2	2	11.6
5	120.5	22.7	173.2	68.0	1.4	965.7	2	10.5
6	169.5	25.2	134.0	76.2	1.2	961.0	2	12.9
7	85.7	27.7	191.5	69.2	1.4	960.3	15	9.9
8	98.3	29.0	254.3	61.2	1.4	961.9	6	6.3
9	97.7	23.4	99.5	73.3	1.3	967.9	4	12.6
10	147.6	17.9	68.1	81.7	1.0	975.0	2	17.0
11	98.0	15.4	44.5	85.6	1.0	974.8	1	15.2
12	28.7	7.6	24.8	81.4	0.9	982.4		13.4

表9.5 环境保护情况（2010－2011年）
ENVIRONMENTAL PROTECTION (2010-2011)

项　目	Item	2010	2011
环保投资（亿元）	Investment in Environmental Protection (100 million yuan)	231.68	275.2
水资源总量（亿立方米）	Total Water Resources (100 million cu.m)	464. 30	514. 58
用水总量（亿立方米）	Total Use of Water (100 million cu.m)	86. 39	86. 80
生活污水排放量（万吨）	Discharged Volume of Domestic Sewage (10 000 tons)	82933.3	97355.6
化学需氧量排放量（万吨）	Discharged Volume of COD (10 000 tons)	23.45	41.68
二氧化硫排放量（万吨）	Discharged Volume of SO_2 (10 000 tons)	71.94	58.69
#生活二氧化硫排放量（万吨）	Discharged Volume of SO_2 from Daily Life (10 000 tons)	14.67	5.56
饮用水源水质达标率（%）	Rate of Drinking Water Sources up to Standard (%)	100.0	100.0
工业污染治理施工项目数（个）	On-going Projects of Industrial Pollution Treatment (unit)	116	253
工业污染治理项目完成投资（万元）	Completed Investment in Projects of Industrial Pollution Treatment (10 000 yuan)	77502	72994
工业污染治理竣工项目数（个）	Completed Projects of Industrial Pollution Treatment (unit)	89	195
工业固体废物综合利用率（%）	Rate of Industrial Solid Wastes Comprehensively Utilized (%)	80.4	76.86
森林覆盖率(%)	Forest Coverage(%)	37.0	39.0
自然保护区数（个）	Number of Nature Reserves (unit)	58	58
自然保护区面积（万公顷）	Area of Nature Reserves (10 000 hectares)	89.23	87.58
保护区面积占土地总面积比重（%）	Percentage of Nature Reserves to Total Land Area (%)	10.8	10.3
主城区区域环境噪声平均值（分贝）	Average Noises in Downtown (db)	54.2	54.0
主城区道路交通噪声（分贝）	Traffic Noises in Downtown (db)	68.0	68.0
主城区大气可吸入颗粒年日均值（毫克/立方米）	Annual Average Daily Inhalable Motes in Atmosphere in Downtown (mg/cu.m)	0.102	0.093
主城区二氧化硫年日均值（毫克/立方米）	Annual Average Daily SO_2 Concentration in Downtown (mg/cu.m)	0.048	0.038
主城区二氧化氮年日均值（毫克/立方米）	Annual Average Daily NO_2 Concentration in Downtown (mg/cu.m)	0.039	0.032
主城区环境空气质量优良天数比例（%）	Proportion of High Air Quality Days in Downtown (%)	85.2	88.8

注：1）森林覆盖率数据为2002年森林资源二类调查基础上的推算数，该调查一般五年一次。
　　2）环境保护数据2011年统计口径变化，与往年不可比（9-5至9-11表）。

Note: a)The data of forest coverage is calculated on the basis of Class II survey of forest resources in 2002, which is carried out every 5 years ordinarily.
b)Due to the adjustment of statistic scope, the data of environment protection in 2011 is not comparable with the data of previous years (from 9-5 to 9-11).

表9.6 工业"三废"排放处理及综合利用情况（1995－2011年）

DISCHARGE, TREATMENT AND COMPREHENSIVE UTILIZATION OF WASTE GAS, WASTE WATER AND SOLID WASTES (1995-2011)

年份 Year	工业废水排放总量（万吨） Total Volume of Industrial Waste Water Discharged(10 000 tons)	工业废气（万吨）Industrial Waste Gas (10 000 tons) 工业废气排放总量（亿标立方米） Total Volume of Industrial Waste Gas Discharged (100 million cu.m)	工业二氧化硫排放量 Volume of SO_2 Discharged	工业烟（粉）尘排放量 Volume of Industrial Dusts Discharged
1995	95590	1979.00	71.45	22.39
1996	93889	1697.00	72.16	22.36
1997	101324	1794.00	71.43	33.18
1998	93997	1712.76	73.64	28.65
1999	90220	1839.33	75.88	26.44
2000	84344	1907.90	66.42	22.01
2001	81214	1856.24	56.94	21.41
2002	79872	1978.89	55.18	20.31
2003	81973	2276.94	59.97	22.23
2004	83031	3540.86	64.11	21.98
2005	84885	3654.55	68.32	21.28
2006	85866	5066.96	71.08	20.01
2007	69003	7616.62	68.31	18.23
2008	67027	7350.73	62.72	15.33
2009	65684	12586.52	58.61	10.77
2010	45180	10943.13	57.27	8.36
2011	33954	9121.07	53.13	17.12

年份 Year	工业固体废物（万吨）Industrial Solid Wastes (10 000 tons) 产生量 Produced Volume	排放量 Discharged Volume	处置量 Treated Volume	综合利用量 Comprehensively Utilized Volume	综合利用率（%） Rate of Comprehensive Utilization（%）
1995	1092	230	68.34	467.79	50.37
1996	1174	229	61.06	510.06	58.10
1997	1279	273	49.16	623.00	54.27
1998	1368	229	43.75	597.00	61.78
1999	1512	291	42.40	655.47	64.32
2000	1305	238	37.64	626.01	71.00
2001	1300	168	87.85	881.64	65.30
2002	1348	160	68.78	960.95	68.20
2003	1336	142	73.54	967.98	68.43
2004	1489	118	62.09	1093.35	70.93
2005	1777	184	122.41	1329.39	72.07
2006	1815	133	123.99	1367.71	73.70
2007	2087	138	162.73	1623.36	76.71
2008	2311	149	73.24	1850.57	79.07
2009	2552	150	126.68	2076.74	79.80
2010	2869	134	155.20	2348.27	80.40
2011	3346	24	561.89	2590.56	76.86

表9.7 重点调查工业废气排放及处理情况（2011年）

WASTE GAS DISCHARGE AND TREATMENT BY THE INDUSTRIAL ENTERPRISES UNDER MAJOR SURVEY (2011)

行　业	Sector	汇总工业企业数（个）Number of Industrial Enterprises (unit)	废气治理设施数（套）Number of Facilities for Waste Gas Treatment (set)
总　计	**Total**	**3212**	**4134**
采矿业	**Mining and Quarrying**		
煤炭开采和洗选业	Mining and Washing of Coal	354	40
石油和天然气开采业	Extraction of Petroleum and Natural Gas	3	2
黑色金属矿采选业	Mining and Processing of Ferrous Metal Ores	11	6
有色金属矿采选业	Mining and Processing of Non-Ferrous Metal Ores	5	
非金属矿采选业	Mining and Processing of Nonmetal Ores	8	6
开采辅助活动	Mining Support Activities	7	8
其他采矿业	Mining of Other Ores		
制造业	**Manufacturing**		
农副食品加工业	Processing of Food from Agricultural Products	335	66
食品制造业	Manufacture of Foods	58	39
酒、饮料和精制茶制造业	Liquor, Beverage and Refined Tea	384	120
烟草制品业	Manufacture of Tobacco	5	11
纺织业	Manufacture of Textile	72	61
纺织服装、服饰业	Textile and Garments	2	
皮革、毛皮、羽毛及其制品和制鞋业	Manufacture of Leather, Fur, Feather and Related Products	20	16
木材加工和木、竹、藤、棕、草制品业	Processing of Timber, Manufacture of Wood, Bamboo,Rattan, Palm and Straw Products	15	18
家具制造业	Manufacture of Furniture	4	7
造纸及纸制品业	Manufacture of Paper and Paper Products	119	103
印刷和记录媒介复制业	Printing, Reproduction of Recording Media	6	5
文教、工美、体育和娱乐用品制造业	Manufacture of Culture, Education, Handicraft, Fine Arts, Sports and Entertainment Articles	1	2
石油加工、炼焦及核燃料加工业	Processing of Petroleum, Coking, Processing of Nuclear Fuel	14	7
化学原料及化学制品制造业	Manufacture of Raw Chemical Materials and Chemical Products	166	332
医药制造业	Manufacture of Medicines	72	69
化学纤维制造业	Manufacture of Chemical Fibers	3	10
橡胶和塑料制品业	Manufacture of Rubber and Plastics	33	52
非金属矿物制品业	Manufacture of Non-metallic Mineral Products	935	1948
黑色金属冶炼及压延加工业	Smelting and Pressing of Ferrous Metals	73	176
有色金属冶炼及压延加工业	Smelting and Pressing of Nonferrous Metals	39	79
金属制品业	Manufacture of Metal Products	95	196
通用设备制造业	Manufacture of General Purpose Machinery	57	106
专用设备制造业	Manufacture of Special Purpose Machinery	18	18
汽车制造业	Manufacture of Motor Vehicles	101	213
铁路、船舶、航空航天和其他运输设备制造业	Manufacture of Railway, Ship, Aviation and Other Transporting Equipment	72	115
电气机械和器材制造业	Manufacture of Electrical Machinery and Equipment	32	68
计算机、通信和其他电子设备制造业	Manufacture of Communication Equipment, Computers and Other Electronic Equipment	18	48
仪器仪表制造业	Manufacture of Measuring Instruments and Machinery	12	17
其他制造业	Other Manufacture	12	18
废弃资源综合利用业	Comprehensive Utilization of Waste Resources	6	
金属制品、机械和设备修理业	Repair of Metal Products, Machinery and Equipment	5	7
电力、热力、燃气及水生产和供应业	**Production and Supply of Electric Power and Heat Power**		
电力、热力的生产和供应业	Production and Supply of Electric Power and Heat Power	38	145
燃气生产和供应业	Production and Supply of Gas		
水的生产和供应业	Production and Supply of Water	2	

工业废气排放总量（亿标立方米） Total Volume of Industrial Waste Gas Discharged (100 million cu.m)	工业二氧化硫产生量（吨） Volume of Sulphur Dioxide Produced (ton)	工业二氧化硫排放量（吨） Volume of Sulphur Dioxide Discharged (ton)	工业烟（粉）尘产生量（吨） Volume of Fume and Dust Produced (ton)	工业烟（粉）尘排放量（吨） Volume of Fume and Dust Discharged (ton)
9121.07	**1526334.14**	**468245.15**	**18008679.73**	**157382.23**
13.82	2733.81	2702.29	2518.41	2282.38
5.34	4273.96	841.86	1.49	1.49
1.66	42.14	42.14	40941.01	445.46
0.78	2.41	2.41	163.19	1.82
5.50	100296.44	1159.55		
9.08	3169.67	3043.85	2998.77	2239.09
69.09	22688.15	10135.98	159531.46	2049.81
13.99	3218.21	2731.42	3328.44	1079.39
3.92	582.65	309.60	1373.84	49.76
22.92	5677.06	5133.57	4709.99	1414.48
0.24	0.36	0.36	0.24	0.24
1.82	553.44	437.84	325.69	65.94
21.53	402.18	401.28	12289.62	518.37
2.86	32.16	32.16	56.81	38.01
88.70	27752.33	13646.87	174012.89	5776.89
0.76	1.14	1.14	0.76	0.76
4.04				
59.98	8101.14	8076.39	11108.44	2878.90
520.73	29393.49	13601.51	139855.18	9659.36
28.60	7990.52	4079.70	12152.82	1505.03
94.88	31412.70	13850.94	336156.38	3427.98
18.03	4848.33	1645.37	8237.06	352.54
3297.95	107122.99	101539.75	7114193.27	55562.13
1825.81	41681.23	41666.83	1308811.30	27399.14
143.47	14315.81	3205.33	52457.11	938.61
44.52	1721.56	793.13	1967.20	788.89
64.86	890.26	890.26	1540.81	677.07
23.17	4.23	4.23	79.85	69.83
401.98	607.54	212.92	3120.54	880.95
182.83	176.95	176.95	5371.58	2306.39
27.20	11.10	11.10	36.07	12.58
17.67	4.93	4.93	98.86	3.66
1.57	8.70	4.36	1.83	0.90
5.50	143.46	143.46	183.49	147.78
11.39			4876.00	28.07
2084.90	1106473.09	237715.67	8606179.34	34778.55

表9.8 重点调查工业固体废物产生及处理利用情况（2011年）

GENERATION, TREATMENT AND UTILIZATION OF SOLID WASTES OF THE INDUSTRIAL ENTERPRISES UNDER MAJOR SURVEY (2011)

行　业	Sector	企业数（个） Number of Enterprises (unit)
总　计	**Total**	**3212**
采矿业	**Mining and Quarrying**	
煤炭开采和洗选业	Mining and Washing of Coal	354
石油和天然气开采业	Extraction of Petroleum and Natural Gas	3
黑色金属矿采选业	Mining and Processing of Ferrous Metal Ores	11
有色金属矿采选业	Mining and Processing of Non-Ferrous Metal Ores	5
非金属矿采选业	Mining and Processing of Nonmetal Ores	8
开采辅助活动	Mining Support Activities	7
其他采矿业	Mining of Other Ores	
制造业	**Manufacturing**	
农副食品加工业	Processing of Food from Agricultural Products	335
食品制造业	Manufacture of Foods	58
酒、饮料和精制茶制造业	Liquor, Beverage and Refined Tea	384
烟草制品业	Manufacture of Tobacco	5
纺织业	Manufacture of Textile	72
纺织服装、服饰业	Textile and Garments	2
皮革、毛皮、羽毛及其制品和制鞋业	Manufacture of Leather, Fur, Feather and Related Products	20
木材加工和木、竹、藤、棕、草制品业	Processing of Timber, Manufacture of Wood, Bamboo, Rattan, Palm and Straw Products	15
家具制造业	Manufacture of Furniture	4
造纸及纸制品业	Manufacture of Paper and Paper Products	119
印刷和记录媒介复制业	Printing, Reproduction of Recording Media	6
文教、工美、体育和娱乐用品制造业	Manufacture of Culture, Education, Handicraft, Fine Arts, Sports and Entertainment Articles	1
石油加工、炼焦及核燃料加工业	Processing of Petroleum, Coking, Processing of Nuclear Fuel	14
化学原料及化学制品制造业	Manufacture of Raw Chemical Materials and Chemical Products	166
医药制造业	Manufacture of Medicines	72
化学纤维制造业	Manufacture of Chemical Fibers	3
橡胶和塑料制品业	Manufacture of Rubber and Plastics	33
非金属矿物制品业	Manufacture of Non-metallic Mineral Products	935
黑色金属冶炼及压延加工业	Smelting and Pressing of Ferrous Metals	73
有色金属冶炼及压延加工业	Smelting and Pressing of Nonferrous Metals	39
金属制品业	Manufacture of Metal Products	95
通用设备制造业	Manufacture of General Purpose Machinery	57
专用设备制造业	Manufacture of Special Purpose Machinery	18
汽车制造业	Manufacture of Motor Vehicles	101
铁路、船舶、航空航天和其他运输设备制造业	Manufacture of Railway, Ship, Aviation and Other Transporting Equipment	72
电气机械和器材制造业	Manufacture of Electrical Machinery and Equipment	32
计算机、通信和其他电子设备制造业	Manufacture of Communication Equipment, Computers and Other Electronic Equipment	18
仪器仪表制造业	Manufacture of Measuring Instruments and Machinery	12
其他制造业	Other Manufacture	12
废弃资源综合利用业	Comprehensive Utilization of Waste Resources	6
金属制品、机械和设备修理业	Repair of Metal Products, Machinery and Equipment	5
电力、热力、燃气及水生产和供应业	**Production and Supply of Electric Power and Heat Power**	
电力、热力的生产和供应业	Production and Supply of Electric Power and Heat Power	38
燃气生产和供应业	Production and Supply of Gas	
水的生产和供应业	Production and Supply of Water	2

工业固体废物产生量（万吨） Volume of Industrial Solid Waste Produced (10 000 tons)	其中 of which #危险废物产生量 Volume of Hazardous Wastes Produced	工业固体废物综合利用量（万吨） Volume of Industrial Solid Wastes Comprehensively Utilized (10 000 tons)	工业固体废物贮存量（万吨） Volume of Industrial Solid Wastes in Stock (10 000 tons)	工业固体废物处置量（万吨） Volume of Industrial Solid Wastes Treated (10 000 tons)	工业固体废物倾倒丢弃量（万吨） Volume of Industrial Solid Wastes Dumped (10 000 tons)
3200.28	**46.50**	**2500.88**	**180.28**	**528.41**	**20.90**
309.27		238.41	26.79	31.86	18.82
1.58		1.53			0.05
9.19		9.83			
5.52		0.96	0.24	4.30	0.03
0.01					
52.56		51.20		0.52	0.85
32.21		31.88		0.32	0.01
28.11		22.66		5.39	0.06
1.26		0.49		0.77	
3.59		3.25	0.06	0.20	0.09
0.01		0.01			
0.24		0.24			
0.68		0.68			
0.06		0.06			
48.87	2.11	44.98	0.01	3.77	0.11
0.13		0.09		0.04	
8.81	0.01	8.80		0.01	
433.63	10.57	155.89	1.18	279.62	0.04
12.27	0.38	7.74	0.01	4.53	
77.88	27.62	50.27		27.61	0.01
6.66	0.02	5.85		0.80	
283.45	0.06	280.65		2.78	0.10
434.75	0.83	380.86	0.49	52.79	0.63
79.85	0.24	23.07	50.07	6.64	0.10
4.77	0.27	4.05		0.72	
6.30	0.09	3.15		3.15	
0.25	0.01	0.23		0.01	
18.81	1.07	13.76		5.05	
2.86	0.08	2.04		0.82	
1.33	0.06	0.22	0.01	1.10	
2.04	0.86	1.15		0.88	
0.14		0.03		0.11	
0.20		0.20			
1.05	1.02			1.05	
0.69		0.69			
1331.23	1.17	1155.94	101.42	93.55	

表9.9 重点调查工业废水排放及处理情况（2011年）

WASTE WATER DISCHARGE AND TREATMENT BY THE INDUSTRIAL ENTERPRISES UNDER MAJOR SURVEY (2011)

单位：万吨(10 000 tons)

行 业	Sector	企业数（个） Number of Enterprises (unit)	工业废水排放总量（万吨） Total Volume of Waste Water Discharged	废水治理设施数（套） Number of Facilities for Waste Water Control (set)
总 计	**Total**	**3212**	**30593.40**	**1507**
采矿业	**Mining and Quarrying**			
煤炭开采和洗选业	Mining and Washing of Coal	354	8032.00	119
石油和天然气开采业	Extraction of Petroleum and Natural Gas	3	4.90	2
黑色金属矿采选业	Mining and Processing of Ferrous Metal Ores	11	24.75	2
有色金属矿采选业	Mining and Processing of Non-Ferrous Metal Ores	5		2
非金属矿采选业	Mining and Processing of Nonmetal Ores	8	2.08	1
开采辅助活动	Mining Support Activities	7	16.97	6
其他采矿业	Mining of Other Ores			
制造业	**Manufacturing**			
农副食品加工业	Processing of Food from Agricultural Products	335	968.92	112
食品制造业	Manufacture of Foods	58	809.65	42
酒、饮料和精制茶制造业	Liquor, Beverage and Refined Tea	384	902.87	75
烟草制品业	Manufacture of Tobacco	5	31.08	3
纺织业	Manufacture of Textile	72	1042.79	39
纺织服装、服饰业	Textile and Garments	2	4.04	2
皮革、毛皮、羽毛及其制品和制鞋业	Manufacture of Leather, Fur, Feather and Related Products	20	48.00	8
木材加工和木、竹、藤、棕、草制品业	Processing of Timber, Manufacture of Wood, Bamboo, Rattan, Palm and Straw Products	15	6.67	3
家具制造业	Manufacture of Furniture	4	4.97	2
造纸及纸制品业	Manufacture of Paper and Paper Products	119	6197.25	90
印刷和记录媒介复制业	Printing, Reproduction of Recording Media	6	6.52	3
文教、工美、体育和娱乐用品制造业	Manufacture of Culture, Education, Handicraft, Fine Arts, Sports and Entertainment Articles	1		
石油加工、炼焦及核燃料加工业	Processing of Petroleum, Coking, Processing of Nuclear Fuel	14	398.89	16
化学原料及化学制品制造业	Manufacture of Raw Chemical Materials and Chemical Products	166	3396.70	133
医药制造业	Manufacture of Medicines	72	692.62	63
化学纤维制造业	Manufacture of Chemical Fibers	3	1431.44	4
橡胶和塑料制品业	Manufacture of Rubber and Plastics	33	155.89	20
非金属矿物制品业	Manufacture of Non-metallic Mineral Products	935	637.21	140
黑色金属冶炼及压延加工业	Smelting and Pressing of Ferrous Metals	73	1801.27	90
有色金属冶炼及压延加工业	Smelting and Pressing of Nonferrous Metals	39	396.02	42
金属制品业	Manufacture of Metal Products	95	548.21	97
通用设备制造业	Manufacture of General Purpose Machinery	57	281.61	53
专用设备制造业	Manufacture of Special Purpose Machinery	18	68.23	18
汽车制造业	Manufacture of Motor Vehicles	101	811.65	116
铁路、船舶、航空航天和其他运输设备制造业	Manufacture of Railway, Ship, Aviation and Other Transporting Equipment	72	487.23	76
电气机械和器材制造业	Manufacture of Electrical Machinery and Equipment	32	138.40	31
计算机、通信和其他电子设备制造业	Manufacture of Communication Equipment, Computers and Other Electronic Equipment	18	190.44	17
仪器仪表制造业	Manufacture of Measuring Instruments and Machinery	12	39.37	12
其他制造业	Other Manufacture	12	31.33	7
废弃资源综合利用业	Comprehensive Utilization of Waste Resources	6	0.69	1
金属制品、机械和设备修理业	Repair of Metal Products, Machinery and Equipment	5	3.03	3
电力、热力、燃气及水生产和供应业	**Production and Supply of Electric Power and Heat Power**			
电力、热力的生产和供应业	Production and Supply of Electric Power and Heat Power	38	973.94	56
燃气生产和供应业	Production and Supply of Gas			
水的生产和供应业	Production and Supply of Water	2	5.77	1

表9.10 工业污染治理项目及投资情况（2010－2011年）
INDUSTRIAL POLLUTION TREATMENT PROJECTS AND INVESTMENT (2010-2011)

项　目	Item	2010	2011
企业数（个）	**Number of Enterprises (unit)**	**98**	**196**
施工项目数（个）	**Number of Projects under Construction (unit)**	**116**	**253**
治理废水	Treatment of Waste Water	63	131
治理废气	Treatment of Waste Gas	39	56
治理固体废物	Treatment of Solid Wastes	3	26
治理噪声	Treatment of Noise Pollution	1	10
治理其他	Treatment of Other Pollution	10	30
资金来源合计（万元）	**Total Funds (10 000 yuan)**	**77502**	**72993**
排污费补助	Pollution Discharge Fees Subsidy	1530	3316
政府其他补助	Other Government Subsidy	7740	2420
企业自筹	Self-raised Fund	67232	67288
资金使用合计（万元）	**Total Expenditures (10 000 yuan)**	**77502**	**72994**
治理废水	Treatment of Waste Water	37761	36494
治理废气	Treatment of Waste Gas	27369	20027
治理固体废物	Treatment of Solid Wastes	3189	14301.3
治理噪声	Treatment of Noise Pollution	500	353.8
治理其他	Treatment of Other Pollution	8684	1817
本年竣工项目数（个）	**Number of Projects Completed in Current Year (unit)**	**89**	**195**
当年竣工项目新增设计处理利用“三废”能力	**Newly Added Designed Capacity of the Projects Completed in Current Year for the Treatment and Utilization of "Three Wastes"**		
废　水（吨/日）	Waste Water (ton/day)	330753	85700
废　气（万标立方米/时）	Waste Gas (10 000 cu.m/hour)	257	884
固体废物（吨/日）	Solid Wastes (ton/day)		0.16

表9.11 生活污染物排放情况（2010－2011年）
DISCHARGE OF DOMESTIC POLLUTANTS (2010-2011)

项　目	Item	2010	2011
生活污水排放量（万吨）	Volume of Domestic Waste Water Discharged (10 000 tons)	82933.3	97355.6
生活污水中化学需氧量排放量（吨）	Discharge of CCD in Domestic Waste Water (ton)	167720.4	230769.5
生活二氧化硫排放量（吨）	Discharge of Sulfur Dioxide from Daily Life (ton)	146657	55584
生活烟尘排放量（吨）	Discharge of Dust from Daily Life (ton)	105570	2463

重/庆/统/计/年/鉴

主要统计指标解释

自然资源

指人类可以直接从自然界获得，并用于生产和生活的物质资源。自然资源一般可以分成可再生资源和非再生资源两大类。可再生资源指在较短时间内可以再生、可以循环利用的资源，包括土地资源、水资源、气候资源、生物资源和海洋资源等。非再生资源指在使用后不能再生的资源，包括矿产资源和地热能源。

土地资源

土地指陆地的表层部分，它主要由岩石、岩石的风化物和土壤构成。土地资源按利用类型可以分为农用地、建筑用地和未利用地。农用地包括耕地、园地、林地、牧草地和水面。建筑用地包括居民点及工矿用地、交通用地和水利设施用地。未利用地指农用地和建筑用地以外的土地，包括滩涂、荒漠、戈壁、冰川和石山等。

耕地面积

指经过开垦用以种植各种农作物并经常进行耕耘的土地面积，包括种有作物的土地面积、休闲地、新开荒地和抛荒未满三年的土地面积。

林业用地面积

指生长乔木、竹类、灌木、沿海红树林等林木的土地面积，包括有林地、灌木林、疏林地、未成林造林地、迹地、苗圃等。

草地面积

指牧区和农区用于放牧牲畜或割草，植被盖度在5%以上的草原、草坡、草山等面积。包括天然的和人工种植或改良的草地面积。

森林资源

指森林、林木、林地以及依托森林、林木、林地生存的野生动物、植物和微生物。林木指树木和竹子。森林指以乔木为主体的植物群落，是集生的乔木及与共同作用的植物、动物、微生物和土壤、气候等的总体。指森林、林木、林地以及依托森林、林木、林地生存的野生动物、植物和微生物。林木指树木和竹子。森林指以乔木为主体的植物群落，是集生的乔木及与共同作用的植物、动物、微生物和土壤、气候等的总体。

活立木总蓄积量

指一定范围内土地上全部树木蓄积的总量，包括森林蓄积、疏林蓄积、散生木蓄积和四旁（村旁、路旁、水旁、宅旁）树蓄积。

森林面积

指由乔木树种构成，郁闭度0.2以上（含0.2）的林地或冠幅宽度10米以上的林带的面积，即有林地面积。森林面积包括天然起源和人工起源的针叶林面积、阔叶林面积、针阔混交林面积和竹林面积，不包括灌木林地面积和疏林地面积。

森林蓄积量

指一定森林面积上存在着的林木树干部分的总材积。它是反映一个国家或地区森林资源总规模和水平的基本指标之一，也是反映森林资源的丰富程度、衡量森林生态环境优劣的重要依据。

森林覆盖率

指一个国家或地区森林面积占土地面积的百分比。森林覆盖率是反映森林资源的丰富程度和生态平衡状况的重要指标。在计算森林覆盖率时，森林面积包括郁闭度0.2以上的乔木林地面积和竹林地面积、国家特别规定的灌木林地面积、农田林网以及四旁（村旁、路旁、水旁、宅旁）林木的覆盖面积。计算公式为：

森林覆盖率（%）=森林面积/土地总面积×100%

水资源

水在自然界中以固体、液体和气态三种聚集状态存在，分布于海洋、陆地（包括土壤）以及大气之中，通过水循环形成水资源。水资源包括经人类控制并直

主要统计指标解释

接可供灌溉、发电、给水、航运、养殖等用途的地表水和地下水，以及江河、湖泊、井、泉、潮汐、港湾气候和养殖水域等。水资源是发展国民经济不可缺少的重要自然资源。

■ 地表水和地下水

陆地上的水因空间分布不同，可以分为地表水和地下水。地表水指分别存在于河流、湖泊、沼泽、冰川和冰盖等水体中水分的总称，又称陆地水。地下水指储存在地面以下饱和岩土孔隙、裂隙及溶洞中的水。

■ 径流

指大气降水扣除损耗外，从地表和地下向流域出口断面汇集的水流。径流可分为地表径流、地下径流和壤中流。地表径流指沿地表向河流、湖泊、沼泽、海洋等汇集的水流；地下径流指沿潜水层或隔水层间的含水层，向河流、湖泊、沼泽、海洋等汇集的地下水水流。

■ 径流量

指在一定时段内通过河流某一过水断面的水量，用以反映一个国家或地区水资源的丰歉程度。计算公式为：径流量=降水量－蒸发量

■ 矿产资源

矿产指由地质作用形成，具有利用价值的，呈固态、液态、气态的自然资源，是社会生产发展的重要物质基础。目前我国已发现矿种有170多种，按其特点和用途，可分为能源矿产（如煤炭、石油、天然气、地热）、金属矿产（如铁矿、锰矿、铜矿、铅矿、铝土矿）、非金属矿产（如金刚石、石灰石、粘土）和水气矿产（如地下水、矿泉水、二氧化碳气）四大类。其中：金属矿产按其物质成份和性质又可分为：黑色金属矿产、有色金属矿产、贵金属矿产、稀有金属矿产、稀土金属矿产、分散元素金属矿产六类。

■ 矿产基础储量

基础储量是查明矿产资源的一部分。它能满足现行采矿和生产所需的指标要求，是控制的、探明的并通过可行性或预可行性研究认为属于经济的、边界经济的部分，用未扣除设计、采矿损失的数量表示。

■ 气候

指地球与大气之间长期能量交换与质量交换所形成的一种自然环境状态，它是多种因素综合作用的结果。气候既是人类生活和生产的环境要素之一，又是供给人类生活和生产的重要资源。气温、降水、湿度等气象要素的多年平均值是用来描述一个地区气候状况的主要参数，而各种气象要素某年、某月的平均值（或总量）则可以反映出该时期天气气候状况的重要特征。

■ 气温

指空气的温度，我国一般以摄氏度（℃）为单位表示。气象观测的温度表是放在离地面约1.5米处通风良好的百叶箱里测量的，因此，通常说的气温指的是离地面1.5米处百叶箱的温度。其统计计算方法为：

月平均气温是全月各日的平均气温相加，除以该月的天数而得。

年平均气温是将12个月的月平均气温累加后除以12而得。

■ 相对湿度

指空气中实际所含水蒸气密度和同温度下饱和水蒸气密度的百分比值。其统计方法与气温相同。

■ 降水量

指从天空降落到地面的液态或固态（经融化后）水，未经蒸发、渗透、流失而在地面上积聚的深度。其统计计算方法为：

月降水量是将全月各日的降水量累加而得。

年降水量是将12个月的月降水量累加而得。

■ 日照时数

指太阳实际照射地面的时间。其统计方法与降水量相同。

■ 化学需氧量(COD)排放量

为工业废水中COD排放量与生活污水中COD排放量之和。化学需氧量指用化学氧化剂氧化水中有机污染物时所需的氧量。一般利用化学氧化剂将废水中可氧化的物质（有机物、亚硝酸盐、亚铁盐、硫化物等）氧化分解，然后根据残留的氧化剂的量计算出氧的消耗量，来表示废水中有机物的含量，反映水体有机物污染程度。COD值越高，表示水中有机污染物污染越重。

主要统计指标解释

二氧化硫排放量

指报告期内工业SO2排放量与生活SO2排放量之和。

工业废水排放量

指经过企业厂区所有排放口排到企业外部的工业废水量。包括生产废水、外排的直接冷却水、超标排放的矿井地下水和与工业废水混排的厂区生活污水，不包括外排的间接冷却水（清污不分流的间接冷却水应计算在内）。

工业废水排放达标量

指报告期内废水中各项污染物指标都达到国家或地方排放标准的外排工业废水量，包括未经处理外排达标的，经废水处理设施处理后达标排放的，以及经污水处理厂处理后达标排放的。

工业废气排放量

指报告期内企业厂区内燃料燃烧和生产工艺过程中产生的各种排入空气的含有污染物的气体的总量，以标准状态（273K，101325Pa）计算。测算公式为：工业废气排放量=燃料燃烧过程中废气排放量+生产工艺过程中废气排放量

工业二氧化硫排放量

指报告期内企业在燃料燃烧和生产工艺过程中排入大气的SO2总量，计算公式为：

工业SO2排放量=燃料燃烧过程中SO2排放量+生产工艺过程中SO2排放量

工业烟尘排放量

指企业厂区内的燃料燃烧过程中产生的烟气中夹带的颗粒物排放量。

工业粉尘排放量

指企业在生产工艺过程中排放的能在空气中悬浮一定时间的固体颗粒物排放量。如钢铁企业的耐火材料粉尘、焦化企业的筛焦系统粉尘、烧结机的粉尘、石灰窑的粉尘、建材企业的水泥粉尘等。不包括电厂排入大气的烟尘。

工业固体废物产生量

指报告期内企业在生产过程中产生的固体状、半固体状和高浓度液体状废弃物的总量，包括危险废物、冶炼废渣、粉煤灰、炉渣、煤矸石、尾矿、放射性废物和其他废物等；不包括矿山开采的剥离废石和掘进废石（煤矸石和呈酸性或碱性的废石除外）。酸性或碱性废石是指采掘的废石其流经水、雨淋水的ＰＨ值小于4或ＰＨ值大于10.5者。

工业固体废物综合利用量

指报告期内企业通过回收、加工、循环、交换等方式，从固体废物中提取或者使其转化为可以利用的资源、能源和其他原材料的固体废物量（包括当年利用往年的工业固体废物累计贮存量），如用作农业肥料、生产建筑材料、筑路等。综合利用量由原产生固体废物的单位统计。

工业固体废物贮存量

指报告期内企业以综合利用或处置为目的，将固体废物暂时贮存或堆存在专设的贮存设施或专设的集中堆存场所内的数量。专设的固体废物贮存场所或贮存设施必须有防扩散、防流失、防渗漏、防止污染大气、水体的措施。

工业固体废物处置量

指报告期内企业将固体废物焚烧或者最终置于符合环境保护规定要求的场所，并不再回取的工业固体废物量（包括当年处置往年的工业固体废物累计贮存量）。处置方法有填埋（其中危险废物应安全填埋）、焚烧、专业贮存场（库）封场处理、深层灌注、回填矿井及海洋处置（经海洋管理部门同意投海处理）等。

工业固体废物排放量

指报告期内企业将所产生的固体废物排到固体废物污染防治设施、场所以外的数量，不包括矿山开采的剥离废石和掘进废石（煤矸石和呈酸性或碱性的废石除外）。

“三废”综合利用产品产值

指报告期内利用“三废”（废液、废气、废渣）作为主要原料生产的产品产值（现行价），已经销售或准备销售的应计算产品产值，留作生产上自用的不应计算产品产值。

主要统计指标解释

■ 城镇生活污水排放量

指城镇居民每年排放的生活污水。用人均系数法测算。测算公式为：

城镇生活污水排放量=城镇生活污水排放系数×市镇非农业人口×365

■ 生活及其他烟尘排放量

指除工业生产活动以外的所有社会、经济活动及公共设施的经营活动中燃烧所排放的烟尘纯重量。以生活及其他煤炭消费量为基础进行测算。

Explanatory Notes on Main Statistical Indicators

Natural Resources

Refer to material resources that could be obtained from the nature by human being and used for production and living. Natural resources in general can be classified as renewable resources and non-renewable resources. Renewable resources refer to resources that could be renewed and recycled during a relatively short period of time, including land resource, water resource, climate resource, biology resource and marine resource. Non-renewable resources include resources that could not be renewed, such as minerals and geothermal resource.

Land Resource

Land refers to the surface of the earth, consisting of mainly rocks and its weathering and earth. Land resource can be classified, by its utilization, as land for agriculture, land for construction and unused land. Land for agriculture included cultivated land, plantation land, forestland, grassland and waters. Land for construction includes land for residential purpose, for manufacturing and mining, for transportation and for water-conservancy projects. Unused land refers to land other than land for agriculture and construction, including beaches, deserts, Gobi glaciers and rock mountains.

Area of Cultivated Land

Refers to area of land reclaimed for the regular cultivation of various farm crops, including crop-cover land, fallow, newly reclaimed land and land laid idle for less than 3 years.

Area of Afforestated Land

Refers to area for Land for trees bamboo, bushes and mangrove, including forest-covered land, bush-covered land, sparse forest land, land planned for afforestation and nurseries of young trees.

Area of Grassland

Refers to areas of grassland, grass-slopes and grass-covered hills with a vegetation-covering rate of over 5% that are used for animal husbandry or harvesting of grass. It includes natural, cultivated and improved grassland areas.

Forest Resource

Refers to forests, trees, forestland and wild animals, plants and microorganism that live on forest and trees. Trees include trees and bamboo. Forest refers to the population of clusters of trees and other plants, animals and microorganism as well as the earth and climate that have interactions with the trees.

Total Standing Stock Volume

Refers to the total stock volume of trees growing in land, including trees in forest, tress in sparse forest, scattered trees and trees planted by the side of villages, farm houses and along roads and rivers.

Forest Area

Refers to the area of forest where trees and bamboo grow with canopy density above 0.2, including land of natural woods and planted woods, but excluding bush land and thin forest land. It reflects the total areas of afforestation.

Stock Volume of Forest

Refers to total stock volume of wood growing in forest area, which shows the total size and level of forest resources of a country or a region. It is also an important indicator illustrating the richness of forest resource and the status of forest ecological environment.

Forest Coverage Rate

Refers to the ratio of area of afforested land to total land area. It is a very important indicator that reflects the status of abundance of forest resource and balance of the ecosystem. Forest area includes the area of trees and bamboo grow with canopy density above 0.2, the area of shrubby tree according to regulations of the government, the area of forest land inside farm land and the area of trees planted by the side of villages, farm houses and along roads and rivers.The formula for calculating forest coverage rate is as follows.

Forestry coverage rate (%) = (Area of Afforested Land / Area of Total Land) × 100%

EXPLANATORY NOTES TO MAJOR STATISTICAL INDICATORS

Water Resource

Water exists in the nature in solid, liquid and gaseous states, is distributed in the ocean, land (including earth) and air, and constitutes the water resource through the circulation of water. Water resource includes the surface water and ground water that is controlled by the human being for irrigation, power-generation, water supply, navigation and cultivation. It also includes rivers, Lakes, wells, springs, tides, and gulf and water area for cultivation. Water resource as an important natural resource is indispensable for the development of the national economy.

Surface Water and Ground Water

Water on earth can be divided into surface water and ground water according to its distribution. Surface water refers to moisture exists in rivers, lakes, swamps, glaciers, icecaps and so on. It is also called land water. The underground water refers to water deposited under-ground in the cranny and the hole of saturated rock soil and in water-eroded cave.

Runoff

Refers to the water gathered at the way out of the cross section of drainage area either from the surface or underground after deducting the wastage of the precipitation. Runoff can be divided into surface runoff, underground runoff and within soil runoff. Surface runoff refers to water flow to the rivers, lakes, swamps, and seas on the surface of the earth. Underground runoff refers to water flow to rivers, swamps, and seas through the water-bearing stratum of confined layer or unconfined layer.

Volume of Runoff

Refers to the total volume of water running through a certain cross section of a river during a certain period of time, reflecting the water resource condition in a country or a region. The formula for calculating volume or runoff is as follows: Runoff=Precipitation-Evaporation

Mineral Resources

Refer to useful minerals, with solid state, liquid state, gaseity, due to the geological process. Minerals are important natural resources, and important material base for social development. At present, there are more than 170 types of minerals discovered in China. They can be categorized into four groups: energy producing minerals (including coal, petroleum, natural gas and terrestrial heat), metallic minerals (including iron, manganese, copper, lead and bauxite), non metallic minerals (including diamond, limestone and clay), and water/gas related minerals (including ground water, mineral water and carbon dioxide). Metallic minerals can be further classified as ferrous, non-ferrous, noble metal, rare metal, rare earth metal and dispersed metals.

Ensured Mineral Reserves

Refer to the actual mineral reserves, which equal to the proven mineral reserves (including industrial reserves and prospective reserves) minus extracted parts and underground losses.

Climate

Refers to the natural environmental status formed by the long-time exchange of energy and mass between the earth and the atmosphere, and is the result of interaction of many factors. Climate is both one of the environment factors and also the important resources for the living and production activities of the human being. The average values across several years of meteorological factors such as temperature, rainfall and humidity are used as important parameters to describe the climate of a region, while the average values (or total values) of a given year of month of meteorological factors reflect the key characteristics of climate for that period of time.

Temperature

Refers to the air temperature. China uses centigrade (°C) as the unit. The thermometry used for weather observation is put in a breezy shutter, which is 1.5 meters high from the ground. Therefore, the commonly used temperature refers to the temperature in the breezy shutter 1.5 meters away from the ground. The calculation method is as follows:

Monthly average temperature is the summation of average daily temperature of one month divided by the actual days of that particular month.

Annual average temperature is the summation of monthly average of a year divided by 12 months.

Relative Humidity

Refers to the ratio of actual water vapor pressure to the saturation water vapor pressure under the current temperature. The calculation method is the same as that of temperature.

Volume of Precipitation

Refers to the deepness of liquid state of solid state (thawed) water falling from the sky to the ground that has not been evaporated, infiltrated or run off. The calculation method is as follows:

Monthly precipitation is the summation of daily precipitation of a month.

Annual precipitation is the summation of 12 months' precipitation of a year.

Sunshine Hours

Refer to the actual hours of sun irradiating the earth. The calculation method is the same as that of the precipitation.

COD Emission

Refers to the total volume of COD emitted from industrial activities and life activities.COD refers to the amount of oxygen required when chemical oxidants are used to oxidize organic pollutants in water. Chemical oxidants are used to oxidize possible material in water, such as organic material, nitrite, ferrous salt, sulfide and so on. Then according to residual amount of oxidants to calculate consumption of oxygen, it is said that how much organic pollutants are in water. A higher value of COD corresponds to more serious pollution by organic pollutants.

SO_2 Emission

Refer to the total volume of SO_2 emitted from industrial activities and life activities within a given period of time.

Volume of Industrial Waste Water Discharged

Refers to the volume of industrial waste water discharged, through all outlets, to the outside of industrial enterprises, including waste water produced, direct - cooling water, underground water from mines that does not meet the standard of discharge, and the domestic sewage mixed up with industrial waste water when discharged, but excluding discharged indirect - cooling water.

Volume of Waste Water up to the Standard for Discharge

Refers to the volume of discharged industrial wastewater that, with or without treatment, has come up to the national or local standards for discharge.

Industrial Waste Air Emission

Refers to discharge into atmosphere of waste air containing pollutants generated from fuel burning and production process in enterprises within a given period of time. It is calculated at standard status (273K, 101325Pa) as:

Industrial waste air emission = emission through fuel burning + emission through production process

Industrial SO_2 Emission

Refers to volume of sulphur dioxide emission from fuel burning and production process in premises of enterprises for a given period of time. Its calculation formula is:

Industrial SO_2 Emission = SO_2 Emission from fuel burning + SO_2 Emission from production process

Industrial Soot Emission

Refers to volume of soot in smoke emitted in process of fuel burning in premises of enterprises.

Industrial Dust Emission

Refers to volume of dust emitted by production process of enterprises and suspended in the air for a given period of time, including dust from refractory material of iron and steel works, dust from coke-screening systems and sintering machines of coke plants, dust from lime kilns and dust from cement production in building material enterprises, but excluding soot and dust emitted from power plants.

Volume of Industrial Solid Wastes Produced

Refers to total volume of solid, semi-solid and high concentration liquid residues produced by industrial enterprises from production process in a given period of time, including hazardous wastes, slag, coal ash, gangue, tailings, radioactive residues and other wastes, but excluding stones stripped or dug out in mining (gangue and acid or alkaline stones not included). A stone is acid or alkaline depending on the pH value of the water below 4 or above 10.5 when the stone is in or soaked by the water.

Volume of Industrial Solid Wastes Utilized in a Comprehensive Way

Refers to volume of solid wastes from which useful materials can be extracted or which can be converted into usable resources, energy or other materials by means of reclamation, processing, recycling and exchange (including utilizing in the year the stocks of industrial solid wastes of the previous year). Examples of such utilizations include fertilizers, building materials and road materials. The information shall be collected by the producing units of the wastes.

EXPLANATORY NOTES TO MAJOR STATISTICAL INDICATORS

□ Volume of Industrial Solid Wastes Stored up

Refers to the volume of industrial solid wastes temporarily stored up or piled with special facilities or piled in the special sites for the purpose of utilization or treatment in future. The special facilities or special sites for storing up solid wastes should have the measures against spreading or being washed away to other places, permeating the soil or causing air pollution or water contamination.

□ Volume of Industrial Solid Wastes Treated

Refers to quantity of industrial solid wastes which are burnt or placed ultimately in the sites meeting the requirements for environmental protection and not salvaged or recycled (including disposition in the year of those wastes of previous years). The disposition includes landfill (Safe landfills should be conducted for hazardous wastes), incineration, containment spaces, deep underground disposal, backfill in mining pits and disposal at sea (accepted by management of sea).

□ Volume of Industrial Solid Wastes Discharged

Refers to volume of industrial solid wastes discharged by producing enterprises to disposal facilities or to other sites. The wastes exclude stones stripped or dug from mining (gangue and acid or alkaline waste stones not included).

□ Output Value of Products Made from Utilization of Waste Gas, Waste Water and Industrial Solid Wastes

Refers to the value of products (calculated at current prices) made by industrial enterprises using recovered waste water, waste gas or solid wastes as main raw materials. Only the value of the products, which have been sold or are ready, to be sold should be included. The value of the products, which will be used in the production of the enterprises, should not be included.

□ Urban Consumption Waste Water Discharge

Refers to annual discharge of consumption waste water by urban households. Its calculation formula is:

Discharge = Discharge of Consumption Wastewater by Urban Households × Urban Non-agricultural Population × 365

□ Soot Emission by Consumption and Others

Refers to net volume of soot emitted by fuel burning from all social and economic activities and operation of public facilities other than industrial activities. It is calculated on the basis of coal consumption by households and others.

第10章

要素市场

MARKETS OF KEY FACTORS

简要说明
BRIEF INTRODUCTION

本章资料中的国有土地使用权出让与划拨、城市房产市场交易情况由市统计局固定资产投资处根据市国土资源和房屋管理局资料整理提供，亿元以上商品市场由市统计局贸易外经处提供，技术市场由市统计局社会科技处根据市科学技术委员会资料整理提供，人才市场、劳动力市场和证券市场情况由市统计局综合处根据市人才交流服务中心、市就业服务管理局、市发展和改革委员会和重庆证监局资料整理编辑。

货币流通、保险业务和有价证券的相关资料详见第十七章金融。

The data on transaction and allotment of the right to use the state-owned land and the real estate markets in urban areas are sorted and compiled by Division of Statistics of Investment in Fixed Assets, Chongqing Municipal Bureau of Statistics on the basis of the data provided by Chongqing Administration of Land, Resources and Housing; the data of the transaction of the commodity markets with transaction value over 100 million yuan are provided by Division of Trade and External Economic Relations Statistics, Chongqing Municipal Bureau of Statistics; the data of transactions of technology exchanges are provided by Division of Social and Technology Statistics, Chongqing Municipal Bureau of Statistics on the basis of the data from Chongqing Science and Technology Commission; the data of the human resource markets, labor force markets and securities markets are sorted and compiled by Division of Comprehensive Statistics, Chongqing Municipal Bureau of Statistics on the basis of the data from Chongqing Human Resource Exchanges Service Center, Chongqing Administration of Employment Services, Chongqing Development and Reform Commission and China Securities Regulatory Commission Chongqing Bureau.

See Chapter 17 Financial Intermediation for the data on currency, insurance and securities.

表10.1 国有土地使用权出让与划拨情况（2010－2011年）
TRANSACTIONS AND ALLOTMENT OF THE RIGHT TO USE THE STATE-OWNED LAND (2010-2011)

指　标	Item	2010	2011
土地使用权出让	**Transaction of Right to Use State-owned Land**		
地　块（宗）	Land Parcel (parcel)	1666	1912
面　积（公顷）	Land Area (hectare)	5759.52	6899.60
出让价款（亿元）	Value of Transaction (100 million yuan)	840	1109.37
土地使用权划拨	**Allotment of Right to Use State-owned Land**		
地　块（宗）	Land Parcel (parcel)	1093	1011
面　积（公顷）	Land Area (hectare)	5732.94	11318.96

表10.2 城市房产市场交易情况（2010－2011年）
REAL ESTATE MARKETS IN URBAN AREA (2010-2011)

指　标	Item	2010	2011
房产转让	**Housing Transactions**		
成交面积（万平方米）	Area of Transactions (10 000 sq.m)	2797.13	1934.43
#住　宅	Residential Buildings	2499.62	1600.58
#商品房	Commercialized Buildings	1984.36	1543.09
存量房	Buildings in Stock	812.77	391.34
成交金额（亿元）	Total Value of Transactions (100 million yuan)	1406.13	1193.46
#住　宅	Residential Buildings	1208.62	934.57
#商品房	Commercialized Buildings	1177.02	1034.30
存量房	Buildings in Stock	229.11	159.16
房产抵押	**Housing Mortgage**		
面积（万平方米）	Area (10 000 sq.m)		
担保金额（亿元）	Amount Assured (100 million yuan)		

注：本表为主城九区的数据。
Note: The table above shows the data of the 9 urban district.

表10.3 亿元以上商品市场交易情况（2010－2011年）

TRANSACTIONS OF COMMODITY MARKETS WITH TRANSACTION VALUE OVER 100 MILLION YUAN (2010-2011)

单位：万元 (10 000 yuan)

指　标	Item	摊位数量（个） Number of Stands (unit)		总成交额 Total Volume of Transactions	
		2010	2011	2010	2011
合　计	**Total**	**80570**	**85298**	**24579490**	**29873359**
食品、饮料、烟酒类	Food, Beverages, Tobacco and Liquor	23447	24824	5095146	6150864
服装鞋帽、针、纺织品类	Clothing, Shoes, Hats and Textiles	19559	20188	2933019	3751979
化妆品类	Cosmetics	570	576	50002	57620
金银珠宝类	Gold,Silver and Jewelry	9	21	3962	7914
日用品类	Articles for Daily Use	4622	5034	295695	719703
五金电料类	Hardwear and Electrical Materials	4796	4175	607848	703868
体育、娱乐用品类	Sports and Entertainment Articles	304	419	9418	47160
书报杂志类	Newspapers and Magazines	51	57	1051	964
电子出版物及音像制品类	E-journal and Video Products	68	83	5582	15073
家用电器和音像制品类	Household Electric Appliances and Video Products	1071	721	310809	383118
中西药品类	Traditional Chinese and Western Medicines	80	285	7914	113434
文化办公用品类	Cultural and Office Articles	2036	3076	897970	1262969
家具类	Furniture	2923	2638	1124320	1365556
通讯器材类	Communication Appliances	779	319	168650	70700
木材及制品类	Wood and Wooden Products	507	400	109834	120009
石油及制品类	Petroleum and Related Products	4	13	3304	330
化工材料及制品类	Chemical Materials and Products	188	289	42296	80739
金属材料类	Metal Materials	3315	3452	7129096	8269185
建筑及装潢材料类	Building and Decoration Materials	5883	6794	1661142	2002983
机电产品及设备类	Mechanical and Electrical Products	3390	3909	1294970	1174897
#农机类	Agricultural Machinery	8	9	1019	1244
汽车类	Automobiles	2064	2512	2078526	2663549
种子饲料类	Seeds and Feedstuff	441	413	162290	162008
棉麻类	Cotton and Hemp	14	31	1495	2043
其他类	Others	4444	5069	585012	746694

表10.4 技术市场交易情况（2011年）
TRANSACTIONS OF TECHNOLOGY EXCHANGES (2011)

单位：项、万元 (item, 10 000 yuan)

指　标	Item	技术买方 Purchases of Technology		技术卖方 Sales of Technology	
		项　数 Number	金　额 Value	项　数 Number	金　额 Value
总　计	**Total**	**3336**	**1010751.57**	**3336**	**1010751.57**
#企业法人	Corporations	1413	816485.45	2419	719260.98
事业法人	Public Institutions	1332	28411.74	871	144602.16
机关法人	Governments	428	87322.26		

表10.5 人才市场人才流动情况（2010－2011年）
HUMAN RESOURCE MARKETS AND EXCHANGES (2010-2011)

指　标	Item	2010	2011
人才流动机构（个）	Number of Agencies of Human Resource Exchanges (unit)	132	137
政府人事部门所属	Under Official Departments	42	42
非政府人事部门所属	Under Un-official Departments	90	95
人才市场（个）	Number of Human Resource Markets (unit)	38	38
举办人才交流会（次）	Number of Job Fairs (time)	2123	2451
登记要求流动人数（人）	Number of Persons Registered for Exchanges (person)	3450000	3855040
参加人才交流会人数（人）	Number of Persons Attending Job Fairs (person)	2845000	3105241
参加人才交流会的招聘单位（个）	Number of Employers Attending Job Fairs (unit)	152200	184320
全年接收人事档案数量（份）	Annual Number of Personnel Files Received (copy)	10500	10831
现存人事档案总量（份）	Number of Personnel Files in Archives (copy)	64500	75331
当年流动人员职称评定（人）	Number of Exchanged Persons Evaluated for Professional Titles in Current Year (person)	2080	2475
评定高级职称人数	Senior Titles	128	286
评定中级职称人数	Medium Titles	725	921
评定初级职称人数	Junior Titles	1227	1268

注：本表指标除人才流动机构为全市口径，其余指标均为人事部门口径。
Note: All the indices of this table are in the scope of personnel departments except the number of agencies of human resource exchanges, which is in the scope of Chongqing.

表10.6 公共就业服务机构介绍情况（2010－2011年）

STATISTICS ON THE PUBLIC JOB SERVICES AND INTERMEDIATION AGENCIES (2010-2011)

单位：人 (person)

指　标	Item	2010	2011
公共就业服务机构（个）	**Number of Job Services Agencies (unit)**	**1051**	**916**
#区县及以上	At District & County Level and above	42	42
登记招聘单位数	**Number of Registered Employers**	**105600**	**120467**
登记招聘人数	**Number of Persons to Be Employed**	**810778**	**1104566**
登记求职人次（人次）	**Number of Registered Job Applicants（person-time)**	**799548**	**897848**
#女　性	Female	376016	384570
#城镇登记失业人员	Registered Unemployed Persons in Urban Areas	290206	380596
#高校毕业生	College Graduates	65402	56157
#农村劳动力	Rural Labor Force	427480	432683
职业指导人数	**Number of Persons under Vocational Guidance**	**722426**	**725011**
介绍成功人次（人次）	**Number of Persons Employed through Job Services (person-times)**	**360006**	**386045**
#女　性	Female	169698	155651
#城镇登记失业人员	Registered Unemployed Persons in Urban Areas	131050	151784
#高校毕业生	College Graduates	36036	28595
#农村劳动力	Rural Labor Force	190025	193583

表10.7 证券市场基本情况（2010－2011年）

GENERAL STATISTICS ON SECURITY MARKETS (2010-2011)

指　标	Item	2010	2011
境内上市公司数（A、B股）(家)	Number of Listed Companies (A and B Shares) in Mainland (unit)	34	36
境内上市外资股（B股）(只)	Number of Listed Companies of Foreign Fund (B Shares) in Mainland (unit)	2	2
境外上市公司数（H股）(家)	Number of Listed Companies (H Shares) Overseas (unit)		
IPO和增发股票量（万股）	Number of Shares of IPO and Additional Equity Offer (10 000 shares)	809055.25	192242.86
股票总发行股本（亿股）	Total Capital Stock (100 million shares)	2301429.47	277.07
#流通股本	Negotiable Capital	1287341.45	164.87
股票市价总值（亿元）	Total Market Capitalization of Shares (100 million yuan)	2645	2028
#股票流通市值	Negotiable Market Capitalization	1434	1029
国债发行额（亿元）	Volume of T-bonds Issued (100 million yuan)		
企业债发行额（亿元）	Volume Enterprise Bonds Issued (100 million yuan)	91	74
股票筹资额（亿元）	Raised Capital of Shares (100 million yuan)	148.7	158.0
投资者开户数（万户）	Total Accounts of Investors (10 000 accounts)	180.38	192.13
期货总成交额（亿元）	Total Future Turnover (100 million yuan)	74806.31	69194.78

注：股票发行量、总发行股本、市价总值和筹资额均不含H股。
Note: H share is not included in the number of shares, total capital stock, total market capitalization and raised capital of shares.

第11章

农业和农村经济

AGRICULTURE AND RURAL ECONOMY

简要说明
BRIEF INTRODUCTION

本章反映全市农业生产和农村经济的基本情况，内容主要包括农村基本情况、农业生产条件与生产情况、农作物播种面积、农林牧渔产品产量、农林牧渔业产值、农业商品产值和商品率、乡镇企业等方面的统计资料。

本章资料由国家统计局重庆调查总队根据市农委、市林业局、市水利局和调查总队等资料整理提供。乡镇企业的有关情况由重庆市统计局综合处根据市乡镇企业管理局提供的资料整理、编辑。

The data in this chapter show the basic conditions of agricultural production and rural economy, including basic statistics on rural areas, basic conditions of agricultural production, sown area of farm crops, output of farming, forestry, animal husbandry and fishery products, gross output value of farming, forestry, animal husbandry and fishery, output value of agricultural commodities and rate of commercialization, and township-owned enterprises.

The data in this chapter are provided by Chongqing Agriculture Commission, Municipal Bureau of Forestry, Municipal Bureau of Water Conservancy and NBS Survey Office in Chongqing, and sorted and compiled by NBS Survey Office in Chongqing. The data of township-owned enterprises are provided by Municipal Administration of Township-owned Enterprises and sorted and compiled by Division of Comprehensive Statistics, Municipal Bureau of Statistics.

表11.1 主要年份农村基本情况
BASIC STATISTICS ON RURAL AREAS IN MAJOR YEARS

年 份 Year	乡村户数 (万户) Number of Rural Households (10 000 households)	乡村人口 (万人) Rural Population (10 000 persons)	乡村从业人员 (万人) Rural Employed Population (10 000 persons)
1949		1446.24	650.59
1952		1546.01	692.81
1957		1685.98	762.15
1962		1506.16	692.19
1965		1676.21	755.99
1970		1977.85	857.78
1975		2264.67	921.67
1978		2316.54	926.32
1980	534.19	2294.08	980.75
1985	573.00	2355.39	1114.34
1986	596.13	2365.34	1154.26
1987	626.70	2391.29	1184.92
1988	650.27	2412.04	1218.03
1989	671.51	2427.70	1249.12
1990	686.26	2446.38	1273.06
1991	697.61	2471.48	1314.79
1992	699.94	2476.10	1350.71
1993	700.88	2463.53	1352.26
1994	710.34	2482.05	1356.59
1995	706.86	2454.17	1349.34
1996	709.86	2464.23	1330.44
1997	708.64	2452.75	1320.91
1998	709.84	2445.12	1316.95
1999	710.99	2442.47	1342.99
2000	710.28	2440.32	1352.60
2001	714.67	2438.79	1345.15
2002	718.31	2443.21	1342.17
2003	718.65	2436.47	1340.25
2004	714.99	2425.25	1361.54
2005	718.84	2430.93	1366.91
2006	714.86	2418.40	1382.62
2007	717.49	2413.95	1378.29
2008	724.06	2405.64	1379.89
2009	723.55	2385.95	1379.94
2010	727.77	2366.66	1379.35
2011	721.14	2324.50	1369.98

表11.2 主要年份农业生产条件
CONDITIONS OF AGRICULTURAL PRODUCTION IN MAJOR YEARS

年 份 Year	有效灌溉面积（万公顷） Irrigated Area (10 000 hectares)	农用机械总动力（万千瓦） Total Agricultural Machinery Power (10 000 kw)	农村用电量（万千瓦时） Electricity Consumption in Rural Areas (10 000 kwh)	农用化肥施用量（折纯）（万吨） Consumption of Chemical Fertilizer (net) (10 000 tons)	农膜使用量（万吨） Consumption of Farm Plastic Film (10 000 tons)	农药使用量（万吨） Consumption of Chemical Pesticides (10 000 tons)
1949	5.48					
1952	6.73					
1957	13.40					
1962	21.31	4	1852			
1965	26.10	10	3791			
1970	31.92	22	12655			
1975	42.84	54	21045			
1978	56.27	101	28542	21.63	0.33	0.64
1980	60.42	155	37953	29.21	0.37	0.71
1985	60.98	219	63309	31.76	0.50	0.73
1986	60.12	240	71471	36.70	0.51	0.79
1987	59.27	259	83229	38.26	0.57	0.78
1988	58.41	278	79637	38.29	0.61	0.81
1989	57.56	291	89611	44.72	0.65	0.81
1990	58.02	300	97091	48.13	0.80	0.87
1991	58.55	316	104430	52.08	0.97	1.01
1992	58.96	324	115831	52.75	1.07	1.05
1993	59.26	343	134027	54.51	1.18	1.27
1994	59.53	366	160197	58.55	1.28	1.29
1995	59.79	386.05	174847	62.02	1.43	1.46
1996	60.08	409.91	196788	65.55	1.53	1.69
1997	61.14	454.07	227302	69.64	1.59	1.68
1998	61.41	506.64	242934	71.18	1.77	1.82
1999	62.05	558.54	260029	71.03	1.86	1.84
2000	62.60	586.47	278728	72.00	1.96	1.85
2001	63.19	628.07	301140	72.58	1.94	1.91
2002	64.12	665.57	338717	73.37	2.53	1.93
2003	64.97	695.67	366535	71.59	2.42	1.95
2004	61.68	728.31	384627	77.02	2.68	1.95
2005	61.81	775.96	428943	79.20	2.75	1.95
2006	62.13	820.01	460291	80.54	2.82	1.96
2007	63.37	860.31	484478	84.32	3.01	2.04
2008	65.89	903.15	550949	88.14	3.09	2.10
2009	67.20	967.41	614832	91.17	3.47	2.20
2010	68.53	1071.09	647738	91.82	3.66	2.10
2011	69.29	1141.00	703706	95.58	3.93	2.03

表11.3 农作物播种面积（1978－2011年）
SOWN AREA (1978-2011)

单位：公顷 (hectare)

年 份 Year	农作物 总播种面积 Total Sown Area	其 中 of which					
		#粮 食 Grain	其 中 of which #稻 谷 Rice	#油 料 Oil-bearing Crops	其 中 of which #油菜籽 Rapeseeds	#蔬 菜 Vegetables	#烟 叶 Tobacco
1978	3498061	3177221	849243	92351	71374	95954	26582
1980	3345304	3048196	828317	116577	89369	78400	10416
1985	3214717	2748498	820140	176866	137367	140569	30956
1986	3232433	2710205	819858	183859	143792	159811	40897
1987	3241258	2697509	807797	180579	143292	160867	41729
1988	3287399	2727164	821305	185171	150612	171444	54056
1989	3381959	2788700	836231	188593	154505	177979	75726
1990	3438950	2847370	821986	203171	168751	183873	66607
1991	3526637	2889404	816684	224412	188989	197049	70859
1992	3522037	2874889	819262	215622	179402	200686	81258
1993	3513064	2870480	804560	184964	147692	222621	82461
1994	3493884	2877837	800342	174643	135505	225902	54997
1995	3526684	2876853	799482	201550	162572	236283	58939
1996	3585745	2889834	802279	202483	159584	257106	77657
1997	3605420	2881902	797955	191800	152222	267203	99482
1998	3614446	2900656	794636	192330	148896	290397	56603
1999	3592496	2862143	788576	197151	151801	301389	63969
2000	3590815	2773404	776636	226384	173185	327094	70775
2001	3555871	2714600	763964	225046	167911	366330	55210
2002	3464566	2606866	757195	236325	173930	359674	56012
2003	3307179	2410369	738486	236724	176836	386990	57237
2004	3435957	2516507	749300	244129	173815	390237	52995
2005	3444733	2501263	747949	252421	187333	399970	51508
2006	3073880	2155500	672300	187290	133680	417414	48879
2007	3134700	2195800	652130	192920	135370	432906	43553
2008	3215064	2215407	673538	215531	150170	481563	47749
2009	3308300	2229493	682041	237025	173643	552233	52579
2010	3359387	2243887	683907	254993	191847	589093	42733
2011	3413088	2259413	686485	257096	196200	618631	46165

表11.4 主要年份农林牧渔产品产量
OUTPUT OF FARMING, FORESTRY, ANIMAL HUSBANDRY AND FISHERY IN MAJOR YEARS

年份 Year	粮食（万吨） Grain (10 000 tons)	其中 of which #稻谷 Rice	#豆类 Beans	油料（万吨） Oil-bearing Crops (10 000 tons)	其中 of which #油菜籽 Rapeseeds	麻类（吨） Fiber Crops (ton)	甘蔗（万吨） Sugarcane (10 000 tons)
1949	402.68	246.57		0.90		1416	8.78
1952	470.97	281.33		3.19		1889	10.61
1957	596.55	316.39		5.13		1811	6.86
1962	378.23	191.26		1.40		598	1.04
1965	566.17	293.32		3.87		1048	14.47
1970	564.37	307.80		2.68		666	9.00
1975	603.72	325.84		4.13		632	24.87
1978	814.71	345.07	29.07	7.71	6.03	1659	31.20
1980	835.43	341.59	22.20	11.57	9.28	6172	36.64
1985	948.97	461.73	22.26	18.12	13.63	25787	30.24
1986	1004.92	493.41	25.02	20.91	15.85	21719	31.42
1987	1004.51	499.56	22.34	20.89	16.14	35995	29.43
1988	958.02	503.00	20.53	19.25	14.94	31013	29.32
1989	1044.88	541.81	17.25	18.78	14.38	18932	24.41
1990	1085.07	550.40	19.93	22.02	17.74	12707	20.55
1991	1115.28	535.90	21.53	26.92	22.81	11487	26.07
1992	1050.24	509.07	18.48	25.18	21.40	9716	14.33
1993	1052.72	479.90	21.90	21.70	17.22	9257	12.30
1994	1134.10	523.13	25.94	19.26	15.31	11471	9.39
1995	1153.68	532.63	30.38	25.12	20.54	11092	8.76
1996	1172.14	542.64	20.10	23.60	18.66	10898	8.27
1997	1184.63	552.44	21.90	23.34	18.34	11175	8.08
1998	1155.36	519.38	22.17	25.11	19.03	7541	7.28
1999	1143.05	533.01	21.93	24.09	17.33	6826	7.59
2000	1131.21	525.43	24.60	31.06	22.61	8406	9.06
2001	1035.35	466.45	23.32	29.96	21.91	8857	10.08
2002	1082.15	484.42	27.78	35.04	25.84	12139	12.06
2003	1087.20	494.29	32.21	38.27	28.51	9620	11.35
2004	1144.57	509.55	38.11	41.75	30.99	10209	11.77
2005	1168.19	521.43	42.16	42.71	31.81	12362	11.46
2006	808.40	344.90	29.24	28.94	23.47	11846	10.16
2007	1088.00	491.59	35.12	30.68	23.19	15399	11.26
2008	1153.20	529.39	37.78	35.68	26.54	16982	11.18
2009	1137.20	511.30	39.83	40.54	30.95	15869	11.57
2010	1156.13	518.57	41.93	44.45	34.22	14700	11.68
2011	1126.90	493.50	43.49	46.51	35.14	14455	11.80

表11.4 续表1 continued1

年 份 Year	烟 叶（吨） Tobacco (ton)	蔬 菜（万吨） Vegetables (10 000 tons)	茶 叶（吨） Tea (ton)	蚕 茧（吨） Silkworm Cocoons (ton)	水 果（万吨） Fruits (10 000 tons)	牛 奶（吨） Cow Milk (ton)	禽 蛋（万吨） Poultry Eggs (10 000 tons)
1949	8535		916	761	6.02	1171	
1952	9238		1059	1236	7.75	1292	
1957	8247		1914	1588	7.14	2621	
1962	2566		1981	1325	8.80	3925	
1965	4654		2369	2306	6.83	6576	
1970	1667		2927	6608	4.54	9651	
1975	8146		4884	10477	7.12	11940	
1978	22528	243.95	8004	15404	7.91	15891	4.46
1980	8098	229.86	9217	25751	15.69	17277	5.51
1985	36239	390.86	16172	33130	24.70	29677	8.77
1986	46724	421.94	16893	32693	28.61	32665	9.44
1987	44992	439.00	18267	35755	29.57	36474	9.98
1988	68928	460.93	18676	41748	20.50	39126	10.17
1989	62093	469.31	18568	42063	37.19	40308	11.24
1990	74393	499.61	18103	43502	35.08	46293	12.01
1991	98156	533.00	18264	47757	40.75	51988	12.94
1992	124705	541.38	17178	50686	41.38	56579	14.61
1993	113208	558.23	19522	54505	56.85	54880	15.71
1994	68904	569.83	21920	57408	52.87	48514	17.32
1995	77981	593.91	17452	27000	59.29	39153	19.18
1996	132355	637.03	15536	27402	56.62	40297	20.85
1997	164736	668.44	14996	28072	60.72	45129	23.50
1998	79970	711.30	15299	29226	74.10	46587	24.46
1999	95653	737.11	14441	24177	71.70	46614	26.29
2000	104082	775.42	14526	29098	81.68	55989	27.89
2001	80064	779.96	14142	32396	82.61	67791	29.79
2002	87052	833.84	14093	33856	113.41	80952	31.58
2003	86048	840.17	14320	27802	128.59	90608	35.36
2004	85036	863.57	16064	29376	137.22	85143	36.55
2005	90173	890.47	16545	31092	154.63	86076	39.15
2006	91945	888.76	17087	27488	145.74	83456	30.30
2007	71513	945.21	18853	29196	175.89	86095	32.30
2008	85513	994.52	21696	24388	193.28	77842	33.11
2009	99905	1177.45	22569	19464	212.87	79422	35.97
2010	81030	1309.54	25237	20321	238.47	79819	37.22
2011	93608	1407.97	27895	20118	261.16	80000	37.42

注：2006年起禽蛋产量已根据第二次农业普查数据重新进行了调整。
Note: Output of Poultry Eggs was adjusted according to the sencond National Agricultural Census since 2006.

表11.4 续表2 continued2

年 份 Year	水产品（吨） Aquatic Products (ton)	肉猪出栏头数（万头） Slaughtered Fattened Hogs (10 000 heads)	猪年末头数（万头） Hogs at Year End (10 000 heads)	大牲畜年末存栏头数（万头） Large Animals at Year End (10 000 heads)	其 中 of which #牛 Cattle and Buffaloes	肉类总产量（万吨） Output of Meat (10 000 tons)	其 中 of which #猪 肉 Pork
1949	3576	174.70		107.90		11.00	
1952	4119	254.80		122.50		16.00	
1957	6515	345.10		131.20		21.70	
1962	3791	76.90		115.60		6.90	
1965	6964	421.50		128.00		25.60	
1970	7649	414.50		150.20		23.10	
1975	10797	489.90		151.10		28.10	
1978	14362	542.70	914.98	142.15	141.58	40.51	37.38
1980	17734	797.63	1165.05	141.75	141.19	59.89	55.92
1985	42838	1140.06	1353.02	128.91	127.62	84.45	79.96
1986	47805	1190.22	1377.37	129.39	128.10	88.56	83.15
1987	51854	1243.78	1418.69	128.24	126.96	92.76	86.89
1988	58419	1345.77	1448.48	128.35	127.07	99.85	94.02
1989	65707	1375.38	1471.66	127.92	126.64	102.41	96.09
1990	65482	1375.79	1429.13	129.18	127.63	102.92	96.12
1991	71813	1429.45	1440.56	129.77	128.21	107.45	99.87
1992	74459	1469.47	1444.16	130.80	128.84	111.47	102.66
1993	89227	1492.99	1438.96	130.54	129.24	113.73	104.30
1994	103492	1555.69	1476.05	132.50	132.41	121.61	108.48
1995	121289	1610.14	1489.55	136.61	135.72	127.22	112.27
1996	140656	1637.51	1477.06	140.43	137.89	133.22	114.18
1997	160692	1699.74	1475.25	144.01	141.04	141.86	119.66
1998	178607	1720.14	1492.95	152.48	149.24	140.00	121.61
1999	191313	1703.19	1512.18	163.88	160.58	140.50	120.61
2000	200345	1724.96	1509.91	167.45	164.05	143.91	122.45
2001	196967	1746.85	1533.03	168.63	165.05	147.88	124.87
2002	211568	1781.69	1548.89	170.52	166.85	152.40	127.48
2003	224893	1828.49	1583.03	172.58	169.31	159.51	131.82
2004	239255	1909.32	1640.75	173.56	170.08	167.01	136.43
2005	250568	2006.39	1708.80	174.48	170.69	178.39	144.46
2006	226129	1732.70	1377.40	97.71	94.00	151.50	124.80
2007	255372	1783.20	1422.94	98.15	94.44	159.27	130.27
2008	190600	1898.67	1566.47	107.36	103.61	177.58	140.65
2009	203900	2003.11	1604.07	122.85	119.39	187.72	146.52
2010	224300	2010.51	1557.87	131.39	128.08	192.46	147.55
2011	275600	2020.87	1540.57	127.86	124.53	196.28	148.55

注：本表中除水产品外，其余数据从2006年起已根据第二次农业普查数据重新进行了调整。
Note: Except the data of aquatic products,the other data in this table have been adjusted according to the Sencend National Agricultural Census since 2006.

表11.5 主要年份农林牧渔业总产值
GROSS OUTPUT VALUE OF FARMING, FORESTRY, ANIMAL HUSBANDRY AND FISHERY IN MAJOR YEARS

单位：万元 (10 000 yuan)

年份 Year	农林牧渔业总产值 Gross Output Value	其中 of which 农业 Farming	林业 Forestry	牧业 Animal Husbandry	渔业 Fishery	农林牧渔服务业 Agricultural Services
1949	142123	111424	3837	26293	568	
1952	186367	140707	6523	38205	932	
1957	240351	176658	10816	51916	961	
1962	153506	120349	4605	28245	307	
1965	165688	122775	5799	36617	497	
1970	269234	192504	11128	64604	998	
1975	295062	210016	18048	65660	1338	
1978	357616	262881	17236	75731	1768	
1980	417925	296840	16160	102514	2411	
1985	739003	477570	43546	208842	9044	
1986	801998	516990	42045	231097	11867	
1987	902072	564063	40932	282816	14262	
1988	1104369	641751	49662	393394	19561	
1989	1243819	706771	49328	463300	24420	
1990	1460003	858133	55308	518757	27805	
1991	1595286	938353	60038	565193	31702	
1992	1713839	995009	70992	612498	35340	
1993	2073607	1197742	77531	749776	48558	
1994	2831816	1552652	86981	1127394	64789	
1995	3778259	2278927	106732	1304229	88371	
1996	4249903	2713807	115493	1311666	108937	
1997	4393508	2678892	117313	1468914	128389	
1998	4288839	2549365	150929	1444758	143787	
1999	4168780	2496237	115588	1409527	147428	
2000	4126272	2447376	108236	1419910	150750	
2001	4311666	2503968	112044	1544041	151613	
2002	4609755	2640760	135143	1661965	171887	
2003	4885655	2701156	145824	1776384	183251	79040
2004	6127723	3329516	184814	2309374	212464	91555
2005	6621943	3583035	199704	2494965	237959	106280
2006	5752428	3230078	223069	2042194	159087	98000
2007	7207260	4095523	178527	2644768	184442	104000
2008	8713871	4730118	217986	3441474	211481	112811
2009	9131080	5311679	258084	3194244	242699	124374
2010	10211328	6233343	304021	3265542	272083	136339
2011	12653319	7512246	380907	4253262	349432	157471

注：1)按照国民经济行业分类标准（GB/T4754-2002），从2003年起增加了农林牧渔服务业（下表同）。
2)2006年以来为第二次农普衔接数。从2007年起，因口径变化，对农业和林业产值进行了调整。
Note: a) According to the national standard of industry classification (GB/T4754-2002), the gross output value has included agricultural services since 2003 (the same below).
b) The numbers after 2006 are the coordinationi numbers of the Second National Agricultural Census. The total output of agriculture and forestry has been modified since 2007 due to the change of statistical scope.

表11.6 主要年份农林牧渔业总产值指数（上年=100）

GROSS OUTPUT VALUE INDICES OF FARMING, FORESTRY, ANIMAL HUSBANDRY AND FISHERY IN MAJOR YEARS (PRECEDING YEAR=100)

年 份 Year	农林牧渔业总产值 Gross Output Value	其 中 of which				
		农 业 Farming	林 业 Forestry	牧 业 Animal Husbandry	渔 业 Fishery	农林牧渔服务业 Agricultural Services
1952	119.9	116.8	123.7	135.7	111.2	
1957	129.0	126.7	144.5	133.4	156.4	
1962	63.9	69.9	58.0	39.4	49.5	
1965	151.1	137.2	125.4	275.5	194.9	
1970	101.5	100.3	88.5	109.7	107.3	
1975	108.2	110.6	129.7	94.6	134.0	
1978	123.2	126.7	119.1	109.7	121.2	
1980	115.3	105.9	99.6	165.8	121.0	
1985	144.1	130.9	210.2	169.8	292.2	
1986	105.8	106.3	83.9	109.3	119.4	
1987	102.7	102.1	89.0	106.3	110.3	
1988	101.8	97.3	99.1	111.7	115.2	
1989	106.4	108.4	99.9	103.0	111.0	
1990	102.7	101.1	96.4	106.4	106.8	
1991	106.2	105.3	102.1	108.2	113.9	
1992	101.9	98.7	110.4	107.3	100.9	
1993	104.1	103.4	104.8	104.6	120.8	
1994	105.6	103.5	101.8	109.0	115.4	
1995	106.3	105.1	106.7	107.7	116.8	
1996	102.8	101.8	101.3	103.6	116.2	
1997	103.3	102.0	95.8	105.4	115.7	
1998	102.4	101.5	117.2	101.6	112.4	
1999	99.8	100.7	75.7	100.4	108.5	
2000	101.0	100.3	86.6	102.9	104.5	
2001	102.1	100.3	109.7	104.1	101.9	
2002	101.7	99.7	102.3	104.2	105.6	
2003	104.6	103.5	119.6	104.8	106.8	
2004	105.7	105.5	108.8	104.9	108.4	116.5
2005	105.2	103.9	100.8	106.9	106.0	113.3
2006	96.8	94.9	99.9	99.6	89.0	105.7
2007	109.5	114.8	105.1	101.6	110.2	106.0
2008	107.1	107.7	104.5	106.7	104.0	104.3
2009	106.4	106.8	106.6	105.7	108.8	104.8
2010	105.9	106.7	110.2	103.8	110.0	104.4
2011	104.8	105.2	110.0	102.5	118.4	105.0

注：本表指数按可比价计算；其中1952年以1949年为100。
Note: Indices of this table are calculated at constant prices. The index of 1952 is calculated with the index of 1949 equal to 100.

表11.7 农林牧渔业总产值（2010－2011年）
GROSS OUTPUT VALUE OF FARMING, FORESTRY, ANIMAL HUSBANDRY AND FISHERY (2010-2011)

单位：万元 (10 000 yuan)

指　标	Item	农林牧渔业总产值 Gross Output Value		指　数 上年=100 Index Preceding Year=100
		2010	2011	
总　计	**Total**	**10211328**	**12653319**	**104.8**
农　业	Farming	6233343	7512246	105.2
谷物及其他作物	Cereal and Other Crops	2901337	3280478	99.6
#谷　物	Cereal	1654862	1854055	97.2
豆　类	Beans	253689	287062	103.7
油　料	Oil Crops	266638	302341	104.6
烟　草	Tobacco	101288	137136	115.5
蔬菜园艺作物	Vegetables and Gardening	2410418	3004006	110.2
#蔬　菜（含菜用瓜）	Vegetables (including Melons as Vegetables)	2202374	2743455	107.5
花　卉	Flowers	47274	54839	108.0
水果、坚果、饮料和香料作物	Fruits, Nuts, Drinks and Spices	802512	1035233	109.4
#水果、坚果（含果用瓜）	Fruits and Nuts (including Melons as Fruits)	581493	767950	109.5
茶及其他饮料	Tea and Other Drinks	83282	102315	110.5
#茶	Tea	83282	102315	110.5
中药材	Traditional Chinese Medical Materials	119075	192528	111.5
林　业	Forestry	304021	380907	110.0
林木的培育和种植	Forest Cultivation	179118	219835	105.2
#造　林	Afforestation	77336	85625	95.9
竹木采运	Bamboo Felling and Transportation	30686	34822	107.8
林产品	Forest Products	94217	126250	119.7
牧　业	Animal Husbandry	3265542	4253262	102.5
牲畜饲养	Livestock Raising	214911	250832	105.6
#牛	Cattle	137530	157098	105.6
奶产品	Milk Products	27138	31200	100.3
猪的饲养	Hog Raising	1787345	2424744	100.5
家禽饲养	Poultry Raising	1055066	1249243	106.0
#禽　蛋	Poultry Eggs	390786	404291	100.5
狩猎和捕捉动物	Animal Hunting	364	420	103.1
其他畜牧业	Others	207857	328024	116.9
#蚕　茧	Silkworm Cocoons	45316	60756	99.0
渔　业	Fishery	272083	349432	118.4
#内陆水域水产品	Aquatic Products in Inland Water Areas	272083	349432	118.4
#养　殖	By Breeding	246478	316080	123.1
#鱼　类	Fish	268445	344527	122.9
农林牧渔服务业	Agricultural Services	136339	157471	105.0

注：本表数据绝对值按现价计算，指数按可比价计算。
Note: The absolute figures in this table are calculated at current prices whereas the indices are calculated at constant prices.

表11.8 农村基本情况（2010－2011年）
BASIC STATISTICS ON RURAL AREAS (2010-2011)

指　标	Item	2010	2011
户　数（万户）	**Number Households (10 000 households)**	**727.77**	**721.14**
人　口（万人）	**Population (10 000 persons)**	**2366.66**	**2324.50**
乡村从业人员（万人）	**Rural Employed Population (10 000 persons)**	**1379.93**	**1369.98**
按性别分	By Sex		
男	Male	747.78	732.45
女	Female	631.57	637.51
按产业分	By Sector		
第一产业	Primary Industry	626.12	604.04
第二产业	Secondary Industry	384.96	
第三产业	Tertiary Industry	368.27	
农村基础设施（个）	**Rural Infrastructure (unit)**		
自来水受益村数	Number of Villages with Access to Tap Water	5612	5864
通汽车村数	Number of Villages with Highways	8660	8569
通电话村	Number of Villages with Telephones	8686	8581

注：从2001年起，民政部门调整乡、镇、村的区划，村个数均比往年减少。
Note: The number of villages is less than that in previous years for the administrative adjustment since 2001.

表11.9 农业生产条件（2010－2011年）
CONDITIONS OF AGRICULTURAL PRODUCTION (2010-2011)

指　标	Item	2010	2011
农业机械化情况	**Agricultural Mechanization**		
农业机械总动力（万千瓦）	Total Agricultural Machinery Power (10 000 kw)	1071.09	1141.00
农用大中型拖拉机数（万台）	Number of Large and Medium-sized Agricultural Tractors (10 000 units)	0.33	0.36
农用大中型拖拉机动力（万千瓦）	Capacity of Large and Medium-sized Agricultural Tractors (10 000 kw)	10.06	
小型拖拉机数（万台）	Number of Small Tractors (10 000 units)	0.68	0.77
小型拖拉机动力（万千瓦）	Capacity of Small Tractors (10 000 kw)	8.78	
农用排灌动力机械台数（万台）	Number of Drainage and Irrigation Engines (10 000 units)	90.43	89.10
农用排灌动力机械动力（万千瓦）	Capacity of Drainage and Irrigation Engines (10 000 kw)	271.30	
农用水泵（万台）	Pumps (10 000 units)	90.43	95.40
机动脱粒机（万台）	Motorized Threshing Machines (10 000 units)	60.77	61.60
农用运输车（万辆）	Farm Tracks (10 000 vehicles)	5.15	3.76
渔用机动船（万艘）	Motorized Fishing Boats (10 000 vessels)	0.58	0.59
农业主要能源及物耗	**Main Agricultural Energy and Material Consumption**		
农村用电量（万千瓦时）	Electricity Consumed in Rural Areas (10 000 kwh)	647738	703706
乡村办电站（个）	Power Stations in Rural Areas (unit)	627	802
乡村办电站发电量（万千瓦时）	Capacity of Power Station in Rural Areas (10 000 kwh)	171502	179263
有效灌溉面积（公顷）	Irrigated Area (hectare)	685250	692880
化肥施用量（折纯量）(万吨)	Consumption of Chemical Fertilizer (net) (10 000 tons)	91.82	95.58
#氮　肥	Nitrogenous Fertilizer	49.31	50.20
磷　肥	Phosphate Fertilizer	17.49	18.21
钾　肥	Potash Fertilizer	5.24	5.61
复合肥	Compound Fertilizer	19.13	21.39
农用塑料薄膜使用量（万吨）	Consumption of Farm Plastic Film (10 000 tons)	3.66	3.93
#地膜使用量	Consumption of Farm Plastic Film	1.94	2.07
地膜覆盖面积（公顷）	Area Covered by Farm Plastic Film (hectare)	285215	299991
农用柴油使用量（万吨）	Consumption of Diesel Oil (10 000 tons)	16.38	17.23
农药使用量（万吨）	Consumption of Chemical Pesticides (10 000 tons)	2.09	2.03

表11.10 主要农作物播种面积及产量（2010－2011年）
SOWN AREA AND OUTPUT OF MAJOR FARM CROPS (2010-2011)

指　标	Item	播种面积（公顷）Sown Area (hectare)		总产量（吨）Total Output (ton)		单位产量（公斤/公顷）Yield Per Unit (kg/ha)	
		2010	2011	2010	2011	2010	2011
粮　食	**Grain**	**2243888**	**2259413**	**11561300**	**11269032**	**5152.4**	**4987.6**
谷　物	Cereal	1319670	1316381	8220861	7991615	6229.5	6070.9
稻　谷	Rice	683904	686485	5185738	4935000	7582.6	7188.8
中　稻	Middle Rice	683904	686485	5185738	4935000	7582.6	7188.8
小　麦	Wheat	150532	138362	459303	423858	3051.2	3063.4
玉　米	Corn	461886	466930	2515596	2570000	5446.4	5504.0
高　粱	Sorghum	14522	15867	39952	46444	2751.1	2927.1
其他谷物	Other Cereal	8826	8737	20272	16314	2296.9	1867.2
豆　类	Beans	213954	224634	419320	434942	1959.9	1936.2
#大　豆	Soybean	91174	95400	181171	186509	1987.1	1955.0
薯　类	Tubers	710264	718398	2921119	2842475	4112.7	3956.7
#马铃薯	Potato	336263	344198	1121316	1161475	3334.6	3374.4
油　料	**Oil-bearing Crops**	**254995**	**257096**	**444499**	**465073**	**1743.2**	**1808.9**
#花　生	Peanut	49295	50379	90527	101123	1836.4	2007.2
油菜籽	Rapeseed	191849	196200	342193	351400	1783.7	1791.0
芝　麻	Sesame Seed	7717	6906	6839	6877	886.2	995.9
麻　类	**Fiber Crops**	**10370**	**9607**	**14700**	**14455**	**1417.6**	**1504.6**
#苎　麻	Ramie	10274	8935	14504	12779	1411.7	1430.2
黄红麻	Jute and Ambary Hemp	72	72	102	100	1416.7	1390.4
糖　料（甘蔗）	**Sugar Crops (sugarcane)**	**3131**	**3382**	**116833**	**118048**	**37314.9**	**34902.7**
烟　叶	**Tobacco**	**42735**	**46165**	**81030**	**93608**	**1896.1**	**2027.7**
#烤　烟	Flue-cured Tobacco	34914	38911	63880	75928	1829.6	1951.3
蔬菜、瓜果	**Vegetables and Melons**	**611799**	**640119**	**13454555**	**14482130**	**21991.8**	**22624.1**
#蔬　菜（含菜用瓜）	Vegetables (including Melons as Vegetables)	589095	618631	13095385	14079653	22229.7	22759.4

表11.11 林牧渔业生产情况（2010－2011年）
OUTPUT OF FORESTRY, ANIMAL HUSBANDRY AND FISHERY (2010-2011)

指 标	Item	2010	2011
林 业（公顷）	**Forestry (hectare)**		
当年造林面积	Increased Forest Area in Current Year	255235	244644
年末封山育林面积	Year-end Area of Hillsides Closed for Afforestation	314726	372116
零星（四旁）植树（万株）	Scattered (Four-side) Tree Planting (10 000 plants)	9892.93	10921.95
育苗面积	Seeding Raising Area	15062	17353
当年苗木产量（万株）	Output of Plants in Current Year (10 000 plants)	81421.88	81989.34
幼林抚育实际面积	Actual Tending Area for Young Stands	80454	102434
成林抚育面积	Tending Area for Mature Plantation	51145	67443
牧 业	**Animal Husbandry**		
年末大牲畜总头数（万头）	Number of Large Animals (year-end, 10 000 heads)	131.39	127.86
#农事劳役头数	Number of Draught Animals	50.86	46.97
年末生猪存栏头数（万头）	Number of Hogs (year-end, 10 000 heads)	1557.87	1540.57
年末羊只数（万只）	Number of Sheep and Goats (year-end, 10 000 heads)	168.41	176.73
年内出栏肥猪头数（万头）	Number of Slaughtered Fattened Hogs (10 000 heads)	2010.51	2020.87
年内出栏羊只数（万只）	Number of Slaughtered Sheep and Goats (10 000 heads)	191.33	202.64
年内出栏家禽（万只）	Number of Slaughtered Poultry (10 000 heads)	19674.24	20863.42
渔 业（公顷）	**Fishery (hectare)**		
水产品养殖面积	Cultured Areas of Aquatic Products	76390	81245
#池 塘	Ponds	41760	45397
水 库	Reservoirs	26552	27425

表11.12 林牧渔业主要产品产量（2010－2011年）
OUTPUT OF THE MAJOR PRODUCTS OF FORESTRY, ANIMAL HUSBANDRY AND FISHERY (2010-2011)

单位：吨 (ton)

指 标	Item	2010	2011
水 果	Fruits	2384711	2611604
#柑 桔	Citrus	1390243	1533332
肉 类	Meat	1924588	1962849
#猪 肉	Pork	1475548	1485523
禽 肉	Meat of Poultry	309659	326209
兔 肉	Meat of Rabbit	44625	50846
奶 类	Milk	79820	80003
#牛 奶	Cow Milk	79819	80000
蜂 蜜	Honey	11915	12386
水产品	Aquatic Products	224300	275600
#养 殖	Cultured Aquatic Products	213345	262645
年末实有茶园面积（公顷）	Area of Tea Plantations (year-end) (hectare)	32276	34663
#本年采摘面积	Picked Area in Current Year	23845	25395
年末果园面积（公顷）	Area of Orchards (year-end) (hectare)	248651	264768
#梨 园	Pear	35207	35897
#柑 桔	Citrus	138032	147496

表11.13 主要农产品产量与建国以来最高年产量的比较（2011年）

OUTPUT OF MAJOR AGRICULTURAL PRODUCTS IN COMPARISON WITH THE PEAK YEAR SINCE THE FOUNDATION OF PRC (2011)

单位：万吨 (10 000 tons)

指 标	Item	2011	建国以来最高产量 Output in the Peak Year Since the Foundation of PRC		2011年为建国以来最高年份的比重（%） 2011 as Percentage of Peak Year
			年 份 Year	产 量 Output	
粮食总产量	Total Output of Grain	1126.90	1997	1184.63	95.1
#稻 谷	Rice	493.50	1997	552.44	89.3
小 麦	Wheat	42.39	1995	156.24	27.1
玉 米	Corn	257.00	2010	251.56	102.2
豆 类	Beans	43.49	1958	45.34	95.9
薯 类	Tubers	284.25	2009	284.40	99.9
油菜籽	Rapeseed	35.14	2010	34.22	102.7
麻 类	Fiber Crops	1.45	1985	2.60	55.6
甘 蔗	Sugarcane	11.80	1980	36.64	32.2
烤 烟	Flue-cured Tobacco	7.59	1997	11.00	69.0
蔬菜类	Vegetables	1407.97	2010	1309.54	107.5
年末生猪存栏头数（万头）	Number of Hogs (year-end, 10 000 heads)	1540.57	2005	1708.80	90.2
肉 类	Meat	196.28	2010	192.46	102.0
#猪 肉	Pork	148.55	2010	147.55	100.7
禽 肉	Meat of Poultry	32.62	2010	30.97	105.3
奶 类	Milk	8.00	2003	9.06	88.3
禽 蛋	Poultry Eggs	37.42	2005	39.15	95.6
水产品	Aquatic Products	27.56	2005	25.06	110.0
蚕 茧	Silkworm Cocoon	2.01	1994	5.74	35.0
茶 叶	Tea	2.79	2010	2.52	110.7
水 果	Fruits	261.16	2010	238.47	109.5

表11.14 农业商品产值和商品率（2010－2011年）

OUTPUT VALUE OF AGRICULTURAL COMMODITIES AND RATE OF COMMERCIALIZATION (2010-2011)

指 标	Item	农业商品产值（万元） Output Value of Agricultural Commodities(10 000 yuan)		农业商品率（%） Rate of Commercialization (%)	
		2010	2011	2010	2011
总 计	**Total**	**6202059**	**7802248**	**60.7**	**62.4**
农 业	Farming	3241338	3928904	52.0	52.3
#粮食作物	Grain Crops	743123	865256	30.6	32.0
经济作物	Cash Crops	314745	381150	79.6	80.0
蔬 菜	Vegetables	1396305	1761298	63.4	64.2
茶、桑、水果	Tea, Mulberry and Fruits	464100	609029	72.1	72.5
林 业	Forestry	199742	257493	65.7	67.6
牧 业	Animal Husbandry	2543857	3334558	77.9	78.4
#猪	Hogs	1347658	1913025	75.4	78.9
活的畜禽产品	Livestocks and Relative Products	383894	416208	77.3	77.0
渔 业	Fishery	217122	281293	79.8	80.5

表11.15 乡镇企业主要指标（2010－2011年）
MAIN INDICATORS OF TOWNSHIP-OWNED ENTERPRISES (2010-2011)

单位：万元 (10 000 yuan)

指　标	Item	2010	2011
企业单位数（个）	Number of Enterprises (unit)	73135	75452
#工　业	Industry	26700	27546
#集体企业	Collective-owned Enterprises	169	154
私有企业	Private Enterprises	26531	27392
从业人数（人）	Employees (person)	2352419	2416043
#集体企业	Collective-owned Enterprises	44036	43227
私有企业	Private Enterprises	2308383	2372816
总产值	Gross Output Value	53206451	64275749
#集体企业	Collective-owned Enterprises	315469	391196
私有企业	Private Enterprises	52890982	63884553
工业总产值	Gross Industrial Output Value	34143085	42339018
#集体企业	Collective-owned Enterprises	143993	134213
私有企业	Private Enterprises	33999092	42204805
乡镇企业增加值	Value-added of Township Enterprises	15201225	17280421
#工　业	Industry	9704555	11410238
营业收入	Business Income	52328504	65281891
#集体企业	Collective-owned Enterprises	315923	394126
私有企业	Private Enterprises	52012581	64887765
利润总额	Total Pre-tax Profits	2354782	2852403
实交税金	Taxes Payed	1831498	2184061
#所得税	Income Tax	272728	328046
工资总额	Total Wages	4612512	5904580
#集体企业	Collective-owned Enterprises	77968	97541
私有企业	Private Enterprises	4534544	5806812
年末固定资产原值	Original Value of Fixed Assets at Year-end	17135817	17678705
#集体企业	Collective-owned Enterprises	185257	183376
私有企业	Private Enterprises	16950559	17495329
银行（信用社）贷款余额	Bank (Credit Cooperative) Loan Balance	3476838	3512060

重/庆/统/计/年/鉴

主要统计指标解释

农林牧渔业总产值

指以货币表现的农、林、牧、渔业全部产品和对农林牧渔业生产活动进行的各种支持性服务活动的价值总量，它反映一定时期内农林牧渔业生产总规模和总成果。1957年以前的农林牧渔业总产值中包括了厩肥和农民自给性手工业(如农民自制衣服、鞋、袜，自己从事粮食初步加工等)。1958年及以后，林业中增加了村及村以下竹木采伐产值；牧业中取消了厩肥产值；副业中取消了农民自给性手工业产值，增加了村及村以下办的工业产值； 渔业中增加了海洋捕捞水产品产值。1980年及以后，在副业中增加了农民家庭兼营工业商品部分的产值。从1984年起村及村以下工业产值划归工业。从1993年起取消副业，将野生动物的捕猎划入牧业、野生植物采集和农民家庭兼营商品性工业划归农业。从2003年起，执行新的国民经济行业分类标准，农林牧渔业总产值中包括了农林牧渔服务业产值。林业中增加了森林采运业产值。农业中取消了家庭兼营商品性工业产值，将野生林产品的采集划归林业。第一次农业普查以后，由于畜牧业产品年报数据与普查数据之间存在一定的差距，国家统计局农调总队对畜牧业年报数据与普查数据进行衔接，相应的畜牧业产值进行调整。第二次农业普查后，国家统计局再次对种植业、畜牧业、林业、渔业、服务业数据进行了衔接与调整。

农林牧渔业总产值的计算方法通常是按农、林、牧、渔业产品及其副产品的产量分别乘以各自单位产品价格求得；少数生产周期较长，当年没有产品或产品产量不易统计的，则采用间接方法匡算其产值；然后将五业产值相加即为农林牧渔业总产值。

粮食产量

指全社会的产量。包括国有经济经营的、集体统一经营的和农民家庭经营的粮食产量，还包括工矿企业办的农场和其他生产单位的产量。粮食除包括稻谷、小麦、玉米、高粱、谷子及其他杂粮外，还包括薯类和豆类。其产量计算方法，豆类按去豆荚后的干豆计算；薯类（包括甘薯和马铃薯，不包括芋头和木薯）1963年以前按每4公斤鲜薯折 1 公斤粮食计算，从1964年开始及以后改为按5公斤鲜薯折 1 公斤粮食计算。城市郊区作为蔬菜的薯类（如：马铃薯等）按鲜品计算，并且不作粮食统计。其他粮食一律按脱粒后的原粮计算。1989年以前全国粮食产量数据主要靠全面报表取得，1989年开始使用抽样调查数据。

油料产量

指全部油料作物的生产量。包括花生、油菜籽、芝麻、向日葵籽，胡麻籽（亚麻籽）和其他油料。不包括大豆，也不包括木本油料和野生油料。花生以带壳干花生计算。

水产品产量

指人工养殖的水产品和天然生长的水产品的捕捞量。包括海水的鱼类、虾蟹类、贝类和藻类以及内陆水域的鱼类、虾蟹类和贝类，不包括淡水生植物。水产品产量是通过各级水产和统计部门逐级上报取得数据。1995年及以前，贝类中牡蛎按鲜肉计算；蚶、蛤、蛙按 5 斤鲜品折 1 斤计算。1996年以后则统一按鲜品计算。

肉产量

指人工养殖的水产品和天然生长的水产品的捕捞量。包括海水的鱼类、虾蟹类、贝类和藻类以及内陆水域的鱼类、虾蟹类和贝类，不包括淡水生植物。水产品产量是通过各级水产和统计部门逐级上报取得数据。1995年及以前，贝类中牡蛎按鲜肉计算；蚶、蛤、蛙按 5 斤鲜品折 1 斤计算。1996年以后则统一按鲜品计算。

期初（末）畜禽存栏头（只）数

指报告期初（末）农村各种合作经济组织和国营农场、农民个人、机关、团体、学校、工矿企业，部队等单位以及城镇居民饲养的大牲畜、猪、羊、家禽等畜禽的存栏头（只）数。

农作物播种面积

指实际播种或移植有农作物的面积，凡是实际种

主要统计指标解释

植有农作物的面积，不论种植在耕地上还是种植在非耕地上，均包括在农作物播种面积中。在播种季节基本结束后，因遭灾而重新改种和补种的农作物面积，也包括在内。它是反映我国耕地面积利用情况的一个重要指标。目前，农作物播种面积主要包括粮食、棉花、油料、糖料、麻类、烟叶、蔬菜和瓜类、药材和其它农作物九大类。

■ 有效灌溉面积

指具有一定的水源，地块比较平整，灌溉工程或设备已经配套，在一般年景下当年能够进行正常灌溉的耕地面积。在一般情况下，有效灌溉面积应等于灌溉工程或设备已经配备，能够进行正常灌溉的水田和水浇地面积之和。它是反映我国耕地抗旱能力的一个重要指标。

农用化肥施用量　指本年内实际用于农业生产的化肥数量，包括氮肥、磷肥，钾肥和复合肥。化肥施用量要求按折纯量计算数量。折纯法化肥施用量是把氮肥、磷肥和钾肥分别按含氮、含五氧化二磷、含氧化钾的百分之一百成份折算后的数量。复合肥按其所含主要成分折算。公式为：

折纯量= 实物量 × 某种化肥有效成份含量的百分比

■ 农用化肥施用量

指本年内实际用于农业生产的化肥数量，包括氮肥、磷肥，钾肥和复合肥。化肥施用量要求按折纯量计算数量。折纯法化肥施用量是把氮肥、磷肥和钾肥分别按含氮、含五氧化二磷、含氧化钾的百分之一百成份折算后的数量。复合肥按其所含主要成分折算。公式为：

折纯量= 实物量 × 某种化肥有效成份含量的百分比

■ 农业机械总动力

指主要用于农、林、牧、渔业的各种动力机械的动力总和。包括耕作机械、排灌机械、收获机械、农用运输机械、植物保护机械、牧业机械、林业机械、渔业机械和其他农业机械［内燃机按引擎马力折成瓦（特）计算，电动机按功率折成瓦（特）计算］。不包括专门用于乡、镇、村、组办工业、基本建设、非农业运输、科学试验和教学等非农业生产方面用的动力机械与作业机械。

■ 乡村从业人员

指乡村人口中劳动年龄在16周岁以上实际参加生产经营活动并取得实物或货币收入的人员，包括劳动年龄内经常参加劳动的人员，也包括超过劳动年龄但经常参加劳动的人员，但不包括户口在家的在外学生、现役军人和丧失劳动能力的人，也不包括待业人员和家务劳动者。从业人员按从事主业时间最长（时间相同按收入）分为农业从业人员、工业从业人员、建筑业从业人员、交通运输业、仓储及邮电通信业从业人员、批零贸易及餐饮业从业人员、其他非农行业从业人员。

Explanatory Notes on Main Statistical Indicators

□ Gross Output Value of Farming Forestry, Animal Husbandry and Fishery

Refers to the total value of products of farming, forestry, animal husbandry and fishery, and total value of services rendered to support farming, forestry, animal husbandry and fishery activities. It reflects the total scale and results of agricultural production during a given period. Prior to 1957, Chinas gross agricultural output value included barnyard manure and handicraft products for self-consumption (clothes, shoes, stockings, and initial grain processing undertaken by peasants). Since 1958, cutting and felling of bamboo and trees by villages and other cooperative organizations under villages have been included in forestry; value of barnyard manure has been excluded from animal husbandry; self consumed handicrafts has been excluded from sideline occupations, while the output value of industries run by villages and cooperative organizations under village had been included in sideline occupations and the output value of fish catches by motor fishing boats has been added to fishery. Since 1980, the value of handicraft products made for sale by individuals in households had been added to sideline occupations. Since 1984, industries run by villages and under villages have been included in the sector of industry. Since 1993, the subdivision of sideline occupations has been canceled, and the hunting of wild animals has been classified into animal husbandry, and the gathering of wild plants and commodity industry run by rural household have been included in farming. A new industrial classification of economic activities was introduced in 2003. Under the new classification, value of services to farming, forestry, animal husbandry and fishery is included in the gross output value of agriculture, value of wood felling and transport is included in forestry, value of industrial output by rural households is not included in agriculture, and the collection of wild forest products is taken from agriculture and included in the forestry. The first agriculture census of China revealed some discrepancy between the production of animal products from the annual reports and that from the census. Efforts were made by the Rural Socio-economic Survey Organization of NBS to adjust the output value of animal husbandry to make the figures from the annual reports consistent with the census data. After the Second Agriculture Census of China, the National Bureau of Statistics adjustment the data of farming, animal husbandry, forestry, fisheries and services once again.

Gross output value of agriculture is obtained by first multiplying the output of each product or by product by its price, resulting in the output value of each single item. For a small number of products, annual output of which is not available or difficult to get due to the long production (growing) process involved, the output value is estimated through an indirect approach. The sum of output value of all products of farming, forestry, animal husbandry and fishery is then equal to the gross output value of agriculture.

□ Grain Yield

Refers to the total output in the whole country including grains produced by state farms, collective units, rural households, as well as by farms affiliated to industrial and mining enterprises and other production units. Grain includes rice, wheat, corn, sorghum, millet and other miscellaneous grains as well as tubers and bean. Output of beans refers to dry beans without pods. The output of tubers (sweet potatoes and potatoes, not including taros and cassava) was converted into that of grain at the ratio 4:1, i.e. 4 kilograms of fresh tubers was equivalent to 1 kilogram of grain up to 1963. Since 1964 the ratio for conversion has been 5:1. Tubers supplied as vegetables (such as potatoes) in cities and suburbs are calculated as fresh vegetables and their output is not included in the output of grain. Output of all other grains refers to husked grain. Data on grain production before 1989 were obtained through Comprehensive Statistical Reporting System. Since 1989, data from sample surveys are used.

□ Yield of Oil-bearing Crops

Refers to the total yield of oil-bearing crops of various kinds, including peanuts, (dry, in shell) rapeseeds, sesame, sunflower seeds, flax seeds, and other oil-bearing crops. Soybeans, oil-bearing woody plants, and oil-bearing crops are not included.

□ Output of Aquatic Products

Refers to catches of both artificially cultured and naturally grown aquatic products, including fish, shrimps, crabs and shellfish in sea and inland water as well as seaweed. Freshwater plants are not included. Data on output of aquatic products are reported by aquatic product and statistical agencies level by level. Before 1995, among the shellfish, the oyster was counted as fresh meat; 5 kilograms of ark shell, clams and frogs are equivalent to 1 kilogram of fresh aquatic products; they are all counted as fresh aquatic products since 1996.

□ Output of Meat

Refers to the total meat of livestock. Data, which refers to the meat of slaughtered hogs, cattle, sheep and goats with head, feet and offal taken away, and refers to the meat of slaughtered animials such as rabbit with feather, visceral taken away.

□ Number of Livestock or Poultry in Hand at the Beginning (or End) of the Reference Period

Refers to the total number of large animals, pigs, sheep, fowls, etc., raised by rural cooperative organizations, state farms, rural individuals, government agencies, schools, industrial and mining enterprises, army, and urban residents at the beginning (or end) of the reference period.

□ Sown Area of Crops

Refers to area of land sown or trans-planted with crops regardless of being in cultivated area or non-cultivated area. Area of land resown due to natural disasters is also included. At present, the sown area of crops mainly include the following 9 categories of crops: grain, cotton, oil-bearing crops, sugar crops, fiber crops, Tobacco, Vegetables and melons, medicinal materials and other farm crops.

□ Irrigated Area

Refers to areas that are effectively irrigated, i.e. level land, which has water source and complete sets of irrigation facilities to lift and move adequate water for irrigation purpose under normal conditions. Under normal conditions, irrigated area is the sum of watered fields and irrigated fields where irrigation systems or equipment have been installed for regular irrigation purpose. This important indicator reflects drought resistance capacity of the cultivated land in China.

□ Consumption of Chemical Fertilizers for Farming

Refers to the quantity of chemical fertilizers applied in agriculture in the year, including nitrogenous fertilizer, phosphate fertilizer, potash fertilizer, and compound fertilizer. The consumption of chemical fertilizers is required in calculation to convert the gross weight into weight containing 100% effective component (e.g. 100% nitrogen content in nitrogenous fertilizer, 100% phosphorous pentoxide content in phosphate fertilizer, 100% potassium oxide content in potash fertilizer). Compound fertilizer is converted with its major component. The formula is:

Volume of effective component= physical quantity × effective component of certain chemical fertilizer (%)

□ Total Power of Farm Machinery

Refers to total mechanical power of machinery used in farming, forestry, animal husbandry, and fishery, including sloughing, irrigation and drainage, harvesting, transport, plant protection, stockbreeding, forestry and fishery. The power of internal combustion engines is required to convert horsepower into watts and the power of electric motors is required to be converted into watts. Machinery employed for non-agricultural purposes, such as the machines used in township-run and village-run industry, construction, non-agricultural transport, scientific experiments and teaching, is excluded.

□ Rural Employed Persons

Refer to rural labor forces aged over 16 years old who are engaged in real production and management activities and receive payment in kind or wages, including those covered within the age frame and regularly participating in production activities, and those who are out of the range of age frame and also participating in production activities regularly. Excluding students studying in other places with their permanent residence registered in local areas, servicemen and persons incapable of working; also excluding those who are waiting for jobs and those engaged in household work. Persons employed are classified as rural employed persons; industrial employed persons; construction industry employed persons; transport, storage and telecommunications industries employed persons; whole sales and retail sales trade and catering industry employed persons and other non-agricalture employed persons according to the longest period of employment in major activities (or using income indicator when period of employment is the same).

第12章

工　业

INDUSTRY

B 简要说明 BRIEF INTRODUCTION

本章资料主要包括工业企业主要指标，规模以上（即指年主营业务收入2000万元及以上）工业企业单位数、主要经济指标和效益指标，国有控股工业企业的主要经济指标和效益指标，私营工业企业的主要经济指标和效益指标，外商投资和港澳台投资企业的主要经济指标和效益指标，大中型工业企业的主要经济指标和效益指标，主要工业产品产量以及占全国当年产量的比重。本章资料由市统计局工业处整理提供。

The data in this chapter cover the main indicators of industrial enterprises; the number, main economic indicators and benefit indicators of enterprises above designated size (enterprises with annual revenue from principal business 20 million yuan and above); the main economic indicators and benefit indicators of state-holding industrial enterprises, private industrial enterprises, industrial enterprises with Hong Kong, Macao, Taiwan and foreign funds and large and medium-sized industrial enterprises; the output of major industrial products and their percentage to nation total in this year. The data in this chapter are sorted and provided by Division of Industry Statistics, Chongqing Municipal Bureau of Statistics.

表12.1 工业企业主要指标（1978－2011年）
MAJOR INDICATORS OF INDUSTRIAL ENTERPRISES (1978-2011)

单位：万元 (10 000 yuan)

年 份 Year	单位数（个） Number of Enterprises (unit)	从业人员平均人数（人） Average Emloyment (person)	工业总产值 Industrial Gross Output Value	
			绝对值 Value	指数（上年=100） Index Preceding Year=100
1978	8037	951217	643444	100.0
1980	10963	998963	772307	104.6
1985	9924	1251649	1408126	117.2
1986	12454	1473491	1604215	104.1
1987	11556	1511086	1921043	112.4
1988	11303	1552189	2529674	116.1
1989	10976	1587712	2991130	102.4
1990	10763	1610473	2993490	100.7
1991	10780	1652984	3424558	111.8
1992	9693	1662144	4191279	116.3
1993	9083	1752822	5847377	118.2
1994	9713	1692108	7185418	115.4
1995	11474	1724173	7651109	115.2
1996	2332	1474400	7304148	
1997	2210	1428600	7947952	114.4
1998	2000	1164200	7667894	100.7
1999	1975	1004400	8585525	118.9
2000	2040	907900	9623226	113.6
2001	2054	841900	10728325	115.5
2002	2072	820103	12283741	119.8
2003	2243	843341	15889928	126.7
2004	2634	900546	21427261	129.9
2005	2946	924204	25258684	118.6
2006	3214	968440	32142340	127.4
2007	3942	1082675	43632489	133.6
2008	6119	1321310	57558984	129.3
2009	6412	1372758	67729015	115.2
2010	7130	1465587	91435532	128.4
2011	4778	1457566	118470581	128.2

注：1）本表统计口径1996年以前为全部独立核算工业企业，1996年-2006年为全部国有及规模以上（即年主营业务收入在500万元及以上）非国有工业企业，2007年-2010年为年主营业务收入在500万元及以上的规模以上工业企业，2011年为年主营业务收入在2000万元及以上的规模以上工业企业（下表同）。
2）工业总产值的绝对值按现价计算，由于工业统计制度变更，工业总产值指数2003年及以前按可比价计算，2004年起按现价计算。
3）由于部分指标无法取得，因此2008年工业总产值指数采用2008年12月快报数代替，其余指标均取自2008年经济普查数。

Note: a) The statistic scope of this table is all the industrial enterprises with independent accounting system before 1996, all the state-owned industrial enterprises and non-state-owned industrial enterprises over designated size with annual revenue from principal business of 5 million yuan and above from 1996 to 2006, the industrial enterprises over designated size with annual revenue from principal business of 5 million yuan and above from 2007 to 2010, and the industrial enterprises over designated size with annual revenue from principal business of 20 million yuan and above in 2011 (the same below).
b) Gross output value of industry is calculated at current prices. As industry statistic system has been changed, the index of industrial gross output value in 2003 and previous years is calculated at constant prices, while the index is calculated at current prices since 2004.
c) Because some of the indices are not available, the index of industrial gross output value in 2008 is replaced by the accumulated value in December 2008, and other indices are the data from the census of economy in 2008.

表12.1 续表 continued

单位：万元 (10 000 yuan)

年　份 Year	年末固定资产 Year-end Fixed Assets		流动资产合计 Total Circulating Assets	主营业务收入 Revenue from Principal Business	利税总额 Total Pre-tax Profits	利润总额 Total Profits
	原　值 Original Value	净　值 Net Value				
1978	706016	475301	298093	595593	119300	
1980	823370	540178	329897	708120	146213	
1985	1339800	923111	604983	1449426	260677	
1986	1445859	970019	743986	1559353	225749	
1987	1635303	1135872	908572	1897962	251220	
1988	1830786	1254850	1062157	2472560	358610	
1989	2063326	1405200	1441939	2734475	365348	
1990	2314886	1490850	1942657	2782262	253309	
1991	2585930	1647544	2418353	3338105	291455	
1992	2947902	1784094	2852708	4167995	365134	
1993	3424857	2106423	3484050	6124846	551046	
1994	4953046	2967592	4631636	6294911	573144	
1995	7307273	4057468	5702467	7524836	580345	
1996	7708153	5398622	5749079	7113430	480449	-49429
1997	8578673	5952377	6959065	7981695	460736	-116702
1998	9866758	6940364	7202796	7809127	393220	-193078
1999	10840971	7604150	7733524	8546131	572648	-67491
2000	11515782	7848443	8157646	9593576	855670	156449
2001	12056356	7958216	8874861	10732455	1016889	238170
2002	12730167	8282507	9228472	12357157	1320260	405426
2003	13424490	8576299	10305605	15950727	1910901	859689
2004	14970250	9738481	11641381	21088433	2420163	1155898
2005	16779752	11001178	13571979	25151726	2564825	1155912
2006	20266728	13551444	15484263	32008042	3192103	1557631
2007	24067348	16421036	18541937	42629860	5025623	2405387
2008	30254424	20829025	24807777	56676087	6017115	3086786
2009	34109428	22757818	28630140	66247114	7105030	3560249
2010	44634155	29639590	36084780	90390303	10118841	5185939
2011	50234507	30341715	45089210	113823442	11643029	6603471

表12.2 主要工业产品产量（1978－2011年）
OUTPUT OF MAJOR INDUSTRIAL PRODUCTS (1978-2011)

年 份 Year	原 煤 （万吨） Coal (10 000 tons)	天然气 （亿立方米） Natural Gas (100 million cu.m)	发电量 （亿千瓦时） Electricity (100 million kwh)	钢 材 （万吨） Steel Products (10 000 tons)	铝 材 （万吨） Aluminum Products (10 000 tons)	水 泥 （万吨） Cement (10 000 tons)	汽 车 （万辆） Motor Vehicles (10 000 units)
1978	1429.30	0.09	29.60	73.09	1.47	96.14	0.16
1980	1519.58	15.78	33.32	76.52	2.27	129.10	0.23
1985	2085.66	24.47	36.67	86.35	4.50	262.78	0.89
1986	2109.01	25.88	41.96	94.99	4.55	269.20	0.61
1987	2255.86	28.39	54.73	111.36	5.00	308.29	0.90
1988	2459.97	29.44	66.38	121.06	5.01	353.43	1.66
1989	2540.03	31.96	72.64	102.59	4.99	345.39	2.02
1990	2332.71	34.59	73.75	109.61	3.97	351.85	2.18
1991	2380.45	35.86	84.05	105.67	5.51	428.56	3.04
1992	2432.44	36.44	91.95	112.24	5.55	517.31	4.56
1993	2624.97	37.14	118.41	162.74	5.79	562.32	6.82
1994	2841.32	41.87	124.36	130.74	6.19	642.62	8.77
1995	3104.83	45.00	127.62	120.68	5.93	820.57	11.47
1996	1498.72	26.10	128.73	117.55	7.36	648.76	12.41
1997	1410.35	30.69	139.88	116.08	9.31	862.10	16.07
1998	2573.99	33.24	158.67	131.01	10.62	1173.59	15.74
1999	1183.22	34.74	158.27	135.10	12.11	1197.60	21.85
2000	1149.90	38.98	167.90	156.98	13.98	1402.78	24.59
2001	1154.67	41.88	170.41	161.42	16.82	1511.18	24.38
2002	1211.73	45.41	184.75	201.48	19.94	1679.52	33.13
2003	1484.20	47.29	188.64	235.24	21.60	1927.00	40.45
2004	1738.19	51.57	232.82	288.10	26.23	1906.23	42.89
2005	1957.79	57.09	234.03	294.70	39.36	2100.69	42.15
2006	2172.19	70.88	275.44	382.87	66.41	2533.84	51.99
2007	2711.65	71.11	325.22	436.57	81.13	2819.92	70.80
2008	3702.86	79.50	396.64	487.20	79.76	3230.51	76.64
2009	4290.79	75.70	428.26	477.44	75.15	3610.99	118.65
2010	4547.03	67.48	456.71	699.91	102.79	4598.04	161.58
2011	4464.61	62.94	529.57	948.17	134.45	4935.15	172.20

表12.2 续表 continued

年 份 Year	其中 of which #轿 车（万辆） Cars (10 000 units)	摩托车（万辆） Motorcycles (10 000 units)	电子计算机整机（万台） Computers (10 000 sets)	维纶纤维（万吨） PVA Fiber (10 000 tons)	硫 酸（万吨） Sulphuric Acid (10 000 tons)	啤 酒（万千升） Beer (1000 kiloliters)	卷 烟（亿支） Cigarettes (100 million pieces)	农用化肥（万吨） Chemical Fertilizer (10 000 tons)
1978					12.76		87.70	20.23
1980		0.27			15.85		115.75	13.10
1985		47.18			15.09	3.47	246.70	15.23
1986		31.94			20.86	4.16	314.90	17.28
1987		27.14			23.25	5.18	346.95	21.70
1988		44.47			25.31	6.26	355.65	21.55
1989		36.85			27.33	5.90	356.20	21.60
1990		38.22			25.24	5.91	357.85	24.58
1991		48.48			33.10	6.67	368.85	28.24
1992		69.37			34.28	7.74	439.10	28.86
1993		120.38			25.96	15.61	437.10	31.73
1994		170.23			25.31	16.69	430.65	35.59
1995		220.17			48.84	18.89	502.25	54.37
1996	1.34	177.36		1.71	51.29	28.54	453.91	78.97
1997	2.89	177.04		1.23	52.00	40.05	507.38	66.07
1998	3.56	126.90		0.90	59.47	50.66	369.35	73.40
1999	4.46	174.93		0.63	61.83	50.81	482.85	74.27
2000	4.82	191.07		0.77	50.65	50.42	343.50	72.26
2001	4.31	253.53		1.03	65.77	39.91	338.50	77.57
2002	6.78	323.42		1.11	85.64	41.36	343.80	82.53
2003	12.06	441.32		1.18	99.18	44.42	387.50	89.97
2004	15.73	473.07		1.30	135.51	46.21	386.32	104.22
2005	15.33	420.84		1.56	150.08	53.87	396.08	121.89
2006	26.30	534.60		1.52	190.44	64.73	406.00	127.82
2007	41.80	638.25		1.57	223.78	76.49	426.00	154.20
2008	40.72	774.90		1.47	172.31	68.01	451.00	127.06
2009	63.30	761.74		1.23	202.29	72.77	476.00	152.00
2010	85.17	849.23	193.43	1.26	222.00	75.20	501.00	181.49
2011	93.67	879.59	2547. 82	1.55	176.76	77.31	516.00	169.52

表12.3 工业企业经济效益指标（1992－2011年）
INDICATORS ON ECONOMIC BENEFIT OF INDUSTRIAL ENTERPRISES (1992-2011)

单位：%（%）

年 份 Year	经济效益综合指数 Comprehensive Index of Economic Benefits	总资产贡献率 Ratio of Total Assets to Industrial Output Value	资本保值增值率 Ratio of Assets Appreciation YOY	资产负债率 Asset-Liability Ratio
1992	76.2			
1993	84.6			
1994	83.9			
1995	73.0			
1996	63.8	2.8	125.7	68.6
1997	60.3	2.7	113.9	68.4
1998	57.3	5.0	103.0	68.3
1999	67.7	5.5	101.4	67.1
2000	87.1	6.3	112.1	64.8
2001	95.2	6.9	108.3	62.7
2002	109.8	7.8	120.7	61.3
2003	129.7	9.9	115.8	60.8
2004	140.9	10.6	120.2	60.8
2005	139.4	10.0	116.2	59.7
2006	153.7	10.5	114.4	59.8
2007	187.7	12.6	118.2	59.7
2008	204.0	12.2	117.6	60.0
2009	204.4	12.1	114.6	60.3
2010	226.0	13.6	125.0	60.3
2011	244.1	13.7	120.5	60.7

年 份 Year	流动资产周转率（次） Turnover Ratio of Circulating Assets (time)	成本费用利润率 Ratio of Profits to Cost	全员劳动生产率（元/人年） Overall Labor Productivity (yuan/person-year)	产品销售率 Sales as Percentage of Output
1992	1.4	3.2	7296	97.0
1993	1.6	3.1	10758	97.1
1994	1.4	2.7	12638	96.4
1995	1.2	0.7	11804	96.3
1996	1.3	-1.2	13546	96.5
1997	1.2	-1.8	14972	95.6
1998	1.1	-2.4	16690	97.2
1999	1.1	-1.1	23385	97.5
2000	1.2	1.7	31081	99.1
2001	1.2	2.3	37750	97.9
2002	1.3	3.4	46464	98.1
2003	1.5	5.7	55957	97.8
2004	1.8	5.8	66148	99.9
2005	1.9	4.9	77511	98.8
2006	2.1	5.2	87750	98.4
2007	2.3	6.1	127993	97.1
2008	2.4	5.8	156167	98.0
2009	2.3	5.8	159484	98.3
2010	2.5	6.1	183031	98.1
2011	2.6	6.0	213463	97.4

注：1）经济效益综合指数1997年前由资金利税率、增加值率、流动资产周转率、成本费用利润率、全员劳动生产率、产品销售率等六项指标构成，从1997年起由总资产贡献率、资本保值增值率、资产负债率、流动资产周转率、成本费用利润率、全员劳动生产率、产品销售率等七项指标构成。

2）由于部分指标无法取得，因此2008年资本保值增值率、全员劳动生产率采用2008年12月快报数代替，其余指标均取自2008年经济普查数。

Note: a) Comprehensive index of economic benefits before 1997 are composed of 6 items, namely ratio of pretax profits to total industrial assets, ratio of value-added to gross industrial output value, turnover ratio of circulating assets, ratio of profits to cost, overall labor productivity and sales as percentage of output, and since 1997 are composed of 7 items, namely ratio of total assets to industrial output value, ratio of assets appreciation YOY, asset-liability ratio, turnover ratio of circulating assets, ratio of profits to cost, overall labor productivity and sales as percentage of output.

b)Because some of the indices are not available, the index of industrial gross output value, value-added of industry and its index in 2008 are replaced by the accumulated value in December 2008, and other indices are the data from the census of economy in 2008.

表12.4 规模以上工业企业单位数（2010－2011年）
NUMBER OF INDUSTRIAL ENTERPRISES ABOVE DESIGNATED SIZE (2010-2011)

单位：个 (unit)

指　标	Item	2010	2011
总　计	**Total**	**7130**	**4778**
＃国有控股企业	State-owned and State-holding Enterprises	547	458
＃亏损企业	Loss-generating Enterprises	736	393
按登记注册类型分	**By Status of Registration**		
内资企业	Domestic-funded Enterprises	6806	4493
国有企业	State-owned Enterprises	141	111
集体企业	Collective-owned Enterprises	143	62
股份合作企业	Cooperative Share Holding Enterprises	43	27
国有联营	State Joint Ownership Enterprises	4	2
集体联营	Collective Joint Ownership Enterprises	5	1
国有与集体联营	Joint State-Collective Enterprises	4	2
其他联营	Other Joint Ownership Enterprises	3	1
国有独资公司	Soly State-funded Corporations	108	90
其他有限责任公司	Other Limited Liability Corporations	948	870
股份有限公司	Share-holding Corporations Ltd.	174	144
私营独资	Soly Private-funded Enterprises	1353	691
私营合作	Cooperative Private Enterprises	286	140
私营有限责任公司	Private Limited Liability Corporations	3191	2050
私营股份有限公司	Private Share-holding Corporations Ltd.	372	234
其他内资	Other Enterprises	31	68
港澳台商投资企业	Enterprises Funded by Hong Kong, Macao and Taiwan	123	109
合资经营	Joint-ventures	59	58
合作经营	Cooperative Enterprises	3	2
独　资	Enterprises with Sole Investment	55	44
投资股份有限公司	Share-holding Corporations Ltd.	6	4
其他	Others		1
外商投资企业	Foreign-funded Enterprises	201	176
中外合资经营	Joint-ventures	125	114
中外合作经营	Cooperative Enterprises	7	3
外资企业	Enterprises with Sole Investment	61	56
外商投资股份有限公司	Share-holding Corporations Ltd.	8	2
其他	Others		1
按轻重工业分	**By Light and Heavy Industries**		
轻工业	Light Industry	2712	1800
重工业	Heavy Industry	4418	2978
按企业规模分	**By Size**		
大型企业	Large	73	174
中型企业	Medium	713	953
小型企业	Small	6344	3532
微型企业	Mini		119

注：2011年，企业规模划分根据国家统计局相关标准变更。
Note: In 2011, the classification of enterprise size is changed according to the related standard of the NBS.

表12.5 规模以上工业企业主要产品产量占全国的比重（2011年）

OUTPUT OF MAJOR INDUSTRIAL PRODUCTS OF INDUSTRIA ENTERPRISES ABOVE DESIGNATED SIZED AS PERCENTAGE OF NATION TOTAL (2011)

产　品	Products	全　国 Nation Total	重　庆 Chongqing	重庆占全国比重（%） Chongqing as % of Nation Total
维纶纤维（吨）	PVA Fiber (ton)	58000.0	15464.0	26.7
布（亿米）	Cloth (100 million m)	837.0	5.1	0.6
蚕　丝（万吨）	Silk (10 000 tons)	10.8	0.4	3.5
合成洗涤剂（万吨）	Synthetic Detergents (10 000 tons)	850.8	4.1	0.5
合成洗衣粉（万吨）	Synthetic Washing Powder (10 000 tons)	373.4	2.1	0.6
原　盐（万吨）	Salt (10 000 tons)	6429.4	224.4	3.5
卷　烟（亿支）	Cigarettes (100 million pieces)	24474.0	516.0	2.1
白　酒（万千升）	Liquor (1000 kiloliters)	1025.8	17.4	1.7
啤　酒（万千升）	Beer (1000 kiloliters)	4898.9	77.3	1.6
软饮料（万吨）	Soft Beverage (10 000 tons)	11762.2	298.4	2.5
乳制品（万吨）	Dairy Products (10 000 tons)	2387.5	12.9	0.5
原　煤（亿吨）	Coal (100 million tons)	35.2	0.5	1.3
发电量（亿千瓦小时）	Electricity (100 million kwh)	47000.7	529.6	1.1
天然气（亿立方米）	Natural Gas (100 million cu.m)	1030.6	62.9	6.1
生　铁（万吨）	Pig Iron (10 000 tons)	62969.3	559.4	0.9
粗　钢（万吨）	Crude Steel (10 000 tons)	68388.3	630.5	0.9
成品钢材（万吨）	Steel Products (10 000 tons)	88258.2	948.2	1.1
铝　材（万吨）	Aluminum Products (10 000 tons)	2742.7	134.5	4.9
水　泥（万吨）	Cement (10 000 tons)	208500.0	4935.2	2.4
硫　酸（万吨）	Sulphuric Acid (10 000 tons)	7466.4	176.8	2.4
纯　碱（万吨）	Soda Ash (10 000 tons)	2308.2	113.7	4.9
烧　碱（万吨）	Caustic Soda (10 000 tons)	2466.2	28.5	1.2
农用化学肥料（万吨）	Chemical Fertilizer (10 000 tons)	6217.2	169.5	2.7
化学农药（万吨）	Chemical Pesticides (10 000 tons)	264.8	0.8	0.3
合成氨（万吨）	Synthetic Ammonia (10 000 tons)	5068.7	152.2	3.0
化学原料药（万吨）	Chemical Raw Material Medicine (10 000 tons)	290.1	0.8	0.3
中成药（万吨）	Traditional Chinese Medicine (10 000 tons)	238.4	6.7	2.8
冰醋酸（万吨）	Glacial Acetic Acid (10 000 tons)	424.8	41.2	9.7
精甲醇（万吨）	Refined Methanol (10 000 tons)	2226.9	72.2	3.2
涂　料（万吨）	Paint (10 000 tons)	1079.3	15.2	1.4
卫生陶瓷（万件）	Toilet Wares (10 000 tons)	20065.4	375.7	1.9
变压器（万千伏安）	Transformers (10 000 kilovolt-amperes)	142977.0	2767.7	1.9
汽　车（万辆）	Motor Vehicles (10 000 units)	1841.6	172.2	9.4
#轿　车	Cars	1012.7	93.7	9.3
摩托车（万辆）	Motorcycles (10 000 units)	2732.8	879.6	32.2
微型计算机设备(万台)	Microcomputers (10 000 sets)	32036.7	2547.8	8.0

表12.6 规模以上工业企业主要经济指标（2011年）

MAIN ECONOMIC INDICATORS OF INDUSTRIAL ENTERPRISES ABOVE DESIGNATED SIZE (2011)

指　标	Item	单位数（个） Number of Enterprises (unit)
总　计	**Total**	**4778**
#国有控股企业	State-owned and State-holding Enterprises	458
按登记注册类型分	**By Status of Registration**	
内资企业	Domestic-funded Enterprises	4493
#国有企业	State-owned	111
集体企业	Collective-owned	62
港澳台投资企业	Funded by Hong Kong, Macao and Taiwan	109
外商投资企业	Foreign-funded	176
按轻、重工业分	**By Light and Heavy Industries**	
轻工业	Light Industry	1800
重工业	Heavy Industry	2978
按企业规模分	**By Size**	
大型企业	Large	174
中型企业	Medium	953
小型企业	Small	3532
微型企业	Mini	119
按行业分	**By Sector**	
煤炭开采和洗选业	Mining and Washing of Coal	394
石油和天然气开采业	Extraction of Petroleum and Natural Gas	1
黑色金属矿采选业	Mining and Processing of Ferrous Metal Ores	28
有色金属矿采选业	Mining and Processing of Non-Ferrous Metal Ores	3
非金属矿采选业	Mining and Processing of Nonmetal Ores	74
开采辅助活动	Mining Support Activities	
其他采矿业	Mining of Other Ores	
农副食品加工业	Processing of Food from Agricultural Products	299
食品制造业	Manufacture of Foods	92
酒、饮料和精制茶制造业	Liquor, Beverage and Refined Tea	64
烟草制品业	Manufacture of Tobacco	4
纺织业	Manufacture of Textile	136
纺织服装、鞋、帽制造业	Manufacture of Textile Wearing Apparel, Footware and Caps	56
皮革、毛皮、羽毛（绒）及其制品业	Manufacture of Leather, Fur, Feather and Related Products	100
木材加工和木竹藤棕草制品业	Processing of Timber, Manufacture of Wood, Bamboo, Rattan, Palm and Straw Products	33
家具制造业	Manufacture of Furniture	40
造纸及纸制品业	Manufacture of Paper and Paper Products	92
印刷业、记录媒介的复制	Printing, Reproduction of Recording Media	50
文教、工美、体育和娱乐用品制造业	Manufacture of Culture, Education, Handicraft, Fine Arts, Sports and Entertainment Articles	15
石油加工、炼焦及核燃料加工业	Processing of Petroleum, Coking, Processing of Nuclear Fuel	25
化学原料及化学制品制造业	Manufacture of Raw Chemical Materials and Chemical Products	231
医药制造业	Manufacture of Medicines	97
化学纤维制造业	Manufacture of Chemical Fibers	2
橡胶和塑料制品业	Manufacture of Rubber and Plastics	167
非金属矿物制品业	Manufacture of Non-metallic Mineral Products	396
黑色金属冶炼及压延加工业	Smelting and Pressing of Ferrous Metals	186
有色金属冶炼及压延加工业	Smelting and Pressing of Nonferrous Metals	92
金属制品业	Manufacture of Metal Products	189
通用设备制造业	Manufacture of General Purpose Machinery	223
专用设备制造业	Manufacture of Special Purpose Machinery	126
汽车制造业	Manufacture of Motor Vehicles	533
铁路、船舶、航空航天和其他运输设备制造业	Manufacture of Railway, Ship, Aviation and Other Transporting Equipment	532
电气机械及器材制造业	Manufacture of Electrical Machinery and Equipment	190
通信设备、计算机及其他电子设备制造业	Manufacture of Communication Equipment, Computers and Other Electronic Equipment	67
仪器仪表及文化、办公用机械制造业	Manufacture of Measuring Instruments and Machinery for Cultural Activity and Office Work	75
其他制造业	Other Manufacture	14
废弃资源综合利用业	Comprehensive Utilization of Waste Resources	11
金属制品、机械和设备修理业	Repair of Metal Products, Machinery and Equipment	8
电力、热力的生产和供应业	Production and Supply of Electric Power and Heat Power	75
燃气生产和供应业	Production and Supply of Gas	37
水的生产和供应业	Production and Supply of Water	21

单位：万元 (10 000 yuan)

从业人员平均人数（万人）Average Employment (10 000 persons)	工业总产值 Gross Industrial Output Value	工业销售产值 Sales Value of Industry	其 中 of which #出口交货值 Value of Export Delivery	实收资本 Paid-in Capital	其 中 of which #国家资本 State Capital	#外商资本 Foreign Capital
145.76	**118470581**	**115345158**	**9224768**	**16999938**	**1991256**	**1529271**
42.70	38990511	38006347	920146	8216248	1884110	562944
126.09	91497058	88597817	3739580	13143857	1784545	168931
6.67	4091730	4134166	62387	1591984	333834	
1.26	378478	370986		35932	54	
8.88	10456362	10263694	4331143	1514737	21260	94104
10.79	16517161	16483647	1154045	2341344	185452	1266236
49.59	33761084	32818305	2437087	3992365	258172	255846
96.16	84709497	82526853	6787681	13007574	1733084	1273426
49.69	52817729	51753317	6800606	7133681	677264	854202
51.75	32843565	31708874	1841471	5251288	799985	373830
43.95	32356051	31428541	582691	4470589	514007	282023
0.37	453236	454425		144380		19217
16.11	3773610	3694395	10964	610252	125147	
0.12	100616	95146		1062	240	
0.47	95201	92038		28095	18845	
0.16	46122	36704		1418		
0.90	667683	653533		83015	1608	
4.66	4674147	4571072	93545	283585	16650	27838
2.03	1264710	1229567	26646	132497	6035	
1.84	1233818	1210294	14192	220689	2166	72211
0.54	1199668	1180462		108763	81959	
2.85	1757205	1720957	142583	152925		18690
2.07	647943	580823	94729	52036	100	1666
2.75	901308	890079	23005	35000		
0.46	255297	245756	7102	32588		1550
0.93	601286	603919		36733		
1.63	1313812	1270701	33994	559261	4469	22576
1.07	636885	611807		100391	3907	10397
0.47	154274	149798	19644	25629		3482
0.60	469719	495931	5463	91090		
7.87	7355197	7173540	131479	1728845	196255	248784
3.31	2197862	2086915	120572	457965	53290	667
0.03	71398	71454		1500		
3.10	2468001	2367369	22476	295678	3879	39564
10.20	6076244	5904071	150323	1473287	63964	265012
4.78	7333177	7172135	3800	599702	14743	
2.74	5006688	4684853	193026	718410	97889	
4.74	2812314	2729645	147657	352295	7810	18204
6.30	4453041	4310936	361471	659667	73232	87026
2.53	1950157	1946715	56241	207007	12209	12165
20.08	21993269	21415626	480451	2472761	212262	483924
17.48	12666364	12390845	1811146	1619743	22853	78171
5.89	6906272	6625844	304499	531311	82673	9740
5.93	8154357	8092545	4705556	550014	13865	54431
2.24	1150147	1112097	61592	157750	1577	18652
1.68	743841	682976	38540	211527	26222	
0.16	841662	790875	164071	10084		
0.23	98700	97093		11161		
4.67	5445536	5416728		1887668	772559	14200
0.82	772365	765433		246167	42333	40321
0.57	180684	174483		252369	32516	

表12.6 续表1 continued1

指 标	Item	资 产 Total Assets
总 计	**Total**	**93210985**
#国有控股企业	State-owned and State-holding Enterprises	47765637
按登记注册类型分	**By Status of Registration**	
内资企业	Domestic-funded Enterprises	74652141
#国有企业	State-owned	7560835
集体企业	Collective-owned	220888
港澳台投资企业	Funded by Hong Kong, Macao and Taiwan	7684894
外商投资企业	Foreign-funded	10873951
按轻、重工业分	**By Light and Heavy Industries**	
轻工业	Light Industry	22144174
重工业	Heavy Industry	71066811
按企业规模分	**By Size**	
大型企业	Large	46458265
中型企业	Medium	26240284
小型企业	Small	20098797
微型企业	Mini	413639
按行业分	**By Sector**	
煤炭开采和洗选业	Mining and Washing of Coal	3532745
石油和天然气开采业	Extraction of Petroleum and Natural Gas	48743
黑色金属矿采选业	Mining and Processing of Ferrous Metal Ores	181155
有色金属矿采选业	Mining and Processing of Non-Ferrous Metal Ores	38807
非金属矿采选业	Mining and Processing of Nonmetal Ores	486251
开采辅助活动	Mining Support Activities	
其他采矿业	Mining of Other Ores	
农副食品加工业	Processing of Food from Agricultural Products	1633036
食品制造业	Manufacture of Foods	815596
酒、饮料和精制茶制造业	Liquor, Beverage and Refined Tea	994768
烟草制品业	Manufacture of Tobacco	723539
纺织业	Manufacture of Textile	667665
纺织服装、鞋、帽制造业	Manufacture of Textile Wearing Apparel, Footware and Caps	269773
皮革、毛皮、羽毛（绒）及其制品业	Manufacture of Leather, Fur, Feather and Related Products	245274
木材加工及木竹藤棕草制品业	Processing of Timber, Manufacture of Wood, Bamboo, Rattan, Palm and Straw Products	87030
家具制造业	Manufacture of Furniture	333512
造纸及纸制品业	Manufacture of Paper and Paper Products	1431133
印刷业、记录媒介的复制	Printing, Reproduction of Recording Media	471427
文教、工美、体育和娱乐用品制造业	Manufacture of Culture, Education, Handicraft, Fine Arts, Sports and Entertainment Articles	123613
石油加工、炼焦及核燃料加工业	Processing of Petroleum, Coking, Processing of Nuclear Fuel	234622
化学原料及化学制品制造业	Manufacture of Raw Chemical Materials and Chemical Products	7543067
医药制造业	Manufacture of Medicines	2813839
化学纤维制造业	Manufacture of Chemical Fibers	14569
橡胶和塑料制品业	Manufacture of Rubber and Plastics	1273120
非金属矿物制品业	Manufacture of Non-metallic Mineral Products	6508633
黑色金属冶炼及压延加工业	Smelting and Pressing of Ferrous Metals	4505049
有色金属冶炼及压延加工业	Smelting and Pressing of Nonferrous Metals	3140816
金属制品业	Manufacture of Metal Products	2234865
通用设备制造业	Manufacture of General Purpose Machinery	3748736
专用设备制造业	Manufacture of Special Purpose Machinery	1380015
汽车制造业	Manufacture of Motor Vehicles	15292688
铁路、船舶、航空航天和其他运输设备制造业	Manufacture of Railway, Ship, Aviation and Other Transporting Equipment	8538789
电气机械及器材制造业	Manufacture of Electrical Machinery and Equipment	3824327
通信设备、计算机及其他电子设备制造业	Manufacture of Communication Equipment, Computers and Other Electronic Equipment	3297243
仪器仪表及文化、办公用机械制造业	Manufacture of Measuring Instruments and Machinery for Cultural Activity and Office Work	1083065
其他制造业	Other Manufacture	1192686
废弃资源综合利用业	Comprehensive Utilization of Waste Resources	147139
金属制品、机械和设备修理业	Repair of Metal Products, Machinery and Equipment	28427
电力、热力的生产和供应业	Production and Supply of Electric Power and Heat Power	12335362
燃气生产和供应业	Production and Supply of Gas	997543
水的生产和供应业	Production and Supply of Water	992321

单位：万元 (10 000 yuan)

其　中 of which	固定资产 Fixed Assets		负　债	其　中 of which
#流动资产 Circulating Assets	原　值 Original Value	净　值 Net Value	Total Liabilities	#流动负债 Total Circulating Liabilities
45089210	**50234507**	**30341715**	**56597445**	**41978045**
19843952	26659035	17255361	30039645	20400565
34701186	41705572	25055143	44709404	32535846
2793783	4459912	2598122	4300174	2862319
107408	85349	48788	121693	110037
3920484	3016502	2178891	5127468	3582801
6467540	5512433	3107682	6760572	5859398
12363665	10824117	6096477	12487148	10241863
32725545	39410389	24245238	44110297	31736182
23040910	22889632	14044838	28357965	22176916
12752249	14834727	8553796	16483648	11927891
9114128	12333108	7593010	11453921	7672834
181922	177040	150071	301910	200404
1112205	1638806	1069635	1612334	1187321
23126	35303	12605	16548	16331
99822	27476	16344	116095	107879
28007	12131	10645	30837	29837
144855	234804	159744	199396	156698
892707	799129	500886	843201	731703
403342	481757	278760	435021	347080
463434	580966	357708	562871	531445
512023	336663	160043	324159	272590
333303	478247	287565	348445	220564
147241	118778	94667	121170	106954
141440	667168	68327	124811	95370
33783	56060	43846	28283	27275
238398	70953	50545	181331	175741
539294	699501	569322	736479	401226
229122	268215	178343	229917	164853
71775	42749	30475	37494	30235
109541	117557	63741	146708	129761
3009292	4575205	2734217	4281390	2885381
1424558	922165	616481	1424632	1186354
8778	6761	3539	4586	4586
632731	1562724	430068	723085	593316
2454361	3900198	2700771	4116730	2759735
2262566	1806391	1283884	3317228	2252811
1308668	1899298	1128064	2257635	1333472
1263251	1051230	686431	1374539	1151223
2532011	1294550	749618	2276880	2029231
902643	582384	290304	779486	695668
8908087	6228086	3250580	8710301	7808928
5417781	3663408	1901236	5205355	4535569
2883173	893231	544026	2454172	2157197
2348451	1320250	714864	2490926	2299229
800449	279725	157507	670448	622607
609214	514216	359314	962893	743850
117945	17903	12967	122370	122320
14652	18684	12924	10372	9515
1985963	11910225	8029017	8260980	3523170
464469	429960	281961	539733	323470
216751	691651	500742	518607	207548

表12.6 续表2 continued2

指 标	Item	所有者权益 Creditors' Equity
总 计	**Total**	**36292183**
#国有控股企业	State-owned and State-holding Enterprises	17656241
按登记注册类型分	**By Status of Registration**	
内资企业	Domestic-funded Enterprises	29675521
#国有企业	State-owned	3262612
集体企业	Collective-owned	99027
港澳台投资企业	Funded by Hong Kong, Macao and Taiwan	2536313
外商投资企业	Foreign-funded	4080349
按轻、重工业分	**By Light and Heavy Industries**	
轻工业	Light Industry	9580438
重工业	Heavy Industry	26711745
按企业规模分	**By Size**	
大型企业	Large	18001880
中型企业	Medium	9665605
小型企业	Small	8513813
微型企业	Mini	110886
按行业分	**By Sector**	
煤炭开采和洗选业	Mining and Washing of Coal	1902799
石油和天然气开采业	Extraction of Petroleum and Natural Gas	32195
黑色金属矿采选业	Mining and Processing of Ferrous Metal Ores	65029
有色金属矿采选业	Mining and Processing of Non-Ferrous Metal Ores	7952
非金属矿采选业	Mining and Processing of Nonmetal Ores	285648
开采辅助活动	Mining Support Activities	
其他采矿业	Mining of Other Ores	
农副食品加工业	Processing of Food from Agricultural Products	773696
食品制造业	Manufacture of Foods	377389
酒、饮料和精制茶制造业	Liquor, Beverage and Refined Tea	431666
烟草制品业	Manufacture of Tobacco	399380
纺织业	Manufacture of Textile	317619
纺织服装、鞋、帽制造业	Manufacture of Textile Wearing Apparel, Footware and Caps	147842
皮革、毛皮、羽毛（绒）及其制品业	Manufacture of Leather, Fur, Feather and Related Products	118582
木材加工和木竹藤棕草制品业	Processing of Timber, Manufacture of Wood, Bamboo, Rattan, Palm and Straw Products	58459
家具制造业	Manufacture of Furniture	150191
造纸及纸制品业	Manufacture of Paper and Paper Products	693249
印刷业、记录媒介的复制	Printing, Reproduction of Recording Media	239425
文教、工美、体育和娱乐用品制造业	Manufacture of Culture, Education, Handicraft, Fine Arts, Sports and Entertainment Articles	85963
石油加工、炼焦及核燃料加工业	Processing of Petroleum, Coking, Processing of Nuclear Fuel	86686
化学原料及化学制品制造业	Manufacture of Raw Chemical Materials and Chemical Products	3242926
医药制造业	Manufacture of Medicines	1376215
化学纤维制造业	Manufacture of Chemical Fibers	9983
橡胶和塑料制品业	Manufacture of Rubber and Plastics	514702
非金属矿物制品业	Manufacture of Non-metallic Mineral Products	2367479
黑色金属冶炼及压延加工业	Smelting and Pressing of Ferrous Metals	1172347
有色金属冶炼及压延加工业	Smelting and Pressing of Nonferrous Metals	882381
金属制品业	Manufacture of Metal Products	852048
通用设备制造业	Manufacture of General Purpose Machinery	1437919
专用设备制造业	Manufacture of Special Purpose Machinery	593799
汽车制造业	Manufacture of Motor Vehicles	6563368
铁路、船舶、航空航天和其他运输设备制造业	Manufacture of Railway, Ship, Aviation and Other Transporting Equipment	3316802
电气机械及器材制造业	Manufacture of Electrical Machinery and Equipment	1329662
通信设备、计算机及其他电子设备制造业	Manufacture of Communication Equipment, Computers and Other Electronic Equipment	775048
仪器仪表及文化、办公用机械制造业	Manufacture of Measuring Instruments and Machinery for Cultural Activity and Office Work	412430
其他制造业	Other Manufacture	229793
废弃资源综合利用业	Comprehensive Utilization of Waste Resources	24706
金属制品、机械和设备修理业	Repair of Metal Products, Machinery and Equipment	18032
电力、热力的生产和供应业	Production and Supply of Electric Power and Heat Power	4062092
燃气生产和供应业	Production and Supply of Gas	464062
水的生产和供应业	Production and Supply of Water	472620

单位：万元 (10 000 yuan)

主营业务收入 Revenue from Principal	主营业务成本 Cost of Principal	主营业务税金及附加 Tax and Extra Charges of	本年应交增值税 VAT Payable	主营业务利润 Profit of Principal	利润总额 Total After-tax	利税总额 Total Pre-tax	工资总额 Total Wages
113823442	**97386148**	**1357255**	**3655797**	**15080038**	**6603471**	**11643029**	**6372570**
37263302	31648359	1009305	1537615	4605638	1631259	4195256	2521675
87278976	74471884	994982	2656470	11812110	5307893	8977230	5348946
4115102	3517828	15544	130028	581730	222249	368897	355416
385890	335061	2954	10413	47876	11978	25462	41143
9997904	9184361	20673	267985	792870	274657	563521	466151
16546562	13729903	341600	730368	2475059	1020921	2102279	557473
32581571	26997613	723908	959880	4860050	2129788	3827663	1938478
81241871	70388535	633347	2695917	10219988	4473683	7815366	4434092
50520608	43508437	1070224	1899454	5941947	2444975	5428824	2767348
31393953	26912860	128606	935986	4352487	2042350	3111647	2107304
31440960	26539819	156746	812143	4744395	2112079	3088494	1484840
467921	425033	1679	8213	41209	4068	14063	13079
3726924	2953597	43246	246142	730081	367062	658202	664516
85453	75029	666	1498	9757	4528	6692	9392
98369	54513	1648	11944	42208	-427	13165	16078
35494	29734	99	3114	5661	4698	7911	5136
654462	541334	12063	22107	101065	47339	81521	30136
4559559	3826839	13549	96004	719171	250171	359920	187324
1299260	1039083	5418	44614	254760	94061	144350	73182
1217794	901049	42901	54783	273844	99041	197229	80140
1155830	397686	551063	135875	207081	135492	822431	68030
1774643	1596649	5203	48698	172790	96730	152474	110959
572200	458396	6169	9810	107635	49818	65806	64587
880211	758689	2988	20324	118534	49941	73414	100821
248215	211078	1013	3215	36125	16750	20981	11609
615990	489803	2332	12157	123856	59287	73862	37566
1250235	1064560	5338	33865	180336	87580	126825	55111
586306	489676	2728	19876	93902	60041	82731	34923
154098	109881	1582	5743	42636	25379	32707	13833
495942	418589	2533	12471	74819	41412	56584	27223
7142444	5905707	27331	245710	1209406	447937	721299	382608
2043675	1502965	9782	91097	530928	183950	285057	191453
65092	62843	518	1221	1731	1631	3370	741
2301004	2026270	7988	50703	266746	146731	205653	112575
5838240	4810025	36167	233328	992048	412528	683056	366969
6993935	6184830	12893	164112	796212	238520	416052	211364
4525715	4182761	10268	73800	332686	231746	316443	140235
2725847	2325026	11310	55079	389512	178277	244668	188853
4404922	3611356	18337	118825	775229	377974	516317	285248
1954822	1593695	10011	33721	351117	164394	208287	93994
20870697	17661257	393679	838517	2815761	1292848	2527322	915976
12128282	10734956	53560	263101	1339767	576099	901258	651864
6494793	5702012	23244	143836	769537	436242	603647	229114
7890518	7464089	6562	205826	419868	80350	292759	292340
1066120	840299	4771	40745	221050	77572	123877	115489
659700	630114	1001	5569	28585	34413	42645	98217
788369	762318	1841	17731	24210	9794	29366	5567
96679	83741	458	3598	12481	6888	10966	13701
5429413	5070995	19369	263081	339049	103283	388308	407807
785726	674564	5584	13172	105579	80282	99463	57402
206463	140141	2043	10784	64278	33110	46411	20491

表12.7 规模以上工业企业经济效益指标（2011年）

INDICATORS ON ECONOMIC BENEFIT OF INDUSTRIAL ENTERPRISES ABOVE DESIGNATED SIZE (2011)

指　标	Item	总资产贡献率 Ratio of Total Assets to Industrial Output Value
总　计	**Total**	**13.7**
#国有控股企业	State-owned and State-holding Enterprises	10.0
按登记注册类型分	**By Status of Registration**	
内资企业	Domestic-funded Enterprises	13.2
#国有企业	State-owned	5.8
集体企业	Collective-owned	11.8
港澳台投资企业	Funded by Hong Kong, Macao and Taiwan	8.8
外商投资企业	Foreign-funded	20.2
按轻、重工业分	**By Light and Heavy Industries**	
轻工业	Light Industry	18.3
重工业	Heavy Industry	12.2
按企业规模分	**By Size**	
大型企业	Large	12.7
中型企业	Medium	13.2
小型企业	Small	16.8
微型企业	Mini	4.4
按行业分	**By Sector**	
煤炭开采和洗选业	Mining and Washing of Coal	19.5
石油和天然气开采业	Extraction of Petroleum and Natural Gas	14.0
黑色金属矿采选业	Mining and Processing of Ferrous Metal Ores	8.5
有色金属矿采选业	Mining and Processing of Non-Ferrous Metal Ores	20.4
非金属矿采选业	Mining and Processing of Nonmetal Ores	18.1
开采辅助活动	Mining Support Activities	
其他采矿业	Mining of Other Ores	
农副食品加工业	Processing of Food from Agricultural Products	23.1
食品制造业	Manufacture of Foods	19.0
酒、饮料和精制茶制造业	Liquor, Beverage and Refined Tea	21.0
烟草制品业	Manufacture of Tobacco	114.5
纺织业	Manufacture of Textile	24.0
纺织服装、鞋、帽制造业	Manufacture of Textile Wearing Apparel, Footware and Caps	25.5
皮革、毛皮、羽毛（绒）及其制品业	Manufacture of Leather, Fur, Feather and Related Products	30.9
木材加工和木竹藤棕草制品业	Processing of Timber, Manufacture of Wood, Bamboo, Rattan, Palm and Straw Products	24.8
家具制造业	Manufacture of Furniture	22.7
造纸及纸制品业	Manufacture of Paper and Paper Products	9.8
印刷业、记录媒介的复制	Printing, Reproduction of Recording Media	18.6
文教、工美、体育和娱乐用品制造业	Manufacture of Culture, Education, Handicraft, Fine Arts, Sports and Entertainment Articles	26.7
石油加工、炼焦及核燃料加工业	Processing of Petroleum, Coking, Processing of Nuclear Fuel	25.7
化学原料及化学制品制造业	Manufacture of Raw Chemical Materials and Chemical Products	11.2
医药制造业	Manufacture of Medicines	11.2
化学纤维制造业	Manufacture of Chemical Fibers	24.4
橡胶和塑料制品业	Manufacture of Rubber and Plastics	17.3
非金属矿物制品业	Manufacture of Non-metallic Mineral Products	12.1
黑色金属冶炼及压延加工业	Smelting and Pressing of Ferrous Metals	11.6
有色金属冶炼及压延加工业	Smelting and Pressing of Nonferrous Metals	11.8
金属制品业	Manufacture of Metal Products	12.0
通用设备制造业	Manufacture of General Purpose Machinery	14.5
专用设备制造业	Manufacture of Special Purpose Machinery	15.6
汽车制造业	Manufacture of Motor Vehicles	16.8
铁路、船舶、航空航天和其他运输设备制造业	Manufacture of Railway, Ship, Aviation and Other Transporting Equipment	11.6
电气机械及器材制造业	Manufacture of Electrical Machinery and Equipment	16.9
通信设备、计算机及其他电子设备制造业	Manufacture of Communication Equipment, Computers and Other Electronic Equipment	9.3
仪器仪表及文化、办公用机械制造业	Manufacture of Measuring Instruments and Machinery for Cultural Activity and Office Work	12.4
其他制造业	Other Manufacture	4.6
废弃资源综合利用业	Comprehensive Utilization of Waste Resources	23.5
金属制品、机械和设备修理业	Repair of Metal Products, Machinery and Equipment	38.4
电力、热力的生产和供应业	Production and Supply of Electric Power and Heat Power	5.3
燃气生产和供应业	Production and Supply of Gas	9.6
水的生产和供应业	Production and Supply of Water	5.5

单位：% (%)

资本保值增值率 Ratio of Assets Appreciation YOY	资产负债率 Asset-Liability Ratio	流动资产周转率（次） Turnover Ratio of Circulating Assets (time)	成本费用利润率 Ratio of Profits to Cost	全员劳动生产率（元/人年） Overall Labor Productivity (yuan/person-year)	产品销售率 Sales as Percentage of Output
120.5	**60.7**	**2.6**	**6.0**	**213463**	**97.4**
118.5	62.9	2.0	4.4	243195	97.5
121.9	59.9	2.6	6.4	196968	96.8
122.8	56.9	1.5	5.4	176724	101.0
136.6	55.1	3.7	3.3	98612	98.0
128.9	66.7	2.6	2.7	233203	98.2
109.8	62.2	2.6	6.5	390010	99.8
135.6	56.4	2.7	7.0	182133	97.2
117.9	62.1	2.5	5.6	229620	97.4
115.8	61.0	2.3	4.9	273007	98.0
127.4	62.8	2.5	6.8	172217	96.6
125.1	57.0	3.5	7.2	193791	97.1
69.0	73.0	2.6	0.9	323528	100.3
147.3	45.6	3.5	10.7	117267	97.9
102.4	34.0	3.7	5.6	363999	94.6
86.3	64.1	1.1	-0.4	131657	96.7
116.2	79.5	1.3	14.3	101294	79.6
123.5	41.0	4.5	8.1	220287	97.9
130.7	51.6	5.2	5.9	197199	97.8
128.6	53.3	3.4	7.6	153143	97.2
109.0	56.6	2.7	8.9	205042	98.1
113.4	44.8	2.3	28.1	1712339	98.4
126.4	52.2	5.4	5.7	161141	97.9
114.7	44.9	3.9	9.5	96841	89.6
133.5	50.9	6.5	5.9	105515	98.8
122.3	32.5	7.4	7.5	133266	96.3
118.2	54.4	2.6	10.9	158187	100.4
136.7	51.5	2.3	7.5	200711	96.7
127.0	48.8	2.6	11.0	163035	96.1
125.9	30.3	2.2	21.3	143301	97.1
141.0	62.5	4.5	9.1	207583	105.6
116.3	56.8	2.4	6.6	270440	97.5
143.3	50.6	1.5	9.8	219350	95.0
100.2	31.5	7.4	2.6	613844	100.1
134.5	56.8	3.7	6.7	204228	95.9
115.9	63.3	2.4	7.6	182083	97.2
108.3	73.6	3.1	3.6	285458	97.8
116.7	71.9	3.7	4.9	420132	93.6
113.4	61.5	2.2	7.0	150431	97.1
111.8	60.7	1.8	9.2	200759	96.8
140.1	56.5	2.2	9.1	204952	99.8
122.9	57.0	2.4	6.4	241739	97.4
111.3	61.0	2.3	4.9	174587	97.8
111.5	64.2	2.3	6.9	231916	95.9
150.4	75.6	3.4	1.0	330321	99.2
132.2	61.9	1.4	7.5	150712	96.7
95.1	80.7	1.3	4.4	123930	91.8
91.7	83.2	6.7	1.3	1016045	94.0
120.0	36.5	6.6	7.7	133396	98.4
117.3	67.0	2.8	1.9	365164	99.5
114.3	54.1	1.8	10.7	219770	99.1
126.3	52.3	1.1	16.2	202634	96.6

表12.7 续表 continued

指 标	Item	销售利润率 Rate of Return on Sale
总 计	**Total**	**5.8**
#国有控股企业	State-owned and State-holding Enterprises	4.4
按登记注册类型分	**By Status of Registration**	
内资企业	Domestic-funded Enterprises	6.1
#国有企业	State-owned	5.4
集体企业	Collective-owned	3.1
港澳台投资企业	Funded by Hong Kong, Macao and Taiwan	2.7
外商投资企业	Foreign-funded	6.2
按轻、重工业分	**By Light and Heavy Industries**	
轻工业	Light Industry	6.5
重工业	Heavy Industry	5.5
按企业规模分	**By Size**	
大型企业	Large	4.8
中型企业	Medium	6.5
小型企业	Small	6.7
微型企业	Mini	0.9
按行业分	**By Sector**	
煤炭开采和洗选业	Mining and Washing of Coal	9.8
石油和天然气开采业	Extraction of Petroleum and Natural Gas	5.3
黑色金属矿采选业	Mining and Processing of Ferrous Metal Ores	-0.4
有色金属矿采选业	Mining and Processing of Non-Ferrous Metal Ores	13.2
非金属矿采选业	Mining and Processing of Nonmetal Ores	7.2
开采辅助活动	Mining Support Activities	
其他采矿业	Mining of Other Ores	
农副食品加工业	Processing of Food from Agricultural Products	5.5
食品制造业	Manufacture of Foods	7.2
酒、饮料和精制茶制造业	Liquor, Beverage and Refined Tea	8.1
烟草制品业	Manufacture of Tobacco	11.7
纺织业	Manufacture of Textile	5.5
纺织服装、鞋、帽制造业	Manufacture of Textile Wearing Apparel, Footware and Caps	8.7
皮革、毛皮、羽毛（绒）及其制品业	Manufacture of Leather, Fur, Feather and Related Products	5.7
木材加工和木竹藤棕草制品业	Processing of Timber, Manufacture of Wood, Bamboo, Rattan, Palm and Straw Products	6.7
家具制造业	Manufacture of Furniture	9.6
造纸及纸制品业	Manufacture of Paper and Paper Products	7.0
印刷业、记录媒介的复制	Printing, Reproduction of Recording Media	10.2
文教、工美、体育和娱乐用品制造业	Manufacture of Culture, Education, Handicraft, Fine Arts, Sports and Entertainment Articles	16.5
石油加工、炼焦及核燃料加工业	Processing of Petroleum, Coking, Processing of Nuclear Fuel	8.4
化学原料及化学制品制造业	Manufacture of Raw Chemical Materials and Chemical Products	6.3
医药制造业	Manufacture of Medicines	9.0
化学纤维制造业	Manufacture of Chemical Fibers	2.5
橡胶和塑料制品业	Manufacture of Rubber and Plastics	6.4
非金属矿物制品业	Manufacture of Non-metallic Mineral Products	7.1
黑色金属冶炼及压延加工业	Smelting and Pressing of Ferrous Metals	3.4
有色金属冶炼及压延加工业	Smelting and Pressing of Nonferrous Metals	5.1
金属制品业	Manufacture of Metal Products	6.5
通用设备制造业	Manufacture of General Purpose Machinery	8.6
专用设备制造业	Manufacture of Special Purpose Machinery	8.4
汽车制造业	Manufacture of Motor Vehicles	6.2
铁路、船舶、航空航天和其他运输设备制造业	Manufacture of Railway, Ship, Aviation and Other Transporting Equipment	4.8
电气机械及器材制造业	Manufacture of Electrical Machinery and Equipment	6.7
通信设备、计算机及其他电子设备制造业	Manufacture of Communication Equipment, Computers and Other Electronic Equipment	1.0
仪器仪表及文化、办公用机械制造业	Manufacture of Measuring Instruments and Machinery for Cultural Activity and Office Work	7.3
其他制造业	Other Manufacture	5.2
废弃资源综合利用业	Comprehensive Utilization of Waste Resources	1.2
金属制品、机械和设备修理业	Repair of Metal Products, Machinery and Equipment	7.1
电力、热力的生产和供应业	Production and Supply of Electric Power and Heat Power	1.9
燃气生产和供应业	Production and Supply of Gas	10.2
水的生产和供应业	Production and Supply of Water	16.0

资本积累率 Rate of Capital Accumulation	流动比率 Current Ratio	速动比率 Quick Ratio	产权比率 Equity Ratio	人均实现利税（元） Per Capita Pre-tax Profits (yuan)	从业人员人均工资（元） Per Capita Wages of Employees (yuan)
20.5	**1.1**	**0.8**	**1.6**	**79880**	**43721**
18.5	1.0	0.7	1.7	98242	59051
21.9	1.1	0.8	1.5	71196	42421
22.8	1.0	0.8	1.3	55302	53281
36.6	1.0	0.6	1.2	20187	32619
28.9	1.1	0.8	2.0	63477	52509
9.8	1.1	0.9	1.7	194870	51675
35.6	1.2	0.9	1.3	77180	39087
17.9	1.0	0.8	1.7	81272	46110
15.8	1.0	0.8	1.6	109257	55694
27.4	1.1	0.8	1.7	60129	40721
25.1	1.2	0.9	1.3	70270	33783
-31.0	0.9	0.8	2.7	38361	35675
47.3	0.9	0.8	0.8	40845	41237
2.4	1.4	1.3	0.5	57052	80068
-13.7	0.9	0.8	1.8	28191	34428
16.2	0.9	0.5	3.9	48835	31704
23.5	0.9	0.7	0.7	90639	33507
30.7	1.2	0.9	1.1	77264	40213
28.6	1.2	0.9	1.2	71263	36129
9.0	0.9	0.6	1.3	106981	43469
13.4	1.9	0.8	0.8	1536679	127112
26.4	1.5	1.0	1.1	53503	38936
14.7	1.4	0.7	0.8	31837	31247
33.5	1.5	0.9	1.1	26728	36706
22.3	1.2	0.8	0.5	46082	25497
18.2	1.4	1.1	1.2	79387	40376
36.7	1.3	1.0	1.1	77830	33821
27.0	1.4	1.1	1.0	77045	32523
25.9	2.4	1.9	0.4	70066	29633
41.0	0.8	0.4	1.7	94670	45546
16.3	1.0	0.8	1.3	91670	48626
43.3	1.2	1.0	1.0	86123	57842
0.2	1.9	1.1	0.5	101515	22322
34.5	1.1	0.7	1.4	66299	36292
15.9	0.9	0.7	1.7	66994	35992
8.3	1.0	0.6	2.8	87038	44217
16.7	1.0	0.6	2.6	115549	51207
13.4	1.1	0.9	1.6	51666	39879
11.8	1.2	1.0	1.6	81901	45247
40.1	1.3	1.0	1.3	82200	37095
22.9	1.1	0.9	1.3	121205	43928
11.3	1.2	1.0	1.6	51566	37296
11.5	1.3	1.0	1.8	102527	38914
50.4	1.0	0.8	3.2	49362	49292
32.2	1.3	1.0	1.6	55379	51629
-4.9	0.8	0.6	4.2	25371	58431
-8.3	1.0	0.8	5.0	183768	34839
20.0	1.5	1.4	0.6	47023	58750
17.3	0.6	0.5	2.0	83226	87405
14.3	1.4	1.4	1.2	121936	70371
26.3	1.0	1.0	1.1	80742	35649

表12.8 国有控股工业企业主要经济指标（2011年）
MAIN ECONOMIC INDICATORS OF STATE-HOLDING INDUSTRIAL ENTERPRISES (2011)

指　标	Item	单位数（个） Number of Enterprises (unit)
总　计	**Total**	**458**
按登记注册类型分	**By Status of Registration**	
内资企业	Domestic-funded Enterprises	430
#国有企业	State-owned	111
集体企业	Collective-owned	
港澳台投资企业	Funded by Hong Kong, Macao and Taiwan	5
外商投资企业	Foreign-funded	23
按轻、重工业分	**By Light and Heavy Industries**	
轻工业	Light Industry	104
重工业	Heavy Industry	354
按企业规模分	**By Size**	
大型企业	Large	74
中型企业	Medium	183
小型企业	Small	197
微型企业	Mini	4
按行业分	**By Sector**	
煤炭开采和洗选业	Mining and Washing of Coal	20
石油和天然气开采业	Extraction of Petroleum and Natural Gas	1
黑色金属矿采选业	Mining and Processing of Ferrous Metal Ores	1
有色金属矿采选业	Mining and Processing of Non-Ferrous Metal Ores	
非金属矿采选业	Mining and Processing of Nonmetal Ores	2
开采辅助活动	Mining Support Activities	
其他采矿业	Mining of Other Ores	
农副食品加工业	Processing of Food from Agricultural Products	21
食品制造业	Manufacture of Foods	7
酒、饮料和精制茶制造业	Liquor, Beverage and Refined Tea	4
烟草制品业	Manufacture of Tobacco	4
纺织业	Manufacture of Textile	2
纺织服装、鞋、帽制造业	Manufacture of Textile Wearing Apparel, Footware and Caps	
皮革、毛皮、羽毛（绒）及其制品业	Manufacture of Leather, Fur, Feather and Related Products	2
木材加工和木竹藤棕草制品业	Processing of Timber, Manufacture of Wood, Bamboo, Rattan, Palm and Straw Products	1
家具制造业	Manufacture of Furniture	
造纸及纸制品业	Manufacture of Paper and Paper Products	2
印刷业、记录媒介的复制	Printing, Reproduction of Recording Media	5
文教、工美、体育和娱乐用品制造业	Manufacture of Culture, Education, Handicraft, Fine Arts, Sports and Entertainment Articles	
石油加工、炼焦及核燃料加工业	Processing of Petroleum, Coking, Processing of Nuclear Fuel	2
化学原料及化学制品制造业	Manufacture of Raw Chemical Materials and Chemical Products	41
医药制造业	Manufacture of Medicines	13
化学纤维制造业	Manufacture of Chemical Fibers	
橡胶和塑料制品业	Manufacture of Rubber and Plastics	6
非金属矿物制品业	Manufacture of Non-metallic Mineral Products	26
黑色金属冶炼及压延加工业	Smelting and Pressing of Ferrous Metals	13
有色金属冶炼及压延加工业	Smelting and Pressing of Nonferrous Metals	17
金属制品业	Manufacture of Metal Products	11
通用设备制造业	Manufacture of General Purpose Machinery	26
专用设备制造业	Manufacture of Special Purpose Machinery	10
汽车制造业	Manufacture of Motor Vehicles	42
铁路、船舶、航空航天和其他运输设备制造业	Manufacture of Railway, Ship, Aviation and Other Transporting Equipment	25
电气机械及器材制造业	Manufacture of Electrical Machinery and Equipment	14
通信设备、计算机及其他电子设备制造业	Manufacture of Communication Equipment, Computers and Other Electronic Equipment	8
仪器仪表及文化、办公用机械制造业	Manufacture of Measuring Instruments and Machinery for Cultural Activity and Office Work	22
其他制造业	Other Manufacture	4
废弃资源综合利用业	Comprehensive Utilization of Waste Resources	
金属制品、机械和设备修理业	Repair of Metal Products, Machinery and Equipment	
电力、热力的生产和供应业	Production and Supply of Electric Power and Heat Power	68
燃气生产和供应业	Production and Supply of Gas	21
水的生产和供应业	Production and Supply of Water	17

单位：万元 (10 000 yuan)

从业人员平均人数（万人）Average Employment (10 000 persons)	工业总产值 Gross Output Value	工业销售产值 Sales Value of Industry	其 中 of which	实收资本 Paid-in Capital	其 中 of which	
			#出口交货值 Value of Export Delivery		#国家资本 State Capital	#外商资本 Foreign Capital
42.70	**38990511**	**38006347**	**920146**	**8216248**	**1884110**	**562944**
36.58	27561451	26575420	577465	6866949	1710574	127189
6.67	4091730	4134166	62387	1591984	333834	
2.00	2920964	2845361	1829	377366	10015	35000
4.12	8508096	8585565	340852	971933	163521	400754
7.46	5157375	4952819	307137	1092358	227838	40426
35.24	33833137	33053528	613009	7123891	1656272	522518
27.93	29202512	28569060	688050	4789936	663628	529071
11.75	6335674	6170366	172835	2002816	758551	12143
2.96	3428011	3242097	59261	1382609	461931	21729
0.07	24315	24824		40888		
6.14	935591	910468		368442	124471	
0.12	100616	95146		1062	240	
0.11	36295	37227		18845	18845	
0.02	23404	22666		1100	100	
0.69	897651	848730	32479	67177	14006	
0.51	323987	315203		45653	6035	
0.18	121468	97737		18049	200	
0.54	1199668	1180462		108763	81959	
0.13	40863	34218	2689	10880		
0.23	44713	43225		6541		
0.01	4820	4231		2000		
0.05	21150	20326		13758		
0.16	25067	25550		6617	3907	388
0.19	170618	207542		21630		
3.44	2765853	2764251	75639	858160	182292	6417
1.21	698481	681559	60978	165639	41094	
0.25	222298	221176		46818	3858	
1.40	756480	749596	119813	391761	54904	72279
2.08	3001344	2972654		262612	14743	
1.20	2004853	1791683	93278	572071	95593	
1.30	618251	604122	12261	154269	3291	
2.46	1997836	1904972	24652	378400	57281	21592
0.57	480641	506287	858	58583	11948	5333
7.50	12452998	12106912	94708	1399860	204566	372612
2.41	1546837	1504544	241622	501741	22853	39920
0.68	466312	415612	15498	98044	58348	
0.52	570496	583653	91009	90939	8369	2150
1.32	659797	639197	31033	80886	1577	7253
1.48	609945	562189	23629	207612	26222	
4.60	5392769	5366126		1837714	772559	
0.70	670961	666766		217841	42333	35000
0.49	128450	122316		202784	32516	

表12.8 续表1 continued1

指 标	Item	资 产 Total Assets
总 计	**Total**	**47765637**
按登记注册类型分	**By Status of Registration**	
内资企业	Domestic-funded Enterprises	39518877
#国有企业	State-owned	7560835
集体企业	Collective-owned	
港澳台投资企业	Funded by Hong Kong, Macao and Taiwan	3299176
外商投资企业	Foreign-funded	4947584
按轻、重工业分	**By Light and Heavy Industries**	
轻工业	Light Industry	5794878
重工业	Heavy Industry	41970759
按企业规模分	**By Size**	
大型企业	Large	32298685
中型企业	Medium	9376343
小型企业	Small	5935759
微型企业	Mini	154850
按行业分	**By Sector**	
煤炭开采和洗选业	Mining and Washing of Coal	2232924
石油和天然气开采业	Extraction of Petroleum and Natural Gas	48743
黑色金属矿采选业	Mining and Processing of Ferrous Metal Ores	83469
有色金属矿采选业	Mining and Processing of Non-Ferrous Metal Ores	
非金属矿采选业	Mining and Processing of Nonmetal Ores	10554
开采辅助活动	Mining Support Activities	
其他采矿业	Mining of Other Ores	
农副食品加工业	Processing of Food from Agricultural Products	318167
食品制造业	Manufacture of Foods	255410
酒、饮料和精制茶制造业	Liquor, Beverage and Refined Tea	146713
烟草制品业	Manufacture of Tobacco	723539
纺织业	Manufacture of Textile	24718
纺织服装、鞋、帽制造业	Manufacture of Textile Wearing Apparel, Footware and Caps	
皮革、毛皮、羽毛（绒）及其制品业	Manufacture of Leather, Fur, Feather and Related Products	38287
木材加工和木竹藤棕草制品业	Processing of Timber, Manufacture of Wood, Bamboo, Rattan, Palm and Straw Products	3664
家具制造业	Manufacture of Furniture	
造纸及纸制品业	Manufacture of Paper and Paper Products	28643
印刷业、记录媒介的复制	Printing, Reproduction of Recording Media	34048
文教、工美、体育和娱乐用品制造业	Manufacture of Culture, Education, Handicraft, Fine Arts, Sports and Entertainment Articles	
石油加工、炼焦及核燃料加工业	Processing of Petroleum, Coking, Processing of Nuclear Fuel	73929
化学原料及化学制品制造业	Manufacture of Raw Chemical Materials and Chemical Products	4061685
医药制造业	Manufacture of Medicines	1277511
化学纤维制造业	Manufacture of Chemical Fibers	
橡胶和塑料制品业	Manufacture of Rubber and Plastics	192472
非金属矿物制品业	Manufacture of Non-metallic Mineral Products	1527167
黑色金属冶炼及压延加工业	Smelting and Pressing of Ferrous Metals	2854309
有色金属冶炼及压延加工业	Smelting and Pressing of Nonferrous Metals	2015217
金属制品业	Manufacture of Metal Products	995116
通用设备制造业	Manufacture of General Purpose Machinery	2325772
专用设备制造业	Manufacture of Special Purpose Machinery	589449
汽车制造业	Manufacture of Motor Vehicles	9112030
铁路、船舶、航空航天和其他运输设备制造业	Manufacture of Railway, Ship, Aviation and Other Transporting Equipment	1774104
电气机械及器材制造业	Manufacture of Electrical Machinery and Equipment	830953
通信设备、计算机及其他电子设备制造业	Manufacture of Communication Equipment, Computers and Other Electronic Equipment	545004
仪器仪表及文化、办公用机械制造业	Manufacture of Measuring Instruments and Machinery for Cultural Activity and Office Work	698405
其他制造业	Other Manufacture	1152616
废弃资源综合利用业	Comprehensive Utilization of Waste Resources	
金属制品、机械和设备修理业	Repair of Metal Products, Machinery and Equipment	
电力、热力的生产和供应业	Production and Supply of Electric Power and Heat Power	12146923
燃气生产和供应业	Production and Supply of Gas	833652
水的生产和供应业	Production and Supply of Water	810445

单位：万元 (10 000 yuan)

其 中 of which	固定资产 Fixed Assets		负 债	其 中 of which
#流动资产 Circulating Assets	原 值 Original Value	净 值 Net Value	Total Liabilities	#流动负债 Total Circulating Liabilities
19843952	**26659035**	**17255361**	**30039645**	**20400565**
15264529	23309212	15045843	24517125	16183776
2793783	4459912	2598122	4300174	2862319
1528233	1023868	896016	2463355	1484139
3051190	2325955	1313503	3059165	2732651
2925855	2594907	1638341	3680669	2895575
16918097	24064128	15617020	26358975	17504990
14334698	17461724	10413830	19524012	14532092
3920233	5076383	3519882	6537525	4290431
1565994	4019902	3226784	3863827	1531943
23028	101026	94865	114281	46099
595417	942911	374649	1027478	754952
23126	35303	22698	16548	16331
32082	13229	4705	60427	60427
1359	10522	1486	6670	3469
138889	150238	36982	135255	124063
97101	148439	36661	177723	119741
87501	51561	13761	115526	111807
512023	336663	176620	324159	272590
13715	9648	2845	10850	5737
29605	11291	6073	21070	11840
1605	3875	2359	1681	1633
11970	16889	2382	29762	26633
23955	24314	11400	19710	15969
45987	48612	29722	45664	42799
1420661	2311904	946576	2351691	1644183
706736	358664	92228	857625	715488
53910	137296	29223	159602	138688
483005	1043649	286192	958575	638072
1411775	851540	104300	2309224	1439329
600450	1230855	370836	1525084	727781
504786	506180	101368	629228	496392
1695925	601221	214138	1471332	1299329
419221	126724	24026	427851	389195
5177590	3479734	1761817	4834993	4425007
1058056	600200	289466	1269202	1095967
671020	133057	53654	598310	510102
380016	154067	56043	271541	254838
526138	168567	77552	464171	426123
581919	501066	152621	945138	731611
1965374	11749981	3835725	8120500	3477565
376225	357847	128987	446948	270936
196812	542990	156583	406111	151969

表12.8 续表2 continued2

指　标	Item	所有者权益 Creditors' Equity
总　计	**Total**	**17656241**
按登记注册类型分	**By Status of Registration**	
内资企业	Domestic-funded Enterprises	14952000
#国有企业	State-owned	3262612
集体企业	Collective-owned	
港澳台投资企业	Funded by Hong Kong, Macao and Taiwan	835822
外商投资企业	Foreign-funded	1868419
按轻、重工业分	**By Light and Heavy Industries**	
轻工业	Light Industry	2110423
重工业	Heavy Industry	15545819
按企业规模分	**By Size**	
大型企业	Large	12716328
中型企业	Medium	2838419
小型企业	Small	2060924
微型企业	Mini	40569
按行业分	**By Sector**	
煤炭开采和洗选业	Mining and Washing of Coal	1205446
石油和天然气开采业	Extraction of Petroleum and Natural Gas	32195
黑色金属矿采选业	Mining and Processing of Ferrous Metal Ores	23042
有色金属矿采选业	Mining and Processing of Non-Ferrous Metal Ores	
非金属矿采选业	Mining and Processing of Nonmetal Ores	3884
开采辅助活动	Mining Support Activities	
其他采矿业	Mining of Other Ores	
农副食品加工业	Processing of Food from Agricultural Products	180224
食品制造业	Manufacture of Foods	77688
酒、饮料和精制茶制造业	Liquor, Beverage and Refined Tea	31187
烟草制品业	Manufacture of Tobacco	399380
纺织业	Manufacture of Textile	13869
纺织服装、鞋、帽制造业	Manufacture of Textile Wearing Apparel, Footware and Caps	
皮革、毛皮、羽毛（绒）及其制品业	Manufacture of Leather, Fur, Feather and Related Products	17217
木材加工和木竹藤棕草制品业	Processing of Timber, Manufacture of Wood, Bamboo, Rattan, Palm and Straw Products	1983
家具制造业	Manufacture of Furniture	
造纸及纸制品业	Manufacture of Paper and Paper Products	-1119
印刷业、记录媒介的复制	Printing, Reproduction of Recording Media	14337
文教、工美、体育和娱乐用品制造业	Manufacture of Culture, Education, Handicraft, Fine Arts, Sports and Entertainment Articles	
石油加工、炼焦及核燃料加工业	Processing of Petroleum, Coking, Processing of Nuclear Fuel	28264
化学原料及化学制品制造业	Manufacture of Raw Chemical Materials and Chemical Products	1697845
医药制造业	Manufacture of Medicines	419882
化学纤维制造业	Manufacture of Chemical Fibers	
橡胶和塑料制品业	Manufacture of Rubber and Plastics	32870
非金属矿物制品业	Manufacture of Non-metallic Mineral Products	568592
黑色金属冶炼及压延加工业	Smelting and Pressing of Ferrous Metals	545075
有色金属冶炼及压延加工业	Smelting and Pressing of Nonferrous Metals	490067
金属制品业	Manufacture of Metal Products	365888
通用设备制造业	Manufacture of General Purpose Machinery	827788
专用设备制造业	Manufacture of Special Purpose Machinery	161201
汽车制造业	Manufacture of Motor Vehicles	4276279
铁路、船舶、航空航天和其他运输设备制造业	Manufacture of Railway, Ship, Aviation and Other Transporting Equipment	505208
电气机械及器材制造业	Manufacture of Electrical Machinery and Equipment	232393
通信设备、计算机及其他电子设备制造业	Manufacture of Communication Equipment, Computers and Other Electronic Equipment	253464
仪器仪表及文化、办公用机械制造业	Manufacture of Measuring Instruments and Machinery for Cultural Activity and Office Work	234234
其他制造业	Other Manufacture	207478
废弃资源综合利用业	Comprehensive Utilization of Waste Resources	
金属制品、机械和设备修理业	Repair of Metal Products, Machinery and Equipment	
电力、热力的生产和供应业	Production and Supply of Electric Power and Heat Power	4014185
燃气生产和供应业	Production and Supply of Gas	392956
水的生产和供应业	Production and Supply of Water	403241

单位：万元 (10 000 yuan)

主营业务收入 Revenue from Principal Business	主营业务成本 Cost of Principal Business	主营业务税金及附加 Tax and Extra Charges of Principal Business	主营业务利润 Profit of Principal Business	利润总额 Total After-tax Profits	利税总额 Total Pre-tax Profits	工资总额 Total Wages
37263302	**31648359**	**1009305**	**4605638**	**1631259**	**4195256**	**2521675**
26040397	22259713	695846	3084838	1133718	2833419	2129955
4115102	3517828	15544	581730	222249	368897	355416
2716168	2562998	4041	149129	-16594	17904	131552
8506738	6825648	309418	1371671	514136	1343933	260168
4896478	3474198	582993	839287	266510	1105920	435480
32366824	28174161	426312	3766351	1364749	3089336	2086196
27758669	23495348	971939	3291382	1235320	3464075	1806138
6241058	5454241	24400	762417	184775	415823	567490
3256115	2693997	12952	549166	210627	314681	145676
7460	4773	14	2673	537	677	2372
961117	825154	11111	124853	26062	126675	294700
85453	75029	666	9757	4528	6692	9392
41118	30029	723	10367	-1667	2772	5157
22770	15104	121	7545	5607	5912	537
837394	642480	981	193933	25574	37081	39601
320201	257462	1341	61399	16364	29078	20841
97643	59678	15249	22716	7039	29407	6533
1155830	397686	551063	207081	135492	822431	68030
57562	43266	309	13988	4913	6038	3020
39352	34502	155	4696	1363	2988	7679
4859	4564	28	267	-7	273	271
21095	20794	26	276	91	328	1899
25419	20544	84	4790	889	2446	3784
207120	180632	1100	25388	8803	15497	13216
2758587	2338381	7001	413205	127352	238931	207758
659297	484269	3506	171522	31469	71033	106036
216299	201855	178	14265	-570	6112	6422
732756	606940	5570	120246	24013	67470	74770
2820834	2702870	2211	115753	-45512	-9968	120710
1762450	1687794	1685	72971	19590	34111	72454
603258	515043	3713	84501	28586	37726	55832
1898006	1480904	8522	408580	231295	314577	147197
505564	397912	5778	101875	65986	82311	35556
11703462	9770412	349370	1583681	602630	1551801	413223
1313726	1199740	8505	105482	31536	79001	107593
514452	459595	1114	53743	250	9834	31296
560451	496815	479	63157	26610	28836	23177
590701	452621	2983	135097	39028	68917	83494
538675	523195	355	15125	25780	29807	89212
5379567	5032067	19124	328377	99772	382665	405475
681744	589652	4854	87238	64429	81127	53026
146544	101373	1401	43769	23966	33349	13783

表12.9 国有控股工业企业经济效益指标（2011年）

INDICATORS ON ECONOMIC BENEFIT OF STATE-HOLDING INDUSTRIAL ENTERPRISES (2011)

指 标	Item	总资产贡献率 Ratio of Total Assets to Industrial Output Value
总 计	**Total**	**10.0**
按轻、重工业分	**By Light and Heavy Industries**	
轻工业	Light Industry	20.2
重工业	Heavy Industry	8.6
按企业规模分	**By Size**	
大型企业	Large	11.7
中型企业	Medium	5.7
小型企业	Small	7.3
微型企业	Mini	1.8
按行业分	**By Sector**	
煤炭开采和洗选业	Mining and Washing of Coal	6.4
石油和天然气开采业	Extraction of Petroleum and Natural Gas	14.0
黑色金属矿采选业	Mining and Processing of Ferrous Metal Ores	5.2
有色金属矿采选业	Mining and Processing of Non-Ferrous Metal Ores	
非金属矿采选业	Mining and Processing of Nonmetal Ores	57.5
开采辅助活动	Mining Support Activities	
其他采矿业	Mining of Other Ores	
农副食品加工业	Processing of Food from Agricultural Products	12.6
食品制造业	Manufacture of Foods	13.7
酒、饮料和精制茶制造业	Liquor, Beverage and Refined Tea	21.5
烟草制品业	Manufacture of Tobacco	114.5
纺织业	Manufacture of Textile	24.9
纺织服装、服饰业	Manufacture of Textile Wearing Apparel, Footware and Caps	
皮革、毛皮、羽毛（绒）及其制品业	Manufacture of Leather, Fur, Feather and Related Products	7.8
木材加工和木竹藤棕草制品业	Processing of Timber, Manufacture of Wood, Bamboo, Rattan, Palm and Straw Products	9.5
家具制造业	Manufacture of Furniture	
造纸及纸制品业	Manufacture of Paper and Paper Products	2.3
印刷业、记录媒介的复制	Printing, Reproduction of Recording Media	8.3
文教、工美、体育和娱乐用品制造业	Manufacture of Culture, Education, Handicraft, Fine Arts, Sports and Entertainment Articles	
石油加工、炼焦及核燃料加工业	Processing of Petroleum, Coking, Processing of Nuclear Fuel	22.9
化学原料及化学制品制造业	Manufacture of Raw Chemical Materials and Chemical Products	7.3
医药制造业	Manufacture of Medicines	7.2
化学纤维制造业	Manufacture of Chemical Fibers	
橡胶和塑料制品业	Manufacture of Rubber and Plastics	3.4
非金属矿物制品业	Manufacture of Non-metallic Mineral Products	6.7
黑色金属冶炼及压延加工业	Smelting and Pressing of Ferrous Metals	2.6
有色金属冶炼及压延加工业	Smelting and Pressing of Nonferrous Metals	2.9
金属制品业	Manufacture of Metal Products	4.8
通用设备制造业	Manufacture of General Purpose Machinery	14.3
专用设备制造业	Manufacture of Special Purpose Machinery	14.1
汽车制造业	Manufacture of Motor Vehicles	16.7
铁路、船舶、航空航天和其他运输设备制造业	Manufacture of Railway, Ship, Aviation and Other Transporting Equipment	5.5
电气机械及器材制造业	Manufacture of Electrical Machinery and Equipment	3.0
计算机、通信和其他电子设备制造业	Manufacture of Communication Equipment, Computers and Other Electronic Equipment	5.3
仪器仪表及文化、办公用机械制造业	Manufacture of Measuring Instruments and Machinery for Cultural Activity and Office Work	10.8
其他制造业	Other Manufacture	3.6
废弃资源综合利用业	Comprehensive Utilization of Waste Resources	
金属制品、机械和设备修理业	Repair of Metal Products, Machinery and Equipment	
电力、热力的生产和供应业	Production and Supply of Electric Power and Heat Power	5.3
燃气生产和供应业	Production and Supply of Gas	9.2
水的生产和供应业	Production and Supply of Water	4.6

单位：% (%)

资本保值增值率 Ratio of Assets Appreciation YOY	资产负债率 Asset-Liability Ratio	流动资产周转率（次） Turnover Ratio of Circulating Assets (time)	成本费用利润率 Ratio of Profits to Cost	全员劳动生产率（元/人年） Overall Labor Productivity (yuan/person-year)	产品销售率 Sales as Percentage of Output
118.5	**62.9**	**2.0**	**4.4**	**243195**	**97.5**
118.1	63.5	1.8	6.0	262310	96.0
119.4	62.8	2.0	4.2	239149	97.7
115.0	60.5	2.0	4.5	278473	97.8
129.9	69.7	1.7	2.9	147640	97.4
128.4	65.1	2.2	6.7	292333	94.6
97.5	73.8	0.3	7.0	118791	102.1
157.7	46.0	1.8	2.5	90037	97.3
102.4	34.0	3.7	5.6	363999	94.6
78.0	72.4	1.5	-3.5	79692	102.6
88.3	63.2	16.8	35.1	352133	96.8
90.0	42.5	6.1	3.3	283474	94.6
122.6	69.6	3.4	5.2	132257	97.3
109.9	78.7	1.1	7.6	213893	80.5
113.4	44.8	2.3	28.1	1712339	98.4
151.4	43.9	4.2	10.9	97063	83.7
103.1	55.0	2.5	1.9	50600	96.7
102.0	45.9	3.0	-0.1	109694	87.8
-23.6	103.9	1.8	0.4	72752	96.1
104.1	57.9	1.1	3.5	41539	101.9
71.0	61.8	4.5	4.5	187129	121.6
120.4	57.9	2.0	4.6	222224	99.9
94.3	67.1	0.9	4.7	193744	97.6
84.7	82.9	4.0	-0.3	187961	99.5
108.6	62.8	1.5	3.4	171606	99.1
82.7	80.9	2.0	-1.6	122434	99.0
123.2	75.7	3.4	1.0	384054	89.4
103.5	63.2	1.3	4.8	112094	97.7
109.8	63.3	1.2	13.2	251566	95.4
121.5	72.6	1.2	14.0	234284	105.3
124.5	53.1	2.4	5.3	367851	97.2
104.1	71.5	1.3	2.2	132509	97.3
187.1	72.0	0.9	0.0	83685	89.1
213.3	49.8	1.5	4.8	281696	102.3
142.5	66.5	1.1	6.6	150928	96.9
93.3	82.0	1.1	3.9	118217	92.2
118.0	66.9	2.8	1.8	366504	99.5
110.2	53.6	1.9	9.8	218478	99.4
129.6	50.1	0.9	15.5	174300	95.2

表12.9 续表 continued

指　标	Item	销售利润率 Rate of Return on Sale
总　计	**Total**	**4.4**
按轻、重工业分	**By Light and Heavy Industries**	
轻工业	Light Industry	5.4
重工业	Heavy Industry	4.2
按企业规模分	**By Size**	
大型企业	Large	4.5
中型企业	Medium	3.0
小型企业	Small	6.5
微型企业	Mini	7.2
按行业分	**By Sector**	
煤炭开采和洗选业	Mining and Washing of Coal	2.7
石油和天然气开采业	Extraction of Petroleum and Natural Gas	5.3
黑色金属矿采选业	Mining and Processing of Ferrous Metal Ores	-4.1
有色金属矿采选业	Mining and Processing of Non-Ferrous Metal Ores	
非金属矿采选业	Mining and Processing of Nonmetal Ores	24.6
开采辅助活动	Mining Support Activities	
其他采矿业	Mining of Other Ores	
农副食品加工业	Processing of Food from Agricultural Products	3.1
食品制造业	Manufacture of Foods	5.1
酒、饮料和精制茶制造业	Liquor, Beverage and Refined Tea	7.2
烟草制品业	Manufacture of Tobacco	11.7
纺织业	Manufacture of Textile	8.5
纺织服装、服饰业	Manufacture of Textile Wearing Apparel, Footware and Caps	
皮革、毛皮、羽毛（绒）及其制品业	Manufacture of Leather, Fur, Feather and Related Products	3.5
木材加工和木竹藤棕草制品业	Processing of Timber, Manufacture of Wood, Bamboo, Rattan, Palm and Straw Products	-0.1
家具制造业	Manufacture of Furniture	
造纸及纸制品业	Manufacture of Paper and Paper Products	0.4
印刷业、记录媒介的复制	Printing, Reproduction of Recording Media	3.5
文教、工美、体育和娱乐用品制造业	Manufacture of Culture, Education, Handicraft, Fine Arts, Sports and Entertainment Articles	
石油加工、炼焦及核燃料加工业	Processing of Petroleum, Coking, Processing of Nuclear Fuel	4.3
化学原料及化学制品制造业	Manufacture of Raw Chemical Materials and Chemical Products	4.6
医药制造业	Manufacture of Medicines	4.8
化学纤维制造业	Manufacture of Chemical Fibers	
橡胶和塑料制品业	Manufacture of Rubber and Plastics	-0.3
非金属矿物制品业	Manufacture of Non-metallic Mineral Products	3.3
黑色金属冶炼及压延加工业	Smelting and Pressing of Ferrous Metals	-1.6
有色金属冶炼及压延加工业	Smelting and Pressing of Nonferrous Metals	1.1
金属制品业	Manufacture of Metal Products	4.7
通用设备制造业	Manufacture of General Purpose Machinery	12.2
专用设备制造业	Manufacture of Special Purpose Machinery	13.1
汽车制造业	Manufacture of Motor Vehicles	5.1
铁路、船舶、航空航天和其他运输设备制造业	Manufacture of Railway, Ship, Aviation and Other Transporting Equipment	2.4
电气机械及器材制造业	Manufacture of Electrical Machinery and Equipment	
计算机、通信和其他电子设备制造业	Manufacture of Communication Equipment, Computers and Other Electronic Equipment	4.7
仪器仪表及文化、办公用机械制造业	Manufacture of Measuring Instruments and Machinery for Cultural Activity and Office Work	6.6
其他制造业	Other Manufacture	4.8
废弃资源综合利用业	Comprehensive Utilization of Waste Resources	
金属制品、机械和设备修理业	Repair of Metal Products, Machinery and Equipment	
电力、热力的生产和供应业	Production and Supply of Electric Power and Heat Power	1.9
燃气生产和供应业	Production and Supply of Gas	9.5
水的生产和供应业	Production and Supply of Water	16.4

单位：% (%)

资本积累率 Rate of Capital Accumulation	流动比率 Current Ratio	速动比率 Quick Ratio	产权比率 Equity Ratio	人均实现利税（元） Per Capita Pre-tax Profits (yuan)	从业人员人均工资（元） Per Capita Wages of Employees (yuan)
18.5	**1.0**	**0.7**	**1.7**	**98242**	**59051**
18.1	1.0	0.7	1.7	148274	58386
19.4	1.0	0.8	1.7	87654	59192
15.0	1.0	0.8	1.5	124024	64665
29.9	0.9	0.7	2.3	35396	48306
28.4	1.0	0.8	1.9	106343	49230
-2.5	0.5	0.4	2.8	10272	35988
57.7	0.8	0.7	0.9	20648	48035
2.4	1.4	1.3	0.5	57052	80068
-22.0	0.5	0.3	2.6	26196	48745
-11.7	0.4	0.3	1.7	273681	24856
-10.0	1.1	0.8	0.8	53492	57128
22.6	0.8	0.6	2.3	57534	41237
9.9	0.8	0.5	3.7	161930	35976
13.4	1.9	0.8	0.8	1536679	127112
51.4	2.4	0.8	0.8	45638	22826
3.1	2.5	1.1	1.2	12906	33169
2.0	1.0	0.4	0.8	18459	18338
-123.6	0.4	0.3	-26.6	6713	38904
4.1	1.5	1.2	1.4	14866	23004
-29.0	1.1	0.4	1.6	79966	68196
20.4	0.9	0.7	1.4	69477	60412
-5.7	1.0	0.9	2.0	58536	87380
-15.3	0.4	0.2	4.9	24036	25254
8.6	0.8	0.6	1.7	48090	53293
-17.3	1.0	0.5	4.2	-4804	58173
23.2	0.8	0.5	3.1	28353	60222
3.5	1.0	0.8	1.7	29049	42991
9.8	1.3	1.0	1.8	128111	59946
21.5	1.1	0.8	2.7	143349	61923
24.5	1.2	1.0	1.1	206838	55078
4.1	1.0	0.6	2.5	32760	44617
87.1	1.3	1.1	2.6	14375	45747
113.3	1.5	1.2	1.1	55167	44342
42.5	1.2	1.0	2.0	52202	63244
-6.7	0.8	0.6	4.6	20178	60393
18.0	0.6	0.5	2.0	83259	88222
10.2	1.4	1.3	1.1	116095	75882
29.6	1.3	1.2	1.0	67631	27953

表12.10 私营工业企业主要经济指标（2011年）
MAIN ECONOMIC INDICATORS OF PRIVATE INDUSTRIAL ENTERPRISES (2011)

指 标	Item	单位数（个） Number of Enterprises (unit)
总 计	**Total**	3115
按登记注册类型分	**By Status of Registration**	
私营独资企业	Solely Private-funded Enterprises	691
私营合伙企业	Private Partnership Enterprises	140
私营有限责任公司	Private Limited Liability Companies	2050
私营股份有限公司	Private Share-holding Companies	234
按轻、重工业分	**By Light and Heavy Industries**	
轻工业	Light Industry	1281
重工业	Heavy Industry	1834
按企业规模分	**By Size**	
大型企业	Large	40
中型企业	Medium	479
小型企业	Small	2498
微型企业	Mini	98
按行业分	**By Sector**	
煤炭开采和洗选业	Mining and Washing of Coal	302
石油和天然气开采业	Extraction of Petroleum and Natural Gas	
黑色金属矿采选业	Mining and Processing of Ferrous Metal Ores	25
有色金属矿采选业	Mining and Processing of Non-Ferrous Metal Ores	2
非金属矿采选业	Mining and Processing of Nonmetal Ores	59
开采辅助活动	Mining Support Activities	
其他采矿业	Mining of Other Ores	
农副食品加工业	Processing of Food from Agricultural Products	218
食品制造业	Manufacture of Foods	57
酒、饮料和精制茶制造业	Liquor, Beverage and Refined Tea	41
烟草制品业	Manufacture of Tobacco	
纺织业	Manufacture of Textile	112
纺织服装、鞋、帽制造业	Manufacture of Textile Wearing Apparel, Footware and Caps	34
皮革、毛皮、羽毛（绒）及其制品业	Manufacture of Leather, Fur, Feather and Related Products	81
木材加工及木竹藤棕草制品业	Processing of Timber, Manufacture of Wood, Bamboo, Rattan, Palm and Straw Products	24
家具制造业	Manufacture of Furniture	33
造纸及纸制品业	Manufacture of Paper and Paper Products	69
印刷业、记录媒介的复制	Printing, Reproduction of Recording Media	27
文教、工美、体育和娱乐用品制造业	Manufacture of Culture, Education, Handicraft, Fine Arts, Sports and Entertainment Articles	9
石油加工、炼焦及核燃料加工业	Processing of Petroleum, Coking, Processing of Nuclear Fuel	17
化学原料及化学制品制造业	Manufacture of Raw Chemical Materials and Chemical Products	111
医药制造业	Manufacture of Medicines	52
化学纤维制造业	Manufacture of Chemical Fibers	2
橡胶和塑料制品业	Manufacture of Rubber and Plastics	119
非金属矿物制品业	Manufacture of Non-metallic Mineral Products	260
黑色金属冶炼及压延加工业	Smelting and Pressing of Ferrous Metals	134
有色金属冶炼及压延加工业	Smelting and Pressing of Nonferrous Metals	53
金属制品业	Manufacture of Metal Products	138
通用设备制造业	Manufacture of General Purpose Machinery	135
专用设备制造业	Manufacture of Special Purpose Machinery	89
汽车制造业	Manufacture of Motor Vehicles	316
铁路、船舶、航空航天和其他运输设备制造业	Manufacture of Railway, Ship, Aviation and Other Transporting Equipment	386
电气机械及器材制造业	Manufacture of Electrical Machinery and Equipment	120
通信设备、计算机及其他电子设备制造业	Manufacture of Communication Equipment, Computers and Other Electronic Equipment	20
仪器仪表及文化、办公用机械制造业	Manufacture of Measuring Instruments and Machinery for Cultural Activity and Office Work	34
其他制造业	Other Manufacture	7
废弃资源综合利用业	Comprehensive Utilization of Waste Resources	9
金属制品、机械和设备修理业	Repair of Metal Products, Machinery and Equipment	5
电力、热力的生产和供应业	Repair of Metal Supply of Electric Power and Heat Power	2
燃气生产和供应业	Production and Supply of Gas	10
水的生产和供应业	Production and Supply of Water	3

单位：万元 (10 000 yuan)

从业人员平均人数（万人）Average Employment (10 000 persons)	工业总产值 Gross Output Value	工业销售产值 Sales Value of Industry	其 中 of which	实收资本 Paid-in Capital	其 中 of which	
			#出口交货值 Value of Export Delivery		#国家资本 State Capital	#外商资本 Foreign Capital
62.38	43143975	42071704	2102554	3673733	15242	7432
9.38	5276481	5144787	10301	351491	2989	
2.72	1002816	963829	11816	75291	183	
44.09	31241345	30445746	1407375	2717006	11120	7432
6.19	5623333	5517342	673062	529944	950	
26.38	15914559	15549194	1206392	1175647	6365	577
36.00	27229417	26522510	896162	2498086	8877	6855
9.13	8210006	8034850	967265	757121	42	
23.22	14561276	14079887	888067	1156319	3045	6855
29.77	20033126	19616589	247222	1683854	12155	577
0.26	339567	340379		76439		
7.27	2170498	2135310	10855	154834		
0.33	53916	50974		8930		
0.13	23855	15231		1330		
0.65	359444	355429		32990	1165	
2.76	2266564	2230285	18225	118862	351	
0.76	418373	401839	6320	35056		
0.68	428794	414913	14192	45455		577
2.20	1347575	1315926	100778	95732		
0.71	259568	244624	23311	16225		
1.79	725332	716416	22480	18180		
0.29	211953	203595		20243		
0.55	312228	305901		17969		
0.78	543215	534604	31738	56234	1469	
0.28	181706	178987		14109		
0.20	82663	81153	12389	9697		
0.33	197306	187556	5463	29559		
2.49	2592661	2499682	37084	303933		
1.13	667223	631499	2608	130487	4545	
0.03	71398	71454		1500		
1.76	1314525	1237700	3566	142587	21	1000
5.91	3092626	3030443	5625	327191		
2.06	3363947	3265044		250719		
1.09	1882901	1800802	75564	87436		
2.62	1679093	1637962	86959	126468	119	5855
2.33	1446643	1422513	141123	109392	2400	
1.27	901381	880311	38970	95772	261	
7.65	5272404	5173320	129989	384516	1695	
10.43	8036530	7902185	908447	729398		
2.26	1932784	1882014	229849	216256	2267	
0.68	448984	430920	7802	21820	950	
0.51	261941	253154	10237	31825		
0.13	81973	69538	14911	3465		
0.13	370899	370680	164071	4224		
0.05	45542	44675		1860		
0.03	9354	9354		7891		
0.08	74551	72154		14552		
0.02	13627	13560		7038		

表12.10 续表1 continued1

指 标	Item	资 产 Total Assets
总 计	**Total**	20428877
按登记注册类型分	**By Status of Registration**	
私营独资企业	Solely Private-funded Enterprises	1787632
私营合伙企业	Private Partnership Enterprises	287697
私营有限责任公司	Private Limited Liability Companies	15097254
私营股份有限公司	Private Share-holding Companies	3256294
按轻、重工业分	**By Light and Heavy Industries**	
轻工业	Light Industry	7464532
重工业	Heavy Industry	12964345
按企业规模分	**By Size**	
大型企业	Large	5539374
中型企业	Medium	6564221
小型企业	Small	8188118
微型企业	Mini	137164
按行业分	**By Sector**	
煤炭开采和洗选业	Mining and Washing of Coal	887201
石油和天然气开采业	Extraction of Petroleum and Natural Gas	
黑色金属矿采选业	Mining and Processing of Ferrous Metal Ores	95565
有色金属矿采选业	Mining and Processing of Non-Ferrous Metal Ores	18063
非金属矿采选业	Mining and Processing of Nonmetal Ores	143914
开采辅助活动	Mining Support Activities	
其他采矿业	Mining of Other Ores	
农副食品加工业	Processing of Food from Agricultural Products	636417
食品制造业	Manufacture of Foods	180285
酒、饮料和精制茶制造业	Liquor, Beverage and Refined Tea	190930
烟草制品业	Manufacture of Tobacco	
纺织业	Manufacture of Textile	457188
纺织服装、鞋、帽制造业	Manufacture of Textile Wearing Apparel, Footware and Caps	92457
皮革、毛皮、羽毛（绒）及其制品业	Manufacture of Leather, Fur, Feather and Related Products	156065
木材加工及木竹藤棕草制品业	Processing of Timber, Manufacture of Wood, Bamboo, Rattan, Palm and Straw Products	58449
家具制造业	Manufacture of Furniture	161266
造纸及纸制品业	Manufacture of Paper and Paper Products	254958
印刷业、记录媒介的复制	Printing, Reproduction of Recording Media	96560
文教、工美、体育和娱乐用品制造业	Manufacture of Culture, Education, Handicraft, Fine Arts, Sports and Entertainment Articles	26560
石油加工、炼焦及核燃料加工业	Processing of Petroleum, Coking, Processing of Nuclear Fuel	116573
化学原料及化学制品制造业	Manufacture of Raw Chemical Materials and Chemical Products	1229370
医药制造业	Manufacture of Medicines	443264
化学纤维制造业	Manufacture of Chemical Fibers	14569
橡胶和塑料制品业	Manufacture of Rubber and Plastics	570372
非金属矿物制品业	Manufacture of Non-metallic Mineral Products	1825023
黑色金属冶炼及压延加工业	Smelting and Pressing of Ferrous Metals	1279693
有色金属冶炼及压延加工业	Smelting and Pressing of Nonferrous Metals	648886
金属制品业	Manufacture of Metal Products	858504
通用设备制造业	Manufacture of General Purpose Machinery	646542
专用设备制造业	Manufacture of Special Purpose Machinery	462851
汽车制造业	Manufacture of Motor Vehicles	2832109
铁路、船舶、航空航天和其他运输设备制造业	Manufacture of Railway, Ship, Aviation and Other Transporting Equipment	4588126
电气机械及器材制造业	Manufacture of Electrical Machinery and Equipment	895736
通信设备、计算机及其他电子设备制造业	Manufacture of Communication Equipment, Computers and Other Electronic Equipment	115875
仪器仪表及文化、办公用机械制造业	Manufacture of Measuring Instruments and Machinery for Cultural Activity and Office Work	157482
其他制造业	Other Manufacture	26084
废弃资源综合利用业	Comprehensive Utilization of Waste Resources	76230
金属制品、机械和设备修理业	Repair of Metal Products, Machinery and Equipment	7179
电力、热力的生产和供应业	Repair of Metal Supply of Electric Power and Heat Power	38165
燃气生产和供应业	Production and Supply of Gas	90386
水的生产和供应业	Production and Supply of Water	49982

单位：万元 (10 000 yuan)

其中 of which	固定资产 Fixed Assets		负债	其中 of which
#流动资产 Circulating Assets	原值 Original Value	净值 Net Value	Total Liabilities	#流动负债 Total Circulating Liabilities
11642197	12167953	5953370	11328982	9343797
818536	1119507	682894	738244	578402
122967	220307	118799	120752	77787
8836954	9077754	4080113	8580349	7083219
1863740	1750384	1071565	1889638	1604388
4279695	4573760	2185579	3817760	3280848
7362503	7594193	3767791	7511222	6062949
3454249	2126672	671208	3293759	2731759
3708872	4811656	2807380	3723053	3067010
4402315	5186934	2724295	4224700	3485923
76762	42691	11700	87470	59105
348598	534321	378673	390257	277702
65746	13903	7747	55188	46972
12983	5363	4926	14419	13419
49575	91820	61347	52559	40364
308481	429977	228200	251636	208646
87427	182159	64220	74031	60462
91286	75687	57903	81254	67213
222693	367288	200913	225297	137808
52830	29151	22226	47194	38894
80393	642129	51864	74058	56203
22449	34104	28445	18158	17577
94742	39144	29915	74247	68867
125298	133289	105006	129189	112788
49805	47826	32422	40330	37650
11620	14292	12002	9015	7218
40130	44927	25761	76228	67093
659867	961469	482574	715645	516292
187648	178980	123554	165243	142602
8778	6761	3539	4586	4586
319283	662441	129726	259421	183293
894731	1172677	699423	1077381	804133
688996	770671	386364	804060	653183
394814	531090	184166	397274	279553
523451	311804	190644	493458	428419
354212	398073	178253	356917	316141
280860	179649	137605	181235	159661
1800246	1361422	658113	1898963	1663457
2948932	2147355	1160049	2587944	2289286
588472	356128	169278	469470	392265
66192	269852	38771	57447	52493
105115	49902	28166	82963	78484
18839	7498	5865	12410	11790
59879	15521	11480	61195	61145
2425	6611	4537	2504	1895
8002	35146	8096	14250	5079
55869	37858	27192	45265	27416
11533	21667	14409	28295	13745

表12.10 续表2 continued2

指　标	Item	所有者权益 Creditors' Equity
总　　计	Total	8951840
按登记注册类型分	By Status of Registration	
私营独资企业	Solely Private-funded Enterprises	1008955
私营合伙企业	Private Partnership Enterprises	161422
私营有限责任公司	Private Limited Liability Companies	6425348
私营股份有限公司	Private Share-holding Companies	1356115
按轻、重工业分	By Light and Heavy Industries	
轻工业	Light Industry	3609085
重工业	Heavy Industry	5342755
按企业规模分	By Size	
大型企业	Large	2232243
中型企业	Medium	2783326
小型企业	Small	3887356
微型企业	Mini	48916
按行业分	By Sector	
煤炭开采和洗选业	Mining and Washing of Coal	479926
石油和天然气开采业	Extraction of Petroleum and Natural Gas	
黑色金属矿采选业	Mining and Processing of Ferrous Metal Ores	40346
有色金属矿采选业	Mining and Processing of Non-Ferrous Metal Ores	3626
非金属矿采选业	Mining and Processing of Nonmetal Ores	90148
开采辅助活动	Mining Support Activities	
其他采矿业	Mining of Other Ores	
农副食品加工业	Processing of Food from Agricultural Products	376593
食品制造业	Manufacture of Foods	103127
酒、饮料和精制茶制造业	Liquor, Beverage and Refined Tea	109444
烟草制品业	Manufacture of Tobacco	
纺织业	Manufacture of Textile	230486
纺织服装、鞋、帽制造业	Manufacture of Textile Wearing Apparel, Footware and Caps	45264
皮革、毛皮、羽毛（绒）及其制品业	Manufacture of Leather, Fur, Feather and Related Products	80203
木材加工及木竹藤棕草制品业	Processing of Timber, Manufacture of Wood, Bamboo, Rattan, Palm and Straw Products	40203
家具制造业	Manufacture of Furniture	85029
造纸及纸制品业	Manufacture of Paper and Paper Products	124364
印刷业、记录媒介的复制	Printing, Reproduction of Recording Media	55619
文教、工美、体育和娱乐用品制造业	Manufacture of Culture, Education, Handicraft, Fine Arts, Sports and Entertainment Articles	17513
石油加工、炼焦及核燃料加工业	Processing of Petroleum, Coking, Processing of Nuclear Fuel	39117
化学原料及化学制品制造业	Manufacture of Raw Chemical Materials and Chemical Products	509137
医药制造业	Manufacture of Medicines	275038
化学纤维制造业	Manufacture of Chemical Fibers	9983
橡胶和塑料制品业	Manufacture of Rubber and Plastics	286938
非金属矿物制品业	Manufacture of Non-metallic Mineral Products	743131
黑色金属冶炼及压延加工业	Smelting and Pressing of Ferrous Metals	460785
有色金属冶炼及压延加工业	Smelting and Pressing of Nonferrous Metals	250918
金属制品业	Manufacture of Metal Products	357009
通用设备制造业	Manufacture of General Purpose Machinery	288081
专用设备制造业	Manufacture of Special Purpose Machinery	278651
汽车制造业	Manufacture of Motor Vehicles	921883
铁路、船舶、航空航天和其他运输设备制造业	Manufacture of Railway, Ship, Aviation and Other Transporting Equipment	1987180
电气机械及器材制造业	Manufacture of Electrical Machinery and Equipment	405187
通信设备、计算机和其他电子设备制造业	Manufacture of Communication Equipment, Computers and Other Electronic Equipment	58428
仪器仪表及文化、办公用机械制造业	Manufacture of Measuring Instruments and Machinery for Cultural Activity and Office Work	74400
其他制造业	Other Manufacture	13674
废弃资源综合利用业	Comprehensive Utilization of Waste Resources	15035
金属制品、机械和设备修理业	Repair of Metal Products, Machinery and Equipment	4653
电力、热力的生产和供应业	Production and Supply of Electric Power and Heat Power	23915
燃气生产和供应业	Production and Supply of Gas	45120
水的生产和供应业	Production and Supply of Water	21687

单位：万元 (10 000 yuan)

主营业务收入 Revenue from Principal Business	主营业务成本 Cost of Principal Business	主营业务税金及附加 Tax and Extra Charges of Principal Business	主营业务利润 Profit of Principal Business	利润总额 Total After-tax Profits	利税总额 Total Pre-tax Profits	工资总额 Total Wages
41680825	35463715	202082	6015028	2755696	4119189	2192250
5126973	4183515	33602	909857	443968	609909	304943
965389	771659	8414	185316	86381	129657	92990
30178775	25844779	129188	4204809	1893527	2825208	1560381
5409688	4663763	30878	715047	331820	554416	233937
15521685	13171222	70180	2280283	929261	1363605	888809
26159139	22292493	131902	3734744	1826435	2755584	1303441
7908779	6770627	35682	1102471	470980	770614	376871
13791425	11753460	61155	1976811	983589	1443761	861894
19624856	16616643	103775	2904438	1293065	1888739	945352
355764	322986	1470	31308	8062	16075	8133
2112449	1634442	23809	454198	268187	411352	272302
52966	23663	859	28444	1015	9514	10093
15231	12706	67	2459	1579	1879	3984
357871	278225	9516	70130	32238	51806	19366
2222737	1885273	10581	326883	135265	180309	100539
409463	323441	1583	84439	25363	36336	24345
406839	318268	4677	83894	42749	60299	29207
1337740	1208510	4058	125172	70758	110740	76573
242495	196906	1170	44419	19749	26811	23058
714125	617988	2049	94088	43052	57004	67636
205230	175029	822	29380	13610	16552	7763
312917	244961	1836	66120	16991	26358	25410
527164	460429	2508	64227	26156	41427	24758
177152	152788	396	23967	11504	15254	8478
86312	66245	335	19733	7318	8669	6471
189429	150706	728	37995	22320	26633	11156
2474474	2027671	13914	432890	169024	273907	89725
619273	464334	2344	152596	63617	86333	37119
65092	62843	518	1731	1631	3370	741
1190593	1009180	5083	176331	100513	131046	61988
3019306	2511970	19438	487898	217149	357450	185026
3237707	2678874	7763	551070	211639	324193	65670
1728489	1620930	5282	102277	76912	113587	46370
1620885	1391549	6286	223050	116458	162354	102312
1436392	1209055	5268	222070	85861	120448	80696
893421	730279	2855	160287	79069	100056	40939
5097381	4419210	22500	655671	358291	535772	277480
7789697	6863657	30257	895783	368713	574025	360965
1887150	1611045	9671	266435	112657	164121	78845
425135	376830	2276	46029	13556	19100	19844
243556	204617	877	38062	14520	23583	16905
69985	60856	537	8593	4397	7936	4957
368989	358186	1651	9152	2668	15489	4486
44675	37299	120	7256	2378	3618	2362
9182	4813	75	4294	3737	4167	711
75186	60581	308	14297	13628	15411	2967
14138	10358	68	3712	1425	2280	1003

表12.11 私营工业企业经济效益指标（2011年）
INDICATORS ON ECONOMIC BENEFIT OF PRIVATE INDUSTRIAL ENTERPRISES (2011)

指 标	Item	总资产贡献率 Ratio of Total Assets to Industrial Output Value
总 计	**Total**	**21.4**
按轻、重工业分	**By Light and Heavy Industries**	
轻工业	Light Industry	19.4
重工业	Heavy Industry	22.6
按企业规模分	**By Size**	
大型企业	Large	14.9
中型企业	Medium	23.6
小型企业	Small	24.2
微型企业	Mini	12.6
按行业分	**By Sector**	
煤炭开采和洗选业	Mining and Washing of Coal	47.3
石油和天然气开采业	Extraction of Petroleum and Natural Gas	
黑色金属矿采选业	Mining and Processing of Ferrous Metal Ores	10.6
有色金属矿采选业	Mining and Processing of Non-Ferrous Metal Ores	10.4
非金属矿采选业	Mining and Processing of Nonmetal Ores	37.5
开采辅助活动	Mining Support Activities	
其他采矿业	Mining of Other Ores	
农副食品加工业	Processing of Food from Agricultural Products	29.4
食品制造业	Manufacture of Foods	22.5
酒、饮料和精制茶制造业	Liquor, Beverage and Refined Tea	32.4
烟草制品业	Manufacture of Tobacco	
纺织业	Manufacture of Textile	25.2
纺织服装、服饰业	Manufacture of Textile Wearing Apparel, Footware and Caps	30.7
皮革、毛皮、羽毛（绒）及其制品业	Manufacture of Leather, Fur, Feather and Related Products	37.8
木材加工和木竹藤棕草制品业	Processing of Timber, Manufacture of Wood, Bamboo, Rattan, Palm and Straw Products	28.8
家具制造业	Manufacture of Furniture	17.6
造纸及纸制品业	Manufacture of Paper and Paper Products	17.3
印刷业、记录媒介的复制	Printing, Reproduction of Recording Media	16.2
文教、工美、体育和娱乐用品制造业	Manufacture of Culture, Education, Handicraft, Fine Arts, Sports and Entertainment Articles	32.9
石油加工、炼焦及核燃料加工业	Processing of Petroleum, Coking, Processing of Nuclear Fuel	24.1
化学原料及化学制品制造业	Manufacture of Raw Chemical Materials and Chemical Products	24.5
医药制造业	Manufacture of Medicines	20.5
化学纤维制造业	Manufacture of Chemical Fibers	24.4
橡胶和塑料制品业	Manufacture of Rubber and Plastics	24.1
非金属矿物制品业	Manufacture of Non-metallic Mineral Products	20.8
黑色金属冶炼及压延加工业	Smelting and Pressing of Ferrous Metals	26.7
有色金属冶炼及压延加工业	Smelting and Pressing of Nonferrous Metals	19.4
金属制品业	Manufacture of Metal Products	20.2
通用设备制造业	Manufacture of General Purpose Machinery	19.4
专用设备制造业	Manufacture of Special Purpose Machinery	22.1
汽车制造业	Manufacture of Motor Vehicles	20.1
铁路、船舶、航空航天和其他运输设备制造业	Manufacture of Railway, Ship, Aviation and Other Transporting Equipment	13.7
电气机械及器材制造业	Manufacture of Electrical Machinery and Equipment	19.7
计算机、通信和其他电子设备制造业	Manufacture of Communication Equipment, Computers and Other Electronic Equipment	17.6
仪器仪表及文化、办公用机械制造业	Manufacture of Measuring Instruments and Machinery for Cultural Activity and Office Work	16.1
其他制造业	Other Manufacture	32.3
废弃资源综合利用业	Comprehensive Utilization of Waste Resources	25.2
金属制品、机械和设备修理业	Repair of Metal Products, Machinery and Equipment	50.9
电力、热力的生产和供应业	Production and Supply of Electric Power and Heat Power	11.1
燃气生产和供应业	Production and Supply of Gas	17.7
水的生产和供应业	Production and Supply of Water	5.7

单位：% (%)

资本保值增值率 Ratio of Assets Appreciation YOY	资产负债率 Asset-Liability Ratio	流动资产周转率（次） Turnover Ratio of Circulating Assets (time)	成本费用利润率 Ratio of Profits to Cost	全员劳动生产率（元/人年） Overall Labor Productivity (yuan/person-year)	产品销售率 Sales as Percentage of Output
126.5	**55.5**	**3.6**	**7.1**	**186460**	**97.5**
142.9	51.2	3.7	6.4	158365	97.7
114.9	57.9	3.6	7.5	207053	97.4
120.2	59.5	2.3	6.2	239400	97.9
131.1	56.7	3.7	7.7	174405	96.7
128.2	51.6	4.5	7.2	178278	97.9
65.2	63.8	4.7	2.4	341585	100.2
135.6	44.0	6.1	14.7	138971	98.4
91.2	57.8	0.8	2.0	149796	94.5
262.4	79.8	1.2	11.6	64741	63.9
137.8	36.5	7.2	10.7	180299	98.9
144.1	39.5	7.3	6.6	171013	98.4
140.7	41.1	4.7	7.0	143836	96.1
121.8	42.6	4.5	11.9	192360	96.8
	49.3	6.0	5.5	159153	97.7
	51.0	4.6	8.9	106417	94.2
137.5	47.5	8.9	6.6	129912	98.8
99.9	31.1	9.1	7.4	165526	96.1
131.3	46.0	3.3	6.0	139777	98.0
120.9	50.7	4.2	5.3	159221	98.4
129.6	41.8	3.6	7.0	172348	98.5
108.8	33.9	7.4	10.6	149129	98.2
227.5	65.4	4.6	13.7	180685	95.1
123.1	58.2	3.8	7.6	291951	96.4
152.8	37.3	3.3	12.1	178257	94.7
100.2	31.5	7.4	2.6	613844	100.1
152.7	45.5	3.8	9.2	205954	94.2
140.2	59.0	3.4	7.8	156886	98.0
144.3	62.8	4.7	7.2	408258	97.1
95.1	61.2	4.5	4.5	370604	95.6
116.1	57.5	3.1	7.8	165769	97.6
136.2	55.2	4.1	6.4	167648	98.3
175.6	39.2	3.2	9.8	182687	97.7
123.8	67.1	2.9	7.4	170250	98.1
111.8	56.4	2.7	4.9	198032	98.3
134.9	52.4	3.2	6.4	198470	97.4
65.9	49.6	6.5	3.4	210720	96.0
112.4	52.7	2.3	6.2	141034	96.7
84.2	47.6	3.8	6.7	150678	84.8
100.7	80.3	6.2	0.7	406035	99.9
137.5	34.9	18.4	6.1	253568	98.1
111.7	37.3	1.2	59.6	130807	100.0
128.4	50.1	1.4	20.5	256116	96.8
128.1	56.6	1.2	11.8	293119	99.5

表12.11 续表 continued

指　标	Item	销售利润率 Rate of Return on Sale
总　计	**Total**	**6.6**
按轻、重工业分	**By Light and Heavy Industries**	
轻工业	Light Industry	6.0
重工业	Heavy Industry	7.0
按企业规模分	**By Size**	
大型企业	Large	6.0
中型企业	Medium	7.1
小型企业	Small	6.6
微型企业	Mini	2.3
按行业分	**By Sector**	
煤炭开采和洗选业	Mining and Washing of Coal	12.7
石油和天然气开采业	Extraction of Petroleum and Natural Gas	
黑色金属矿采选业	Mining and Processing of Ferrous Metal Ores	1.9
有色金属矿采选业	Mining and Processing of Non-Ferrous Metal Ores	10.4
非金属矿采选业	Mining and Processing of Nonmetal Ores	9.0
开采辅助活动	Mining Support Activities	
其他采矿业	Mining of Other Ores	
农副食品加工业	Processing of Food from Agricultural Products	6.1
食品制造业	Manufacture of Foods	6.2
酒、饮料和精制茶制造业	Liquor, Beverage and Refined Tea	10.5
烟草制品业	Manufacture of Tobacco	
纺织业	Manufacture of Textile	5.3
纺织服装、服饰业	Manufacture of Textile Wearing Apparel, Footware and Caps	8.1
皮革、毛皮、羽毛（绒）及其制品业	Manufacture of Leather, Fur, Feather and Related Products	6.0
木材加工和木竹藤棕草制品业	Processing of Timber, Manufacture of Wood, Bamboo, Rattan, Palm and Straw Products	6.6
家具制造业	Manufacture of Furniture	5.4
造纸及纸制品业	Manufacture of Paper and Paper Products	5.0
印刷业、记录媒介的复制	Printing, Reproduction of Recording Media	6.5
文教、工美、体育和娱乐用品制造业	Manufacture of Culture, Education, Handicraft, Fine Arts, Sports and Entertainment Articles	8.5
石油加工、炼焦及核燃料加工业	Processing of Petroleum, Coking, Processing of Nuclear Fuel	11.8
化学原料及化学制品制造业	Manufacture of Raw Chemical Materials and Chemical Products	6.8
医药制造业	Manufacture of Medicines	10.3
化学纤维制造业	Manufacture of Chemical Fibers	2.5
橡胶和塑料制品业	Manufacture of Rubber and Plastics	8.4
非金属矿物制品业	Manufacture of Non-metallic Mineral Products	7.2
黑色金属冶炼及压延加工业	Smelting and Pressing of Ferrous Metals	6.5
有色金属冶炼及压延加工业	Smelting and Pressing of Nonferrous Metals	4.4
金属制品业	Manufacture of Metal Products	7.2
通用设备制造业	Manufacture of General Purpose Machinery	6.0
专用设备制造业	Manufacture of Special Purpose Machinery	8.9
汽车制造业	Manufacture of Motor Vehicles	7.0
铁路、船舶、航空航天和其他运输设备制造业	Manufacture of Railway, Ship, Aviation and Other Transporting Equipment	4.7
电气机械及器材制造业	Manufacture of Electrical Machinery and Equipment	6.0
计算机、通信和其他电子设备制造业	Manufacture of Communication Equipment, Computers and Other Electronic Equipment	3.2
仪器仪表及文化、办公用机械制造业	Manufacture of Measuring Instruments and Machinery for Cultural Activity and Office Work	6.0
其他制造业	Other Manufacture	6.3
废弃资源综合利用业	Comprehensive Utilization of Waste Resources	0.7
金属制品、机械和设备修理业	Repair of Metal Products, Machinery and Equipment	5.3
电力、热力的生产和供应业	Production and Supply of Electric Power and Heat Power	40.7
燃气生产和供应业	Production and Supply of Gas	18.1
水的生产和供应业	Production and Supply of Water	10.1

单位：% (%)

资本积累率 Rate of Capital Accumulation	流动比率 Current Ratio	速动比率 Quick Ratio	产权比率 Equity Ratio	人均实现利税（元） Per Capita Pre-tax Profits (yuan)	从业人员人均工资（元） Per Capita Wages of Employees (yuan)
26.5	**1.2**	**1.0**	**1.3**	**66035**	**35144**
42.9	1.3	1.0	1.1	51684	33688
14.9	1.2	0.9	1.4	76554	36211
20.2	1.3	1.0	1.5	84413	41282
31.1	1.2	0.9	1.3	62176	37118
28.2	1.3	1.0	1.1	63445	31755
-34.8	1.3	1.1	1.8	62019	31377
35.6	1.3	1.1	0.8	56598	37466
-8.8	1.4	1.3	1.4	29096	30864
162.4	1.0	0.2	4.0	14331	30387
37.8	1.2	1.0	0.6	79800	29831
44.1	1.5	1.1	0.7	65374	36452
40.7	1.4	1.0	0.7	48057	32199
21.8	1.4	0.9	0.7	89147	43180
	1.6	1.1	1.0	50266	34757
	1.4	0.9	1.0	37687	32412
37.5	1.4	1.0	0.9	31759	37682
-0.1	1.3	0.9	0.5	57393	26919
31.3	1.4	0.8	0.9	47941	46216
20.9	1.1	0.9	1.0	53125	31749
29.6	1.3	1.1	0.7	53902	29959
8.8	1.6	1.4	0.5	43476	32453
127.5	0.6	0.4	1.9	81098	33971
23.1	1.3	1.0	1.4	109813	35972
52.8	1.3	0.9	0.6	76394	32846
0.2	1.9	1.1	0.5	101515	22322
52.7	1.7	1.2	0.9	74437	35210
40.2	1.1	0.9	1.4	60448	31290
44.3	1.1	0.8	1.7	157536	31911
-4.9	1.4	0.9	1.6	103855	42397
16.1	1.2	0.9	1.4	61969	39052
36.2	1.1	0.8	1.2	51806	34708
75.6	1.8	1.4	0.7	78488	32114
23.8	1.1	0.9	2.1	70033	36271
11.8	1.3	1.1	1.3	55014	34594
34.9	1.5	1.1	1.2	72671	34912
-34.1	1.3	0.9	1.0	28254	29356
12.4	1.3	1.0	1.1	45882	32888
-15.8	1.6	0.5	0.9	60260	37642
0.7	1.0	0.8	4.1	120440	34883
37.5	1.3	1.1	0.5	68530	44741
11.7	1.6	1.6	0.6	160273	27331
28.4	2.0	2.0	1.0	193845	37319
28.1	0.8	0.8	1.3	111229	48922

表12.12 内资工业企业主要经济指标（2011年）

MAIN ECONOMIC INDICATORS OF INDUSTRIAL ENTERPRISES WITH HONG KONG, MACAO, TAIWAN AND FOREIGN FUNDS (2011)

指 标	Item	单位数（个） Number of Enterprises (unit)
总 计	**Total**	**4493**
#国有控股企业	State-owned and State-holding Enterprises	430
按登记注册类型分	**By Status of Registration**	
#国有企业	State-owned	111
集体企业	Collective-owned	62
按轻、重工业分	**By Light and Heavy Industries**	
轻工业	Light Industry	1716
重工业	Heavy Industry	2777
按企业规模分	**By Size**	
大型企业	Large	134
中型企业	Medium	866
小型企业	Small	3379
微型企业	Mini	114
按行业分	**By Sector**	
煤炭开采和洗选业	Mining and Washing of Coal	394
石油和天然气开采业	Extraction of Petroleum and Natural Gas	1
黑色金属矿采选业	Mining and Processing of Ferrous Metal Ores	28
有色金属矿采选业	Mining and Processing of Non-Ferrous Metal Ores	3
非金属矿采选业	Mining and Processing of Nonmetal Ores	74
开采辅助活动	Mining Support Activities	
其他采矿业	Mining of Other Ores	
农副食品加工业	Processing of Food from Agricultural Products	287
食品制造业	Manufacture of Foods	90
酒、饮料和精制茶制造业	Liquor, Beverage and Refined Tea	58
烟草制品业	Manufacture of Tobacco	4
纺织业	Manufacture of Textile	131
纺织服装、鞋、帽制造业	Manufacture of Textile Wearing Apparel, Footware and Caps	47
皮革、毛皮、羽毛（绒）及其制品业	Manufacture of Leather, Fur, Feather and Related Products	100
木材加工和木竹藤棕草制品业	Processing of Timber, Manufacture of Wood, Bamboo, Rattan, Palm and Straw Products	31
家具制造业	Manufacture of Furniture	37
造纸及纸制品业	Manufacture of Paper and Paper Products	84
印刷业、记录媒介的复制	Printing, Reproduction of Recording Media	47
文教、工美、体育和娱乐用品制造业	Manufacture of Culture, Education, Handicraft, Fine Arts, Sports and Entertainment Articles	13
石油加工、炼焦及核燃料加工业	Processing of Petroleum, Coking, Processing of Nuclear Fuel	25
化学原料及化学制品制造业	Manufacture of Raw Chemical Materials and Chemical Products	211
医药制造业	Manufacture of Medicines	93
化学纤维制造业	Manufacture of Chemical Fibers	2
橡胶和塑料制品业	Manufacture of Rubber and Plastics	152
非金属矿物制品业	Manufacture of Non-metallic Mineral Products	373
黑色金属冶炼及压延加工业	Smelting and Pressing of Ferrous Metals	183
有色金属冶炼及压延加工业	Smelting and Pressing of Nonferrous Metals	86
金属制品业	Manufacture of Metal Products	181
通用设备制造业	Manufacture of General Purpose Machinery	207
专用设备制造业	Manufacture of Special Purpose Machinery	115
汽车制造业	Manufacture of Motor Vehicles	476
铁路、船舶、航空航天和其他运输设备制造业	Manufacture of Railway, Ship, Aviation and Other Transporting Equipment	518
电气机械及器材制造业	Manufacture of Electrical Machinery and Equipment	177
通信设备、计算机及其他电子设备制造业	Manufacture of Communication Equipment, Computers and Other Electronic Equipment	41
仪器仪表及文化、办公用机械制造业	Manufacture of Measuring Instruments and Machinery for Cultural Activity and Office Work	64
其他制造业	Other Manufacture	14
废弃资源综合利用业	Comprehensive Utilization of Waste Resources	11
金属制品、机械和设备修理业	Repair of Metal Products, Machinery and Equipment	8
电力、热力的生产和供应业	Production and Supply of Electric Power and Heat Power	74
燃气生产和供应业	Production and Supply of Gas	34
水的生产和供应业	Production and Supply of Water	19

单位：万元 (10 000 yuan)

从业人员平均人数（万人） Average Employment (10 000 persons)	工业总产值 Gross Output Value	工业销售产值 Sales Value of Industry	其　中 of which	实收资本 Paid-in Capital	其　中 of which	
			#出口交货值 Value of Export Delivery		#国家资本 State Capital	#外商资本 Foreign Capital
126.09	**91497058**	**88597817**	**3739580**	**13143857**	**1784545**	**168931**
36.58	27561451	26575420	577465	6866949	1710574	127189
6.67	4091730	4134166	62387	1591984	333834	
1.26	378478	370986		35932	54	
44.91	29743783	28871882	2071219	3061488	252516	41566
81.18	61753275	59725935	1668361	10082369	1532028	127365
37.62	33256516	32263503	2075836	4923219	508064	127137
46.40	27828458	26772349	1228577	4255226	779439	13211
41.71	30015584	29164178	435167	3841559	497042	28583
0.36	396500	397787		123852		
16.11	3773610	3694395	10964	610252	125147	
0.12	100616	95146		1062	240	
0.47	95201	92038		28095	18845	
0.16	46122	36704		1418		
0.90	667683	653533		83015	1608	
4.42	3956261	3860955	82489	237655	14856	
1.75	1041719	1010866	26646	110235	6035	
1.13	777925	736353	14192	109336	1300	6881
0.54	1199668	1180462		108763	81959	
2.66	1587899	1553092	114864	131185		
1.31	459410	424425	23311	22115	100	
2.75	901308	890079	23005	35000		
0.44	245486	236082		32218		1510
0.61	329629	323129		22130		
1.10	711771	701896	31738	94198	4469	
0.95	505587	480011		77626	3907	
0.26	109821	105517	12578	12147		
0.60	469719	495931	5463	91090		
7.42	6230935	6085335	111330	1371846	178441	
3.21	2148470	2039081	79641	446397	53290	
0.03	71398	71454		1500		
2.42	1953043	1858370	3636	222658	3879	1000
8.97	5165247	5045718	18172	938341	62448	
3.15	4809734	4675289	3800	424789	14743	
2.61	4504458	4199412	169217	684466	97889	
4.53	2727437	2646668	109506	324106	7810	5855
5.45	3526978	3391091	161316	484179	38801	712
2.12	1442048	1453541	53567	168974	12209	
16.73	13921609	13268080	429634	1593412	69400	114426
16.84	11924365	11653632	1615416	1526848	22853	33174
5.42	6480018	6253387	279273	471437	80391	
1.64	1246583	1207949	143646	178377	8719	
1.55	630435	596367	13565	99838	1577	52
1.68	743841	682976	38540	211527	26222	
0.16	841662	790875	164071	10084		
0.23	98701	97093		11161		
4.65	5422392	5395749		1871668	772559	
0.52	493401	486469		104517	42333	5321
0.51	134871	128669		190193	32516	

表12.12 续表1 continued1

指 标	Item	资 产 Total Assets
总 计	**Total**	**74652141**
#国有控股企业	State-owned and State-holding Enterprises	39518877
按登记注册类型分	**By Status of Registration**	
#国有企业	State-owned	7560835
集体企业	Collective-owned	220888
按轻、重工业分	**By Light and Heavy Industries**	
轻工业	Light Industry	18720653
重工业	Heavy Industry	55931488
按企业规模分	**By Size**	
大型企业	Large	34250059
中型企业	Medium	22181262
小型企业	Small	17858136
微型企业	Mini	362684
按行业分	**By Sector**	
煤炭开采和洗选业	Mining and Washing of Coal	3532745
石油和天然气开采业	Extraction of Petroleum and Natural Gas	48743
黑色金属矿采选业	Mining and Processing of Ferrous Metal Ores	181155
有色金属矿采选业	Mining and Processing of Non-Ferrous Metal Ores	38807
非金属矿采选业	Mining and Processing of Nonmetal Ores	486251
开采辅助活动	Mining Support Activities	
其他采矿业	Mining of Other Ores	
农副食品加工业	Processing of Food from Agricultural Products	1244977
食品制造业	Manufacture of Foods	640322
酒、饮料和精制茶制造业	Liquor, Beverage and Refined Tea	494851
烟草制品业	Manufacture of Tobacco	723539
纺织业	Manufacture of Textile	587447
纺织服装、鞋、帽制造业	Manufacture of Textile Wearing Apparel, Footware and Caps	176545
皮革、毛皮、羽毛（绒）及其制品业	Manufacture of Leather, Fur, Feather and Related Products	245274
木材加工和木竹藤棕草制品业	Processing of Timber, Manufacture of Wood, Bamboo, Rattan, Palm and Straw Products	79611
家具制造业	Manufacture of Furniture	168256
造纸及纸制品业	Manufacture of Paper and Paper Products	389748
印刷业、记录媒介的复制	Printing, Reproduction of Recording Media	368478
文教、工美、体育和娱乐用品制造业	Manufacture of Culture, Education, Handicraft, Fine Arts, Sports and Entertainment Articles	58063
石油加工、炼焦及核燃料加工业	Processing of Petroleum, Coking, Processing of Nuclear Fuel	234622
化学原料及化学制品制造业	Manufacture of Raw Chemical Materials and Chemical Products	6456674
医药制造业	Manufacture of Medicines	2744066
化学纤维制造业	Manufacture of Chemical Fibers	14569
橡胶和塑料制品业	Manufacture of Rubber and Plastics	958329
非金属矿物制品业	Manufacture of Non-metallic Mineral Products	4547645
黑色金属冶炼及压延加工业	Smelting and Pressing of Ferrous Metals	1918383
有色金属冶炼及压延加工业	Smelting and Pressing of Nonferrous Metals	2856136
金属制品业	Manufacture of Metal Products	2159468
通用设备制造业	Manufacture of General Purpose Machinery	3086057
专用设备制造业	Manufacture of Special Purpose Machinery	1156235
汽车制造业	Manufacture of Motor Vehicles	10825217
铁路、船舶、航空航天和其他运输设备制造业	Manufacture of Railway, Ship, Aviation and Other Transporting Equipment	8177659
电气机械及器材制造业	Manufacture of Electrical Machinery and Equipment	3548303
通信设备、计算机及其他电子设备制造业	Manufacture of Communication Equipment, Computers and Other Electronic Equipment	901346
仪器仪表及文化、办公用机械制造业	Manufacture of Measuring Instruments and Machinery for Cultural Activity and Office Work	662327
其他制造业	Other Manufacture	1192686
废弃资源综合利用业	Comprehensive Utilization of Waste Resources	147139
金属制品、机械和设备修理业	Repair of Metal Products, Machinery and Equipment	28427
电力、热力的生产和供应业	Production and Supply of Electric Power and Heat Power	12291035
燃气生产和供应业	Production and Supply of Gas	480283
水的生产和供应业	Production and Supply of Water	800724

单位：万元 (10 000 yuan)

其 中 of which	固定资产 Fixed Assets		负 债	其 中 of which
#流动资产 Circulating Assets	原 值 Original Value	净 值 Net Value	Total Liabilities	#流动负债 Total Circulating Liabilities
34701186	**41705572**	**25055143**	**44709404**	**32535846**
15264529	23309212	15045843	24517125	16183776
2793783	4459912	2598122	4300174	2862319
107408	85349	48788	121693	110037
10623047	9229207	4979419	10618905	8808194
24078138	32476365	20075724	34090500	23727653
16171485	18102490	10709608	20292289	15790223
10429668	12471626	7387553	13967676	9855399
7938576	10979646	6826563	10188741	6727647
161457	151810	131420	260699	162577
1112205	1638806	1069635	1612334	1187321
23126	35303	12605	16548	16331
99822	27476	16344	116095	107879
28007	12131	10645	30837	29837
144855	234804	159744	199396	156698
577834	711594	443203	544145	437530
304851	407614	238662	366900	278959
261737	248894	159477	271618	246754
512023	336663	160043	324159	272590
295895	429088	248016	294970	193465
89679	78649	65352	83833	70962
141440	667168	68327	124811	95370
28856	52459	41636	25396	24481
98219	41326	31525	76123	70533
202678	175980	140125	220164	191582
189861	188998	120614	179216	125832
33366	29787	19680	22528	17931
109541	117557	63741	146708	129761
2622814	3691906	2115279	3789207	2563140
1385893	899620	599870	1389771	1152684
8778	6761	3539	4586	4586
473850	1067389	317238	526530	411920
1816325	2555929	1811438	2834038	1958701
1019981	1062539	590711	1185250	975623
1099459	1843451	1084930	2039262	1121469
1227180	984069	653923	1320805	1098420
2073152	1086785	615921	1872840	1643250
763273	332496	257986	680222	611278
5976190	4390659	2280545	6054236	5384558
5162272	3525353	1832867	4975748	4324382
2685834	808071	483436	2338673	2053469
477706	646334	324665	648366	487748
467770	184190	107879	433108	393209
609214	514216	359314	962893	743850
117945	17903	12967	122370	122320
14652	18684	12924	10372	9515
1980421	11880864	8008438	8219494	3502997
258984	249024	164434	261772	162415
205499	505036	347467	384086	156497

表12.12 续表2 continued2

指　标	Item	所有者权益 Creditors' Equity
总　计	**Total**	**29675521**
#国有控股企业	State-owned and State-holding Enterprises	14952000
按登记注册类型分	**By Status of Registration**	
#国有企业	State-owned	3262612
集体企业	Collective-owned	99027
按轻、重工业分	**By Light and Heavy Industries**	
轻工业	Light Industry	8028762
重工业	Heavy Industry	21646760
按企业规模分	**By Size**	
大型企业	Large	13889350
中型企业	Medium	8139192
小型企业	Small	7545837
微型企业	Mini	101143
按行业分	**By Sector**	
煤炭开采和洗选业	Mining and Washing of Coal	1902799
石油和天然气开采业	Extraction of Petroleum and Natural Gas	32195
黑色金属矿采选业	Mining and Processing of Ferrous Metal Ores	65029
有色金属矿采选业	Mining and Processing of Non-Ferrous Metal Ores	7952
非金属矿采选业	Mining and Processing of Nonmetal Ores	285648
开采辅助活动	Mining Support Activities	
其他采矿业	Mining of Other Ores	
农副食品加工业	Processing of Food from Agricultural Products	687448
食品制造业	Manufacture of Foods	270236
酒、饮料和精制茶制造业	Liquor, Beverage and Refined Tea	223001
烟草制品业	Manufacture of Tobacco	399380
纺织业	Manufacture of Textile	290877
纺织服装、鞋、帽制造业	Manufacture of Textile Wearing Apparel, Footware and Caps	92354
皮革、毛皮、羽毛（绒）及其制品业	Manufacture of Leather, Fur, Feather and Related Products	118582
木材加工和木竹藤棕草制品业	Processing of Timber, Manufacture of Wood, Bamboo, Rattan, Palm and Straw Products	53927
家具制造业	Manufacture of Furniture	90143
造纸及纸制品业	Manufacture of Paper and Paper Products	168179
印刷业、记录媒介的复制	Printing, Reproduction of Recording Media	187177
文教、工美、体育和娱乐用品制造业	Manufacture of Culture, Education, Handicraft, Fine Arts, Sports and Entertainment Articles	35379
石油加工、炼焦及核燃料加工业	Processing of Petroleum, Coking, Processing of Nuclear Fuel	86686
化学原料及化学制品制造业	Manufacture of Raw Chemical Materials and Chemical Products	2648716
医药制造业	Manufacture of Medicines	1341303
化学纤维制造业	Manufacture of Chemical Fibers	9983
橡胶和塑料制品业	Manufacture of Rubber and Plastics	399976
非金属矿物制品业	Manufacture of Non-metallic Mineral Products	1699184
黑色金属冶炼及压延加工业	Smelting and Pressing of Ferrous Metals	717660
有色金属冶炼及压延加工业	Smelting and Pressing of Nonferrous Metals	816075
金属制品业	Manufacture of Metal Products	830362
通用设备制造业	Manufacture of General Purpose Machinery	1184624
专用设备制造业	Manufacture of Special Purpose Machinery	469987
汽车制造业	Manufacture of Motor Vehicles	4752761
铁路、船舶、航空航天和其他运输设备制造业	Manufacture of Railway, Ship, Aviation and Other Transporting Equipment	3185279
电气机械及器材制造业	Manufacture of Electrical Machinery and Equipment	1168604
通信设备、计算机及其他电子设备制造业	Manufacture of Communication Equipment, Computers and Other Electronic Equipment	252895
仪器仪表及文化、办公用机械制造业	Manufacture of Measuring Instruments and Machinery for Cultural Activity and Office Work	229033
其他制造业	Other Manufacture	229793
废弃资源综合利用业	Comprehensive Utilization of Waste Resources	24706
金属制品、机械和设备修理业	Repair of Metal Products, Machinery and Equipment	18032
电力、热力的生产和供应业	Production and Supply of Electric Power and Heat Power	4059253
燃气生产和供应业	Production and Supply of Gas	224763
水的生产和供应业	Production and Supply of Water	415544

单位：万元 (10 000 yuan)

主营业务收入 Revenue from Principal Business	主营业务成本 Cost of Principal Business	主营业务税金及附加 Tax and Extra Charges of Principal Business	主营业务利润 Profit of Principal Business	利润总额 Total After-tax Profits	利税总额 Total Pre-tax Profits	工资总额 Total Wages
87278976	**74471884**	**994982**	**11812110**	**5307893**	**8977230**	**5348946**
26040397	22259713	695846	3084838	1133718	2833419	2129955
4115102	3517828	15544	581730	222249	368897	355416
385890	335061	2954	47876	11978	25462	41143
28537809	23588308	692491	4257011	1812916	3326097	1741299
58741167	50883575	302492	7555100	3494977	5651132	3607647
31382451	26974530	730064	3677856	1682520	3513887	2072978
26360614	22512861	114828	3732924	1663994	2579624	1877477
29138412	24626573	148501	4363338	1951843	2865206	1386946
397500	357919	1589	37992	9536	18512	11545
3726924	2953597	43246	730081	367062	658202	664516
85453	75029	666	9757	4528	6692	9392
98369	54513	1648	42208	-427	13165	16078
35494	29734	99	5661	4698	7911	5136
654462	541334	12063	101065	47339	81521	30136
3837534	3141831	13389	682313	211297	290358	175107
1024851	812150	4328	208373	76002	111631	56408
719924	547300	24651	147974	72773	127327	45539
1155830	397686	551063	207081	135492	822431	68030
1593022	1429374	5134	158513	89671	137847	91661
415413	336218	5726	73469	31932	44955	42958
880211	758689	2988	118534	49941	73414	100821
238542	203427	979	34136	15610	19554	10470
330140	258783	1953	69404	17833	27652	26802
687136	588644	3124	95369	31098	49354	35172
455678	384401	2209	69067	43265	60408	28472
109817	83931	1171	24716	11236	14750	7868
495942	418589	2533	74819	41412	56584	27223
6061799	5075903	23405	962491	346810	583637	358105
1998619	1473284	9499	515836	175572	273280	185743
65092	62843	518	1731	1631	3370	741
1802206	1563681	6753	231712	127708	177784	85207
4959748	4144556	31790	783403	379451	610894	303734
4633166	3914547	11238	707381	286128	432182	105824
4040274	3789476	9405	241394	144896	214814	134119
2635569	2244854	11173	379542	176839	242294	182275
3436799	2858417	13841	564541	236720	344420	239269
1462799	1165638	8675	288485	147285	186817	82595
12704730	11107745	86527	1510457	761955	1193788	688692
11403722	10071389	48124	1284209	562886	860795	634141
6124527	5391694	21924	710909	395159	549097	210449
1198709	1050895	5063	142751	36399	61247	57194
598443	484243	2546	111654	43924	64764	65482
659700	630114	1001	28585	34413	42645	98217
788369	762318	1841	24210	9794	29366	5567
96679	83741	458	12481	6888	10966	13701
5408943	5052098	19369	337477	102754	386997	407025
500695	422464	3395	74836	54484	68646	34675
153647	106756	1466	45426	25435	35670	14402

表12.13 内资工业企业经济效益指标（2011年）
INDICATORS ON ECONOMIC BENEFIT OF INDUSTRIAL ENTERPRISES WITH HONG KONG, MACAO, TAIWAN AND FOREIGN FUNDS (2011)

指　标	Item	总资产贡献率 Ratio of Total Assets to Industrial Output Value
总　计	**Total**	**13.2**
按轻、重工业分	**By Light and Heavy Industries**	
轻工业	Light Industry	18.8
重工业	Heavy Industry	11.3
按企业规模分	**By Size**	
大型企业	Large	11.2
中型企业	Medium	13.0
小型企业	Small	17.5
微型企业	Mini	6.1
按行业分	**By Sector**	
煤炭开采和洗选业	Mining and Washing of Coal	19.5
石油和天然气开采业	Extraction of Petroleum and Natural Gas	14.0
黑色金属矿采选业	Mining and Processing of Ferrous Metal Ores	8.5
有色金属矿采选业	Mining and Processing of Non-Ferrous Metal Ores	20.4
非金属矿采选业	Mining and Processing of Nonmetal Ores	18.1
开采辅助活动	Mining Support Activities	
其他采矿业	Mining of Other Ores	
农副食品加工业	Processing of Food from Agricultural Products	24.6
食品制造业	Manufacture of Foods	19.4
酒、饮料和精制茶制造业	Liquor, Beverage and Refined Tea	26.8
烟草制品业	Manufacture of Tobacco	114.5
纺织业	Manufacture of Textile	24.6
纺织服装、服饰业	Manufacture of Textile Wearing Apparel, Footware and Caps	27.0
皮革、毛皮、羽毛（绒）及其制品业	Manufacture of Leather, Fur, Feather and Related Products	30.9
木材加工和木竹藤棕草制品业	Processing of Timber, Manufacture of Wood, Bamboo, Rattan, Palm and Straw Products	25.1
家具制造业	Manufacture of Furniture	17.7
造纸及纸制品业	Manufacture of Paper and Paper Products	13.7
印刷业、记录媒介的复制	Printing, Reproduction of Recording Media	17.3
文教、工美、体育和娱乐用品制造业	Manufacture of Culture, Education, Handicraft, Fine Arts, Sports and Entertainment Articles	26.1
石油加工、炼焦及核燃料加工业	Processing of Petroleum, Coking, Processing of Nuclear Fuel	25.7
化学原料及化学制品制造业	Manufacture of Raw Chemical Materials and Chemical Products	10.6
医药制造业	Manufacture of Medicines	11.1
化学纤维制造业	Manufacture of Chemical Fibers	24.4
橡胶和塑料制品业	Manufacture of Rubber and Plastics	19.6
非金属矿物制品业	Manufacture of Non-metallic Mineral Products	14.7
黑色金属冶炼及压延加工业	Smelting and Pressing of Ferrous Metals	23.7
有色金属冶炼及压延加工业	Smelting and Pressing of Nonferrous Metals	9.1
金属制品业	Manufacture of Metal Products	12.3
通用设备制造业	Manufacture of General Purpose Machinery	12.0
专用设备制造业	Manufacture of Special Purpose Machinery	16.6
汽车制造业	Manufacture of Motor Vehicles	11.4
铁路、船舶、航空航天和其他运输设备制造业	Manufacture of Railway, Ship, Aviation and Other Transporting Equipment	11.6
电气机械及器材制造业	Manufacture of Electrical Machinery and Equipment	16.5
计算机、通信和其他电子设备制造业	Manufacture of Communication Equipment, Computers and Other Electronic Equipment	8.0
仪器仪表及文化、办公用机械制造业	Manufacture of Measuring Instruments and Machinery for Cultural Activity and Office Work	10.5
其他制造业	Other Manufacture	4.6
废弃资源综合利用业	Comprehensive Utilization of Waste Resources	23.5
金属制品、机械和设备修理业	Repair of Metal Products, Machinery and Equipment	38.4
电力、热力的生产和供应业	Production and Supply of Electric Power and Heat Power	5.3
燃气生产和供应业	Production and Supply of Gas	14.3
水的生产和供应业	Production and Supply of Water	4.8

单位：% (%)

资本保值增值率 Ratio of Assets Appreciation YOY	资产负债率 Asset-Liability Ratio	流动资产周转率（次） Turnover Ratio of Circulating Assets (time)	成本费用利润率 Ratio of Profits to Cost	全员劳动生产率（元/人年） Overall Labor Productivity (yuan/person-year)	产品销售率 Sales as Percentage of Output
121.9	**59.9**	**2.6**	**6.4**	**196968**	**96.8**
132.5	56.7	2.7	6.8	180516	97.1
118.9	61.0	2.5	6.1	206068	96.7
115.4	59.2	2.0	5.4	240108	97.0
129.7	63.0	2.6	6.6	166931	96.2
128.5	57.1	3.7	7.2	190699	97.2
72.5	71.9	2.5	2.5	285243	100.3
147.3	45.6	3.5	10.7	117267	97.9
102.4	33.9	3.7	5.6	363999	94.6
86.3	64.1	1.1	-0.4	131657	96.7
116.2	79.5	1.3	14.3	101294	79.6
123.5	41.0	4.5	8.1	220287	97.9
128.4	43.7	6.7	6.0	188273	97.6
132.7	57.3	3.4	8.1	147747	97.0
108.4	54.9	2.8	11.3	206978	94.7
113.4	44.8	2.3	28.1	1712339	98.4
136.2	50.2	5.4	5.9	154351	97.8
101.1	47.5	4.6	8.4	103054	92.4
133.5	50.9	6.5	5.9	105515	98.8
122.2	31.9	8.3	7.2	131928	96.2
130.5	45.2	3.4	6.0	133611	98.0
116.5	56.5	3.4	4.9	148170	98.6
126.5	48.6	2.4	10.0	147084	94.9
113.0	38.8	3.3	12.7	156954	96.1
141.0	62.5	4.5	9.1	207583	105.6
122.1	58.7	2.4	5.9	237095	97.7
143.8	50.6	1.5	9.5	220317	94.9
100.2	31.5	7.4	2.6	613844	100.1
145.6	54.9	3.8	7.6	217332	95.2
123.3	62.3	2.8	8.3	175149	97.7
136.6	61.8	4.6	6.7	377763	97.2
115.2	71.4	4.0	3.3	390176	93.2
114.6	61.2	2.2	7.2	153067	97.0
122.5	60.7	1.7	7.2	180577	96.2
148.4	58.8	1.9	11.0	183068	100.8
122.7	55.9	2.2	6.1	182290	95.3
111.6	60.8	2.2	5.1	175576	97.7
111.0	65.9	2.4	6.6	228934	96.5
83.7	71.9	2.5	3.2	215481	96.9
126.3	65.4	1.3	7.6	120604	94.6
95.1	80.7	1.3	4.4	123930	91.8
91.7	83.2	6.7	1.3	1016045	94.0
120.0	36.5	6.6	7.7	133396	98.4
118.1	66.9	2.8	1.9	364485	99.5
113.3	54.5	2.0	11.5	228482	98.6
129.6	48.0	0.9	16.1	174414	95.4

表12.13 续表 continued

指　标	Item	销售利润率 Rate of Return on Sale
总　计	**Total**	**6.1**
按轻、重工业分	**By Light and Heavy Industries**	
轻工业	Light Industry	6.4
重工业	Heavy Industry	5.9
按企业规模分	**By Size**	
大型企业	Large	5.4
中型企业	Medium	6.3
小型企业	Small	6.7
微型企业	Mini	2.4
按行业分	**By Sector**	
煤炭开采和洗选业	Mining and Washing of Coal	9.8
石油和天然气开采业	Extraction of Petroleum and Natural Gas	5.3
黑色金属矿采选业	Mining and Processing of Ferrous Metal Ores	-0.4
有色金属矿采选业	Mining and Processing of Non-Ferrous Metal Ores	13.2
非金属矿采选业	Mining and Processing of Nonmetal Ores	7.2
开采辅助活动	Mining Support Activities	
其他采矿业	Mining of Other Ores	
农副食品加工业	Processing of Food from Agricultural Products	5.5
食品制造业	Manufacture of Foods	7.4
酒、饮料和精制茶制造业	Liquor, Beverage and Refined Tea	10.1
烟草制品业	Manufacture of Tobacco	11.7
纺织业	Manufacture of Textile	5.6
纺织服装、服饰业	Manufacture of Textile Wearing Apparel, Footware and Caps	7.7
皮革、毛皮、羽毛（绒）及其制品业	Manufacture of Leather, Fur, Feather and Related Products	5.7
木材加工和木竹藤棕草制品业	Processing of Timber, Manufacture of Wood, Bamboo, Rattan, Palm and Straw Products	6.5
家具制造业	Manufacture of Furniture	5.4
造纸及纸制品业	Manufacture of Paper and Paper Products	4.5
印刷业、记录媒介的复制	Printing, Reproduction of Recording Media	9.5
文教、工美、体育和娱乐用品制造业	Manufacture of Culture, Education, Handicraft, Fine Arts, Sports and Entertainment Articles	10.2
石油加工、炼焦及核燃料加工业	Processing of Petroleum, Coking, Processing of Nuclear Fuel	8.4
化学原料及化学制品制造业	Manufacture of Raw Chemical Materials and Chemical Products	5.7
医药制造业	Manufacture of Medicines	8.8
化学纤维制造业	Manufacture of Chemical Fibers	2.5
橡胶和塑料制品业	Manufacture of Rubber and Plastics	7.1
非金属矿物制品业	Manufacture of Non-metallic Mineral Products	7.7
黑色金属冶炼及压延加工业	Smelting and Pressing of Ferrous Metals	6.2
有色金属冶炼及压延加工业	Smelting and Pressing of Nonferrous Metals	3.6
金属制品业	Manufacture of Metal Products	6.7
通用设备制造业	Manufacture of General Purpose Machinery	6.9
专用设备制造业	Manufacture of Special Purpose Machinery	10.1
汽车制造业	Manufacture of Motor Vehicles	6.0
铁路、船舶、航空航天和其他运输设备制造业	Manufacture of Railway, Ship, Aviation and Other Transporting Equipment	4.9
电气机械及器材制造业	Manufacture of Electrical Machinery and Equipment	6.5
计算机、通信和其他电子设备制造业	Manufacture of Communication Equipment, Computers and Other Electronic Equipment	3.0
仪器仪表及文化、办公用机械制造业	Manufacture of Measuring Instruments and Machinery for Cultural Activity and Office Work	7.3
其他制造业	Other Manufacture	5.2
废弃资源综合利用业	Comprehensive Utilization of Waste Resources	1.2
金属制品、机械和设备修理业	Repair of Metal Products, Machinery and Equipment	7.1
电力、热力的生产和供应业	Production and Supply of Electric Power and Heat Power	1.9
燃气生产和供应业	Production and Supply of Gas	10.9
水的生产和供应业	Production and Supply of Water	16.6

资本积累率 Rate of Capital Accumulation	流动比率 Current Ratio	速动比率 Quick Ratio	产权比率 Equity Ratio	人均实现利税（元） Per Capita Pre-tax Profits (yuan)	从业人员人均工资（元） Per Capita Wages of Employees (yuan)
21.9	**1.1**	**0.8**	**1.5**	**71196**	**42421**
32.5	1.2	0.9	1.3	74067	38776
18.9	1.0	0.8	1.6	69609	44438
15.4	1.0	0.8	1.5	93403	55102
29.7	1.1	0.8	1.7	55601	40467
28.5	1.2	0.9	1.4	68691	33251
-27.5	1.0	0.9	2.6	50998	31806
47.3	0.9	0.8	0.8	40845	41237
2.4	1.4	1.3	0.5	57052	80068
-13.7	0.9	0.8	1.8	28191	34428
16.2	0.9	0.5	3.9	48835	31704
23.5	0.9	0.7	0.7	90639	33507
28.4	1.3	1.0	0.8	65622	39575
32.7	1.1	0.8	1.4	63749	32213
8.4	1.1	0.7	1.2	113180	40479
13.4	1.9	0.8	0.8	1536679	127112
36.2	1.5	1.0	1.0	51846	34475
1.1	1.3	0.8	0.9	34401	32873
33.5	1.5	0.9	1.1	26728	36706
22.2	1.2	0.8	0.5	44940	24063
30.5	1.4	0.8	0.8	45235	43845
16.5	1.1	0.8	1.3	44904	32000
26.5	1.5	1.2	1.0	63608	29979
13.0	1.9	1.5	0.6	55914	29826
41.0	0.8	0.4	1.7	94670	45546
22.1	1.0	0.8	1.4	78659	48263
43.8	1.2	1.0	1.0	85174	57891
0.2	1.9	1.1	0.5	101515	22322
45.6	1.2	0.7	1.3	73422	35189
23.3	0.9	0.8	1.7	68083	33851
36.6	1.0	0.8	1.7	137345	33630
15.2	1.0	0.6	2.5	82450	51477
14.6	1.1	0.9	1.6	53474	40228
22.5	1.3	1.0	1.6	63243	43935
48.4	1.2	0.9	1.4	88109	38954
22.7	1.1	0.9	1.3	71363	41169
11.6	1.2	1.0	1.6	51127	37665
11.0	1.3	1.0	2.0	101347	38843
-16.3	1.0	0.7	2.6	37393	34919
26.3	1.2	0.9	1.9	41837	42301
-4.9	0.8	0.6	4.2	25371	58431
-8.3	1.0	0.8	5.0	183768	34839
20.0	1.5	1.4	0.6	47023	58750
18.1	0.6	0.5	2.0	83222	87529
13.3	1.6	1.5	1.2	131355	66352
29.6	1.3	1.2	0.9	70633	28519

表12.14 外商投资和港澳台投资工业企业主要经济指标（2011年）

MAIN ECONOMIC INDICATORS OF INDUSTRIAL ENTERPRISES WITH HONG KONG, MACAO, TAIWAN AND FOREIGN FUNDS (2011)

指 标	Item	单位数（个） Number of Enterprises (unit)
总 计	**Total**	**285**
#国有控股企业	State-owned and State-holding Enterprises	28
按登记注册类型分	**By Status of Registration**	
#港澳台投资企业	Funded by Hong Kong, Macao and Taiwan	109
外商投资企业	Foreign-funded	176
按轻、重工业分	**By Light and Heavy Industries**	
轻工业	Light Industry	84
重工业	Heavy Industry	201
按企业规模分	**By Size**	
大型企业	Large	40
中型企业	Medium	87
小型企业	Small	153
微型企业	Mini	5
按行业分	**By Sector**	
煤炭开采和洗选业	Mining and Washing of Coal	
石油和天然气开采业	Extraction of Petroleum and Natural Gas	
黑色金属矿采选业	Mining and Processing of Ferrous Metal Ores	
有色金属矿采选业	Mining and Processing of Non-Ferrous Metal Ores	
非金属矿采选业	Mining and Processing of Nonmetal Ores	
开采辅助活动	Mining Support Activities	
其他采矿业	Mining of Other Ores	
农副食品加工业	Processing of Food from Agricultural Products	12
食品制造业	Manufacture of Foods	2
酒、饮料和精制茶制造业	Liquor, Beverage and Refined Tea	6
烟草制品业	Manufacture of Tobacco	
纺织业	Manufacture of Textile	5
纺织服装、鞋、帽制造业	Manufacture of Textile Wearing Apparel, Footware and Caps	9
皮革、毛皮、羽毛（绒）及其制品业	Manufacture of Leather, Fur, Feather and Related Products	
木材加工和木竹藤棕草制品业	Processing of Timber, Manufacture of Wood, Bamboo, Rattan, Palm and Straw Products	2
家具制造业	Manufacture of Furniture	3
造纸及纸制品业	Manufacture of Paper and Paper Products	8
印刷业、记录媒介的复制	Printing, Reproduction of Recording Media	3
文教、工美、体育和娱乐用品制造业	Manufacture of Culture, Education, Handicraft, Fine Arts, Sports and Entertainment Articles	2
石油加工、炼焦及核燃料加工业	Processing of Petroleum, Coking, Processing of Nuclear Fuel	
化学原料及化学制品制造业	Manufacture of Raw Chemical Materials and Chemical Products	20
医药制造业	Manufacture of Medicines	4
化学纤维制造业	Manufacture of Chemical Fibers	
橡胶和塑料制品业	Manufacture of Rubber and Plastics	15
非金属矿物制品业	Manufacture of Non-metallic Mineral Products	23
黑色金属冶炼及压延加工业	Smelting and Pressing of Ferrous Metals	3
有色金属冶炼及压延加工业	Smelting and Pressing of Nonferrous Metals	6
金属制品业	Manufacture of Metal Products	8
通用设备制造业	Manufacture of General Purpose Machinery	16
专用设备制造业	Manufacture of Special Purpose Machinery	11
汽车制造业	Manufacture of Motor Vehicles	57
铁路、船舶、航空航天和其他运输设备制造业	Manufacture of Railway, Ship, Aviation and Other Transporting Equipment	14
电气机械及器材制造业	Manufacture of Electrical Machinery and Equipment	13
通信设备、计算机及其他电子设备制造业	Manufacture of Communication Equipment, Computers and Other Electronic Equipment	26
仪器仪表及文化、办公用机械制造业	Manufacture of Measuring Instruments and Machinery for Cultural Activity and Office Work	11
其他制造业	Other Manufacture	
废弃资源综合利用业	Comprehensive Utilization of Waste Resources	
金属制品、机械和设备修理业	Repair of Metal Products, Machinery and Equipment	
电力、热力的生产和供应业	Production and Supply of Electric Power and Heat Power	1
燃气生产和供应业	Production and Supply of Gas	3
水的生产和供应业	Production and Supply of Water	2

单位：万元 (10 000 yuan)

从业人员平均人数（万人） Average Employment (10 000 persons)	工业总产值 Gross Output Value	工业销售产值 Sales Value of Industry	其 中 of which	实收资本 Paid-in Capital	其 中 of which	
			#出口交货值 Value of Export Delivery		#国家资本 State Capital	#外商资本 Foreign Capital
19.67	**26973523**	**26747341**	**5485189**	**3856082**	**206711**	**1360340**
6.12	11429061	11430926	342681	1349299	173536	435754
8.88	10456362	10263694	4331143	1514737	21260	94104
10.79	16517161	16483647	1154045	2341344	185452	1266236
4.69	4017300	3946423	365868	930877	5655	214280
14.98	22956222	22800918	5119321	2925205	201056	1146061
12.07	19561213	19489814	4724770	2210462	169200	727064
5.35	5015107	4936525	612894	996062	20547	360618
2.24	2340467	2264363	147525	629030	16965	253440
	56736	56638		20527		19217
0.23	717886	710117	11056	45930	1793	27838
0.27	222991	218702		22261		
0.72	455893	473942		111353	866	65329
0.19	169306	167865	27719	21740		18690
0.76	188533	156398	71419	29921		1666
0.02	9811	9674	7102	370		40
0.32	271657	280790		14603		
0.53	602040	568805	2256	465063		22576
0.12	131298	131796		22764		10397
0.20	44454	44281	7066	13482		3482
0.45	1124262	1088205	20150	356999	17815	248784
0.10	49392	47834	40931	11569		667
0.68	514958	508998	18840	73019		38564
1.22	910997	858353	132152	534946	1516	265012
1.63	2523443	2496847		174913		
0.13	502231	485441	23810	33945		
0.20	84877	82977	38151	28190		12349
0.86	926064	919845	200155	175488	34431	86314
0.41	508109	493174	2674	38033		12165
4.12	8071660	8147546	50817	879349	142862	369499
0.64	741999	737213	195730	92896		44997
0.47	426255	372456	25226	59875	2283	9740
4.29	6907774	6884597	4561909	371637	5146	54431
0.69	519712	515729	48027	57912		18601
0.02	23143	20979		16000		14200
0.29	278965	278965		141650		35000
0.07	45814	45814		62176		

表12.14 续表1 continued1

指 标	Item	资 产 Total Assets
总 计	**Total**	**18558844**
#国有控股企业	State-owned and State-holding Enterprises	8246760
按登记注册类型分	**By Status of Registration**	
#港澳台投资企业	Funded by Hong Kong, Macao and Taiwan	7684894
外商投资企业	Foreign-funded	10873951
按轻、重工业分	**By Light and Heavy Industries**	
轻工业	Light Industry	3423521
重工业	Heavy Industry	15135324
按企业规模分	**By Size**	
大型企业	Large	12208206
中型企业	Medium	4059022
小型企业	Small	2240661
微型企业	Mini	50956
按行业分	**By Sector**	
煤炭开采和洗选业	Mining and Washing of Coal	
石油和天然气开采业	Extraction of Petroleum and Natural Gas	
黑色金属矿采选业	Mining and Processing of Ferrous Metal Ores	
有色金属矿采选业	Mining and Processing of Non-Ferrous Metal Ores	
非金属矿采选业	Mining and Processing of Nonmetal Ores	
开采辅助活动	Mining Support Activities	
其他采矿业	Mining of Other Ores	
农副食品加工业	Processing of Food from Agricultural Products	388060
食品制造业	Manufacture of Foods	175273
酒、饮料和精制茶制造业	Liquor, Beverage and Refined Tea	499918
烟草制品业	Manufacture of Tobacco	
纺织业	Manufacture of Textile	80218
纺织服装、鞋、帽制造业	Manufacture of Textile Wearing Apparel, Footware and Caps	93228
皮革、毛皮、羽毛（绒）及其制品业	Manufacture of Leather, Fur, Feather and Related Products	
木材加工和木竹藤棕草制品业	Processing of Timber, Manufacture of Wood, Bamboo, Rattan, Palm and Straw Products	7419
家具制造业	Manufacture of Furniture	165256
造纸及纸制品业	Manufacture of Paper and Paper Products	1041385
印刷业、记录媒介的复制	Printing, Reproduction of Recording Media	102949
文教、工美、体育和娱乐用品制造业	Manufacture of Culture, Education, Handicraft, Fine Arts, Sports and Entertainment Articles	65551
石油加工、炼焦及核燃料加工业	Processing of Petroleum, Coking, Processing of Nuclear Fuel	
化学原料及化学制品制造业	Manufacture of Raw Chemical Materials and Chemical Products	1086393
医药制造业	Manufacture of Medicines	69773
化学纤维制造业	Manufacture of Chemical Fibers	
橡胶和塑料制品业	Manufacture of Rubber and Plastics	314791
非金属矿物制品业	Manufacture of Non-metallic Mineral Products	1960989
黑色金属冶炼及压延加工业	Smelting and Pressing of Ferrous Metals	2586666
有色金属冶炼及压延加工业	Smelting and Pressing of Nonferrous Metals	284680
金属制品业	Manufacture of Metal Products	75397
通用设备制造业	Manufacture of General Purpose Machinery	662678
专用设备制造业	Manufacture of Special Purpose Machinery	223779
汽车制造业	Manufacture of Motor Vehicles	4467471
铁路、船舶、航空航天和其他运输设备制造业	Manufacture of Railway, Ship, Aviation and Other Transporting Equipment	361130
电气机械及器材制造业	Manufacture of Electrical Machinery and Equipment	276024
通信设备、计算机及其他电子设备制造业	Manufacture of Communication Equipment, Computers and Other Electronic Equipment	2395896
仪器仪表及文化、办公用机械制造业	Manufacture of Measuring Instruments and Machinery for Cultural Activity and Office Work	420738
其他制造业	Other Manufacture	
废弃资源综合利用业	Comprehensive Utilization of Waste Resources	
金属制品、机械和设备修理业	Repair of Metal Products, Machinery and Equipment	
电力、热力的生产和供应业	Production and Supply of Electric Power and Heat Power	44327
燃气生产和供应业	Production and Supply of Gas	517260
水的生产和供应业	Production and Supply of Water	191597

单位：万元 (10 000 yuan)

其 中 of which	固定资产 Fixed Assets		负 债	其 中 of which
#流动资产 Circulating Assets	原 值 Original Value	净 值 Net Value	Total Liabilities	#流动负债 Total Circulating Liabilities
10388024	**8528935**	**5286573**	**11888040**	**9442199**
4579423	3349823	2209519	5522519	4216789
3920484	3016502	2178891	5127468	3582801
6467540	5512433	3107682	6760572	5859398
1740618	1594910	1117058	1868243	1433669
8647406	6934025	4169515	10019797	8008529
6869426	4787142	3335231	8065676	6386692
2322581	2363101	1166243	2515973	2072492
1175552	1353462	766448	1265180	945187
20466	25230	18651	41212	37827
314874	87535	57683	299057	294173
98491	74144	40097	68120	68120
201697	332072	198232	291253	284692
37408	49160	39549	53476	27099
57562	40129	29315	37337	35992
4927	3601	2210	2887	2794
140179	29627	19020	105208	105208
336617	523521	429197	516315	209644
39261	79217	57729	50701	39021
38410	12962	10795	14967	12305
386478	883300	618938	492183	322241
38665	22545	16611	34861	33670
158882	495335	112830	196555	181396
638036	1344269	889333	1282693	801034
1242585	743851	693173	2131978	1277188
209209	55847	43135	218374	212003
36070	67161	32509	53734	52804
458860	207765	133697	404040	385981
139370	249888	32318	99265	84390
2931896	1837428	970036	2656065	2424370
255509	138055	68369	229607	211187
197339	85160	60589	115498	103729
1870745	673916	390199	1842561	1811482
332678	95535	49628	237340	229398
5542	29361	20579	41487	20173
205485	180936	117527	277961	161055
11252	186616	153276	134521	51051

表12.14 续表2 continued2

指 标	Item	所有者权益 Creditors' Equity
总 计	**Total**	**6616662**
#国有控股企业	State-owned and State-holding Enterprises	2704241
按登记注册类型分	**By Status of Registration**	
#港澳台投资企业	Funded by Hong Kong, Macao and Taiwan	2536313
外商投资企业	Foreign-funded	4080349
按轻、重工业分	**By Light and Heavy Industries**	
轻工业	Light Industry	1551676
重工业	Heavy Industry	5064986
按企业规模分	**By Size**	
大型企业	Large	4112530
中型企业	Medium	1526412
小型企业	Small	967976
微型企业	Mini	9744
按行业分	**By Sector**	
煤炭开采和洗选业	Mining and Washing of Coal	
石油和天然气开采业	Extraction of Petroleum and Natural Gas	
黑色金属矿采选业	Mining and Processing of Ferrous Metal Ores	
有色金属矿采选业	Mining and Processing of Non-Ferrous Metal Ores	
非金属矿采选业	Mining and Processing of Nonmetal Ores	
开采辅助活动	Mining Support Activities	
其他采矿业	Mining of Other Ores	
农副食品加工业	Processing of Food from Agricultural Products	86248
食品制造业	Manufacture of Foods	107153
酒、饮料和精制茶制造业	Liquor, Beverage and Refined Tea	208665
烟草制品业	Manufacture of Tobacco	
纺织业	Manufacture of Textile	26743
纺织服装、鞋、帽制造业	Manufacture of Textile Wearing Apparel, Footware and Caps	55488
皮革、毛皮、羽毛（绒）及其制品业	Manufacture of Leather, Fur, Feather and Related Products	
木材加工和木竹藤棕草制品业	Processing of Timber, Manufacture of Wood, Bamboo, Rattan, Palm and Straw Products	4532
家具制造业	Manufacture of Furniture	60049
造纸及纸制品业	Manufacture of Paper and Paper Products	525070
印刷业、记录媒介的复制	Printing, Reproduction of Recording Media	52248
文教、工美、体育和娱乐用品制造业	Manufacture of Culture, Education, Handicraft, Fine Arts, Sports and Entertainment Articles	50584
石油加工、炼焦及核燃料加工业	Processing of Petroleum, Coking, Processing of Nuclear Fuel	
化学原料及化学制品制造业	Manufacture of Raw Chemical Materials and Chemical Products	594209
医药制造业	Manufacture of Medicines	34912
化学纤维制造业	Manufacture of Chemical Fibers	
橡胶和塑料制品业	Manufacture of Rubber and Plastics	114727
非金属矿物制品业	Manufacture of Non-metallic Mineral Products	668295
黑色金属冶炼及压延加工业	Smelting and Pressing of Ferrous Metals	454687
有色金属冶炼及压延加工业	Smelting and Pressing of Nonferrous Metals	66307
金属制品业	Manufacture of Metal Products	21686
通用设备制造业	Manufacture of General Purpose Machinery	253295
专用设备制造业	Manufacture of Special Purpose Machinery	123813
汽车制造业	Manufacture of Motor Vehicles	1810607
铁路、船舶、航空航天和其他运输设备制造业	Manufacture of Railway, Ship, Aviation and Other Transporting Equipment	131523
电气机械及器材制造业	Manufacture of Electrical Machinery and Equipment	161058
通信设备、计算机及其他电子设备制造业	Manufacture of Communication Equipment, Computers and Other Electronic Equipment	522153
仪器仪表及文化、办公用机械制造业	Manufacture of Measuring Instruments and Machinery for Cultural Activity and Office Work	183398
其他制造业	Other Manufacture	
废弃资源综合利用业	Comprehensive Utilization of Waste Resources	
金属制品、机械和设备修理业	Repair of Metal Products, Machinery and Equipment	
电力、热力的生产和供应业	Production and Supply of Electric Power and Heat Power	2840
燃气生产和供应业	Production and Supply of Gas	239299
水的生产和供应业	Production and Supply of Water	57076

单位：万元 (10 000 yuan)

主营业务收入 Revenue from Principal Business	主营业务成本 Cost of Principal Business	主营业务税金及附加 Tax and Extra Charges of Principal Business	主营业务利润 Profit of Principal Business	利润总额 Total After-tax Profits	利税总额 Total Pre-tax Profits	工资总额 Total Wages
26544465	**22914264**	**362273**	**3267928**	**1295578**	**2665799**	**1023624**
11222905	9388646	313460	1520800	497542	1361837	391720
9997904	9184361	20673	792870	274657	563521	466151
16546562	13729903	341600	2475059	1020921	2102279	557473
4043761	3409304	31417	603040	316872	501565	197179
22500704	19504960	330855	2664889	978706	2164234	826445
19138158	16533907	340160	2264091	762455	1914936	694370
5033339	4399998	13778	619563	378356	532024	229827
2302547	1913245	8245	381057	160236	223288	97894
70421	67114	90	3217	-5469	-4449	1533
722026	685008	160	36858	38874	69561	12217
274409	226932	1090	46387	18059	32719	16774
497870	353750	18250	125870	26268	69902	34601
181622	167275	69	14277	7059	14627	19298
156787	122178	443	34166	17886	20852	21629
9674	7651	34	1989	1140	1427	1139
285850	231020	379	54452	41454	46210	10764
563099	475917	2214	84968	56482	77471	19939
130628	105275	519	24835	16776	22322	6451
44281	25950	411	17920	14143	17956	5964
1080645	829805	3926	246915	101126	137662	24503
45056	29682	282	15092	8378	11777	5709
498798	462589	1235	34974	19023	27869	27368
878491	665470	4377	208645	33077	72163	63235
2360770	2270283	1655	88831	-47608	-16131	105539
485441	393285	863	91292	86850	101629	6116
90278	80172	137	9970	1437	2374	6578
968123	752939	4496	210688	141254	171898	45979
492023	428056	1336	62632	17110	21470	11399
8165967	6553511	307152	1305304	530893	1333534	227284
724560	663567	5436	55558	13212	40463	17723
370266	310318	1321	58628	41082	54549	18664
6691809	6413193	1499	277117	43951	231512	235146
467677	356056	2225	109396	33649	59113	50007
20470	18897		1573	529	1310	781
285031	252100	2189	30742	25799	30817	22726
52815	33386	577	18853	7676	10741	6089

表12.15 外商投资和港澳台投资工业企业经济效益指标（2011年）
INDICATORS ON ECONOMIC BENEFIT OF INDUSTRIAL ENTERPRISES WITH HONG KONG, MACAO, TAIWAN AND FOREIGN FUNDS (2011)

指 标	Item	总资产贡献率 Ratio of Total Assets to Industrial Output Value
总 计	**Total**	**15.5**
按轻、重工业分	**By Light and Heavy Industries**	
轻工业	Light Industry	15.4
重工业	Heavy Industry	15.5
按企业规模分	**By Size**	
大型企业	Large	16.8
中型企业	Medium	14.3
小型企业	Small	11.2
微型企业	Mini	-7.7
按行业分	**By Sector**	
煤炭开采和洗选业	Mining and Washing of Coal	
石油和天然气开采业	Extraction of Petroleum and Natural Gas	
黑色金属矿采选业	Mining and Processing of Ferrous Metal Ores	
有色金属矿采选业	Mining and Processing of Non-Ferrous Metal Ores	
非金属矿采选业	Mining and Processing of Nonmetal Ores	
开采辅助活动	Mining Support Activities	
其他采矿业	Mining of Other Ores	
农副食品加工业	Processing of Food from Agricultural Products	18.4
食品制造业	Manufacture of Foods	17.7
酒、饮料和精制茶制造业	Liquor, Beverage and Refined Tea	15.3
烟草制品业	Manufacture of Tobacco	
纺织业	Manufacture of Textile	20.2
纺织服装、服饰业	Manufacture of Textile Wearing Apparel, Footware and Caps	22.6
皮革、毛皮、羽毛（绒）及其制品业	Manufacture of Leather, Fur, Feather and Related Products	
木材加工和木竹藤棕草制品业	Processing of Timber, Manufacture of Wood, Bamboo, Rattan, Palm and Straw Products	21.0
家具制造业	Manufacture of Furniture	27.8
造纸及纸制品业	Manufacture of Paper and Paper Products	8.4
印刷业、记录媒介的复制	Printing, Reproduction of Recording Media	23.4
文教、工美、体育和娱乐用品制造业	Manufacture of Culture, Education, Handicraft, Fine Arts, Sports and Entertainment Articles	27.2
石油加工、炼焦及核燃料加工业	Processing of Petroleum, Coking, Processing of Nuclear Fuel	
化学原料及化学制品制造业	Manufacture of Raw Chemical Materials and Chemical Products	14.9
医药制造业	Manufacture of Medicines	17.3
化学纤维制造业	Manufacture of Chemical Fibers	
橡胶和塑料制品业	Manufacture of Rubber and Plastics	10.5
非金属矿物制品业	Manufacture of Non-metallic Mineral Products	5.9
黑色金属冶炼及压延加工业	Smelting and Pressing of Ferrous Metals	2.6
有色金属冶炼及压延加工业	Smelting and Pressing of Nonferrous Metals	39.1
金属制品业	Manufacture of Metal Products	5.3
通用设备制造业	Manufacture of General Purpose Machinery	26.1
专用设备制造业	Manufacture of Special Purpose Machinery	10.1
汽车制造业	Manufacture of Motor Vehicles	29.9
铁路、船舶、航空航天和其他运输设备制造业	Manufacture of Railway, Ship, Aviation and Other Transporting Equipment	11.7
电气机械及器材制造业	Manufacture of Electrical Machinery and Equipment	20.8
计算机、通信和其他电子设备制造业	Manufacture of Communication Equipment, Computers and Other Electronic Equipment	9.9
仪器仪表及文化、办公用机械制造业	Manufacture of Measuring Instruments and Machinery for Cultural Activity and Office Work	15.4
其他制造业	Other Manufacture	
废弃资源综合利用业	Comprehensive Utilization of Waste Resources	
金属制品、机械和设备修理业	Repair of Metal Products, Machinery and Equipment	
电力、热力的生产和供应业	Production and Supply of Electric Power and Heat Power	6.0
燃气生产和供应业	Production and Supply of Gas	5.2
水的生产和供应业	Production and Supply of Water	8.4

单位：% (%)

资本保值增值率 Ratio of Assets Appreciation YOY	资产负债率 Asset-Liability Ratio	流动资产周转率（次） Turnover Ratio of Circulating Assets (time)	成本费用利润率 Ratio of Profits to Cost	全员劳动生产率（元/人年） Overall Labor Productivity (yuan/person-year)	产品销售率 Sales as Percentage of Output
114.8	**64.1**	**2.6**	**5.0**	**319223**	**99.2**
147.4	54.6	2.4	8.2	197617	98.2
111.3	66.2	2.6	4.4	357281	99.3
117.3	66.1	2.8	4.0	375569	99.6
117.0	62.0	2.2	7.7	218018	98.4
103.2	56.5	2.0	7.3	251367	96.8
20.6	80.9	3.4	-7.8	4183916	99.8
152.2	77.1	2.3	5.5	366274	98.9
119.9	38.9	3.2	6.1	187569	98.1
109.7	58.3	2.5	5.6	202012	104.0
81.6	66.7	4.9	4.0	255663	99.2
155.5	40.0	2.7	12.2	86159	83.0
124.3	38.9	2.0	13.4	162084	98.6
106.9	63.7	2.1	16.8	205269	103.4
144.2	49.6	1.7	10.6	309585	94.5
128.6	49.2	3.3	14.7	285098	100.4
135.2	22.8	1.2	46.3	125559	99.6
96.4	45.3	2.8	10.5	821955	96.8
128.6	50.0	1.2	21.8	188752	96.9
103.5	62.4	3.2	3.8	157603	98.8
101.3	65.4	1.4	3.9	232953	94.2
80.8	82.4	1.9	-2.0	107634	99.0
139.7	76.7	2.3	21.2	1006087	96.7
81.7	71.3	2.6	1.6	92025	97.8
80.5	61.0	2.1	16.6	328835	99.3
118.9	44.4	3.5	3.7	317134	97.1
123.6	59.5	2.9	7.0	482935	100.9
105.3	63.6	2.9	1.8	148646	99.4
115.4	41.8	1.9	12.2	266321	87.4
211.3	76.9	3.6	0.6	374137	99.7
140.3	56.4	1.4	7.3	218367	99.2
107.0	93.6	3.8	2.4	568862	90.7
189.7	53.7	1.4	9.3	204236	100.0
103.2	70.2	4.7	16.6	406805	100.0

表12.15 续表 continued

指 标	Item	销售利润率 Rate of Return on Sale
总 计	**Total**	**4.9**
按轻、重工业分	**By Light and Heavy Industries**	
轻工业	Light Industry	7.8
重工业	Heavy Industry	4.3
按企业规模分	**By Size**	
大型企业	Large	4.0
中型企业	Medium	7.5
小型企业	Small	7.0
微型企业	Mini	-7.8
按行业分	**By Sector**	
煤炭开采和洗选业	Mining and Washing of Coal	
石油和天然气开采业	Extraction of Petroleum and Natural Gas	
黑色金属矿采选业	Mining and Processing of Ferrous Metal Ores	
有色金属矿采选业	Mining and Processing of Non-Ferrous Metal Ores	
非金属矿采选业	Mining and Processing of Nonmetal Ores	
开采辅助活动	Mining Support Activities	
其他采矿业	Mining of Other Ores	
农副食品加工业	Processing of Food from Agricultural Products	5.4
食品制造业	Manufacture of Foods	6.6
酒、饮料和精制茶制造业	Liquor, Beverage and Refined Tea	5.3
烟草制品业	Manufacture of Tobacco	
纺织业	Manufacture of Textile	3.9
纺织服装、服饰业	Manufacture of Textile Wearing Apparel, Footware and Caps	11.4
皮革、毛皮、羽毛（绒）及其制品业	Manufacture of Leather, Fur, Feather and Related Products	
木材加工和木竹藤棕草制品业	Processing of Timber, Manufacture of Wood, Bamboo, Rattan, Palm and Straw Products	11.8
家具制造业	Manufacture of Furniture	14.5
造纸及纸制品业	Manufacture of Paper and Paper Products	10.0
印刷业、记录媒介的复制	Printing, Reproduction of Recording Media	12.8
文教、工美、体育和娱乐用品制造业	Manufacture of Culture, Education, Handicraft, Fine Arts, Sports and Entertainment Articles	31.9
石油加工、炼焦及核燃料加工业	Processing of Petroleum, Coking, Processing of Nuclear Fuel	
化学原料及化学制品制造业	Manufacture of Raw Chemical Materials and Chemical Products	9.4
医药制造业	Manufacture of Medicines	18.6
化学纤维制造业	Manufacture of Chemical Fibers	
橡胶和塑料制品业	Manufacture of Rubber and Plastics	3.8
非金属矿物制品业	Manufacture of Non-metallic Mineral Products	3.8
黑色金属冶炼及压延加工业	Smelting and Pressing of Ferrous Metals	-2.0
有色金属冶炼及压延加工业	Smelting and Pressing of Nonferrous Metals	17.9
金属制品业	Manufacture of Metal Products	1.6
通用设备制造业	Manufacture of General Purpose Machinery	14.6
专用设备制造业	Manufacture of Special Purpose Machinery	3.5
汽车制造业	Manufacture of Motor Vehicles	6.5
铁路、船舶、航空航天和其他运输设备制造业	Manufacture of Railway, Ship, Aviation and Other Transporting Equipment	1.8
电气机械及器材制造业	Manufacture of Electrical Machinery and Equipment	11.1
计算机、通信和其他电子设备制造业	Manufacture of Communication Equipment, Computers and Other Electronic Equipment	0.7
仪器仪表及文化、办公用机械制造业	Manufacture of Measuring Instruments and Machinery for Cultural Activity and Office Work	7.2
其他制造业	Other Manufacture	
废弃资源综合利用业	Comprehensive Utilization of Waste Resources	
金属制品、机械和设备修理业	Repair of Metal Products, Machinery and Equipment	
电力、热力的生产和供应业	Production and Supply of Electric Power and Heat Power	2.6
燃气生产和供应业	Production and Supply of Gas	9.1
水的生产和供应业	Production and Supply of Water	14.5

资本积累率 Rate of Capital Accumulation	流动比率 Current Ratio	速动比率 Quick Ratio	产权比率 Equity Ratio	人均实现利税（元） Per Capita Pre-tax Profits (yuan)	从业人员人均工资（元） Per Capita Wages of Employees (yuan)
14.8	**1.1**	**0.8**	**1.8**	**135556**	**52051**
47.4	1.2	0.9	1.2	107001	42065
11.3	1.1	0.8	2.0	144492	55177
17.3	1.1	0.8	2.0	158681	57539
17.0	1.1	0.9	1.6	99364	42924
3.2	1.2	1.0	1.3	99682	43703
-79.4	0.5	0.5	4.2	-1235833	425861
52.2	1.1	0.7	3.5	297780	52299
19.9	1.4	1.3	0.6	119194	61107
9.7	0.7	0.4	1.4	97275	48151
-18.4	1.4	1.1	2.0	76582	101038
55.5	1.6	0.5	0.7	27429	28451
24.3	1.8	1.0	0.6	70663	56396
6.9	1.3	1.3	1.8	144813	33732
44.2	1.6	1.2	1.0	146061	37592
28.6	1.0	0.8	1.0	179873	51984
35.2	3.1	2.4	0.3	88455	29381
-3.6	1.2	1.0	0.8	306870	54621
28.6	1.1	0.9	1.0	116146	56306
3.5	0.9	0.6	1.7	40954	40218
1.3	0.8	0.6	1.9	59005	51705
-19.2	1.0	0.5	4.7	-9875	64613
39.7	1.0	0.8	3.3	762980	45917
-18.3	0.7	0.4	2.5	11611	32164
-19.5	1.2	0.9	1.6	200300	53576
18.9	1.7	1.1	0.8	51911	27561
23.6	1.2	0.9	1.5	323422	55123
5.3	1.2	1.0	1.7	63076	27628
15.4	1.9	1.4	0.7	116136	39736
111.3	1.0	0.9	3.5	53929	54776
40.3	1.5	1.2	1.3	85808	72590
7.0	0.3	0.2	14.6	84542	50413
89.7	1.3	1.2	1.2	105141	77538
3.2	0.2	0.2	2.4	153878	87236

表12.16 大中型工业企业主要经济指标（2011年）

MAIN ECONOMIC INDICATORS OF LARGE & MEDIUM-SIZED INDUSTRIAL ENTERPRISES (2011)

指　标	Item	单位数（个） Number of Enterprises (unit)	从业人员平均人数（万人） Average Employment (10 000 persons)	工业总产值 Gross Output Value
总　计	**Total**	**1127**	**101.44**	**85661294**
#国有控股企业	State-holding Enterprises	257	39.68	35538186
按登记注册类型分	**By Status of Registration**			
内资企业	Domestic-funded Enterprises	1000	84.02	61084974
#国有企业	State-owned	60	5.89	3597064
集体企业	Collective-owned	10	0.66	109389
港澳台投资企业	Funded by Hong Kong, Macao and Taiwan	48	8.03	9603033
外商投资企业	Foreign-funded	79	9.39	14973287
按轻、重工业分	**By Light and Heavy Industries**			
轻工业	Light Industry	412	33.00	23330422
重工业	Heavy Industry	715	68.44	62330873

指　标	Item	固定资产净值 Net Value of Fixed Assets	负　债 Total Liabilities	其　中 of which #流动负债 Total Circulating Liabilities
总　计	**Total**	**22598634**	**44841613**	**34104807**
#国有控股企业	State-holding Enterprises	13933712	26061537	18822523
按登记注册类型分	**By Status of Registration**			
内资企业	Domestic-funded Enterprises	18097160	34259964	25645623
#国有企业	State-owned	2159166	3808801	2642889
集体企业	Collective-owned	15739	52121	50444
港澳台投资企业	Funded by Hong Kong, Macao and Taiwan	2013967	4758756	3278542
外商投资企业	Foreign-funded	2488076	5823112	5180861
按轻、重工业分	**By Light and Heavy Industries**			
轻工业	Light Industry	4660637	10001778	8188735
重工业	Heavy Industry	17937997	34839835	25916072

单位：万元 (10 000 yuan)

工业销售产值 Sales Value of Industry	其 中 of which #出口交货值 Value of Export Delivery	实收资本 Paid-in Capital	其 中 of which #国家资本 State Capital	外商资本 Foreign Capital	资 产 Total Assets	其 中 of which #流动资产 Circulating Assets	固定资产原值 Original Value of Fixed Assets
83462191	**8642077**	**12384969**	**1477249**	**1228031**	**72698549**	**35793159**	**37724359**
34739426	860885	6792752	1422179	541214	41675028	18254931	22538107
59035852	3304413	9178445	1287503	140348	56431321	26601153	30574116
3655485	30414	1321097	200406		6632389	2507731	3876254
108159		15544			86838	30146	32488
9445156	4289584	1378267	14684	92378	7029472	3499844	2566542
14981183	1048080	1828369	175062	995304	9239428	5692191	4584744
22652696	2181865	2977531	203507	210858	17227945	9795509	7863987
60809495	6460212	9407438	1273742	1017173	55470604	25997650	29860372

所有者权益 Creditors' Equity	主营业务收入 Revenue from Principal Business	主营业务成本 Cost of Principal Business	主营业务税金及附加 Tax and Extra Charges of Principal Business	主营业务利润 Profit of Principal Business	利润总额 Total After-tax Profits	利税总额 Total Pre-tax Profits	工资总额 Total Wages
27667484	**81914561**	**70421297**	**1198830**	**10294434**	**4487325**	**8540471**	**4874651**
15554748	33999727	28949589	996339	4053800	1420095	3879898	2373628
22028542	57743064	49487392	844892	7410780	3346514	6093511	3950454
2823496	3635279	3126217	13198	495865	187146	320002	319871
34626	107315	87975	444	18896	1500	5348	19563
2250313	9168972	8479026	16657	673288	212650	475073	431903
3390083	15009865	12460606	337399	2211860	929299	1973664	493202
7188361	22320262	18311121	670118	3339023	1491091	2910724	1420709
20479124	59594299	52110176	528712	6955411	2996234	5629748	3453942

表12.17 大中型工业企业经济效益指标（2011年）
INDICATORS ON ECONOMIC BENEFIT OF LARGE & MEDIUM-SIZED INDUSTRIAL ENTERPRISES (2011)

指 标	Item	总资产贡献率 Ratio of Total Assets to Industrial Output Value
总 计	**Total**	**12.8**
#国有控股企业	State-holding Enterprises	10.4
按登记注册类型分	**By Status of Registration**	
内资企业	Domestic-funded Enterprises	11.9
#国有企业	State-owned	5.8
集体企业	Collective-owned	6.2
港澳台投资企业	Funded by Hong Kong, Macao and Taiwan	8.3
外商投资企业	Foreign-funded	22.1
按轻、重工业分	**By Light and Heavy Industries**	
轻工业	Light Industry	17.8
重工业	Heavy Industry	11.3

指 标	Item	销售利润率 Rate of Return on Sale
总 计	**Total**	**5.5**
#国有控股企业	State-holding Enterprises	4.2
按登记注册类型分	**By Status of Registration**	
内资企业	Domestic-funded Enterprises	5.8
#国有企业	State-owned	5.1
集体企业	Collective-owned	1.4
港澳台投资企业	Funded by Hong Kong, Macao and Taiwan	2.3
外商投资企业	Foreign-funded	6.2
按轻、重工业分	**By Light and Heavy Industries**	
轻工业	Light Industry	6.7
重工业	Heavy Industry	5.0

单位：%（%）

资本保值增值率 Ratio of Assets Appreciation YOY	资产负债率 Asset-Liability Ratio	流动资产周转率（次） Turnover Ratio of Circulating Assets (time)	成本费用利润率 Ratio of Profits to Cost	全员劳动生产率（元/人年） Overall Labor Productivity (yuan/person-year)	产品销售率 Sales as Percentage of Output
119.6	**61.7**	**2.4**	**5.6**	**221588**	**97.4**
117.5	62.5	1.9	4.2	239737	97.8
120.2	60.7	2.2	6.0	199746	96.7
121.7	57.4	1.5	5.1	179339	101.6
139.8	60.0	3.6	1.6	66084	98.9
115.3	67.7	2.6	2.2	232364	98.4
118.4	63.0	2.7	6.5	406878	100.1
137.1	58.1	2.3	7.1	194109	97.1
117.9	62.8	2.4	5.1	234840	97.6

资本积累率 Rate of Capital Accumulation	流动比率 Current Ratio	速动比率 Quick Ratio	产权比率 Equity Ratio	人均实现利税（元） Per Capita Pre-tax Profits (yuan)	从业人员人均工资（元） Per Capita Wages of Employees (yuan)
19.6	**1.0**	**0.8**	**1.6**	**84194**	**48055**
17.5	1.0	0.7	1.7	97784	59822
20.2	1.0	0.8	1.6	72540	47031
21.7	0.9	0.7	1.3	54332	54309
39.8	0.6	0.3	1.5	8074	29533
15.3	1.1	0.7	2.1	59179	53802
18.4	1.1	0.9	1.7	209236	52286
37.1	1.2	0.9	1.4	88197	43048
17.9	1.0	0.8	1.7	82263	50470

表12.18 规模以上工业企业主要产品产量（2010－2011年）

OUTPUT OF MAJOR PRODUCTS OF INDUSTRIAL ENTERPRISES ABOVE DESIGNATED SIZE (2010-2011)

产　品	Products	2010	2011
化学纤维（万吨）	Chemical Fiber (10 000 tons)	6.71	6.32
纱（吨）	Yarn (ton)	140713	132705
布（万米）	Cloth (10 000 m)	84335.42	51254.56
印染布（万米）	Printed and Dyed Fabric (10 000 m)	44149.36	16230.47
毛　线（吨）	Knitting Wool (ton)	1920	3213
蚕丝（吨）	Silk (ton)	8339	3811
丝织品(蚕丝及交织机织物（含蚕丝≥50%)）(万米）	Silk Products (silk and mixture fabric (with content of silk ≥50%)) (10 000 m)	1717.53	1398.21
电视机（万部）	TV Sets (10 000 units)	65.87	85.05
#彩色电视机	Color TV Sets	65.87	85.05
微型计算机设备（台）	Microcomputers (units)	1891864	25478229
#笔记本计算机	Laptops	848138	24073940
摩托车（万辆）	Motorcycles (10 000 units)	849.23	879.59
机制纸及纸板（吨）	Machine-made Paper and Paperboard (ton)	1892304	1779975
日用陶瓷制品（万件）	Daily-use Ceramic Products (10 000 pcs)	17222.50	
日用玻璃制品（吨）	Daily-use Glassware (ton)	540769	545864
合成洗涤剂（吨）	Synthetic Detergents (ton)	71755	40951
肥　皂（吨）	Soap (ton)	609	
干电池（折一号电池）（万只）	Dry Cells (equivalent to No.1 battery) (10 000 units)	7780.74	7846.25
卷　烟（亿支）	Cigarettes (100 million pieces)	501.00	516.00
白　酒（万千升）	Liquor (1000 kiloliters)	15.48	17.35
啤　酒（万千升）	Beer (1000 kiloliters)	75.19	77.31
罐　头（吨）	Canned Food (ton)	62042	44467
食用植物油（吨）	Edible Vegetable Oil (ton)	197797	486440
皮　鞋（万双）	Leather Shoes (10 000 pairs)	4165.43	4462.73
服　装（万件）	Garments (10 000 pcs)	9537.08	8636.75
乳制品（万吨）	Dairy Products (10 000 tons)	12.58	12.85
无酒精饮料（软饮料）（吨）	Non-alcoholic Beverage (soft) (ton)	3499660	2983523
原　煤（万吨）	Coal (10 000 tons)	4547.03	4464.61
洗精煤（万吨）	Washed and Fine Coal (10 000 tons)	1045.02	1155.07
焦　炭（万吨）	Coke (10 000 tons)	359.17	397.01
发电量（万千瓦时）	Electricity (10 000 kwh)	4567098.90	5295687.08
天然气（万立方米）	Natural Gas (10 000 cu.m)	674767.71	629384.17
生　铁（万吨）	Pig Iron (10 000 tons)	417.41	559.36
粗　钢（万吨）	Crude Steel (10 000 tons)	456.09	630.45
钢　材（万吨）	Steel Products (10 000 tons)	699.92	948.17
#大型钢材	Large	15.05	11.50
中小型钢材	Medium	52.33	51.57
中厚钢板	Medium Rolled-steel	211.88	205.53
无缝钢管	Seamless Steel Pipe	22.05	23.57

表12.18 续表 continued

产　品	Products	2010	2011
铝（吨）	Aluminum (ton)	160486	1344489
硫　酸（吨）	Sulphuric Acid (ton)	2219975	1767635
盐　酸（吨）	Hydrochloric Acid (ton)	109863	71998
烧　碱（吨）	Caustic Soda (ton)	243469	285230
精甲醇（商品量）（吨）	Fine Methyl Alcohol (commodities) (ton)	583855	722128
涂　料（吨）	Paint (ton)	218141	152084
塑料制品（吨）	Plastics (ton)	597507	772890
合成橡胶（吨）	Synthetic Rubber (ton)	27334	27714
化学原料药（吨）	Chemical Raw Material (ton)	8035	8153
中成药（吨）	Traditional Chinese Medicine (ton)	57583	66746
轮胎外胎（万条）	Tire (10 000 units)	1751.89	2502.97
水　泥（万吨）	Cement (10 000 tons)	4598.04	4935.15
人造板（立方米）	Artificial Boards (cu.m)	329711.30	416747.08
矿山设备（吨）	Mining Equipment (ton)	39883	68420
起重设备（起重机）（吨）	Hoist and Derrick (ton)	57684	57254
房间空气调节器（台）	Air-Conditioners (unit)	5733924	8674009
发电设备（千瓦）	Generating Equipment (kw)	1435344	1727027
交流电动机（万千瓦）	AC Motors(10 000 kw)	576.13	333.83
电力变压器（万千伏安）	Electric Transformer Products (10 000 kva)	4024.57	2767.72
金属切削机床（台）	Metal-cutting Machines (unit)	7010	7013
汽　车（辆）	Motor Vehicles (unit)	1615766	1722047
#轿　车	Cars	851664	936682
内燃机（发动机）（万千瓦）	Internal Combustion Engines (10 000 kw)	5258.68	6664.21
泵（台）	Industry Pumps (unit)	520213	537974
风　机（台）	Air Pumps (unit)	13525	42108
气体压缩机（台）	Gas Compressors (unit)	344	256061
轴　承（万套）	Bearings (10 000 sets)	9241.01	9001.98
工业锅炉（蒸吨）	Industry Boilers (ton)	838.00	787.57
民用钢质船舶（载重吨）	Civil Steel Ships (ton)	933367	1395618
合成氨（吨）	Synthetic Ammonia (ton)	1451003	1521920
化　肥（100%）（吨）	Chemical Fertilizer (100%) (ton)	1814895	1695241
#氮　肥	Nitrogen Fertilizer	1055161	1045605
磷　肥	Phosphate Fertilizer	747170	646839
配混合饲料（吨）	Mingled Forage (ton)	277175	2254663
化学农药原药（吨）	Chemical Pesticides (ton)	1293	78307

主要统计指标解释

■ 工业

指从事自然资源的开采，对采掘品和农产品进行加工和再加工的物质生产部门。具体包括：（1）对自然资源的开采，如采矿、晒盐、森林采伐等（不包括禽兽捕猎和水产捕捞）；（2）对农副产品的加工、再加工，如粮油加工、食品加工、轧花、缫丝、纺织、制革等；（3）对采掘品的加工、再加工，如炼铁、炼钢、化工生产、石油加工、机器制造、木材加工等，以及电力、自来水、煤气的生产和供应等；（4）对工业品的修理、翻新，如机器设备的修理、交通运输工具（包括小卧车）的修理等。

工业统计调查单位为独立核算法人工业企业。

独立核算法人工业企业指从事工业生产经营活动的单位。独立核算法人工业企业应同时具备以下条件：①依法成立，有自己的名称、组织机构和场所，能够承担民事责任；②独立拥有和使用资产，承担负债，有权与其他单位签订合同；③独立核算盈亏，并能够编制资产负债表。

本年鉴中涉及的企业登记注册类型：

（1）国有企业：指企业全部资产归国家所有，并按《中华人民共和国企业法人登记管理条例》规定登记注册的非公司制的经济组织。不包括有限责任公司中的国有独资公司。

（2）集体企业：指企业资产归集体所有，并按《中华人民共和国企业法人登记管理条例》规定登记注册的经济组织。

（3）股份合作企业：指以合作制为基础，由企业职工共同出资入股，吸收一定比例的社会资产投资组建，实行自主经营，自负盈亏，共同劳动，民主管理，按劳分配与按股分红相结合的一种集体经济组织。

（4）联营企业：两个及两个以上相同或不同所有制性质的企业法人或事业单位法人，按自愿、平等、互利的原则，共同投资组成的经济组织称为联营企业。联营企业包括国有联营企业、集体联营企业、国有与集体联营企业和其他联营企业。

国有联营企业：指所有联营单位均为国有。

集体联营企业：指所有联营单位均为集体。

国有与集体联营企业：指联营单位既有国有也有集体。

其他联营企业：指上述三种联营企业之外的其他联营形式的企业。

（5）有限责任公司：根据《中华人民共和国公司登记管理条例》规定登记注册，由两个以上，五十个以下的股东共同出资，每个股东以其所认缴的出资额对公司承担有限责任，公司以其全部资产对其债务承担责任的经济组织称为有限责任公司。有限责任公司分为国有独资公司以及其他有限责任公司。

国有独资公司：指国家授权的投资机构或者国家授权的部门单独投资设立的有限责任公司。

其他有限责任公司：指国有独资公司以外的其他有限责任公司。

（6）股份有限公司：指根据《中华人民共和国公司登记管理条例》规定登记注册，其全部注册资本由等额股份构成并通过发行股票筹集资本，股东以其认购的股份对公司承担有限责任，公司以其全部资产对其债务承担责任的经济组织。

（7）私营企业：指由自然人投资设立或由自然人控股，以雇佣劳动为基础的营利性经济组织。包括按照《公司法》、《合伙企业法》、《私营企业暂行条例》以及《个人独资企业法》规定登记注册的私营有限责任公司、私营股份有限公司、私营合伙企业、私营独资企业和个人独资企业。

（8）其他内资企业：指上述第（1）至第（7）之外的其他内资经济组织。

（9）与港澳台商合资经营企业：指港澳台地区投资者与内地企业依照《中华人民共和国中外合资经营企业法》及有关法律的规定，按合同规定的比例投资设立、分享利润和分担风险的企业。

（10）与港澳台商合作经营企业：指港澳台地区投资者与内地企业依照《中华人民共和国中外合作经营企业法》及有关法律的规定，依照合作合同的约定进行投资或提供条件设立、分配利润和分担风险的企业。

（11）港澳台商独资经营企业：指依照《中华人民共和国外资企业法》及有关法律的规定，在内地由

主要统计指标解释

港澳台地区投资者全额投资设立的企业。

（12）港澳台商投资股份有限公司：指根据国家有关规定，经外经贸部依法批准设立，其中港、澳、台商的股本占公司注册资本的比例达25%以上的股份有限公司。凡其中港、澳、台商的股本占公司注册资本的比例小于25%的，属于内资企业中的股份有限公司。

（13）中外合资经营企业：指外国企业或外国人与中国内地企业依照《中华人民共和国中外合资经营企业法》及有关法律的规定，按合同规定的比例投资设立、分享利润和分担风险的企业。

（14）中外合作经营企业：指外国企业或外国人与中国内地企业依照《中华人民共和国中外合作经营企业法》及有关法律的规定，依照合作合同的约定进行投资或提供条件设立、分配利润和分担风险的企业。

（15）外资企业：指依照《中华人民共和国外资企业法》及有关法律的规定，在中国内地由外国投资者全额投资设立的企业。

（16）外商投资股份有限公司：指根据国家有关规定，经外经贸部依法批准设立，其中外资的股本占公司注册资本的比例达25%以上的股份有限公司。凡其中外资股本占公司注册资本的比例小于25%的，属于内资企业中的股份有限公司。

国有控股企业

是指在企业的全部实收资本中，国有经济成分的出资人拥有的实收资本(股本)所占企业全部实收资本(股本)的比例大于50%的国有绝对控股。

在企业的全部实收资本中，国有经济成分的出资人拥有的实收资本(股本)所占比例虽未大于50%，但相对大于其他任何一方经济成分的出资人所占比例的国有相对控股；或者虽不大于其他经济成分，但根据协议规定拥有企业实际控制权的国有协议控股。

投资双方各占50%，且未明确由谁绝对控股的企业，若其中一方为国有经济成分的，一律按国有控股处理。

轻工业

指主要提供生活消费品和制作手工工具的工业。按其所使用的原料不同，可分为两大类：(1)以农产品为原料的轻工业，是指直接或间接以农产品为基本原料的轻工业。主要包括食品制造、饮料制造、烟草加工、纺织、缝纫、皮革和毛皮制作、造纸以及印刷等工业；(2)以非农产品为原料的轻工业，是指以工业品为原料的轻工业。主要包括文教体育用品、化学药品制造、合成纤维制造、日用化学制品、日用玻璃制品、日用金属制品、手工工具制造、医疗器械制造、文化和办公用机械制造等工业。

重工业

指为国民经济各部门提供物质技术基础的主要生产资料的工业。按其生产性质和产品用途，可以分为下列三类：(1)采掘(伐)工业，是指对自然资源的开采，包括石油开采、煤炭开采、金属矿开采、非金属矿开采等工业；(2)原材料工业，指向国民经济各部门提供基本材料、动力和燃料的工业。包括金属冶炼及加工、炼焦及焦炭、化学、化工原料、水泥、人造板以及电力、石油和煤炭加工等工业；(3)加工工业，是指对工业原材料进行再加工制造的工业。包括装备国民经济各部门的机械设备制造工业、金属结构、水泥制品等工业，以及为农业提供的生产资料如化肥、农药等工业。

根据上述划分原则，修理业中以重工业产品为修理作业对象的划为重工业，反之划为轻工业。

工业总产值

指工业企业在本年内生产的以货币形式表现的工业最终产品和提供工业劳务活动的总价值量。

(1)工业总产值计算应遵循的原则

①工业生产的原则。即凡是企业在本年内生产的最终产品和提供的劳务，均应包括在内。其中的最终产品，不管是否在本年内销售，只要是本年内生产的，就应包括在内。凡不是工业生产的产品，均不得计入工业总产值。

②最终产品的原则。即企业生产的成品价值必须是本企业生产的，经检验合格不需再进行任何加工的最终产品。企业对外销售的半成品也应视为最终产品计入工业总产值。而在本企业内各车间转移的半成品和在制品只能计算其期末期初差额价值。

③“工厂法”原则。即以法人工业企业作为一个整体计算工业总产值，是其本年内生产的最终产品和提供劳务的总价值量。

(2)工业总产值的内容

包括三部分：生产的成品价值、对外加工费收入、自制半成品在制品期末期初差额价值。

①成品价值：指企业在本年内生产，并在本年内不再进行加工，经检验合格、包装入库的已经销售和

主要统计指标解释

准备销售的全部工业成品(包括半成品)价值合计。成品价值中包括企业生产的自制设备及提供给本企业在建工程、其他非工业部门和生活福利部门等单位使用的成品价值，但不包括用订货者来料加工的成品(半成品)价值。

工业总产值是按现行价格计算的。成品价值按成品实物量乘以本年不含应交增值税(销项税额)的产品实际销售平均单价计算。会计核算中按成本价格转帐的自制设备和自产自用的成品，按成本价格计算生产成品价值。

②对外加工费收入：指企业在本年内完成的对外承做的工业品加工(包括用订货者来料加工生产)的加工费收入和对外工业品修理作业所收取的加工费收入。对外加工费收入按不含应交增值税(销项税额)的价格计算，可根据会计“产品销售收入”科目的有关资料取得。

对于以对外加工生产为主，对外加工费收入所占比重较大的企业，如果对外加工费收入出现跨年度支付的情况，为保证总产值生产口径计算的准确性，则应将对外加工费收入按实际情况调整，记录本年应实际收取的对外加工费收入。

③自制半成品在制品期末期初差额价值。为了使工业总产值与工业中间投入中的物耗价值一致，以便同口径地计算工业增加值，规定本指标的计算原则是：凡是企业会计产品成本核算中计算半成品、在制品成本，则工业总产值中必须包括自制半成品在制品期末期初差额价值。反之则不包括。

自制半成品在制品期末期初差额价值等于自制半成品在制品期末价值减去期初价值后的余额，如果期末价值小于期初价值，该指标为负值，企业在计算产值时，应按负值计算，不能作为零处理。

(3)工业总产值计算的几种具体规定

①凡自备原材料，不论其加工繁简程度如何，一律按全价，即包括自备原材料的价值，计算工业总产值。

②凡来料加工，加工企业一律按财务上结算的加工费计算工业总产值，即不包括定货者来料的价值。一般分两种情况：a、工业企业之间的来料加工，加工企业(即承包单位)按财务上结算的加工费计算工业总产值；委托加工的企业(即发包单位)按全价计算工业总产值。b、工业企业与非工业企业之间的来料加工，当工业企业作为加工企业时一律按加工费计算工业总产值。

③自制半成品、在制品期末期初差额价值，原则上应计入工业总产值，但如果会计产品成本核算中不计算自制半成品、在制品成本，则不计入工业总产值；如果会计产品成本核算中计算自制半成品、在制品成本的，则计入工业总产值。

■ 工业销售产值

指以货币形式表现的，工业企业在本年内销售的本企业生产的工业产品或提供工业性劳务价值的总价值量。工业销售产值包括的内容为：(1)销售成品价值；(2)对外加工费收入。区分来料加工与自备原材料生产的依据同工业总产值中的规定。

■ 出口交货值

指工业企业交给外贸部门或自营（委托）出口（包括销往香港、澳门、台湾），用外汇价格结算的产品价值，以及外商来样、来料加工、来件装配和补偿贸易等生产的产品价值。在计算出口交货值时，要把外汇价格按交易时的汇率折算成人民币计算。

■ 资产合计

指企业拥有或控制的能以货币计量的经济资源，包括各种财产、债权和其他权利。资产按其流动性(即资产的变现能力和支付能力)划分为：流动资产、长期投资、固定资产、无形资产、递延资产和其他资产。根据会计“资产负债表”中“资产总计”项的期末数填列。

（1）流动资产：指企业可以在一年内或者超过一年的一个生产周期内变现或者耗用的资产，包括现金及各种存款、短期投资，应收及预付款项、存货等。根据会计“资产负债表”中“流动资产合计”项的期末数填列。

（2）固定资产：指企业使用期限超过一年的房屋、建筑物、机器、机械、运输工具以及其他与生产、经营有关的设备、器具、工具等。不属于生产经营主要设备的物品，单位价值在2000元以上，并且使用年限超过2年的，也应当作为固定资产。“固定资产合计”根据会计“资产负债表”中“固定资产合计”项的期末数填列。

主要统计指标解释

■ 负债合计

指企业所承担的能以货币计量，将以资产或劳务偿付的债务，偿还形式包括货币、资产或提供劳务。

负债一般按偿还期长短分为流动负债和长期负债。根据会计“资产负债表”中“负债合计”的期末数填列。

（1）流动负债：指企业在一年内或超过一年的一个营业周期内需要偿还的债务，包括短期借款、应付票据、应付帐款、预收帐款、应付工资、应交税金、应付利润、预提费用等。根据企业会计“资产负债表”中“流动负债合计”的期末数填报。

（2）长期负债：指企业偿还期在一年以上或者超过一年的一个营业周期以上的债务，包括长期借款、长期应付款、应付债券等。根据会计“资产负债表”中的“长期负债合计”的期末数填报。

■ 所有者权益

指所有者在企业资产中享有的经济利益，它等于企业资产减去负债后的余额。包括实收资本（或股本）、资本公积、盈余公积、未分配利润等。根据会计“资产负债表”中的“所有者权益合计”项的期末数填列。

■ 主营业务收入

指企业经营主要业务所取得的收入总额。根据会计“利润表”中对应指标的本年累计数填列。若执行2006年《企业会计制度》的企业，用“营业收入”的本期累计数代替。

■ 土营业务成本

指企业经营主要业务发生的实际成本。根据会计“利润表”中对应指标的本年累计数填列。若执行2006年《企业会计制度》的企业，用“营业成本”的本期累计数代替。

■ 主营业务税金及附加

指企业经营主要业务应负担的营业税、消费税、城市维护建设税、资源税、土地增值税、教育费附加。根据会计“利润表”中对应指标的本年累计数填列。若执行2006年《企业会计制度》的企业，用“营业税金及附加”的本期累计数代替。

■ 营业利润

指企业从事生产经营活动所取得的利润，即主营业务收入减主营业务成本和主营业务税金及附加，加其他业务利润，减去营业费用、管理费用、财务费用后的金额。本指标根据会计“利润表”中对应指标的“本年累计数”填列。

■ 应交增值税

指企业按税法规定，从事货物销售或提供加工、修理修配劳务等增加货物价值的活动本期应交纳的税金。指企业在报告期应交增值税额。计算公式为：

本年应交增值税=销项税额-(进项税额-进项税额转出)-出口抵减内销产品应纳税额-减免税款+出口退税

■ 利润总额

指企业在生产经营过程中各种收入扣除各种耗费后的盈余，反映企业在报告期内实现的亏盈总额，包括营业利润、补贴收入、投资净收益和营业外收支净额。根据会计“利润表”中的对应指标的本期累计数填列。

■ 利税总额

指企业利润总额、产品销售税金及附加、应交增值税之和。

■ 工业经济效益综合指数

是综合衡量地区工业经济效益总体水平的一种特殊相对数，是反映一定时期工业经济运行质量的主要指标。工业经济效益综合指数由总资产贡献率、资本保值增值率、资产负债率、流动资产周转率、成本费用利润率、全员劳动生产率和产品销售率的实际数值分别除以该项指标的全国标准值，并乘以各自的权数，加总后除以总权数求得。该指标可从静态水平和动态趋势上较为全面地反映各地区工业经济效益的变化情况，并可在一定程度上消除地区对比的不可比因素。

■ 总资产贡献率

反映企业全部资产的获利能力，是企业经营业绩和管理水平的集中体现，是评价和考核企业盈利能力的核心指标。计算公式为：

总资产贡献率（%）=（利润总额+税金总额+利息支出）/平均资产总额×100%

■ 资本保值增值率

反映企业净资产的变动状况，是企业发展能力的集中体现。计算公式为：

资本保值增值率（%）=报告期期末所有者权益/上年同期期末所有者权益×100%

主要统计指标解释

资产负债率

该指标既反映企业经营风险的大小，也反映企业利用债权人提供的资金从事经营活动的能力。计算公式为：

资产负债率（%）=负债总额/资产总额×100%

流动资产周转次数

指在一定时期内流动资产完成的周转次数，反映流动资产的周转速度。计算公式为：

流动资产周转次数＝产品销售收入/全部流动资产平均余额

成本费用利润率

指在一定时期内实现的利润与成本费用之比，是反映工业生产成本及费用投入的经济效益指标，同时也是反映降低成本的经济效益的指标。计算公式为：

成本费用利润率（%）＝利润总额/成本费用总额×100%

成本费用利润率

指在一定时期内实现的利润与成本费用之比，是反映工业生产成本及费用投入的经济效益指标，同时也是反映降低成本的经济效益的指标。计算公式为：

成本费用利润率（%）＝利润总额/成本费用总额×100%

全员劳动生产率

指根据产品的价值量指标计算的平均每一就业人员在单位时间内的产品生产量。是考核企业经济活动的重要指标，是企业生产技术水平、经营管理水平、职工技术熟练程度和劳动积极性的综合表现。目前，我国的全员劳动生产率是将工业企业的增加值除以同一时期全部就业人员的平均人数来计算的。计算公式为：

全员劳动生产率＝工业增加值/全部从业人员平均人数

产品销售率

指工业销售产值与同期全部工业总产值之比，反映工业产品已实现销售的程度，分析工业产销衔接情况，研究工业产品满足社会需求程度的指标。计算公式为：

产品销售率（%）＝现价工业销售产值/报告期现价工业总产值×100%

销售利润率

指企业利润与销售收入的比率。计算公式为：

销售利润率（%）＝利润/销售收入×100%

资本积累率

指企业所有者权益增长额与年初所有者权益的比率。计算公式为：

资本积累率（%）＝所有者权益增长额/年初所有者权益×100%

流动比率

指流动资产与流动负债的比率，它表明每一元流动负债有多少流动资产作为偿还的保证，反映企业用可在短期内转变为现金的流动资产偿还到期流动负债的能力。计算公式为：

流动比率＝流动资产/流动负债

速动比率

指企业速动资产与流动负债的比率。计算公式为：

速动比率＝速动资产/流动负债

产权比率

指企业负债总额与所有者权益的比率，是企业财务结构稳健与否的重要标志，也称资本负债率。计算公式为：

产权比率＝负债总额/所有者权益

CHONGQING STATISTICAL YEARBOOK

Explanatory Notes on Main Statistical Indicators

Industry

Refers to the material production sector which is engaged in extraction of natural resources and processing and reprocessing of minerals and agricultural products, including;(I)extraction of natural resources, such as mining, salt production, logging (but not including hunting and fishing);(II)processing and reprocessing of farm and sideline produces, such as rice husking, flour milling, wine making, oil pressing, cotton ginning, silk reeling, spinning and weaving, and leather making;(III)manufacture of industrial products, such as steel making, iron smelting, chemicals manufacturing, petroleum processing, machine building, timber processing; water and gas production and electricity generation and supply; 4) repairing of industrial products such as the repairing of machinery and means of transport (including cars). Prior to 1984, the rural industry run by villages and cooperative organizations under village was classified into agriculture. Since 1984, it has been grouped into industry.

In industrial statistics surveys, the units of enquiry are corporate industrial enterprises with independent accounting systems.

Corporate industrial enterprises with independent accounting systems refer to enterprises engaging in industrial production activities, which meet the following requirements:(I)They are established legally, having their own names, organizations, location and able to take civil liability; (II)They possess and use their assets independently, assume liabilities and are entitled to sign contracts with other units;(III)They are financially independent and compile their own balance sheets.

Types of enterprise registration involved in this yearbook are as the following:

(I) State-owned Enterprises: refer to non-corporation economic units where the entire assets are owned by the state and which have registered in accordance with the Regulation of the People's Republic of China on the Management of Registration of Corporate Enterprises. Excluded from this category are sole state-funded corporations in the limited liability corporations.

(II) Collective-owned Enterprises: refer to economic units where the assets are owned collectively and which have registered in accordance with the Regulation of the People's Republic of China on the Management of Registration of Corporate Enterprises.

(III) Cooperative Enterprises: refer to a form of collective economic units (enterprises) where capitals come mainly from employees as their shares, with certain proportion of capital from the outside, where production is organized on the basis of independent operation, independent accounting for profits and losses, joint work, democratic management, and a distribution system that integrates remuneration according to work with dividend according to capital share.

(IV) Joint Ownership Enterprises: refer to economic units established by two or more corporate enterprises or corporate institutions of the same or different ownership, through joint investment on the basis of equality, voluntary participation and mutual benefits. They include state joint ownership enterprises, collective joint ownership enterprises, joint state-collective enterprises, other joint ownership enterprises. They include:

a) State-owned joint-operation enterprises (joint operation between State-owned enterprises);

b) Collective joint-operation enterprises (joint operation between collective enterprises);

c) State-collective joint-operation enterprises (joint operation between state and collective enterprises);

d)Other joint-operation enterprises(joint operation exclude state and collective enterprises).

(V) Limited Liability Corporations: refer to economic units established with investment from 2-50 investors and registered in accordance with the Regulation of the People's Republic of China on the Management of Registration of Corporations, each investor bearing limited liability to the corporation depending on its share of investment, and the corporation bearing liability to its debt to the maximum of its total assets. Limited liability corporations include exclusive state-funded limited liability corporations and other limited liability corporations.

Exclusive state-funded limited liability corporations: State-authorized investment institutions or departments of State has authorized the establishment of a separate investment in the limited liability company.

Other limited liability corporations:corporation exclude exclusive state-funded limited liability company.

(Ⅵ) Share holding Corporations Ltd.: refer to economic units registered in accordance with the Regulation of the People's Republic of China on the Management of Registration of Corporations, with total registered capitals divided into equal shares and raised through issuing stocks. Each investor bears limited liability to the corporation depending on the holding of shares, and the corporation bears liability to its debt to the maximum of its total assets.

(Ⅶ) Private Enterprises: refer to profit-making economic units invested and established by natural persons, or controlled by natural persons using employed labor. Included in this category are private limited liability corporations, private share-holding corporations Ltd., private partnership enterprises and private-funded enterprises registered in accordance with the Corporation Law, Partnership Enterprises Law and Interim Regulations on Private Enterprise.

(Ⅷ) Other Domestic-funded Enterprises: refer to domestic-funded economic units other than those mentioned above.

(Ⅸ) Joint-venture Enterprises with Funds from Hong Kong, Macao and Taiwan: refer to enterprises jointly established by invertors from Hong Kong, Macao and Taiwan with enterprises in the mainland of China in accordance with the Law of the People's Republic of China on Sino-foreign Joint Venture Enterprises and other relevant laws, where the share of investment, profits and risks is stipulated in the contract.

(Ⅹ) Cooperative Enterprises with Funds from Hong Kong Macau and Taiwan: established by investors from Hong Kong, Macau and Taiwan with enterprises in the mainland of China in accordance with the Law of the People's Republic of China on Sino-foreign Cooperative Enterprises and other relevant laws, where the investment or provision of facilities, and the share of profits and risks is stipulated in the cooperative contract.

(Ⅺ) Enterprises with Sole (exclusive) Investment from Hong Kong, Macau and Taiwan: refer to enterprises established in the mainland of China with exclusive investment from investors from Hong Kong, Macau and Taiwan in accordance with the Law of the People's Republic of China on Foreign-Funded Enterprises and other relevant laws.

(Ⅻ) Share-holding Corporations Ltd. with Investment from Hong Kong, Macau and Taiwan: refer to share-holding corporations Ltd. established with the approval from the former Ministry of Foreign Trade and Economic Relations in line with relevant state regulations, where the share of investment from Hong Kong, Macau or Taiwan businessmen exceeds 25% of the total registered capital of the corporation. In case the share of investment from Hong Kong, Macau or Taiwan is less than 25% of the total registered capital, the enterprise is to be classified as domestic-funded share-holding corporation Ltd.

(XⅢ) Joint-venture Enterprises with Foreign Investment: refer to enterprises jointly established by foreign enterprises or foreigners with enterprises in the mainland of China in accordance with the Law of the People's Republic of China on Sino-foreign Joint Venture Enterprises and other relevant laws, where the share of investment, profits and risks is stipulated in the contract.

(XⅣ) Cooperation Enterprises with Foreign Investment: refer to enterprises jointly established by foreign enterprises or foreigners with enterprises in the mainland of China in accordance with the Law of the People's Republic of China on Sino-foreign Cooperative Enterprises and other relevant laws, where the investment or provision of facilities, and the share of profits and risks is stipulated in the cooperative contract.

(XⅤ) Enterprises with Sole (exclusive) Foreign Investment: refer to enterprises established in the mainland of China with exclusive investment from foreign investors in accordance with the Law of the People's Republic of China on Foreign-Funded Enterprises and other relevant laws.

(XⅥ) Share-holding Corporations Ltd. with Foreign Investment: refer to share-holding corporations Ltd. established with the approval from the Ministry of Foreign Trade and Economic Relations in line with relevant state regulations, where the share of investment from foreign investors exceeds 25% of the total registered capital of the corporation. In case the share of foreign investment is less than 25% of the total registered capital, the enterprise is to be classified as domestic-funded share-holding corporation Ltd.

□ State-holding Enterprises

Refer to a classification of enterprises of mixed ownership. It means the state-owned asset of total assets is more than that of other owners. The classification shows the status of share held by state-owned economy.

□ Light Industry

Refers to the industry that produces consumer goods and hand tools. It consists of two categories, depending on the materials used:

(Ⅰ) Industries using farm products as raw materials. These are the branches of light industry which directly or indirectly use farm products as basic raw materials, including the manufacture of

EXPLANATORY NOTES TO
MAJOR STATISTICAL INDICATORS

food and beverages, tobacco processing, textile, clothing, fur and leather manufacturing, paper making, printing, etc.

(Ⅱ) Industries using non-farm products as raw materials. These are the branches of light industry which use manufactured goods as raw materials, including the manufacture of cultural, educational articles and sports goods, chemicals, synthetic fibre, chemical products for daily use, glass products for daily use, metal products for daily use, hand tools, medical apparatus and instruments, and the manufacture of cultural and office machinery.

□ Heavy Industry

Refers to the industry which produces capital goods, and provides various sectors of the national economy with necessary material and technical basis for production. It consists of the following three branches according to the purpose of production or the use of products:

(Ⅰ) Mining, quarrying and logging industry, which refers to the industry that extracts natural resources, including extraction of petroleum, coal, metal and non-metal ores.

(Ⅱ) Raw materials industry refers to the industry that provides various sectors of the national economy with raw materials, fuels and power. It includes smelting and processing of metals, coking and coke chemistry, chemical materials and building materials such as cement, plywood, and power, petroleum refining and coal dressing.

(Ⅲ) Manufacturing industry which refers to the industry that processes raw materials. It includes machine-building industries which equip sectors of the national economy; industries producing metal structure and cement products; and industries producing means of agricultural production, such as chemical fertilizers and pesticides.

In accordance with the above principles of classification, the repairing trades, which are engaged primarily in repairing products of heavy industry, are classified as heavy industry while those which are engaged in repairing products of light industry are classified as light industry.

□ Gross Industrial Output Value

Refers to the total volume of final industrial products produced and industrial services provided in this year.

(Ⅰ) Principles for calculations

①Statistics on industrial production follow the principle that all products produced by the enterprises and accepted through quality check during the reference period are to be included no matter whether they are sold or not during the reference period.

②Determination of final products follows the principle that all products that are included in the calculation of gross industrial output value are the final products of the enterprise which have been accepted through quality check and require no further processing. If an enterprise has semi-finished products to sell, these intermediate products are considered as the final products of the enterprise.

Finished and semi-finished products which tranfer in the workshop can only calculate the difference value between the end and the beginning.

③Gross industrial output value is calculated following the principle of factory approach, i.e. industrial enterprise is used as the basic accounting unit in calculating the gross industrial output value. By this approach, value of the same product is not to be double-counted, and the output value of different workshops (branch factories) within the enterprise should not be added. However, this approach allows the possibility of double counting between enterprises.

(Ⅱ) Content

Gross industrial output value consists of 3 components: value of the finished products during the reference period, income from processing for external parties, and value of change in semi-finished products between the end and the beginning of the reference period.

①Value of finished products during the reference period: refers to the value of all finished (semi-finished) industrial products that are produced during the reference period without the need for further processing, checked for acceptance, packed and put into the warehouse of the enterprise, including the value of own-produced equipment and the value of products provided to the projects under construction of the enterprise, and to other non-industrial or welfare units. Value of finished products does not include the value of finished products (semi-finished products) that are produced using the materials from the clients who place the orders.

Value of finished products during the reference period is calculated by the quantity of products produced using own materials multiplied by the average unit prices at which products are sold (excluding value-added tax). Own-produced equipment and products produced for own use are valued at cost prices as in the case of enterprise accounting.

②Income from external processing: refers to income from contracted external processing of industrial products (including processing of industrial products using materials from the clients), and the income from industrial repairing work provided to other parties. Income from external processing is calculated using information from the item "products sales income" in the enterprise accounting at the prices with value-added tax excluded.

If the income from external processing is paid beyond one year, Enterprises which the share of income from processing service is significant should adjust and record actual income from external processing this year.

③Value of change in semi-finished products between the end and the beginning of the reference period.If the enterprise accounting excludes the cost of semi-finished products,then it should not be included in the gross industrial output value,and the reverse if otherwise.

Value of change in semi-finished products between the end and the beginning of the reference period:refers to the value of change in semi-finished products between the end and the beginning of the reference period. If the value of the end is less than the beginning, the index is negative and not dealted as zero.

(III) Method of calculation

①All products produced using own materials are to be calculated with full value in reporting the gross industrial output value irrespective of the complexity of production.

②For external processing, it allows calculate using processing fee.There are two cases: a、Between industrial enterprises.For gross industrial output value, processing enterprises calculate using processing fee and Commissioned processing calculate using full price.b、Between industrial enterprise and non-industrial enterprise.When industrial enterprise is processing enterprise,it allows caluculate using processing fee.

③The value of change in semi-finished products should be included in the gross industrial output value if it is included in the accounting record of the enterprise, otherwise it should not be included.

□ Industrial Sales Value

Is the total volume of industrial products produced and sold by industrial enterprises in a given period in monetary terms. It includes: (I) the value of finished-products; (II) the value for external processing. The difference between all products produced using own materials and external processing for calculation of industrial sales value is as same as the calculation of gross industry output value.

□ Value Added of Industry

Refers to the final results of industrial trade in money terms during the reference period. The value added is the balance that the total results of industrial production deduct the used or transferred products and their value. It is the newly increased value.

□ Value of Export Delivery

Refers to the value of products exported via foreign trade agencies or by the industrial enterprises on their own (including the export to Hong Kong, Macao and Taiwan), as well as the value of products in the productions like processing with foreign designs, processing on given materials, assembling of supplied parts and compensation trade, which is settled by foreign exchanges. The value of export delivery should be calculated in RMB according to the exchange rate at the time of trade.

□ Total Assets

Refer to all assets which are owned or controlled by enterprises, including circulating assets, long-term investment, fixed assets, intangible assets and deferred assets, other long-term assets, and deferred taxes, etc. The summation of above items is equal to total assets shown in the balance sheets of the enterprises. Total assets correspond to the summation item of total assets shown in the balance sheets of the enterprises

(I) Circulating assets (working capital) refer to assets which can be cashed in or spent or consumed in an operating cycle of one year or over one year, including cash, all kinds of deposits, short term investment, receivables, advance payment, stock, etc. Circulating assets correspond to the summation item of circulation assets shown in the balance sheets of the enterprises.

(II) Fixed assets refer to the assets with high unit value can keep its original body in use and last for a long period. Refers to the use of more than one year of housing, buildings, machines, machinery, transport equipment and other production and business-related equipment, apparatus, tools, etc. Some items which are not belong to the production and operation of major equipment, but the unit value of more than 2,000 yuan, and the use of more than two years, should also be as fixed assets. Fixed assets correspond to the summation item of fixed assets shown in the balance sheets of the enterprises.

(III) Intangible assets refer to the assets without material form used by enterprises over a long time, such as patents, non-patent technologies, trade marks, copyright, land use right, business reputation, etc.

□ Total Liabilities

Refer to the debts that enterprises are responsible for repayment, including liquid liabilities and long-term liabilities. The forms of reimbursement are including currency,assets and

EXPLANATORY NOTES TO MAJOR STATISTICAL INDICATORS

providing labor services.Total liabilities correspond to the summation item of liabilities shown in the balance sheets of the enterprises.

(Ⅰ)Liquid liabilities (also called quick liabilities or immediate liabilities) refer to enterprises total debt payable within an operating cycle of one year or over one year, including short term loans, payables and advance payments, wages payable, taxes payable and profit payable, etc. Liquid liabilities correspond to the summation item of liquid liabilities shown in the balance sheets of the enterprises.

(Ⅱ)Long-term liabilities refers to total debt payable within an operating cycle of one year or over one year, including long-term loans, payable liabilities, long-term payables, etc. Long-term liabilities correspond to the summation item of long-term shown in the balance sheets of the enterprises.

□ Creditors' Equity

Refers to investors' ownership of net assets of the enterprise. It is equal to the total assets of the enterprise minus its total liabilities, including the primary input from investors, capital accumulation fund, surplus accumulation fund and undistributed profit.It is the last digital of "creditors' equity" in "balance sheet". Creditors equity correspond to the summation item of creditors' equity shown in the balance sheets of the enterprises.

□ Revenue from Principal Business

Refers to the toal of revenue from principal business. It is the annual accumulation of the corresponding item in the "profit table" of the accountant. For enterprises that follow the 2006 Enterprise Accounting Standards, the year-end accumulation of Operating income is used as a substitute.

□ Cost of Principal Business

Refers to real costs from principal business. It is the annual accumulation of the corresponding item in the "profit table" of the accountant. For enterprises that follow the 2006 Enterprise Accounting Standards, the year-end accumulation of Operating costs is used as a substitute.

□ Tax and Extra Charges from Principal Business

Refer to the tax and charges including the business tax, consumption tax, city maintenance and construction tax, resources tax, land increasing value tax and extra charges for education and etc. It is the annual accumulation of the corresponding item in the "profit table" of the accountant. For enterprises that follow the 2006 Enterprise Accounting Standards, the year-end accumulation of tax and extra charges from the sales of products is used as a substitute.

□ Profit from business

Refers to the profits from operation activities, that is the main business income minus the cost of main business and main business tax and surcharges, add other business profits, minus operating expenses, management fees, finance charges. It is the annual accumulation of the corresponding item in the "profit table" of the accountant.

□ Value Added Tax Payable

Refers to the amount of the value-added tax, which should be paid by the enterprises in the reporting period.According to the tax laws, increasing the activities of the current value of the goods,such as the sale of goods or the provision of processing, repair workshop and other services should pay taxes.It is calculated as follows:

Value added tax payable=tax on sales-(tax on purchases-transferred tax on purchases)- Tax credits-tax cut +export rebate

□ Total Profits

Refers to the annual accumulation of the corresponding item in the "profit table" of the accountant. It is the profits gained from the revenues in the reference period, including business profits, subsidies, net income of investment and net income of other business.

□ Total Value of Profit and Tax (Pre-tax Profits)

Refers to the sum of the total profits, products sales tax and surcharges and the value added tax payable of industrial enterprises. It is also called Pre-tax profits.

□ Industrial Comprehensive Index of Economic Efficiency

Is a special kind of relative figure to comprehensively measure overall economic efficiency of regional industry, showing the quality of industrial economic efficiency of the reference period. Industrial comprehensive index of economic efficiency is calculated with 7 items of ratio of total assets to industrial output value, ratio of creditors' equity of current year to that of previous year, ratio of liabilities to assets, turnover ratio of output value, circulating funds, ratio of profits to cost, overall labor productivity, ratio of sales to products. The actual figure of every indicator above is divided by responding national standard numerical value, and the results multiply correlative weight coefficients, then the total number is divided by general weight coefficient. The index comprehensively reflects the changes of regional industrial economic efficiency in static and dynamic status, eliminating the incomparable factors at a certain extent.

□ Ratio of Total Assets to Industrial Output Value

Reflects the profit-making capability of all assets of the enterprise and is a key indicator manifesting the performance and management and evaluating the profit-making potential of the enterprise. It is calculated as follows:

Ratio of Total Assets to Industrial Output (%) = [(Total profits + Total taxes + Interest payment) / average assets] × 100%

□ Capital Maintenance and Appreciation Rate

Reflects the changes of an enterprise's net assets. It epitomizes the growth capability of an enterprise. Its calcuating formula is:

Capital Maintenance and appreciation rate = Ownership equity at the end of the reporting period/Ownership equity at the same period of the previous year.

□ Ratio of Liabilities to Assets

Reflect both the operation risk and the capability of the enterprise in making use of the capital from the creditors. It is calculated as follows:

Ratio of liabilities to assets (%) = Total liabilities/total assets×100%

□ Turnover Ratio of Circulating Funds

Refers to times of turnover of circulating funds in a given period of time, which reflects the speed of the turnover of working capital and is calculated as follows:

Turnover Ratio of Circulating Funds (%) = Sales Revenue of Products/Average Balance of Total Circulating Funds×100%

□ Ratio of Profits to Costs

Refers to the ratio of profits realized in a given period to the total costs in the same period, which reflects the economic efficiency of input cost and is calculated as follows:

Ratio of Profits to Cost (%) =Total Profits/Total Costs×100%

□ Overall Labor Productivity

Refers to the average output per employed person in industrial enterprises in value terms. At present, the value added and the average number of staff and workers of an industrial enterprises in a given period are used to calculate the overall labor productivity. The formula used is:

Overall Labor Productivity = (Value Added of Industry) / (Average Number of Staff and Workers)

□ Ratio of Sales to Products

Refers to the ratio of total sales in a given period to the gross output value in the same period, which reflects the extent of industrial output sold and is calculated as follows:

Ratio of Sales to Products (%) =Total Sales (at Current Prices) / Gross Output Value (at Current Prices) ×100%

□ Ratio of Profits to Sales

Refers to the ratio of total profits to the sales revenue in a given period and is calculated as follows:

Ratio of Profits to Sales (%) =Total Profits /Sales Revenue×100%

□ Ratio of Accumulated Capital to Original Capital

Refers to the ratio of the increased volume of creditors' equity to the creditors' equity at the year's beginning. The formula used is:

Ratio of Accumulated Capital to Original Capital (%) = Increased Volume of Creditors' Equity / Creditors' Equity at Year's Beginning×100%

□ Current Ratio

Refers to the ratio of the circulating assets to the circulating liabilities, i.e. the amount of circulating assets as the guarantee to pay off each yuan of circulating liabilities, which reflects the ability of the enterprise to pay off the due circulating liabilities with the circulating assets realizable in a short period of time. The formula is:

Current Ratio (%) = Circulating Assets / Circulating Liabilities

EXPLANATORY NOTES TO MAJOR STATISTICAL INDICATORS

□ Quick Ratio

Refers to the ratio of quick assets to circulating liabilities of the enterprise, and is calculated as the follows:

Quick Ratio = Quick Assets / Circulating Liabilities

□ Ratio of Equity to Production

Refers to the ratio of total liabilities to creditors' equity. It is the sign of financial stability of the enterprises, and also called ratio of total liabilities to total capital. The formula is:

Ratio of Equity to Production = Total Liabilities / Creditors' Equity

第13章

建筑业

CONSTRUCTION

简要说明
BRIEF INTRODUCTION

本章资料包括全市按登记注册地统计的建筑业基本情况、建筑企业房屋施工及竣工面积和劳务分包建筑业企业主要指标、各类建筑施工企业主要经济指标等，由市统计局固定资产投资处提供。全市建筑业增加值情况参见本书第二章国民经济核算。

The data in this chapter include the general information of all the construction enterprises with the place of registration in Chongqing, the main indicators on the floor space of buildings under construction and completed of construction enterprises and on the labor subcontractors in construction industry, as well as the main economic indicators on various construction enterprises. The data in this chapter are provided by Division of Statistics of Investment in Fixed Assets, Chongqing Municipal Bureau of Statistics. See Chapter 2 National Economic Accounting of this book for the value added of construction industry.

表13.1 建筑业基本情况（1985－2011年）
BASIC STATISTICS ON CONSTRUCTION INDUSTRY (1985-2011)

年 份 Year	企业数（个） Number of Enterprises (unit)	年末从业人数（万人） Number of Employees at Year-end (10 000 persons)	总产值（万元） Gross Output Value (10 000 yuan)	房屋建筑施工面积（万平方米） Floor Space of Buildings under Construction (10 000 sq.m)	房屋建筑竣工面积（万平方米） Floor Space of Buildings Completed (10 000 sq.m)
1985	298	14.12	96201	684.85	340.18
1986	291	17.12	112719	674.54	345.37
1987	303	18.08	138515	740.55	350.79
1988	399	20.71	183070	866.76	372.69
1989	400	20.60	196510	853.54	391.35
1990	445	20.89	220685	905.58	450.19
1991	465	21.50	262155	915.31	458.23
1992	482	23.58	340256	1015.59	490.88
1993	607	22.47	426228	1238.22	537.78
1994	561	26.61	656959	1456.78	577.22
1995	556	28.24	810548	1678.02	656.38
1996	1473	64.43	2052964	4065.24	2276.97
1997	1501	68.98	2440552	4451.06	2562.73
1998	1655	80.46	2896198	5275.68	2837.02
1999	1735	75.49	3175927	5481.86	2974.82
2000	1785	73.37	3486579	6088.49	3083.72
2001	1721	83.99	4368064	7962.27	4341.38
2002	1778	82.05	5015839	8707.39	4711.06
2003	1760	81.80	5862095	9754.10	4939.62
2004	2442	86.91	6902774	10184.46	5167.65
2005	2310	83.10	7835658	10722.57	5155.18
2006	2455	86.72	8950918	11522.42	5309.27
2007	2486	96.97	11287118	13866.76	5750.65
2008	2483	105.42	14963195	15618.93	6485.30
2009	2465	118.88	19152495	16475.84	7473.16
2010	2467	139.33	25343196	19489.39	8292.00
2011	2530	134.84	33288252	21976.19	8989.56

注：1）1993年实行一套表制度，附营建筑企业有所增加；1996年以前口径范围包括全民、城镇集体建筑安装企业，1996年-2001年为资质等级四级以上的建筑安装企业(下表同)。
2）2002年起建筑业执行新建筑资质，2002年房屋建筑施工、竣工面积和2003年起所有数据不含劳务分包企业(下表同)。

Note: a) As the system of one suit of tables was implemented in 1993, the affiliated construction enterprises increased. The statistics scope before 1996 included the whole people-owned, collective-owned construction and installation enterprises; while the statistics scope from 1996 to 2001 included the construction and installation enterprises of qualification Grade-4 and above (the same below).
b) The new grade system was carried out in construction in 2002. The data of floor space under construction and completed in 2002, and all the data since 2003 exclude the data of labor subcontractors (the same below).

表13.2 建筑业企业房屋施工及竣工面积（2010－2011年）
FLOOR SPACE OF BUILDINGS UNDER CONSTRUCTION AND COMPLETED BY CONSTRUCTION ENTERPRISES (2010-2011)

指 标	Item	2010	2011
房屋建筑施工面积（万平方米）	**Floor Space of Buildings under Construction (10 000 sq.m)**	**19489.39**	**21976.19**
#本年新开工面积	Floor Space of Buildings Newly Started in This Year	11095.49	11099.31
#实行投标承包面积	Floor Space Contracted by Bidding	13981.37	15024.28
#本年新开工	Newly Started in This Year	8485.49	8369.53
房屋建筑竣工面积（万平方米）	**Floor Space of Buildings Completed (10 000 sq.m)**	**8292.00**	**8989.56**
住宅房屋	Residential Buildings	6239.93	6433.18
商业及服务用房屋	Buildings for Business and Services	244.33	414.54
#批发和零售用房	Buildings for Wholesale and Retail	103.93	147.68
住宿和餐饮用房	Buildings for Hotels and Catering Services	84.53	79.84
居民服务业用房	Buildings for Residential Services	55.87	186.26
办公用房	Office Buildings	383.68	438.35
科研、教育、医疗用房屋	Buildings for Scientific Research、Education、Medical	272.31	303.11
#科学研究用房屋	Buildings for Scientific Research	5.43	8.52
教育用房屋	Buildings for Education	218.59	205.58
医疗用房屋（卫生医疗用房）	Buildings for Health and Medical Cares	48.29	89.01
文化、体育和娱乐用房	Buildings for Culture, Sports and Entertainment	63.11	52.53
厂房及建筑物	Works and Buildings	795.46	1048.61
#厂房	Works	795.46	560.53
仓库	Warehouses		48.61
其他未列明的房屋建筑物	Other Buildings	293.18	250.64

表13.3 劳务分包建筑业企业主要指标（2010－2011年）
MAIN INDICATORS ON LABOR SUBCONTRACTORS IN CONSTRUCTION INDUSTRY (2010-2011)

单位：万元 (10 000 yuan)

指 标	Item	2010	2011
企业数（个）	Number of Enterprises (unit)	336	357
年末从业人数（人）	Number of Persons Employed at Year-end (person)	152736	178931
企业总收入	Total Revenue	434615	641448
#劳务收入	Revenue from Labor Services	434005	636427
税 金	Taxes	14276	26173
利润总额	Total Profits	10720	6719
从业人员劳动报酬	Earnings of Employed	286368	497810

表13.4 建筑施工企业主要经济指标（2010－2011年）
MAIN ECONOMIC INDICATORS ON CONSTRUCTION ENTERPRISES (2010-2011)

指　标	Type	2010	2011
企业数（个）	**Number of Enterprises (unit)**	**2467**	**2530**
年末从业人数（万人）	**Number of Employees at Year-end (10 000 persons)**	**139.33**	**134.84**
总产值（万元）	**Gross Output Value (10 000 yuan)**	**25343196**	**33288252**
按登记注册类型分	By Status of Registration		
内资企业	Domestic-funded Enterprises	25320550	33270244
#国　有	State-owned Enterprises	3625083	5562847
其他有限责任	Other Limited Liability Enterprises	11136396	13470225
私　营	Private Enterprises	8767261	10739874
按构成分	By Constitution		
#建筑工程	Construction	22771825	30134042
安装工程	Installation	1628910	2110554
按行业分	By Sector		
#房屋和土木工程建筑业	Construction of Buildings and Civil Engineering	23249018	30577940
#房屋工程建筑业	Buildings	17901489	22636724
建筑安装业	Construction Installation	1137677	1294830
建筑装饰业	Construction Decoration	534265	824357
按资质等级分	By Grade		
施工总承包	General Contractors of Construction	22987429	30361775
#一　级	First Grade	11820982	15651065
二　级	Second Grade	7151579	9324563
专业承包	Specialized Contractors of Construction	2355767	2926477
#一　级	First Grade	1001080	1379312
二　级	Second Grade	748942	813165
竣工产值（万元）	**Output Value of Completed Construction (10 000 yuan)**	**14577910**	**16961126**
按登记注册类型分	By Status of Registration		
内资企业	Domestic-funded Enterprises	14565546	16944557
#国　有	State-owned Enterprises	1888708	2378852
其他有限责任	Other Limited Liability Enterprises	5681315	6193823
私　营	Private Enterprises	5904104	6592252
按行业分	By Sector		
#房屋和土木工程建筑业	Construction of Buildings and Civil Engineering	13294822	15403304
#房屋工程建筑业	Buildings	11084527	12502131
建筑安装业	Construction Installation	661639	760734
建筑装饰业	Construction Decoration	301444	454021
按资质等级分	By Grade		
施工总承包	General Contractors of Construction	13419493	15671044
#一　级	First Grade	5926692	6779753
二　级	Second Grade	4799267	5934382
专业承包	Specialized Contractors of Construction	1158417	1290082
#一　级	First Grade	326053	327357
二　级	Second Grade	481341	526218
房屋建筑施工面积（万平方米）	**Floor Space of Buildings under Construction (10 000 sq.m)**	**19489.39**	**21976.19**
房屋建筑竣工面积（万平方米）	**Floor Space of Buildings Completed (10 000 sq.m)**	**8292.00**	**8989.56**
年末自有机械设备台数（万台）	**Number of Machinery and Equipment Self-owned (year-end)(10 000 sets)**	**17.76**	**18.78**
年末自有机械设备总功率（万千瓦）	**Total Power of Machinery and Equipment Self-owned (year-end)(10 000 kw)**	**337.66**	**463.87**

表13.5 国有建筑施工企业主要经济指标（2010－2011年）
MAIN ECONOMIC INDICATORS ON STATE-OWNED CONSTRUCTION ENTERPRISES (2010-2011)

指　标	Type	2010	2011
企业数（个）	**Number of Enterprises (unit)**	**125**	**130**
年末从业人数（万人）	**Number of Employees at Year-end (10 000 persons)**	**13.30**	**12.56**
总产值（万元）	**Gross Output Value (10 000 yuan)**	**3625083**	**5562847**
按构成分	By Constitution		
#建筑工程	Construction	3265411	5145443
安装工程	Installation	214716	260522
按行业分	By Sector		
#房屋和土木工程建筑业	Construction of Buildings and Civil Engineering	3368912	5282976
#房屋工程建筑业	Buildings	1150831	1657383
建筑安装业	Construction Installation	62747	56576
建筑装饰业	Construction Decoration	28647	47804
按资质等级分	By Grade		
施工总承包	General Contractors of Construction	3317737	5186169
#一　级	First Grade	1941762	3122955
二　级	Second Grade	845888	1229004
专业承包	Specialized Contractors of Construction	307346	376678
#一　级	First Grade	203139	229137
二　级	Second Grade	51971	99265
竣工产值（万元）	**Output Value of Completed Construction (10 000 yuan)**	**1888708**	**2378852**
按行业分	By Sector		
#房屋和土木工程建筑业	Construction of Buildings and Civil Engineering	1701384	2179422
#房屋工程建筑业	Buildings	662214	783184
建筑安装业	Construction Installation	36537	31810
建筑装饰业	Construction Decoration	1281	15690
按资质等级分	By Grade		
施工总承包	General Contractors of Construction	1762445	2203374
#一　级	First Grade	999158	1057237
二　级	Second Grade	569098	964715
专业承包	Specialized Contractors of Construction	126263	175478
#一　级	First Grade	58564	88517
二　级	Second Grade	48628	73628
房屋建筑施工面积（万平方米）	**Floor Space of Buildings under Construction (10 000 sq.m)**	**1491.24**	**1837.28**
房屋建筑竣工面积（万平方米）	**Floor Space of Buildings Completed (10 000 sq.m)**	**526.34**	**542.28**
年末自有机械设备台数（万台）	**Number of Machinery and Equipment Self-owned (year-end)(10 000 sets)**	**1.42**	**1.85**
年末自有机械设备总功率（万千瓦）	**Total Power of Machinery and Equipment Self-owned (year-end)(10 000 kw)**	**53.60**	**65.24**

表13.6 其他有限责任制建筑施工企业主要经济指标（2010－2011年）
MAIN ECONOMIC INDICATORS ON OTHER CONSTRUCTION ENTERPRISES OF LIMITED LIABILITY (2010-2011)

指 标	Ttpe	2010	2011
企业数（个）	**Number of Enterprises (unit)**	**728**	**781**
年末从业人数（万人）	**Number of Employees at Year-end (10 000 persons)**	**57.12**	**56.00**
总产值（万元）	**Gross Output Value (10 000 yuan)**	**11136396**	**13470225**
按构成分	By Constitution		
#建筑工程	Construction	9851772	12060670
安装工程	Installation	833597	943473
按行业分	By Sector		
#房屋和土木工程建筑业	Construction of Buildings and Civil Engineering	10266010	12235936
#房屋工程建筑业	Buildings	7716485	9648453
建筑安装业	Construction Installation	533370	726379
建筑装饰业	Construction Decoration	197564	338230
按资质等级分	By Grade		
施工总承包	General Contractors of Construction	9978424	12034845
#一 级	First Grade	6869610	7794809
二 级	Second Grade	2120829	2939287
专业承包	Specialized Contractors of Construction	1157972	1435380
#一 级	First Grade	588197	860057
二 级	Second Grade	335724	307477
竣工产值（万元）	**Output Value of Completed Construction (10 000 yuan)**	**5681315**	**6193823**
按行业分	By Sector		
#房屋和土木工程建筑业	Construction of Buildings and Civil Engineering	5219007	5544644
#房屋工程建筑业	Buildings	4374704	5033309
建筑安装业	Construction Installation	302118	412214
建筑装饰业	Construction Decoration	83761	178729
按资质等级分	By Grade		
施工总承包	General Contractors of Construction	5162672	5646348
#一 级	First Grade	3125694	2879409
二 级	Second Grade	1368080	1850801
专业承包	Specialized Contractors of Construction	518643	547476
#一 级	First Grade	190605	145794
二 级	Second Grade	213539	223097
房屋建筑施工面积（万平方米）	**Floor Space of Buildings under Construction (10 000 sq.m)**	**8659.86**	**9649.04**
房屋建筑竣工面积（万平方米）	**Floor Space of Buildings Completed (10 000 sq.m)**	**3022.60**	**3624.99**
年末自有机械设备台数（万台）	**Number of Machinery and Equipment Self-owned (year-end)(10 000 sets)**	**8.08**	**7.30**
年末自有机械设备总功率（万千瓦）	**Total Power of Machinery and Equipment Self-owned (year-end)(10 000 kw)**	**130.47**	**213.12**

表13.7 私营建筑施工企业主要经济指标（2010－2011年）

MAIN ECONOMIC INDICATORS ON PRIVATE CONSTRUCTION ENTERPRISES (2010-2011)

指 标	Type	2010	2011
企业数（个）	**Number of Enterprises (unit)**	**1377**	**1368**
年末从业人数（万人）	**Number of Employees at Year-end (10 000 persons)**	**57.91**	**56.13**
总产值（万元）	**Gross Output Value (10 000 yuan)**	**8767261**	**10739874**
按构成分	By Constitution		
#建筑工程	Construction	7975776	9699855
安装工程	Installation	489295	671698
按行业分	By Sector		
#房屋和土木工程建筑业	Construction of Buildings and Civil Engineering	7920900	9755739
#房屋工程建筑业	Buildings	7583380	9339337
建筑安装业	Construction Installation	465788	437468
建筑装饰业	Construction Decoration	262566	313550
按资质等级分	By Grade		
施工总承包	General Contractors of Construction	8024192	9854044
#一 级	First Grade	2687327	3338155
二 级	Second Grade	3501234	4294795
专业承包	Specialized Contractors of Construction	743069	885830
#一 级	First Grade	134387	158995
二 级	Second Grade	328520	362183
竣工产值（万元）	**Output Value of Completed Construction (10 000 yuan)**	**5904104**	**6592252**
按行业分	By Sector		
#房屋和土木工程建筑业	Construction of Buildings and Civil Engineering	5351588	5997992
#房屋工程建筑业	Buildings	5113097	5726327
建筑安装业	Construction Installation	273275	274136
建筑装饰业	Construction Decoration	185170	195207
按资质等级分	By Grade		
施工总承包	General Contractors of Construction	5444753	6111196
#一 级	First Grade	1665957	2095551
二 级	Second Grade	2394388	2597998
专业承包	Specialized Contractors of Construction	459351	481057
#一 级	First Grade	61918	62424
二 级	Second Grade	199317	195320
房屋建筑施工面积（万平方米）	**Floor Space of Buildings under Construction (10 000 sq.m)**	**8020.91**	**7871.68**
房屋建筑竣工面积（万平方米）	**Floor Space of Buildings Completed (10 000 sq.m)**	**4095.68**	**3947.67**
年末自有机械设备台数（万台）	**Number of Machinery and Equipment Self-owned (year-end)(10 000 sets)**	**6.97**	**8.09**
年末自有机械设备总功率（万千瓦）	**Total Power of Machinery and Equipment Self-owned (year-end)(10 000 kw)**	**130.06**	**145.42**

表13.8 施工总承包建筑施工企业主要经济指标（2010－2011年）
MAIN ECONOMIC INDICATORS ON GENERAL CONTRACTORS OF CONSTRUCTION (2010-2011)

指　标	Type	2010	2011
企业数（个）	**Number of Enterprises (unit)**	**1463**	**1530**
年末从业人数（万人）	**Number of Employees at Year-end (10 000 persons)**	**129.13**	**125.46**
总产值（万元）	**Gross Output Value (10 000 yuan)**	**22987429**	**30361775**
按登记注册类型分	By Status of Registration		
内资企业	Domestic-funded Enterprises	22985466	30353678
#国　有	State-owned Enterprises	3317737	5186169
其他有限责任	Other Limited Liability Enterprises	9978424	12034845
私　营	Private Enterprises	8024193	9854044
按构成分	By Constitution		
#建筑工程	Construction	21494759	28551845
安装工程	Installation	769108	1030240
按行业分	By Sector		
#房屋和土木工程建筑业	Construction of Buildings and Civil Engineering	22356512	29343308
#房屋工程建筑业	Buildings	17722981	22519619
建筑安装业	Construction Installation	339735	514920
建筑装饰业	Construction Decoration	52327	187310
按资质等级分	By Grade		
#一　级	First Grade	11820982	15651065
二　级	Second Grade	7151579	9324563
竣工产值（万元）	**Output Value of Completed Construction (10 000 yuan)**	**13419493**	**15671044**
按登记注册类型分	By Status of Registration		
内资企业	Domestic-funded Enterprises	13419493	15664386
#国　有	State-owned Enterprises	1762445	2203374
其他有限责任	Other Limited Liability Enterprises	5162672	5646348
私　营	Private Enterprises	5444753	6111196
按行业分	By Sector		
#房屋和土木工程建筑业	Construction of Buildings and Civil Engineering	12986452	15048520
#房屋工程建筑业	Buildings	10985896	12432950
建筑安装业	Construction Installation	178553	238180
建筑装饰业	Construction Decoration	36576	113701
按资质等级分	By Grade		
#一　级	First Grade	5926692	6779753
二　级	Second Grade	4799267	5934382
房屋建筑施工面积（万平方米）	**Floor Space of Buildings under Construction (10 000 sq.m)**	**19042.45**	**21667.70**
房屋建筑竣工面积（万平方米）	**Floor Space of Buildings Completed (10 000 sq.m)**	**8142.75**	**8894.93**
年末自有机械设备台数（万台）	**Number of Machinery and Equipment Self-owned (year-end)(10 000 sets)**	**13.96**	**16.01**
年末自有机械设备总功率（万千瓦）	**Total Power of Machinery and Equipment Self-owned (year-end)(10 000 kw)**	**302.26**	**412.83**

表13.9 专业承包建筑施工企业主要经济指标（2010－2011年）
MAIN ECONOMIC INDICATORS ON SPECIALIZED CONTRACTORS OF CONSTRUCTION (2010-2011)

指　标	Type	2010	2011
企业数（个）	**Number of Enterprises (unit)**	**1004**	**1000**
年末从业人数（万人）	**Number of Employees at Year-end (10 000 persons)**	**10.20**	**9.38**
总产值（万元）	**Gross Output Value (10 000 yuan)**	**2355767**	**2926477**
按登记注册类型分	By Status of Registration		
内资企业	Domestic-funded Enterprises	2335084	2916566
#国　有	State-owned Enterprises	307346	376678
其他有限责任	Other Limited Liability Enterprises	1157972	1435380
私　营	Private Enterprises	743069	885830
按构成分	By Constitution		
#建筑工程	Construction	1277066	1582197
安装工程	Installation	859802	1080314
按行业分	By Sector		
#房屋和土木工程建筑业	Construction of Buildings and Civil Engineering	892506	1234632
#房屋工程建筑业	Buildings	178508	117105
建筑安装业	Construction Installation	797942	779910
建筑装饰业	Construction Decoration	481938	637047
按资质等级分	By Grade		
#一　级	First Grade	1001080	1379312
二　级	Second Grade	748942	813165
竣工产值（万元）	**Output Value of Completed Construction (10 000 yuan)**	**1158417**	**1290082**
按登记注册类型分	By Status of Registration		
内资企业	Domestic-funded Enterprises	1146053	1280171
#国　有	State-owned Enterprises	126263	175478
其他有限责任	Other Limited Liability Enterprises	518643	547476
私　营	Private Enterprises	459351	481057
按行业分	By Sector		
#房屋和土木工程建筑业	Construction of Buildings and Civil Engineering	308370	354784
#房屋工程建筑业	Buildings	98631	69182
建筑安装业	Construction Installation	483085	522554
建筑装饰业	Construction Decoration	264868	340320
按资质等级分	By Grade		
#一　级	First Grade	326053	327357
二　级	Second Grade	481341	526218
房屋建筑施工面积（万平方米）	**Floor Space of Buildings under Construction (10 000 sq.m)**	**446.94**	**308.50**
房屋建筑竣工面积（万平方米）	**Floor Space of Buildings Completed (10 000 sq.m)**	**149.25**	**94.63**
年末自有机械设备台数（万台）	**Number of Machinery and Equipment Self-owned (year-end)(10 000 sets)**	**3.80**	**2.77**
年末自有机械设备总功率（万千瓦）	**Total Power of Machinery and Equipment Self-owned (year-end)(10 000 kw)**	**35.40**	**51.04**

表13.10 房屋和土木工程建筑施工企业主要经济指标（2010－2011年）
MAIN ECONOMIC INDICATORS ON CONSTRUCTION ENTERPRISES OF BUILDINGS AND CIVIL ENGINEERING (2010-2011)

指 标	Type	2010	2011
企业数（个）	**Number of Enterprises (unit)**	**1505**	**1571**
年末从业人数（万人）	**Number of Employees at Year-end (10 000 persons)**	**129.07**	**123.44**
总产值（万元）	**Gross Output Value (10 000 yuan)**	**23249018**	**30577940**
按登记注册类型分	By Status of Registration		
内资企业	Domestic-funded Enterprises	23247055	30576040
#国 有	State-owned Enterprises	3368912	5282976
其他有限责任	Other Limited Liability Enterprises	10266010	12235936
私 营	Private Enterprises	7920900	9755739
按构成分	By Constitution		
#建筑工程	Construction	21867968	28996172
安装工程	Installation	744753	847397
按资质等级分	By Grade		
施工总承包	General Contractors of Construction	22356512	29343308
#一 级	First Grade	11792735	15365238
二 级	Second Grade	6785619	8905049
专业承包	Specialized Contractors of Construction	892506	1234632
#一 级	First Grade	536566	896767
二 级	Second Grade	189150	144218
竣工产值（万元）	**Output Value of Completed Construction (10 000 yuan)**	**13294822**	**15403304**
按登记注册类型分	By Status of Registration		
内资企业	Domestic-funded Enterprises	13294822	15402843
#国 有	State-owned Enterprises	1701384	2179422
其他有限责任	Other Limited Liability Enterprises	5219007	5544644
私 营	Private Enterprises	5351588	5997992
按资质等级分	By Grade		
施工总承包	General Contractors of Construction	12986452	15048520
#一 级	First Grade	5926291	6738064
二 级	Second Grade	4554082	5618404
专业承包	Specialized Contractors of Construction	308370	354784
#一 级	First Grade	90957	130693
二 级	Second Grade	105206	106628
房屋建筑施工面积（万平方米）	**Floor Space of Buildings under Construction (10 000 sq.m)**	**18996.76**	**21447.90**
房屋建筑竣工面积（万平方米）	**Floor Space of Buildings Completed (10 000 sq.m)**	**8124.58**	**8751.19**
年末自有机械设备台数（万台）	**Number of Machinery and Equipment Self-owned (year-end)(10 000 sets)**	**15.14**	**16.14**
年末自有机械设备总功率（万千瓦）	**Total Power of Machinery and Equipment Self-owned (year-end) (10 000 kw)**	**304.92**	**430.17**

表13.11 建筑安装企业主要经济指标（2010－2011年）

MAIN ECONOMIC INDICATORS ON CONSTRUCTION ENTERPRISES OF INSTALLATION (2010-2011)

指 标	Type	2010	2011
企业数（个）	**Number of Enterprises (unit)**	**380**	**344**
年末从业人数（万人）	**Number of Employees at Year-end (10 000 persons)**	**5.26**	**5.17**
总产值（万元）	**Gross Output Value (10 000 yuan)**	**1137677**	**1294830**
按登记注册类型分	By Status of Registration		
内资企业	Domestic-funded Enterprises	1127061	1288633
#国 有	State-owned Enterprises	62747	56576
其他有限责任	Other Limited Liability Enterprises	533370	726379
私 营	Private Enterprises	465788	437468
按构成分	By Constitution		
#建筑工程	Construction	360168	229158
安装工程	Installation	730495	1026250
按资质等级分	By Grade		
施工总承包	General Contractors of Construction	339735	514920
#一 级	First Grade	28246	190516
二 级	Second Grade	192034	133528
专业承包	Specialized Contractors of Construction	797942	779910
#一 级	First Grade	140918	126424
二 级	Second Grade	367881	321734
竣工产值（万元）	**Output Value of Completed Construction (10 000 yuan)**	**661639**	**760734**
按登记注册类型分	By Status of Registration		
内资企业	Domestic-funded Enterprises	661499	754537
#国 有	State-owned Enterprises	36537	31810
其他有限责任	Other Limited Liability Enterprises	302118	412214
私 营	Private Enterprises	273275	274136
按资质等级分	By Grade		
施工总承包	General Contractors of Construction	178553	238180
#一 级	First Grade	401	4796
二 级	Second Grade	102701	80219
专业承包	Specialized Contractors of Construction	483085	522554
#一 级	First Grade	85324	57707
二 级	Second Grade	262423	262769
房屋建筑施工面积（万平方米）	**Floor Space of Buildings under Construction (10 000 sq.m)**	**376.83**	**256.91**
房屋建筑竣工面积（万平方米）	**Floor Space of Buildings Completed (10 000 sq.m)**	**121.87**	**108.18**
年末自有机械设备台数（万台）	**Number of Machinery and Equipment Self-owned (year-end)(10 000 sets)**	**1.13**	**0.92**
年末自有机械设备总功率（万千瓦）	**Total Power of Machinery and Equipment Self-owned (year-end) (10 000 kw)**	**17.31**	**11.78**

表13.12 建筑装饰企业主要经济指标（2010－2011年）
MAIN ECONOMIC INDICATORS ON CONSTRUCTION ENTERPRISES OF DECORATION (2010-2011)

指　标	Type	2010	2011
企业数（个）	**Number of Enterprises (unit)**	**487**	**497**
年末从业人数（万人）	**Number of Employees at Year-end (10 000 persons)**	**3.60**	**4.34**
总产值（万元）	**Gross Output Value (10 000 yuan)**	**534265**	**824357**
按登记注册类型分	By Status of Registration		
内资企业	Domestic-funded Enterprises	524198	814446
#国　有	State-owned Enterprises	28647	47804
其他有限责任	Other Limited Liability Enterprises	197564	338230
私　营	Private Enterprises	262566	313550
按构成分	By Constitution		
#建筑工程	Construction	272371	513484
安装工程	Installation	125112	1151474
按资质等级分	By Grade		
施工总承包	General Contractors of Construction	52327	187310
#一　级	First Grade		67506
二　级	Second Grade	14215	107109
专业承包	Specialized Contractors of Construction	481938	637047
#一　级	First Grade	238238	269571
二　级	Second Grade	137817	209592
竣工产值（万元）	**Output Value of Completed Construction (10 000 yuan)**	**301444**	**454021**
按登记注册类型分	By Status of Registration		
内资企业	Domestic-funded Enterprises	289220	444110
#国　有	State-owned Enterprises	1281	15690
其他有限责任	Other Limited Liability Enterprises	83761	178729
私　营	Private Enterprises	185170	195207
按资质等级分	By Grade		
施工总承包	General Contractors of Construction	36576	113701
#一　级	First Grade		28969
二　级	Second Grade	1476	75645
专业承包	Specialized Contractors of Construction	264868	340320
#一　级	First Grade	99358	111475
二　级	Second Grade	91641	134047
房屋建筑施工面积（万平方米）	**Floor Space of Buildings under Construction (10 000 sq.m)**	**19.97**	**91.37**
房屋建筑竣工面积（万平方米）	**Floor Space of Buildings Completed (10 000 sq.m)**	**10.36**	**62.02**
年末自有机械设备台数（万台）	**Number of Machinery and Equipment Self-owned (year-end)(10 000 sets)**	**0.84**	**1.05**
年末自有机械设备总功率（万千瓦）	**Total Power of Machinery and Equipment Self-owned (year-end) (10 000 kw)**	**7.62**	**12.66**

表13.13 建筑施工企业按资质等级分主要财务和经济效益指标（2011年）

MAIN INDICATORS ON FINANCE AND ECONOMIC BENEFIT OF CONSTRUCTION ENTERPRISES BY GRADE (2011)

单位：万元 (10 000 yuan)

指 标	Item	合 计 Total	其 中 of which 施工总承包 General Contractors	专业承包 Specialized Contractors
企业数（个）	Number of Enterprises (unit)	2530	1530	1000
年末从业人数（万人）	Number of Employees at Year-end (10 000 persons)	134.84	125.46	9.38
自有固定资产原价	Original Value of Fixed Assets Owned	3215219	2701290	513929
自有固定资产净价	Net Value of Fixed Assets Owned	2103124	1778489	324635
自有机械设备年末台数（万台）	Number of Machinery and Equipment Self-owned (year-end) (10 000 sets)	18.78	16.01	2.77
自有机械设备年末净值	Net Value of Machinery and Equipment Self-owned (year-end)	932919	824605	108314
自有机械设备年末总功率（万千瓦）	Total Power of Machinery and Equipment Self-owned (year-end) (10 000 kw)	463.87	412.83	51.04
总产值	Gross Output Value	33288252	30361775	2926477
实收资本	Paid-in Capital	6551511	4889432	1662079
资产合计	Total Assets	26787597	23744927	3042670
#流动资产	Current Assets	20708265	18304095	2404170
固定资产	Fixed Assets	2916615	2530257	386358
负债合计	Total Liabilities	17677942	15745685	1932257
流动负债	Current Liabilities	15897608	14067941	1829667
非流动负债	Non-current Liabilities	1780335	1677745	102590
所有者权益	Creditors' Equity	9109654	7999241	1110413
利税总额	Total Pre-tax Profits	2720913	2455101	265812
#利润总额	Total Profits	1559532	1411036	148496
营业收入	Operating Revenue	33172444	30137823	3034621
#主营业务收入	Revenue from Major Business	33002031	29996366	3005665
房屋建筑施工面积（万平方米）	Floor Space of Buildings under Construction (10 000 sq.m)	21976.19	21667.70	308.49
房屋建筑竣工面积（万平方米）	Floor Space of Buildings Completed (10 000 sq.m)	8989.56	8894.93	94.63
全员劳动生产率：	Overall Labor Productivity			
按总产值计算（元/人）	In Terms of Gross Output Value (yuan/person)	175331	167934	322882
技术装备率（元/人）	Value of Machines Per Laborer (yuan/person)	6919	6573	11547
动力装备率（千瓦/人）	Power of Machines Per Laborer (kw/person)	3	3	5
房屋建筑面积竣工率（%）	Rate of Floor Space of Buildings Completed (%)	41.2	41.4	30.7
资产负债率（%）	Asset-Liability Ratio (%)	66.0	66.3	63.5

表13.14 建筑施工企业按行业分主要财务和经济效益指标（2011年）
MAIN INDICATORS ON FINANCE AND ECONOMIC BENEFIT OF CONSTRUCTION ENTERPRISES BY SECTOR (2011)

单位：万元 (10 000 yuan)

指 标	Item	合 计 Total	其 中 of which		
			房屋和土木工程建筑业 Building and Civil Engineering	建筑安装业 Construction Installation	建筑装饰业 Construction Decoration
企业数（个）	Number of Enterprises (unit)	2530	1571	344	497
年末从业人数（万人）	Number of Employees at Year-end (10 000 persons)	134.84	123.44	5.17	4.34
自有固定资产原价	Original Value of Fixed Assets Owned	3215219	2812073	175437	96048
自有固定资产净价	Net Value of Fixed Assets Owned	2103124	1833229	110533	56838
自有机械设备年末台数（万台）	Number of Machinery and Equipment Self-owned (year-end) (10 000 sets)	18.78	16.14	0.92	1.05
自有机械设备年末净值	Net Value of Machinery and Equipment Self-owned (year-end)	932919	870252	16599	22254
自有机械设备年末总功率（万千瓦）	Total Power of Machinery and Equipment Self-owned (year-end) (10 000 kw)	463.87	430.17	11.78	12.66
总产值	Gross Output Value	33288252	30577940	1294830	824357
实收资本	Paid-in Capital	6551511	4919537	340000	1170032
资产合计	Total Assets	26787597	23885424	1582047	718841
#流动资产	Circulat Assets	20708265	18383834	1256523	623045
固定资产	Fixed Assets	2916615	2601625	138697	70584
负债合计	Total Liabilities	17677942	15780043	1066957	423906
流动负债	Circulat Liabilities	15897608	14258658	875556	386160
非流动负债	Non-current Liabilities	1780335	1521385	191401	37746
所有者权益	Creditors' Equity	9109654	8105381	515091	294935
利税总额	Total Pre-tax Profits	2720913	2465716	140189	65889
#利润总额	Total Profits	1559532	1410950	89590	28165
营业收入	Operating Revenue	33172444	30315486	1423852	838184
#主营业务收入	Revenue from Major Business	33002031	30177814	1410177	829536
房屋建筑施工面积（万平方米）	Floor Space of Buildings under Construction (10 000 sq.m)	21976.19	21447.90	256.91	91.37
房屋建筑竣工面积（万平方米）	Floor Space of Buildings Completed (10 000 sq.m)	8989.56	8751.19	108.18	62.02
全员劳动生产率：	Overall Labor Productivity				
按总产值计算（元/人）	In Terms of Gross Output Value (yuan/person)	175331	171145	254898	206647
技术装备率（元/人）	Value of Machines Per Laborer (yuan/person)	6919	7050	3211	5128
动力装备率（千瓦/人）	Power of Machines Per Laborer (kw/person)	3	3	2	3
房屋建筑面积竣工率（%）	Rate of Floor Space of Buildings Completed (%)	41.2	41.1	42.1	67.9
资产负债率（%）	Asset-Liability Ratio (%)	66.0	66.1	67.4	59.0

重/庆/统/计/年/鉴

主要统计指标解释

建筑业统计单位

指从事房屋、构筑物建造和设备安装活动的法人企业。建筑业法人企业应具有建筑业资质并能够独立核算，同时其应具备以下条件：①依法成立，有自己的名称、组织机构和场所，能够承担民事责任；②独立拥有和使用资产，承担负债，有权与其他单位签订合同；③独立核算盈亏，能够编制资产负债表。

建筑业总产值

是以货币形式表现的建筑业企业在一定时期内生产的建筑业产品和提供的服务的总和。建筑业总产值包括：

⑴建筑工程产值：指列入建筑工程预算内的各种工程价值。

⑵安装工程产值：指设备安装工程价值，不包括被安装设备本身的价值。

⑶其他产值：建筑业总产值中除建筑工程、安装工程以外的产值。包括房屋构筑物修理产值、非标准设备制造产值、总包企业向分包企业收取的管理费以及不能明确划分的施工活动所完成的产值。

a. 房屋构筑物修理产值：指房屋和构筑物修理所完成的产值，但不包括被修理房屋、构筑物本身价值和生产设备的修理产值。

b. 非标准设备制造产值：指加工制造没有定型的非标准生产设备的加工费和原材料价值(如化工厂、炼油厂用的各种罐、槽，矿井生产统一使用的各种漏斗、三角槽、阀门等)以及附属加工厂为本企业承建工程制作的非标准设备的价值。

建筑业增加值

指建筑业企业在报告期内以货币形式表现的建筑业生产经营活动的最终成果。

从2004年第一次全国经济普查开始，建筑业现价增加值按生产法和分配法(收入法)两种方法计算，以收入法的计算结果为准，即从收入的角度出发，根据生产要素在生产过程中应得的收入份额计算。具体计算方法：经济普查年度建筑业增加值按照《经济普查年度GDP核算方案》计算，非经济普查年度建筑业增加值按照《非经济普查年度GDP核算方案》计算。

房屋建筑施工面积

指在报告期内施过工的全部房屋建筑面积，包括本期新开工的房屋面积、上期施工跨入本期继续施工的房屋面积、上期停缓建在本期恢复施工的房屋面积、本期竣工的房屋面积及本期施工后又停缓建的房屋面积。

房屋建筑竣工面积

指在报告期内房屋建筑按照设计要求全部完工，达到了使用条件，经验收鉴定合格，正式移交使用单位的房屋建筑面积。

CHONGQING STATISTICAL YEARBOOK

Explanatory Notes on Main Statistical Indicators

□ Statistical Unit in the Construction Industry

Refers to a corporate enterprise engaged in the construction of buildings and structures and in the installation of equipment. A corporate construction enterprise should have qualification certificates with independent accounting system, and should meet the following 3 requirements: a) being set up in line with relevant legal basis, having its full name, organization and location, and capable of taking civil liabilities; b) independently possessing and using its assets and assuming its liabilities, and entitled to sign contracts with other institutions; and c) making independent accounts of its profits and losses, and capable of compiling its own balance sheet.

□ Gross Output Value of Construction

Refers to total of construction products and services, expressed in money terms, produced or rendered by construction and installation enterprises during a given period of time. It includes:

(Ⅰ) Output value of construction projects: the value of projects covered by the project budgets;

(Ⅱ) Output value of installation projects: the value of the installation of equipment, (excluding the value of the equipment to be installed);

(Ⅲ) Other output values: the output value of construction industry apart from that of construction projects and installation projects. It includes: output value of repair of buildings and structures; output value of non-standard equipment manufacturing; overhead expenses received by contracted enterprises from the sub-contracted enterprises and the completed output value of construction activities for which there is no clear definition.

a. Output value of repair of buildings and structures: the value created through the repairs of buildings or structures. It does not include the value of buildings or structures being repaired and the value of the repair of production equipment;

b. Output value of manufactured non-standard equipment: the value of non-standard production equipment, including raw materials and manufacturing cost, made for the construction project (i.e., chemical plant; kettles or tanks used by refineries; various fillers, triangle tanks, valves used by mines). It also includes the output value of equipment manufactured by subsidiary workshops.

□ Value-added of Construction

Refers to the final result of the activities of production and operation of enterprises of the construction industry in monetary terms during the reference period.

Starting from the 2004 economic census, value-added of construction is calculated by both production approach and income approach, with the figures from the income approach as the final figures., Under the income approach,, calculation starts from the perspective of income and is based on the share of income derived from the production process by the relevant factors of production.. Specifically, value-added of construction for the Census years is calculated in accordance with the Programme of Compilation of GDP and National Accounts for the Year of Economic Census, and value-added of construction for other years is calculated in accordance with the Programme of Compilation of GDP and National Accounts for the Non Economic Census Years.

□ Floor Space of Buildings Under Construction

Refers to floor space of buildings under construction during the reference period, including the floor space of buildings for which construction has newly started; buildings for which construction has started earlier and is continuing during the reference period; and buildings for which construction has been suspended earlier but has restarted during the reference period; buildings completed during the reference period; and buildings under construction but construction has subsequently been during the reference period.

□ Floor Space of Buildings Completed

Refers to the floor space of buildings that are completed in the reference period in accordance with the requirements of the design, up to the standard for being put into use, and having been checked and accepted by departments concerned as qualified ones.

第14章

运输和邮电

TRANSPORT,POSTAL AND TELECOMMUNICATION SERVICES

B 简要说明
BRIEF INTRODUCTION

本章反映全市交通运输业和邮电通信业情况，主要包括货物和旅客运输量、港口吞吐量、交通基础设施和运输营运工具、民用车辆和船舶、主要港口码头泊位和仓库、邮电业务、电信主要通信能力和邮电通信水平。本章资料由市统计局服务业统计处负责整理编辑。

交通运输有关资料来源于市交通委员会、市公安局、成都铁路局、民航重庆安全监督管理局和市统计局。邮电通信业资料来源于市邮政局和市通信管理局。

The data in this chapter show the conditions of transport, postal and telecommunication services, mainly covering the data of freight and passenger traffic, freight handled at ports, transport infrastructure and means, civil motor vehicles and transport vessels, berths and warehouses at major ports, business volume of postal and telecommunication services, main communication capacity of telecommunications and level of postal and telecommunication services. The data in this chapter are sorted and compiled by Division of Service Statistics, Chongqing Municipal Bureau of Statistics.

The data of transport are provided by Communications Commission of Chongqing Municipality, Chongqing Public Security Bureau, Chengdu Railway Bureau, CAAC Chongqing Safety Supervision and Administrative Bureau and Chongqing Municipal Bureau of Statistics. The data of postal and telecommunication services are provided by Post Bureau of Chongqing and Chongqing Communications Administration.

表14.1 主要年份客货运输量及周转量
FREIGHT AND PASSENGER VOLUME AND TURNOVER IN MAJOR YEARS

年份 Year	客运量（万人） Passenger Traffic (10 000 persons)	旅客周转量（万人公里） Passenger-kilometers (10 000 person-km)	货运量（万吨） Freight Traffic (10 000 tons)	货物周转量（万吨公里） Freight ton-kilometers (10 000 ton-km)
1952	82		134	31531
1957	121		842	632103
1962	965	12619	808	147390
1965	1707	23268	2365	141406
1970	2136	27461	2536	111415
1975	3602	40180	3226	276337
1978	5294	293741	4816	1189803
1980	7846	417025	4469	1106294
1985	16923	975571	13513	2004938
1986	18308	1119673	14860	2184266
1987	21002	1160714	15618	2296505
1988	21119	1206942	22881	2470614
1989	22692	1185786	20764	2676052
1990	20332	1068775	15546	2452448
1991	26598	1176783	16186	2702591
1992	32924	1543492	17419	3005694
1993	34025	1724473	18841	3282548
1994	36340	1890785	21130	3077590
1995	39731	2104270	22796	3359847
1996	42370	2094740	24339	3150421
1997	46199	2242533	23979	2972254
1998	49020	2346281	25328	2684566
1999	52442	2434000	25190	2742000
2000	56969	2577859	26852	3063900
2001	59244	2662900	28212	3253200
2002	61918	2776900	29787	3376300
2003	58290	2526100	32565	3680300
2004	63495	2994200	36434	5180300
2005	60436	3018038	39200	6248968
2006	61228	3015761	42808	8213853
2007	77187	3938936	49973	10497955
2008	107191	4430156	63651	14864332
2009	114598	4814394	68491	16442995
2010	126804	5497718	81385	20103977
2011	141204	6402511	96779	25297609

注：1996年起铁路数据按重庆现地域进行了调整。
Note: The data of railway have been adjusted according to present administrative divisions of Chongqing since 1996.

表14.2 主要年份港口吞吐量和公路线路里程
VOLUME OF FREIGHT HANDLED AT PORTS AND LENGTH OF HIGHWAYS IN MAJOR YEARS

年 份 Year	港口货物吞吐量（万吨） Freight Handled at Ports (10 000 tons)	其 中 of which		公路线路里程（公里） Length of Highways (km)	其 中 of which
		进 港 In-port	出 港 Out-port		高速公路 Expressways
1952	61.80	26.60	35.20	743	
1957	356.10	73.10	283.00	1021	
1962	173.50	93.40	80.10	6044	
1965	217.10	115.70	101.40	7221	
1970	267.00	161.00	106.00	7538	
1975	228.90	108.90	120.00	9753	
1978	369.80	184.10	185.70	15421	
1980	378.20	194.10	184.10	16811	
1985	438.30	195.40	242.90	19377	
1986	532.70	303.40	229.30	19666	
1987	553.70	292.28	261.42	19942	
1988	570.30	296.14	274.16	20609	
1989	651.93	330.74	321.19	20944	
1990	572.50	275.70	296.80	21162	
1991	566.10	262.77	303.33	21474	
1992	664.90	326.80	338.10	21804	
1993	687.70	299.50	388.20	21990	
1994	665.65	289.26	376.39	22148	
1995	853.00	390.00	463.00	22556	
1996	1076.00	492.00	584.00	26892	114
1997	2548.70	977.20	1571.50	27045	114
1998	2477.30	1186.60	1290.70	27210	134
1999	2599.84	1610.44	989.40	28086	134
2000	2448.00	1485.00	963.00	30354	232
2001	2839.87	1690.39	1149.48	30654	320
2002	3004.00	1718.41	1285.59	31060	399
2003	3243.76	1796.24	1447.52	31407	580
2004	4539.00	2337.09	2201.91	32344	714
2005	5251.30	2758.11	2493.19	98218	748
2006	5420.43	2747.65	2672.78	100299	778
2007	6433.54	3330.46	3103.08	104705	1049
2008	7892.80	4349.38	3543.42	108632	1165
2009	8611.62	4833.29	3778.33	110951	1577
2010	9668.42	5682.24	3986.18	116949	1861
2011	11605.67	7338.72	4266.95	118562	1861

注：2006年起，公路线路里程包括村道，2005年数据按同口径进行了调整。
Note: The length of highways has included village roads since 2006, and the data of 2005 has been adjusted according to the same scope.

表14.3 主要年份邮电通信指标
INDICATORS OF POSTAL AND TELECOMMUNICATION SERVICES IN MAJOR YEARS

年 份 Year	邮政局、所 （个） Number of Postal Offices (unit)	邮电业务总量 （万元） Total Business Volume of Postal and Telecommunication Services (10 000 yuan)	其 中 of which #电 信 Telecommunication Services	邮电业务收入 （万元） Business Revenue from Postal and Telecommunication Services (10 000 yuan)	其 中 of which #电 信 Telecommunication Services
1952	1023	12		133	
1957	1846	33		874	
1962	1747	102		1000	
1965	1751	245		1461	
1970	2166	267		1371	
1975	1933	2190		1726	
1978	1925	2650		2103	
1980	1917	5071		2650	
1985	1853	7268		5796	
1986	1862	8264		6840	
1987	1896	9719		7675	
1988	1918	11853		10120	
1989	2025	14351		11734	
1990	2056	18999		14222	
1991	2047	23708		20585	
1992	2075	31305		27608	
1993	2041	47627		41653	
1994	1957	70543		71212	
1995	2220	109627		157568	
1996	2314	159929		167313	
1997	1821	233471	211458	223052	184899
1998	1958	345932	319375	264846	219493
1999	1958	519537	490494	401767	349001
2000	2018	858200	822824	544369	482075
2001	2154	706000	635041	663200	593050
2002	2202	867600	791573	770500	695409
2003	2218	1213062	1128172	870787	788000
2004	2121	1686491	1592416	1006050	918555
2005	2068	2101467	1996000	1121730	1030130
2006	2008	2761750	2634708	1197759	1099750
2007	1981	3658095	3505910	1315347	1194089
2008	1927	4247535	4065296	1518100	1397500
2009	1838	4898417	4646833	1633300	1477100
2010	1775	1997363	1795756	1790807	1598773
2011	1678	2426432	2167301	2023921	1776624

注：1996年前邮政电信合营，1996年前电信数据包含在邮电通信指标中；邮电业务总量2001年前为1990年不变价，2001年至2009年为2000年不变价口径；2010年及以后为2010年不变价口径。

Note: Before 1996, postal services and telecommunication services are managed together, so the data of telecommunication service before 1996 is included in the postal and telecommunication services. The data of total business volume of postal and telecommunication services before 2001 is calculated at 1990 constant price, and since 2001 it is calculated at 2000constant price.

表14.4 邮电业务主要指标（1985－2011年）

MAIN INDICATORS OF POSTAL AND TELECOMMUNICATION SERVICES (1985-2011)

年 份 Year	函 件（万件） Number of Letters (10 000pcs)	特快专递（万件） Pieces of Express Mail Services (10 000pcs)	邮政部门报刊累计数（万份） Accumulated Issue of Newspapers and Magazines (10 000 copies)	长途电话（万分钟） Long-distance Calls (10 000 minutes)	移动电话用户（万户） Mobile Telephone Subscribers (10 000 subscribers)	固定互联网络用户（万户） Subscribers of Internet Services (10 000 subscribers)	本地电话年末用户（万户） Subscribers of Local Telephone at Year-end (10 000 subscribers)	其中 of which #城市电话用户 Urban Telephone Subscribers
1985	8961		32750	477			3.80	3.10
1986	10210		34696	515			4.83	3.42
1987	11755	1	36902	595			5.39	3.93
1988	12432	1	40591	707			6.07	4.58
1989	11609	2	16162	724			6.62	5.17
1990	11544	2	16037	873	0.08		7.25	5.70
1991	11539	3	17540	1227	0.09		8.87	7.15
1992	13618	7	18216	2132	0.15		12.63	10.69
1993	16013	22	18464	3519	0.59		18.53	16.30
1994	16519	40	15491	7022	1.73		29.00	25.39
1995	14633	52	16453	11650	3.62		37.24	32.10
1996	14100	63	15572	18288	9.00	0.03	66.50	56.33
1997	12159	68	28025	23527	19.15	0.20	126.25	108.91
1998	12715	97	30922	23912	40.73	0.76	156.28	123.52
1999	13266	145	33532	22210	79.90	2.49	197.88	148.22
2000	11542	210	31232	23424	160.00	10.00	268.43	186.93
2001	13561	260	27506	22555	245.80	28.60	337.70	221.40
2002	18038	235	27177	23607	424.70	55.60	413.63	262.34
2003	20497	272	25945	23408	619.40	88.65	533.40	343.80
2004	18426	334	19833	26115	811.61	122.16	642.39	425.49
2005	12499	348	22369	27450	943.40	128.66	688.91	456.51
2006	9553	386	22455	27018	1064.60	140.60	725.50	469.07
2007	6579	520	22178	28379	1176.90	169.30	723.13	459.27
2008	5476	1608	23475	233680	1281.70	189.57	688.10	435.10
2009	5218	2240	25281	254955	1440.92	203.80	627.73	397.80
2010	4927	2829	24942	386223	1664.40	263.10	582.70	376.40
2011	6146	4068	31217	582024	1801.19	326.78	571.25	384.54

注：1）2008年起对长途电话通话时长统计口径作了调整，同时长途电话计量单位改为通话时长计量（万分钟）。1985年-2007年长途电话计量单位为（万次）；
2）2009年起特快专递包括快递公司数据，2008年数据按同口径进行了调整。

Note:a) Since 2008, the data of long-distance calls has been calculated by hold-on time (10 000 min). From 1985 to 2007, the data of long-distance.calls is calculated at 10 000 times.
b) Since 2009, the data of express mail services has included the data of express delivery companies and the data of 2008 has been adjusted according to the same scope.

表14.5 交通基础设施和交通运输营运工具（2010－2011年）
TRANSPORT INFRASTRUCTURE AND TRANSPORT MEANS (2010-2011)

指　标	Item	2010	2011
交通基础设施	**Transport Infrastructure**		
公路线路里程（公里）	Length of Highways (km)	116949	118562
按行政等级分	By Administrative Level		
#国　道	National	3109	3109
省　道	Provincial	8155	8153
按技术等级分	By Technical Level		
等级公路	Expressway and Class I-IV Highways	80006	83614
#高速公路	Expressway	1861	1861
一级公路	First Class	562	565
二级公路	Second Class	7489	7522
等外公路	Highways Below Class IV	36943	34948
公路桥梁数量（座）	Number of Highway-bridges (unit)	9722	9796
公路桥梁总延米（延米）	Extended Length of Highway-bridges (extended meter)	598892	606928
铁路营运里程（公里）	Length of Railways in Operation (km)	1396	1386
内河航道里程（公里）	Length of Navigable Inland Waterways (km)	4451	4451
#等级航道	Standard Waterways	1866	1866
与重庆正班通航城市（个）	Number of Navigable Citys from Chongqing (city)	82	98
国　内	Domestic Routes	74	85
国　际（地区）	International (regional) Routes	8	13
交通运输营运工具	**Transport Means**		
公路营运载货汽车（辆）	Business Trucks (unit)	259600	212008
公路营运载客汽车（辆）	Business Buses and Cars(unit)	47712	46940
运输船舶实有数（艘）	Transportation Vessels(unit)	4368	4160
#交通部门	Transportation Department	2757	2541
机动船	Motor Vessels	2356	2395
驳　船	Barges	401	146
重庆机场飞行起降架次（万架次）	Throughput of Civil Aircrafts in Chongqing Airport (10 000 flights)	15.01	17.05

表14.6 民用车辆、船舶拥有量（2010－2011年）
POSSESSION CIVIL MOTOR VEHICLES AND TRANSPORT VESSELS (2010-2011)

指　标	Item	2010	2011
民用车辆拥有量（辆）	**Possession of Civil Motor Vehicles (unit)**	**2759728**	**3379098**
#私人民用车辆拥有量	Private Vehicles	2339836	2955312
#载客汽车	Buses and Cars	598637	782994
载货汽车	Trucks	139966	114533
#汽　车	Motor Vehicles	1175631	1299457
载客汽车	Buses and Cars	785437	993083
载货汽车	Trucks	340328	283381
其它汽车	Others	49866	22993
摩托车	Motorcycles	1551441	2044328
民用船舶拥有量（艘）	**Possession of Civil Transport Vessels (unit)**	**4368**	**4160**
#私人船舶拥有量	Private Vessels	1611	1619
#机动船	Motor Vessels	1585	1585
#客　船	Passenger Vessels	820	792
货　船	Cargo Vessels	755	788
驳　船	Barges	26	34
#机动船	Motor Vessels	3941	3980
#客　船	Passenger Vessels	1385	1333
货　船	Cargo Vessels	2482	2612
驳　船	Barges	427	180

表14.7 客货运输量、周转量及港口吞吐量（2010－2011年）
FREIGHT AND PASSENGER VOLUME AND TURNOVER AND THROUGHPUT OF PORTS (2010-2011)

指　标	Item	2010	2011
客运量总计（万人）	**Total Passenger Traffic (10 000 persons)**	**126804**	**141204**
铁　路	Railway	2663	2933
公　路	Highway	122125	136142
水　路	Waterway	1277	1322
民　航	Civil Aviation	739	807
旅客周转量总计（亿人公里）	**Total Passenger-kilometers (100 million person-km)**	**549.77**	**640.25**
铁　路	Railway	95.11	116.02
公　路	Highway	351.03	408.91
水　路	Waterway	10.21	11.07
民　航	Civil Aviation	93.42	104.25
货运量总计（万吨）	**Total Freight Traffic (10 000 tons)**	**81384.99**	**96778.51**
铁　路	Railway	2279.50	2190.81
公　路	Highway	69438.00	82818.00
水　路	Waterway	9660.00	11762.04
民　航	Civil Aviation	7.49	7.66
货物周转量总计（亿吨公里）	**Total Freight Ton-kilometers (100 million ton-km)**	**2010.39**	**2529.76**
铁　路	Railway	179.80	191.27
公　路	Highway	610.31	779.77
水　路	Waterway	1219.27	1557.67
民　航	Civil Aviation	1.01	1.05
港口货物吞吐量（万吨）	**Total Cargo Handled at Ports (10 000 tons)**	**9668.42**	**11605.67**
其中：集装箱	In Which: Containers	662.00	789.00
进港量	In-port	5682.24	7338.72
出港量	Out-port	3986.18	4266.95
空港吞吐量	**Throughput of Airports**		
旅　客（万人）	Passengers (10 000 persons)	1604.63	1930.39
货　物（万吨）	Cargo (10 000 tons)	19.78	23.96

表14.8 主要港口码头泊位数（2010－2011年）
NUMBER OF BERTHS AT MAJOR PORTS (2010-2011)

指 标	Item	2010	2011
码头岸线长度（米）	**Length of Quay Line (m)**	**15977**	**16355**
生产用	For Productive Use	13237	13915
非生产用	For Non-Productive Use	2740	2440
泊位个数（个）	**Number of Berths (unit)**	**166**	**190**
生产用	For Productive Use	144	149
非生产用	For Non-Productive Use	22	21

表14.9 主要港口码头仓库（2010－2011年）
WAREHOUSES AT MAJOR PORTS (2010-2011)

指 标	Item	2010	2011
年末职工人数（人）	Number of Staff and Workers at Year-end (person)	8850	8492
仓库总面积（平方米）	Total Area of Warehouses (sq.m)	264200	264200
堆场总面积（平方米）	Total Area of Stacking Yard (sq.m)	769130	856269
集装箱吞吐量（吨）	Containers Handled at Ports (ton)	6066380	7289894
国际集装箱	International Containers	2575865	3175217
国内集装箱	Domestic Containers	3490515	4114677
集装箱吞吐量（TEU）	Containers Handled at Ports (TEU)	500068	620565
国际集装箱	International Containers	264891	321591
国内集装箱	Domestic Containers	235177	298974

注：TEU是“折合20英尺标准箱”的英文缩写。
Note: TEU is the abbreviation of “Twenty-foot Equivalent Unit”.

表14.10 邮电业务基本情况（2010－2011年）
STATISTICS ON POSTAL AND TELECOMMUNICATION SERVICES (2010-2011)

指 标	Item	2010	2011
邮政局（所）数（处）	Number of Postal Offices (unit)	1775	1678
邮路总长度（公里）	Total Length of Postal Routes (km)	38727	35229
农村投递线路（公里）	Rural Delivery Routes (km)	63110	53280
邮电业务总量（万元）	Business Volume of Postal and Telecommunication Services (10 000 yuan)	1997363	2426432
邮 政	Postal Services	201607	259131
电 信	Telecommunication Services	1795756	2167301
函 件（万件）	Number of Letters (10 000 pcs)	4927	6146
包 件（万件）	Number of Parcels (10 000 pcs)	101	106
特快专递（万件）	Pieces of Express Mail Services (10 000 pcs)	2829	4068
邮政部门报刊累计数（万份）	Accumulated Issue of Newspapers and Magazines (10 000 copies)	24942	31217
集邮业务（万枚）	Stamps for Collection (10 000 pcs)	777.70	1054
长途电话（万分钟）	Long-distance Calls (10 000 min)	386223	582024
本地电话年末用户（万户）	Number of Fixed Telephone Subscribers at Year-end (10 000 subscribers)	582.70	571.25
城市电话用户	Urban Telephone Subscribers	376.40	384.54
#住宅电话	Householde Fixed Telephone Subscribers	261.80	267.37
乡村电话用户	Rural Telephone Subscribers	206.30	186.71
#住宅电话	Householde Fixed Telephone Subscribers	186.30	168.05
公用电话（万户）	Public Telephones (10 000 subscribers)	39.90	33.36
移动电话年末用户（万户）	Mobile Telephone Subscribers at Year-end (10 000 subscribers)	1664.40	1801.19
固定互联网络用户（万户）	Internet Subscribers (10 000 subscribers)	263.10	326.78

注：邮电业务总量2010年起为2010年不变价口径。
Note:The data of total business volume of postal and telecommunication services in 2010 is calculated at 2010 constant price.

表14.11 电信主要通信能力（2010－2011年）
MAIN COMMUNICATION CAPACITY OF TELECOMMUNICATIONS (2010-2011)

项 目	Item	2010	2011
长话业务电路（2M）	Capacity of Long-distance Telephone Lines (2M)	27446	43662
固定交换机容量（万门）	Capacity of Local Telephone Exchanges (10 000 lines)	1150	1101
移动用户交换机容量（万户）	Capacity of Mobile Telephone Exchanges (10 000 subscribers)	2746	2976
移动电话基站数（个）	Number of Base Stations of Mobile Telephones (unit)	30672	38103
移动电话信道数（万个）	Number of Signal Channels of Mobile Telephones (10 000 lines)	133	168
短信息中心容量（万条）	Capacity of SMS Center (10 000 messages)	9396	10764
光缆线路长度（公里）	Length of Long-distance Optical Cable Lines (km)	26	31

表14.12 邮电通信水平（2010－2011年）
LEVEL OF POSTAL AND TELECOMMUNICATION SERVICES (2010-2011)

项 目	Item	2010	2011
平均每一邮政局所服务面积（平方公里）	Average Area Served by Every Post Office (sq.m)	46.35	49.03
平均每一邮政局所服务人口（万人）	Average Population Served by Every Post Office (10 000 persons)	1.63	1.74
平均每百人邮电业务总量（元）	Total Business Volume of Postal and Telecommunication Services per 100 Persons (yuan)	69242	83125
平均每人每年发函件数（件）	Annual Average Number of Letters Mailed Per Capita (piece)	1.71	2.11
平均每人每年自邮政部门订报刊数（份）	Annual Average Number of Newspapers and Magazines Subscribed from Postal Departments Per Capita (piece)	8.65	10.69
平均每百人拥有电话机（含移动）(部)	Number of Telephone Sets (including mobile phones) Owned Per 100 Persons (unit)	77.90	81.28
平均每百人拥有移动电话（部）	Number of Mobile Telephones Owned Per 100 Persons (unit)	57.70	61.71

注：人均指标按年末常住人口计算。
Note: The per capital indicators are calculated upon the permanent population at year-end.

重/庆/统/计/年/鉴

主要统计指标解释

货（客）运量

指在一定时期内，各种运输工具实际运送的货物（旅客）数量。是反映运输业为国民经济和人民生活服务的数量指标，也是制定和检查运输生产计划，研究运输发展规模和速度的重要指标。货运按吨计算，客运按人计算。货物不论运输距离长短或货物类别，均按实际重量统计；旅客不论行程远近或票价多少，均按一人一次作为客运量统计。半价票，小孩票也按一人统计。

货物（旅客）周转量

指在一定时期内，由各种运输工具运送的货物（旅客）数量与其相应运输距离的乘积之总和。是反映运输业生产总成果的重要指标，也是编制和检查运输生产计划，计算运输效率、劳动生产率以及核算运输单位成本的主要基础资料。通常以吨公里和人公里为计算单位。计算货物周转量通常按发出站与到达站之间的最短距离，也就是计费距离计算。计算公式为：

货物（旅客）周转量=Σ货物（旅客）运输量×运输距离

公路里程

指在一定时期内实际达到《公路工程技术标准JTG B01-2003》规定的等级公路，并经公路主管部门正式验收交付使用的公路里程数。包括大中城市的郊区公路以及通过小城镇街道部分的公路里程和公路桥梁长度、隧道长度、渡口宽度等，不包括大中城市的街道、厂矿、林区生产用道和农业生产用道的里程。两条或多条公路共同经由同一路段，只计算一次，不得重复计算里程长度。它是反映公路建设发展规模的重要指标，也是计算运输网密度等指标的基础资料。

内河航道里程

也称内河通航里程，指在一定时期内，能通航运输船舶及排筏的天然河流、湖泊水库、运河及通航渠道的长度。包括全年季节性通航累计三个月以上的航道，不包括仅供零散流放竹、木排的河道。它是反映内河水运网规模、水平和发展情况的主要指标。

民用汽车拥有量

指报告期末，在公安交通管理部门按照《机动车注册登记工作规范》，已注册登记领有民用车辆牌照的全部汽车数量。汽车拥有量统计的主要分类：根据汽车结构分为载客汽车、载货汽车及其他汽车；根据汽车所有者不同分为个人（私人）汽车、单位汽车；根据汽车的使用性质分为营运汽车、非营运汽车和特种汽车；根据汽车大小规格不同载客汽车分为大型、中型、小型和微型，载货汽车分为重型、中型、轻型和微型。

邮电业务总量

指以货币表现的邮电通信企业为社会提供各类邮电通信服务的总数量。邮电业务量按专业分类包括函件、包件、汇票、报刊发行、邮政快件、特快专递、邮政储蓄、集邮、传真、长途电话、出租电路、移动电话、分组交换数据通信、出租代维等。计算方法为各类产品乘以相应的平均单价（不变价）之和，再加上出租电路和设备、代用户维护电话交换机和线路等的服务收入。它综合反映了一定时期邮电业务发展的总成果，是研究邮电业务量构成和发展趋势的重要指标。计算公式为：

邮电业务总量=Σ（各类邮电业务量×不变单价）＋出租代维及其他业务收入=邮政业务总量＋电信业务总量

本地电话用户

指接入本地电信运营商固定电话网上的电话用户。包括：住宅用户、单位用户、公用电话用户等。按电话用户位置又分为城市电话用户和乡村电话用户。1997年以前，“市内电话用户”是指接入县城及县以上城市的电话网上的电话用户；“农村电话用户”是指接入县邮电局农话台及县以下农村电话交换点，以县城为中心（除市话用户外）联通县、乡

主要统计指标解释

（镇）、行政村、村民小组的用户。从1997年起，电话用户数分组调整为以用户所在区域划分为“城市电话用户”和“乡村电话用户”，与过去的按市内电话和农村电话划分方法不同。而电话用户总数、电话机总部数统计范围不变。

■ 城市电话用户

指直辖市、省辖市、地级市、县级市的市区、市郊区及县城（包括县人民政府所在地的县城关区或行政建制相当于县人民政府所在地的镇）范围内接入局用交换机的电话用户数，包括分布在农村地区的独立工矿区、林区、驻军等接入局用交换机的电话用户数。

■ 乡村电话用户

指县城关区以下的集镇和农村接入局用交换机的电话用户数。

■ 住宅电话用户

指安装在居民住宅或农民家里并按照住宅电话用户登记注册和收费的电话用户。包括私人付费、单位付费和按规定免费的住宅电话用户。

■ 移动电话用户

指通过移动电话交换机进入移动电话网、占用移动电话号码的各类电话用户。包括签约用户和智能网预付费用户。一个移动电话号码统计为一户。

■ 局用交换机容量

是指安装在电信运营企业内用于接续本地固定电话的电话交换机容量、有倍增设备按倍增后的数量计数。包括现用和备用的人工或自动交换机的全部容量。不包括用户交换机容量。

■ 移动电话交换机容量

指移动电话交换机根据一定话务模型和交换机处理能力计算出来的最大同时服务用户的数量。

Explanatory Notes on Main Statistical Indicators

□ Freight (Passenger) Traffic

Refers to the volume of freight (passenger) transported with various means. Freight transport is calculated in tons and passenger traffic is calculated in the number of persons. Despite the type of freight and traveling distance, the freight transport is calculated in the actual weight of the goods; and despite the traveling distance and ticket price, the passenger traffic is calculated by the principle that one person can be counted only once in one travel. The passenger who travels with a half-price ticket or a child ticket is also calculated as one person. The freight (passenger) traffic provides a quantitative measure to show how the transport industry serves the national economy and people, and is also an important indicator for planning the transport industry and for studying the development scale and speed of the transport industry.

□ Freight Ton-kilometers (Passenger-kilometers)

Refer to the sum of the products of the volume of transported cargo (passengers) multiplying by the transport distance. It is an important indicator to reflect the achievement of transportation industry. Normally, the shortest distance between the departure station and the destination station (i.e., the payable distance) is the basis to calculate the freight ton-kilometers. This is an important indicator to show the total results of the transport industry, to prepare and examine the transport plan and to measure the efficiency, the labour productivity and the unit cost of transport. The formula is as follows:

Freight Ton-kilometers (Passenger-Kilometers) = ∑ [Freight (Passenger) Traffic × Distance of Transportation]

□ Length of Highways

Refers to the length of highways which are built in conformity with the grades specified by the highway engineering standard formulated by the Ministry of Communications, and have been formally checked and accepted by the departments of highways and put into use. The length of highways includes that of the suburb highways at large and medium-sized cities, highways passing through streets at small cities and towns, and also the length of bridge and ferries. It does not include the length of streets in big and medium-sized cities and highways built for the production purpose at factories, mines, forest areas and agricultural areas. If two more highways go the same section of the way, the length of the section is only calculated for once and no duplication is allowed. The length of highways is an important indicator to show the development of the highway construction and to provide essential information to calculate the transport network density.

□ Length of Navigable Inland Waterways

An indicator reflecting the size and development of inland water network, it refers to the length of the natural rivers, lakes, reservoirs, canals, and ditches open to navigation during a given period, which enables the transport by ships and rafts. It includes the channels open to navigation for over an accumulative 3 months in a year, yet this does not include the river courses which are only used to float odd logs and bamboo rafts.

□ Possession of Civil Motor Vehicles

Refer to the total numbers of vehicles that are registered and received vehicles' license tags according to the Work Standard for Motor Vehicles Registration formulated by transport management office under department of public security at the end of reference period. They are divided into following categories according to the structure of motor vehicles: passenger vehicles, trucks and others; and private vehicles and vehicles for units use according to ownerships; working vehicles, non-working vehicles and special motor vehicles according to kind of usage; large passenger vehicles, medium passenger vehicles and small passenger vehicles, heavy trucks, light-heavy trucks and light trucks according to sizes of vehicles.

□ Business Volume of Postal and Telecommunication Services

Refers to the total amount of post and telecommunications services, expressed in value terms, provided by the post and telecommunications departments for the society. Postal and telecommunication services can be classified as letters, parcels, remittance, issue of newspapers and magazines, fast mail service, express mail service, saving deposits, stamps for collection, public and individual telegraph service, facsimiles, long-distance telephone service, leasing of telephone lines, urban paging service, mobile telephone service, data transfer and transmission, etc.. The accounting approach is to multiply the service products of all types with their average unit price (constant price) to get sum of business value, plus income from other services such as leasing of telephone lines and equipment, maintenance of telephone switchboards and lines on behalf of customers. This indicator reflects the overall results of post and telecommunications service during a given period, and is important to study the composition of business service and the development of post and telecommunications service. The formula is as follows:

Business Volume of Postal and Telecommunication Services = ∑ (Transaction of Post and Telecommunication Services × Constant Price) + Income from Leasing, Maintenance and other Services = Business Volume of Postal Services + Business Volume of Telecommunication Services

□ Local Telephone Subscribers

Refer to subscribers that are connected to the local telecommunication service provider through fix line network, including household subscribers, institutional subscribers and public telephones. They are also classified as city subscribers and rural subscribers according to locations. Before 1997, city subscribers referred to those connected to city telephone networks in county towns and cities, while village subscribers referred to those connected to village telephone stations at and below counties. Since 1997, the classification of telephone subscribers was modified on the basis of physical location of the subscribers as urban telephone subscribers and rural telephone subscribers, which is different from the previous classification of categorizing local telephones and rural telephones, while the definition of total subscribers and total number of telephones remain unchanged.

□ Urban Telephone Subscribers

Refer to subscribers telephone subscribers, located at municipalities, cities under the jurisdiction of province, cities at prefectural level, downtown and suburb of city at county level town and county towns (including country towns where county government located, and towns of county level according to the administrative organizational system), that are connected to the public line telephone network, including rural mineral area, forest area, military area.

□ Rural Telephone Subscribers

Refer to telephone subscribers, located at counties (towns) and villages outside the range of cities according to administrative jurisdiction.

□ Household Telephone Subscribers

Refer to telephone sets installed in resident dwellings, including those with telephone charges paid by individuals, by public units and free of charge.

□ Mobile Telephone Subscribers

Refer to the persons who own mobile telephone numbers and are connected with the mobile telephone communication network through the mobile telephone switchboards, including contracted subscribers and pre-paid subscribers for intelligent network. One mobile telephone is taken as a subscriber.

□ Capacity of Office Telephone Exchanges

Refers to the capacity (measured in gate) of telephone exchanges installed in the offices of telecommunication service providers for communication between fixed telephones. It includes the capacity of both manual and automatic exchanges in use and for stand-by purpose, excluding the capacity of subscribers exchanges.

□ Capacity of Mobile Telephone Exchanges

Refers to the capacity of the maximum services provided to subscribers at one time basing on a certain model and transacting capacity of the mobile telephone exchanges.

第 15 章

国内贸易

DOMESTIC TRADE

简要说明

BRIEF INTRODUCTION

本章主要内容有社会消费品零售总额，批发和零售业商品销售总额，限额以上批发零售和住宿餐饮业企业财务状况、限额以上住宿业和限额以上餐饮业基本经营情况，以及限额以上批发和零售业、住宿和餐饮业连锁经营情况。本章资料由市统计局贸易外经处提供。

The data in this chapter cover the total sales of the consumer goods, total sales of wholesale and retail trade, the financial indicators of wholesale and retail, hotel and catering enterprises above designated size, the operation of hotels and the enterprises in catering trade above designated size, and the operation of chain enterprises above designated size in wholesale, retail, hotel and catering trade. All the data in this chapter are provided by Division of Trade and External Economic Relations Statistics, Municipal Bureau of Statistics.

表15.1 社会消费品零售总额（1949－2011年）
TOTAL RETAIL SALES OF CONSUMER GOODS (1949-2011)

单位：万元 (10 000 yuan)

年 份 Year	社会消费品零售总额 Total Retail Sales of Consumer Goods	其中 of which 国有经济 State-owned	集体经济 Collective -owned	个体及私营经济 Individual and Private	外资及港澳台经济 Funded by Hong Kong,Macao, Taiwan & Foreign Entrepreneurs	其 他 Others
1949	46167					
1950	50695					
1951	55644					
1952	61973	19332	9941	32009		691
1953	77007	28033	13017	34889		1068
1954	83302	38415	19862	23381		1644
1955	84015	37910	18769	25264		2072
1956	98852	50892	39094	4648		4218
1957	108061	55533	43171	4458		4899
1958	119981	72248	40787	2705		4241
1959	141591	106899	26508	3006		5178
1960	156655	116749	28958	7877		3071
1961	133022	101961	20412	8403		2246
1962	124248	87477	27335	6987		2449
1963	112094	74490	31651	3913		2040
1964	122995	85845	32817	2405		1928
1965	134722	94009	35935	2318		2460
1966	147697	103011	38259	3585		2842
1967	155358	110170	40829	1502		2857
1968	132702	91591	37960	535		2616
1969	152531	110384	38638	638		2871
1970	163612	118044	40460	2120		2988
1971	172626	124688	42034	2739		3165
1972	191113	135637	45994	5863		3619
1973	195825	141100	48694	2376		3655
1974	197474	140839	50050	2682		3903
1975	217537	148811	53318	11876		3532
1976	218022	111129	95330	8200		3363
1977	233979	118830	102849	8402		3898
1978	250188	126981	112537	6599		4071

表15.1 续表 continued

单位：万元 (10 000 yuan)

年 份 Year	社会消费品零售总额 Total Retail Sales of Consumer Goods	其 中 of which				
		国有经济 State-owned	集体经济 Collective -owned	个体及私营经济 Individual and Private	外资及港澳台经济 Funded by Hong Kong,Macao, Taiwan & Foreign Entrepreneurs	其 他 Others
1979	301563	156918	130798	8043		5804
1980	366349	178516	162400	17649		7784
1981	405952	193060	180443	24020		8429
1982	431269	201845	188198	30649		10577
1983	466704	212294	190909	53632		9869
1984	538909	229611	202957	93137		13204
1985	690779	256981	261103	155266		17429
1986	780787	290656	260816	207041		22274
1987	926227	343448	302177	253031		27571
1988	1191747	430347	372593	350032		38775
1989	1332450	445314	380342	344338		162456
1990	1371244	464257	370361	352587		184039
1991	1569138	524150	448634	359098		237256
1992	2031140	661857	554059	494300		320924
1993	2573768	933913	704291	492283	2372	440909
1994	3343325	1079062	664616	880747	3166	715734
1995	4161295	1004126	752266	1223620	23727	1157556
1996	4986299	1106800	792017	1550975	25224	1511283
1997	5681890	1137394	853410	1529836	34914	2126336
1998	6193991	1029384	710562	2103320	82477	2268248
1999	6670104	1129936	643832	2562478	115128	2218730
2000	7199508	1075849	675284	2855855	163455	2429065
2001	7823114	1190283	634269	3243281	205648	2549633
2002	8535962	1166478	544491	3717999	208733	2898261
2003	9346711	1117167	406950	4449249	221716	3151629
2004	10683290	864210	201479	7404246	210630	2002725
2005	12278119	1062661	210209	8242314	266333	2496602
2006	14315133	1741735	235363	9545634	345925	2446476
2007	17111165	1446490	254185	11391396	523912	3495182
2008	21471209	1215973	366449	13829885	751017	5307885
2009	24790110	1113998	310118	16949474	1807967	4608553
2010	29386000	1881433	435520	18017116	835625	8216306
2011	34878070	3150573	480803	21006935	2756570	7483189

表15.2 社会消费品零售总额（2010－2011年）
TOTAL RETAIL SALES OF CONSUMER GOODS (2010-2011)

单位：万元 (10 000 yuan)

指　标	Item	2010	2011
总　计	**Total**	**29386000**	**34878070**
按销售单位所在地分	**By Location**		
城　镇	City	27925962	33171110
其中：城区	County	19599589	23343110
乡　村	Under County Level	1460038	1706960
按登记注册类型分	**By Type of Registration**		
国有经济	State-owned	1881433	3150573
集体经济	Collective-owned	435520	480803
个体及私营经济	Individual and Private	18017116	21006935
外资及港澳台经济	Funded by Hong Kong, Macao, Taiwan & Foreign Entrepreneurs	835625	2756570
其他经济	Others	8216306	7483189
按行业分	**By Sector**		
批发和零售业	Wholesale and Retail Services	24307510	28941620
住宿和餐饮业	Catering Trade	4472923	5217341
其他行业	Others	605567	719110

表15.3 限额以上住宿和餐饮业法人企业基本经营情况（2010－2011年）
BASIC CONDITIONS OF ENTERPRISES ABOVE DESIGNATED SIZE IN HOTELS AND CATERING SERVICES (2010-2011)

单位：万元 (10 000 yuan)

指　标	Item	2010	2011
营业收入	Business Revenue	1343668	1825091
客房收入	From Hotel Rooms	250639	339128
餐费收入	From Meals	979787	1344744
商品销售收入	From Commodities	45707	59900
其他收入	Other Income	67535	81319
住宿餐饮设施	Infrastructure of Hotels and Catering Services		
床位数（个）	Number of Beds (unit)	77351	80269
餐位数（位）	Number of Catering Seats (unit)	585061	595402

表15.4 批发和零售业商品销售总额（2011年）

TOTAL SALES OF ENTERPRISES IN WHOLESALE AND RETAIL TRADE (2011)

单位：万元 (10 000 yuan)

指 标	Item	销售总额 Total Sales	其 中 of which	
			批 发 Wholesale	零 售 Retail
总 计	**Total**	**100010887**	**71404298**	**28606589**
限额以上批发和零售法人企业	**Enterprises above Designated Size in Wholesales and Retail Trade**	**77408479**	**55253801**	**22154678**
按登记注册类型分	**By Type Registration**			
内资企业	Domestic-funded Enterprises	66219537	46679892	19539645
#国有企业	State-owned Enterprises	11328372	8817216	2511156
集体企业	Collective-owned Enterprises	815794	755771	60023
股份合作企业	Cooperative Enterprises	640132	468332	171800
联营企业	Joint-owned Enterprises	198405	107473	90932
有限责任公司	Limited-liability Companies	28978081	22205487	6772594
股份有限公司	Share Holding Corporation Ltd.	7120422	3967670	3152752
私营企业	Private Enterprises	15223007	9171263	6051743
港澳台商投资企业	Enterprises Funded by Hong Kong, Macao and Taiwan	7427722	5549114	1878608
外商投资企业	Foreign-funded Enterprises	3761221	3024795	736426
按行业分	**By Sector**			
农畜产品批发业	Wholesale of Farm Produce and Livestock Products	655087	564480	90608
食品、饮料及烟草制品批发业	Wholesale of Food, Beverages and Tobaccos	7508259	7162444	345815
纺织、服装及日用品批发业	Wholesale of Textiles, Garments and Daily Consumer Articles	694512	554913	139599
文化、体育用品及器材批发业	Wholesale of Culture, Sports Appliances and Equipment	288398	284275	4123
医药及医疗器材批发业	Wholesale of Medicines and Medical Appliances	3645058	2827748	817311
矿产品、建材及化工产品批发业	Wholesale of Mineral Products, Building Materials and Chemical Products	24723441	21866286	2857155
机械设备、五金交电及电子产品批发业	Wholesale of Machinery, Hardware and Electronic Products	19283774	18797071	486703
贸易经纪与代理业	Trade Broker and Agency	53238	51000	2238
其他批发业	Other Wholesale not Classified Elsewhere	1055481	1040663	14818
综合零售业	Retail Trade	4855682	159153	4696529
食品、饮料及烟草制品专门零售业	Special Retail of Food, Beverages and Tobaccos	1354784	77083	1277701
纺织、服装及日用品专门零售业	Special Retail of Textiles, Garments and Daily Consumer Articles	573885	55336	518549
文化、体育用品及器材专门零售业	Retail of Culture, Sports Appliances and Equipment	489085	197490	291595
医药及医疗器材专门零售业	Retail of Medicines and Medical Appliances	690864	151104	539760
汽车、摩托车、燃料及零配件专门零售业	Retail of Motor Vehicles, Motorcycles, Fuel and Parts	7305454	888905	6416549
家用电器及电子产品专门零售业	Special Retail of Household Electric Appliances and Electronic Products	1837658	136805	1700853
五金、家具及室内装修材料专门零售业	Special Retail of Hardware, Furniture and Decoration Materials	2057549	418620	1638930
无店铺及其他零售业	Non-shop and Other Retails	336272	20426	315846
其他批发零售贸易业	**Other Wholesales and Retail Trade**	**22602407**	**16150497**	**6451911**

表15.5 限额以上批发和零售业主要商品分类销售额（2010－2011年）
SALES OF MAIN COMMODITIES OF THE ENTERPRISES ABOVE DESIGNATED SIZE IN WHOLESALE AND RETAIL TRADE BY CATEGORY (2010-2011)

单位：亿元 (100 million yuan)

指　标	Item	销售额 Total Sales		其　中 of which 批　发 Wholesale		零　售 Retail	
		2010	2011	2010	2011	2010	2011
总　计	**Total**	**5695.95**	**7883.30**	**4147.70**	**5490.19**	**1548.25**	**2393.11**
食品、饮料、烟酒类	Food, Beverages, Tobacco and Liquor	796.80	1211.82	580.17	840.64	216.63	371.18
肉禽蛋类	Meat, Poultry and Eggs	40.85	69.95	19.35	28.39	21.50	41.55
其他食品类	Other Food	323.81	524.08	175.35	273.52	148.46	250.56
饮料类	Beverages	25.97	34.39	9.26	10.30	16.71	24.09
烟酒类	Tobacco and Liquor	406.17	583.41	376.21	528.43	29.96	54.98
服装鞋帽、针、纺织品类	Clothing, Shoes, Hats and Textiles	214.95	290.45	33.45	34.32	181.50	256.14
服装类	Clothing	149.72	219.26	19.33	20.06	130.39	199.20
鞋帽类	Shoes and Hats	38.69	39.45	2.55	1.32	36.14	38.13
针、纺织品类	Knitwear and Textiles	26.54	31.74	11.57	12.93	14.97	18.81
化妆品类	Cosmetics	22.02	27.92	2.71	4.10	19.31	23.82
金银珠宝类	Gold, Silver and Jewelry	36.10	59.82	12.15	23.10	23.95	36.72
日用品类	Articles for Daily Use	80.71	127.83	19.88	33.76	60.83	94.07
#洗涤用品类	Washing Articles	18.33	36.04	7.58	8.19	10.75	27.86
儿童玩具类	Children Toys	2.65	4.49	0.47	1.43	2.18	3.06
五金、电料类	Hardware and Electrical Materials	31.72	44.53	13.50	19.94	18.22	24.59
体育、娱乐用品类	Sports and Recreation Articles	5.81	7.43	0.45	0.74	5.36	6.68
书报杂志类	Newspapers and Magazines	34.29	38.54	18.77	21.23	15.52	17.31
电子出版物及音像制品类	E-journal and Video Products	4.82	4.25	2.10	1.41	2.72	2.84
家用电器和音像器材类	Household Appliances and Video Appliances	1034.42	1274.09	896.59	1072.72	137.83	201.38
中西药品类	Traditional Chinese and Western Medicines	332.06	402.57	220.99	259.97	111.07	142.60
#西　药	Western Medicines	267.52	309.15	179.91	202.25	87.61	106.89
中草药及中成药	Traditional Chinese Medicines	46.30	61.71	31.58	42.35	14.72	19.36
文化办公用品类	Cultural and Office Articles	43.43	87.79	13.91	32.08	29.52	55.71
家具类	Furniture	93.79	141.41	25.36	33.03	68.43	108.38
通讯器材类	Communication Appliances	48.21	57.31	26.13	25.36	22.08	31.96
煤炭及制品类	Coal and Related Products	157.35	260.66	153.61	248.39	3.74	12.27
木材及制品类	Wood and Wooden Products	9.55	17.85	9.55	17.85		
石油及制品类	Petroleum and Related Products	500.79	677.22	372.59	435.23	128.20	241.99
化工材料及制品类	Chemical Materials and Related Products	269.10	363.11	269.10	363.11		
#化肥类	Fertilizer	108.87	124.16	108.87	124.16		
金属材料类	Metal Materials	623.68	888.68	623.68	888.68		
建筑及装潢材料类	Building and Decoration Materials	266.55	414.33	182.81	286.63	83.74	127.70
机电产品设备类	Mechanical and Electrical Products	287.86	363.11	269.52	322.85	18.34	40.26
#农机类	Agricultural Machinery	4.02	8.55	4.02	8.55		
汽车类	Automobiles	650.00	887.88	273.63	334.97	376.37	552.91
种子饲料类	Seed and Feedstuff	3.70	7.37	3.70	7.37		
棉麻类	Cotton, Hemp	8.24	9.50	8.10	9.04	0.14	0.46
其他类	Others	140.00	217.83	115.25	173.70	24.75	44.14

表15.6 限额以上批发业法人企业财务状况（2011年）

FINANCIAL INDICATORS OF WHOLESALE ENTERPRISES ABOVE DESIGNATED SIZE (2011)

指 标	Item	企业数（个）Number of Enterprises (unit)	流动资产合计 Total Circulating Assets	固定资产原价 Original Value of Fixed Assets
总 计	**Total**	**1623**	**13763107**	**1684890**
#国有控股	State Holding	226	4148040	1185629
按登记注册类型分组	**By Type of Registration**			
内资企业	Domestic-funded Enterprises	1597	10970463	1653634
国有企业	State-owned Enterprises	122	2151865	733822
集体企业	Collective-owned Enterprises	20	211420	7951
股份合作企业	Cooperative Enterprises	17	132712	8702
联营企业	Joint-owned Enterprises	5	13117	6712
国有联营企业	State Joint-owned Enterprises	3	3632	3918
集体联营企业	Collective Joint-owned Enterprises	1		
国有与集体联营企业	State-Collective Joint-owned Enterprises			
其他联营企业	Other Joint-owned Enterprises	1	9485	2795
有限责任公司	Limited Liability Corporations	639	5349901	326818
国有独资公司	Solely State-owned Corporations	28	658722	59421
其他有限责任公司	Other Limited Liability Corporations	611	4691180	267397
股份有限公司	Share-holding Corporations Ltd.	65	890257	370207
私营企业	Private Enterprises	635	1994890	164296
私营独资企业	Private-funded Enterprises	79	44882	11335
私营合伙企业	Private Partnership Enterprises	10	20297	2032
私营有限责任公司	Private Limited Liability Corporations	512	1886316	141581
私营股份有限公司	Private Share-holding Corporatinos Ltd.	34	43395	9348
其他企业	Other Enterprises	94	226300	35125
港澳台商投资企业	Enterprises Funded by Hong Kong, Macao and Taiwan	9	686780	4993
合资经营企业	Joint-venture Enterprises	2	53965	699
合作经营企业	Cooperative Enterprises			
独资经营企业	Enterprises with Sole Fund	7	632815	4294
投资股份有限公司	Share-holding Corporations Ltd.			
外商投资企业	Foreign-funded Enterprises	17	2105864	26263
中外合资经营企业	Joint-venture Enterprises	8	40920	6797
中外合作经营企业	Cooperative Enterprises	1	7330	214
外资企业	Enterprises with Sole Fund	6	2044336	18701
外商投资股份有限公司	Share-holding Corporations Ltd.	2	13277	551
按批发行业小类分组	**By Wholesale Sector**			
农畜产品批发	Wholesale of Farm Produce and Livestock Products	46	100604	41162
谷物、豆及薯类批发	Wholesale of Cereal, Bean and Tuber	14	29777	25322
种子、饲料批发	Wholesale of Seed and Feedstuff	13	15388	4332
棉、麻批发	Wholesale of Cotton and Fiber Crops	6	13134	7309
牲畜批发	Wholesale of Livestocks	4	1850	1897
其他农畜产品批发	Wholesale of Other Farm Produce and Livestock Products	9	40455	2302
食品、饮料及烟草制品批发	Wholesale of Food, Beverages and Tobaccos	210	1806798	514665
米、面制品及食用油批发	Wholesale of Rice, Flour and Edible Oil	37	479895	74007
糕点、糖果及糖批发	Wholesale of Cake, Candy and Sugar	11	33658	4300
果品、蔬菜批发	Wholesale of Fruits and Vegetables	33	12798	14665
肉、禽、蛋及水产品批发	Wholesale of Meat, Poultry, Eggs and Aquatic Products	8	12692	5311
盐及调味品批发	Wholesale of Salts and Condiments	9	163457	21598

单位：万元 (10 000 yuan)

累计折旧 Total Depreciation	资产总计 Total Assets	负债合计 Total Liabilities	实收资本 Paid-in Capital	主营业务收入 Revenue of Principal Business	主营业务成本 Cost of Principal Business	主营业务税金及附加 Taxes and Extra Charges on Principal Business
572616	**18009654**	**13142187**	**2228908**	**51585441**	**46184367**	**314987**
439664	6173172	3560395	1163475	17078499	15272741	213764
565933	15110987	10983964	2126120	43870970	39160176	311897
276240	3308737	1633284	634690	8791672	7493900	200332
2765	227375	205207	7247	650993	630312	1723
1595	144230	131025	7284	439709	414337	964
2797	55052	34034	11130	99072	79138	44
2424	12494	11292	1006	38651	37306	20
	13000	12950	50	18445		
373	29558	9792	10075	41977	41832	24
97500	6108503	5111486	541600	19830343	18592486	61021
22004	893192	629135	106467	1528487	1413635	10666
75496	5215311	4482351	435132	18301856	17178851	50355
135958	1526531	810657	418794	4643266	4295032	8896
38965	3452457	2860521	445035	8469838	6794822	26899
4397	66853	46470	15177	551756	515636	4454
365	24414	22118	1993	62506	57995	149
32189	3304435	2756168	413276	7619789	6005541	20370
2014	56755	35765	14589	235787	215649	1926
10114	288103	197750	60341	946076	860149	12018
1865	741769	716630	45661	4747120	4688278	2693
429	54330	10555	14130	44382	42294	58
1436	687439	706075	31531	4702738	4645983	2635
4818	2156899	1441594	57127	2967352	2335914	397
1555	66676	34262	26306	151731	138625	212
165	7633	9603	415	10348	7663	44
2979	2067058	1386291	26906	2754037	2143934	116
119	15532	11439	3500	51235	45692	25
13041	194517	113681	39057	484142	452176	1212
9831	91397	40542	21819	177560	164647	207
661	23444	13130	6742	39078	31125	729
1502	27656	16298	5530	108407	104403	146
58	3719	2069	1050	7337	6877	1
990	48301	41641	3917	151761	145125	130
219360	2597403	1244548	268063	6511814	5240779	212785
18233	727739	426008	79467	723024	674915	1584
1176	42770	35435	3234	140293	129954	353
1531	133444	97264	26751	508004	376364	5897
2627	18111	5618	5692	92901	82425	697
8652	252138	157998	51760	295047	264604	421

表15.6 续表1 continued1

指 标	Item	企业数（个） Number of Enterprises (unit)	流动资产合计 Total Circulating Assets	固定资产原价 Original Value of Fixed Assets
饮料及茶叶批发	Wholesale of Beverages and Tea	17	18404	3780
烟草制品批发	Wholesale of Tobaccos	39	969299	371474
其他食品批发	Wholesale of other Food	56	116595	19531
纺织、服装及日用品批发	Wholesale of Textiles, Garments and Daily Consumer Articles	48	196061	17302
纺织品、针织品及原料批发	Wholesale of Textiles, Knitwear and Raw Materials	10	32355	601
服装批发	Wholesale of Garments	12	67073	9555
鞋帽批发	Wholesale of Shoes and Hats			
厨房、卫生间用具及日用杂货批发	Wholesale of Kitchen Utensils, Toilet Ware and Daily Consumer Articles Sundry Goods	2	2442	241
化妆品及卫生用品批发	Wholesale of Cosmetics and Sanitary Articles	4	13997	1234
其他日用品批发	Wholesale of Other Daily Consumer Articles	20	80193	5670
文化、体育用品及器材批发	Wholesale of Cultural and Sports Articles and Equipment	13	174783	12827
文具用品批发	Wholesale of Cultural Articles	1	2747	47
体育用品批发	Wholesale of Sports Articles			
图书批发	Wholesale of Books	2	31841	580
报刊批发	Wholesale of Newspapers and Magazines	1	5502	551
音像制品及电子出版物批发	Wholesale of E-journals and Video Products			
首饰、工艺品及收藏品批发	Wholesale of Jewelry, Handicrafts and Collections	6	129393	10799
其他文化用品批发	Wholesale of Other Cultural Goods	3	5300	851
医药及医疗器材批发	Wholesale of Medicines and Medical Appliances	127	1373677	92695
西药批发业	Wholesale of Western Medicines	100	874297	60973
中药材及中成药批发	Wholesale of Traditional Chinese Medicines	19	181637	23925
医疗用品及器材批发	Wholesale of Medical Articles and Appliances	8	317743	7797
矿产品、建材及化工产品批发	Wholesale of Mineral Products, Building Materials and Chemical Products	763	4329586	848507
煤炭及制品批发	Wholesale of Coal and Related Products	141	839752	62822
石油及制品批发	Wholesale of Petroleum and Related Products	84	503470	614019
非金属矿及制品批发	Wholesale of Nonmetal Mineral and Related Products	11	154554	5062
金属及金属矿批发	Wholesale of Metal and Metal Mineral	144	1253804	58364
建材批发	Wholesale of Building Materials	220	902569	44933
化肥批发	Wholesale of Fertilizers	61	264383	28174
农药批发	Wholesale of Pesticides	1	1109	445
农用薄膜批发	Wholesale of Films for Agriculture	2	7384	121
其他化工产品批发	Wholesale of Other Chemical Products	99	402561	34568
机械设备、五金交电及电子产品批发	Wholesale of Machinery, Hardware and Electronic Products	314	5605039	121088
农业机械批发	Wholesale of Agricultural Machinery	14	31134	5499
汽车、摩托车及零配件批发	Wholesale of Automobiles, Motorcycles and Parts	155	1187123	55004
五金、交电批发	Wholesale of Hardware	27	41719	9870
家用电器批发	Wholesale of Household Electric Appliances	36	1927421	8709
计算机、软件及辅助设备批发	Wholesale of Computers, Software and Assistant Equipment	7	2173249	9741
通讯及广播电视设备批发	Wholesale of Communication, Broadcast and TV Equipment	14	38404	10880
其他机械设备及电子产品批发	Wholesale of Other Machinery and Electronic Products	61	205989	21386
贸易经纪与代理	Trade Broker and Agency	4	14273	4315
其他批发业	Other Wholesales	98	162287	32330
再生物资回收与批发	Wholesale of Recycled Materials	79	87919	27043
其他未列明的批发	Other Wholesale not Classified Elsewhere	19	74367	5286

单位：万元 (10 000 yuan)

累计折旧 Total Depreciation	资产总计 Total Assets	负债合计 Total Liabilities	实收资本 Paid-in Capital	主营业务收入 Revenue of Principal Business	主营业务成本 Cost of Principal Business	主营业务税金及附加 Taxes and Extra Charges on Principal Business
1002	26151	17821	6898	128860	118127	340
181815	1255963	402194	82520	4178675	3211580	201182
4324	141086	102210	11740	445009	382810	2311
6561	249416	211086	23932	552758	456429	8686
316	35658	30985	3355	81889	78019	31
3992	80571	65603	12736	200514	131021	7941
119	2565	1181	350	22346	20809	146
535	15122	13699	1130	38788	35420	45
1600	115500	99618	6361	209221	191160	524
2709	187588	142557	16845	305632	234578	1922
37	2814	2340	500	8407	7837	11
157	32933	24734	10000	31273	18362	156
232	6418	6157	2000	30249	18134	1485
1960	138925	104029	3747	219087	175334	242
323	6498	5298	598	16617	14912	27
37837	1661826	1164153	194422	3223201	3042050	3839
23202	988040	768449	96617	2355553	2231995	2414
12131	243783	191877	45805	441325	417965	447
2504	430002	203827	52000	426323	392091	978
255580	6874115	5197943	1247487	22661695	20326676	62445
19382	962382	763288	123111	2467849	2273589	14854
192479	1459783	664504	718426	6874089	6326618	6442
1207	170533	155434	5389	318225	286478	2911
16347	1462481	1175352	159331	5382419	5250523	7019
8035	2009501	1839083	124939	4428463	3146754	23586
8163	340504	240065	66018	1188095	1136915	5877
2	2304	815	336	9918	9799	1
48	7518	6414	600	14351	13793	10
9917	459110	352989	49337	1978287	1882207	1746
28039	6001504	4902750	389502	16814839	15462118	15082
1229	46693	29335	5104	92539	85660	133
9685	1389117	1195038	115247	3583081	3381444	2300
2045	52514	30617	4819	211259	183968	1896
2895	1958104	2029495	20192	9333184	8880652	7042
2539	2253916	1420091	188279	2596700	2002623	357
2469	52396	38811	8753	86706	77629	269
7176	248764	159363	47108	911371	850141	3086
1314	18099	11097	1568	47453	45425	233
8175	225185	154373	48032	983908	924135	8783
6028	145511	88731	42844	927983	876506	8268
2147	79674	65642	5187	55925	47629	516

表15.6 续表2 continued2

指　标	Item	其他业务利润 Profits from Other Business	销售费用 Selling Expense	管理费用 Overhead
总　计	**Total**	**78256**	**1455941**	**1538435**
#国有控股	State Holding	19899	476774	325359
按登记注册类型分组	**By Type of Registration**			
内资企业	Domestic-funded Enterprises	72304	1382213	998470
国有企业	State-owned Enterprises	9176	223745	276421
集体企业	Collective-owned Enterprises	240	8901	2806
股份合作企业	Cooperative Enterprises	123	10689	2933
联营企业	Joint-owned Enterprises		1556	6549
国有联营企业	State Joint-owned Enterprises		1486	199
集体联营企业	Collective Joint-owned Enterprises			5990
国有与集体联营企业	State-Collective Joint-owned Enterprises			
其他联营企业	Other Joint-owned Enterprises		70	360
有限责任公司	Limited Liability Corporations	39662	735561	199178
国有独资公司	Solely State-owned Corporations	2491	40301	30394
其他有限责任公司	Other Limited Liability Corporations	37171	695261	168784
股份有限公司	Share-holding Corporations Ltd.	15588	182120	16741
私营企业	Private Enterprises	6848	194022	475711
私营独资企业	Private-funded Enterprises	1014	11077	7604
私营合伙企业	Private Partnership Enterprises		2707	903
私营有限责任公司	Private Limited Liability Corporations	5608	171990	463736
私营股份有限公司	Private Share-holding Corporatinos Ltd.	227	8249	3468
其他企业	Other Enterprises	667	25618	18132
港澳台商投资企业	Enterprises Funded by Hong Kong, Macao and Taiwan	5860	83785	13941
合资经营企业	Joint-venture Enterprises	35	709	386
合作经营企业	Cooperative Enterprises			
独资经营企业	Enterprises with Sole Fund	5825	83076	13555
投资股份有限公司	Share-holding Corporations Ltd.			
外商投资企业	Foreign-funded Enterprises	92	-10057	526024
中外合资经营企业	Joint-venture Enterprises	12	5749	3310
中外合作经营企业	Cooperative Enterprises		2272	423
外资企业	Enterprises with Sole Fund	77	-18660	522067
外商投资股份有限公司	Share-holding Corporations Ltd.	2	582	224
按批发行业小类分组	**By Wholesale Sector**			
农畜产品批发	Wholesale of Farm Produce and Livestock Products	1858	7183	7457
谷物、豆及薯类批发	Wholesale of Cereal, Bean and Tuber	1308	2629	3535
种子、饲料批发	Wholesale of Seed and Feedstuff	76	1693	1798
棉、麻批发	Wholesale of Cotton and Fiber Crops	44	1210	1296
牲畜批发	Wholesale of Livestocks		356	119
其他农畜产品批发	Wholesale of Other Farm Produce and Livestock Products	430	1296	710
食品、饮料及烟草制品批发	Wholesale of Food, Beverages and Tobaccos	10336	193435	279719
米、面制品及食用油批发	Wholesale of Rice, Flour and Edible Oil	1621	17066	12255
糕点、糖果及糖批发	Wholesale of Cake, Candy and Sugar	725	5290	2883
果品、蔬菜批发	Wholesale of Fruits and Vegetables		2737	3657
肉、禽、蛋及水产品批发	Wholesale of Meat, Poultry, Eggs and Aquatic Products	49	1764	2162
盐及调味品批发	Wholesale of Salts and Condiments	845	15055	11349

单位：万元 (10 000 yuan)

营业利润 Business Profit	利润总额 Total Profits	应交所得税 Payable Income Tax	应付职工薪酬 Payroll Payable	应交增值税 VAT Payable	从业人员期末人数(人) Number of Persons Employed at Year-end(person)	土地和固定资产支出 Expenditure on Land and Fixed Assests	其 中 of which 土地购置 Purchase of Land	房屋和建筑物 Houing and Building
2033812	**1277619**	**212884**	**592875**	**751656**	**102108**	**199447**	**84128**	**33566**
761855	618003	107457	374932	408458	36767	155705	71047	16164
1990331	1075471	163793	574137	708189	98675	195907	84128	30226
594240	480294	87872	262653	326341	18734	65060	14325	11428
6140	5595	363	3115	2878	1153	154	7	
10112	8615	18	1503	2093	1145			
11384	-1029	631	988	200	218	4351	2987	
-371	-367	9	919	121	151	4351	2987	
12455			40	55	12			
-700	-662	622	29	25	55			
238210	233749	38661	142687	224818	37114	35385	6976	10773
24002	36987	8512	19598	6175	2989	13950	323	6766
214208	196762	30148	123088	218643	34125	21435	6653	4007
142536	84253	7380	85089	30085	14051	81203	59823	2902
959843	238783	26324	60734	111690	22954	7050	10	3072
11896	8705	546	4977	4787	2061	151		82
566	498	85	918	278	507	142		55
941348	224965	25212	51233	103406	18408	6447	10	2934
6034	4615	482	3606	3220	1978	311		
27867	25211	2544	17368	10084	3306	2704		2052
-37861	-37769	7488	5393	22808	648	38		
863	861	136	296	247	52			
-38724	-38630	7352	5097	22561	596	38		
81343	239918	41603	13346	20660	2785	3502		3340
2948	2809	646	1917	946	684	419		289
-87	-57	118	1140	398	468			
74210	236828	40745	10101	18003	1558	3083		3051
4271	338	95	188	1313	75			
14116	7882	570	5614	4998	46	1120		587
6218	1348	41	2070	474	14	178		65
3071	1483	55	805	732	13	199		
885	2647	321	1572	2905	6	553		385
-192	546		290	14	4	150		138
4134	1857	153	877	874	9	40		
592776	566369	83046	264012	108386	210	27136	875	16057
7955	14140	584	7829	4449	37	4645	310	3526
1602	2138	265	2792	1357	11	71		
119095	104246	38	2563	1681	33	163		84
5790	5842	109	1721	521	8	534		
5965	8320	341	10137	3526	9	8854	14	3698

表15.6 续表3 continued3

指 标	Item	其他业务利润 Profits from Other Business	销售费用 Selling Expense	管理费用 Overhead
饮料及茶叶批发	Wholesale of Beverages and Tea	83	4703	1714
烟草制品批发	Wholesale of Tobaccos	3931	108277	237031
其他食品批发	Wholesale of other Food	3082	38543	8668
纺织、服装及日用品批发	Wholesale of Textiles, Garments and Daily Consumer Articles	2461	38295	15013
纺织品、针织品及原料批发	Wholesale of Textiles, Knitwear and Raw Materials		2365	642
服装批发	Wholesale of Garments	410	26252	11288
鞋帽批发	Wholesale of Shoes and Hats			
厨房、卫生间用具及日用杂货批发	Wholesale of Kitchen Utensils, Toilet Ware and Daily Consumer Articles Sundry Goods		1073	209
化妆品及卫生用品批发	Wholesale of Cosmetics and Sanitary Articles	125	2138	929
其他日用品批发	Wholesale of Other Daily Consumer Articles	1926	6468	1946
文化、体育用品及器材批发	Wholesale of Cultural and Sports Articles and Equipment	733	36037	7401
文具用品批发	Wholesale of Cultural Articles		386	170
体育用品批发	Wholesale of Sports Articles			
图书批发	Wholesale of Books	7	6712	2481
报刊批发	Wholesale of Newspapers and Magazines	280	9891	882
音像制品及电子出版物批发	Wholesale of E-journals and Video Products			
首饰、工艺品及收藏品批发	Wholesale of Jewelry, Handicrafts and Collections	82	18124	2819
其他文化用品批发	Wholesale of Other Cultural Goods	364	925	1049
医药及医疗器材批发	Wholesale of Medicines and Medical Appliances	12124	75517	56148
西药批发业	Wholesale of Western Medicines	4896	46219	41050
中药材及中成药批发	Wholesale of Traditional Chinese Medicines	117	9007	8531
医疗用品及器材批发	Wholesale of Medical Articles and Appliances	7111	20290	6568
矿产品、建材及化工产品批发	Wholesale of Mineral Products, Building Materials and Chemical Products	23419	523961	532782
煤炭及制品批发	Wholesale of Coal and Related Products	9953	102650	29029
石油及制品批发	Wholesale of Petroleum and Related Products	1827	247644	9660
非金属矿及制品批发	Wholesale of Nonmetal Mineral and Related Products	334	7326	3629
金属及金属矿批发	Wholesale of Metal and Metal Mineral	2122	57391	26303
建材批发	Wholesale of Building Materials	1007	58663	422459
化肥批发	Wholesale of Fertilizers	6460	19492	16655
农药批发	Wholesale of Pesticides		64	46
农用薄膜批发	Wholesale of Films for Agriculture	21	83	107
其他化工产品批发	Wholesale of Other Chemical Products	1695	30647	24895
机械设备、五金交电及电子产品批发	Wholesale of Machinery, Hardware and Electronic Products	19973	568346	629739
农业机械批发	Wholesale of Agricultural Machinery	302	3432	1470
汽车、摩托车及零配件批发	Wholesale of Automobiles, Motorcycles and Parts	13320	128966	27197
五金、交电批发	Wholesale of Hardware	137	5490	4709
家用电器批发	Wholesale of Household Electric Appliances	3150	425387	57997
计算机、软件及辅助设备批发	Wholesale of Computers, Software and Assistant Equipment	12	-27931	521208
通讯及广播电视设备批发	Wholesale of Communication, Broadcast and TV Equipment	738	3577	4119
其他机械设备及电子产品批发	Wholesale of Other Machinery and Electronic Products	2315	29426	13039
贸易经纪与代理	Trade Broker and Agency	7	1157	282
其他批发业	Other Wholesales	7346	12011	9896
再生物资回收与批发	Wholesale of Recycled Materials	6979	8217	7951
其他未列明的批发	Other Wholesale not Classified Elsewhere	367	3795	1945

单位：万元 (10 000 yuan)

营业利润 Business Profit	利润总额 Total Profits	应交所得税 Payable Income Tax	应付职工薪酬 Payroll Payable	应交增值税 VAT Payable	从业人员期末人数(人) Number of Persons Employed at Yearend(person)	土地和固定资产支出 Expenditure on Land and Fixed Assests	其中 of which 土地购置 Purchase of Land	 房屋和建筑物 Houing and Building
3573	3597	208	1831	2367	912	156		
433873	415537	80030	226897	88168	7328	12264	552	8750
14923	12549	1471	10243	6319	3804	449		
34968	33738	8978	12379	17458	5107	2655		2214
282	268	37	957	485	437			
24599	24063	7341	7529	14826	2817	156		
77	70		98	151	184			
66	40	18	1565	280	430	30		
9945	9298	1583	2231	1717	1239	2469		2214
26014	27315	3441	23817	5466	4964	1881		1680
4	4	1	307	12	298			
3793	3761		1578	1545	244			
123	313		7410	-182	1843	168		
22066	22897	3438	13914	3954	2259	1713		1680
28	339	3	608	137	320			
49243	58917	7762	39353	32918	12497	12778	7758	908
23852	29381	4586	28371	29198	9434	3351		760
1206	1256	331	6588	1908	2086	314		
24185	28279	2846	4395	1813	977	9113	7758	148
1151377	273561	44389	172683	408829	37432	147883	73582	11184
35924	37114	5059	18005	19136	6179	1706		248
269334	116437	12645	105635	258822	18469	131705	69147	4699
12083	9499	1119	2013	37505	476	257		195
24117	26327	4695	14059	23928	3269	3909	1005	1700
766563	46737	15257	11149	53000	3683	5550	3410	1651
8178	8954	1011	9930	6713	2766	385		83
6	6	2	46		12			
260	283	48	45	75	13			
34912	28205	4555	11801	9650	2565	4372	20	2608
131783	284456	62431	66854	140419	16539	5345	1905	867
1662	1981	230	1500	270	441	392		
57827	55719	8326	24025	8119	6414	1147	577	
13604	11991	1169	3192	1981	1043	162		
-25192	-27434	11083	23862	70943	4562	565		156
67682	230321	39948	2275	15998	494			
637	1101	314	2544	2553	923	48		
15563	10776	1361	9457	40555	2662	3032	1328	711
154	170	29	982	384	396	306		
33382	25211	2238	7181	32798	3164	344	7	69
32317	24980	1780	5347	31900	2589	158		61
1066	231	457	1834	897	575	185	7	8

表15.7 限额以上零售业法人企业财务状况（2011年）

FINANCIAL INDICATORS OF RETAIL ENTERPRISES ABOVE DESIGNATED SIZE (2011)

指 标	Item	企业数（个）Number of Enterprises (unit)	流动资产合计 Total Circulating Assets	固定资产原价 Original Value of Fixed Assets
总 计	**Total**	**1807**	**4623364**	**1390328**
#国有控股	State Holding	110	1486361	535968
按登记注册类型分	**By Type of Registration**			
内资企业	Domestic-funded Enterprises	1775	3670213	1052698
国有企业	State-owned Enterprises	49	191554	74571
集体企业	Collective-owned Enterprises	22	5651	3390
股份合作企业	Cooperative Enterprises	32	38668	10275
联营企业	Joint-owned Enterprises	9	16988	10166
国有联营企业	State Joint-owned Enterprises	4	14904	8801
集体联营企业	Collective Joint-owned Enterprises	2	123	500
国有与集体联营企业	State-Collective Joint-owned Enterprises	2	536	813
其他联营企业	Other Joint-owned Enterprises	1	1425	53
有限责任公司	Limited Liability Corporations	513	1879138	383420
国有独资公司	Solely State-owned Corporations	7	94193	17317
其他有限责任公司	Other Limited Liability Corporations	506	1784945	366103
股份有限公司	Share-holding Corporations Ltd.	55	399232	186484
私营企业	Private Enterprises	975	1017013	358173
私营独资企业	Private-funded Enterprises	277	83158	36486
私营合伙企业	Private Partnership Enterprises	33	13300	3654
私营有限责任公司	Private Limited Liability Corporations	627	898621	311809
私营股份有限公司	Private Share-holding Corporatinos Ltd.	38	21933	6224
其他企业	Other Enterprises	120	121970	26218
港澳台商投资企业	Enterprises Funded by Hong Kong, Macao and Taiwan	16	607912	155052
合资经营企业	Joint-venture Enterprises	4	70424	11891
合作经营企业	Cooperative Enterprises			
独资经营企业	Enterprises with Sole Fund	10	71757	13478
投资股份有限公司	Share-holding Corporations Ltd.	1	9337	124
外商投资企业	Foreign-funded Enterprises	16	345240	182578
中外合资经营企业	Joint-venture Enterprises	4	70424	11891
中外合作经营企业	Cooperative Enterprises			
外资企业	Enterprises with Sole Fund	10	71757	13478
外商投资股份有限公司	Share-holding Corporations Ltd.	1	9337	124
按零售行业小类分	**By Retail Sector**			
综合零售	Comprehensive Retails	207	1410497	614822
百货零售	Department Stores	94	1194449	547827
超级市场零售	Supermarkets	64	135978	52375
其他综合零售	Other Comprehensive Retails	49	80069	14621
食品、饮料及烟草制品专门零售	Special Retail of Food, Beverages and Tobaccos	133	189645	98868
粮油零售	Retail of Grains and Edible Oil	29	33165	23612
糕点、面包零售	Retail of Cakes and Bread	6	5546	2115
果品、蔬菜零售	Retail of Fruits and Vegetables	8	14461	3989
肉、禽、蛋及水产品零售	Retail of Meat, Poultry, Eggs and Aquatic Products	22	4618	7767
饮料及茶叶零售	Retail of Beverages and Tea	26	20125	7619
烟草制品零售	Retail of Tobaccos	3	1729	351
其他食品零售	Retail of Other Food	39	110002	53415

单位：万元 (10 000 yuan)

累计折旧 Total Depreciation	资产总计 Total Assets	负债合计 Total Liabilities	实收资本 Paid-in Capital	主营业务收入 Revenue of Principal Business	主营业务成本 Cost of Principal Business	主营业务税金及附加 Taxes and Extra Charges on Principal Business
441101	**6950052**	**4525504**	**1209383**	**17193803**	**15294461**	**139624**
176357	2249065	1514074	256724	5128449	4560381	26940
302132	5652149	3612775	985586	15104610	13520106	123978
25710	327435	249657	63964	1115910	1021376	2813
1460	8351	4928	2320	38248	32291	479
1714	53136	32396	9423	150395	126678	1475
2953	27776	17486	6891	108265	97574	576
2659	24401	17079	4700	93300	83989	487
25	623	20	600	1683	1451	72
259	1271	181	791	10028	9449	7
10	1482	205	800	3254	2685	10
112411	2621575	1862754	407985	5987845	5415406	24992
3950	124715	106736	11399	292463	283995	2944
108461	2496860	1756018	396586	5695383	5131411	22048
66356	685876	395987	65393	1460411	1275589	10461
87435	1764208	932739	401740	5376440	4736593	79902
6780	142634	83757	35497	675461	587192	13709
941	18504	13039	3753	67736	56804	499
78563	1570419	818911	352083	4490184	3972618	64371
1152	32651	17032	10407	143059	119980	1323
4093	163794	116829	27872	867097	814600	3280
40099	751325	562204	94902	1626939	1419892	11680
6014	79357	54695	8483	112354	86232	1607
2050	93128	73213	25802	198771	177004	1444
73	9540	293	10248	2384	1929	18
98870	546578	350525	128895	462254	354463	3966
6014	79357	54695	8483	112354	86232	1607
2050	93128	73213	25802	198771	177004	1444
73	9540	293	10248	2384	1929	18
231996	2414933	1507865	390727	4250378	3657848	32616
213044	1842307	1230214	276404	3149006	2685082	26875
16175	253783	203776	37212	603669	530132	3463
2777	318843	73875	77111	497704	442634	2278
29474	321624	140140	97628	1175384	974455	9102
8879	57774	35850	5866	147894	128399	829
479	8135	5054	277	22646	10532	1000
1624	33495	12858	2866	27201	23868	164
2213	14364	6298	5382	82018	73214	537
1873	27521	12897	4865	104641	83983	999
36	2153	2031	109	7851	6856	84
14370	178183	65153	78263	783134	647603	5488

表15.7 续表1 continued1

指　标	Item	企业数（个） Number of Enterprises (unit)	流动资产合计 Total Circulating Assets	固定资产原价 Original Value of Fixed Assets
纺织、服装及日用品专门零售	Special Retail of Textile, Garments and Daily Consumer Articles	110	111233	28235
纺织品及针织品零售	Retail of Textiles and Knitwear	14	9528	8383
服装零售	Retail of Garments	51	62264	5654
鞋帽零售	Retail of Shoes and Hats	14	5641	2231
钟表、眼镜零售	Retail of Clocks, Watches and Glasses	12	26538	8916
化妆品及卫生用品零售	Retail of Cosmetics and Sanitary Articles	4	481	627
其他日用品零售	Retail of Other General Merchandise	15	6780	2425
文化、体育用品及器材专门零售	Special Retail of Cultural and Sports Articles	50	295709	69417
文具用品零售	Retail of Cultural Articles	20	9025	1592
体育用品零售	Retail of Sports Articles	2	2214	74
图书零售	Retail of Books	8	261244	65802
报刊零售	Retail of Newspapers and Magazines			
音像制品及电子出版物零售	Retail of Video Products and E-journals			
珠宝首饰零售	Retail of Jewelry	13	19598	1638
工艺美术品及收藏品零售	Retail of Handicrafts and Collections	2	588	159
照相器材零售	Retail of Cameras	1	1045	11
其他文化用品零售	Retail of Other Cultural Goods	4	1996	141
医药及医疗器材专门零售	Special Retail of Medicine and Medical Appliances	120	173232	39023
药品零售	Retail of Medicine	115	169794	38832
医疗用品及器材零售	Retail of Medical Articles and Appliances	5	3438	191
汽车、摩托车、燃料及零配件专门零售	Special Retail of Automobiles, Motorcycles, Fuel and Spare Parts	639	1661354	333601
汽车零售	Retail of Automobiles	381	1432022	245141
汽车零配件零售	Retail of Automobile Fittings	25	52109	6976
摩托车及零配件零售业	Retail of Motorcycles and Parts	138	57654	8785
机动车燃料零售	Retail of Motor Fuel	95	119570	72699
家用电器及电子产品专门零售	Special Retail of Household Electric Appliances and Electronic Products	300	481122	81748
家用电器零售业	Retail of Household Electric Appliances	179	334725	66333
计算机、软件及辅助设备零售	Retail of Computers, Software and Assistant Equipment	81	118748	7236
通信设备零售	Retail of Communication Equipment	33	23451	8007
其他电子产品零售	Retail of Other Electronic Products	7	4198	172
五金、家具及室内装修材料专门零售	Special Retail of Hardware, Furniture and Decoration Materials	199	173278	109322
五金零售	Retail of Hardware	31	47085	15266
家具零售	Retail of Furniture	48	86500	53564
涂料零售	Retail of Paint	3	965	568
其他室内装修材料零售	Retail of Other Indoor Decoration Materials	117	38728	39924
无店铺及其他零售业	Non-shop and Other Retails	49	127294	15291
流动货摊零售	Retail by Mobile Stalls			
邮购及电子销售	Distribution of Post and E-commerce	1	27	
生活用燃料零售	Retail of Fuel for Daily Use	16	8273	3303
花卉零售	Retail of Flowers	6	39575	5644
旧货零售	Retail of Used Goods	1	1211	80
其他未列明的零售	Other Retails not Classified Elsewhere	25	78208	6264

单位：万元 (10 000 yuan)

累计折旧 Total Depreciation	资产总计 Total Assets	负债合计 Total Liabilities	实收资本 Paid-in Capital	主营业务收入 Revenue of Principal Business	主营业务成本 Cost of Principal Business	主营业务税金及附加 Taxes and Extra Charges on Principal Business
9344	178712	125228	42347	505591	417062	3532
3878	19638	10656	2127	37827	32116	525
1864	85218	80225	10520	262406	214734	1695
402	7858	3573	1926	53038	37388	435
2557	55641	23283	25489	44359	29209	471
243	1059	461	558	3270	2330	67
401	9299	7031	1728	104692	101285	341
25598	452271	258855	42393	360142	281880	2074
474	10814	7009	1725	32260	26754	280
29	2259	1800	550	4010	3319	5
24465	412143	229276	34913	264777	203774	913
507	21365	16184	4028	46743	37122	841
27	721	203	78	2428	1753	14
1	1055	955	100	5338	4978	3
95	3913	3428	1000	4587	4180	18
14306	220659	158600	42539	639272	552799	3000
14218	216509	156355	41182	629834	545199	2875
88	4151	2245	1358	9438	7600	124
80568	2286147	1629407	405488	6687757	6208782	16070
54866	1916434	1395720	310945	5145860	4794481	12136
2128	58614	42581	6907	164553	149675	409
2828	70728	37839	11864	250604	225070	1443
20745	240371	153267	75772	1126742	1039556	2082
16835	609229	423830	94555	1590537	1430388	9016
13169	435451	282317	66088	1151417	1021057	5721
2266	133171	112642	20039	332413	314081	2391
1309	36248	25317	7588	89124	79070	878
92	4359	3555	840	17582	16179	25
27185	301391	174720	54525	1653853	1461195	62785
3112	62773	44482	15684	219285	195540	6948
19605	154054	72993	17178	1088524	963435	46399
103	1430	250	1180	33501	30151	1156
4366	83134	56995	20483	312543	272069	8283
5794	165087	106859	39180	330888	310053	1429
	45		10	102	79	1
933	11743	7460	2081	36287	31157	352
2086	46450	20198	16428	41029	34286	594
41	1251	943	300	7500	6716	10
2735	105598	78258	20362	245970	237815	471

表15.7 续表2 continued2

指　标	Item	其他业务利润 Profits from Other Business	销售费用 Selling Expense	管理费用 Overhead
总　计	**Total**	**181053**	**882150**	**394439**
#国有控股	State Holding	80607	333834	120917
按登记注册类型分	**By Type of Registration**			
内资企业	Domestic-funded Enterprises	135158	687125	332840
国有企业	State-owned Enterprises	6851	51095	14457
集体企业	Collective-owned Enterprises	154	1750	1795
股份合作企业	Cooperative Enterprises	22	7443	5102
联营企业	Joint-owned Enterprises	271	3608	2581
国有联营企业	State Joint-owned Enterprises	271	3170	2392
集体联营企业	Collective Joint-owned Enterprises		13	33
国有与集体联营企业	State-Collective Joint-owned Enterprises		290	-30
其他联营企业	Other Joint-owned Enterprises		136	185
有限责任公司	Limited Liability Corporations	44436	231368	134375
国有独资公司	Solely State-owned Corporations	873	1545	2067
其他有限责任公司	Other Limited Liability Corporations	43563	229823	132308
股份有限公司	Share-holding Corporations Ltd.	47476	121639	52726
私营企业	Private Enterprises	35796	252922	112153
私营独资企业	Private-funded Enterprises	1231	22233	13401
私营合伙企业	Private Partnership Enterprises	304	4559	1786
私营有限责任公司	Private Limited Liability Corporations	33102	222530	92324
私营股份有限公司	Private Share-holding Corporatinos Ltd.	1159	3600	4642
其他企业	Other Enterprises	152	17300	9651
港澳台商投资企业	Enterprises Funded by Hong Kong, Macao and Taiwan	32114	137940	39506
合资经营企业	Joint-venture Enterprises	4463	8655	6086
合作经营企业	Cooperative Enterprises			
独资经营企业	Enterprises with Sole Fund	4185	10316	15327
投资股份有限公司	Share-holding Corporations Ltd.	100		863
外商投资企业	Foreign-funded Enterprises	13781	57085	22093
中外合资经营企业	Joint-venture Enterprises	4463	8655	6086
中外合作经营企业	Cooperative Enterprises			
外资企业	Enterprises with Sole Fund	4185	10316	15327
外商投资股份有限公司	Share-holding Corporations Ltd.	100		863
按零售行业小类分	**By Retail Sector**			
综合零售	Comprehensive Retails	106203	384777	142848
百货零售	Department Stores	86180	307240	98547
超级市场零售	Supermarkets	19754	57659	30633
其他综合零售	Other Comprehensive Retails	269	19878	13668
食品、饮料及烟草制品专门零售	Special Retail of Food, Beverages and Tobaccos	20003	103661	27053
粮油零售	Retail of Grains and Edible Oil	1388	4554	4861
糕点、面包零售	Retail of Cakes and Bread	37	6101	1794
果品、蔬菜零售	Retail of Fruits and Vegetables	39	200	579
肉、禽、蛋及水产品零售	Retail of Meat, Poultry, Eggs and Aquatic Products	64	1756	1217
饮料及茶叶零售	Retail of Beverages and Tea	62	6095	2464
烟草制品零售	Retail of Tobaccos		501	206
其他食品零售	Retail of Other Food	18413	84456	15932

单位：万元 (10 000 yuan)

营业利润 Business Profit	利润总额 Total Profits	应交所得税 Payable Income Tax	应付职工薪酬 Payroll Payable	应交增值税 VAT Payable	从业人员期末人数(人) Number of Persons Employed at Yearend(person)	土地和固定资产支出 Expenditure on Land and Fixed Assests	其中 of which	
							土地购置 Purchase of Land	房屋和建筑物 Houing and Building
619838	**514821**	**71745**	**383147**	**263720**	**150871**	**153853**	**21785**	**73585**
181328	179161	18481	136122	80123	42525	23389	4284	9638
537047	418929	50992	357622	221150	132414	121163	21785	44879
30758	19502	640	18136	10471	6137	4508	3229	368
1895	1292	90	1204	255	1467	482		
8586	6223	879	2340	1692	1143	117	36	
3239	3161	516	2695	1335	586	210		
2578	2609	399	2340	1170	414	210		
109			30	10	27			
316	316	59	162	57	59			
236	236	59	163	98	86			
219133	201642	20806	130602	78829	43383	82182	9252	33406
937	1594	431	1858	227	515	982		870
218197	200048	20375	128744	78603	42868	81201	9252	32536
47430	44833	7529	64257	26588	15358	543		35
206058	129649	18282	129544	99505	59993	24980	4137	10692
37457	23605	1376	12282	18233	6215	1220	215	206
4124	2693	129	2119	985	1243	154		60
150329	100037	16121	112769	77416	51374	23279	3921	10298
14148	3314	656	2373	2872	1161	328		129
19948	12628	2250	8845	2475	4347	8140	5130	378
50584	57297	10893	14782	33087	13147	17336		13846
12594	12632	2140	4117	3430	1329	131		
-2024	3081	802	3756	3427	924	9587		8945
-326	-328		211		55	3		
32207	38595	9860	10744	9483	5310	15355		14860
12594	12632	2140	4117	3430	1329	131		
-2024	3081	802	3756	3427	924	9587		8945
-326	-328		211		55	3		
125180	123175	25510	127642	75483	55947	40391	2726	30678
107982	115979	23825	92988	63083	36614	35069	71	30431
-988	-4666	1024	29885	6963	16860	4961	2655	110
18187	11862	662	4769	5436	2473	361		137
77063	65605	9357	45101	18270	21853	3021	737	1037
9531	10144	786	3196	1600	1579	1486	617	748
3227	3226	694	731	24	454	14		
1977	2043	85	522	352	210	27		9
5198	2755	229	2780	843	1120	1335	120	280
9155	6894	658	2798	1607	1435	156		
113	113	35	110	111	44			
47862	40430	6870	34964	13733	17011	5		

表15.7 续表3 continued3

指 标	Item	其他业务利润 Profits from Other Business	销售费用 Selling Expense	管理费用 Overhead
纺织、服装及日用品专门零售	Special Retail of Textile, Garments and Daily Consumer Articles	4197	37523	31323
纺织品及针织品零售	Retail of Textiles and Knitwear	28	1071	2013
服装零售	Retail of Garments	3695	19255	20840
鞋帽零售	Retail of Shoes and Hats		8574	4576
钟表、眼镜零售	Retail of Clocks, Watches and Glasses	474	7409	2746
化妆品及卫生用品零售	Retail of Cosmetics and Sanitary Articles		393	198
其他日用品零售	Retail of Other General Merchandise		821	951
文化、体育用品及器材专门零售	Special Retail of Cultural and Sports Articles	2177	25009	12344
文具用品零售	Retail of Cultural Articles	175	1653	1724
体育用品零售	Retail of Sports Articles	2	459	295
图书零售	Retail of Books	1735	16480	9201
报刊零售	Retail of Newspapers and Magazines			
音像制品及电子出版物零售	Retail of Video Products and E-journals			
珠宝首饰零售	Retail of Jewelry	48	5585	611
工艺美术品及收藏品零售	Retail of Handicrafts and Collections		281	271
照相器材零售	Retail of Cameras	2	274	74
其他文化用品零售	Retail of Other Cultural Goods	216	278	168
医药及医疗器材专门零售	Special Retail of Medicine and Medical Appliances	2091	42256	25189
药品零售	Retail of Medicine	2091	41521	24811
医疗用品及器材零售	Retail of Medical Articles and Appliances		736	378
汽车、摩托车、燃料及零配件专门零售	Special Retail of Automobiles, Motorcycles, Fuel and Spare Parts	18552	153273	91400
汽车零售	Retail of Automobiles	16882	106642	74319
汽车零配件零售	Retail of Automobile Fittings	900	4365	3132
摩托车及零配件零售业	Retail of Motorcycles and Parts	187	6748	4383
机动车燃料零售	Retail of Motor Fuel	583	35518	9567
家用电器及电子产品专门零售	Special Retail of Household Electric Appliances and Electronic Products	25139	85051	27833
家用电器零售业	Retail of Household Electric Appliances	20643	72436	18337
计算机、软件及辅助设备零售	Retail of Computers, Software and Assistant Equipment	2552	7131	4985
通信设备零售	Retail of Communication Equipment	1842	5149	3643
其他电子产品零售	Retail of Other Electronic Products	102	336	869
五金、家具及室内装修材料专门零售	Special Retail of Hardware, Furniture and Decoration Materials	1904	44734	31805
五金零售	Retail of Hardware	402	5973	5430
家具零售	Retail of Furniture	1419	27749	17652
涂料零售	Retail of Paint		878	702
其他室内装修材料零售	Retail of Other Indoor Decoration Materials	83	10134	8021
无店铺及其他零售业	Non-shop and Other Retails	787	5866	4644
流动货摊零售	Retail by Mobile Stalls			
邮购及电子销售	Distribution of Post and E-commerce			2
生活用燃料零售	Retail of Fuel for Daily Use	12	1839	995
花卉零售	Retail of Flowers	7		1003
旧货零售	Retail of Used Goods		795	137
其他未列明的零售	Other Retails not Classified Elsewhere	767	3232	2506

单位：万元 (10 000 yuan)

营业利润 Business Profit	利润总额 Total Profits	应交所得税 Payable Income Tax	应付职工薪酬 Payroll Payable	应交增值税 VAT Payable	从业人员期末人数(人) Number of Persons Employed at Year-end(person)	土地和固定资产支出 Expenditure on Land and Fixed Assests	其中 of which 土地购置 Purchase of Land	房屋和建筑物 Houing and Building
16620	14557	2536	17143	8991	7638	278	8	70
1753	1608	217	1289	429	615	8		8
7757	7303	1256	8095	5590	3612	76	8	2
1551	1091	130	3118	555	1383	75		60
4222	3823	822	3505	1926	1415	114		
212	56	8	326	123	137			
1126	677	104	810	368	476	5		
62941	68196	696	17846	9679	5033	676		210
1933	1515	17	1264	372	1542	400		
-68	-68		360	52	185			
59023	65736	402	14270	7859	2524			
1803	906	254	1437	1187	567	273		210
106	106	17	57	147	24			
10	10	3	161	28	84			
135	-9	4	298	34	107	3		
14552	9970	2386	24275	10320	10310	3399		1376
14103	9512	2318	23807	9528	10209	3342		1376
449	458	69	468	792	101	58		
206072	160851	21706	97171	86397	26026	103205	18199	39462
147770	132060	18809	78010	74114	19687	88150	16604	38660
7135	6477	1577	2849	1844	818	1516		2
12021	6618	403	4256	4362	2076	42	1	
39145	15697	917	12057	6077	3445	13496	1594	799
59176	28882	3022	29322	21926	13881	794	10	244
52139	23264	2591	19191	17314	8775	481	10	
5205	4208	266	6108	3379	3039	301		244
1636	1284	128	3593	1019	1881	10		
195	125	38	431	214	186	3		
49820	37846	5720	20748	29770	7156	1432	26	474
4063	3842	559	2468	1878	1028	335		277
32918	24138	4562	8851	24249	3091	595	26	86
614	614		346	332	82			
12225	9252	600	9083	3311	2955	503		111
8413	5738	812	3899	2885	3027	657	80	34
21	21		2	1	3			
1681	1245	108	807	874	361	429	50	20
4658	2471	285	1265	212	2014	32	30	
-253	-197		35	92	127			
2307	2199	418	1790	1706	522	196		14

表15.8 限额以上住宿业法人企业财务状况（2011年）
FINANCIAL INDICATORS OF HOTELS ABOVE DESIGNATED SIZE (2011)

指　标	Item	企业数（个） Number of Enterprises (unit)	流动资产合计 Total Circulating Assets	固定资产原价 Original Value of Fixed Assets
总　计	**Total**	**298**	**573333**	**878903**
#国有控股	State Holding	54	44454	202544
按住宿行业小类分组	**By Classification of Hotels**			
旅游饭店	Tourist Hotels	193	514590	781688
一般旅店	General Hotels	79	53893	81473
其他住宿服务	Other Accommodation Services	26	4849	15743
按登记注册类型分	**By Type of Registration**			
内资企业	Domestic-funded Enterprises	287	461950	664951
国有企业	State-owned Enterprises	37	25593	112102
集体企业	Collective-owned Enterprises	12	4906	11099
股份合作企业	Cooperative Enterprises	1	600	1700
联营企业	Joint-owned Enterprises			
有限责任公司	Limited Liability Corporations	95	213250	370056
国有独资公司	Solely State-owned Corporations	2	1677	14723
其他有限责任公司	Other Limited Liability Corporations	93	211574	355333
股份有限公司	Share-holding Corporations Ltd.	18	29295	34564
私营企业	Private Enterprises	99	113338	101351
私营独资企业	Private-funded Enterprises	21	15725	15536
私营合伙企业	Private Partnership Enterprises	9	2114	5946
私营有限责任公司	Private Limited Liability Corporations	60	70675	67487
私营股份有限公司	Private Share-holding Corporatinos Ltd.	9	24825	12382
其他企业	Other Enterprises	25	74968	34080
港澳台商投资企业	Enterprises Funded by Hong Kong, Macao and Taiwan	5	33618	87035
合资经营企业	Joint-venture Enterprises	2	646	4122
合作经营企业	Cooperative Enterprises			
独资经营企业	Enterprises with Sole Fund	3	32972	82913
投资股份有限公司	Share-holding Corporations Ltd.			
外商投资企业	Foreign-funded Enterprises	6	77765	126917
中外合资经营企业	Joint-venture Enterprises	1	72	485
中外合作经营企业	Cooperative Enterprises			
外资企业	Enterprises with Sole Fund	4	77651	126304
外商投资股份有限公司	Share-holding Corporations Ltd.			

单位：万元 (10 000 yuan)

累计折旧 Total Depreciation	其 中 of which 本年折旧 Depreciation in Current Year	资产总计 Total Assets	负债合计 Total Liabilities	实收资本 Paid-in Capital	主营业务收入 Revenue of Principal Business	主营业务成本 Cost of Principal Business	主营业务税金及附加 Taxes and Extra Charges on Principal Business
326255	**46524**	**1487472**	**1151022**	**389731**	**596991**	**261707**	**28211**
79343	7587	251751	148966	98817	104511	43672	5191
299093	41158	1284995	1015992	322440	493712	203113	23982
24105	4774	178107	110353	63007	80629	45391	3079
3057	593	24370	24678	4284	22650	13203	1150
213862	41039	1221412	932540	327968	531571	245883	24776
47106	4291	137599	75305	61928	64483	29997	3072
4827	610	13121	12770	2797	13288	6081	675
500	11	1800	800	350	404	283	14
103738	25873	625986	516528	171399	235128	106565	11080
5276	525	19843	23773	4130	6070	1974	294
98462	25349	606143	492755	167269	229058	104591	10786
10707	1929	63872	45780	10154	44567	23101	2185
35945	5839	240235	169182	58497	126542	58900	5715
5771	561	40727	28754	5830	16318	9187	716
2687	269	6288	3442	2213	9074	5451	304
22807	4022	131552	90956	39706	88723	40205	4015
4680	988	61668	46030	10750	12427	4057	680
11040	2486	138799	112175	22843	47158	20956	2034
44236	379	89496	81293	28639	16956	3184	919
2436	98	4561	1546	3525	2760	384	136
41800	281	84936	79746	25114	14196	2800	783
68157	5106	176563	137190	33124	48464	12641	2515
		562	483	18	401	378	22
68076	5082	175396	136101	32606	47684	11890	2472

表15.8 续表 continued

指　标	Item	其他业务利　润 Profits from Other Business	销售费用 Selling Expense	管理费用 Overhead
总　计	**Total**	**1829**	**137490**	**142241**
#国有控股	State Holding	-660	27302	31339
按住宿行业小类分组	**By Classification of Hotels**			
旅游饭店	Tourist Hotels	2380	119645	122719
一般旅店	General Hotels	-575	13265	16771
其他住宿服务	Other Accommodation Services	24	4580	2752
按登记注册类型分	**By Type of Registration**			
内资企业	Domestic-funded Enterprises	1699	120934	120368
国有企业	State-owned Enterprises	-656	13453	16809
集体企业	Collective-owned Enterprises	127	3001	2810
股份合作企业	Cooperative Enterprises		15	2
联营企业	Joint-owned Enterprises			
有限责任公司	Limited Liability Corporations	1125	56620	61173
国有独资公司	Solely State-owned Corporations		1703	4022
其他有限责任公司	Other Limited Liability Corporations	1125	54916	57151
股份有限公司	Share-holding Corporations Ltd.	49	8231	7277
私营企业	Private Enterprises	943	27426	23911
私营独资企业	Private-funded Enterprises	76	3297	3683
私营合伙企业	Private Partnership Enterprises	25	2024	411
私营有限责任公司	Private Limited Liability Corporations	789	18498	16691
私营股份有限公司	Private Share-holding Corporatinos Ltd.	52	3606	3127
其他企业	Other Enterprises	113	12188	8386
港澳台商投资企业	Enterprises Funded by Hong Kong, Macao and Taiwan		3845	15311
合资经营企业	Joint-venture Enterprises		1443	1155
合作经营企业	Cooperative Enterprises			
独资经营企业	Enterprises with Sole Fund		2402	14156
投资股份有限公司	Share-holding Corporations Ltd.			
外商投资企业	Foreign-funded Enterprises	129	12711	6562
中外合资经营企业	Joint-venture Enterprises		8	
中外合作经营企业	Cooperative Enterprises			
外资企业	Enterprises with Sole Fund	129	12694	6561
外商投资股份有限公司	Share-holding Corporations Ltd.			

单位：万元 (10 000 yuan)

营业利润 Business Profit	利润总额 Total Profits	应交所得税 Payable Income Tax	应付职工薪酬 Payroll Payable	应交增值税 VAT Payable	从业人员期末人数(人) Number of Persons Employed at Year-end(person)	土地和固定资产支出 Expenditure on Land and Fixed Assests	其 中 of which	
							土地购置 Purchase of Land	房屋和建筑物 Houing and Building
473	**-437**	**5571**	**98621**	**3108**	**39786**	**40497**	**4226**	**26079**
-8025	-6520	218	22713	67	8410	1782		774
-2321	-2608	5214	86310	1143	33859	32020	4226	18982
1891	1802	235	9616	1899	4479	8351		7098
903	369	122	2694	65	1448	126		
-2530	-3526	3322	88323	2999	36881	39238	4226	26079
-999	-308	139	14965	47	5331	164		
677	609	96	2418	660	1036	459		53
89	89		29		16			
-14864	-14412	786	38211	2043	15278	29325	2200	21358
-2700	-2644		1625	2	545	167		
-12164	-11767	786	36586	2041	14733	29158	2200	21358
2747	2531	86	7132	7	2658	3347		3182
6507	4824	985	17675	242	8538	3041	26	1461
-1293	-1418	52	2634		1302	1787	26	1230
882	387	18	946	11	465	217		
6597	5479	801	12161	219	5675	1038		231
321	376	115	1935	11	1096			
3312	3141	1231	7893	1	4024	2903	2000	26
-7164	-7113		2597	12	948	13		
-419	-420		838	8	291	13		
-6745	-6693		1759	4	657			
10167	10201	2249	7701	96	1957	1246		
-10	-11		53		23			
10203	10238	2258	7648	96	1909	1246		

表15.9 限额以上餐饮业法人企业财务状况（2011年）

FINANCIAL INDICATORS OF CATERING ENTERPRISES ABOVE DESIGNATED SIZE (2011)

指　标	Item	企业数（个）Number of Enterprises (unit)	流动资产合计 Total Circulating Assets	固定资产原价 Original Value of Fixed Assets
总　计	**Total**	**762**	**362109**	**394535**
#国有控股	State Holding	21	36892	74506
按登记注册类型分组	**By Type of Registration**			
内资企业	Domestic-funded Enterprises	753	343366	360019
国有企业	State-owned Enterprises	10	24228	18745
集体企业	Collective-owned Enterprises	24	2496	4186
股份合作企业	Cooperative Enterprises	7	615	1055
联营企业	Joint-owned Enterprises			
有限责任公司	Limited Liability Corporations	139	111067	96995
国有独资公司	Solely State-owned Corporations	2	638	6541
其他有限责任公司	Other Limited Liability Corporations	137	110430	90454
股份有限公司	Share-holding Corporations Ltd.	15	93475	95442
私营企业	Private Enterprises	478	94130	130012
私营独资企业	Private-funded Enterprises	203	15232	35634
私营合伙企业	Private Partnership Enterprises	29	2809	5281
私营有限责任公司	Private Limited Liability Corporations	219	70046	81492
私营股份有限公司	Private Share-holding Corporatinos Ltd.	27	6044	7606
其他企业	Other Enterprises	80	17354	13584
港澳台商投资企业	Enterprises Funded by Hong Kong, Macao and Taiwan	4	3506	16704
合资经营企业	Joint-venture Enterprises	1	971	11577
合作经营企业	Cooperative Enterprises			
独资经营企业	Enterprises with Sole Fund	3	2535	5127
投资股份有限公司	Share-holding Corporations Ltd.			
外商投资企业	Foreign-funded Enterprises	5	15238	17813
中外合资经营企业	Joint-venture Enterprises			
中外合作经营企业	Cooperative Enterprises			
外资企业	Enterprises with Sole Fund	5	15238	17813
外商投资股份有限公司	Share-holding Corporations Ltd.			
按餐饮行业中类分组	**By Sector**			
正餐服务	Dinner Services	696	289249	304630
快餐服务	Fast Food Services	17	58544	54692
饮料及冷饮服务业	Beverage and Cold Beverage Services	2	146	253
其他餐饮服务	Other Catering Services	47	14171	34962

单位：万元 (10 000 yuan)

累计折旧 Total Depreciation	其 中 of which 本年折旧 Depreciation in Current Year	资产总计 Total Assets	负债合计 Total Liabilities	实收资本 Paid-in Capital	主营业务收入 Revenue of Principal Business	主营业务成本 Cost of Principal Business	主营业务税金及附加 Taxes and Extra Charges on Principal Business
136364	**22972**	**852254**	**445934**	**225468**	**1149968**	**726174**	**47418**
42113	3087	76112	55857	16568	38691	20083	1742
120653	18184	786036	411034	203929	1064586	690702	42813
6525	911	40756	32116	7329	13249	9321	495
938	113	6458	1918	3184	16726	14558	196
309	103	2783	2725	668	6424	4939	228
23895	4510	259120	148897	63512	217122	123480	9599
2039	394	5552	743	612	1650	634	92
21856	4116	253568	148154	62900	215471	122847	9506
48953	5638	188556	88064	41332	121250	79025	6865
37237	6505	249789	119654	78196	602261	401801	22314
8021	1511	50649	16489	23637	127072	90971	4554
1342	117	9411	2552	4795	36514	24414	907
25002	4396	176133	93256	47514	411247	268729	15481
2872	481	13596	7357	2250	27428	17687	1373
2797	405	38574	17660	9708	87555	57579	3116
2410	2036	30651	20284	9681	13424	3688	756
846	744	17590	11467	6123	3733	374	228
1564	1292	13062	8817	3558	9691	3315	528
13302	2753	35566	14616	11859	71958	31784	3850
13302	2753	35566	14616	11859	71958	31784	3850
114344	15701	642084	338286	138979	975680	607636	39397
17343	5875	119087	51081	59717	127230	85604	6879
138	24	260	69	50	1866	1738	11
4539	1372	90822	56498	26723	45192	31196	1132

表15.9 续表 continued

指　标	Item	其他业务利　润 Profits from Other Business	销售费用 Selling Expense	管理费用 Overhead
总　计	**Total**	**8974**	**178032**	**88818**
#国有控股	State Holding	219	9227	9500
按登记注册类型分组	**By Type of Registration**			
内资企业	Domestic-funded Enterprises	6300	145031	80696
国有企业	State-owned Enterprises	7	2510	3612
集体企业	Collective-owned Enterprises	65	365	426
股份合作企业	Cooperative Enterprises		864	562
联营企业	Joint-owned Enterprises			
有限责任公司	Limited Liability Corporations	2232	43993	22715
国有独资公司	Solely State-owned Corporations	5	1036	178
其他有限责任公司	Other Limited Liability Corporations	2227	42957	22537
股份有限公司	Share-holding Corporations Ltd.	1393	5777	6904
私营企业	Private Enterprises	2011	79527	40496
私营独资企业	Private-funded Enterprises	907	10151	7548
私营合伙企业	Private Partnership Enterprises	27	5206	3352
私营有限责任公司	Private Limited Liability Corporations	1077	59166	27557
私营股份有限公司	Private Share-holding Corporatinos Ltd.		5004	2039
其他企业	Other Enterprises	592	11996	5981
港澳台商投资企业	Enterprises Funded by Hong Kong, Macao and Taiwan	2674	6893	3744
合资经营企业	Joint-venture Enterprises		1125	1997
合作经营企业	Cooperative Enterprises			
独资经营企业	Enterprises with Sole Fund	2674	5768	1748
投资股份有限公司	Share-holding Corporations Ltd.			
外商投资企业	Foreign-funded Enterprises		26108	4378
中外合资经营企业	Joint-venture Enterprises			
中外合作经营企业	Cooperative Enterprises			
外资企业	Enterprises with Sole Fund		26108	4378
外商投资股份有限公司	Share-holding Corporations Ltd.			
按餐饮行业中类分组	**By Sector**			
正餐服务	Dinner Services	6140	158818	75282
快餐服务	Fast Food Services	2674	15434	8272
饮料及冷饮服务业	Beverage and Cold Beverage Services		49	16
其他餐饮服务	Other Catering Services	160	3732	5248

单位：万元 (10 000 yuan)

营业利润 Business Profit	利润总额 Total Profits	应交所得税 Payable Income Tax	应付职工薪酬 Payroll Payable	应交增值税 VAT Payable	从业人员期末人数(人) Number of Persons Employed at Year-end(person)	土地和固定资产支出 Expenditure on Land and Fixed Assests	其 中 of which	
							土地购置 Purchase of Land	房屋和建筑物 Houing and Building
111711	**64773**	**13090**	**137773**	**3774**	**70178**	**14723**	**430**	**11264**
-856	165	55	14666	2514	2629	782		
105036	58838	11744	125744	3773	62074	5058	110	2386
-1439	-859	25	2941	85	1382			
1055	488	204	1518	87	975	106		90
-216	-251	33	593		369			
18003	6098	1850	30471	973	13416	1038	16	380
-294	-263		383		149	2		
18297	6361	1850	30089	973	13267	1036	16	380
22752	23541	4167	22150	1755	9637	617		
55731	25903	4954	58125	642	31365	3239	94	1916
13800	8070	1714	11434	313	5889	532	63	89
2352	1727	117	2790	120	1383	1006		606
38410	15371	2943	41719	179	22768	1681	31	1216
1169	735	179	2181	29	1325	20		6
9150	3919	512	9947	231	4930	59		
1035	229	26	1231	1	1182	9371	320	8878
10	10		676	1	310	9371	320	8878
1026	219	26	555		872			
5640	5706	1321	10798		6922	294		
5640	5706	1321	10798		6922	294		
94767	49882	8951	123781	3009	60569	4925	94	2286
13033	12250	4009	8468	1	7095			
49	49	12	43		15			
3862	2592	118	5480	764	2499	9799	336	8978

表15.10 限额以上批发和零售业、餐饮业连锁经营情况（2010－2011年）

OPERATION OF CHAIN ENTERPRISES ABOVE DESIGNATED SIZE IN WHOLESALE, RETAIL AND CATERING TRADE (2010-2011)

单位：万元 (10 000 yuan)

指 标	Item	合计 Total		其中 of which #直营店 Regular Chain	
		2010	2011	2010	2011
门店总数（个）	Number of Stores (unit)	12710	13604	2834	3582
#百货店	Department Stores	254	376	254	376
超级市场	Supermarkets	3510	3275	451	430
营业面积（平方米）	Business Areas (sq.m)	4159270	4818785	2596985	3356188
#百货店	Department Stores	1207668	1224809	1207668	1224809
超级市场	Supermarkets	779990	958770	418087	819237
从业人数（人）	Employment (person)	195557	213334	69659	92708
#百货店	Department Stores	19161	20285	19161	20285
超级市场	Supermarkets	28107	30583	12660	26842
商品购进总额	Total Purchases	5947592	9079128	5026650	8370089
#百货店	Department Stores	1848916	2464005	1848916	2464005
超级市场	Supermarkets	906257	1445248	423814	1409961
统一配送商品购进额	Purchases of Centralized Delivery	2630932	5205915	2407638	5000251
#百货店	Department Stores	1163728	1629757	1163728	1629757
超级市场	Supermarkets	347079	1442727	311291	1407441
自有配送中心配送商品购进额	Purchases of Self-owned Delivery Center	1824205	3150505	1660855	3010855
#百货店	Department Stores	816598	1140014	816598	1140014
超级市场	Supermarkets	287682	339310	256902	310496
非自有配送中心配送商品购进额	Purchases of Non-self-owned Delivery Center	393955	663461	366549	629777
#百货店	Department Stores	347131	489743	347131	489743
超级市场	Supermarkets	5252	79164	780	75000
营业收入（餐饮业）	Business Revenue (Catering Trade)	992347	1254168	243369	351704
#正 餐	Restaurant	582171	1129320	87843	230675
快 餐	Fast Food	332072	111025	151885	111025
销售总额（批发和零售业）	Total Sales (Wholesale & Retail)	6148367	8625278	5486378	8430422
#百货店	Department Stores	2278672	2692252	2278672	2692252
超级市场	Supermarkets	993156	1250011	435427	1217272
#零售额	Retail	4053419	6406208	3958926	6271742
#百货店	Department Stores	2231707	2643041	2231707	2643041
超级市场	Supermarkets	481450	1243733	434275	1210994

重/庆/统/计/年/鉴

主要统计指标解释

社会消费品零售总额

指批发和零售业、餐饮业、新闻出版业、邮政业和其他服务业等，售予城乡居民用于生活消费的商品和社会集团用于公共消费的商品之总量。社会消费品零售总额包括：

一、批发和零售业企业（单位）售予城乡居民用于生活消费和社会集团用于公共消费的商品。包括：

1.售予城乡居民的各种生活消费品；

2.售予入境旅游的外国人、华侨、港澳台同胞的各类商品；

3.售予行政事业单位、社会团体、军队和武警等机构的商品，以及以零售方式售予各类企业的商品。具体包括：用于非生产和社会交往的办公用品，如通讯设备、计算器具和设备、电讯网络设备、文印设备、音像视听器材和设备、纸张、本册、文具及装订文印材料、家具、日用电器、针纺织品、清洁卫生用品、文体用品、奖品、纪念品、礼品等；供内部人员乘坐的交通工具和燃料；用于办公设施修缮的各类配件、材料、工具等；用于取暖和防暑降温的设备、燃料、材料及食品等；专用于教学的用品和设备；非营利医疗机构的中、西药品、中药材和医疗设备器材；非专用的劳动保护用品；不对外营业的内部食堂用的餐具、炊具、设备、清洁卫生工具和食品、燃料等；军队、武警用于其人员生活的衣着品和个人用品；其他各类非生产性设备和用品。

二、餐饮业出售的主食、菜肴、烟酒饮料和其他商品。

三、新闻出版业、邮政业售予城乡居民、企事业单位、军队和武警等机构的书报杂志、音像制品、邮品等。

四、其他服务业出售的食品、烟酒饮料、服装鞋帽、日常生活用品、医药保健用品、艺术品、工艺美术品、玩具、殡葬用品以及其他消费品。

批发和零售业商品购进、销售、库存总额

指各种登记注册类型的批发和零售业企业(单位)以本企业(单位)为总体的，从国内、国外市场购进的商品总量，销售和出口的商品总量、库存的商品总量等情况。该指标可以反映商品流转过程中商品的购进、销售、库存之间的比例关系和存在的问题。

销售总额

指对本企业(单位)以外的单位和个人出售(包括对境外直接出口)的商品总额。它反映批发和零售业在国内市场上销售商品以及出口商品的总量。商品销售包括：(1)售给城乡居民和社会集团消费用的商品；(2)售给工业、农业、建筑业、运输邮电业、批发和零售业、住宿和餐饮业、其他服务业等作为生产、经营使用的商品；(3)售给批发和零售业作为转卖或加工后转卖的商品；(4)对国(境)外直接出口的商品。不包括出售本企业(单位)自用的废旧包装用品，未通过买卖行为付出的商品，经本单位介绍、由买卖双方直接结算、本单位只收取手续费的业务，购货退出的商品以及商品损耗和损失等。

住宿和餐饮业营业额

指住宿和餐饮业法人企业（单位）在经营活动中因提供服务或销售商品等取得的收入。包括：客房收入、餐费收入、商品销售额和其他收入。客房收入指住宿和餐饮业法人企业（单位）在经营活动中因提供住宿服务取得的收入。餐费收入指住宿和餐饮业法人企业、（单位）因为顾客提供就餐服务取得的收入，包括经烹饪、调制加工后出售的各种食品，如主食、炒菜、凉拌菜等的收入。商品销售额指住宿和餐饮业法人企业（单位）伴随服务而出售商品所取得的收入（含增值税）。其他收入指营业收入中除客房收入、餐费收入、商品销售额以外的其他收入，包括娱乐、健身和商务服务等。

连锁企业（或称连锁店、连锁公司）

指在核心企业或总店的领导下，由分散的、经营同类商品或服务的企业或活动单位，采取共同方针，实行集中采购和分散销售的有机结合，通过规范化经营，实现规模效益的经济联合组织形式。一般连锁店

主要统计指标解释

应由若干个分店组成。其经营特征：(1)经营同类商品；(2)使用统一商号；(3)统一采购配送，采购与销售相分离（部分商品可根据物流合理和保质保鲜原则，由供应商直接送货到门店，其余均由总部统一配送）。

连锁门店的形式分为直营连锁和加盟连锁。

直营连锁也叫正规连锁。指连锁门店均由总部独资或控股开设，在总部的直接领导下统一经营。总部采取纵深似的管理方式，直接下令掌管所有的零售门店，零售门店也必须完全接受总部指挥。这是大型垄断商业资本通过吞并、兼并或独资、控股等途径，发展壮大自身实力和规模的一种形式。

加盟连锁包括特许连锁和自由连锁两种形式。

特许连锁指各连锁门店（被特许人）通过合同形式，取得使用总部（特许人）商标、商号、经营技术和销售总部开发的商品的特许权，各加盟连锁门店为独立法人，在总部指导下统一经营。

自由连锁也称自愿连锁。指连锁公司的门店均为独立法人，各自的资产所有权关系不变，在公司总部的指导下共同经营。各成员店使用共同的店名，与总部订阅有关购、销、宣传等方面的合同，并按合同开展经营活动。在合同规定的范围之外，各成员店可以自由活动。根据自愿原则，各成员店可自由加入连锁体系，也可自由退出。

■ 限额以上批发业

是指年主营业务收入在2000万元及以上的批发业。

■ 限额以上零售业

是指年主营业务收入在500万元以上的零售业。

■ 限额以上住宿业

是指年主营业务收入在200万元以上的住宿业。

■ 限额以上餐饮业

是指年主营业务收入在200万元以上的餐饮业。

CHONGQING STATISTICAL YEARBOOK

Explanatory Notes on Main Statistical Indicators

□ Total Retail Sales of Consumer Goods

refer to the sum of retail sales of commodities sold by wholesale and retail trades, catering services, publishing, post and telecommunications and other service industries to urban and rural households for household consumption and to social institutions for public consumption. Retail sales of consumer goods include:

(I) Sales sold by wholesale and retail trades to urban and rural households for household consumption and to social institutions for public consumption.

a) of commodities to urban and rural households;

b) of commodities to foreigners, overseas Chinese and Chinese compatriots from Hong Kong, Macao and Taiwan visiting China;

c) of commodities to government agencies, institutions, social organizations, military and armed police units, and commodities to enterprises in the form of retail sales. More specifically, they include: office facilities and articles for non-production purposes such as communications equipment, computing equipment and instruments, TV and network equipment, printing and copying equipment, audio-visual equipment and instruments, paper, notebooks, stationeries, furniture, electric appliances, knitwear, sanitation and cleaning articles, cultural and sport articles, articles for prizes, souvenirs, etc.; transport vehicles and fuels for employees; materials, spare parts and tools for the maintenance of office facilities; equipment, fuels, materials and food for winter heating or summer cooling purposes; articles and equipment for teaching purpose; Chinese and western medicines and medical equipment and facilities purchased by non profit-making medical institutes; non-specialized work safety articles; cooking utensils, tableware, equipment, cleaning articles, food and fuels purchased by in-house cafeterias; clothes and personal articles purchased by military or armed police units for their officials and soldiers; and other equipment and articles for non-production purposes.

(II) Sales of stable food, cooked dishes, beverages, tobaccos and other articles by catering units.

(III) Sales of books, newspapers, magazines, audio-visual products and post products by publishing, post and telecommunications departments to urban and rural households and to enterprises, institutions, military and armed police units.

(IV) Sales of food, beverages, tobaccos, clothing, hats, footwear, articles for daily use, medicines, medical and health articles, work of art, handicrafts, toys, funeral articles and other articles by other service industries.

□ Purchase, Sales and Stock of Commodities by Wholesale and Retail Trades

Refer to the total volume of commodities purchased, total volume of sales and exports, and the stock of commodities by wholesale and retail enterprises (establishments) of different status of registration from domestic and overseas markets. This indicator reflects the relationship among purchase, sales and stock of commodities in the circulation of goods and reveals the existing problems.

□ Total Sales of Commodities

Refer to value of commodities sold by the establishments to other establishments and individuals (including direct export to abroad). This indicator is used to show the total value of sales of commodities at domestic markets and export. The sales include: (I) commodities sold to urban and rural residents and social groups for their consumption; (II) commodities sold to establishments in industry, agriculture, construction, transportation, post and telecommunications, wholesale and retail trades, hotels and catering services, and public utility for their production and operation; (III) commodities sold to wholesale and retail establishments for re-selling, with or without further processing; and; (IV) commodities for direct export to abroad. Excluded are selling of waste packaging materials used by the establishments (units) themselves, commodities transferred without buying or selling procedures, commission income from brokerage in transactions for which settlement is directly handled by buyers and sellers, rejected commodities in the purchase, loss in commodities, etc.

□ Business Revenue of Hotels and Catering Services

Refers to revenue received from providing services or selling commodities by corporate enterprises and establishments engaged in hotels and catering services, including income from hotels, from catering services, from selling of commodities and from other services. Income from hotels refers to income of corporate enterprises and establishments engaged in hotels and catering services by providing lodging services. Income from catering services refers to income of corporate enterprises and establishments engaged in hotels and catering services by providing catering services, including selling of cooked or prepared foods such as staple food, cooked dishes or cold dishes. Income from selling of commodities refers to income of corporate enterprises and establishments engaged in hotels and catering services by selling commodities (including value-added tax) that accompany the services they provide. Income from other activities refers to income received other than income from hotels, catering services or selling of commodities, such as income from providing recreation, fitness or business services.

□ Chain Enterprises (also called chain stores or chain corporations)

Refer to a form of joint economic entities under which scattered enterprises or establishments engaged in providing homogeneous commodities or services, with the central leadership of core enterprise or headquarters and guided by common policies, conduct centralized purchase and distributed selling of commodities, in order to gain better efficiency through standardized operation. Consisting of a number of branch stores, the chain stores have in general the following features; (Ⅰ) homogeneous commodities; (Ⅱ) unique name of stores; (Ⅲ) centralized purchase and delivery which is separated from distributed selling operation (most commodities are delivered from the headquarters except some items which, for logistics, quality or freshness considerations, might be delivered by suppliers directly).

The modes of chain operation include Regular Chain and Franchise Operation.

Regular Chain: refers to chain that are invested or controlled by the headquarters. They operate under direct and unified management from the headquarters. Adopting a direct management approach, the headquarters gives orders and controls all retail stores, which follow completely the directives from the headquarters. Large monopolized commercial companies develop and expand their business through purchasing, merging, direct investment and controlling of shares.

Franchise Operation includes Franchise Chain and Voluntary Chain.

Franchise Chain: Through contracts, chain stores (or their owners) obtain licenses from the headquarters (franchisee) to use designated trade marks, names, operation know-how, and to sell commodities developed by the headquarters. Under this arrangement, each store in the chain is an independent legal entity and operates under the guidance from the headquarters.

Voluntary Chain: Under this arrangement, all stores operate together under the guidance of the headquarters, while maintaining their status of independent legal entities with full ownership of their assets. They use the same store name and sign contracts with the headquarters concerning purchase, sale, and promotion. They will operate under the contracts. They are free to engage in other activities which are not bounded in the contract. They are free to join in or leave the chain.

□ Wholesale Enterprises above Designated Size

Refers to the wholesale enterprises with the annual revenue from the major business of 20 million yuan and above.

□ Retail Enterprises above Designated Size

Refers to the retail enterprises with the annual revenue from the major business of 5 million yuan and above.

□ Hotels above Designated Size

Refers to the hotels with the annual revenue from the major business of 2 million yuan and above.

□ Catering Enterprises above Designated Size

Refers to the catering enterprises with the annual revenue from the major business of 2 million yuan and above.

第16章

对外经济贸易和旅游业

FOREIGN ECONOMIC RELATIONS,TRADE AND TOURISM

简要说明 BRIEF INTRODUCTION

本章内容包括全市进出口、利用外资、对外承包工程和劳务合作、旅游情况，以及利用内资方面的资料。进出口、利用外资、国外友好城市交流和旅游资料由市统计局贸易外经处分别根据重庆海关、市对外贸易经济委员会、市政府外事办公室和市旅游局的有关资料加工整理，利用内资数据由市统计局贸易外经处提供。

The data in this chapter include the statistics on imports & exports, utilization of foreign capital, contracted projects and labor cooperation with foreign countries (territories) and tourism as well as the utilization of domestic capital. The data of imports & exports, utilization of foreign capital, communications with foreign twin cities and tourism are provided by Chongqing Customs, Chongqing Foreign Trade and Economic Relations Commission, Foreign Affairs Office of Chongqing Municipal Government and Chongqing Tourism Administration, and sorted and compiled by Division of Trade and External Economic Relations Statistics, Chongqing Municipal Bureau of Statistics. The data of utilization of domestic capital are provided by Division of Trade and External Economic Relations Statistics of Municipal Bureau of Statistics.

表16.1 进出口总值（1987－2011年）
TOTAL VALUE OF IMPORTS AND EXPORTS (1987-2011)

单位：万美元 (USD 10 000)

年 份 Year	进出口总值 Total Imports and Exports	其 中 of which		进出口差额 Balance of Imports and Exports
		进 口 Imports	出 口 Exports	
1987	29681	12235	17446	5211
1988	41078	18907	22171	3264
1989	60299	31247	29052	-2195
1990	68095	35366	32729	-2637
1991	61950	22701	39249	16548
1992	74244	33377	40867	7490
1993	85470	44310	41160	-3150
1994	123957	52430	71527	19097
1995	141859	57126	84733	27607
1996	158543	99178	59365	-39813
1997	167843	89828	78015	-11813
1998	103386	51975	51411	-564
1999	121044	72005	49039	-22966
2000	178547	79025	99522	20497
2001	183384	73136	110248	37112
2002	179401	70282	109119	38837
2003	259488	100979	158509	57530
2004	385735	176616	209119	32503
2005	429283	177229	252054	74825
2006	547013	211821	335192	123371
2007	744546	293774	450772	156998
2008	952121	379939	572182	192243
2009	770859	342851	428008	85157
2010	1242634	493759	748875	255116
2011	2921786	937973	1983813	1045840

表16.2 利用外资基本情况（1985－2011年）
BASIC STATISTICS ON UTILIZATION OF FOREIGN CAPITAL (1985-2011)

单位：万美元 (USD 10 000)

年 份 Year	新签利用外资协议（合同）数(个) Number of Newly Signed Agreements (Contracts) of Foreign Capital Utilization (unit)	其 中 of which #外商直接投资 Foreign Direct Investment	协议合同金额 Value of Agreements and Contracts	其 中 of which #外商直接投资 Foreign Direct Investment	实际利用外资额 Foreign Capital Actually Utilized	其 中 of which #外商直接投资 Foreign Direct Investment
1985	28		3991		2499	427
1986	21	6	2957	1528	3596	790
1987	31	10	3320	774	4509	1924
1988	72	18	54862	1913	13153	2069
1989	39	15	3887	7141	22479	756
1990	81	55	19133	6245	14489	332
1991	110	80	12074	4252	16143	977
1992	516	443	59665	37919	29745	10247
1993	795	681	106629	72892	41970	25915
1994	453	364	65266	47932	65644	44953
1995	341	280	112473	74567	61554	37926
1996	233	160	35873	24232	44151	21878
1997	289	229	77109	46017	98208	38466
1998	263	222	75099	47577	55163	43107
1999	199	169	70115	50688	32699	23893
2000	237	190	86888	35716	34532	24436
2001	191	172	71884	44261	42442	25649
2002	169	148	64824	50215	45034	28089
2003	218	187	71397	55301	56654	31112
2004	281	258	66621	66315	40752	40508
2005	266	208	81877	80213	52127	51575
2006	252	223	112960	111558	70217	69595
2007	263	240	407369	406799	108912	108534
2008	197	135	283124	279513	273735	272913
2009	220	161	379861	371427	404383	401643
2010	261	232	628902	625891	636956	634397
2011	361	326	1361151	1352112	1057862	1052948

注：1) 2004年及以后年份均不包括对外借款。
2) 2010年及2011年“外商直接投资”的数据口径为“外商投资”。

Note:a) Foreign loans have been excluded since 2004.
b) The data of "Foreign Direct Investment" in 2010 and 2011 are "Foreign Investment".

表16.3 国际旅游人数和外汇收入（1983－2011年）
NUMBER OF INTERNATIONAL TOURISTS AND FOREIGN EXCHANGE EARNINGS (1983-2011)

年 份 Year	接待旅游人数（人次） Number of Tourists (person-time)	其 中 of which		旅游外汇收入（万美元） Foreign Exchange Earnings from Tourism (USD 10 000)	平均每人逗留天数（天） Average Staying Period Per Capita (day)
		#外国人 Foreigners	#港澳台同胞 Compatriots from Hong Kong, Macao and Taiwan		
1983	23032	18706	3997	26	1.3
1984	28094	21110	6505	259	1.7
1985	49508	40460	8370	527	2.1
1986	55152	44290	8904	860	1.7
1987	60894	52177	8253	1063	1.5
1988	64181	45193	18711	1281	1.5
1989	41248	21454	19595	1027	1.6
1990	69609	19913	49570	1823	1.3
1991	81745	29625	51950	2354	1.6
1992	141165	52949	88050	3997	1.3
1993	135596	59140	76025	4819	1.4
1994	138593	93408	44180	5432	1.5
1995	142892	93625	48942	6333	2.0
1996	161761	108163	53238	7090	2.3
1997	259414	154919	103720	10548	2.7
1998	163738	116288	47211	8837	3.2
1999	184936	133629	51173	9726	3.2
2000	266081	192863	73218	13837	3.2
2001	313254	219214	94040	16341	3.1
2002	461484	310934	150550	21802	2.7
2003	234521	181744	52777	11323	2.8
2004	434423	338892	95531	20308	2.7
2005	523872	418076	105796	26436	3.0
2006	603239	488249	114990	30872	3.2
2007	761676	622427	139249	38231	3.2
2008	871907	742792	129115	44977	3.0
2009	1048125	847967	200158	53721	3.0
2010	1370231	1039598	330633	70320	3.4
2011	1864016	1326135	537881	96806	3.9

表16.4 对外承包工程和劳务合作（1985－2011年）

CONTRACTED PROJECTS AND LABOR COOPERATION WITH FOREIGN COUNTRIES AND TERRITORIES (1985-2011)

单位：万美元 (USD 10 000)

年 份 Year	签订合同数（个） Number of Contracts (unit)	合同金额 Value of Contracts	实际完成营业额 Value of Turnover Fulfilled
1985	9	2109	572
1986	18	1571	337
1987	15	1540	572
1988	13	2640	2683
1989	27	2605	2574
1990	14	2971	2189
1991	16	4329	2436
1992	19	3765	2896
1993	13	9440	2704
1994	45	4106	4132
1995	33	4032	3757
1996	35	6654	3160
1997	22	2607	2725
1998	24	1969	3203
1999	235	4591	3842
2000	231	9232	5806
2001	232	11590	6700
2002	117	12200	7959
2003	94	13450	8810
2004	81	14805	10078
2005	70	18498	12138
2006	72	21447	16050
2007	67	30714	20585
2008	55	86398	30673
2009	80	104463	36885
2010	48	81560	45074
2011	93	67494	44517

表16.5 按商品类别分的进出口总值（2010－2011年）
TOTAL IMPORTS AND EXPORTS BY COMMODITY CATEGORY (2010-2011)

单位：万美元 (USD 10 000)

商品类别	Categories of Commodities	进口 Imports		出口 Exports	
		2010	2011	2010	2011
总　值	**Total Value**	**493759**	**937973**	**748875**	**1983813**
#初级产品	Primary Products	112139	139688	19756	25435
工业制成品	Mamufactured Products	381620	798285	729119	1958378
按进出口商品类章分	By Category of Imported and Exported Goods				
活动物、动物产品	Live Animals and Animal Products	152	637	9233	10631
植物产品	Vegetable Products	22294	37936	2023	3450
动植物油脂及分解产品、精制食用油脂，动植物蜡	Animal or Vegetable Fats and Oils and Their Cleavage Products, Prepared Edible Fats, Animal or Vegetable Waxes	1232	2419	168	124
食品、饮料、酒及醋；烟草及烟草代用品的制品	Prepared Foodstuffs; Beverages, Spirits and Vinegar; Tobacco and Manufactured Tobacco Substitutes	1333	1031	3788	6299
矿产品	Mineral Products	55250	68219	1473	1263
化学工业及其相关工业的产品	Products of the Chemical or Industries Allied	48755	64780	70820	89012
塑料及其制品、橡胶及其制品	Plastics and Articles Thereof Rubber and Articles Thereof	23561	30299	15637	80014
生皮、皮革、毛皮及制品；鞍具及挽具；旅行用品、手提包及类似品；动物肠线（蚕胶丝除外）制品	Raw Hides and Skins, Leather, Fur Skins and Articles Thereof; Saddlery and Harness; Travel Goods, Handbags and Similar Containers; Articles of Animal Gut (Other Than Silk-Worm Gut)	483	784	16184	69398
木及木制品；木炭；软木及软木制品；稻草、秸杆、针茅或其他编结材料制品；蓝筐及柳条编结品	Wood and Articles of Wood; Wood Charcoal; Cork and Articles of Cork; Manufactures of Straw, of Esparto or of Other Plaiting Materials; Basket Ware and Wickerwork	352	296	413	565
木浆及其他纤维状纤维素浆；回收（废碎）纸或纸板；纸、纸板及其制品	Pulp of Wood or of Other Fibrous Cellulosic Material; Waste and Scrap of Paper or Paperboard; Paper and Paperboard and Articles Thereof	7146	11328	3109	26741

表16.5 续表 continued

单位：万美元 (USD 10 000)

商品类别	Categories of Commodities	进口 Imports		出口 Exports	
		2010	2011	2010	2011
纺织原料及纺织制品	Textiles and Textile Articles	3930	5574	45520	130807
鞋、帽、伞、杖、鞭及其零件；已加工的羽毛及其制品；人造花；人发制品	Footwear, Headgear, Umbrellas, Sun Umbrellas, Walking-Sticks, Seat-Sticks, Whips, Riding-Crops and Parts Thereof; Prepared Feathers and Articles Made Therewith; Artificial Flowers; Articles of Human Hair	42	171	7750	37890
石料、石膏、水泥、石棉、云母及类似材料的制品；陶瓷产品；玻璃及其制品	Articles of Stone, Plaster, Cement, Asbestos, Mica or Similar Materials; Ceramic Products; Glass and Glassware	1306	1495	35621	94201
天然或养殖珍珠、宝石或半宝石、贵金属、包贵金属	Natural or Cultured Pearls, Precious or Semi-Precious Stones, Precious Metals, Metals Clad With Precious Metal	278	469	1026	493
贱金属及其制品	Base Metals and Articles of Base Metal	44262	42938	51441	160890
机器、机械器具、电气设备及其零件；录音机及放声机、电视图象、声音的录制和重放设备及其零件、附件	Machinery and Mechanical Appliances; Electrical Equipment; Parts Thereof; Sound Recorders and Reproducers, Television Image and Sound Recorders and Reproducers; and Parts and Accessories of Such Articles	163148	506189	234861	825822
车辆、航空器、船舶及运输设备	Vehicles, Aircraft, Vessels and Associated Transport Equipment	77265	88597	226173	312697
光学、照相、电影、计量、检验、医疗或外科用仪器及设备、精密仪器及设备；钟表；乐器；上述物品的零件、附件	Optical, Photographic, Cinematographic, Measuring, Checking, Precision, Medical or Surgical Instruments and Apparatus; Clocks And Watches; Musical Instruments; Parts and Accessories Thereof	41897	73361	12330	31827
武器、弹药及其零件、附件	Arms and Ammunition; Parts and Accessories Thereof			1	17
杂项制品	Miscellaneous Manufactured Articles	1072	1449	11040	100730
艺术品、收藏品及古玩	Works of Art, Collectors' Pieces and Antiques	1	1	216	934
特殊交易品及未分类商品	Commodities and Transactions not Classified According to Kind			48	8

表16.6 按贸易方式分的进出口总值（2010－2011年）

TOTAL VALUE OF IMPORTS AND EXPORTS BY CUSTOMS REGIME (2010-2011)

单位：万美元 (USD 10 000)

指　标	Item	进出口总值 Total Imports and Exports		其　中 of which 进　口 Imports		出　口 Exports	
		2010	2011	2010	2011	2010	2011
总　计	**Total**	**1242634**	**2921786**	**493759**	**937973**	**748875**	**1983813**
一般贸易	Ordinary Trade	1017609	1478799	431408	555297	586201	923502
国家间国际组织无偿援助和赠送的物资	Donations by Foreign Countries and International Associations	197	311			197	311
其他境外捐赠物资	Other Donations from Abroad	37		37			
加工贸易	Processing Trade	158656	691231	38574	74491	120082	616740
补偿贸易	Compensation Trade						
来料加工装配贸易	Processing and Assembling Trade	2833	11017	268	8453	2565	2564
进料加工贸易	Feeding Processing Trade	155823	680214	38306	66038	117517	614176
加工贸易进口设备	Equipment Importation for Processing Trade	57	54	57	54		
寄售代销贸易	Consignment Trade						
边境小额贸易	Petty Trade in Border Areas	3				3	
对外承包工程出口货物	Goods Exportation for Contracted Projects with Foreign Countries	151	814			151	814
租赁贸易	Leasing Trade	23	10010		10010	23	
外商投资企业作为投资进口的设备物品	Imported Equipment and Materials as Investment of Foreign-Funded Enterprises	4320	9355	4320	9355		
出料加工贸易	Outward Processing Trade						
易货贸易	Barter Trade						
免税外汇商品	Tax-Free Commodities on Foreign Exchange						
保税监管所进出境货物	Inbound and Outbound Goods in Bonded Warehouses	5568	2411	4311	2390	1257	21
海关特殊监管区域物流货物	Transit Goods in Specialized Bonded Warehouses	31777	286962	14242	270167	17535	16795
海关特殊监管区域进口设备	Imported Equipment in Specialized Bonded Warehouses	153	15057	153	15057		
其　他	Others	24083	426782	657	1152	23426	425630

表16.7 按国别（地区）分的进出口总值（2010－2011年）

IMPORTS AND EXPORTS BY COUNTRY OR REGION (2010-2011)

单位：万美元 (USD 10 000)

国别（地区）	Country(Region)	进出口总额 Total Imports and Exports		其中 of which 进口 Imports		出口 Exports	
		2010	2011	2010	2011	2010	2011
进出口贸易总值	**Total**	**1242634**	**2921786**	**493759**	**937973**	**748875**	**1983813**
亚　洲	**Asia**	**552273**	**1236660**	**250167**	**561876**	**302106**	**674784**
#阿富汗	Afghanistan	159	233			159	233
巴　林	Bahrain	149	577			149	577
孟加拉国	Bangladesh	2743	6509	120	299	2623	6211
文　莱	Brunei	140	690			140	690
缅　甸	Myanmar	23122	31964			23122	31964
柬埔寨	Cambodia	1937	16485	2		1934	16485
塞浦路斯	Cyprus	79	333			79	333
香　港	Hong Kong	23530	26418	332	755	23198	25662
印　度	India	33552	79418	4471	4945	29081	74473
印度尼西亚	Indonesia	21396	40460	8380	10076	13016	30384
伊　朗	Iran	22178	76491	1771	9749	20407	66742
伊拉克	Iraq	2895	12193			2895	12193
以色列	Israel	2298	11269	664	568	1633	10701
日　本	Japan	164033	193295	126511	149540	37522	43756
约　旦	Jordan	650	9447			650	9447
科威特	Kuwait	1849	2307	467		1382	2307
老　挝	Laos	3590	3695			3590	3695
黎巴嫩	Lebanon	602	4042			602	4042
澳　门	Macao	189	791			189	791
马来西亚	Malaysia	27152	175469	17544	137256	9608	38213
蒙　古	Mongolia	1172	2074			1172	2074
阿　曼	Oman	4896	2031	4803	1457	93	574
巴基斯坦	Pakistan	17965	32425	13	39	17952	32386
菲律宾	Philippines	13187	44040	1837	15842	11349	28199
卡塔尔	Qatar	1461	1610	512	254	949	1357
沙特阿拉伯	Saudi Arabia	6503	23237	2691	1693	3812	21543
新加坡	Singapore	10822	42593	5120	8169	5701	34424
韩　国	South Korea	52270	82133	33416	59951	18854	22182
斯里兰卡	Sri Lanka	2134	4537		15	2134	4522
叙利亚	Syria	3510	6246			3510	6246
泰　国	Thailand	22076	56026	9836	28291	12240	27734
土耳其	Turkey	9917	23914	1596	1661	8321	22253
阿拉伯联合酋长国	UAE	11073	31542	23	64	11051	31478
也门共和国	Yemen	1145	5363			1145	5363
越　南	Vietnam	22499	47330	1245	14371	21253	32959
中华人民共和国	China	19254	56656	19254	56656		
台　湾	Taiwan	17102	77219	9020	59207	8082	18013
非洲	**Africa**	**62841**	**186553**	**1354**	**1480**	**61487**	**185073**
#阿尔及利亚	Algeria	7449	20117			7449	20117
安哥拉	Angola	3055	9492			3055	9492
贝　宁	Benin	425	3152	62		363	3152
博茨瓦纳	Botswana	70	536			70	536
喀麦隆	Cameroun	482	2756	3	9	480	2747
佛得角	Cape Verde	11	527			11	527
刚　果	Congo	58	1318			58	1318
吉布提	Djibouti	213	2566			213	2566
埃　及	Egypt	4072	20155	163	158	3909	19997
赤道几内亚	Equatorial Guinea	54	740			54	740
埃塞俄比亚	Ethiopia	935	1136		3	935	1133

表16.7 续表1 continued1

单位：万美元 (USD 10 000)

国别（地区）	Country(Region)	进出口总额 Total Imports and Exports		其中 of which 进口 Imports		出口 Exports	
		2010	2011	2010	2011	2010	2011
加　蓬	Gabon	168	953	125		42	953
冈比亚	Gambia	36	304			36	304
加　纳	Ghana	2062	8989	2	4	2060	8985
几内亚	Guinea	751	1838			751	1838
科特迪瓦(象牙海岸)	Cote d'ivoire	372	1556			372	1556
肯尼亚	Kenya	3184	10991	23	4	3161	10987
利比利亚	Liberia	443	1091			443	1091
利比亚	Libya	594	1528	39		556	1528
马达加斯加	Madagascar	343	1784	1	3	342	1781
毛里塔尼亚	Mauritania	84	1579		1	84	1578
毛里求斯	Mauritius	239	1254		1	239	1253
摩洛哥	Morocco	2320	5821	27	259	2293	5563
莫桑比克	Mozambique	2125	4641			2125	4640
纳米比亚	Namibia	79	1314			79	1314
尼日利亚	Nigeria	13046	22747	85	831	12961	21915
留尼汪	Reunion	28	451			28	451
塞内加尔	Senegal	354	2790			354	2790
塞拉利昂	Sierra Leone	69	248			69	248
索马里	Somalia	115	624			115	624
南非(阿扎尼亚)	South Africa	7032	21213	811	185	6221	21028
苏　丹	Sudan	1172	5563			1172	5563
坦桑尼亚	Tanzania	2486	6248			2486	6247
多　哥	Togo	5645	11169			5645	11169
突尼斯	Tunisia	1161	2991	13	22	1148	2969
乌干达	Uganda	268	1304			268	1304
布基纳法索	Burkina Faso	545	219			545	219
扎伊尔	Zaire	445	2037		1	445	2036
津巴布韦	Zimbabwe	606	1888			606	1888
欧洲	**Europe**	**266469**	**693594**	**108121**	**203815**	**158348**	**489779**
#比利时	Belgium	11205	22457	779	1227	10426	21230
丹　麦	Denmark	2120	6866	1108	2739	1012	4127
英　国	UK	17829	39970	8599	11566	9230	28404
德　国	Germany	77529	152793	46277	77766	31252	75027
法　国	France	16019	117174	5558	23876	10461	93298
爱尔兰	Ireland	873	1097	415	101	458	996
意大利	Italy	19605	37247	4932	10432	14673	26816
荷　兰	Holland	43396	118907	13525	14518	29871	104389
希　腊	Greece	2478	4930	134	35	2345	4895
葡萄牙	Portugal	1230	4861	83	171	1146	4690
西班牙	Spain	15510	44702	9652	22347	5858	22355
阿尔巴尼亚	Albania	298	1638	38		260	1638
奥地利	Austria	3044	8567	1227	6392	1818	2175
保加利亚	Bulgaria	480	2019	145	44	336	1975
芬　兰	Finland	2593	15242	807	5430	1787	9811
匈牙利	Hungary	1897	3849	943	955	953	2894
马耳他	Malta	3360	2866	2	77	3358	2790
挪　威	Norway	3022	2015	1328	1054	1694	961
波　兰	Poland	6556	9658	910	1319	5647	8339
罗马尼亚	Romania	1278	5435	519	146	759	5289
瑞　典	Sweden	7726	8225	5077	3503	2649	4721
瑞　士	Switzerland	3486	10000	2522	8429	964	1571

表16.7 续表2 continued2

单位：万美元 (USD 10 000)

国别（地区）	Country(Region)	进出口总值 Total Imports and Exports		其中 of which 进口 Imports		出口 Exports	
		2010	2011	2010	2011	2010	2011
爱沙尼亚	Estonia	129	271	30	27	99	244
拉脱维亚	Latvia	278	604	9	9	269	596
立陶宛	Lithuania	261	1116		1	261	1115
格鲁吉亚	Georgia	72	1696			72	1696
阿塞拜疆	Azerbaijan	158	941			158	941
俄罗斯	Russia	15956	37274	1324	2696	14632	34578
乌克兰	Ukraine	3235	10555	253	3	2982	10552
斯洛文尼亚共和国	Slovenia	724	3478	50	196	674	3282
克罗地亚共和国	Croatia	879	2754	3	1	876	2753
捷克共和国	Czech	1719	3998	891	758	827	3240
斯洛伐克共和国	Slovakia	632	8070	596	7872	37	198
塞尔维亚	Serbia	283	1471	101	7	182	1463
黑　山	Montenegro	164	347	111		53	347
拉丁美洲	**Latin America**	**139074**	**293677**	**31379**	**48931**	**107695**	**244746**
#阿根廷	Argentina	28115	43946	5634	3707	22481	40238
伯利兹	Belize	57	240			57	240
玻利维亚	Bolivia	262	641		135	262	506
巴　西	Brazil	35506	78015	18825	36098	16681	41918
智　利	Chile	7558	30699	823	5455	6735	25245
哥伦比亚	Columbia	5507	14930	181	21	5325	14909
哥斯达黎加	Costa Rica	2666	2506	2340	1417	327	1089
古　巴	Cuba	99	308			99	308
多米尼加共和国	Dominica	1926	2817	80	36	1846	2781
厄瓜多尔	Ecuador	3651	5880	32		3618	5880
危地马拉	Guatemala	1706	3702	47	4	1659	3697
圭亚那	Guyana	263	1383	3		259	1383
海　地	Haiti	639	698			639	698
洪都拉斯	Honduras	664	1659	26		638	1659
牙买加	Jamaica	214	1064	130	67	84	997
墨西哥	Mexico	19642	49564	3112	1931	16530	47634
尼加拉瓜	Nicaragua	505	796	13	3	493	793
巴拿马	Panama	4487	11783	14		4473	11783
巴拉圭	Paraguay	7282	7454			7282	7454
秘　鲁	Peru	7401	13810	35	55	7366	13755
波多黎各	Porto Rico	80	229	10		69	229
萨尔瓦多	El Salvador	254	1187	38		216	1187
苏里南	Suriname	156	892			156	892
特立尼达和多巴哥	Trinidad and Tobago	89	600	5		85	600
乌拉圭	Uruguay	8240	10304			8240	10303
委内瑞拉	Venezuela	2032	7746	32		2001	7746
北美洲	**North America**	**184945**	**444085**	**73141**	**85021**	**111804**	**359064**
#加拿大	Canada	13076	38487	6112	6246	6964	32241
美　国	USA	171868	405594	67029	78775	104839	326819
大洋洲	**Oceania**	**37031**	**67211**	**29597**	**36844**	**7435**	**30367**
#澳大利亚	Australia	35598	54905	29529	36701	6069	18204
斐　济	Fiji	25	397			25	397
新西兰	New Zealand	1020	3747	68	143	953	3604
巴布亚新几内亚	Papua New Guinea	249	2121			249	2121
马绍尔群岛共和国	Marshall Islands	2	5186			2	5186

表16.8 出口主要商品数量和金额（2010－2011年）
MAIN EXPORT COMMODITIES IN VOLUME AND VALUE (2010-2011)

单位：万美元 (USD 10 000)

品 名	Name	数 量 Volume		金 额 Value	
		2010	2011	2010	2011
肉及杂碎（吨）	Meat and Sweetbread (ton)	11768	8485	5574	5027
#猪肉（吨）	Pork (ton)	8224	5056	2305	1788
粮食（吨）	Cereals (ton)	574	137	146	41
蔬菜（吨）	Vegetables (ton)	17999	18948	1945	2543
茶叶（吨）	Tea (ton)	6210	4221	548	366
猪肉罐头（吨）	Dried Capsicum (ton)	3980	4530	734	984
蘑菇罐头（吨）	Canned Mushroom (ton)	1365	1073	201	182
肠衣（吨）	Casings (ton)	2859	3096	3015	3050
填充用羽毛；羽绒（吨）	Feathers and Down for Stuffing (ton)	610	902	1907	3578
药材（吨）	Medical Materials (ton)	118	65	380	1826
烤烟（吨）	Tobacco (ton)		1751		639
肥料（吨）	Fertilizer (ton)	100813	106223	3492	3869
印刷品（吨）	Presswork (ton)	469	4907	200	2503
生丝（吨）	Raw Silk (ton)	366	246	1448	1195
粘土及其他耐火矿物（吨）	Clay and Other Fire-resisting Minerals (ton)	38929	19411	877	406
稀土及其制品（吨）	Rare Earth and Products (ton)	52	41	164	266
碳酸钠(纯碱)（吨）	Sodium Carbonate (ton)	96915	107294	1771	2769
合成有机染料（吨）	Synthetic Organic Dyestuffs (ton)	286	918	196	529
医药品（吨）	Medical and Pharmaceutical Products (ton)	3665	5825	13584	12846
农 药（吨）	Pesticide (ton)	2062	3095	1009	1315
新的充气橡胶轮胎（吨）	Rubber Tyres (ton)	7356	9669	1961	3041
纸及纸板(未切成形的)（吨）	Paper and Paperboard(Unchopped in shape)(ton)	416	7176	170	4485
纺织纱线、织物及制品	Yarn, Textile and Products			37904	64143
#亚麻及苎麻机织物（万米）	Flax and Ramie Textile (10 000meters)	1585	1149	6811	5420
塑料编织袋(周转袋除外)（万条）	PP Bags (10,000 pcs)	256	3520	68	1237

单位：万美元 (USD 10 000)

品　名	Name	数　量 Volume		金　额 Value	
		2010	2011	2010	2011
花岗岩石材及制品（吨）	Granite and Products (ton)	128	1352	199	1852
平板玻璃（吨）	Sheet Glass	37	555	6	120
玻璃制品（吨）	Glass Products (ton)	19977	98452	3832	35424
家用陶瓷器皿（吨）	Porcelain and Pottery Ware for Household Use (ton)	4187	2366	1076	1532
铁合金（吨）	Ferro-Alloys (ton)	8575	6624	1058	881
钢材（吨）	Rolled Steel (ton)	15742	27826	1848	5594
#钢铁板材（吨）	Sheet Iron and Steel (ton)	8286	11308	799	1557
未锻造的铜及铜材（吨）	Unwrought Copper and Rolled Copper (ton)	300	880	266	697
未锻造的铝及铝材（吨）	Unwrought Aluminum and Rolled Aluminum (ton)	76280	84492	20499	25088
#铝材（吨）	Rolled Aluminum (ton)	67993	67516	18768	21120
未锻造的锰（吨）	Unwrought Manganese (ton)	16644	7881	4845	2886
钢铁或铜制标准紧固件（吨）	Iron or Copper Nails, Bolts, etc. (ton)	1879	10659	663	3675
不锈钢厨具、餐具等家用器具（吨）	Household Utensils like Stainless Steel Cookers and Tableware (ton)	1606	2469	547	943
手用或机用工具（吨）	Tools for Manual or Mechanical Use (ton)	8640	42744	3117	15090
电扇（百台）	Electric Fan (100 sets)	744	1353	203	266
空气调节器（百台）	Air Conditioner (100 sets)	287	147	376	235
纺织机械及零件	Textile Machinery			420	810
金属加工机床（台）	Machine Tools (set)	337116	230739	877	790
电子计算器(包括袖珍数据记录机)（千台）	Electronic Calculator (including mini data recorder) (1,000 sets)	687	11489	142	1177
自动数据处理设备及其部件（千台）	Automatic Data Processing Machines and Components (1,000 sets)	2313	21035	52539	527835
#便携式电脑（千台）	Notebook Computer (1,000 sets)	972	15741	44231	514506
液晶显示器（千台）	LCD (1,000 sets)	783	1063	8119	10850
自动数据处理设备的零件（吨）	Parts for Auto Data Processing Equipment (ton)	34	302	333	1772
液晶显示板（万个）	LCD Panel (10,000 pcs)	11	4	40	188
轴承（万套）	Bearing (10,000 sets)	385	575	296	701

表16.8 续表 continued

单位：万美元 (USD 10 000)

品　名	Name	数　量 Volume		金　额 Value	
		2010	2011	2010	2011
电动机及发电机（万台）	Electric Motors and Generators (10 000 sets)	256	539	1914	2721
变压器（万个）	Transformer (10 000 units)	9444	9186	3528	5466
静止式变流器（万个）	Static Converters (10 000 units)	219	1058	915	1992
原电池（万个）	Primary Cells and Batteries (10 000 units)	12394	13733	728	748
蓄电池（万个）	Battery (10,000 pcs)	13	38	140	653
电话机（万台）	Telephone (10,000 sets)	5	12	512	837
#手持或车载无线电话机（万台）	Mobile Phone or Car Phone (10,000 sets)	5	6	503	686
扬声器（万个）	Speaker (10,000 pcs)	128	470	32	117
录、放像机（百台）	Video Recorder and Player (100 sets)	16	3241	26	1269
#DVD播放机（百台）	DVD Player (100 sets)	1	2621	1	1183
收音设备(包括收录音机及散件)（百台）	Radio Sets (including Sound Recording Apparatus) (100 sets)	4445	78556	309	1706
录放音、像机及唱机的零附件	Components and Accessories of Sound and Video Recorder and Player			1194	663
电视、收音机及电讯设备零附件（吨）	Parts of TV sets, Radio Sets and Telecommunication Equipment (ton)	130	2310	238	1164
印刷电路（万块）	Printed Circuit Board (10,000 pcs)	94	105	186	128
通断保护电路装置及零件	Electrical Apparatus for Switching or Protecting Electrical Circuits			1016	2027
节能灯（万只）	Compact Fluorescent Lamp (10,000 pcs)	20	36	24	105
二极管及类似半导体器件（百万个）	Diode and Semi Conductors (1 million pcs)	708	1078	829	1361
集成电路（百万个）	IC (1 million pcs)	28	26	1377	5604
#处理器及控制器（万个）	Processor and Controller (10,000 pcs)	7	389	937	5008
电线和电缆（吨）	Insulated Wire or Cable (ton)	3036	2228	1453	1434
集装箱（个）	Container (unit)	2	8309		3534
汽车(包括整套散件)（辆）	Motor Vehicles (including parts) (unit)	56258	97934	30882	52477
#小轿车（辆）	Car (unit)	21744	46557	12917	29007
货车（辆）	Truck (unit)	28643	43182	11775	17812
汽车零件	Parts of Motor Vehicles			15666	23196

单位：万美元 (USD 10 000)

品　名	Name	数　量 Volume		金　额 Value	
		2010	2011	2010	2011
摩托车（辆）	Motorcycles (unit)	3657351	4553976	141208	190358
摩托车及自行车的零件	Parts of Motorcycles and Bicycles			18318	25225
船舶（艘）	Ships (unit)	99	12490	12844	10584
眼镜及其零件	Glasses and Parts			573	4546
医疗仪器及器械	Medical Instruments and Appliances			1073	1784
手表（万只）	Watch (10,000 pcs)	214	1976	640	2171
日用钟（万只）	Clocks (10 000 sets)	281	3265	661	6998
家具及其零件	Furniture			4137	25511
床垫、寝具及类似品	Mattress and Bed Linens			217	2995
灯具、照明装置及类似品	Lights, Illumination Devices and Similar Products			1246	6080
箱包及类似容器	Suitcases, Bags and Similar Containers			16008	68247
体育用品及设备	Sports Appliances and Equipment			1180	10939
服装及衣着附件	Garments and Accessories			24699	95059
#织物制服装	Textile Garments			19704	50090
鞋类	Footwear			5453	8190
#鞋（吨）	Shoes (ton)	4439	5033	5239	7140
塑料制品（吨）	Plastic Articles (ton)	9269	104787	5650	49856
玩具	Toys			652	1054
游戏机（万台）	Video Game Consoles (10,000 sets)	34	339	300	1845
圣诞用品（吨）	Articles for Christmas（ton）	798	20085	344	12069
足球、篮球、排球（万个）	Football, Basketball and Volleyball (10,000 pcs)	64	732	84	1301
艺术品、收藏品及古董	Artworks, Collections and Antiques			216	934
伞（吨）	Umbrella (ton)	863	10892	284	3983
机电产品	Mechanical and Electrical Products			500241	1319384
高新技术产品	High and New-tech Products			79483	589420

表16.9 进口主要商品数量和金额（2010－2011年）

MAIN IMPORT COMMODITIES IN VOLUME AND VALUE (2010-2011)

单位：万美元 (USD 10 000)

品 名	Name	数 量 Volume		金 额 Value	
		2010	2011	2010	2011
大 豆（吨）	Soybean (ton)	477554	659956	22237	37349
食用植物油（吨）	Edible Vegetable Oil (ton)	12079	20403	1111	2348
酒 类（升）	Liquor (liter)	317450	694024	105	378
饲料用鱼粉（吨）	Fish Meal as Feedstuff (ton)	4113	1180	517	124
天然橡胶(包括胶乳)（吨）	Natural Rubber (including Latex) (ton)	2680	2016	876	1008
合成橡胶(包括胶乳)（吨）	Synthetic Rubber (including Latex) (ton)	9620	4495	3078	1976
锯 材（立方米）	Sawn Timber (cubic meter)	12856	9766	253	235
纸 浆（吨）	Paper Pulp (ton)	3968	6484	388	586
棉 花（吨）	Cotton (ton)	11082	9414	2660	3389
铁矿砂及其精矿（万吨）	Iron Ore (10 000 tons)	274	319	35531	53852
铬矿砂及其精矿（吨）	Chrome Ore and Its Concentrate (ton)	30975	7427	916	230
氧化铝（吨）	Alumina (ton)	5	43	17	213
成品油（吨）	Petroleum Products Refined (ton)	568	533	262	263
二甲苯（吨）	Xylene (ton)	324091	308673	34556	48468
医药品（吨）	Pharmaceutical Products (ton)	33	93	1775	2658
#抗菌素(制剂除外)（吨）	Bacteriophage (excluding preparation agent) (ton)	12	16	1325	1948
钛白粉（吨）	Titanium Dioxide Powder (ton)	231	627	60	198
聚合物油漆及清漆（吨）	Polymer Paint and Varnish (ton)	728	451	215	190
初级形状的塑料（吨）	Primary-Shaped Plastics (ton)	55915	64100	9390	11479
非泡沫塑料的板、片、膜、箔（吨）	Non-Foam-Plastic Plates, Sheets, Films and Foils (ton)	1668	2234	691	1969
废 纸（吨）	Waste Paper (ton)	217350	240086	5345	6757
纸及纸板(未切成形的)（吨）	Paper and Paperboard (Unchopped in Shape) (ton)	2938	2290	1069	808
纺织纱线、织物及制品	Yarn, Textile and Products			879	1411
服装及衣着附件	Garment and Accessories			398	806
玻璃纤维及其制品（吨）	Glass Fiber and Products (ton)	99	391	116	248
废金属（吨）	Waste Metal (ton)	96571	80203	19119	15381
钢 材（吨）	Rolled Steel (ton)	92462	76896	9490	8551
#钢铁板材（吨）	Sheet Iron and Steel (ton)	89428	71832	8463	7143
钢铁制标准坚固件（吨）	Iron Nails, Bolts, etc. (ton)	6913	6841	5051	5357
未锻造的铝及铝材（吨）	Unwrought Aluminum and Rolled Aluminum (ton)	366	416	153	203
#铝材（吨）	Rolled Aluminum (ton)	339	379	144	187
钢铁或铝制结构体及其部件（吨）	Iron and Steel or Aluminum Structure and Parts (ton)	15	108	21	167
活塞式内燃机的零件（吨）	Parts of Piston Combustion Engines (ton)	10616	15079	18917	24588
液泵及液体提升机（台）	Liquid Pump and Liquid Lifter (unit)	805588	850576	9143	10569
制冷设备用压缩机（台）	Compressors for Refrigeration (unit)	21756	11098	293	152
非家用型水的过滤.净化机器（台）	Water Filter and Purification Machines Not for Home Use (unit)	60	124	151	457
饮料及液体食品灌装设备（台）	Beverage and Liquid Food Filling Equipment (set)	3	4	135	326
机械提升搬运装卸设备及零件	Mechanical Lifting, Handling, Loading and Unloading Equipment and Parts			1521	4527
建筑及采矿用机械及零件	Building and Mining Machinery and Parts			1020	1655
食品、饮料工业用加工机械及零件	Food and Beverage Processing Machinery and Parts			126	186

表16.9 续表 continued

单位：万美元 (USD 10 000)

品 名	Name	数 量 Volume		金 额 Value	
		2010	2011	2010	2011
制造纸及纸制品用机械及零件	Paper and Paper Products Manufacture Machinery and Parts			652	15302
印刷、装订机械及零件	Printing and Binding Machinery and Parts			903	2332
纺织机械及零件	Textile Machinery and Parts			822	873
金属加工机床（台）	Machine Tools (set)	358	532	10783	17347
#数控机床（台）	CNC Machine Tools (set)	104	125	4033	9587
金属轧机及零件	Rolling Mill and Parts			233	370
橡胶或塑料加工机械及零件	Rubber or Plastic Processing Machinery and Parts			1808	4999
型模及金属铸造用型箱	Dies and Boxes for Metal Casting			786	1567
阀 门（万套）	Valves (10 000 sets)	286	262	3988	3703
自动数据处理设备及其部件（千台）	Automatic Data Processing Machines and Components (1 000 sets)	2546	23502	6409	58302
#存储部件（千台）	Memory Unit (1 000 sets)	2370	18821	5844	56094
自动数据处理设备的零件（吨）	Parts for Auto Data Processing Equipment (ton)	66	344	9322	25785
制造单晶柱或晶圆用的机器及装置（台）	Crystal Column or Wafer Manufacturing Machines and Devices (set)	37	103	1865	3495
制造半导体或电路用的机器及装置（台）	Machines and Devices for the Manufacture of Semiconductor Devices and IC (set)	150	35	1328	206
电动机及发电机（万台）	Electric Motors and Generators (10 000 sets)	508	383	1613	2170
发电机组及旋转式变流机（台）	Generating Units and Rotary Converters (set)	166	52	195	145
变压、整流、电感器及零件	Transformers, Rectifiers, Inductors and Parts			828	7536
蓄电池（万个）	Battery (10 000 pcs)		4209	1	7405
无线电导航雷达及遥控设备（台）	Radio Navigation Radars and Remote Control Equipment (set)	357269	214563	668	533
摄像机、数字照相机及摄录一体机（百台）	Video Camera and Digital Camera (100 sets)		38578	54	1260
收音设备(包括收录音机及散件)（百台）	Radio Sets (including Sound Recording Apparatus) (100 sets)	165	154	343	306
电视、收音机及电讯设备的零附件（吨）	Parts of TV sets, Radio Sets and Telecommunication Equipment (ton)	30	20	159	303
电容器（吨）	Capacitors (ton)	18	178	488	4629
电阻器（吨）	Resistor (ton)	11	10	94	221
印刷电路（万块）	Printed Circuit (10 000 units)	3398	7249	452	1800
通断保护电路装置及零件	Electrical Apparatus for Switching or Protecting Electrical Circuits			5268	8513
二极管及类似半导体器件（百万个）	Diode and Semi Conductors (1 million pcs)	239	1500	696	4404
集成电路（百万个）	IC (1 million pcs)	61	631	23075	187521
电线和电缆（吨）	Insulated Wire or Cable (ton)	447	839	856	1624
汽车(包括整套散件)（辆）	Motor Vehicles (including parts) (unit)	10414	1320	15231	3577
#四轮驱动轻型越野车（辆）	4×4 SUV (unit)	571	612	2217	2336
汽车零件	Parts of Motor Vehicles			64280	69234
飞机（架）	Plane (unit)		3		15283
液晶显示板（万个）	LCD Panel (10 000 units)	16	282	135	9374
医疗仪器及器械	Medical Instruments and Appliances			7492	12227
计量检测分析自控仪器及器具	Metering, Testing, Analyzing and Auto Controlling Instruments and Appliances			31542	47818
印刷品（吨）	Printed Matters (ton)	26	75	28	2523
塑料制品（吨）	Plastic Articles (ton)	1545	2404	2366	2701
机电产品	Mechanical and Electrical Products			294535	685016
高新技术产品	High and New-tech Products			96636	394184

表16.10 利用外资情况（2010－2011年）
UTILIZATION OF FOREIGN CAPITAL (2010-2011)

单位：万美元 (USD 10 000)

指　标	Item	2010	2011
新签利用外资协议（合同）数(个)	**Number of Newly Signed Agreements (Contracts) of Foreign Capital Utilization (unit)**	**261**	**361**
外商投资	Foreign Investment	232	326
外商其他投资	Other Foreign Investment	29	35
协议（合同）额	**Value of Agreements (Contracts)**	**628902**	**1361151**
外商投资	Foreign Investment	625891	1352112
外商其他投资	Other Foreign Investment	3011	9039
实际利用外资额	**Foreign Capital Actually Utilized**	**636956**	**1057862**
外商投资	Foreign Investment	634397	1052948
外商其他投资	Other Foreign Investment	2559	4914

表16.11 对外承包工程、劳务合作和设计咨询（2010－2011年）
CONTRACTED PROJECTS, LABOR SERVICES AND DESIGN & CONSULTATION WITH FOREIGN COUNTRIES AND TERRITORIES (2010-2011)

指　标	Item	2010	2011
签订合同数（个）	**Number of Contracts (unit)**	**48**	**93**
对外承包工程	Contracted Projects	29	36
对外劳务合作	Labor Services	14	44
设计咨询	Design and Consultation	5	13
合同金额（万美元）	**Value of Contracts (USD 10 000)**	**81560**	**67494**
对外承包工程	Contracted Projects	80504	65265
对外劳务合作	Labor Services	700	697
设计咨询	Design and Consultation	356	1532
实际完成营业额（万美元）	**Value of Turnover Fulfilled (USD 10 000)**	**45074**	**44517**
对外承包工程	Contracted Projects	38951	42934
对外劳务合作	Labor Services	6016	779
设计咨询	Design and Consultation	107	804
劳务输出（人）	**Labor Exported (person)**	**12092**	**10032**

表16.12 外商直接投资项目（企业）数和投资额（2010－2011年）

NUMBER AND VALUE OF FOREIGN DIRECT INVESTMENT PROJECTS (ENTERPRISES) (2010-2011)

指　标	Item	签定项目（合同）数（个） Number of Projects (Contracts) Signed (unit)		
		2010	2011	至当年底累计 Year-end Accumulation
总　计	**Total**	**232**	**326**	**5273**
按投资方式分	**By Investment Mode**			
合资经营	Joint Venture	77	95	2585
合作经营	Cooperative Operation	5	3	290
独资经营	Solely Foreign-Funded	146	225	2384
股份制	Share Holding	2	1	10
合作开发	Cooperative Operation	1		1
其　他	Others	1	2	3
按行业分	**By Sector**			
第一产业	Primary Industry	11	12	139
第二产业	Secondary Industry	107	139	3149
工　业	Industry	105	136	2924
建筑业	Construction	2	3	225
第三产业	Tertiary Industry	114	175	1985
交通运输、仓储及邮电通讯业	Transport, Storage, Post and Communication	9	7	103
信息传输、计算机服务和软件业	Information Transmission, Computer Services and Softwares	9	12	62
批发和零售业	Wholesale and Retail Trades	25	36	151
住宿和餐饮业	Hotels and Catering Services	4	14	233
金融业	Financial Intermediation	2	3	10
房地产业	Real Estate	13	13	615
租赁和商务服务业	Leasing and Business Services	42	72	699
科学研究、技术服务和地质勘测业	Scientific Research, Technical Service and Geologic Prospecting		4	23
水利、环境和公共设施管理业	Management of Water Conservancy, Environment and Public Facilities	4	4	23
居民服务和其他服务业	Services to Households and Other Services	4	8	26
教　育	Education	1	1	22
文化、体育与娱乐业	Culture, Sports and Entertainment	1	1	12
其　他	Others			6
按主要国别（地区）分	**By Country (Region)**			
澳　门	Macao	2		49
台　湾	Taiwan	22	43	846
日　本	Japan	12	4	240
美　国	USA	10	9	517
加拿大	Canada	4	6	114
香　港	Hong Kong	108	139	2338
新西兰	New Zealand			17
新加坡	Singapore	14	20	196
马来西亚	Malaysia	1	5	62
澳大利亚	Australia	5	2	68
法　国	France	4	4	37
英　国	UK	2	4	67
瑞　典	Sweden	1	1	10
韩　国	South Korea	4	6	98
印度尼西亚	Indonesia		1	15
泰　国	Thailand	1	1	49
比利时	Belgium			4
瑞　士	Switzerland			6

注：1）本表当年底累计数据除实际利用外资累计数按行业分组和按主要国别分组为1998年开始的累计数外，其余均为1979年开始的累计数。
2）2010年、2011年数据口径为“外商投资”。

单位：万美元 (USD 10 000)

外商协议投资额 Contracted Foreign Investment			实际利用外资额 Foreign Capital Actually Utilized		
2010	2011	至当年底累计 Year-end Accumulation	2010	2011	至当年底累计 Year-end Accumulation
625891	**1352112**	**3911604**	**634397**	**1052948**	**2960260**
159904	377374	1303472	184758	240454	995432
6865	15441	212597	4241	5565	97183
267962	870022	2079770	254325	698264	1537000
37026	4841	73497	36939	32330	96323
6334	11679	18013	6334	3580	9914
147800	72755	224255	147800	72755	224408
571	16957	62439	827	2938	9090
225344	511201	1578510	190635	356204	987646
218357	505332	1515645	189349	352543	974984
6987	5869	62865	1286	3661	12662
399976	823954	2270655	442935	693806	1811663
4114	40450	78367	1536	25075	36025
768	2866	7616	474	590	2430
-1708	157153	215632	8109	116004	150018
7233	7093	51933	7200	6010	31085
149676	51741	250270	156075	50421	249812
186704	337973	1221958	239887	306675	1029534
43476	150761	323216	24116	123503	219790
	2514	3663	4	522	648
5200	20746	45102	4638	8176	24326
5007	52597	63490	596	56759	60664
1	55	6292		71	6116
-495	5	2351	300		550
		765			665
367	186	8329	199	269	2033
410	-3907	78721	990	17229	46854
7689	5155	97414	8615	6207	72154
7118	57736	155832	7817	30509	80885
829	2958	14050	348	885	8636
529730	745099	2397098	544495	619328	1774274
		2449			198
9427	295093	364715	2799	194567	239352
57	508	10435	22	350	3231
3840	96	13115	3961	18	7390
3498	4142	12107	3000	4205	9828
1113	6237	33210	58	5919	23228
-61	2130	4552		1342	2858
11663	5984	30230	2150	14062	20576
	966	2017	116		191
7	37	8708			1325
69	-54	185			107
	473	1543		473	5013

Note: a) In terms of the data of "Year-end Accumulation" in the table above, except the data of "Foreign Capital Actually Utilized" by sector and by country (region) which are accumulated since 1998, all the other data are accumulated since 1979.
b) The data of 2010 and 2011 refer to "Foreign Investment".

表16.13 实际利用内资项目资金来源情况（2010－2011年）
ACTUAL UTILIZATION OF DOMESTIC CAPITAL BY SOURCE (2010-2011)

单位：万元 (10 000 yuan)

项　目	Item	2010	2011
总　计	**Total**	**26382949**	**49198400**
按资金来源分组	**By Source of Domestic Capital**		
#北　京	Beijing	5666209	10922070
天　津	Tianjin	138789	251996
河　北	Hebei	209983	320422
山　西	Shanxi	204947	448984
内蒙古	Inner Mongolia	46046	89811
辽　宁	Liaoning	282247	582240
吉　林	Jilin	28939	63897
黑龙江	Heilongjiang	231505	445240
上　海	Shanghai	2603960	3527985
江　苏	Jiangsu	1652952	3492692
浙　江	Zhejiang	3040140	4545787
安　徽	Anhui	287623	850540
福　建	Fujian	1543318	2774310
江　西	Jiangxi	124069	443697
山　东	Shandong	661351	873490
河　南	Henan	151409	536098
湖　北	Hubei	662246	1583667
湖　南	Hunan	384901	621421
广　东	Guangdong	4304826	7468188
广　西	Guangxi	29213	92359
海　南	Hainan	49016	132248
四　川	Sichuan	2888314	6506696
贵　州	Guizhou	238482	714106
云　南	Yunnan	596516	941394
西　藏	Tibet	13803	43663
陕　西	Shaanxi	196234	707591
甘　肃	Gansu	40440	6941
青　海	Qinghai	3180	28239
宁　夏	Ningxia	1083	35247
新　疆	Xinjiang	101208	147381
#东部地区	Eastern Region	20152791	34891428
中部地区	Middle Region	2075639	4993544
西部地区	Western Region	4154519	9313428

表16.14 实际利用内资项目资金行业分布情况（2010－2011年）
ACTUAL UTILIZATION OF DOMESTIC CAPITAL BY SECTOR (2010-2011)

单位：万元 (10 000 yuan)

项　目	Item	2010	2011
总　计	**Total**	**26382949**	**49198400**
按行业分	**By Sector**		
第一产业	Primary Industry	730882	1598697
第二产业	Secondary Industry	11385667	22073414
采矿业	Mining and Quarrying	774522	1300623
制造业	Manufacturing	7699978	16386211
电力、燃气及水的生产和供应业	Production and Supply of Electricity, Gas and Water	1035409	1443789
建筑业	Construction	1875758	2942791
第三产业	Tertiary Industry	14266400	25526289
交通运输、仓储及邮政业	Transport, Storage and Post	1199475	2134687
信息传输、计算机服务和软件业	Information Transmission, Computer Services and Software	84075	486021
批发与零售业	Wholesale and Retail Trades	1194332	2141518
住宿和餐饮业	Hotels and Catering Services	297677	630192
金融业	Financial Intermediation	413079	1981392
房地产业	Real Estate	9838473	14711594
租赁与商务服务业	Leasing and Business Services	291226	655347
科学研究、技术服务与地质勘查业	Scientific Research, Technical Service and Geologic Prospecting	72193	503593
水利、环境和公共设施管理业	Management of Water Conservancy, Environment and Public Facilities	331735	897576
居民服务和其他服务业	Services to Households and Other Services	80235	343976
教　育	Education	153214	315655
卫生、社会保障和社会福利业	Health, Social Security and Social Welfare	53532	190894
文化、体育与娱乐业	Culture, Sports and Entertainment	257154	533844
公共管理与社会组织	Public Administration and Social Organizations		

表16.15 1000万元以上利用内资项目合同（协议、计划）资金来源情况（2010－2011年）

UTILIZATION OF CONTRACTED (AGREED, PLANNED) DOMESTIC CAPITAL ABOVE 10 MILLION YUAN BY SOURCE (2010-2011)

单位：万元 (10 000 yuan)

项 目	Item	项目合同（协议、计划）总资金 Total Contracted (Agreed, Planned) Capital		其中 of which #外省投入 From Outside Chongqing	
		2010	2011	2010	2011
总 计	**Total**	**109302362**	**175500959**	**98649723**	**159463165**
按资金来源分	**By Source of Domestic Capital**				
#北 京	Beijing	27709031	41990425	23229127	37580448
天 津	Tianjin	751536	1540127	866861	1350586
河 北	Hebei	618989	935873	520116	870480
山 西	Shanxi	1639400	2187161	1636400	2183361
内蒙古	Inner Mongolia	72500	287400	66000	282200
辽 宁	Liaoning	1198803	1439303	1067903	1291963
吉 林	Jilin	53558	143858	48658	92212
黑龙江	Heilongjiang	307879	734048	288509	725648
上 海	Shanghai	10210779	14268003	9356161	12794062
江 苏	Jiangsu	6463645	10139957	5655089	8714794
浙 江	Zhejiang	11801888	17017921	10952344	15869659
安 徽	Anhui	890787	2375352	857087	2299952
福 建	Fujian	5080724	7570361	4868974	7094988
江 西	Jiangxi	236978	802072	236198	697342
山 东	Shandong	2422221	3583464	2014819	3168772
河 南	Henan	493329	1594289	476179	1220789
湖 北	Hubei	2327187	5255360	2317838	4585318
湖 南	Hunan	656010	1808793	801185	1929145
广 东	Guangdong	17990935	28107486	16108035	25965276
广 西	Guangxi	81800	252113	81800	252113
海 南	Hainan	110500	438619	102500	263119
四 川	Sichuan	12950664	23824925	12049832	20860768
贵 州	Guizhou	535100	1765015	801720	2036923
云 南	Yunnan	2946942	4681173	2994339	4678573
西 藏	Tibet	20866	83000	13559	42235
陕 西	Shaanxi	783356	2063003	684645	1870531
甘 肃	Gansu	627355	25000	228453	17000
青 海	Qinghai	6900	51208	17692	200508
宁 夏	Ningxia	3500	85350	3000	79350
新 疆	Xinjiang	309200	450300	304700	445050
#东部地区	Eastern Region	84359051	127031539	75253508	115187761
中部地区	Middle Region	6605128	14900933	6463909	13763013
西部地区	Western Region	18338183	33568487	16932306	30512391

表16.16 1000万元以上实际利用内资项目资金来源情况（2010－2011年）
ACTUALLY UTILIZATION OF DOMESTIC CAPITAL ABOVE 10 MILLION YUAN BY SOURCE (2010-2011)

单位：万元 (10 000 yuan)

项　目	Item	实际利用内资 Domestic Capital Actually Utilized	
		2010	2011
总　计	**Total**	**24678441**	**46274338**
按资金来源分	**By Source of Domestic Capital**		
#北　京	Beijing	5594926	10777320
天　津	Tianjin	122010	203749
河　北	Hebei	180342	256309
山　西	Shanxi	190140	406773
内蒙古	Inner Mongolia	43440	43928
辽　宁	Liaoning	271207	546953
吉　林	Jilin	26800	52354
黑龙江	Heilongjiang	205695	437705
上　海	Shanghai	2513937	3347993
江　苏	Jiangsu	1581319	3265283
浙　江	Zhejiang	2722424	4146108
安　徽	Anhui	261424	802484
福　建	Fujian	1307565	2566524
江　西	Jiangxi	102664	373567
山　东	Shandong	628486	817822
河　南	Henan	124292	469317
湖　北	Hubei	597380	1480301
湖　南	Hunan	337447	526906
广　东	Guangdong	4143656	7135490
广　西	Guangxi	25160	87620
海　南	Hainan	40740	114749
四　川	Sichuan	2562542	6013108
贵　州	Guizhou	190670	609964
云　南	Yunnan	572326	894388
西　藏	Tibet	11959	37788
陕　西	Shaanxi	185241	664903
甘　肃	Gansu	38189	2000
青　海	Qinghai	2518	20654
宁　夏	Ningxia	933	34906
新　疆	Xinjiang	93009	137372
#东部地区	Eastern Region	19106612	33178300
中部地区	Middle Region	1845842	4549407
西部地区	Western Region	3725987	8546631

表16.17 1000万元以上利用内资项目合同（协议、计划）资金行业分布及登记注册类型情况（2010－2011年）

UTILIZATION OF CONTRACTED (AGREED, PLANNED) DOMESTIC CAPITAL ABOVE 10 MILLION YUAN BY SECTOR AND BY REGISTRATION (2010-2011)

单位：万元 (10 000 yuan)

项 目	Item	项目合同（协议、计划）总资金 Total Contracted (Agreed, Planned) Capital		其中 of which #外省投入 From Outside Chongqing	
		2010	2011	2010	2011
总 计	**Total**	**109302362**	**175500959**	**98649723**	**159463165**
按行业分	**By Sector**				
第一产业	Primary Industry	2438754	5613835	2340077	5299075
第二产业	Secondary Industry	51419756	73137012	47418487	68431666
采矿业	Mining and Quarrying	2342454	4279244	2326254	4197205
制造业	Manufacturing	35465700	50041468	33907588	47509535
电力、燃气及水的生产和供应业	Production and Supply of Electricity, Gas and Water	5964906	7305870	4548054	6074368
建筑业	Construction	7646696	11510430	6636591	10650558
第三产业	Tertiary Industry	55443852	96750112	48891159	85732424
交通运输、仓储及邮政业	Transport, Storage and Post	5451012	8280843	4681567	7383242
信息传输、计算机服务和软件业	Information Transmission, Computer Services and Software	153510	4132200	148510	4126350
批发与零售业	Wholesale and Retail Trades	2495217	6496595	2435217	4765433
住宿和餐饮业	Hotels and Catering Services	1673050	2233155	1631750	2149786
金融业	Financial Intermediation	942302	2890246	487232	2424719
房地产业	Real Estate	40029717	59165706	35328914	52219717
租赁与商务服务业	Leasing and Business Services	470380	3130835	470380	3129635
科学研究、技术服务与地质勘查业	Scientific Research, Technical Service and Geologic Prospecting	136000	1524963	125900	1378963
水利、环境和公共设施管理业	Management of Water Conservancy, Environment and Public Facilities	2302500	3744998	1869900	3270098
居民服务和其他服务业	Services to Households and Other Services	264700	852929	194700	747954
教 育	Education	476700	788094	470200	777394
卫生、社会保障和社会福利业	Health, Social Security and Social Welfare	57492	203005	56492	198290
文化、体育与娱乐业	Culture, Sports and Entertainment	991272	3306543	990397	3160843
公共管理与社会组织	Public Administration and Social Organizations				
按登记注册类型分	**By Registration**				
国有企业	State-owned Enterprises	4353105	10787218	3843911	10168903
集体企业	Collective-owned Enterprises	33360	590848	33360	590348
股份合作企业	Cooperative Enterprises	89366	1295363	81309	1070663
联营企业	Joint-owned Enterprises	41418	175558	35978	168658
有限责任公司	Limited Liabilities Corporation	57500332	93512765	51713182	84140030
股份有限公司	Share-holding Ltd.	35665554	47102682	33377294	44387316
私营企业	Private Enterprises	7432829	11268161	7043898	10599266
其他企业	Other Enterprises	506300	596759	506300	594759
港、澳、台商投资企业	Enterprises Funded by Hong Kong, Macao and Taiwan	3032607	3304202	1485424	1751629
外商投资企业	Foreign-funded Enterprises	239421	193224	141267	166014
个 人	Individual	123200	6592254	123200	5745854
其 他	Others	284870	81925	264600	79725

表16.18 1000万元以上利用内资项目资金行业分布及登记注册类型情况（2010－2011年）

UTILIZATION OF DOMESTIC CAPITAL ABOVE 10 MILLION YUAN BY SECTOR AND BY REGISTRATION (2010-2011)

单位：万元 (10 000 yuan)

项 目	Item	实际利用内资 Domestic Capital Actually Utilized	
		2010	2011
总 计	**Total**	**24678441**	**46274338**
按行业分	**By Sector**		
第一产业	Primary Industry	541444	1366535
第二产业	Secondary Industry	10836278	21001071
采矿业	Mining and Quarrying	715551	1193124
制造业	Manufacturing	7348903	15665777
电力、燃气及水的生产和供应业	Production and Supply of Electricity, Gas and Water	1003787	1409908
建筑业	Construction	1768037	2732262
第三产业	Tertiary Industry	13300719	23906732
交通运输、仓储及邮政业	Transport, Storage and Post	1164542	2004815
信息传输、计算机服务和软件业	Information Transmission, Computer Services and Software	53010	444739
批发与零售业	Wholesale and Retail Trades	660325	1532113
住宿和餐饮业	Hotels and Catering Services	217440	452868
金融业	Financial Intermediation	409927	1949067
房地产业	Real Estate	9711724	14489747
租赁与商务服务业	Leasing and Business Services	226938	508776
科学研究、技术服务与地质勘查业	Scientific Research, Technical Service and Geologic Prospecting	65171	473413
水利、环境和公共设施管理业	Management of Water Conservancy, Environment and Public Facilities	319989	806468
居民服务和其他服务业	Services to Households and Other Services	43790	282356
教 育	Education	148449	285505
卫生、社会保障和社会福利业	Health, Social Security and Social Welfare	47422	156428
文化、体育与娱乐业	Culture, Sports and Entertainment	231992	520437
公共管理与社会组织	Public Administration and Social Organizations		
按登记注册类型分	**By Registration**		
国有企业	State-owned Enterprises	1029110	3588888
集体企业	Collective-owned Enterprises	12784	149114
股份合作企业	Cooperative Enterprises	44221	369013
联营企业	Joint-owned Enterprises	14920	88430
有限责任公司	Limited Liabilities Corporation	13304921	23566505
股份有限公司	Share-holding Ltd.	7202892	11717762
私营企业	Private Enterprises	2294543	3356435
其他企业	Other Enterprises	34303	295629
港、澳、台商投资企业	Enterprises Funded by Hong Kong, Macao and Taiwan	479752	497570
外商投资企业	Foreign-funded Enterprises	76103	105920
个 人	Individual	86296	2527199
其 他	Others	98596	11873

表16.19 旅游基本情况（2010－2011年）
BASIC STATISTICS ON TOURISM (2010-2011)

指　标	Item	2010	2011
国际旅游者人数（人次）	**International Tourists (person-time)**	**1370231**	**1864016**
外国人	Foreigners	1039598	1326135
#日　本	Japan	142581	151728
新加坡	Singapore	70639	88553
泰　国	Thailand	43307	39928
美　国	United States	192408	218709
加拿大	Canada	47158	63292
法　国	France	17139	87602
英　国	United Kingdom	34476	73298
德　国	Germany	102841	177102
意大利	Italy	7261	25683
澳大利亚	Australia	28213	65304
香港同胞	Compatriots from Hong Kong	175091	283794
澳门同胞	Compatriots from Macao	4565	8572
台湾同胞	Compatriots from Taiwan	150977	245515
来渝旅游者平均逗留天数（天）	Average Period Tourists Staying in Chongqing (day)	3.4	3.9
旅行社组织国内居民出境旅游人数（万人天）	**Number of Outbound Chinese Tourists Organized by Travel Agencies (10 000 person-days)**	**113.26**	**200.15**
国内旅游者人数（万人次）	**Domestic Tourists (10 000 person-times)**	**16036.57**	**22019.93**
旅游收入	**Earnings from Tourism**		
国际旅游外汇收入（万美元）	Foreign Exchange Earnings from International Tourism (USD 10 000)	70320	96806
国内旅游收入（亿元）	Earnings from Domestic Tourism (100 million yuan)	868.36	1202.76
星级饭店数（个）	**Number of Star-Rated Hotel (unit)**	**271**	**263**
年末旅行社数（个）	**Number of Travel Agencies at Year-end (unit)**	**406**	**457**
出境旅行社	International Travel Agencies	24	27
一般旅行社	Domestic Travel Agencies	382	430
年末旅行社从业人员（人）	**Number of Employees of Travel Agencies at Year-end (person)**	**7123**	**7102**
出境旅行社	International Travel Agencies	2521	3600
一般旅行社	Domestic Travel Agencies	4602	3502

表16.20 星级饭店基本情况（2010－2011年）
BASIC STATISTICS ON STAR-RATED HOTELS (2010-2011)

指　标	Item	2010	2011
星级饭店数（个）	**Number of Star-rated Hotels (unit)**	**271**	**263**
按星级分	By Star Level		
#五星级	5-star	14	19
四星级	4-star	60	56
三星级	3-star	128	123
按注册类型分	By Registration		
内　资	Domestic Funded	261	254
#国　有	State-owned	81	75
集　体	Collective-owned	17	17
私　营	Private	100	94
股份制	Share-holding	28	31
外商及港澳台投资	Foreign-funded and Funded by Hong Kong, Macao and Taiwan	10	9
按饭店客房规模分	By Capacity		
300间以上	With 300 Rooms and Above	12	14
200-299间	With 200-299 Rooms	21	20
100-199间	With 100-199 Rooms	91	88
99间以下	With Less Than 100 Rooms	147	141
星级饭店客房数（间）	**Number of Rooms in Star-rated Hotels (unit)**	**31242**	**30781**
#五星级	5-star	4713	6306
四星级	4-star	9911	8803
三星级	3-star	12264	11685
星级饭店床位数（张）	**Number of Beds in Star-rated Hotels (unit)**	**53578**	**50699**
#五星级	5-star	6989	9249
四星级	4-star	16240	14470
三星级	3-star	22236	20987

表16.21 重庆与国外友好城市交流（2010－2011年）
COMMUNICATIONS WITH FOREIGN TWIN CITIES (2010-2011)

指　标	Item	2010	2011
与国外结成友好城市累计数（个）	**Total Number of Foreign Twin Cities with Chongqing (unit)**	**23**	**26**
出访交流考查	**People Sent for Study Tour**		
批　数（批）	Number of Groups (group)	36	47
人（人次）	Number of People (person-time)	284	382
派出进修生	**People Sent Abroad for Further Studies**		
批　数（批）	Number of Groups (group)	2	4
人（人次）	Number of People (person-time)	4	47
接待来访团组	**Visitor Groups Received**		
批　数（批）	Number of Groups (group)	18	36
人（人次）	Number of People (person-time)	183	192

重/庆/统/计/年/鉴

主要统计指标解释

进出口总额

指实际进出我国国境的货物总金额。包括对外贸易实际进出口货物，来料加工装配进出口货物，国家间、联合国及国际组织无偿援助物资和赠送品，华侨、港澳台同胞和外籍华人捐赠品，租赁期满归承租人所有的租赁货物，进料加工进出口货物，边境地方贸易及边境地区小额贸易进出口货物(边民互市贸易除外)，中外合资企业、中外合作经营企业、外商独资经营企业进出口货物和公用物品，到、离岸价格在规定限额以上的进出口货样和广告品(无商业价值、无使用价值和免费提供出口的除外)，从保税仓库提取在中国境内销售的进口货物，以及其他进出口货物。该指标可以观察一个国家在对外贸易方面的总规模。我国规定出口货物按离岸价格统计，进口货物按到岸价格统计。

商品经营单位所在地进、出口额

指在所在地海关注册登记的有进出口经营权的企业实际进、出口额。

利用外资

指我国各级政府、部门、企业和其他经济组织通过对外借款、吸收外商直接投资以及用其他方式筹措的境外现汇、设备、技术等。

外商直接投资

指外国企业和经济组织或个人(包括华侨、港澳台胞以及我国在境外注册的企业)按我国有关政策、法规，用现汇、实物、技术等在我国境内开办外商独资企业、与我国境内的企业或经济组织共同举办中外合资经营企业、合作经营企业或合作开发资源的投资(包括外商投资收益的再投资)，以及经政府有关部门批准的项目投资总额内企业从境外借入的资金。

外商其他投资

指除对外借款和外商直接投资以外的各种利用外资的形式。包括企业在境内外股票市场公开发行的以外币计价的股票（目前主要是在香港证券市场发行的H股和在境内证券市场发行的B股）发行价总额，国际租赁进口设备的应付款，补偿贸易中外商提供的进口设备、技术、物料的价款，加工装配贸易中外商提供的进口设备、物料的价款。

入境游客

指来中国（大陆）观光、度假、探亲访友、就医疗养、购物、参加会议或从事经济、文化、体育、宗教活动的外国人、港澳台同胞等游客（即入境旅游人数）。统计时，入境游客按每入境一次统计。

旅游外汇收入

指入境旅游者在中国（大陆）境内旅行、游览过程中用于交通、参观展览、住宿、餐饮、购物、娱乐等全部花费。

对外承包工程

指各对外承包公司以招标议标承包方式承揽的下列业务：(1)承包国外工程建设项目；(2)承包我国对外经援项目；(3)承包我国驻外机构的工程建设项目；(4)承包我国境内利用外资进行建设的工程项目；(5)与外国承包公司合营或联合承包工程项目时我国公司分包部分；(6)对外承包兼营的房屋开发业务。对外承包工程的营业额是以货币表现的本期内完成的对外承包工程的工作量，包括以前年度签订的合同和本年度新签订的合同在报告期内完成的工作量。

对外劳务合作

指以收取工资的形式向业主或承包商提供技术和劳动服务的活动。我国对外承包公司在境外开办的合营企业，中国公司同时又提供劳务的，其劳务部分也纳入劳务合作统计。劳务合作营业额按报告期内向雇主提交的结算数(包括工资、加班费和奖金等)统计。

对对外设计咨询

指以服务成果向业主收费的技术服务项目。包括承担地形地貌测绘，地质资源勘探与普查，建设区域规划，提供设计文件、图纸、生产工艺技术资料和工程技术经济咨询，工程项目的可行性考察、研究和评

主要统计指标解释

估，进行技术指导和培训人员等；也包括承担国(境)内利用外资建设工程项目中的设计咨询项目内收取外币部分。

■ 内资

指重庆市以外中华人民共和国境内（不包括港、澳、台地区）的企、事业单位、社会团体及其他投资者，来渝以从事经济社会活动为主要目的，遵循市场机制法则，本着互利互惠的原则进行的独资、合资、参股合作等而流入的资金。它不包括中央和各级政府无偿捐赠等。

Explanatory Notes on Main Statistical Indicators

□ Total Imports and Exports at Customs

Refer to the real value of commodities imported and exported across the border of China. They include the actual imports and exports through foreign trade, imported and exported goods under the processing and assembling trades and materials, supplies and gifts as aid given gratis between governments and by the United Nations and other international organizations, and contributions donated by overseas Chinese, compatriots in Hong Kong and Macao and Chinese with foreign citizenship, leasing commodities owned by tenant at the expiration of leasing period, the imported and exported commodities processed with imported materials, commodities trading in border areas (excluding mutual exchange goods), the imported and exported commodities and articles for public use of the Sino-foreign joint ventures, cooperative enterprises and ventures with sole foreign investment. Also included is import or export of samples and advertising goods for which CIF or FOB value are beyond the permitted ceiling (excluding goods of no trading or use value and free commodities for export), imported goods sold in China from bonded warehouses and other imported or exported goods. The indicator of the total imports and exports at customs can be used to observe the total size of external trade in a country. In accordance with the stipulation of the Chinese government, imports are calculated at CIF, while exports are calculated at FOB.

□ Import Export Value by Location of China's Foreign Trade Managing Units

Refers to actual value of imports and exports carried out by corporations which have been registered by the local Customs house and are vested with right to run import export business.

□ Utilization of Foreign Capital

Refers to remittance, equipment and technology financed from abroad, by loans, foreign direct investment and other forms undertaken by the Chins governments at all levels, by various departments, enterprises and other economic units.

□ Foreign Direct Investment

Refers to the investments inside China by foreign enterprises and economic organizations or individuals (including overseas Chinese, compatriots from Hong Kong and Macao, and Chinese enterprises registered abroad), following the relevant policies and laws of China, for the establishment of ventures exclusively with foreign own investment, Sino-foreign joint ventures and cooperative enterprises or for co-operative exploration of resources with enterprises or economic organizations in China. It includes the re-investment of the foreign entrepreneurs with the profits gained from the investment and the funds that enterprises borrow from abroad in the total investment of projects which are approved by the relevant department of the government.

□ Other Foreign Investment

Refers to all forms of utilization of foreign capitals other than foreign borrowings and foreign direct investment. It includes the total value of stock shares in foreign currencies issued by enterprises at domestic or foreign stock exchanges (now mainly consisting of K shares issued at Hong Kong Security Market and B shares issued at domestic security markets), rent payable for the imported equipment through international leasing arrangement, cost of imported equipment, technology and materials provided by foreign counterparts in compensation trade and processing and assembly trade.

□ Visitor arrivals

Refer to the number of foreigners, Chinese compatriots from Hong Kong, Macao and Taiwan Chinese (mainland) who come to China (mainland) for sight-seeing, vacation, visiting relatives, medical treatment, shopping, attending conference, or to engage in economic, cultural, sports and religious activities. In compiling statistics, each time of entering China is counted as one person-time.

□ Foreign Exchange Earnings from Tourism

Refer to the total expenditures cost in the process of foreigners' tourism in the mainland of China, including traffic, visit, accommodation, table, shopping and amusement expenditures.

EXPLANATORY NOTES TO MAJOR STATISTICAL INDICATORS

□ Overseas Contracted Project

Refers to projects undertaken by Chinese contractors (project contracting companies) through bidding process. They include: (Ⅰ) overseas civil engineering construction projects financed by foreign investors; (Ⅱ) overseas projects financed by the Chinese government through its foreign aid programs; (Ⅲ) construction projects of Chinese diplomatic missions, trade offices and other institutions stationed abroad; (Ⅳ) construction projects in China financed by foreign investment; (Ⅴ) sub-contracted projects to be taken by Chinese contractors through a joint umbrella project with foreign contractor(s); (Ⅵ) housing development projects. The business income from international contracted projects is the work volume of contracted projects completed during the reference period, expressed in monetary terms, including completed work on projects signed in previous years.

□ Overseas Labour Services

Refer to the activities of providing technology and labour services to employers or contractors in the forms of receiving salaries and wages. Labour services providing by contractual joint ventures of Chinese international contracting corporations should be included in the statistics of service co-operation with foreign countries. The business income of labour service cooperation is the income in the form of wages and salaries, overtime pay, bonuses and other remuneration received from the employers during the reference period.

□ Overseas Design and Consultation Services

Refer to projects with income for technical services provided to overseas operators. It includes geographic and topographic mapping, geological resource prospecting and survey, planning of construction areas, provision of design documents, blueprints, materials on production process and techniques, as well as engineering, technical and economic consultation, and feasibility study, research and evaluation of projects. Also included under this category are the above-mentioned services of foreign-financed projects in China that are paid in foreign currencies.

□ Domestic Capital

Refers to capital inpoured by the way of sole investment, joint venture and cooperative operation from the corporations, social unions and other investors within China boundaries but outside Chongqing municipality (excluding Hong Kong, Macao, Taiwan) who consider engaging economic and social activities as their main destination in Chongqing, and follow the market system on behalf of equality. It excludes the subscription for no payment of central and local governments.

第 17 章

金 融 业

FINANCIAL STATISTICS

简要说明 BRIEF INTRODUCTION

本章资料包括全市金融机构信贷收支、证券和保险业情况，由市统计局综合处根据有关部门资料整理编辑。资料分别来源于中国人民银行重庆营业部、重庆市发展和改革委员会、重庆证监局、重庆保监局和重庆保险行业协会。

The data in this chapter include the statistics on credit funds balance of financial institutions, securities and insurance, which are sorted and compiled by Division of Comprehensive Statistics, Chongqing Municipal Bureau of Statistics. The data are provided by Chongqing Business Department of the People's Bank of China, Chongqing Development and Reform Commission, China Securities Regulatory Commission Chongqing Bureau, China Insurance Regulatory Commission Chongqing Bureau and Insurance Association of Chongqing.

表17.1 主要金融机构数（2010－2011年）
NUMBER OF MAIN FINANCIAL INSTITUTIONS (2010-2011)

单位:个 (unit)

指　标	Item	2010	2011
银行机构	**Banks**		
法人/市级分行	Corporate Entity / Branch at Municipal Level		72
#法人	Corporate Entity		29
#村镇银行	Village and Township Bank		19
#市级分行	Branches at Municipal Level		43
中资	Domestic Funded		32
外资	Foreign Funded		11
支行	Sub-branches		2013
分理处	Banking Offices		2100
储蓄所	Saving Offices		54
保险机构	**Insurance Institutions**		
保险公司法人机构	Corporate Entity of Insurance Companies	3	3
内资保险公司	Dometic-funded Insurance Companies		
省（市）级分公司	Branches at Provincial (Municipal) Level	29	33
中心支公司	Central Sub-branches	45	60
支公司	Sub-branches	310	376
营销服务部	Marketing & Service Departments	791	570
中外合资、外资保险公司	Insurance Joint-venturse with Foreign Investment and Wholly Foreign-owned Insurance Companies	5	5
外资保险公司代表处	Agencies of Foreign-funded Insurance Companies	1	1
专业保险中介机构	Professional Insurance Intermediary Institutions		
保险代理公司	Insurance Agent Companies	25	28
保险公估公司	Insurance Assessment Companies	9	9
保险经纪公司	Insurance Broker Companies	14	15
证券机构	**Security Institutions**		
内资证券公司	Dometic-funded Security Companies		
法人机构	Corporate Entity	1	1
营业部	Business Departments	96	112
服务部	Service Departments		
中外合资、外资证券公司分公司	Security Branches of Joint-ventures with Foreign Investment and Wholly Foreign-owned Security Companies		

注：1）中外合资、外资金融机构数只统计到省（市）级。
　　2）保险机构数不含中国出口信用保险公司重庆营业管理部。

Note: a) Joint-venture financial institutions with foreign investment and wholly foreign-owned financial institutions are accounted up to provincial(municipal) level only.
　　b) Chongqing Business Department of China Export & Credit Insurance Corporation is not incuded in the number of insurance institutions.

表17.2 金融机构（含外资）存贷款年末余额（1980－2011年）

YEAR-END DEPOSIT AND LOAN BALANCE OF FINANCIAL INSTITUTIONS (INCLUDING FOREIGN-FUNDED INSTITUTIONS) (1980-2011)

单位：亿元 (100 million yuan)

年 份 Year	本外币存款余额 Total Deposit Balance of RMB and Foreign Currencies	人民币存款余额 Total Deposit Balance of RMB	其 中 of which: #企业存款 Enterprise Deposits	#储蓄存款 Urban and Rural Saving Deposits	本外币贷款余额 Total Loan Balance of RMB and Foreign Currencies	人民币贷款余额 Total Loan Balance of RMB	其 中 of which: 短期贷款 Short-term Loans	中长期贷款 Medium & Long-term Loans
1980		29.15	11.32	6.22		42.19	40.96	1.23
1981		33.98	11.86	8.35		50.29	47.69	2.21
1982		38.66	12.44	10.56		55.30	51.50	3.05
1983		45.22	15.29	13.34		63.25	58.14	4.32
1984		70.86	25.40	18.39		84.53	70.42	11.76
1985		62.38	22.87	25.41		101.56	84.85	14.89
1986		84.57	27.94	34.79		131.70	110.61	18.86
1987		110.37	31.84	44.46		163.63	125.85	22.99
1988		123.47	38.22	50.50		183.32	141.01	25.90
1989		146.71	39.27	68.17		214.41	167.66	29.65
1990		198.00	48.51	92.17		268.40	205.63	38.30
1991		253.57	63.76	121.95		336.85	249.51	58.82
1992		315.70	83.75	154.45		408.64	294.63	78.75
1993		386.86	89.57	198.05		495.71	357.59	98.88
1994		518.27	143.26	285.40		596.96	409.16	136.46
1995		676.70	193.38	401.45		755.39	501.66	185.89
1996	885.91	846.43	266.42	500.71	968.71	913.93	601.10	219.05
1997	1147.92	1098.67	429.42	580.67	1224.01	1156.13	873.14	248.06
1998	1359.52	1306.04	483.80	724.54	1443.65	1358.61	978.51	299.59
1999	1638.21	1580.80	544.00	909.10	1693.64	1611.68	1093.09	398.22
2000	1982.21	1904.71	645.54	1085.36	1966.40	1881.29	1246.81	470.70
2001	2377.99	2294.05	750.81	1317.17	1969.97	1871.98	1043.84	631.26
2002	2903.42	2821.04	909.43	1595.01	2338.17	2244.72	1191.70	754.57
2003	3512.82	3438.61	1098.15	1896.56	2976.67	2774.81	1378.85	1010.69
2004	4105.09	4039.61	1230.85	2189.73	3309.13	3246.28	1362.75	1346.91
2005	4784.76	4727.72	1337.05	2545.85	3779.28	3719.52	1471.86	1810.83
2006	5587.50	5519.75	1551.98	2949.05	4443.84	4388.28	1510.73	2392.26
2007	6662.36	6576.68	1997.71	3228.15	5197.08	5131.69	1597.12	3220.70
2008	8102.00	8021.95	2377.48	3988.96	6384.03	6320.81	1617.52	4093.50
2009	11084.82	10933.00	3770.43	4908.68	8856.56	8766.06	1499.85	6563.63
2010	13613.97	13454.98	4666.88	5839.66	10999.87	10888.15	1686.11	8705.32
2011	16128.87	15832.81	8254.56	6990.25	13195.16	13001.39	2529.81	9968.14

注：2011年“企业存款”更名为“单位存款”。
Note:The index of "enterprise deposit" is replaced by "corporate deposit" in 2011.

表17.3 金融机构（含外资）本外币信贷收支表（2010—2011年）

SOURCES AND USES OF RMB AND FOREIGN CURRENCIES CREDIT FUNDS OF FINANCIAL INSTITUTIONS (INCLUDING FOREIGN-FUNDED INSTITUTIONS) (2010-2011)

单位：亿元 (100 million yuan)

项 目	Item	2010	2011
各项存款余额	Total Deposit Balance	13613.97	16128.87
企事业单位存款	Deposits of Enterprises and Public Institutions	4794.18	8522.82
活期存款	Demand Deposits	3739.11	4406.43
定期存款	Fixed Deposits	1055.07	1525.59
储蓄存款	Urban and Rural Saving Deposits	5863.07	7011.74
各项贷款余额	Total Loan Balance	10999.87	13195.16
短期贷款	Short-term Loans	1693.48	2669.83
中长期贷款	Medium & Long-term Loans	8738.47	10017.40
有价证券及投资	Securities and Investment	1070.65	972.34
有价证券	Securities		477.30
股权及其他投资	Equity and Other Investment		495.04

注：1）外币折本币所用汇率为当年最后一个交易日的中间汇率。
2）2011年“企事业单位存款”更名为“单位存款”。

Note: a) The exchange rates between foreign currencies and RMB are the middle rates on the last trading day in current year.
b) The index of "deposits of enterprises and public institutions" is replaced by "corporate deposit" in 2011.

表17.4 金融机构（含外资）人民币信贷收支表（2010－2011年）

SOURCES AND USES OF RMB CREDIT FUNDS OF FINANCIAL INSTITUTIONS (INCLUDING FOREIGN-FUNDED INSTITUTIONS)(2010-2011)

单位：亿元 (100 million yuan)

项　目	Item	2010	2011
各项存款余额	Total Deposit Balance	13454.98	15832.81
单位存款	Corporate Deposits		8254.56
#活期存款	Demand Deposits		4227.74
定期存款	Fixed Deposits		1492.73
通知存款	Call Deposits		138.74
保证金存款	Margine Deposits		932.64
个人存款	Personal Deposits		7045.99
储蓄存款	Savings Deposits		6990.25
保证金存款	Margine Deposits		5.46
结构性存款	Structured Deposits		50.28
财政性存款	Fiscal Deposits		135.11
临时性存款	Temporary Deposits		30.57
委托存款	Trusted Deposits		60.04
其他存款	Other Deposits		306.54
各项贷款余额	Total Loan Balance	10888.15	13001.39
#短期贷款	Short-term Loans	1686.11	2529.81
#个人短期消费贷款	Personal Short-term Consumer Loans	72.53	106.41
中长期贷款	Medium & Long-term Loans	8705.32	9968.14
#个人中长期消费贷款	Personal Medium & Long-term Consumer Loans	2142.69	2658.28
票据融资	Bill Financing	423.24	346.25
#贴　现	Discount	423.24	346.25
有价证券及投资	Securities and Investment	1070.06	477.21
同业往来	Inter-bank Loans	33.66	8.48
外汇占款	Purchase of Foreign Exchanges		529.42
固定资产	Fixed Assets	142.83	178.02
库存现金	Cash on Hand	86.94	100.92

表17.5 按行业分金融机构（不含外资）本外币贷款结构（2010－2011年）

LOAN COMPOSITION OF RMB AND FOREIGN CURRENCIES OF FINANCIAL INSTITUTIONS (EXCLUDING FOREIGN-FUNDED INSTITUTIONS) (BY SECTOR) (2010-2011)

单位：亿元 (100 million yuan)

项　目	Item	2010	2011
贷款总计	**Total Loans**	**10509.25**	**12765.13**
按行业分	**By Sector**		
#农、林、牧、渔业	Farming, Forestry, Animal Husbandry and Fishery	209.14	234.24
采矿业	Mining and Quarrying	69.48	160.80
制造业	Manufacturing	1323.99	1696.48
电力、燃气及水的生产和供应业	Production and Supply of Electricpower,Gas & Water	416.58	466.22
建筑业	Construction	479.47	751.59
交通运输、仓储和邮政业	Transport, Storage and Post	1180.28	1355.16
信息传输、计算机服务和软件业	Data Transmission, Computer Services and Software	25.28	25.86
批发和零售业	Wholesale and Retail Trades	370.48	602.06
住宿和餐饮业	Hotels and Catering Services	49.68	68.83
金融业	Financial Intermediation	5.55	13.01
房地产业	Real Estate	1087.51	1181.96
租赁和商务服务业	Leasing and Business Services	751.56	1006.55
科学研究、技术服务和地质勘查业	Scientific Research, Technical Services and Geological Prospecting	10.16	14.29
水利、环境和公共设施管理业	Administration of Water Conservancy, Environment and Public Utilities	1658.33	1661.82
居民服务和其他服务业	Household Services and Other Services	41.31	32.86
教育	Education	135.43	111.16
卫生、社会保障和社会福利业	Public Health, Social Security and Social Welfare	34.29	36.34
文化、体育和娱乐业	Culture, Sports and Entertainment	34.3	35.11
公共管理和社会组织	Public Administration and Social Organizations	53.56	15.29
国际组织	International Organizations		
对境外贷款	Loans Abroad	0.35	4.10
个人贷款	Individual Loans	2573.52	3291.40

注：1）委托贷款与信托贷款为金融机构的表外业务，因此，金融机构一般不对此类贷款进行细分。
　　2）2011年统计制度调整后取消“农户贷款”项目。

Note: a) Entrusted loans and trusted loans are the off-balance-sheet business of financial institutions, so those loans will not be further classified.
　　b) The index of "loans to farmers" is cancelled after the adjustment of statistic regulations in 2011.

表17.6 金融机构（含外资）房地产贷款投向表（2010－2011年）
LOANS TO REAL ESTATE FROM FINANCIAL INSTITUTIONS (INCLUDING FOREIGN-FUNDED INSTITUTIONS) (2010-2011)

单位：亿元 (100 million yuan)

项 目	Item	2010	2011
合 计	Total Loans	2981.29	3669.47
房地产开发贷款	Loans to Real Estate Development	936.00	1111.04
地产开发贷款	Loans to Land Development	316.07	277.17
#政府土地储备机构贷款	Loans to Government Land Reserve Institutions	192.53	181.46
房产开发贷款	Loans to Housing Development	619.92	833.87
住房开发贷款	Loans to Residential Housing Development	508.14	674.69
#保障性住房开发贷款	Loans to Low-income Housing Development	22.69	147.16
集资、合作建房贷款	Loans to Cooperative Housing Construction		
商业用房开发贷款	Loans to Housing for Commercial Use	80.23	138.68
其他房产开发贷款	Loans to Other Housing Development	31.55	20.50
购房贷款	Housing Purchase Loan	2045.29	2558.42
企业购房贷款	Enterprise Housing Purchase Loan	1.00	3.44
商业用房贷款	Loan for Housing for Commercial Use	0.95	1.03
住房贷款	Loan for Housing for Residential Use	0.05	2.40
个人购房贷款	Individual Housing Loan	2044.29	2554.99
个人商业用房贷款	Loan for Housing for Commercial Use	58.25	82.57
个人住房贷款	Loan for Housing for Residential Use	1986.04	2472.42
新建房贷款	Loan for Newly Built Housing	1684.29	2068.38
#抵押贷款	Mortgage Loan	1600.12	2004.52
再交易房贷款	Loan for Second-hand Housing	301.75	404.04
证券化的房地产贷款	Securitized Loan to Real Estate		
证券化个人住房贷款	Securitized Individual Housing Loan for Residential Use		
其他证券化房地产贷款	Other Securitized Loan to Real Estate		
个人购买保障性住房贷款	Individual Loan for Purchasing Low-income Housing	11.62	15.67

注：“保障性住房开发贷款”在2012年之前为“经济适用房开发贷款”。
Note: The index of "loans to low-income housing development" was formerly "loans to affordable housing development" before 2012.

表17.7 金融机构（含外资）—境内大中小型企业人民币贷款情况统计表（2010–2011年）

STATISTICS ON THE RMB LOANS TO THE DOMESTIC LARGE, MEDIUM AND SMALL ENTERPRISES FROM FINANCIAL INSTITUTIONS (INCLUDING FOREIGN-FUNDED INSTITUTIONS) (2010-2011)

单位：亿元 (100 million yuan)

项　目	Item	大型企业贷款		中型企业贷款		小型企业贷款	
		2010	2011	2010	2011	2010	2011
境内企业贷款合计	**Total Loans to Domestic Enterprises**	**3228.87**	**3527.76**	**2840.96**	**3124.64**	**1244.70**	**1994.21**
农、林、牧、渔业	Farming, Forestry, Animal Husbandry and Fishery	17.45	13.72	24.76	47.14	163.48	168.02
采矿业	Mining and Quarrying	46.20	56.39	14.23	56.86	8.93	35.36
制造业	Manufacturing	551.13	637.89	485.18	586.83	194.27	289.04
电力、燃气及水的生产和供应业	Production and Supply of Electricpower,Gas & Water	221.84	224.91	151.67	142.72	39.55	81.96
建筑业	Construction	149.50	200.61	171.57	234.26	149.50	310.01
交通运输、仓储和邮政业	Transport, Storage and Post	787.36	808.37	313.40	250.40	45.53	102.90
信息传输、计算机服务和软件业	Data Transmission, Computer Services and Software	16.43	13.98	2.94	4.75	3.13	6.44
批发和零售业	Wholesale and Retail Trades	80.73	102.51	124.32	190.36	129.64	269.78
住宿和餐饮业	Hotels and Catering Services	9.38	1.82	24.71	46.75	16.44	19.74
金融业	Financial Intermediation	2.20	4.95	0.00	0.44	2.50	6.43
房地产业	Real Estate	265.67	328.36	589.19	619.97	137.86	163.75
租赁和商务服务业	Leasing and Business Services	362.80	454.11	237.88	390.62	142.78	150.47
科学研究、技术服务和地质勘查业	Scientific Research, Technical Services and Geological Prospecting	3.30	3.78	2.07	3.47	1.78	1.85
水利、环境和公共设施管理业	Administration of Water Conservancy, Environment and Public Utilities	617.25	642.26	641.02	506.62	194.37	375.90
居民服务和其他服务业	Household Services and Other Services	13.00	8.14	14.43	8.79	4.21	4.46
教育业	Education	25.72	9.97	19.09	15.75	7.14	3.95
卫生、社会保障和社会福利业	Public Health, Social Security and Social Welfare	5.79	1.93	10.77	6.70	1.93	1.35
文化、体育和娱乐业	Culture, Sports and Entertainment	15.18	12.38	4.66	6.95	1.37	1.28
公共管理和社会组织	Public Administration and Social Organizations	37.95	1.67	9.06	5.27	0.28	1.53
国际组织	International Organizations						
境内企业贷款合计	**Total Loans to Domestic Enterprises**	**3228.87**	**3527.76**	**2840.96**	**3124.64**	**1244.70**	**1994.21**
正常类贷款	Pass Loan	3147.97	3453.07	2639.40	2945.05	1121.27	1867.15
关注类贷款	Special Mention Loan	66.05	71.27	178.83	160.79	101.13	103.41
次级类贷款	Substandard Loan	9.98	0.69	11.69	12.54	8.09	12.27
可疑类贷款	Doubtful Loan	1.69	0.97	9.09	5.07	11.29	9.03
损失类贷款	Loss Loan	3.18	1.77	1.95	1.19	2.90	2.36
境内企业贷款合计	**Total Loans to Domestic Enterprises**	**3228.87**	**3527.76**	**2840.96**	**3124.64**	**1244.70**	**1994.21**
信用贷款	Fiduciary Loan	1231.57	1156.23	492.54	447.18	109.46	330.45
保证贷款	Guaranteed Loan	597.58	606.92	675.19	781.77	312.41	500.50
抵（质）押贷款	Mortgage Loan	1399.72	1764.61	1673.22	1895.68	822.82	1163.26
境内企业贷款合计	**Total Loans to Domestic Enterprises**	**3228.87**	**3527.76**	**2840.96**	**3124.64**	**1244.70**	**1994.21**
国有控股企业	State-holding Enterprise	2618.83	2873.69	1737.98	1755.00	699.68	1089.24
集体控股企业	Collective-holding Enterprise	157.59	123.60	188.30	223.78	56.12	101.81
私人控股企业	Private-holding Enterprise	299.40	358.90	778.32	999.66	454.57	745.09
港澳台商控股企业	Hong Kong, Macao or Taiwan-holding Enterprise	48.62	70.52	91.98	102.18	18.70	28.00
外商控股企业	Foreign-holding Enterprise	104.43	101.04	44.37	44.02	15.63	30.07

注：境内企业授信户数仅在单家法人机构表中列示。
Note: The nubmer of domestic enterprise accounts is only listed in the table of single corporate entity.

表17.8 上市公司情况（1993－2011年）
STATISTICS ON LISTED COMPANIES (1993-2011)

单位:个 (unit)

年份 Year	全市总计 Total	其中 of which					
		上交所 Shanghai Stock Exchange	深交所 Shenzhen Stock Exchange	仅发A股公司 A Share Only	发A、B股公司 A&B Shares	仅发B股公司 B Share Only	发A、H股公司 A&H Shares
1993	3	1	2	3			
1994	5	2	3	5			
1995	7	3	4	6		1	
1996	11	4	7	10		1	
1997	19	8	11	17	1	1	
1998	19	8	11	17	1	1	
1999	22	9	13	20	1	1	
2000	25	11	14	23	1	1	
2001	26	12	14	24	1	1	
2002	27	13	14	25	1	1	
2003	27	13	14	25	1	1	
2004	29	14	15	27	1	1	
2005	29	14	15	27	1	1	
2006	29	14	15	27	1	1	
2007	30	15	15	27	1	1	1
2008	31	15	16	28	1	1	1
2009	31	15	16	28	1	1	1
2010	34	16	18	31	1	1	1
2011	36	16	20	33	1	1	1

注：本表不包括仅发H股的公司。
Note: Companies with H share only are not included in this tables.

表17.9 有价证券发行情况（1981－2011年）
ISSUANCE OF SECURITIES (1981-2011)

单位：亿元 (100 million yuan)

年 份 Year	企业债券发行额 Issued Value of Corporate Bonds	股票发行量（万股） Amount of Issued Shares（10 000shares）	其 中 of which A 股 A Shares	 B 股 B Shares	股票筹资额 Raised Capital	其 中 of which A 股 A Shares	 B 股 B Shares
1981							
1982							
1983							
1984							
1985							
1986	1.50						
1987	0.59						
1988	1.85						
1989	0.39						
1990	1.95						
1991	3.90						
1992	5.45						
1993	4.18	7220	7220		2.08	2.08	
1994	1.17	3000	3000		1.13	1.13	
1995		17200	5200	12000	5.30	0.52	4.78
1996	3.60	50610	15610	35000	10.41	4.56	5.85
1997	4.85	42039	42039		26.76	26.76	
1998	3.40	5000	5000		3.75	3.75	
1999	4.10	10000	10000		7.21	7.21	
2000		29600	29600		22.63	22.63	
2001		3108	3108		4.73	4.73	
2002	15.00	2000	2000		3.16	3.16	
2003		3275	3275		3.74	3.74	
2004		22285	22285		15.65	15.65	
2005	17.00						
2006	30.00	31133	31133		14.63	14.63	
2007	20.00	51929	51929		26.37	26.37	
2008	45.00	22062	22062		12.73	12.73	
2009	105.00	237708	237708		17.56	17.56	
2010	91.00	809055	809055		149.00	149.00	
2011	74.00	192243	192243		158.02	158.02	

注：股票发行量和筹资额均不含H股。
Note: The amount of issued shares and raised capital don't include H share.

表17.10 保险业务基本情况（1996－2011年）

BASIC STATISTICS ON INSURANCE BUSINESS (1996-2011)

单位：亿元 (100 million yuan)

年 份 Year	保费收入 Premium	其 中 of which 财产保险 Property Insurance	人身保险 Life Insurance	赔款及给付 Claim and Payments	其 中 of which 财产保险 Property Insurance	人身保险 Life Insurance
1996	12.82	8.05	4.77	6.48	4.44	2.04
1997	19.52	9.03	10.49	7.18	4.39	2.79
1998	22.77	9.31	13.46	10.64	6.55	4.09
1999	25.39	10.04	15.35	8.91	4.96	3.95
2000	27.71	10.72	16.99	8.27	5.28	2.99
2001	33.72	11.32	22.40	11.25	5.91	5.34
2002	46.17	13.31	32.86	14.20	7.57	6.63
2003	57.93	15.24	42.69	14.53	8.56	5.97
2004	66.51	17.45	49.06	16.25	9.43	6.82
2005	73.10	19.46	53.64	17.59	10.54	7.05
2006	93.24	24.17	69.07	20.51	12.08	8.43
2007	124.68	33.10	91.58	35.25	18.44	16.81
2008	200.55	37.76	162.80	45.64	22.59	23.05
2009	244.70	47.05	197.65	56.63	28.88	27.75
2010	321.08	65.96	255.12	62.10	32.05	30.05
2011	311.81	81.63	230.19	73.98	39.31	34.66

表17.11 按险种分的保险业务指标（2010－2011年）

STATISTICS ON INSURANCE BUSINESS BY CLASSIFICATION (2010-2011)

单位：万元 (10 000 yuan)

项 目	Item	保 费 Premium 2010	2011	赔款及给付 Claim and Payment 2010	2011
合 计	**Total**	**3210769**	**3118127**	**621013**	**739784**
财产保险	**Property Insurance**	**659596**	**816272**	**320496**	**393137**
企业财产保险	Enterprise Property Insurance	33060	38242	14740	11370
家庭财产保险	Family Property Insurance	972	1381	312	250
机动车辆保险	Motor Vehicle Insurance	539316	663951	268410	338912
工程保险	Engineering Insurance	18610	12777	4380	3838
责任保险	Liability Insurance	25406	35279	12418	13106
信用保险	Export Credit Insurance	5699	7950	1325	3629
保证保险	Guarantee Insurance	5953	13512	960	781
船舶保险	Ship Insurance	10382	11753	6490	5960
货物运输保险	Freight Transport Insurance	13045	15695	5810	7848
特殊风险保险	Special Risks Insurance	420	260	74	57
农业保险	Agriculture Insurance	6712	15434	5578	7384
其他保险	Other Insurances	21	38	1	2
人身保险	**Life Insurance**	**2551173**	**2301855**	**300518**	**346647**
人寿保险	Life Insurance	2357666	2061873	219349	262223
健康保险	Health Insurance	116345	136979	55707	53722
意外伤害保险	Personal Accident Insurance	77163	103004	25462	30701

重/庆/统/计/年/鉴

主要统计指标解释

■ 信贷资金

指金融机构以信用方式积聚和分配的货币资金。金融机构信贷资金的来源有各项存款、金融债券发行、应付及暂收款、对国际金融机构负债、流通中货币、各项准备、所有者权益和其他项目等；信贷资金的运用有各项贷款、有价证券及投资、应收及预付款、委托投资、金银占款、外汇占款、库存现金、财政借款及在国际金融机构中的资产等。

■ 存款

指企业、机关、团体或居民根据资金必须收回的原则，把货币资金存入银行或其他信贷机构保管并取得一定利息的一种信用活动形式。根据存款对象或性质的不同可划分为企业存款、财政存款、机关团体存款、基本建设存款、储蓄存款、农村存款、委托存款、其他存款等科目。它是银行信贷资金的主要来源。

■ 贷款

指银行或其他信贷机构根据资金必须归还的原则，按一定利率，为企业、个人等提供资金的一种信用活动形式。我国银行贷款分为短期贷款、委托及信托类贷款、其他类贷款等。

■ 金融机构往来

指各金融机构之间的资金往来，包括同业存放款和同业拆借款。

■ 准备金

指各金融机构在中央银行的存款及缴存中央银行的法定准备金。

■ 证券

由债券购买者承购的或因销售产品而拥有的，可在金融市场上交易并代表一定债权的书面证明。包括政府债券、金融债券、企业债券、商业票据、股票、支付固定收入但不提供法人企业残余价值分享权的优先股等。

■ 股票

指股票购买者及直接投资者对其投资企业净资产所拥有的权益。股票是股份公司签发的证明股东投资并按其所持股份享有权益和承担义务的权益性证券。

■ 保险公司

在中国境内的、经过保险监督部门批准设立，并依法登记注册的各类商业保险公司。

■ 保费

指投保人为取得保险人在约定范围内所承担赔偿责任而支付给保险人的费用。

■ 赔款

指保险人根据保险合同的规定，向被保险人支付的赔偿保险责任损失的金额。

■ 给付

包括死伤医疗给付和满期给付。死伤医疗给付是指保险人根据人寿保险及长期健康保险合同的规定，因被保险人在保险期内发生保险责任范围内的保险事故支付给被保险人（或受益人）的金额。满期给付是指被保险人生存期满，保险人按人寿保险合同规定支付给被保险人的满期保险金额。

Explanatory Notes on Main Statistical Indicators

□ Credit Funds

Refer to the funds issued as loans by banking institutions. The sources of credit funds of the banking institutions included deposits, issue of financial bonds, account-payable and temporary gathering, liabilities to international financial institutions, currency in circulation, various reserves, owners rights and interests and other items. The credit funds can be used in forms of loans, securities and investment, account receivable and advance payment, entrusted investment, gold, foreign exchange, cash on hand, government debt and assets in the international financial institutions.

□ Deposit

Is a form of credit by which enterprises, institutions, organizations or households can put money into banks and other credit institutions for safekeeping and interest earning under the principle of free withdrawal. According to different depositors, deposits are divided into enterprise deposits, treasury deposits, deposits of government agencies and organizations, capital construction deposits, savings deposits, rural saving deposits, entrusted deposits and other deposits. Deposits are major sources of the credit funds of banks.

□ Loan

Is a form of credit by which banks and other credit institutions provide funds at certain interest rate to enterprises and individuals in the light of the principle of unconditional repayment. Loans from Chinese banks include short-term loan, medium-term and long-term loans, entrusted loans, and other loans.

□ Transactions between Financial Institutions

Refer to flow of capital between financial institutions, including inter-bank deposits and loans.

□ Reserve Funds

Refer to savings of financial institutions in the central bank and designated reserves to the central bank.

□ Securities

Refer to written certificates representing creditors' rights, purchased by bond holders or owned by selling products, which can be transacted at the financial markets. They include government bonds, financial bonds, corporation bonds, commercial drafts, stocks, preferential stocks that provide fixed income without the right to share the residual value of corporations, etc.

□ Stocks

Refer to the rights by stockholders and direct investors on the net assets of corporations they invested in. Stocks refer to negotiable securities on creditor's rights, issued by stock companies certifying the investment by stockholders and their rights and duties depending on their stocks.

□ Insurance Companies

Refer to commercial insurance companies of various forms registered by law and established in China with the approval of insurance regulatory agencies.

□ Premium

Is the fee paid by the insurant based on a proportion of the benefit he or she may get from the insurance plus the insurance value. It includes the income from the deposit of property insurance and personal insurance.

□ Settled Claim

Is the compensation paid by the insurer to the insurant in accordance with the insurance contract.

□ Payment

Includes payment for death, injury or medical treatment and mature payment. Payment for death, injury or medical treatment refers to the money paid to the insurant (of the beneficiary) in accordance with the life of health insurance contract when the insurant encounters accidents within the insured period covered in the contract. Mature payment refers to the mature payment to the insurant in accordance with the life insurance contract at the end of the insured period for the loss which has been checked and found to be in the range of liability of the insurance after an accident has happened to the insured property or to a person who has insured his life. It is further divided into settled and unsettled claim.

第18章

教育、科技和文化业

EDUCATION,SCIECE,TECHNOLOGY AND CULTURE

简要说明
BRIEF INTRODUCTION

本章资料主要包括全市教育事业、科学技术活动和文化事业的基本情况，由市统计局社会科技统计处根据调查资料和有关部门资料整理编辑。

教育部分包括各类教育的学校、教师和学生情况，由市教育委员会提供；专利资料由市知识产权局提供；商标申请注册来源于市工商行政管理局；产品质量监督抽查由市质量技术监督局提供；文化部分主要包括图书馆、文物、群众艺术文化、广播电视、新闻出版等情况，资料主要来自市文化广播电视局、市新闻出版局。

The data in this chapter include the basic statistics on education, scientific & technological activities and culture undertakings. All the data are compiled by Division of Social and Technology Statistics, Chongqing Municipal Bureau of Statistics on the basis of the data from survey and related departments.

The statistics of education cover the data of schools, teachers and students of various kinds, which were provided by Chongqing Education Commission. The data of patent are provided by Chongqing Intellectual Property Office. The data of trademark application and registration are provided by Chongqing Administration for Industry and Commerce. The data of sampling supervision & check on quality of products are provided by Chongqing Bureau of Quality and Technical Supervision. The data of culture mainly include public libraries, cultural relics, mass arts & culture, radio and television, and press and publication, which are provided by Chongqing Administration of Culture, Radio and Television and Chongqing Press and Publication Bureau.

表18.1 主要年份各级各类学校数
NUMBER OF SCHOOLS BY LEVEL AND TYPE IN MAJOR YEARS

单位：所 (unit)

年 份 Year	普通高等学校 Regular Institutions of Higher Education	普通中学 Regular Secondary Schools	小 学 Primary Schools	特殊教育学校 Special Schools	幼儿园 Kindergartens
1952	7	128	12920		
1957	9	249	16201		
1962	10	402	14148		
1965	11	696	31503		
1970	11	1700	21253		
1975	8	1366	25465		
1978	13	2948	25002		
1980	16	1989	25120		
1985	18	1788	22793	7	5800
1986	19	1739	22486	19	5230
1987	19	1759	22094	18	5542
1988	20	1753	21629	20	5009
1989	20	1751	20972	23	4726
1990	20	1753	20248	24	5232
1991	20	1762	19829	29	4486
1992	20	1766	19496	32	4814
1993	20	1746	18849	30	4061
1994	20	1725	18175	31	4094
1995	22	1638	19637	30	6046
1996	22	1651	16779	36	5538
1997	22	1606	16261	37	5741
1998	22	1555	15737	37	5412
1999	23	1552	15223	42	6007
2000	22	1568	14730	42	6659
2001	29	1607	13076	44	3726
2002	29	1574	12031	38	3477
2003	33	1564	10966	41	3093
2004	34	1511	10409	43	3408
2005	35	1414	9558	43	3287
2006	38	1373	8754	44	3376
2007	38	1361	7990	43	3351
2008	47	1325	7575	41	3582
2009	51	1304	7096	36	3700
2010	53	1273	5544	36	4105
2011	59	1259	5248	36	4114

注：1）2001年起幼儿园资料按教育部对幼儿园数的认定标准统计，与以往年数不可比（下表同）。
2）2008年学校数含“独立学院”数。

Note: a) The data of kindergartens have been in accordance with the definition by Ministry of Education since 2001, not comparable with that of previous years (the same below).
b) Number of schools in 2008 includes the number of "non-university tertiary".

表18.2 主要年份各级各类学校在校学生数
NUMBER OF STUDENTS ENROLLMENT BY LEVEL AND TYPE IN MAJOR YEARS

单位：人 (person)

年份 Year	普通高等学校 Regular Institutions of Higher Education	普通中学 Regular Secondary Schools	小学 Primary Schools	特殊教育学校 Special Schools	幼儿园 Kindergartens
1952	6437	61345	1524145		
1957	15211	181423	1539805		
1962	21173	163628	1640036		
1965	17408	266504	1967997		
1970	4235	651232	2130534		
1975	10194	963304	3415196		
1978	16357	1631581	4035934		
1980	25349	1323181	4316902		
1985	39871	1102702	3857331	418	296336
1986	44454	1107545	3610433	543	306591
1987	47644	1122462	3279059	571	409209
1988	49981	1124510	2858642	669	389185
1989	48449	1111706	2581889	831	351175
1990	49331	1080755	2393235	803	413552
1991	49964	978204	2314986	1179	505799
1992	54121	868431	2361261	1966	549271
1993	63795	790396	2500362	1850	445940
1994	71118	876008	2595400	1415	534177
1995	73398	977079	2638555	1783	577162
1996	79929	1012654	2737051	1832	588854
1997	83764	1002915	2854307	1706	590464
1998	86913	1083691	2884385	2325	613298
1999	101601	1282599	2802741	9007	625666
2000	132512	1477861	2761308	21160	640804
2001	170006	1540317	2777859	18383	599282
2002	211221	1574357	2797557	17199	587645
2003	255266	1663728	2779441	14483	572538
2004	303913	1707489	2718999	15973	544759
2005	357926	1735166	2609754	12463	536266
2006	405118	1794129	2523824	12151	530842
2007	445800	1834364	2384527	11773	535457
2008	485013	1907856	2243916	12172	574187
2009	523279	1920158	2081367	13189	632170
2010	565868	1908158	1999407	14618	708711
2011	613026	1838917	1954818	16978	842846

注：本章普通高等学校数据均含研究生（以下各表同）。
Note: The data of regular institutions of higher education in this chapter include the postgraduates (the same applies to the following tables).

表18.3 主要年份各级各类学校专任教师数

NUMBER OF FULL-TIME TEACHERS BY LEVEL AND TYPE IN MAJOR YEARS

单位：人 (person)

年 份 Year	普通高等学校 Regular Institutions of Higher Education	普通中学 Regular Secondary Schools	小 学 Primary Schools	特殊教育学校 Special Schools	幼儿园 Kindergartens
1952	839	3385	41698		
1957	2193	7940	52530		
1962	3297		55213		
1965	3336		78503		
1970	3177	24970	73695		
1975	3574	42893			
1978	3914				
1980	5025	60953	125304		
1985	8061	58886	119119	74	11937
1986	8236	55071	113724	101	12054
1987	8622	57044	112163	113	15090
1988	8823	60450	111596	145	15873
1989	8726	61938	109691	186	15898
1990	8677	64056	110580	186	17443
1991	8596	64934	111305	277	19313
1992	8696	65030	111667	321	19244
1993	8777	63555	113834	326	18388
1994	9186	65316	116603	360	19729
1995	9409	67498	117497	353	19948
1996	9400	69503	117711	383	20111
1997	9432	70661	119881	411	20665
1998	9498	72333	121062	400	20962
1999	9987	76158	120229	469	21088
2000	10449	81766	119014	569	22598
2001	12125	85030	118623	474	12067
2002	13954	87427	117543	510	11666
2003	16013	89560	115212	543	12141
2004	18214	92051	114007	541	12351
2005	20184	93997	114326	556	13220
2006	23717	95782	113724	584	13615
2007	26089	99807	119831	652	14270
2008	28398	103111	119161	670	15507
2009	29883	106544	117460	699	16579
2010	31070	109303	116057	715	19966
2011	33110	110951	115343	763	22807

表18.4 研究生基本情况（1996－2011年）
BASIC STATISTICS ON POSTGRADUATES (1996-2011)

单位：人 (person)

年 份 Year	在校学生数 Total Enrollment	招生数 New Enrollment	毕业生数 Graduates
1996	2953	1052	762
1997	3199	1108	847
1998	3726	1389	862
1999	5032	2132	991
2000	6233	2686	1084
2001	8358	3410	1401
2002	11110	4423	1616
2003	14763	6392	2715
2004	19367	8202	3426
2005	24363	9436	4193
2006	29000	10475	5492
2007	32145	11312	7483
2008	35005	12376	8925
2009	39080	14159	9759
2010	43149	14851	10347
2011	45213	15341	12351

表18.5 主要年份文化机构数
NUMBER OF CULTURAL INSTITUTIONS IN MAJOR YEARS

单位：个 (unit)

年　份 Year	专业剧团 Specialized Troupes	文化馆、艺术馆 Cultural Centers and Art Centers	图书馆 Libraries
1975	54	33	10
1978	54	36	10
1980	55	35	21
1985	54	35	25
1986	52	35	26
1987	51	35	26
1988	45	35	27
1989	44	35	35
1990	42	39	36
1991	42	39	38
1992	42	39	38
1993	41	39	41
1994	36	40	41
1995	36	40	42
1996	39	46	42
1997	39	47	42
1998	39	47	42
1999	36	46	42
2000	35	44	42
2001	36	44	42
2002	32	44	43
2003	32	44	44
2004	29	44	44
2005	29	42	43
2006	78	41	43
2007	84	41	43
2008	177	41	43
2009	160	41	43
2010	381	41	43
2011	282	41	43

注：专业剧团数据2006年起统计口径调整为含系统内、系统外两部分。
Note: The data of specialized troupes has included the units either inside or outside the public-owned system since 2006.

表18.6 教育事业基本情况（2010－2011年）
BASIC STATISTICS ON EDUCATION (2010-2011)

单位：人、所 (person，unit)

指 标	Item	2010	2011
学校数	**Number of Schools**		
高等学校	Higher Education	58	64
普通高等学校	Regular Institutions of Higher Education	53	59
本科院校	Universities with Full Undergraduate Courses	22	22
#独立学院	Non-university Tertiary	7	7
专科院校	Colleges with Specialized Courses	31	37
成人高等学校	Institutions of Higher Education for Adult	5	5
高中阶段学校	Senior Secondary Education	516	499
普通高中	Regular Senior Secondary Schools	268	263
中等职业学校	Vocational Secondary Schools	248	236
义务教育学校	Compulsory Education	6549	6244
普通初中	Regular Jnior Secondary Schools	1005	996
普通小学	Regular Primary Schools	5544	5248
特殊教育学校	Special Education	36	36
幼儿园	Kindergartens	4105	4114
工读学校	Schools for Juvenile Delinquents	5	4
成人中学	Secondary Schools for Adult	103	147
成人小学	Primary Schools for Adult	684	414
#扫盲班	Literacy Courses	222	164
在校学生数	**Total Enrollment**		
高等教育	Higher Education	805291	849955
研究生	Postgraduates	43149	45213
博 士	Doctor's Degree	5024	5245
硕 士	Master's Degree	38125	39968
普通本专科	Regular Undergraduates and College Students	522719	567813
本 科	Enrolled in Full Undergraduate Courses	328741	361532
专 科	Enrolled in Specialized Courses	193978	206281
成人本专科	Adult Undergraduates and College Students	124068	114642
本 科	Enrolled in Full Undergraduate Courses	31741	30015
专 科	Enrolled in Specialized Courses	92327	84627
在职人员攻读博硕士学位	Employees Enrolled in Graduate Programs Leading to Doctor and Master Degree	11418	11721
网络本专科	Students Enrolled in Internet-based Courses	103937	110566
本 科	Enrolled in Full Undergraduate Courses	52237	51656
专 科	Enrolled in Specialized Courses	51700	58910
高中阶段教育	Senior Secondary Education	1141729	1148840
普通高中	Regular Senior Secondary Schools	626434	648720

表18.6 续表1 continued1

单位：人、所 (person，unit)

指　标	Item	2010	2011
中等职业教育	Vocational Secondary Education	515295	500120
义务教育	Compulsory Education	3281131	3145015
普通初中	Regular Jnior Secondary Schools	1281724	1190197
普通小学	Regular Primary Schools	1999407	1954818
特殊教育	Special Education	14618	16978
学前教育	Pre-school Education	708711	842846
工读学校	Schools for Juvenile Delinquents	111	70
成人中学	Secondary Schools for Adult	74705	79932
成人小学	Primary Schools for Adult	63985	38561
#扫盲班	Literacy Courses	9174	3925
招生数	**New Enrollment**		
高等教育	Higher Education	285300	300692
研究生	Postgraduates	14851	15341
博　士	Doctor's Degree	1175	1217
硕　士	Master's Degree	13676	14124
普通本专科	Regular Undergraduates and College Students	166222	181077
本　科	Enrolled in Full Undergraduate Courses	96434	105129
专　科	Enrolled in Specialized Courses	69788	75948
成人本专科	Adult Undergraduates and College Students	49728	44230
本　科	Enrolled in Full Undergraduate Courses	12625	12088
专　科	Enrolled in Specialized Courses	37103	32142
在职人员攻读博硕士学位	Employees Enrolled in Graduate Programs Leading to Doctor and Master Degree	3792	3749
网络本专科	Students Enrolled in Internet-based Courses	50707	56295
本　科	Enrolled in Full Undergraduate Courses	23246	24508
专　科	Enrolled in Specialized Courses	27461	31787
高中阶段教育	Senior Secondary Education	393269	413957
普通高中	Regular Senior Secondary Schools	227567	226743
中等职业教育	Vocational Secondary Education	165702	187214
义务教育	Compulsory Education	738264	710766
普通初中	Regular Jnior Secondary Schools	408525	372073
普通小学	Regular Primary Schools	329739	338693
特殊教育	Special Education	2348	3485
学前教育	Pre-school Education	455958	481527
工读学校	Schools for Juvenile Delinquents	64	41
成人中学	Secondary Schools for Adult		
成人小学	Primary Schools for Adult		
#扫盲班	Literacy Courses		

表18.6 续表2 continued2

单位：人 (person)

指 标	Item	2010	2011
毕业生数	**Graduates**		
高等教育	Higher Education	220026	235062
研究生	Postgraduates	10347	12351
博 士	Doctor's Degree	779	875
硕 士	Master's Degree	9568	11476
普通本专科	Regular Undergraduates and College Students	122811	130702
本 科	Enrolled in Full Undergraduate Courses	66490	70019
专 科	Enrolled in Specialized Courses	56321	60683
成人本专科	Adult Undergraduates and College Students	55109	49994
本 科	Enrolled in Full Undergraduate Courses	19411	12516
专 科	Enrolled in Specialized Courses	35698	37478
在职人员攻读博硕士学位	Employees Enrolled in Graduate Programs Leading to Doctor and Master Degree		
网络本专科	Students Enrolled in Internet-based Courses	31759	42015
本 科	Enrolled in Full Undergraduate Courses	17080	21190
专 科	Enrolled in Specialized Courses	14679	20825
高中阶段教育	Senior Secondary Education	327598	342359
普通高中	Regular Senior Secondary Schools	169522	189625
中等职业教育	Vocational Secondary Education	158076	152707
义务教育	Compulsory Education	814953	791896
普通初中	Regular Jnior Secondary Schools	416604	428823
普通小学	Regular Primary Schools	398349	363073
特殊教育	Special Education	2426	1585
学前教育	Pre-school Education	242987	299037
工读学校	Schools for Juvenile Delinquents	67	61
成人中学	Secondary Schools for Adult	75284	80360
成人小学	Primary Schools for Adult	80408	48224
#扫盲班	Literacy Courses	6693	3139
教职工数	**Teachers and Staff**		
高等学校	Higher Education	50140	51892
普通高等学校	Regular Institutions of Higher Education	48356	50119
本科院校	Universities with Full Undergraduate Courses	35399	35767
#独立学院	Non-university Tertiary	5688	6022
专科院校	Colleges with Specialized Courses	12957	14352
成人高等学校	Institutions of Higher Education for Adult	1784	1773
高中阶段、义务教育学校	Senior Secondary Education and Compulsory Education	274557	273252
普通中学	Regular Secondary Schools	124404	132969
中等职业	Vocational Secondary Schools	24294	23886

表18.6 续表3 continued3

单位：人 (person)

指　标	Item	2010	2011
普通小学	Regular Primary Schools	125859	116397
特殊教育学校	Special Education	846	895
幼儿园	Pre-school Education	35701	43725
工读学校	Schools for Juvenile Delinquents	75	56
成人中学	Secondary Schools for Adult	289	308
成人小学	Primary Schools for Adult	1004	952
#扫盲班	Literacy Courses	407	354
专任教师数	**Full-time Teachers**		
高等学校	Higher Education	32147	34127
普通高等学校	Regular Institutions of Higher Education	31070	33110
本科院校	Universities with Full Undergraduate Courses	22420	23486
#独立学院	Non-university Tertiary	3732	4151
专科院校	Colleges with Specialized Courses	8650	9624
成人高等学校	Institutions of Higher Education for Adult	1077	1017
高中阶段学校	Senior Secondary Education	50343	52858
普通高中	Regular Senior Secondary Schools	32214	34234
中等职业教育	Vocational Secondary Schools	18129	18624
义务教育	Compulsory Education	193146	192060
普通初中	Regular Jnior Secondary Schools	77089	76717
普通小学	Regular Primary Schools	116057	115343
特殊教育学校	Special Education	715	763
幼儿园	Kindergartens	19966	22807
工读学校	Schools for Juvenile Delinquents	54	42
成人中学	Secondary Schools for Adult	138	202
成人小学	Primary Schools for Adult	476	427
#扫盲班	Literacy Courses	242	199
每一教师负担学生数	**Student-Teacher Ratio**		
小　学	Primary Schools	17.2	17.0
普通初中	Regular Jnior Secondary Schools	16.6	15.5
普通高中	Regular Senior Secondary Schools	19.4	19.0
中　职（不含技工校）	Secondary Vocational Schools (not including technical schools)	30.7	27.3
普通高等学校	Regular Institutions of Higher Education	16.8	16.6
每十万人口在校学生数	**Student Enrollment per 100 000 population**		
高等教育	Higher Education	2817	2523
高中阶段	Senior Secondary Education	3993	3983
初中阶段	Jnior Secondary Education	4483	4126
小　学	Primary Education	6993	6777
幼儿园	Kindergartens	2479	2922

表18.7 各级学校入学率及升学率（2010－2011年）
NET ENROLLMENT RATIO AND PROMOTION RATE OF SCHOOLS BY LEVEL (2010-2011)

单位：% (%)

指 标	Item	2010	2011
小学学龄儿童入学率	Net Enrollment Ratio of Primary Schools	99.94	99.96
初中适龄人口入学率	Net Enrollment Ratio of Junior Secondary Schools	99.1	99.2
高中阶段毛入学率	Gross Enrollment Ratio of Senior Secondary Schools	80.0	84.0
高等教育毛入学率	Gross Enrollment Ratio of Higher Education	30.0	32.0
初中毕业生升学率	Promotion Rate of Junior Secondary School Graduates	90.3	92.3
#升普通高中	To Regular Senior Secondary Schools	54.6	52.9
小学毕业生升学率	Promotion Rate of Primary School Graduates	102.6	102.5

表18.8 普通高等学校分科学生数（2011年）
STUDENT ENROLLMENT IN REGULAR INSTITUTIONS OF HIGHER EDUCATION BY FIELD OF STUDY (2011)

单位：人 (person)

项 目	Item	在校学生数 Total Enrollment	其 中 of which #本 科 Undergratudat Courses	招生数 New Enrollment	其 中 of which #本 科 Undergratudat Courses	毕业生数 Graduates	其 中 of which #本 科 Undergratudat Courses
总 计	**Total**	**406745**	**361532**	**120470**	**105129**	**82370**	**70019**
哲 学	Philosophy	627	172	218	83	170	13
经济学	Economics	22440	21401	6825	6448	4132	3815
法 学	Law	28424	21824	8073	5821	6912	4669
教育学	Education	12677	9530	3826	2812	2989	1996
文 学	Literature	87599	82598	26048	24378	18714	17192
历史学	History	2080	1786	577	486	511	435
理 学	Science	33965	30690	9323	8256	7697	6761
工 学	Engineering	114093	99543	34171	29370	22234	18629
农 学	Agriculture	8084	6763	2415	1979	1724	1441
医 学	Medicine	20416	16254	5724	4129	3829	2741
管理学	Management	76340	70971	23270	21367	13458	12327
专业学位	Special Degrees						

表18.9 中等职业教育学校分科学生情况（2011年）
STUDENTS IN VOCATIONAL SECONDARY SCHOOLS BY FIELD OF STUDY (2011)

单位：人 (person)

项 目	Item	毕业生数 Graduates	招生数 New Enrollment	在校学生数 Total Enrollment
总 计	**Total**	**118634**	**146484**	**379534**
农林类	Agriculture and Forestry	2700	10651	22592
资源与环境类	Resources and Environment	675	972	2199
能源类	Energy	205	362	1156
土木水利工程类	Civil and Hydraulic Engineering	2747	7752	16006
加工制造类	Manufacturing	35391	27023	84952
石油化工类	Petroleum and Chemicals	558	450	1253
轻纺食品类	Textile & Light and Food	785	1191	3964
交通运输类	Communication & Transportation	4399	9876	24712
信息技术类	Information Technology	32919	29472	81316
医药卫生类	Medicine and Health	9318	11895	34276
休闲保健类	Leisure and Health Care	221	555	1303
财经商贸类	Finance, Economy and Trade	10667	12224	31703
旅游类	Tourism	4710	6792	16297
文化艺术	Culture and Art	7651	5778	17643
体育类	Sports	198	282	693
教育类	Education	3586	19191	33765
司法类	Judicature	323	593	1623
社会公共事务类	Social and Public Affairs	1337	925	3107
其 他	Others	244	500	974

注：本表不含技工学校。
Note: The data of vestibule schools are not included in this table.

表18.10 各级学校在校女学生和女专任教师数（2010—2011年）

NUMBER OF FEMALE STUDENTS AND FEMALE FULL-TIME TEACHERS BY SCHOOL LEVEL (2010-2011)

单位：人 (person)

项　目	Item	2010	2011
女学生数	**Number of Female Students**	**2899230**	**2925056**
高等教育	Higher Education	392136	417495
研究生	Postgraduate	20783	22049
普通本专科学校	Institutions of Higher Education	266236	292259
高中教育阶段	High School Education	544763	560758
普通高中	Regular High School	316528	330330
中等职业教育	Vocational Secondary Schools	228235	230428
义务教育	Compulsory Education	1555220	1486755
普通初中	Regular Junior Secondary School	615473	568176
普通小学	Regular Primary School	939747	918579
女学生占学生总数的百分比(%)	**Percentage of Female Students to Total Students (%)**	**47.6**	**47.8**
高等教育	Higher Education	48.7	49.1
研究生	Postgraduate	48.2	48.8
普通本专科学校	Institutions of Higher Education	50.9	51.5
高中教育阶段	High School Education	47.7	48.8
普通高中	Regular High School	50.5	50.9
中等职业教育	Vocational Secondary Schools	44.3	46.1
义务教育	Compulsory Education	47.4	47.3
普通初中	Regular Junior Secondary School	48.0	47.7
普通小学	Regular Primary School	47.0	47.0
女专任教师数	**Number of Female Full-time Teachers**	**152888**	**158179**
普通高等学校	Institutions of Higher Education	13700	14694
高中阶段学校	High School Education	21985	23535
普通高中	Regular High School	13799	15200
中等职业学校	Vocational Secondary Schools	8186	8335
义务教育学校	Compulsory Education	96512	96726
普通初中	Regular Junior Secondary School	34839	35082
普通小学	Regular Primary School	61673	61644
女专任教师占专任教师总数的百分比(%)	**Percentage of Female Full-time Teachers to Total Full-time Teachers(%)**	**51.5**	**52.2**
普通高等学校	Institutions of Higher Education	44.1	44.4
高中阶段学校	High School Education	43.7	44.5
普通高中	Regular High School	42.8	44.4
中等职业学校	Vocational Secondary Schools	45.2	44.8
义务教育学校	Compulsory Education	50.0	50.4
普通初中	Regular Junior Secondary School	45.2	45.7
普通小学	Regular Primary School	53.1	53.4

表18.11 科技经费、科技奖励情况（2010－2011年）

FUNDS AND REWARDS FOR SCIENTIFIC AND TECHNOLOGICAL RESEARCH (2010-2011)

单位：项(item)

指　标	Item	2010	2011
科学支出(万元)	**Expenditure of Scientific Research (10 000 yuan)**	**178968**	**241932**
市　级	Municipal	64560	91434
区　县	District and Country	114408	150498
科技奖励情况	**Rewards for Scientific and Technological Research**		
科技进步奖	Award for Science and Technology Progress	169	166
国家级	National	14	13
一等奖	1st Prize	1	1
二等奖	2nd Prize	13	12
市　级	Municipal	155	153
一等奖	1st Prize	12	9
二等奖	2nd Prize	49	47
三等奖	3rd Prize	94	97
自然科学奖	Award for Natural Sciences	21	16
市　级	Municipal	21	16
一等奖	1st Prize	4	3
二等奖	2nd Prize	6	5
三等奖	3rd Prize	11	8
技术发明奖	Award for Technological Invention	6	11
国家级	National	2	
市　级	Municipal	4	11
一等奖	1st Prize	1	1
二等奖	2nd Prize		5
三等奖	3rd Prize	3	5

表18.12 科学技术协会活动情况（2011年）
ACTIVITIES OF SCIENCE AND TECHNOLOGY ASSOCIATIONS (2011)

指　标	Item	合　计 Total	其　中 of which 市级科协 Science and Technology Associations at Municipal Level	市级学会 Learned Societies at Municipal Level	区县科协 Science and Technology Associations below Municipal Level
国内学术会议	**Domestic Academic Meetings**				
举办次数（次）	Number of Meetings (time)	826	33	578	215
参加人数（人次）	Number of Participants (person-times)	90622	8800	55457	26365
交流论文数（篇）	Number of Theses Presented (piece)	10584	1835	8749	
国际学术会议	**International Academic Conference**				
会议次数	Number of Conferences	58	9	49	
中方参加人数（人次）	Number of Chinese Participants (person-times)	6364	1788	4576	
中方交流论文（篇）	Number of Chinese Theses Presented (piece)	1356	295	1061	
外方参加人数（人次）	Number of Foreign Participants (person-times)	937	212	725	
外方交流论文（篇）	Number of Foreign Theses Presented (piece)	573	125	448	
科普活动	**Science Popularization Activities**				
举办科普讲座（次）	Number of Lectures (time)	1601	67	802	732
科普讲座受众人数（万人次）	Number of Audience (10 000 person-times)	333	122	140	72
举办科普展览（次）	Number of Exhibitions (time)	835	18	167	650
科普展览受众人数（万人次）	Number of Participants (10 000 person-times)	517	83	197	236
举办青少年科技夏（冬）令营（次）	Number of Science and Technology Summer (Winter) Camps for Teenagers (time)	54	17	10	27
举办青少年科技竞赛（次）	Number of Teenagers Science and Technology Competitions (time)	220	11	27	182
科学考察	**Scientific Study Tour**				
派往国外科技团组（个）	Outbound Science and Technology Delegations	67	13	53	1
总人数（人次）	Number of Delegates (person-times)	563	344	218	1
咨　询	**Consultancy**				
完成技术咨询合同数（项）	Number of Technological Consultancy Contracts Completed (item)	497	360	92	45
技术咨询合同实现金额（万元）	Actually Received Contract Amount of Technological Consultancy (10 000 yuan)	33900	30218	486	3196
#技术交易额（万元）	Technology Transaction Value (10 000 yuan)	33715	30218	320	3177

表18.13 研究与试验发展（R&D）活动基本情况（2011年）

BASIC STATISTICS ON R&D ACTIVITIES (2011)

指　标	Item	合　计 Total	科研机构 Research Institutes	高等院校 Colleges & Universities
有R&D活动的单位数（个）	Units Engaged in R&D Activities (unit)	626	28	78
R&D经费内部支出（万元）	Inner Expenditure of R&D Funds (10 000 yuan)	1283560	154242	116172
#基础研究	Basic Research	89403	40621	47294
应用研究	Application Research	206511	81062	49910
试验发展	Testing Development	987649	32558	18971
#日常性支出	Daily Expenditure	1037142	101945	91313
#人员劳务费	Remuneration for Personnel	265470	16766	26232
#资产性支出	Expenditure for Assets	246419	52297	24859
#仪器和设备	Facilities	217047	38182	19523
#政府资金	Funds from Government	201425	79569	61121
企业资金	Funds from Enterprises	1014756	37572	41867
国外资金	Foreign Funds	5416	75	498
其他资金	Others	61971	37027	12692
R&D人员（人）	R&D Personnel (person)	65287	4227	15706
#女　性	Female	17468	1456	5474
#全时人员	Full-time Employees	39748	3195	4973
#博士毕业	With Doctor's Degree	4430	187	3732
硕士毕业	With Master's Degree	10270	1086	6053
本科毕业	With Bachelor's Degree	21117	1801	4831
R&D人员全时当量（人年）	Full-time Personnel (person-year)	40698	3657	6303
#研究人员	Researchers	19883	2426	5299
#基础研究	Personnel of Basic Research	4187	942	3171
应用研究	Personnel of Application Research	6232	1828	2658
试验发展	Personnel of Testing Development	30281	887	477
R&D项目（课题）数（项）	Number of R&D Projects (Topics)	19375	1054	13111
R&D项目（课题）人员全时当量（人年）	Number of Full-time Persons for Each R&D Project (Topic) (person-year)	36095	3316	6291
R&D项目（课题）经费支出（万元）	Expenditure for R&D Projects (Topics) (RMB 10 000)	985769	98497	88481
研究机构机构数（个）	Number of Research Institutions (unit)	698	30	266
研究机构R&D人员（人）	R&D Personnel in Research Institutions (person)	32924	4227	3528
#博士和硕士	With Doctor's Degree and Master's Degree	6653	1273	2781
研究机构R&D经费支出（万元）	Research Institutions' Expenditure for R&D (RMB 10 000)	636109	154242	37445
研究机构仪器设备原价（万元）	Original Price of Instruments and Equipment in Research Institutions (RMB 10 000)	707834	82248	140020
#进　口	Imported	232232	22633	36640
专利申请数（件）	Number of Patent Applications (pcs)	10345	216	1624
#发明申请	Invention Patent	3575	129	1214
有效发明专利数（件）	Number of Effective Invention Patents (pcs)	6443	226	3492
专利所有权转让及许可数（件）	Number of Patent Right Transfers and Permissions (pcs)	892	5	102
专利所有权转让及许可收入（万元）	Income from Patent Right Transfers and Permissions (RMB 10 000)	4497	67	1550
形成国家或行业标准数（项）	Number of National or Industrial Standards Newly Formed (items)	520	20	
发表科技论文（篇）	Number of Scientific and Technical Theses Published (theses)	34166	1432	28572
出版科技著作（种）	Scientific and Technical Works Published (kind)	1020	51	936

表18.13 续表 continued

指　标	Item	企　业 Enterprises	其中 of which #工业企业 Industrial Enterprises	其　他 Others
有R&D活动的单位数（个）	Units Engaged in R&D Activities (unit)	460	431	60
R&D经费内部支出（万元）	Inner Expenditure of R&D Funds (10 000 yuan)	998370	943975	14776
#基础研究	Basic Research	342	342	1146
应用研究	Application Research	69859	39296	5680
试验发展	Testing Development	928169	904337	7951
#日常性支出	Daily Expenditure	831956	787888	11928
#人员劳务费	Remuneration for Personnel	214604	200663	7868
#资产性支出	Expenditure for Assets	166415	156087	2849
#仪器和设备	Facilities	157432	150903	1911
#政府资金	Funds from Government	49593	45124	11142
企业资金	Funds from Enterprises	932863	885922	2454
国外资金	Foreign Funds	4843	4843	
其他资金	Others	11072	8086	1180
R&D人员（人）	R&D Personnel (person)	42511	40490	2843
#女　性	Female	9522	9084	1016
#全时人员	Full-time Employees	30742	29816	838
#博士毕业	With Doctor's Degree	374	268	137
硕士毕业	With Master's Degree	2511	2069	620
本科毕业	With Bachelor's Degree	13812	13190	673
R&D人员全时当量（人年）	Full-time Personnel (person-year)	29232	27652	1506
#研究人员	Researchers	11223	10527	936
#基础研究	Personnel of Basic Research	38	38	36
应用研究	Personnel of Application Research	1021	675	725
试验发展	Personnel of Testing Development	28172	26938	745
R&D项目（课题）数（项）	Number of R&D Projects (Topics)	4781	4524	429
R&D项目（课题）人员全时当量（人年）	Number of Full-time Persons for Each R&D Project (Topic) (person-year)	25299	23893	1189
R&D项目（课题）经费支出（万元）	Expenditure for R&D Projects (Topics) (RMB 10 000)	789752	761360	9040
研究机构机构数（个）	Number of Research Institutions (unit)	379	365	23
研究机构R&D人员（人）	R&D Personnel in Research Institutions (person)	24630	24296	539
#博士和硕士	With Doctor's Degree and Master's Degree	2410	2264	189
研究机构R&D经费支出（万元）	Research Institutions' Expenditure for R&D (RMB 10 000)	439180	431731	5241
研究机构仪器设备原价（万元）	Original Price of Instruments and Equipment in Research Institutions (RMB 10 000)	479834	469000	5732
#进　口	Imported	170292	168400	2667
专利申请数（件）	Number of Patent Applications (pcs)	8447	8121	58
#发明申请	Invention Patent	2204	2089	28
有效发明专利数（件）	Number of Effective Invention Patents (pcs)	2722	2532	3
专利所有权转让及许可数（件）	Number of Patent Right Transfers and Permissions (pcs)	785	780	
专利所有权转让及许可收入（万元）	Income from Patent Right Transfers and Permissions (RMB 10,000)	2880	2858	
形成国家或行业标准数（项）	Number of National or Industrial Standards Newly Formed (items)	486	454	14
发表科技论文（篇）	Number of Scientific and Technical Theses Published (theses)	2160	1318	2002
出版科技著作（种）	Scientific and Technical Works Published (kind)	6		27

表18.14 大中型工业企业科技机构情况（2011年）

SCIENTIFIC AND TECHNOLOGICAL INSTITUTIONS OF LARGE & MEDIUM-SIZED INDUSTRIAL ENTERPRISES (2011)

项　目	Item	科技机构数（个）Number of Institutions (unit)	科技机构科技活动人数（人）Personnel of Institutions (person)	科技机构经费内部支出（万元）Inner Expenditures for Science and Technology (10 000 yuan)
总　计	**Total**	**353**	**29230**	**691574**
按隶属关系分	**By Relationship**			
中　央	Central	68	11794	310590
地　方	Local	285	17436	380983
按登记注册类型分	**By Registration**			
内资企业	Domestic-funded	306	24948	590905
国有企业	State-owned	38	1798	43609
集体企业	Collective-owned	1	14	23
股份合作企业	Cooperative Enterprise	1	12	200
联营企业	Joint Ownership Enterprises	1	40	99
有限责任公司	Limited Liability Corporations	142	9885	222376
股份有限公司	Share Holding Limited Corporations	42	7813	176942
私营企业	Private Enterprises	79	5333	146576
其他企业	Private Limited Liability Corporations	2	53	1081
港、澳、台商投资企业	Enterprises Funded by Hong Kong, Macao and Taiwan	26	1342	19817
合资经营企业	Joint-venture Enterprises	17	552	6997
合作经营企业	Cooperative Enterprises			
独资经营企业	Enterprises with Sole Funded from Hong Kong,Macao and Taiwan	5	463	8676
投资股份有限公司	Share-holding Corporations Ltd. with Investment from Hong Kong, Macao and Taiwan	4	327	4144
外商投资企业	Foreign Funded Enterprises	21	2940	80852
中外合资经营企业	Joint-venture Enterprises	17	2439	76311
中外合作经营企业	Cooperation Enterprises			
外资企业	Enterprises with Sole Fund	3	314	3043
外商投资股份有限公司	Share-holding Corporations Ltd.	1	187	1498
按行业分	**By Industrial Sector**			
采矿业	Mining and Quarrying	4	22	4794
煤炭开采和洗选业	Coal Mining and Dressing	3	18	77
石油和天然气开采业	Petroleum and Natural Gas Extraction			
黑色金属矿采选业	Ferrous Metals Mining and Dressing			
有色金属矿采选业	Nonferrous Metals Mining and Dressing			
非金属矿采选业	Nonmetal Minerals Mining and Dressing	1	4	4717
其他采矿业	Other Minerals Mining			
制造业	Manufacturing	345	28357	684831
农副食品加工业	Farm Products and By-food Processing	8	288	2872
食品制造业	Food Production	6	154	2951
饮料制造业	Beverage Production	6	404	3164

表18.14 续表 continued

项　目	Item	科技机构数（个）Number of Institutions (unit)	科技机构科技活动人数（人）Personnel of Institutions (person)	科技机构经费内部支出（万元）Inner Expenditures for Science and Technology (10 000 yuan)
烟草制品业	Tobacco Products	1	20	5
纺织业	Textile Industry	6	129	3409
纺织服装、鞋、帽制造业	Garments, Shoes and Hats Production	2	21	291
皮革、毛皮、羽毛（绒）及其制品业	Leather, Furs, Down and Related Products			
木材加工及木竹藤棕草制品业	Timber Processing,Bamboo,Cane,Palm, Straw Products			
家具制造业	Furniture Manufacturing			
造纸及纸制品业	Papermaking and Paper Products	1	8	200
印刷业、记录媒介的复制	Printing and Record Medium Reproduction	1	15	10
文教体育用品制造业	Cultural Educational and Sports Goods			
石油加工、炼焦及核燃料加工业	Petroleum, Coking and Nuclear Fuel Processing	1	86	1095
化学原料及化学制品制造业	Raw Chemical Materials and Chemical Products	30	1928	47185
医药制造业	Medical and Pharmaceutical Products	28	1464	24439
化学纤维制造业	Chemical Fiber			
橡胶制品业	Rubber Products	3	94	1087
塑料制品业	Plastic Products			
非金属矿物制品业	Nonmetal Mineral Products	16	505	2682
黑色金属冶炼及压延加工业	Smelting and Pressing of Ferrous Metals	5	196	2462
有色金属冶炼及压延加工业	Smelting and Pressing of Nonferrous Metals	11	709	32666
金属制品业	Metal Products	8	153	1217
通用设备制造业	Ordinary Equipment	32	2119	82793
专用设备制造业	Special Equipment	12	608	6889
交通运输设备制造业	Transportation Equipment	102	15586	409796
电气机械及器材制造业	Electric Equipment and Machinery	29	1162	21206
通信设备、计算机及其他电子设备制造业	Communication, Computers and Other Electronic Equipment	11	553	6108
仪器仪表及文化、办公用机械制造业	Instruments, Meters,Cultural and Office Machinery	16	1078	16067
工艺品及其他制造业	Handicraft and Other Production	10	1077	16236
废弃资源和废旧材料回收加工业	Recovery and Processing of Waste Resources and Materials			
电力、燃气及水的生产和供应业	Electricpower, Gas & Water Production and Supply	4	851	1949
电力、热力的生产和供应业	Electricpower and Hot Power Production and Supply	4	851	1949
燃气生产和供应业	Gas Production and Supply			
水的生产和供应业	Water Production and Supply			

表18.15 规模以上工业企业科技机构情况（2011年）

SCIENTIFIC AND TECHNOLOGICAL INSTITUTIONS OF INDUSTRIAL ENTERPRISES ABOVE DESIGNATED SIZE (2011)

项　目	Item	科技机构数（个）Number of Institutions (unit)	科技机构科技活动人数（人）Personnel of Institutions (person)	科技机构经费内部支出（万元）Inner Expenditures for Science and Technology (10 000 yuan)
总　计	**Total**	**488**	**31428**	**711996**
按隶属关系分	**By Relationship**			
中　央	Central	69	11806	310688
地　方	Local	419	19622	401308
按登记注册类型分	**By Registration**			
内资企业	Domestic-funded	426	26774	608334
国有企业	State-owned	41	1876	44273
集体企业	Collective-owned	2	17	28
股份合作企业	Cooperative Enterprise	1	12	200
联营企业	Joint Ownership Enterprises	1	40	99
有限责任公司	Limited Liability Corporations	175	10541	229449
股份有限公司	Share Holding Limited Corporations	50	7986	178320
私营企业	Private Enterprises	152	6217	154674
其他企业	Private Limited Liability Corporations	4	85	1291
港、澳、台商投资企业	Enterprises Funded by Hong Kong, Macao and Taiwan	36	1645	22277
合资经营企业	Joint-venture Enterprises	22	707	7978
合作经营企业	Cooperative Enterprises			
独资经营企业	Enterprises with Sole Funded from Hong Kong,Macao and Taiwan	9	591	9934
投资股份有限公司	Share-holding Corporations Ltd. with Investment from Hong Kong, Macao and Taiwan	5	347	4365
外商投资企业	Foreign Funded Enterprises	26	3009	81385
中外合资经营企业	Joint-venture Enterprises	21	2490	76798
中外合作经营企业	Cooperation Enterprises			
外资企业	Enterprises with Sole Fund	4	332	3090
外商投资股份有限公司	Share-holding Corporations Ltd.	1	187	1498
按行业分	**By Industrial Sector**			
采矿业	Mining and Quarrying	5	25	4799
煤炭开采和洗选业	Coal Mining and Dressing	3	18	77
石油和天然气开采业	Petroleum and Natural Gas Extraction			
黑色金属矿采选业	Ferrous Metals Mining and Dressing			
有色金属矿采选业	Nonferrous Metals Mining and Dressing			
非金属矿采选业	Nonmetal Minerals Mining and Dressing	2	7	4722
其他采矿业	Other Minerals Mining			
制造业	Manufacturing	479	30552	705248
农副食品加工业	Farm Products and By-food Processing	14	331	3299
食品制造业	Food Production	7	159	2952
饮料制造业	Beverage Production	14	460	3723

表18.15 续表 continued

项　目	Item	科技机构数（个） Number of Institutions (unit)	科技机构科技活动人数（人） Personnel of Institutions (person)	科技机构经费内部支出（万元） Inner Expenditures for Science and Technology (10 000 yuan)
烟草制品业	Tobacco Products	1	20	5
纺织业	Textile Industry	6	129	3409
纺织服装、鞋、帽制造业	Garments, Shoes and Hats Production	3	39	342
皮革、毛皮、羽毛（绒）及其制品业	Leather, Furs, Down and Related Products			
木材加工及木竹藤棕草制品业	Timber Processing,Bamboo,Cane,Palm, Straw Products	1	18	10
家具制造业	Furniture Manufacturing	1	2	16
造纸及纸制品业	Papermaking and Paper Products	1	8	200
印刷业、记录媒介的复制	Printing and Record Medium Reproduction	1	15	10
文教体育用品制造业	Cultural Educational and Sports Goods			
石油加工、炼焦及核燃料加工业	Petroleum, Coking and Nuclear Fuel Processing	3	144	1636
化学原料及化学制品制造业	Raw Chemical Materials and Chemical Products	39	2084	47784
医药制造业	Medical and Pharmaceutical Products	53	1776	28640
化学纤维制造业	Chemical Fiber			
橡胶制品业	Rubber Products	4	109	1187
塑料制品业	Plastic Products	1	13	2
非金属矿物制品业	Nonmetal Mineral Products	21	616	3739
黑色金属冶炼及压延加工业	Smelting and Pressing of Ferrous Metals	6	220	2862
有色金属冶炼及压延加工业	Smelting and Pressing of Nonferrous Metals	14	762	33895
金属制品业	Metal Products	11	197	1840
通用设备制造业	Ordinary Equipment	45	2451	83959
专用设备制造业	Special Equipment	20	674	7380
交通运输设备制造业	Transportation Equipment	123	15992	415117
电气机械及器材制造业	Electric Equipment and Machinery	37	1274	22665
通信设备、计算机及其他电子设备制造业	Communication, Computers and Other Electronic Equipment	19	734	7338
仪器仪表及文化、办公用机械制造业	Instruments, Meters,Cultural and Office Machinery	24	1248	17001
工艺品及其他制造业	Handicraft and Other Production	10	1077	16236
废弃资源和废旧材料回收加工业	Recovery and Processing of Waste Resources and Materials			
电力、燃气及水的生产和供应业	Electricpower, Gas & Water Production and Supply	4	851	1949
电力、热力的生产和供应业	Electricpower and Hot Power Production and Supply	4	851	1949
燃气生产和供应业	Gas Production and Supply			
水的生产和供应业	Water Production and Supply			

表18.16 大中型工业企业R&D人员情况（2011年）

STATISTICS ON R&D PERSONNEL IN LARGE & MEDIUM-SIZED INDUSTRIAL ENTERPRISES (2011)

项　目	Item	R&D人员数（人） R&D Personnel (person)	其中 of which #参加项目人员 Researchers	#R&D全时人员 Full-time Employees	R&D人员折合全时当量（人年） Full-time Personnel (person-year)	其中 of which #试验发展人员 Personnel of Testing Development
总　计	**Total**	**37611**	**32366**	**27816**	**25937**	**25236**
按隶属关系分	**By Relationship**					
中　央	Central	10673	9176	8999	9136	8769
地　方	Local	26938	23190	18817	16802	16467
按登记注册类型分	**By Registration**					
内资企业	Domestic-funded	32282	27827	23697	21886	21199
国有企业	State-owned	4506	3698	3336	3412	3259
集体企业	Collective-owned	84	76	12	53	53
股份合作企业	Cooperative Enterprise	12	12	12	8	8
联营企业	Joint Ownership Enterprises					
有限责任公司	Limited Liability Corporations	13654	11528	9179	8782	8487
股份有限公司	Share Holding Limited Corporations	6176	5304	5651	5289	5177
私营企业	Private Enterprises	7781	7163	5501	4272	4145
其他企业	Private Limited Liability Corporations	69	46	6	69	69
港、澳、台商投资企业	Enterprises Funded by Hong Kong, Macao and Taiwan	1436	1280	1154	1169	1169
合资经营企业	Joint-venture Enterprises	804	694	675	572	572
合作经营企业	Cooperative Enterprises					
独资经营企业	Enterprises with Sole Funded from Hong Kong,Macao and Taiwan	374	346	336	357	357
投资股份有限公司	Share-holding Corporations Ltd. with Investment from Hong Kong, Macao and Taiwan	258	240	143	240	240
外商投资企业	Foreign Funded Enterprises	3893	3259	2965	2883	2869
中外合资经营企业	Joint-venture Enterprises	3577	2996	2812	2706	2692
中外合作经营企业	Cooperation Enterprises					
外资企业	Enterprises with Sole Fund	181	150	66	105	105
外商投资股份有限公司	Share-holding Corporations Ltd.	135	113	87	72	72
按行业分	**By Sector**					
采矿业	Mining and Quarrying	883	676	544	376	355
煤炭开采和洗选业	Coal Mining and Dressing	500	475	195	205	203
石油和天然气开采业	Petroleum and Natural Gas Extraction					
黑色金属矿采选业	Ferrous Metals Mining and Dressing	298	119	298	119	100
有色金属矿采选业	Nonferrous Metals Mining and Dressing					
非金属矿采选业	Nonmetal Minerals Mining and Dressing	85	82	51	52	52
其他采矿业	Other Minerals Mining					

表18.16 续表 continued

项　目	Item	R&D人员数（人） R&D Personnel (person)	其中 of which #参加项目人员 Researchers	#R&D全时人员 Full-time Employees	R&D人员折合全时当量（人年） Full-time Personnel (person-year)	其中 of which #试验发展人员 Personnel of Testing Development
制造业	Manufacturing	35845	30902	27117	25086	24418
农副食品加工业	Farm Products and By-food Processing	439	410	180	286	268
食品制造业	Food Production	591	262	403	219	219
饮料制造业	Beverage Production	547	504	267	293	252
烟草制品业	Tobacco Products	22	15	22	4	4
纺织业	Textile Industry	580	548	517	540	540
纺织服装、鞋、帽制造业	Garments, Shoes and Hats Production	40	39	40	27	27
皮革毛皮羽毛（绒）及其制品业	Leather, Furs, Down and Related Products					
木材加工及木竹藤棕草制品业	Timber Processing,Bamboo, Cane,Palm,Straw Products	23	20	7	5	5
家具制造业	Furniture Manufacturing	290	290	290	58	58
造纸及纸制品业	Papermaking and Paper Products	23	21	19	20	20
印刷业、记录媒介的复制	Printing and Record Medium Reproduction	85	71	18	16	16
文教体育用品制造业	Cultural Educational and Sports Goods					
石油加工、炼焦及核燃料加工业	Petroleum, Coking and Nuclear Fuel Processing	55	43	35	55	55
化学原料及化学制品制造业	Raw Chemical Materials and Chemical Products	2377	2019	1603	1544	1513
医药制造业	Medical and Pharmaceutical Products	2513	2270	1847	1962	1955
化学纤维制造业	Chemical Fiber					
橡胶制品业	Rubber Products	244	197	193	61	61
塑料制品业	Plastic Products	22	15	22	2	2
非金属矿物制品业	Nonmetal Mineral Products	1153	1014	396	558	558
黑色金属冶炼及压延加工业	Smelting and Pressing of Ferrous Metals	249	244	47	165	165
有色金属冶炼及压延加工业	Smelting and Pressing of Nonferrous Metals	911	757	409	660	651
金属制品业	Metal Products	639	602	194	80	80
通用设备制造业	Ordinary Equipment	3697	3072	2597	2715	2702
专用设备制造业	Special Equipment	1404	1082	1292	1243	1055
交通运输设备制造业	Transportation Equipment	14543	12768	12457	10601	10443
电气机械及器材制造业	Electric Equipment and Machinery	1569	1382	893	880	758
通信设备、计算机及其他电子设备制造业	Communication, Computers and Other Electronic Equipment	758	649	722	555	555
仪器仪表及文化、办公用机械制造业	Instruments, Meters,Cultural and Office Machinery	1765	1442	1369	1504	1504
工艺品及其他制造业	Handicraft and Other Production	1306	1166	1278	1032	952
废弃资源和废旧材料回收加工业	Recovery and Processing of Waste Resources and Materials					
电力、燃气及水的生产和供应业	Electricpower, Gas & Water Production and Supply	883	788	155	475	463
电力、热力的生产和供应业	Electricpower and Hot Power Production and Supply	862	768	155	465	453
燃气生产和供应业	Gas Production and Supply	21	20		11	11
水的生产和供应业	Water Production and Supply					

表18.17 规模以上工业企业R&D人员情况（2011年）

STATISTICS ON R&D PERSONNEL IN INDUSTRIAL ENTERPRISES ABOVE DESIGNATED SIZE (2011)

项 目	Item	R&D人员数（人） R&D Personnel (person)	其 中 of which #参加项目人员 Researchers	#R&D全时人员 Full-time Employees	R&D人员折合全时当量（人年） Full-time Personnel (person-year)	其 中 of which #试验发展人员 Personnel of Testing Development
总 计	**Total**	**40490**	**34918**	**29816**	**27652**	**26938**
按隶属关系分	**By Relationship**					
中 央	Central	10736	9235	9035	9182	8816
地 方	Local	29754	25683	20781	18469	18122
按登记注册类型分	**By Registration**					
内资企业	Domestic-funded	34838	30081	25463	23458	22758
国有企业	State-owned	4628	3804	3426	3492	3339
集体企业	Collective-owned	91	82	16	54	54
股份合作企业	Cooperative Enterprise	12	12	12	8	8
联营企业	Joint Ownership Enterprises					
有限责任公司	Limited Liability Corporations	14652	12376	9816	9357	9055
股份有限公司	Share Holding Limited Corporations	6351	5466	5811	5443	5330
私营企业	Private Enterprises	9035	8295	6376	5036	4903
其他企业	Private Limited Liability Corporations	69	46	6	69	69
港、澳、台商投资企业	Enterprises Funded by Hong Kong, Macao and Taiwan	1613	1445	1290	1251	1251
合资经营企业	Joint-venture Enterprises	929	821	765	623	623
合作经营企业	Cooperative Enterprises					
独资经营企业	Enterprises with Sole Funded from Hong Kong,Macao and Taiwan	406	375	365	371	371
投资股份有限公司	Share-holding Corporations Ltd. with Investment from Hong Kong, Macao and Taiwan	278	258	160	256	256
外商投资企业	Foreign Funded Enterprises	4039	3392	3063	2943	2929
中外合资经营企业	Joint-venture Enterprises	3710	3118	2900	2753	2739
中外合作经营企业	Cooperation Enterprises					
外资企业	Enterprises with Sole Fund	194	161	76	118	118
外商投资股份有限公司	Share-holding Corporations Ltd.	135	113	87	72	72
按行业分	**By Sector**					
采矿业	Mining and Quarrying	886	678	544	378	357
煤炭开采和洗选业	Coal Mining and Dressing	500	475	195	205	203
石油和天然气开采业	Petroleum and Natural Gas Extraction					
黑色金属矿采选业	Ferrous Metals Mining and Dressing	298	119	298	119	100
有色金属矿采选业	Nonferrous Metals Mining and Dressing					
非金属矿采选业	Nonmetal Minerals Mining and Dressing	88	84	51	53	53
其他采矿业	Other Minerals Mining					

表18.17 续表 continued

项　目	Item	R&D人员数（人）R&D Personnel (person)	其　中 of which #参加项目人员 Researchers	#R&D全时人员 Full-time Employees	R&D人员折合全时当量（人年）Full-time Personnel (person-year)	其　中 of which #试验发展人员 Personnel of Testing Development
制造业	Manufacturing	38721	33452	29117	26799	26118
农副食品加工业	Farm Products and By-food Processing	578	527	282	384	361
食品制造业	Food Production	619	290	414	241	241
饮料制造业	Beverage Production	685	636	356	382	341
烟草制品业	Tobacco Products	22	15	22	4	4
纺织业	Textile Industry	580	548	517	540	540
纺织服装、鞋、帽制造业	Garments, Shoes and Hats Production	40	39	40	27	27
皮革毛皮羽毛（绒）及其制品业	Leather, Furs, Down and Related Products					
木材加工及木竹藤棕草制品业	Timber Processing,Bamboo, Cane,Palm,Straw Products	44	39	12	10	10
家具制造业	Furniture Manufacturing	300	300	290	65	65
造纸及纸制品业	Papermaking and Paper Products	26	23	21	21	21
印刷业、记录媒介的复制	Printing and Record Medium Reproduction	104	87	34	31	31
文教体育用品制造业	Cultural Educational and Sports Goods					
石油加工、炼焦及核燃料加工业	Petroleum, Coking and Nuclear Fuel Processing	85	72	63	78	78
化学原料及化学制品制造业	Raw Chemical Materials and Chemical Products	2621	2233	1722	1671	1639
医药制造业	Medical and Pharmaceutical Products	2868	2566	2093	2131	2116
化学纤维制造业	Chemical Fiber					
橡胶制品业	Rubber Products	274	222	214	62	62
塑料制品业	Plastic Products	57	48	50	8	8
非金属矿物制品业	Nonmetal Mineral Products	1315	1171	541	696	696
黑色金属冶炼及压延加工业	Smelting and Pressing of Ferrous Metals	379	366	144	292	292
有色金属冶炼及压延加工业	Smelting and Pressing of Nonferrous Metals	984	824	457	699	691
金属制品业	Metal Products	830	767	351	242	242
通用设备制造业	Ordinary Equipment	3906	3241	2706	2836	2822
专用设备制造业	Special Equipment	1520	1189	1380	1326	1138
交通运输设备制造业	Transportation Equipment	14829	13026	12703	10713	10554
电气机械及器材制造业	Electric Equipment and Machinery	1865	1658	1025	1017	895
通信设备、计算机及其他电子设备制造业	Communication, Computers and Other Electronic Equipment	893	766	833	616	616
仪器仪表及文化、办公用机械制造业	Instruments, Meters,Cultural and Office Machinery	1991	1633	1569	1677	1677
工艺品及其他制造业	Handicraft and Other Production	1306	1166	1278	1032	952
废弃资源和废旧材料回收加工业	Recovery and Processing of Waste Resources and Materials					
电力、燃气及水的生产和供应业	Electricpower, Gas & Water Production and Supply	883	788	155	475	463
电力、热力的生产和供应业	Electricpower and Hot Power Production and Supply	862	768	155	465	453
燃气生产和供应业	Gas Production and Supply	21	20		11	11
水的生产和供应业	Water Production and Supply					

表18.18 大中型工业企业R&D活动经费支出与项目情况（2011年）

EXPENDITURES AND PROJECTS OF SCIENTIFIC & TECHNOLOGICAL ACTIVITIES OF LARGE & MEDIUM-SIZED INDUSTRIAL ENTERPRISES (2011)

单位：万元 (10 000 yuan)

项　目	Item	R&D项目数（项） Projects (unit)	研究与发展经费内部支出 Internal Expenses for R&D	技术改造经费支出 Expendi-tures for Technical Transfor -mation	技术引进经费支出 Expendi-tures for Technical Recom-mendation	购买国内技术用款 Purchases of Civil Techno -logy
总　计	**Total**	**4162**	**904484**	**579858**	**179765**	**47295**
按隶属关系分	**By Relationship**					
中　央	Central	1252	341709	163171	146768	22944
地　方	Local	2910	562775	416687	32997	24351
按登记注册类型分	**By Registration**					
内资企业	Domestic-funded	3438	738239	253646	35976	32525
国有企业	State-owned	535	88937	24754	15566	456
集体企业	Collective-owned	11	380	29		
股份合作企业	Cooperative Enterprise	1	800			
联营企业	Joint Ownership Enterprises					
有限责任公司	Limited Liability Corporations	1624	282807	164251	6197	4305
股份有限公司	Share Holding Limited Corporations	583	136152	18561	11866	22900
私营企业	Private Enterprises	674	228844	46052	2347	4865
其他企业	Private Limited Liability Corporations	10	320			
港、澳、台商投资企业	Enterprises Funded by Hong Kong, Macao and Taiwan	258	28304	27401	1655	4325
合资经营企业	Joint-venture Enterprises	54	14223	4407	1650	2448
合作经营企业	Cooperative Enterprises					
独资经营企业	Enterprises with Sole Funded from Hong Kong,Macao and Taiwan	14	8947	18357	5	22
投资股份有限公司	Share-holding Corporations Ltd. with Investment from Hong Kong, Macao and Taiwan	190	5135	4638		1855
外商投资企业	Foreign Funded Enterprises	466	137941	298811	142135	10445
中外合资经营企业	Joint-venture Enterprises	263	131006	296769	140845	7110
中外合作经营企业	Cooperation Enterprises					
外资企业	Enterprises with Sole Fund	187	4125	1940		
外商投资股份有限公司	Share-holding Corporations Ltd.	16	2810	102	1290	3335
按行业分	**By Sector**					
采矿业	Mining and Quarrying	130	8039	12737		723
煤炭开采和洗选业	Coal Mining and Dressing	125	2451	12261		723
石油和天然气开采业	Petroleum and Natural Gas Extraction					
黑色金属矿采选业	Ferrous Metals Mining and Dressing	4	150			
有色金属矿采选业	Nonferrous Metals Mining and Dressing					
非金属矿采选业	Nonmetal Minerals Mining and Dressing	1	5439	476		
其他采矿业	Other Minerals Mining					

表18.18 续表 continued

单位：万元 (10 000 yuan)

项　目	Item	R&D项目数（项） Projects (unit)	研究与发展经费内部支出 Internal Expenses for R&D	技术改造经费支出 Expendi-tures for Technical Transfor -mation	技术引进经费支出 Expendi-tures for Technical Recom-mendation	购买国内技术用款 Purchases of Civil Techno -logy
制造业	Manufacturing	3978	890142	554794	179765	46572
农副食品加工业	Farm Products and By-food Processing	37	8941	354		260
食品制造业	Food Production	18	4884	107		20
饮料制造业	Beverage Production	24	6828	4324	1290	3335
烟草制品业	Tobacco Products	3	31			
纺织业	Textile Industry	95	10101	14807	240	216
纺织服装、鞋、帽制造业	Garments, Shoes and Hats Production	3	2236			
皮革毛皮羽毛（绒）及其制品业	Leather, Furs, Down and Related Products					
木材加工及木竹藤棕草制品业	Timber Processing,Bamboo, Cane,Palm,Straw Products	5	33			
家具制造业	Furniture Manufacturing	2	1235			
造纸及纸制品业	Papermaking and Paper Products	5	1357	35		
印刷业、记录媒介的复制	Printing and Record Medium Reproduction	5	2908	5705		
文教体育用品制造业	Cultural Educational and Sports Goods					
石油加工、炼焦及核燃料加工业	Petroleum, Coking and Nuclear Fuel Processing	6	2741	300	500	
化学原料及化学制品制造业	Raw Chemical Materials and Chemical Products	176	74209	14772	16650	2954
医药制造业	Medical and Pharmaceutical Products	493	34268	12958	10	3367
化学纤维制造业	Chemical Fiber					
橡胶制品业	Rubber Products	16	1969			
塑料制品业	Plastic Products	3	224	611		
非金属矿物制品业	Nonmetal Mineral Products	93	13858	9089	269	5290
黑色金属冶炼及压延加工业	Smelting and Pressing of Ferrous Metals	11	24636	8313		1855
有色金属冶炼及压延加工业	Smelting and Pressing of Nonferrous Metals	126	41469	37308	500	
金属制品业	Metal Products	19	6635	510		30
通用设备制造业	Ordinary Equipment	604	80559	57961	2381	2186
专用设备制造业	Special Equipment	113	25231	10081	45	20
交通运输设备制造业	Transportation Equipment	1520	456959	365290	157528	26405
电气机械及器材制造业	Electric Equipment and Machinery	114	24344	4110	300	500
通信设备、计算机及其他电子设备制造业	Communication, Computers and Other Electronic Equipment	120	7575	804		
仪器仪表及文化、办公用机械制造业	Instruments, Meters,Cultural and Office Machinery	253	19290	1668	53	135
工艺品及其他制造业	Handicraft and Other Production	114	37623	5687		
废弃资源和废旧材料回收加工业	Recovery and Processing of Waste Resources and Materials					
电力、燃气及水的生产和供应业	Electricpower, Gas & Water Production and Supply	54	6303	12327		
电力、热力的生产和供应业	Electricpower and Hot Power Production and Supply	53	6194	12327		
燃气生产和供应业	Gas Production and Supply	1	109			
水的生产和供应业	Water Production and Supply					

表18.19 规模以上工业企业R&D活动经费支出与项目情况（2011年）

EXPENDITURES AND PROJECTS OF SCIENTIFIC & TECHNOLOGICAL ACTIVITIES OF INDUSTRIAL ENTERPRISES ABOVE DESIGNATED SIZE (2011)

单位：万元 (10 000 yuan)

项 目	Item	R&D项目数（项） Projects (unit)	研究与发展经费内部支出 Internal Expenses for R&D	技术改造经费支出 Expendi-tures for Technical Transfor -mation	技术引进经费支出 Expendi-tures for Technical Recom-mendation	购买国内技术用款 Purchases of Civil Techno -logy
总 计	**Total**	**4524**	**943975**	**672935**	**181504**	**50483**
按隶属关系分	**By Relationship**					
中 央	Central	1262	342673	163405	146768	22944
地 方	Local	3262	601301	509530	34736	27539
按登记注册类型分	**By Registration**					
内资企业	Domestic-funded	3758	773557	345651	35976	35693
国有企业	State-owned	552	90638	24906	15566	716
集体企业	Collective-owned	12	417	29		
股份合作企业	Cooperative Enterprise	1	800	420		
联营企业	Joint Ownership Enterprises					
有限责任公司	Limited Liability Corporations	1777	293855	169780	6197	4308
股份有限公司	Share Holding Limited Corporations	591	140224	20829	11866	22910
私营企业	Private Enterprises	815	247303	129687	2347	7760
其他企业	Private Limited Liability Corporations	10	320			
港、澳、台商投资企业	Enterprises Funded by Hong Kong, Macao and Taiwan	278	31498	27993	1655	4345
合资经营企业	Joint-venture Enterprises	65	16415	4492	1650	2448
合作经营企业	Cooperative Enterprises					
独资经营企业	Enterprises with Sole Funded from Hong Kong,Macao and Taiwan	18	9528	18806	5	22
投资股份有限公司	Share-holding Corporations Ltd. with Investment from Hong Kong, Macao and Taiwan	195	5555	4695		1875
外商投资企业	Foreign Funded Enterprises	488	138921	299292	143874	10445
中外合资经营企业	Joint-venture Enterprises	281	131863	297250	142584	7110
中外合作经营企业	Cooperation Enterprises					
外资企业	Enterprises with Sole Fund	191	4248	1940		
外商投资股份有限公司	Share-holding Corporations Ltd.	16	2810	102	1290	3335
按行业分	**By Sector**					
采矿业	Mining and Quarrying	131	8221	40153		2023
煤炭开采和洗选业	Coal Mining and Dressing	125	2451	39111		2023
石油和天然气开采业	Petroleum and Natural Gas Extraction					
黑色金属矿采选业	Ferrous Metals Mining and Dressing	4	150	566		
有色金属矿采选业	Nonferrous Metals Mining and Dressing					
非金属矿采选业	Nonmetal Minerals Mining and Dressing	2	5621	476		
其他采矿业	Other Minerals Mining					

表18.19 续表 continued

单位：万元 (10 000 yuan)

项　目	Item	R&D项目数（项） Projects (unit)	研究与发展经费内部支出 Internal Expenses for R&D	技术改造经费支出 Expendi-tures for Technical Transfor -mation	技术引进经费支出 Expendi-tures for Technical Recom-mendation	购买国内技术用款 Purchases of Civil Techno -logy
制造业	Manufacturing	4339	929451	618828	181504	48460
农副食品加工业	Farm Products and By-food Processing	54	10538	490		260
食品制造业	Food Production	21	5028	107		20
饮料制造业	Beverage Production	31	8783	7829	1290	3335
烟草制品业	Tobacco Products	3	31			
纺织业	Textile Industry	95	10101	14807	240	216
纺织服装、鞋、帽制造业	Garments, Shoes and Hats Production	3	2236			
皮革毛皮羽毛（绒）及其制品业	Leather, Furs, Down and Related Products					
木材加工及木竹藤棕草制品业	Timber Processing,Bamboo, Cane,Palm,Straw Products	7	464			
家具制造业	Furniture Manufacturing	3	1425			
造纸及纸制品业	Papermaking and Paper Products	7	1364	2855		
印刷业、记录媒介的复制	Printing and Record Medium Reproduction	6	2987	5705		
文教体育用品制造业	Cultural Educational and Sports Goods					
石油加工、炼焦及核燃料加工业	Petroleum, Coking and Nuclear Fuel Processing	9	3048	300	500	
化学原料及化学制品制造业	Raw Chemical Materials and Chemical Products	200	78867	14984	16650	2964
医药制造业	Medical and Pharmaceutical Products	559	39864	13682	10	3387
化学纤维制造业	Chemical Fiber					
橡胶制品业	Rubber Products	19	2144			
塑料制品业	Plastic Products	8	837	611		
非金属矿物制品业	Nonmetal Mineral Products	115	17721	11189	269	6810
黑色金属冶炼及压延加工业	Smelting and Pressing of Ferrous Metals	22	25975	30842		2115
有色金属冶炼及压延加工业	Smelting and Pressing of Nonferrous Metals	136	43141	38084	500	
金属制品业	Metal Products	30	8825	510		76
通用设备制造业	Ordinary Equipment	632	82983	58203	2381	2189
专用设备制造业	Special Equipment	125	26345	10686	1756	47
交通运输设备制造业	Transportation Equipment	1552	461844	390158	157556	26405
电气机械及器材制造业	Electric Equipment and Machinery	139	26215	4374	300	500
通信设备、计算机及其他电子设备制造业	Communication, Computers and Other Electronic Equipment	146	9158	839		2
仪器仪表及文化、办公用机械制造业	Instruments, Meters,Cultural and Office Machinery	303	21903	1687	53	135
工艺品及其他制造业	Handicraft and Other Production	114	37623	10187		
废弃资源和废旧材料回收加工业	Recovery and Processing of Waste Resources and Materials			700		
电力、燃气及水的生产和供应业	Electricpower, Gas & Water Production and Supply	54	6303	13955		
电力、热力的生产和供应业	Electricpower and Hot Power Production and Supply	53	6194	12455		
燃气生产和供应业	Gas Production and Supply	1	109	1500		
水的生产和供应业	Water Production and Supply					

表18.20 大中型工业企业新产品开发情况（2011年）

NEW PRODUCTS DEVELOPMENT OF LARGE & MEDIUM-SIZED INDUSTRIAL ENTERPRISES (2011)

单位：万元 (10 000 yuan)

项 目	Item	新产品项目数（项） Projects of New Products (unit)	新产品开发经费支出 Development fund of New Products	新产品产值 Output Value of New Products	新产品销售收入 Sales Revenue of New Products	其中 of which #新产品出口 Exports of New Products
总 计	**Total**	**4207**	**1027439**	**29988840**	**28709744**	**3841620**
按隶属关系分	**By Relationship**					
中 央	Central	1508	498764	8468225	8481844	185074
地 方	Local	2699	528674	21520614	20227900	3656546
按登记注册类型分	**By Registration**					
内资企业	Domestic-funded	3483	733718	19194274	18212721	1700730
国有企业	State-owned	529	86313	750741	701392	8256
集体企业	Collective-owned	11	380	2989	2985	
股份合作企业	Cooperative Enterprise			1845	1661	1317
联营企业	Joint Ownership Enterprises	1	4518			
有限责任公司	Limited Liability Corporations	1456	284976	7487625	7292166	556972
股份有限公司	Share Holding Limited Corporations	835	175706	3837748	3597726	90065
私营企业	Private Enterprises	631	180551	7064525	6571038	1026999
其他企业	Private Limited Liability Corporations	20	1274	48801	45753	17122
港、澳、台商投资企业	Enterprises Funded by Hong Kong, Macao and Taiwan	146	58469	2864733	2849927	2011578
合资经营企业	Joint-venture Enterprises	67	18221	389568	362890	3044
合作经营企业	Cooperative Enterprises					
独资经营企业	Enterprises with Sole Funded from Hong Kong,Macao and Taiwan	22	10322	2180026	2197713	1977596
投资股份有限公司	Share-holding Corporations Ltd. with Investment from Hong Kong, Macao and Taiwan	57	29926	295139	289324	30937
外商投资企业	Foreign Funded Enterprises	578	235252	7929833	7647096	129312
中外合资经营企业	Joint-venture Enterprises	342	230579	6854852	6660450	114569
中外合作经营企业	Cooperation Enterprises					
外资企业	Enterprises with Sole Fund	223	2200	1025373	937046	14743
外商投资股份有限公司	Share-holding Corporations Ltd.	13	2472	49608	49600	
按行业分	**By Sector**					
采矿业	Mining and Quarrying	2	55			
煤炭开采和洗选业	Coal Mining and Dressing	2	55			
石油和天然气开采业	Petroleum and Natural Gas Extraction					
黑色金属矿采选业	Ferrous Metals Mining and Dressing					
有色金属矿采选业	Nonferrous Metals Mining and Dressing					
非金属矿采选业	Nonmetal Minerals Mining and Dressing					
其他矿采选业	Other Minerals Mining and Dressing					

表18.20 续表 continued

单位：万元 (10 000 yuan)

项　目	Item	新产品项目数（项） Projects of New Products (unit)	新产品开发经费支出 Development fund of New Products	新产品产值 Output Value of New Products	新产品销售收入 Sales Revenue of New Products	其中 of which #新产品出口 Exports of New Products
制造业	Manufacturing	4161	1020635	29982160	28703064	3841620
木材及竹材采运业	Logging and Transport of Timber and Bamboo	27	4522	404949	403511	3921
农副食品加工业	Farm Products and By-food Processing	17	4615	70588	62488	
食品制造业	Food Production	18	5215	170866	152961	
饮料制造业	Beverage Production	2	233	328838	301177	
烟草加工业	Tobacco Processing	94	3492	320939	300546	16440
纺织业	Textile Industry	2	2016	1000	1236	
服装及其他纤维制品制造业	Garments and other Fiber Products					
皮革、毛皮、羽绒及其制品业	Leather, Furs, Down and Related Products	5	33	246	243	
木材加工及竹藤棕草制品业	Timber Processing, Bamboo, Cane, Palm Fiber and Straw Products	2	1235	53781	50726	
家具制造业	Furniture Manufacturing	7	1407	175315	155236	
造纸及纸制品业	Papermaking and Paper Products	4	2798	9436	9436	
印刷业、记录媒介的复制	Printing and Record Medium Reproduction					
文教体育用品制造业	Cultural Educational and Sports Goods	8	3658	40374	38000	
石油加工及炼焦业	Petroleum Refining and Coking	138	44075	2353575	1977149	28293
化学原料及化学制品制造业	Raw Chemical Materials and Chemical Products	403	30449	558678	412165	47519
医药制造业	Medical and Pharmaceutical Products					
化学纤维制造业	Chemical Fiber	16	3176	153514	127660	1368
橡胶制品业	Rubber Products	13	718	53280	52824	
塑料制品业	Plastic Products	85	15732	373526	358849	84605
非金属矿物制品业	Nonmetal Mineral Products	26	45291	465192	450700	53992
黑色金属冶炼及压延加工业	Smelting and Pressing of Ferrous Metals	99	44915	1175825	1107241	62206
有色金属冶炼及压延加工业	Smelting and Pressing of Nonferrous Metals	20	5252	166615	165599	90164
金属制品业	Metal Products	689	90699	1362568	1236995	22743
通用设备制造业	Odinary Equipment	108	16310	111277	115888	9306
专用设备制造业	Special Purpose Equipment	1713	578745	14632792	14515568	1300872
交通运输设备制造业	Transport Equipment	145	32779	3623526	3300762	107381
电气机械及器材制造业	Electric Equipment and Machinery	141	16522	2982187	3006930	1998860
电子及通信设备制造业	Electronic and Telecommunication Equipment	276	25292	235022	235748	11532
仪器仪表及文化、办公用机械制造业	Instruments Meters Cultural and Clerical Machinery	103	41457	158255	163427	2418
其他制造业	Other Manufacturing					
电力、蒸汽、热水的生产和供应业	Electricity Steam & Hot Water Production and Supply	44	6749	6680	6680	
煤气生产和供应业	Gas Production and Supply	43	6640	6680	6680	
自来水的生产和供应业	Tap Water Production and Supply	1	109			
水的生产和供应业	Water Production and Supply					

表18.21 规模以上工业企业新产品开发情况（2011年）

NEW PRODUCTS DEVELOPMENT OF INDUSTRIAL ENTERPRISES ABOVE DESIGNATED SIZE (2011)

单位：万元 (10 000 yuan)

项 目	Item	新产品项目数（项） Projects of New Products (unit)	新产品开发经费支出 Development fund of New Products	新产品产值 Output Value of New Products	新产品销售收入 Sales Revenue of New Products	其 中 of which #新产品出口 Exports of New Products
总　计	**Total**	**4612**	**1073308**	**31697481**	**30280328**	**3928448**
按隶属关系分	**By Relationship**					
中　央	Central	1520	500344	8476045	8489629	185074
地　方	Local	3092	572964	23221436	21790699	3743374
按登记注册类型分	**By Registration**					
内资企业	Domestic-funded	3840	774490	20772640	19676694	1776470
国有企业	State-owned	541	88071	763951	713566	8256
集体企业	Collective-owned	11	380	4870	4864	
股份合作企业	Cooperative Enterprise			1845	1661	1317
联营企业	Joint Ownership Enterprises	1	4518			
有限责任公司	Limited Liability Corporations	1602	298197	8015963	7745665	559354
股份有限公司	Share Holding Limited Corporations	850	180873	4079581	3835356	93967
私营企业	Private Enterprises	808	200786	7847769	7329830	1096454
其他企业	Private Limited Liability Corporations	27	1665	58661	45753	17122
港、澳、台商投资企业	Enterprises Funded by Hong Kong, Macao and Taiwan	167	62377	2950772	2912411	2018510
合资经营企业	Joint-venture Enterprises	80	20983	434790	389760	9721
合作经营企业	Cooperative Enterprises					
独资经营企业	Enterprises with Sole Funded from Hong Kong,Macao and Taiwan	30	11467	2220723	2233209	1977744
投资股份有限公司	Share-holding Corporations Ltd. with Investment from Hong Kong, Macao and Taiwan	57	29926	295259	289442	31045
外商投资企业	Foreign Funded Enterprises	605	236441	7974069	7691223	133468
中外合资经营企业	Joint-venture Enterprises	363	231213	6880578	6686066	116429
中外合作经营企业	Cooperation Enterprises					
外资企业	Enterprises with Sole Fund	229	2756	1043883	955557	17038
外商投资股份有限公司	Share-holding Corporations Ltd.	13	2472	49608	49600	
按行业分	**By Sector**					
采矿业	Mining and Quarrying	2	55	4257	4257	
煤炭开采和洗选业	Coal Mining and Dressing	2	55			
石油和天然气开采业	Petroleum and Natural Gas Extraction					
黑色金属矿采选业	Ferrous Metals Mining and Dressing					
有色金属矿采选业	Nonferrous Metals Mining and Dressing					
非金属矿采选业	Nonmetal Minerals Mining and Dressing			4257	4257	
其他矿采选业	Other Minerals Mining and Dressing					

表18.21 续表 continued

单位：万元 (10 000 yuan)

项 目	Item	新产品项目数（项） Projects of New Products (unit)	新产品开发经费支出 Development fund of New Products	新产品产值 Output Value of New Products	新产品销售收入 Sales Revenue of New Products	其 中 of which #新产品出口 Exports of New Products
制造业	Manufacturing	4566	1066504	31686544	30269391	3928448
木材及竹材采运业	Logging and Transport of Timber and Bamboo	40	5755	452290	449165	3921
农副食品加工业	Farm Products and By-food Processing	17	4615	87119	69159	
食品制造业	Food Production	22	6018	190402	172275	5900
饮料制造业	Beverage Production	2	233	328838	301177	
烟草加工业	Tobacco Processing	94	3492	333406	323237	16440
纺织业	Textile Industry	3	2099	1000	1236	
服装及其他纤维制品制造业	Garments and other Fiber Products					
皮革、毛皮、羽绒及其制品业	Leather, Furs, Down and Related Products	7	464	6495	6491	
木材加工及竹藤棕草制品业	Timber Processing, Bamboo, Cane, Palm Fiber and Straw Products	4	1458	75104	72027	
家具制造业	Furniture Manufacturing	10	1421	182911	162999	50
造纸及纸制品业	Papermaking and Paper Products	5	2878	15113	15113	
印刷业、记录媒介的复制	Printing and Record Medium Reproduction					
文教体育用品制造业	Cultural Educational and Sports Goods	11	3812	63386	60540	
石油加工及炼焦业	Petroleum Refining and Coking	158	51116	2477498	2080241	28293
化学原料及化学制品制造业	Raw Chemical Materials and Chemical Products	487	36409	624070	475504	50881
医药制造业	Medical and Pharmaceutical Products					
化学纤维制造业	Chemical Fiber	16	3176	153514	127660	1368
橡胶制品业	Rubber Products	17	1540	85219	64746	
塑料制品业	Plastic Products	106	19191	517802	483444	88775
非金属矿物制品业	Nonmetal Mineral Products	30	46117	571344	555788	53992
黑色金属冶炼及压延加工业	Smelting and Pressing of Ferrous Metals	108	45708	1370336	1271421	62581
有色金属冶炼及压延加工业	Smelting and Pressing of Nonferrous Metals	31	6515	264769	262388	90164
金属制品业	Metal Products	732	93552	1501826	1358604	65840
通用设备制造业	Odinary Equipment	129	18405	177389	181525	9687
专用设备制造业	Special Purpose Equipment	1768	588766	14823722	14681455	1302145
交通运输设备制造业	Transport Equipment	175	35066	3914876	3597420	119010
电气机械及器材制造业	Electric Equipment and Machinery	177	19587	3004268	3028947	2005687
电子及通信设备制造业	Electronic and Telecommunication Equipment	314	27655	304661	303404	21297
仪器仪表及文化、办公用机械制造业	Instruments Meters Cultural and Clerical Machinery	103	41457	159183	163427	2418
其他制造业	Other Manufacturing					
电力、蒸汽、热水的生产和供应业	Electricity Steam & Hot Water Production and Supply	44	6749	6680	6680	
煤气生产和供应业	Gas Production and Supply	43	6640	6680	6680	
自来水的生产和供应业	Tap Water Production and Supply	1	109			
水的生产和供应业	Water Production and Supply					

表18.22 专利申请受理量及专利授权量（2010－2011年）
PATENT APPLICATIONS ACCEPTED AND GRANTED (2010-2011)

单位：件 (pcs)

项　目	Item	申请受理量 Applications Accepted		专利授权量 Applications Granted	
		2010	2011	2010	2011
总　计	**Total**	**22825**	**32039**	**12080**	**15525**
按种类分	**By Type**				
发　明	Inventions	5150	8839	1143	1865
实用新型	Utility Models	11985	16786	6704	8749
外观设计	Designs	5690	6414	4233	4911
按对象分	**By Applicant**				
个　人	Individuals	12371	15834	4242	5849
大专院校	Universities and Colleges	1501	2020	825	1138
科研单位	Research Institutions	413	451	170	240
工矿企业	Industrial and Mineral Enterprises	8094	12689	6517	7653
机关团体	Government Agencies and Organizations	446	1045	326	645

表18.23 图书发行流转及销售情况（2010－2011年）
STATISTICS ON PUBLICATION, CIRCULATION AND SALES OF BOOKS (2010-2011)

单位：万册、万元 (10 000 copies, 10 000 yuan)

指　标	Item	册 数 Number of Books		金 额 Value	
		2010	2011	2010	2011
购　进	**Purchases**	**90719**	**88763**	**438290**	**479720**
销　售	**Sales**	**91587**	**92811**	**516429**	**519465**
零　售	Retail	33036	32924	191924	192283
区　县	Districts and Counties	21069	20964	114278	114987
县以下	Below Counties	11967	11960	77646	77296
批　发	Wholesale	58550	59887	324505	327182
区　县	Districts and Counties	38783	39004	252679	267013
县以下	Below Counties	19767	20883	71826	60169
库　存	**Inventory**	**8170**	**4122**	**88498**	**48753**

表18.24 规模以上工业企业专利主要指标（2010－2011年）

MAJOR INDICATORS ON THE PATENTS OF INDUSTRIAL ENTERPRISES ABOVE DESIGNATED SIZE (2010-2011)

指　标	Item	2010	2011
有专利申请的企业数（个）	Number of Enterprises with Patent Application (unit)	378	409
有专利授权的企业数（个）	Number of Enterprises with Patent Granted (unit)	294	334
拥有有效专利的企业数（累计值）（个）	Number of Enterprises with Valid Patent (cumulative value) (unit)	397	423
专利授权量（项）	Number of Patents Granted (unit)	3962	5398
专利投入（亿元）	Investment in Patent (100 million yuan)	11.87	43.19
专利许可收入（亿元）	Revenue from Patent License (100 million yuan)	2.64	12.43
专利转让收入（亿元）	Revenue from Patent Transfer (100 million yuan)	0.78	0.89
专利产品类别数量（类）	Number of Patent Categories (category)	8080	10063
专利产品产值（亿元）	Output Value of Patented Products (100 million yuan)	997.03	1324.20
#自主研发专利产品产值	Output Value of Self-developed Patented Products	974.68	1251.45
技术引进专利产品产值	Output Value of Imported Patented Products	22.35	72.75
#出口专利产品产值	Output Value of Exported Patented Products	20.97	55.46
专利产品销售收入（亿元）	Sales Revenue of Patented Products (100 million yuan)	952.80	1195.29
#自主研发专利产品销售收入	Sales Revenue of Self-developed Patented Products	931.65	1167.29
技术引进专利产品销售收入	Sales Revenue of Imported Patented Products	21.15	28.00
#出口专利产品销售收入	Sales Revenue of Exported Patented Products	19.29	71.46
被许可的有效专利量（项）	Number of Licensed Patents (unit)	236	626
被许可生产的专利产品产值（当年价格）（亿元）	Output Value of the Patented Products Permitted for Production (current price) (100 million yuan)	20.76	55.18
被许可生产的专利产品销售收入（亿元）	Sales Revenue of the Patented Products Permitted for Production (100 million yuan)	18.94	49.72

表18.25 各类技术合同签定及执行情况（2011年）
SIGNING AND IMPLEMENTATION OF TECHNICAL CONTRACTS BY TYPE (2011)

项　目	Item	合同数（项）Number of Contracts (item)	合同成交金额（万元）Value of Contracts (10 000 yuan)	其　中 of which	
				#技术交易额（万元）Technology Transaction Value (10 000 yuan)	技术交易额比重（%）As Percentage of Contract Value (%)
总　计	**Total**	**3336**	**1010751.57**	**801822.87**	**79.3**
技术开发	Technical Development	2550	566749.46	461756.54	81.5
技术转让	Technical Transfer	196	115711.47	103579.18	89.5
技术咨询	Technical Consultation	125	25360.89	25249.46	99.6
技术服务	Technical Services	465	302929.74	211237.69	69.7

表18.26 新闻出版机构和人员数（2010－2011年）
NUMBER OF INSTITUTIONS AND PERSONS ENGAGED IN PRESS AND PUBLICATION(2010-2011)

单位：个、人 (unit，person)

指　标	Item	2010	2011
书刊出版社	**Publishing Houses**		
机构数	Institutions	3	3
从业人员	Personnel	1098	1773
书刊印刷厂	**Printing Houses**		
机构数	Institutions	41	86
从业人员	Personnel	4758	8256
国有书店	**State-owned Book Stores**		
机构数	Institutions	271	271
从业人员	Personnel	2439	2577

注：印刷厂增幅较大原因，专项厂改为印刷。
Note: The reason for the rapid increase of printing houses is that the specialized factories are switched to printing.

表18.27 图书、杂志和报纸出版情况（2010－2011年）

PUBLICATION OF BOOKS, MAGAZINES AND NEWSPAPERS (2010-2011)

指　标	Item	2010	2011
图　书	**Books Published**		
种　数（种）	Number of Publications (kind)	4691	5651
总印数（万册、万张）	Printed Copies (10 000 copies)	15694	15597
总印张数（万印张）	Printed Sheets (10 000 sheets)	103442	100865
期　刊	**Magazines Published**		
种　数（种）	Number of Publications (kind)	135	134
每期平均印数（万册）	Average Printed Copies Per Issue (10 000 copies)	271	265
总印数（万册）	Printed Copies (10 000 copies)	5409	5183
总印张数（万印张）	Printed Sheets (10 000 sheets)	36068	32964
报　纸	**Newspapers Published**		
种　数（种）	Number of Publications (kind)	26	26
每期平均印数（万份）	Average Printed Copies Per Issue (10 000 copies)	300	316
总印数（万份）	Printed Copies (10 000 copies)	76484	66057
总印张数（万印张）	Printed Sheets (10 000 sheets)	427185	3680310

注：报纸发行总数去除了19种校报。
Note:19 kinds of school newspaper are removed from the total newspaper publications.

表18.28 文化机构和人员数（2010－2011年）

NUMBER OF INSTITUTIONS AND PERSONNEL IN CULTURE (2010-2011)

项　目	Item	2010	2011
机构数(个)	**Number of Institutions (unit)**	**1656**	**1559**
艺术业	Art	427	329
#艺术表演团体	Art Performance Troupes	381	282
艺术表演场所	Art Performance Places	46	46
文物业	Cultural Relics	89	92
图书馆业	Public Libraries	43	43
群众文化服务业	Mass Culture	1041	1037
艺术教育业	Art Education	1	1
文艺科研	Art Research Institutions	1	1
其　他	Others	54	56
从业人员数(人)	**Number of Employed Persons (person)**	**13115**	**12956**
艺术业	Art	5248	4817
#艺术表演团体	Art Performance Troupes	4423	3901
艺术表演场所	Art Performance Places	825	906
文物业	Cultural Relics	1895	1995
图书馆业	Public Libraries	854	848
群众文化服务业	Mass Culture	3726	3872
艺术教育业	Art Education	241	272
文艺科研	Art Research Institutions	29	36
其　他	Others	1122	1116

注：艺术教育机构统计口径为含教育部门和文化部门的艺术教育机构。
Note:The scope of art education institutions include the institutions in educational sector and cultural sector.

表18.29 公共图书馆情况（2010－2011年）
PUBLIC LIBRARIES (2010-2011)

项 目	Item	总 计 Total		其 中 of which #市 级 At Municipal Level	
		2010	2011	2010	2011
总藏量（万册、件）	Total Collections (10 000 volumes)	1031	1149	369	399
书架总长度（万米）	Total Monolayer Length of Bookshelves (10 000 meters)	13	23	4	4
有效借书证数（万个）	Number of Valid Library Cards (10 000 units)	16	29	4	18
图书流通情况	Circulation of Books				
总流通人次（万人次）	Total Number of Circulation (10 000 person-times)	621	777	150	204
书刊外借册次（万册次）	Number of Books Borrowed by Readers (10 000 volume-times)	705	721	132	163
为读者举办各种活动服务次数（次）	Number of Service Activities Provided for Readers (time)	1471	1428	397	380
总支出（万元）	Total Expenditures (10 000 yuan)	9335	13866	4943	6448
#藏量购置费	Purchase Expenses	1626	2291	1010	1569
本年新购藏量（万册）	Number of Books Purchased During Current Year (10 000 volumes)	52	53	22	20
公用房屋建筑面积（万平方米）	Floor Space of Public Buildings (10 000 sq.m)	20	23	5	6
#书 库	Stack Rooms	5	5	1	1
阅览室座席（个）	Seating Capacity of Reading Rooms (seat)	13568	13001	2482	2482

注：指标发放借书证数今年改为有效借书证数，故增幅较大。
Note:The index of "number of library cards distributed" is replaced by "number of valid library cards", so the growth rate is high.

表18.30 文物业情况（2011年）
STATISTICS ON CULTURAL RELICS (2011)

项 目	Item	文物业 Cultural Relics	其 中 of which #博物馆 Museums	#文物保护管理机构 Protection and Management Agencies
藏 品(件)	Number of Collections (pcs)	620620	519143	77415
#一级品	Grade One	1091	1072	19
经费支出（万元）	Total Expenditure(10 000 yuan)	66496	54503	3277

表18.31 群众艺术馆和文化馆（站）情况（2011年）
MASS ART CENTERS AND CULTURAL CENTERS (2011)

项　目	Item	合　计 Total	其　中 of which		
			群众艺术馆 Mass Art Centers	文化馆 Cultural Centers	文化站 Cultural Stations
单位数（个）	Number of Units (unit)	1037	1	40	996
举办展览个数（个）	Conducting Exhibitions (unit)	2869	3	376	2490
组织文艺活动次数（次）	Art Performances (time)	16235	28	2602	13605
举办培训班班次(次）	Training Courses (time)	8188	12	2580	5596

表18.32 艺术表演团体演出情况（2011年）
BASIC STATISTICS ON PERFORMANCE OF ART TROUPES (2011)

种　类	Item	国内演出场数（场） Number of Performances in China (show)	国内演出观众人数（千人次） Number of Spectators of the Performances in China （1000 person-times)
总　计	**Total**	**35900**	**15310**
按登记注册类型分	**By Registration**		
国　有	State-owned	2700	4720
集　体	Collective-owned	200	330
其　他	Others	33000	10260
按剧种分	**By Art Troupes**		
话剧、儿童剧、滑稽剧团	Drama, Plays for Children and Comedy Troupes	300	200
歌剧、舞剧、歌舞剧团	Opera, Dance Drama and Song and Dance Drama Troupes	500	680
歌舞团、轻音乐团	Song and Dance Troupes, Light Music Troupes	2600	2380
文工团、宣传队、乌兰牧骑	Cultural and Performance Troupes and Ulanmuchi (equestrian art troupes)	300	390
乐团、合唱团	Philharmonic and Chorus Troupes	200	160
戏曲剧团	Local Opera Troupes	600	730
#京　剧	Beijing Opera Troupes	200	180
曲艺、杂技、木偶、皮影团	Recitation and Ballad Troupes, Acrobatics and Circus Troupes, Puppet Show Troupes, and Shadow Play Troupes	400	480
综合性艺术表演团体	General Art Performing Troupes	31000	10290

注：艺术表演团体统计口径调整为含系统内、系统外两部分。
Note:The scope of art performance troupes includes the troupes either inside or outside the public-owned system.

表18.33 广播电台、电视台情况（2010－2011年）
STATISTICS ON RADIO AND TV STATIONS (2010-2011)

项　目	Item	2010	2011
广播电台情况	**Statistics on Radio Stations**		
广播节目套数（套）	Number of Programs (set)	26	32
广播人口覆盖率（%）	Radio Coverage of Population (%)	95.71	98.02
中短波转播发射台（座）	Transmission and Relaying Stations of of Medium and Short Wave Broadcast(unit)	5	5
中短波广播发射功率（千瓦）	Power of Transmitters of Medium and Short Wave Broadcast (kw)	120	120
调频转播发射台（座）	Number of Transmission and Relaying Stations of Frequency Modulation Broadcast (unit)	61	60
调频发射功率（千瓦）	Power of Transmitters of Frequency Modulation Broadcast (kw)	155	163
全年公共广播节目播出时间（小时）	Public Programs Broadcasting Hours of the Year (hour)	108811	132849
#新闻资讯	News	30522	32035
专题服务	Special Subject	25936	31596
综　艺	General Entertainment	23360	24108
广播剧	Radio Drama	9011	13251
广　告	Advertising	6303	5587
电视台情况	**Statistics on TV Stations**		
电视节目套数（套）	Number of Programs (unit)	45	45
电视人口覆盖率（%）	TV Coverage of Population (%)	97.39	98.56
电视转播发射台（座）	Number of Broadcast-Television Stations (unit)	47	47
电视发射功率（千瓦）	Power of Television Transmitters (kw)	100	100
全年公共电视节目播出时间（小时）	Public Programs Broadcasting Hours of the Year (hour)	250503	261657
#新闻资讯	News	31632	40517
专题服务	Special Subject	44115	40548
综艺益智	General Entertainment	32586	22768
影视剧	Films and TV plays	93129	112991
广　告	Advertising	33565	26955

重/庆/统/计/年/鉴

主要统计指标解释

普通高等学校

是指按照国家规定的设置标准和审批程序批准举办的，通过全国普通高等学校统一招生考试，招收高中毕业生为主要培养对象，实施高等教育的全日制大学、独立设置的学院和高等专科学校、高等职业学校和其他机构。

大学、独立设置的学院主要实施本科层次以上教育，高等专科学校、高等职业学校实施专科层次教育，其他机构是承担国家普通招生计划任务不计校数的机构。包括普通高等学校分校和批准筹建的普通高等学校等。

成人高等学校

指按照国家规定的设置标准和审批程序批准举办的，通过全国成人高等学校统一招生考试，招收具有高中毕业或同等学历的在职从业人员为主要培养对象，利用函授、业余、脱产等多种形式对其实施高等学历教育的学校。包括职工高等学校、农民高等学校、管理干部学院、教育学院、独立函授学院、广播电视大学、其他机构等。其他机构是承担国家成人招生计划任务不计校数的机构。

小学学龄儿童入学率

指调查范围内已入小学学习的学龄儿童占校内外学龄儿童总数（包括弱智儿童在内，但不包括盲聋哑儿童）的比重。计算公式：

小学学龄儿童入学率＝已入学的小学学龄儿童数/校内外小学学龄儿童总数×100%

专利

是专利权的简称，是对发明人的发明创造经审查合格后，由专利局依据专利法授予发明人和设计人对该项发明创造享有的专有权。包括发明、实用新型和外观设计。反映拥有自主知识产权的科技和设计成果情况。

有专利申请的企业

指在报告年内向国家知识产权局或中国以外的国家知识产权局（地区专利组织）提交专利申请，并收到《专利申请受理通知书》和缴纳相关费用的工业企业。

有专利授权的企业

指报告年内获得国家知识产权局或中国以外的国家知识产权局（地区专利组织）《专利授权通知书》并缴纳相关费用的工业企业。

拥有有效专利的企业（累计值）

指截至报告年末，有专利权处于维持状态的工业企业。

专利产品产值（当年价格）

工业企业在报告年度内生产的以货币形式表现的工业最终专利产品的总价值量。专利产品产值计算参照国家关于“工业总产值”的计算方法。

专利产品销售收入

工业企业在报告期内销售专利产品的货币收入总额。

发明

指对产品、方法或其改进所提出的新的技术方案。是国际通行的反映拥有自主知识产权技术的核心指标。

实用新型

指对产品的形状、构造或者其结合所提出的适于实用的新的技术方案。反映具有一定技术含量的技术成果情况。

外观设计

指对产品的形状、图案、色彩或者其结合所做出的富有美感并适于工业上应用的新设计。反映拥有自主知识产权的外观设计成果情况。

主要统计指标解释

■ 驰名商标

是指在市场上享有较高声誉并为相关公众所熟知的注册商标，也是一种法律保护手段。

■ 著名商标

著名商标的知名度介于驰名商标和普通商标之间的商标群落，是驰名商标坚实的后备力量。

■ 文化事业机构

指从事专业文化工作和为专业文化工作服务的独立建制的单位。不包括这些单位另外举办独立核算的其他机构和各部门的业余文化组织。

■ 艺术表演团体

指从事戏曲、音乐、舞蹈、杂技等专业艺术表演，有独立帐户。不包括半工半艺、半农半艺和民间职业剧团。

■ 艺术表演观众人数（人次）

指售票、包场演出或民族地区免费演出的艺术表演观众人次数，不包括彩排审查和内部观摩演出的观看人次数。

Explanatory Notes on Main Statistical Indicators

□ Regular Institutions of Higher Education

Refer to educational establishments set up according to the government evaluation and approval procedures, enrolling graduates from senior secondary schools and providing higher education courses and training for senior professionals. They include full-time universities, colleges, high professional schools, high professional vocational schools and others.

Universities and colleges are mainly providing undergraduate courses; those high professional schools and high professional vocational schools are mainly providing professional trainings; and others refer to educational establishments, which are responsible for enrolling students but not covered in the total number of schools, including: branch schools of universities and colleges, and universities and colleges that have been proved and prepared to construct.

□ Institutions of Higher Learning for Adults

Refer to educational establishments, set up in line with relevant rules approved by the government, enrolling staff and workers with senior secondary school or equivalent education, and providing higher education courses in many forms of correspondence, spare time, or full time for adults. Professionals thus trained receive a qualification equivalent to graduates studying regular courses at regular universities, colleges and professional colleges. Institutions of higher learning for adults include schools of high education for staff and workers, schools of high education for peasants, colleges for management cadres, pedagogical colleges, independent correspondence colleges, Radio and TV universities and other educational establishments. Other educational establishments are responsible for enrolling adult students but not covered in the number of schools.

□ Enrollment Rate of Primary School-aged Children

Refers to the proportion of school-aged children enrolled at schools to the total number of school-age children both in and outside schools (including retarded children, but excluding blind, deaf and mute children). The formula is:

Enrollment Rate of Primary School-aged Children =Total Primary School-aged Children at Schools/Total Primary School-age Children Both at and Outside Schools×100%

□ Patent

Is an abbreviation for the patent right and refers to the exclusive right of ownership by the inventors or designers for the creation or inventions, given from the patent offices after due process of assessment and approval in accordance with the Patent Law. Patents are granted for inventions, utility models and designs. This indicator reflects the achievements of S&T and design with independent intellectual property.

□ Enterprise with Patent Application

Refers to the industrial enterprise which has submitted patent application to the State Intellectual Property Office or the national intellectual property administration outside China (regional patent organization), received the “Notification of Patent Application Acceptance” and paid off the related fees within the year of report.

□ Enterprise with Patent Granted

Refers to the industrial enterprise which has received the “Notification of Patent Granted” from the State Intellectual Property Office or the national intellectual property administration outside China (regional patent organization) and paid off the related fees within the year of report.

□ Enterprise with Valid Patents (Cumulative Value)

Refers to the industrial enterprise with patents in the status of maintenance by the end of the year of report.

□ Output Value of Patented Products (Current Price)

Refers to the total value of the final patented industrial products produced by the industrial enterprises in the year of report in the form of currency. Refer to the calculation method of “gross industrial output value” stipulated by the state for the calculation of the output value of patented products

EXPLANATORY NOTES TO MAJOR STATISTICAL INDICATORS

Sales Revenue of Patented Products

Refers to the total revenue of currency from the sales of the patented products by the industrial enterprises within the year of report.

Inventions

Refer to the new technical proposals to the products or methods or their modifications. This is universal core indicator reflecting the technologies with independent intellectual property.

Utility Models

Refer to the practical and new technical proposals on the shape and structure of the product or the combination of both. This indicator reflects the condition of technological results with certain technical content.

Designs

Refer to the aesthetics and industrially applicable new designs for the shape, pattern and color of the product, or their combinations. This indicator reflects the appearance design achievements with independent intellectual property.

Famous Trade Marks

Refer to trade marks publicly known with higher honors. It is also a legal protection.

Well-known Trade Marks

Their fames are between famous trade marks and ordinary trade marks. And they are tough reserve force of famous trade marks.

Cultural Institutions

Refer to units which have their own organizational system and independent accounting system and specialize in or serve cultural development. They exclude other establishments run by these cultural institutions and amateur cultural groups established by various departments.

Art Troupe

Refers to the troupe who is engaged in drama, opera, music, dance, acrobatics or other art performance, opens independent accounts with banks and has self-supporting accounting system; excluding the troupes who are engaged partly in industrial or agricultural activities, partly in art performance and the professional troupes organized by the people.

Number of Spectators at Art Performance

Refers to the number of attendants at commercial shows, completely booked shows of free shows given in minority national areas, and does not include the number of spectators at rehearsals for examination and internal shows for study.

第19章

卫生、体育和其他社会活动

PUBLIC HEAITH,SPORTS AND OTHER SOCIAL ACTIVITIES

简要说明
BRIEF INTRODUCTION

本章资料主要包括卫生事业、体育事业、民政事业、劳动和社会保障事业、公检法司情况、安全生产情况、火灾事故和道路交通事故等内容，由市统计局社会科技统计处根据有关部门资料整理提供。

卫生资料来自市卫生局，体育资料来源于市体育局，民政和劳动社会保障有关资料分别由市民政局、市人力资源和社会保障局提供，公检法司资料分别由市公安局、市人民检察院、市高级人民法院和市司法局提供，安全生产情况来自于市安全生产监督管理局，火灾事故和道路交通事故分别由市消防总队和市公安交通管理局提供。

The data in this chapter mainly cover public health, sports, civil affairs, labor & social securities, public security, procuratorial, legal & judicial affairs, work safety, and fires & highway traffic accidents. The data are sorted and compiled by Division of Social and Technology Statistics, Chongqing Municipal Bureau of Statistics on the basis of the data provided by other related departments.

The data on public health are provided by Chongqing Municipal Health Bureau; the data on sports are provided by Chongqing Administration of Sports; the data on civil affairs and labor & social securities are provided by Chongqing Civil Affairs Bureau and Chongqing Administration of Labor and Social Security; the data on public security, procuratorial and legal affairs are provided by Chongqing Public Security Bureau, Chongqing People's Procuratorate, Higher People's Court and Chongqing Justice Bureau; the data on work safety are provided by Chongqing Administration of Work Safety; and the data on fires & highway traffic accidents are provided by Chongqing Fire Brigade and Chongqing Bureau of Traffic Administration.

表19.1 主要年份卫生事业情况
STATISTICS ON PUBLIC HEALTH CARE IN MAJOR YEARS

年份 Year	机构数（个） Number of Institutions (unit)	其中 of which #医院、卫生院 Hospitals and Health Centers	床位数（张） Number of Beds in Health Care Institutions(bed)	卫生技术人员（人） Medical Technical Personnel (person)	其中 of which #执业（助理）医师 Licensed(Assistant) Doctors	#注册护士 Registered Nurses
1952	742		5031	19807		
1957	2185		10255	30290		
1962	3591		22971	35681		
1965	3938		20314	36762	10234	
1970	3579	2183	25038	39813	10475	
1975	4221	2286	37300	51536	12442	
1978	4789	2294	48948	59934	12870	
1980	4686	2316	51194	65441	12806	
1985	4796	2170	54054	76486	12577	11724
1986	5095	2140	54801	77437	12895	11921
1987	5136	2136	57178	78382	13201	12156
1988	5148	2151	59514	80153	21004	13688
1989	5229	2152	61912	81219	27789	16027
1990	5248	2154	62568	82690	28824	16929
1991	5326	2153	64057	83973	28652	17163
1992	5328	2160	64978	85204	28643	17557
1993	4807	2114	65859	84125	29516	17714
1994	4795	2590	66891	85586	30915	18298
1995	4801	2505	67243	86041	31169	18692
1996	4777	2567	66339	87542	30733	19289
1997	4743	2553	69591	88423	43178	19593
1998	4643	2438	65934	83696	43423	19804
1999	4552	2351	66003	88569	44453	20263
2000	4382	2250	65666	88619	44940	20773
2001	4151	2020	64981	86430	44666	20533
2002	2725	1717	61875	79850	37873	20729
2003	2705	1682	63287	78628	37122	20629
2004	2539	1574	63899	77516	36603	20249
2005	2447	1463	64674	78780	37321	20842
2006	2478	1450	68298	79805	37511	21269
2007	2410	1447	74785	83736	38739	23972
2008	2258	1396	81950	88746	39417	26799
2009	2425	1404	92689	97199	41943	31756
2010	17495	1449	103624	111079	47969	37611
2011	17660	1407	115627	120169	49585	42767

注：1）本表机构数不含个体办诊所。
2）2002年起卫生统计制度变更，其指标名称和统计口径变化，与往年不可比：从2002年起卫生机构、床位、卫生技术人员统计范围均不含“医学院校”、“卫生学校”和“计生站”。卫生技术人员中，2002年前为医生和护师（士），2002年后改为执业(助理)医师和注册护士(表19-1至19-5同）。
3）2011年卫生统计口径变化，与往年不可比：从2010年起卫生机构、卫生技术人员、执业（助理医师）、注册护士统计范围均含“村卫生室”。

Note: a) The number of institutions in this table exclude individual-run clinics.
b) Due to the change of health care statistic system in 2002, the indicators and statistic scopes were changed, not comparable with the previous years: since 2002, the scope of the number of health care institutions, the number of beds and the number of medial technical personnel has not included the data of “medical universities”, “health schools” and “family plan service stations”. The indicators of“doctor” and “nurse” before 2002 have been replaced by “licensed (assistant) doctors” and “registered nurses” since 2002 (the same applies to the tables from 19-1 to 19-5).
c) Due to the change of statistic scope, the date are not comparable with the previous years. The data of "village health station" are included in the data of health institutions, medical technical personnel, licensed (assistant) doctors and registered nurses since 2010.

表19.2 卫生事业情况（2010－2011年）
STATISTICS ON PUBLIC HEALTH CARE (2010-2011)

指　标	Item	2010	2011
执业（助理）医师数（人）	Number of Licensed (Assistant) Doctors (person)	47969	49585
医院床位数（张）	Number of Beds in Hospitals (bed)	64827	74827
孕产妇死亡率（1/10万）	Mortality Rate of Pregnant Women (per 100 000 persons)	23.0	21.6
新生儿死亡率（‰）	Mortality Rate of New Infants (‰)	5.2	4.1
甲乙类传染病发病率（1/10万）	Incidence Disease Rate of Class A and B Infections Diseases (per 100 000 persons)	240.8	245.2
农村自来水普及率（%）	Rate of Access to Tap Water in Rural Area (%)	87.5	90.3

注：卫生统计口径发生变化，2010年执业（助理）医师为调整数，含村卫生室执业（助理）医师人数。
Note: Due to the change of the statistic scope, the data of "number of licensed (assistant) doctors" in 2010 is adjusted data, with the data of village health stations included.

表19.3 医院、卫生院、社区诊疗情况（2011年）
STATISTICS ON VISITS AND INPATIENTS IN HOSPITALS, HEALTH STATIONS AND COMMUNITY HEALTH CENTERS (2011)

机构类别	Type of Institution	诊疗人次（万人次） Number of Visits (10 000 person-times)	其中of which #门诊急诊 Outpatients and Emergency Treatment	健康检查人数（万人） Medical Examination (10 000 patients)	住院人数（万人） Number of Inpatients (10 000 patients)	每百门急诊次的入院人数（人） Number of Inpatients per 100 Visits (person)	治愈率（%） Rate of Fully Recovery (%)	好转率（%） Rate of Improvement (%)	病死率（%） Rate of Mortality (%)
医　院	**Hospitals**	**3877.72**	**3781.90**	**272.43**	**211.66**	**5.60**	**48.92**	**47.64**	**0.88**
#综合医院	General Hospitals	2745.34	2676.05	227.26	159.45	6.00	48.96	47.26	0.94
中医医院	Hospitals Specialized in Traditional Chinese Medicine	555.72	545.31	31.43	28.85	5.30	41.53	56.02	0.71
中西医结合医院	Hospitals of Traditional Chinese and Western Medicine	95.19	95.01	0.99	3.14	3.30	54.52	42.85	1.21
口腔医院	Stomatological Hospitals	52.90	52.90		0.12	0.20	91.73	8.18	
肿瘤医院	Cancer Hospitals	17.86	17.86	1.75	1.90	10.70	28.76	64.72	
胸科医院	Chest Hospitals								
妇产（科）医院	OB/GYN Hospitals	20.07	14.80	1.49	0.79	5.40	96.59	3.38	
儿科医院	Children's Hospital	140.54	140.54		5.35	3.80	68.98	29.82	
精神病院	Mental Hospitals	101.92	95.45	1.37	4.67	4.90	41.82	55.23	
传染病院	Hospitals for Infectious Diseases	7.95	7.95	0.77	0.55	6.90	8.25	87.94	
社区卫生服务中心（站）	Community Health Ser--vice Center (Station)	569.82	544.99	61.80	14.21	2.60	66.47	31.32	0.31
卫生院	**Health Centers**	**2521.34**	**2468.03**	**303.04**	**130.27**	**5.30**	**75.53**	**22.69**	**0.12**
#乡镇卫生院	Township Health Centers	2466.92	2413.68	302.13	128.96	5.30	75.63	22.60	0.11

表19.4 卫生机构、床位、人员数（2011年）
NUMBER OF HEALTH CARE INSTITUTIONS, BEDS AND PERSONNEL (2011)

机构类别	Type of Institutions	机构数（个）Health Care Institutions (unit)	床位数（张）Beds (bed)	人员合计（人）Total Personnel (person)	其中 of which			
					卫生技术人员 Medical Technical Personnel	其他技术人员 Other Technical Personnel	管理人员 Managem-ent Personnel	工勤人员 Logistic Workers
总　计	**Total**	**17660**	**115627**	**171060**	**120169**	**4899**	**8240**	**13337**
医院、卫生院	Total Number of Hospitals	1407	107142	115194	92887	4234	6778	11295
医　院	Hospitals	433	74827	83480	66653	3088	5480	8259
#综合医院	General Hospitals	307	52318	60225	48382	2142	3973	5728
中医医院	Hospitals Specialized in Traditional Chinese Medicine	43	9460	10947	9082	334	550	981
中西医结合医院	Hospitals of Traditional Chinese and Western Medicine	8	935	1190	986	35	65	104
口腔医院	Stomatological Hospitals	3	57	692	538	46	75	33
肿瘤医院	Cancer Hospitals	1	961	985	803	80	42	60
胸科医院	Chest Hospitals							
妇产（科）医院	OB/GYN Hospitals	7	185	664	382	17	53	212
儿科医院	Children's Hospital	1	1050	1662	1375	106	106	75
精神病院	Mental Hospitals	20	6449	2514	1905	69	181	359
传染病院	Hospitals for Infectious Diseases	3	642	467	348	25	26	68
卫生院	Health Centers	974	32315	31714	26234	1146	1298	3036
城市街道卫生院	Urban Subdistrict Health Centers	8	677	507	396	9	31	71
乡镇卫生院	Township Health Centers	966	31638	31207	25838	1137	1267	2965
门诊部	Outpatient Department	163	295	926	762	35	61	68
采供血机构	Blood Centers	11		498	361	24	47	66
妇幼保健院（所、站）	Women and Children Care Centers	41	2557	4239	3424	128	299	388
专科疾病防治院（所）	Specialized Disease Prevention & Treatment Institutions	16	127	369	253	18	37	61
疾病预防控制中心	CDC (Epidemic Preventation Stations)	43		2508	1847	134	266	261
医学科学研究机构	Research Institutes of Medical Sciences	1		64	10	38	11	5
医学在职培训机构	Training Institutes for Medical Staff and Workers	6		134	88	6	25	15
健康教育所（中心）	Health Care Training Centers	3		49	17	14	9	9
疗养院	Sanatoriums	4	920	185	94	6	35	50
社区卫生服务中心(站)	Community Health Service Centers	468	4586	7416	5364	201	380	721
卫生监督所	Health Supervision Institutes	42		1182	916	4	219	43
其他卫生机构	Other Health Care Institutions	20	920	693	241	107	142	203
村卫生室	Village Health Stations	10584		27503	3088			
诊所、卫生保健所、室	Clinics and Hygienic Centers	4858		10462	10240			222

注：本表机构数包含个体办诊所、村卫生室。
Note: The number of institutions in this table includes individual-run clinics.

表19.5 卫生机构各类人员数（2010－2011年）
NUMBER OF EMPLOYED PERSONS IN HEALTH INSTITUTIONS (2010-2011)

单位：人、% (person, %)

人员分类	Type of Personnel	人 数 Personnel		构 成 Composition	
		2010	2011	2010	2011
总 计	**Total**	**160055**	**171060**	**100.0**	**100.0**
卫生技术人员	Medical Technical Personnel	111079	120169	69.4	70.2
执业医师	Licensed Doctors	35417	36666	22.1	21.4
执业助理医师	Licensed Assistant Doctors	12552	12919	7.8	7.6
注册护士	Registered Nurses	37611	42767	23.5	25.0
药剂人员	Pharmacists	6267	6438	3.9	3.8
技师（士）	Technical Workers	5433	5793	3.4	3.4
其他人员	Others	13799	15586	8.6	9.1
其他技术人员	Other Technical Personnel	4277	4899	2.7	2.9
管理人员	Management Personnel	7886	8240	4.9	4.8
工勤人员	Logistics Workers	12203	13337	7.6	7.8
每万人口拥有卫生技术人员	**Number of Medical Technical Personnel per 10 000 Population**	**33.36**	**36.09**		
#执业（助理）医师	Licensed (Assistant) Doctors	14.41	14.89		

注：2011年卫生统计口径变化，卫生技术人员、执业医师、执业助理医师、注册护士、每万人口拥有卫生技术人员和执业(助理)医师范围均含村卫生室，2010年以上指标数据为调整数。

Note: Due to the change of statistic scope, the data of medical technical personnel, licensed doctors, licensed assistant doctors, registered nurses, number of medical technical personnel per 10 000 population and licensed (assistant) doctors include the data of village health stations in 2011. The data above in 2010 are adjusted data.

表19.6 结婚登记和离婚登记情况（2010－2011年）
STATISTICS ON MARRIAGES AND DIVORCES (2010-2011)

项 目	Item	2010	2011
结婚登记件数（件）	Registered Marriages (couple)	313393	304848
内地居民	Registered Marriages in Mainland	312517	303924
涉外及华侨、港澳台居民	Registered Marriages with Foreigner or Citizen of Hong Kong, Macao and Taiwan	876	924
结婚登记人数（人）	Registered Newly Married People (person)	626786	609696
初 婚	First Marriages	475845	449840
再 婚	Remarriages	150941	159856
登记离婚件数（件）	Registered Divorces (couple)	95052	105518
#内地居民	Registered Divorces in Mainland	94919	105390
离婚率（‰）	Divorce Rate (‰)	2.9	3.2

表19.7 民政事业情况（2010－2011年）
STATISTICS ON CIVIL AFFAIRS (2010-2011)

指 标	Item	2010	2011
民政经费支出（万元）	Expenditure for Civil Affairs (10 000 yuan)	674873	783120
城市居民最低生活保障人数（万人）	Number of Persons Receiving Minimum Living Allowance in Urban Areas (10 000 persons)	60.77	56.85
农村居民最低生活保障人数（万人）	Number of Persons Receiving Minimum Living Allowance in Rural Areas (10000 persons)	116.88	101.34
农村五保供养人数（万人）	Number of Persons Receiving Livelihood Guaranteed in Five Aspects in Rural Areas (10 000person)	15.92	15.68
享受城镇居民最低生活保障人数占非农业人口比重（%）	Number of Persons Receiving Minimum Living Allowance in Urban Areas as Percentage to Total Non-agricultural Population (%)	5.5	4.4
收养性单位床位数（张）	Number of Beds in Adoption Institutions (bed)	90139	106217
福利企业职工人数（人）	Number of Staff and Workers in Welfare Enterprises (person)	59211	67549
#残疾职工	Disabled Staff and Workers	25421	26857
城镇社区服务设施数（个）	Number of Urban Welfare Facilities (unit)	1718	2124
城镇便民、利民服务网点（个）	Number of Service Stations for Urban Residents (unit)	9668	9880
福利彩票销售额（万元）	Sales of Welfare Lotteries (10 000 yuan)	218965	345860

表19.8 优抚对象基本情况（2010－2011年）
STATISTICS ON SPECIAL CARES FOR SERVICEMEN (2010-2011)

单位：人 (person)

项 目	Item	2010	2011
优抚对象	**Residents Receiving Special Cares for Serviceman**	**224105**	**271234**
享受定期抚恤金人数	Persons Receiving Regular Pensions	6282	6412
享受定期补助人数	Persons Receiving Regular Subvention	196583	243464
#在乡复员军人	Demobilized Soldiers in the Countryside	41234	39712
在乡退伍军人	Veterans in the Country	69246	71724
红军失散人员	Scattered Red Army Soldiers	4	1
伤残人员	Wounded and Disabled Servicemen	21240	21358

表19.9 社会福利事业、企业单位数和工作人员数（2010－2011年）

NUMBER OF SOCIAL WELFARE INSTITUTIONS & ENTERPRISES AND EMPLOYED PERSONS (2010-2011)

单位：个、人 (unit, person)

项　目	Item	机　构 Number of Institutions and Enterprises		工作人员 Number of Personnel	
		2010	2011	2010	2011
收养性单位	Residential Institutions	2196	2241	6366	7641
优抚类	For Servicemen	11	10	174	164
福利类	For Welfares	2185	2231	6192	7477
社会福利企业单位	Social Welfare Enterprises	748	758	59211	67549
福利工厂	Welfare Factories	429	413	30020	33572
假肢厂	Prosthesis Factories				
其他福利企业	Others	319	345	29191	33977
优抚事业单位	Agencies for Servicemen	63	47	438	398
救助管理站	Salvation Management Stations	44	42	333	330
殡葬事业单位	Funeral and Interment Institutions	114	114	1810	1869
福利彩票发行单位	Welfare Lottery Issuing Units	1	1	124	126
募捐单位	Donation Soliciting Units				
社区服务单位	Community Service Institutions	232	300	1199	1883

表19.10 收养性单位基本情况（2011年）

BASIC STATISTICS ON RESIDENTIAL SOCIAL WELFARE INSTITUTIONS (2011)

项　目	Item	院　数（个） Number of Institutions (unit)	工作人员（人） Number of Staff and Workers (person)	床位数（张） Number of Beds (bed)	年末收养人数（人） Number of Residents at Year-end (person)
收养性单位	**Residential Institutions**	**2241**	**7641**	**106217**	**78600**
优抚类	For Servicemen	10	164	676	425
荣誉军人康复医院	Convalescent Hospitals for Honorable Servicemen	2	129	258	179
复退军人精神病院	Mental Hospitals for Ex-servicemen				
光荣院	Homes for Disabled Veterans	8	35	418	246
福利类	For Welfares	2231	7477	105541	78175
社会福利院	Social Welfare Homes	41	1089	9043	6747
儿童福利院	Baby Welfare Homes	7	288	2550	1306
社会福利医院	Social Welfare Hospitals	12	475	1813	1687
城镇老年性福利机构	Urban Welfare Homes for the Aged Persons	141	1563	15054	10347
农村五保供养服务机构	Welfare Homes for Rural Households with Livelihood Guaranteed in Five Aspects	2025	4006	76692	57788
其它福利机构	Others	5	56	389	300

表19.11 社会活动参与情况（2010－2011年）
PARTICIPATION IN SOCIAL ACTIVITIES (2010-2011)

单位：人、个 (person, unit)

指　标	Item	2010	2011
省级人大代表人数	Number of Municipal Deputies of People's Congress	867	864
#女　性	Female	200	200
省级政协委员人数	Number of Municipal Deputies of People's Political Consultative Conferences	869	868
#女　性	Female	173	175
基层地方妇联组织数	Number of Local Women's Federation Unions	11911	11995
工会基层组织数	Number of Grassroots Trade Unions	32885	45828
工会会员人数	Membership of Trade Unions	5230353	6958500

表19.12 基本养老保险情况（2010－2011年）
STATISTICS ON BASIC PENSION INSURANCE (2010-2011)

单位：万元、万人 (10 000 yuan, 10 000 persons)

指　标	Item	2010	2011
城镇企业基本养老保险参保人数	Number of Contributors to Urban Enterprise Basic Pension Insurance	569.77	633.22
#参保职工	Employees	380.54	416.28
#企　业	Enterprises	266.96	293.94
城镇企业基本养老保险实际缴纳保险金	Actually Received Premium of Urban Enterprise Basic Pension Insurance	2251429	3214294
城镇企业基本养老保险金当年支出额	Expenditure of Urban Enterprise Basic Pension Insurance	2608512	3321497
城镇企业基本养老保险当年末结余额	Year-end Balance of Urban Enterprise Basic Pension Insurance	2472918	3261778
应发养老金额	Pension Payable	2608512	3217962
实发养老金额	Pension Actually Paid	2608512	3217962
社会化发放人数	Number of Social Beneficiaries	189.23	216.94
社会化发放养老金额	Actually Paid Social Pension	2608512	3062259
离休、退休、退职人员年末人数	Number of Retires at Year-end	189.23	216.94
机关事业单位社会养老保险参保人数	Number of Contributors to Social Pension Insurance in Government and Public Institutions	14.59	14.34
城乡居民社会养老保险参保人数	Number of Urban and Rural Residents Participating in Social Pension Insurance	807.36	1125.12

注：1）城镇企业基本养老保险统计口径发生变化。农民工养老保险整体并入城镇企业职工养老保险。
2）机关事业单位社会养老保险参保人数含市级、区县级机关事业单位参保人数。

Note:a) Due to the change of statistic scope of urban enterprise basic pension insurance, the off-farm worker pension insurance is included in the urban enterprise worker pension insurance.
b) The number of contributors to social pension insurance in government and public institutions include the contributors from the governments and public institutions at municipal, district and county levels.

表19.13 失业保险基本情况（2010－2011年）

STATISTICS ON UNEMPLOYMENT INSURANCE (2010-2011)

指　标	Item	2010	2011
年末失业保险参保人数（万人）	Unemployment Insurance Contributors at Year-end (10 000 persons)	237.37	268.61
企　业	Enterprises	192.45	229.52
事业单位	Institutions	36.54	32..82
其　他	Others	8.38	6.27
失业保险当年实际缴纳保险金（万元）	Actual Received Premium of Unemployment Insurance in Current Year (10 000 yuan)	91037.25	117910.17
失业保险实际支付人数（万人）	Actual Beneficiaries of Unemployment Insurance (10 000 persons)	8.82	6.32
失业保险基金当年支出额（万元）	Expenses of Unemployment Insurance in Current Year (10 000 yuan)	49537.10	31960.49
失业保险基金当年末结余额（万元）	Year-end Balance of Unemployment Insurance (10 000 yuan)	276907.41	365004.58
年末城镇登记失业人员数（万人）	Year-end Registered Urban Unemployment (10 000persons)	13.02	12.96
城镇登记失业人员就业人数（万人）	Registered Urban Unemployment Reemployed (10 000 persons)	19.58	25.52
本年领取失业保险金人次数（万人次）	Person-times of Reception of Unemployment Insurance in Current Year (10 000 person-times)	53.60	41.20

表19.14 基本医疗保险情况（2010－2011年）

STATISTICS ON BASIC MEDICAL CARE INSURANCE (2010-2011)

单位：万元、万人 (10 000 yuan, 10 000 persons)

指　标	Item	2010	2011
城镇职工基本医疗保险参保人数	Basic Urban Workers Medical Care Insurance Contributors at Year-end	406.21	458.48
在职职工	Staff and Workers	280.60	325.41
退休人员	Retirees	125.61	133.07
城镇职工基本医疗保险基金总收入	Total Revenue of Urban Workers Basic Medical Care Insurance	691176.70	917793.83
城镇职工基本医疗保险基金总支出	Total Expenses of Urban Workers Basic Medical Care Insurance	552431.00	706963.58

表19.15 体育事业基本情况（2010－2011年）
STATISTICS ON MASS SPORTS (2010-2011)

项　目	Item	2010	2011
体育经费（万元）	Sports Expenditures (10 000 yuan)	55595.6	82004.2
体育彩票销售额（万元）	Sales Value of Sports Lotteries (10 000 yuan)	101410	146027.7
体育场地数（个）	Stadiums and Gymnasiums (unit)	17351	17351
#体育场	Stadiums	73	74
体育馆	Gymnasiums	39	40
游泳馆	Natatoriums	8	8
室内外游泳池	Indoor and Outdoor Swimming Pools	122	122
有固定看台的灯光球场	Illuminated Fields with Fixed Seating	70	70
等级运动员	Graded Athletes		
国际级运动健将	International Masters of Sports		3
运动健将	Masters of Sports		16
一级运动员	First Grade	145	186
二级运动员	Second Grade	885	1146
等级裁判员	Graded Referees		
国际裁判	International Referees		
国家级裁判	National Referees		6
一级裁判	First Grade Referees	477	731
二级裁判	Second Grade Referees	1207	415

注：1）体育经费包括体育事业费和体育基建支出。
　　2）体育场地数为2003年普查数。
Note: a) Sports expenditures include sports funds and expenditure for sports infrastructure.
　　b) The number of stadiums and gyms are the data in the census in 2003.

表19.16 律师、公证、调解工作基本情况（2010－2011年）
STATISTICS ON LAWYERS, NOTARIZATION AND MEDIATION (2010-2011)

项　目	Item	2010	2011
律师工作	**Lawyers**		
律师事务所（所）	Number of Law Offices (unit)	453	498
律师工作者（人）	Number of Lawyers (person)	4834	5467
#专　职	Full-time Lawyers	4338	4919
聘请担任法律顾问单位（处）	Number of Units with Permanent Legal Advisors (unit)	8665	9385
民事诉讼代理（件）	Agent of Civil Cases (case)	36329	39558
刑事辩护（件）	Defender of Criminal Cases (case)	7794	16952
行政诉讼代理（件）	Agent of Administrative Action (case)	2296	1775
非诉讼法律事务（件）	Cases of Non-litigious Legal Affairs (case)	7011	8204
解答法律询问（件）	Advisory Services of Legal Affairs (case)	180224	209337
代写法律事务文书（件）	Legal Documents Written on Behalf of Clients (case)	19536	52354
公证工作	**Notarization**		
公证处（个）	Number of Notarial Offices (unit)	41	41
公证员（人）	Public Notaries (person)	189	189
办理公证书（件）	Notarized Documents (case)	193629	161669
人民调解工作	**Number of People's Mediation**		
专职司法助理员（人）	Number of Full-time Judicial Assistants (person)	3023	3008
人民调解委员会（个）	Number of People's Mediation Committees (unit)	13340	13369
调解员（人）	Number of Mediators (person)	116026	104952
调解纠纷（件）	Number of Disputes Mediated (case)	416417	520450
婚姻家庭	Family Disputes	76645	92322
房屋、宅基地	Housing and Housing Sites	16230	25756
合　同	Contract Disputes	14186	18350
劳　动	Labor Disputes	13625	12735
邻　里	Neighbor Disputes	123441	157164
赔　偿	Compensation Disputes	37085	45665
其　他	Others	135205	168458

注：1)律师事务所统计口径发生变化。增加律师事务所境外分所。
2)“行政诉讼代理（件）”2010年数据为司法局调整确认数。

Note: a) Due to the change of the statistic scope of law offices, the data of overseas branches is added.
b) The data of "agent of administrative action" in 2010 is adjusted and confirmed by the Municipal Judicial Bureau.

表19.17 国内外公证文书（2010－2011年）
DOMESTIC AND FOREIGN-RELATED NOTARIAL DOCUMENTS (2010-2011)

单位：件、% (case, %)

项　目	Item	国内公证文书 Domestic Notarial Documents			
		办证件数 Number of Notarial Documents Issued		比　重 Percentage	
		2010	2011	2010	2011
经济公证合计	**Total Notarized Documents on Economic Affairs**	**21255**	**16026**	**100.0**	**100.0**
#购　销	Purchases and Sales of Products	1031	63	4.9	0.4
建筑工程承包	Construction Project Contracts	213	95	1.0	0.6
农林牧渔承包	Farming, Forestry, Animal Husbandry and Fishery Contracts	17	8	0.1	
财产租赁	Property Leasing	16	8	0.1	
劳务合同	Labor Contracts	5	61		0.4
贷款合同	Loan Contracts	13232	9396	62.3	58.6
民事公证合计	**Total Notarized Documents on Civil Affairs**	**135325**	**107265**	**100.0**	**100.0**
#收　养	Child Adoption	164	141	0.1	0.1
继承权	Right of Inheritance	14744	15459	10.9	14.4
遗　嘱	Testament	1160	1261	0.9	1.2
房屋买卖	Purchases and Sales of Houses	1004	892	0.7	0.8
产　权	Property Right	28	35		
民事协议	Civil Agreements	2201	1026	1.7	1.0

项　目	Item	涉外公证文书 Foreign-related Notarial Documents			
		办证件数 Number of Notarial Documents Issued		比　重 Percentage	
		2010	2011	2010	2011
合　计	**Total**	**32864**	**34888**	**100.0**	**100.0**
#出　生	Births	4747	4909	14.4	14.1
学　历	Schooling	1206	157	3.7	0.5
死　亡	Deaths	71	74	0.2	0.2
婚姻状况	Marital Status	434	336	1.3	1.0
亲属关系	Kinship Confirmation	3076	3198	9.4	9.2
受刑事处分	Criminal Records	3537	3527	10.8	10.1
委托书	Proxy	295	477	0.9	1.4
声明书	Announcement	1077	754	3.3	2.2
经　历	Personal Histories	44	44	0.1	0.1
副本与原本相符	Conformation of Copies and Photo-offset Copies to Originals	13547	14015	41.2	40.2
商标注册	Trademark Registrations				
其他经济合同	Other Business Contracts	4	156		0.4

表19.18 公安机关受理查处治安案件情况（2011年）
OFFENSE CASES AGAINST PUBLIC ORDER HANDLED BY PUBLIC SECURITY ORGANS (2011)

单位：起 (case)

案件类别	Category of Cases	受 理 Number of Cases Accepted to be Treated	查 处 Number of Cases Investigated and Treated
合 计	**Total**	**668009**	**658854**
扰乱公共秩序	**Disturbing Public Order**	**230822**	**230139**
#扰乱公共场所秩序	Disturbing the Orders in Public Places	161574	161390
寻衅滋事	Causing Quarrels and Making Troubles	2086	1994
利用邪教、会道门、迷信或冒用宗教气功名义危害社会	Imperil the Society through Evil Cult and Superstition or in the name of Religion and Qigong	92	88
妨害公共安全	**Disturbing Public Safety**	**30281**	**30014**
#违反危险物质管理规定	Violation of Explosives Control Regulations	1009	980
非法携带枪支、弹药及管制刀具	Violation of Firearms Control Regulations	5459	5426
盗窃损毁公共设施	Stealing and Damaging Public Facilities	527	482
侵犯他人人身权利、财产权利	**Infringing the Personal Right and Property Right of Others**	**159193**	**152277**
#殴打他人	Battering Other Persons	64402	61423
故意伤害	Willfully Injuring Others	5647	5305
盗 窃	Stealing Property	15470	14079
诈 骗	Swindling, Seizing and Extorting Property	2476	2192
抢 夺	Robbery and Snatch	152	143
敲诈勒索	Extortion and Blackmail	124	112
妨害社会管理秩序	**Disturbing Order Social Administration**	**247713**	**246424**
#违反旅店业管理	Violating the Hotel Management Regulations	4800	4767
卖淫、嫖娼	Prostitution or Soliciting Prostitutes	3599	3590
赌博或为赌博提供条件	Gambling or Offering Conditions for Gambling	3393	3333
毒品违法案件	Illegal Drug Related Action	8013	7961

表19.19 公安机关立案的刑事案件情况（2011年）

CRIMINAL CASES REGISTERED IN PUBLIC SECURITY ORGANS (2011)

指 标	Item	2011
人民警察数（人）	**Number of Police (person)**	**37544**
刑事案件立案数（起）	**Total Registered Criminal Cases (case)**	**184653**
杀 人	Homicide	264
伤 害	Injury	2277
抢 劫	Robbery	3721
强 奸	Rape	1083
拐卖妇女儿童	Abducting Women or Children	3180
盗 窃	Larceny	117799
诈 骗	Fraud	20645
走 私	Smuggling	
伪造、变造货币，出售、购买、运输、持有、使用假币	Forging Currency, Selling, Buying, Transporting, Holding and Using Counterfeit Currency	53
其 他	Others	35631
刑事案件破案率（%）	**Rate of Solved Criminal Cases (%)**	**32.77**

表19.20 检察机关直接立案侦查案件情况（2011年）

CASES UNDER DIRECT INVESTIGATION BY PEOPLE'S PROCURATORATE (2011)

案件分类	Category of Cases	受案（件） Cases Accepted (case)	立案件数（件） Registered Cases (case)	其中of which #大案 Large Cases	立案人数（人） Person of Cases Registered (person)	其中of which #要案 Key Cases	结案合计 Total Settled Cases 件 (case)	人 (person)
合 计	**Total**	**1232**	**726**	**575**	**951**	**170**	**780**	**1019**
贪污贿赂案件	**Cases on Corruption and Bribery**	**1057**	**610**	**519**	**818**	**153**	**663**	**884**
贪 污	Corruption	375	110	98	246	12	133	281
贿 赂	Bribery	647	481	405	539	136	504	562
挪用公款	Misappropriation of Public Funds	17	14	14	18	4	18	23
集体私分	Collective Illegal Possession of Public Funds	4	5	2	15	1	8	18
巨额财产来源不明	Unstated Source of Large Amount of Properties	14						
其 他	Others							
渎职案件	**Cases on Abuse and Dereliction of Duty**	**175**	**116**	**56**	**133**	**24**	**117**	**135**
滥用职权	Abuse of Power	58	41	21	51	9	41	51
玩忽职守	Dereliction of Duty	65	45	23	47	6	47	49
徇私舞弊	Fraudulent Practice	37	26	12	29	8	23	27
其 他	Others	15	4		6	1	6	8

表19.21 检察机关审查批准、决定逮捕犯罪嫌疑人和提起公诉被告人情况（2011年）
ARRESTS OF CRIMINAL SUSPECTS AND DEFENDANTS UNDER PUBLIC PROSECUTION APPROVED BY PEOPLE'S PROCURATORATE (2011)

案件类别	Category of Cases	批捕、决定逮捕合计 Total Arrests		决定起诉合计 Total Public Prosecutions	
		件 (case)	人 (person)	件 (case)	人 (person)
合　计	**Total**	**16604**	**21688**	**25986**	**35083**
公安、安全、监狱机关侦查	**Handled by Departments of State, Public Security and Prisons**	**16137**	**21159**	**25311**	**34206**
危害国家安全案	Offences Against State Security	1	1		
危害公共安全案	Offences Against Public Security	803	871	4493	4648
破坏社会主义市场经济秩序案	Offences Against Socialist Economic Order	703	1128	829	1379
侵犯公民人身、民主权利案	Offences Against Citizens' Personal and Democratic Rights	2709	3256	3757	4947
侵犯财产案	Offences Against Properties	6073	8394	7885	11692
妨害社会管理秩序案	Offences Against Social Management of Order	5845	7506	8344	11537
危害国防利益案	Offences Against National Defense	3	3	3	3
军人违反职责案	Offences on Dereliction of Duty by Servicemen				
检察机关侦查	**Handled by Procuratorates**	**467**	**509**	**675**	**877**
贪污贿赂案	Offences on Corruption and Bribery	442	481	597	783
渎职案	Offences on Abuse and Dereliction of Duty	25	28	78	94

表19.22 人民法院刑事一审案件收结案情况（2010－2011年）
FIRST TRIAL CRIMINAL CASES ACCEPTED AND SETTLED BY COURTS (2010-2011)

单位：件 (case)

类　别	Category of Cases	收　案 Accepted Cases		结　案 Settled Cases	
		2010	2011	2010	2011
合　计	**Total**	**20942**	**27124**	**21964**	**26154**
#自诉案件	Private Prosecution	221	224	259	191
危害公共安全罪	Offences against Public Security	3858	4544	3940	4476
破坏社会主义市场经济秩序罪	Offences against Socialist Economic Order	468	772	491	686
侵犯公民人身权利、民主权利罪	Offences against Citizens' Personal and Democratic Rights	3903	4226	4244	3997
侵犯财产罪	Offences against Properties	6651	8082	7036	7826
妨害社会管理秩序罪	Offences against social Management of Order	5306	8742	5481	8523
危害国防利益罪	Offences against National Defense	7	5	7	4
贪污贿赂罪	Offences on Corruption and Bribery	656	680	683	571
渎职罪	Offences on Dereliction of Duty	83	71	73	68
危害国家安全罪	Offences against Country Safety	3	1	2	1
其　它	Others	7	1	7	2

注：收结案中含上年结转。
Note: The numbers of accepted and settled cases include the cases turned over from the previous year.

表19.23 人民法院民事、行政一审案件收结案情况（2010－2011年）

FIRST TRIAL CIVIL AND ADMINISTRATIVE CASES ACCEPTED AND SETTLED BY COURTS (2010-2011)

单位：件 (case)

类　别	Category of Cases	收　案 Accepted Cases		结　案 Settled Cases	
		2010	2011	2010	2011
民事一审案件	**First Trial of Civil Cases**	**166570**	**217829**	**179199**	**198895**
婚姻家庭纠纷案件	Disputes of Marriages and Family Affairs	36754	43773	39959	42017
继承纠纷案件	Disputes of Inheritance	1698	2669	1790	2459
合同纠纷案件	Disputes of Contracts	95280	119779	102245	108236
权属、侵权纠纷案件	Disputes of Ownership and Infrigement of Right	32838	51608	35205	46183
行政一审案件	**First Trial of Administrative Cases**	**4590**	**4944**	**5134**	**4683**

注：收案中含上年结转。
Note: The number of accepted cases includes the cases turned over from the previous year.

表19.24 安全生产情况（2002－2011年）

BASIC STATISTICS ON WORK SAFETY (2002-2011)

年　份 Year	亿元地区生产总值生产安全事故死亡率 Mortality Rate of Work Safety Accident per 100 Billion Yuan GDP	工矿商贸企业从业人员十万人生产安全事故死亡率 Mortality Rate of Work Safety Accident per 100 000 Employees of Enterprises	煤炭生产百万吨死亡率 Mortality Rate per 1 Million Tons of Coal Procuction	道路交通万车死亡率 Mortality Rate of Highway Traffic Accident per 10 000 Vehicles
2002	1.44	9.90	21.08	37.50
2003	1.41	13.43	17.82	30.70
2004	0.89	10.24	12.24	18.30
2005	0.75	10.62	13.73	14.51
2006	0.61	8.49	9.30	10.83
2007	0.47	8.05	7.64	9.26
2008	0.34	7.13	6.82	7.60
2009	0.30	6.39	5.44	6.00
2010	0.23	5.05	4.00	4.45
2011	0.18	4.51	3.00	3.13

表19.25 安全生产事故死亡情况（2001－2011年）
BASIC STATISTICS ON DEATH TOLL OF WORK SAFETY ACCIDENTS (2001-2011)

年 份 Year	生产安全事故死亡起数（起） Safety Accidents with Death Toll (case)	其 中 of which			生产安全事故死亡人数（人） Death Toll in Safety Accidents (person)	其 中 of which		
		道路交通事故 Traffic Accidents	煤矿事故 Coal Mine Accidents	火灾事故 Fires		道路交通事故 Traffic Accidents	煤矿事故 Coal Mine Accidents	火灾事故 Fires
2001	2225	1767	241	44	2794	2083	309	53
2002	2535	1872	323	39	3208	2245	460	43
2003	2732	1989	315	44	3613	2317	446	56
2004	2237	1434	342	56	2694	1707	419	63
2005	2117	1333	349	54	2596	1616	455	57
2006	2002	1175	288	42	2381	1424	357	44
2007	1813	1105	257	35	2197	1331	321	40
2008	1681	1063	212	35	1982	1219	280	39
2009	1679	1109	160	35	1928	1209	234	43
2010	1576	1079	136	22	1793	1215	174	28
2011	1444	983	105	24	1656	1098	135	29

表19.26 火灾事故情况（2011年）
BASIC STATISTICS ON FIRES (2011)

项 目	Item	合 计 Total	按事故发生程度分 By Serious Degree of Fires			
			特 大 Extra-Serious	重 大 Serious	较 大 Large	一 般 Ordinary
发 生（起）	Fires (case)	3777			2	3775
死 亡（人）	Deaths (person)	32			7	25
受 伤（人）	Injuries (person)	22				22
损失折款（万元）	Losses Converted into Cash (10 000 yuan)	4345.6			80.70	4264.90
平均每起事故损失（万元）	Average Loss per Fire (10 000 yuan)	1.15			40.35	1.13

注：损失折款指直接经济损失（下表同）。
Note: Losses converted into cash refer to direct losses (the same below).

表19.27 道路交通事故情况（2011年）
BASIC STATISTICS ON TRAFFIC ACCIDENTS (2011)

类 别	Type	发生数（起） Number of Traffic Accidents (case)	死亡人数（人） Number of Deaths (person)	受伤人数（人） Number of Injuries (person)	损失折款（万元） Losses Converted into Cash (10 000 yuan)
总 计	**Total**	**5729**	**985**	**8528**	**1363.53**
#死亡事故	In Which: Deaths	901	985	650	298.11
伤人事故	Injuries	4745		7878	961.71
财产损失事故	Assets Losses	83			103.71
#机动车	Motor Vehicles	5601	954	8390	1359.53
#汽 车	Automobiles	3126	621	4839	1065.65
摩托车	Motorcycles	2093	282	3125	232.28
拖拉机	Tractors	86	25	96	12.48
非机动车	Non-motor-driven Vehicles	81	8	113	2.71
#自行车	Bicycles	25	2	33	0.18
行人乘车人	Pedestrians and Passengers	47	23	25	1.29

注：本表数据不含高速公路交通事故。
Note: The data in this table excludes traffic accidents on expressway.

重/庆/统/计/年/鉴

主要统计指标解释

等级运动员人数

指经考核正式批准授予等级运动员称号的人数。运动员等级分为国际级运动健将、运动健将、一级运动员、二级运动员、三级运动员、少年级运动员。

等级裁判员人数

指经考核正式批准授予等级裁判员称号的人数。裁判员等级分为国际裁判、国家级裁判、一级裁判、二级裁判、三级裁判。

体育场

指有400米跑道（中心含足球场），有固定道牙，跑道6条以上，并有固定看台的室外田径场地。体育场按看台容纳观众人数分为：甲级25000人以上，乙级15000-25000人，、丙级5000-15000人，丁级5000人以下。

体育馆

指有固定看台，可供篮球、排球、羽毛球、乒乓球、体操等项目训练比赛活动用的室内运动场地。体育馆按看台容纳观众人数分为：甲级6000人以上，乙级4000-6000人，丙级2000-4000人，丁级2000人以下。

卫生机构

包括医疗机构、疾病预防控制中心（防疫站）、采供血机构、卫生监督及监测（检验）机构、医学科研和在职培训机构、健康教育所等。

医疗机构

包括医院、社区卫生服务中心（站）、疗养院、卫生院、门诊部、诊所（卫生所、医务室）、妇幼保健院（所、站）、专科疾病防治院（所、站）、急救中心（站）和临床检验中心。医疗机构分为非赢利性医疗机构和赢利性医疗机构。

医院

包括综合医院、中医医院、中西医结合医院、民族医院、各类专科医院和护理院。

卫生技术人员

指卫生机构中医生、护理人员 、药剂人员、检验人员等卫生技术人员。

医生

指在医疗、预防保健机构工作且取得《执业医师证书》的执业医师和执业助理医师。

社会福利企业单位

指以安置城镇有一定劳动能力的盲、聋、哑和肢体残疾人员就业为目的，享受国家减免税待遇的国有或集体企业。包括福利工厂、福利商业和服务业、假肢厂和安置农场等单位。该指标主要反映我国对残疾人照顾的特殊政策。

基本养老保险

（1）参加保险人数：指报告期末按照国家法律、法规和有关政策规定参加基本养老保险的职工人数。包括不能正常缴费、已中断缴费但未终止保险关系的职工人数。

（2）社会统筹基金收入：指根据国家规定，由纳入基本养老保险范围的单位，按照国家规定的缴费基数和缴费比例缴纳的社会统筹基金，以及通过其他方式取得的形成基金来源的收入，包括：单位缴纳的社会统筹基金收入、财政补贴收入、利息收入、其他收入。

（3）社会统筹基金支出：指按照国家政策规定的开支范围和开支标准从社会统筹基金中支付给参加基本养老保险的离休、退休、退职人员个人的养老金、丧葬抚恤补助，以及由于保险关系转移、上下级之间调剂资金等原因而发生的支出。包括：基础性养老金、过渡性养老金、离休金、退休金、退职金、补贴、丧葬抚恤补助、其他支出。

（4）社会统筹基金结余：指截止报告期末基本养老保险的社会统筹基金结余金额。包括银行存款、财政专户、债券投资和其他。

主要统计指标解释

■ 离休、退休、退职人员

指正式办理了离休、退休、退职手续，并享受相应的离休、退休、退职待遇的人员。

■ 失业保险

（1）参加保险人数：指报告期末按照国家法律、法规和有关政策规定参加了失业保险的城镇企业事业单位的职工及地方政府规定参加失业保险的其他人员的人数。

（2）失业保险金：指为保障失业人员的基本生活而按规定支付的失业保险金金额。

■ 基本医疗保险

（1）参加保险人数：指报告期末按国家有关规定参加基本医疗保险的人数。包括参加保险的职工人数和退休人员人数。

（2）社会统筹基金收入：指根据国家有关规定，由纳入基本医疗保险范围的缴费单位，按国家规定的缴费基数和缴费比例缴纳的社会统筹基金，以及通过其他方式取得的形成基金来源的款项，包括：单位缴纳的社会统筹基金收入、财政补贴收入、利息收入、其他收入。

（3）社会统筹基金支出：指按照国家政策规定的开支范围和开支标准从社会统筹基金中支付给参加基本医疗保险的职工和退休人员的医疗保险待遇支出及其他支出。包括：住院医疗费用支出、门急诊医疗费用支出、其他支出。

（4）社会统筹基金结余：指截止报告期末基本医疗保险的社会统筹基金结余金额。包括银行存款、财政专户、债券投资和其他。

■ 律师

指依法取得律师执业证书，担任法律顾问，民事（刑事、行政）案件代理人、刑事案件辩护人、办理非诉讼业务，解答法律询问，代写法律事务文书等，为社会提供法律服务的人员。

■ 公证人员

指在公证处工作的人员总称，包括公证处主任、副主任、公证员、公证员助理（助理公证员）和其他从事辅助性工作的人员。

■ 公证文书

指公证处根据当事人申请，依照事实和法律，按照法定程序制作的，具有法律效力的司法证明文书。

■ 调解员

指在人民调解委员会担负调解民间纠纷工作的人员，包括调解委员会的委员和调解小组的调解员。

■ 调解民间纠纷

指调解委员会按照法律规定，根据自愿原则，用说服教育的方法调解民间发生的有关民事权利和义务争执的件数，包括调解成功数和调解未成功数。

■ 立案

指人民检察院对受理的报案、控告、举报或自首及自行发现的犯罪线索、犯罪嫌疑人进行初步调查后，认为存在职务犯罪事实和应追究刑事责任，并决定作为刑事案件进行侦查的诉讼活动，是追究犯罪的开始。该指标主要反映人民检察院依法将职务犯罪线索作为刑事案件进行侦查的诉讼活动。

■ 大案

指贪污、贿赂案数额在5万元以上，挪用公款案数额在10万元以上，集体私分、巨额财产来源不明、隐瞒境外存款案数额在50万元以上以及按照《人民检察院直接受理的渎职、侵权重、特大案件标准（试行）》认定的案件。该指标主要反映人民检察院立案查办的职务犯罪案件中经济损失大、社会危害严重的案件。

■ 要案

指县、处级以上干部的犯罪案件。该指标主要反映国家工作人员中县、处级以上干部因职务犯罪被人民检察院依法立案侦查的情况。

■ 决定逮捕

指人民检察机关对直接受理、自行侦查的案件，认为需要逮捕犯罪嫌疑人时，依据法律作出的逮捕决定。

■ 批准逮捕

指人民检察机关对公安机关、国家安全机关、监狱

主要统计指标解释

管理机关提出逮捕的犯罪嫌疑人进行审查，根据事实，依法作出逮捕决定。

■ 决定起诉

指人民检察机关对公安机关、国家安全机关、监狱管理机关和检察机关内设机构反贪污贿赂部门移送起诉的刑事犯罪嫌疑人进行审查，根据事实，依法向人民法院提起公诉。

Explanatory Notes on Main Statistical Indicators

Number of Athletes in Grades

Refers to the number of athletes who have been given titles through examination. The titles of athletes include international masters of sports, masters of sports, first-grade, second-grade and third-grade sportsmen and young athletes.

Number of Referees in Grades

Refers to the number of referees who have been given titles after examination. They are classified as international referees, national referees and referees of the first, second and third grades.

Stadiums

Refer to stadiums for track and field events with six lane 400-meter tracks around soccer fields, permanent track marks and permanent bleachers. Stadiums are classified according to seating capacity. They include: Class A stadiums seating 25000 people each, Class B stadiums seating 15000 to 25000 people each, Class C stadiums seating 5000 to 15000 people each, and Class D stadiums seating fewer than 5000 people.

Gymnasiums

Refer to indoor sports grounds with permanent seats in which basketball, volleyball, badminton, table tennis and gymnastics competitions can be held. Gymnasiums are classified according to seating capacity. They include Class A gymnasiums seating over 6000 people, Class B gymnasiums seating 4000 to 6000 people, Class C gymnasiums seating 2000 to 4000 people, and Class D gymnasiums seating fewer than 2000 people.

Health Care Institutions

Include medical institutions, disease prevention and control centers (epidemic prevention stations), blood gathering and supplying institutions, health supervision and inspection (check up) institutions, medicinal scientific research and on-job training institutions, health education and so on.

Medical Organizations

Include hospitals, health service centers (stations) of communities, nursing homes, health centers, clinics, clinics (health stations and infirmaries), maternity and child care agencies (centers and stations), special disease prevention and curing agencies (centers and stations), first aid centers (stations) and clinical inspection centers. Medical organizations are grouped by two types: profit-making and non-profit-making medical organizations.

Hospitals

Include polyclinics, traditional Chinese medical hospitals, hospitals integrated with traditional Chinese therapeutics and western therapeutics, ethical hospitals, various specialties hospitals and nursing hospitals.

Medical Technical Personnel

Refers to doctors, assistant nurses, pharmacists, and laboratory technicians working in medical institutions.

Doctors

Refer to certified physicians and certified assistant physicians with certifications working in medical and health care and prevention agencies.

Social Welfare Enterprises

Are collective owned enterprises which employ the blind, deaf-mute, and other handicapped people who are able to work in cities and towns and enjoy exemption from state taxes, including welfare plants, welfare commercial services, artificial limb plants and farms, etc. This indicator reflects the preferential policies toward disabled persons.

Basic Endowment Insurance

(Ⅰ) Number of people participating in the insurance program: by the end of reference period, number of staff and workers participating in the insurance program in line with national laws, regulations and related policies, including those who can not make regular payment or interrupt payment but not terminate the insurance program.

(Ⅱ) Revenue of social comprehensive funds: according to national provision, payments made by units covered in basic endowment insurance program, and income from other resources, including: income of social comprehensive funds paid by unites, financial subsidies, interest income and others.

EXPLANATORY NOTES TO MAJOR STATISTICAL INDICATORS

(Ⅲ) Expenditure of social comprehensive funds: refer to payment made to those retired and resigned people covered in endowment insurance program in terms of pension or compensation within the expenditure scope and standards according to related national policies, and the expenditure occurred due to shift of the insurance relationship or adjustment funds among agencies, including: basic pension, transitional pension, pension for resigned people, pension for retired people, pension for people quitting jobs, subsidies, funeral subsidies and other expenditure.

(Ⅳ) Balance of social comprehensive funds: refer to the balance of basic endowment insurance of social comprehensive funds at the end of the reference period, including: bank savings, special fiscal account, investment in bonds and others.

□ Retired or Resigned Personnel

Refers to people who have formally gone through the formalities for their retirement or quitting work and enjoy the corresponding treatments.

□ Unemployment Insurance

(Ⅰ) Number of people participated in unemployment insurance program: number of staff and workers in urban enterprises or institutions and other people according to local government regulations participated in unemployment insurance program in line with national law, regulations and related policies by the end of the reference period.

(Ⅱ) Sum of Unemployment Insurance: refer to total amount of insurance paid to un-employees to guarantee their basic lives according to related regulations.

□ Basic Medical Care Insurance

(Ⅰ) Number of people participated in the insurance program: refer to number of people participated in the basic medical care insurance program according to related regulation by the end of reference period, including: number of staff and workers and retired persons participated in this insurance program.

(Ⅱ) Revenue of social comprehensive funds: according to national provision, payments made by units covered in basic medical care insurance program, and income from other resources, including: income of social comprehensive funds paid by unites, financial subsidies, interest income and others.

(Ⅲ) Expenditure of social comprehensive funds: refer to payment made to those retired and resigned people covered in basic medical care insurance within the expenditure scope and standards according to related national policies, including: expenditure on fee-for-service in hospital, expenditure on fee-for-service in clinic and other expenditure.

(Ⅳ) Balance of social comprehensive funds: refer to the balance of medical care insurance of social comprehensive funds at the end of the reference period, including: bank savings, special fiscal account, investment in bonds and others.

□ Lawyers

Are certified legal workers according to law, and who are employed by legal counseling firms to act as legal advisers, agents in criminal or civil lawsuits, or defenders in criminal lawsuits, or to handle non-litigious legal affairs, to advise on matters of law or to write legal papers for others, and provide service to the public.

□ Notary Personnel

Refers to people working for notary offices including: directors, deputy director, notaries, assistant notaries, and other people providing assistance.

□ Notary Documents

Refer to the judicatory notary documents drawn up by the request of the party and are in accordance with facts and laws and following certain legal proceedings.

□ Mediators

Refer to workers on people mediation committees responsible for mediating in civil disputes and cases of slight infraction of the law. They include members of the mediation committees and mediators of mediation groups.

□ Mediation of Civil Disputes

Refers to number of cases made by mediation committees in mediating in civil disputes concerning civil rights and duties through persuasion and education in accordance with the provisions of law on a voluntary basis, so as to solve disputes by helping the parties involved come to an agreement and understanding, including those unsuccessful ones.

□ Acceptance of Case

Refers to the decision made by the people's procuratorate office on reported cases, prosecution, impeachment, surrender, self-found criminal clues or suspects after initial investigation to

Confirm the act of crime and to start legal proceedings of the case as criminal case.

EXPLANATORY NOTES TO MAJOR STATISTICAL INDICATORS

□ Large Cases

Refer to cases involving a corruption or bribery of over 50,000 yuan, or a misappropriation of over 100,000 yuan, Cases of collectively illegal possession of public funds, unstated sources of large properties, or disguised overseas savings deposits involving 500,000 yuan, or a case that has been defined by Standard on Serious and Large Cases of Misconduct and Tortious that Directly Accepted by People's Procurators Office (trial). This indicator mainly reflects number of accepted cases of job-related criminals that caused serious economic losses or extremely harmful to the society.

□ Key Cases

Refer to cases committed by government officials with a ranking of division director or county administrator. This indicator mainly reflects the recorded and spied on cases by the people's procurators offices toward government official with a ranking of division director or county administrator.

□ Decision of Arrest

Refers to decision made by procurators office, in accordance with laws, to arrest the suspect(s) in the cases that are accepted and to be investigated by procurators office.

□ Approval for Arrest

Refers to the decision made by procurators office, in accordance with laws and relevant facts, to approve the arrest of the suspect(s) that is proposed by the public security departments, state security departments or authority of prisons.

□ Decision on Prosecution

Refers to the decision made by procurators office, in accordance with laws and relevant facts, to institute proceedings to the people court against the suspect(s) of criminal cases handed over by the public security departments, state security departments or authority of prisons, or by the anti-corruption departments within the procurators office.

第 20 章

区　县

DISTRICTS,COUNTIES

简要说明 BRIEF INTRODUCTION

本章资料包括按“都市经济发达圈、渝西经济走廊和三峡库区生态经济区”和“一圈两翼”分组的全市38个区县（自治县）的主要经济社会统计资料。

“都市经济发达圈”包括渝中区、大渡口区、江北区、沙坪坝区、九龙坡区、南岸区、北碚区、渝北区、巴南区，即主城九区。

“渝西经济走廊”包括江津区、合川区、永川区、南川区、綦江区、大足区、潼南县、铜梁县、荣昌县和璧山县。

“三峡库区生态经济区”包括除都市经济发达圈和渝西经济走廊以外的19个区县。

“一圈两翼”的多数统计数据经过评估和测算取得，其合计数不等于各区县数据直接相加。2008年原来的北部新区、经济技术开发区以及高新技术产业开发区三区合一，组建成新的北部新区。

本市自治县包括石柱土家族自治县、秀山土家族苗族自治县、酉阳土家族苗族自治县和彭水苗族土家族自治县。

本章资料分别由市统计局人口就业处、核算处、工业处、服务业处、固定资产投资处、贸易外经处、社会科技处、能源资源统计处、普查中心、综合处和国家统计局重庆调查总队根据有关专业统计资料、各区县统计局资料和市级有关部门的区县资料整理编辑。

This chapter includes the main economic and social indicators of 38 districts and counties (autonomous counties) grouped by the “Metropolitan Developed Economic Circle, West Chongqing Economic Corridor and Ecological Economic Zone in the Three Gorges Reservoir Area” and the “One Circle and Two Wings”.

The “Metropolitan Developed Economic Circle” covers the 9 central urban districts, namely Yuzhong, Dadukou, Jiangbei, Shapingba, Jiulongpo, Nan’an, Beibei, Yubei and Banan.

The “West Chongqing Economic Corridor” includes the districts of Jiangjin, Hechuan, Yongchuan, Nanchuan, Qijiang and Dazu, and the counties of Tongnan, Tongliang, Rongchang and Bishan.

The “Ecological Economic Zone in the Three Gorges Reservoir Area” includes the 19 districts and counties other than the Metropolitan Developed Economic Circle and the West Chongqing Economic Corridor.

The data of the “One Circle and Two Wings” are mostly obtained by evaluation and calculation, which are not equal to the sums of all the districts and counties. In 2008, the former New Northern Zone, Economic and Technical Development Zone and High-Tech Industrial Zone were combined into the present New Northern Zone.

The autonomous counties in Chongqing include Shizhu Tujia Autonomous County, Xiushan Tujia and Miao Autonomous County, Youyang Miao Autonomous County and Pengshui Miao and Tujia Autonomous County.

The data in this chapter are prepared and compiled by Division of Population and Employment Statistics, Division of National Economic Accounting, Division of Industry Statistics, Division of Service Statistics, Division of Statistics of Investment in Fixed Assets, Division of Trade and Foreign Economic Relations Statistics, Division of Social and Technology Statistics, Division of Energy and Natural Resources Statistics, Census Center, Division of Comprehensive Statistics of Chongqing Municipal Bureau of Statistics as well as the NBS Survey Office in Chongqing on the basis of the data provided by the related divisions of Municipal Bureau of Statistics, the statistical bureaus of districts and counties and the related municipal departments.

表20.1 各区县户数和人口（2011年）
HOUSEHOLDS AND POPULATION BY REGION (2011)

区　县	Region	年末总户数（户籍统计）（万户） Year-end Households (registration statistics) (10 000 households)	年末总人口（户籍统计）（万人） Year-end Population (registration statistics) (10 000 persons)	其　中 of which		按年龄组分 By Age			
				#非农业人口 Non-agricultural	#女　性 Female	0-18岁 Aged 0-18	18-35岁 Aged 18-35	35-60岁 Aged 35-60	60岁以上 Aged 60 and Over
全　市	**Total**	**1205.20**	**3329.81**	**1277.64**	**1609.28**	**654.72**	**725.12**	**1387.21**	**562.76**
#都市发达经济圈	**Metropolitan Developed Economic Circle**	**241.20**	**622.85**	**451.29**	**309.45**	**86.96**	**152.18**	**267.04**	**116.67**
渝西经济走廊	**West Chongqing Economic Corridor**	**376.08**	**1036.74**	**341.25**	**500.47**	**191.19**	**214.77**	**448.62**	**182.16**
三峡库区生态经济区	**Ecological Economic Zone in Three GorgesReservoir Area**	**587.92**	**1670.22**	**485.10**	**799.36**	**376.57**	**358.17**	**671.55**	**263.93**
#一小时经济圈	**One -Hour Economic Circle**	**699.13**	**1866.74**	**869.41**	**911.51**	**316.53**	**407.36**	**807.02**	**335.83**
渝中区	Yuzhong District	21.80	56.40	56.40	28.48	5.22	14.49	24.34	12.35
大渡口区	Dadukou District	10.35	24.07	20.81	12.09	3.42	5.29	10.83	4.53
江北区	Jiangbei District	23.20	56.06	52.78	27.88	6.92	14.32	23.94	10.88
沙坪坝区	Shapingba District	27.54	79.87	66.95	39.92	10.52	23.41	32.24	13.70
九龙坡区	Jiulongpo District	33.15	83.75	64.53	41.65	12.07	19.72	36.40	15.56
南岸区	Nan'an District	22.86	62.61	55.20	31.34	8.94	16.82	25.98	10.87
北碚区	Beibei District	24.78	63.42	34.64	31.56	8.12	14.19	28.10	13.01
渝北区	Yubei District	42.55	107.61	63.08	53.29	18.77	24.86	46.49	17.49
巴南区	Ba'nan District	34.97	89.06	36.90	43.24	12.98	19.08	38.72	18.28
涪陵区	Fuling District	45.89	116.50	47.88	57.11	21.98	22.67	51.27	20.58
长寿区	Changshou District	35.96	90.65	28.99	44.48	16.40	17.74	40.09	16.42
江津区	Jiangjin District	60.55	150.41	55.56	72.46	26.50	27.17	67.72	29.02
合川区	Hechuan District	58.22	155.92	49.48	75.06	26.69	30.61	69.77	28.85
永川区	Yongchuan District	37.99	112.88	36.04	55.02	21.84	24.09	48.65	18.30
南川区	Nanchuan District	25.07	67.99	17.44	33.20	13.90	11.88	30.81	11.40
綦江区	Qijiang District	46.85	121.31	50.77	59.19	21.98	25.17	51.96	22.20
大足区	Dazu District	31.49	103.40	32.62	49.14	20.68	24.90	41.58	16.24
潼南县	Tongnan County	31.17	94.15	15.06	44.40	18.50	22.81	37.60	15.24
铜梁县	Tongliang County	30.64	83.64	19.12	40.25	15.16	16.13	36.96	15.39
荣昌县	Rongchang County	30.05	83.53	38.29	40.68	14.76	19.25	35.57	13.95
璧山县	Bishan County	24.05	63.51	26.87	31.07	11.18	12.76	28.00	11.57
渝东北翼	**Northeast of Chongqing**	**382.30**	**1095.63**	**298.47**	**524.08**	**241.16**	**237.98**	**443.77**	**172.72**
万州区	Wanzhou District	70.47	174.56	77.11	85.49	30.73	36.04	77.63	30.16
梁平县	Liangping County	31.52	92.13	18.49	43.92	19.35	17.86	40.48	14.44
城口县	Chengkou County	8.69	24.72	6.40	11.54	5.82	6.27	9.07	3.56
丰都县	Fengdu County	27.47	84.21	22.21	40.46	20.79	15.44	34.24	13.74
垫江县	Dianjiang County	33.17	96.52	21.29	46.26	22.79	20.04	38.41	15.28
忠　县	Zhongxian County	34.14	100.52	22.41	48.15	21.22	20.46	41.72	17.12
开　县	Kaixian County	55.46	164.74	48.68	78.16	39.16	37.03	64.00	24.55
云阳县	Yunyang County	44.03	134.29	34.40	63.90	30.97	30.73	52.02	20.57
奉节县	Fengjie County	34.85	106.26	20.95	50.38	24.55	25.37	40.64	15.70
巫山县	Wushan County	23.13	63.76	14.63	30.29	14.25	15.41	24.68	9.42
巫溪县	Wuxi County	19.37	53.92	11.90	25.53	11.53	13.33	20.88	8.18
渝东南翼	**Southeast of Chongqing**	**123.77**	**367.44**	**109.76**	**173.69**	**97.03**	**79.78**	**136.42**	**54.21**
黔江区	Qianjiang District	20.13	54.13	23.03	25.57	13.91	12.78	20.03	7.41
武隆县	Wulong County	13.95	41.32	11.31	19.61	9.26	7.60	17.08	7.38
石柱县	Shizhu County	19.03	54.45	15.73	26.30	13.75	11.06	21.65	7.99
秀山县	Xiushan County	21.15	65.06	21.59	31.09	17.01	15.97	22.76	9.32
酉阳县	Youyang County	27.24	83.94	22.00	39.38	24.22	18.36	29.53	11.83
彭水县	Pengshui County	22.27	68.54	16.10	31.74	18.88	14.01	25.37	10.28

表20.1 续表 continued

区 县	Region	出 生（户籍统计）Birth (registration statistics) 人 数（万人）Population (10 000 persons)	出生率(‰) Birth Rate (‰)	死 亡（户籍统计）Mortality (registration statistics) 人 数（万人）Population (10 000 persons)	死亡率(‰) Mortality Rate (‰)	自然增长（户籍统计）Natural Growth (registration statistics) 人 数（万人）Population (10 000 persons)	自然增长率(‰) Natural Growth Rate (‰)	常住人口（万人）Resident Popolation (10 000 persons)	其中 of which 城镇人口 Urban (10 000 persons)	城镇化率(%) Urban Rate (%)
全 市	**Total**	**41.27**	**12.44**	**19.55**	**5.90**	**21.72**	**6.54**	**2919.00**	**1605.96**	**55.0**
#都市发达经济圈	**Metropolitan Developed Economic Circle**	**5.87**	**9.52**	**2.99**	**4.84**	**2.88**	**4.68**	**772.31**	**661.21**	**85.6**
渝西经济走廊	**West Chongqing Economic Corridor**	**13.58**	**13.13**	**7.12**	**6.89**	**6.46**	**6.24**	**845.58**	**428.72**	**50.7**
三峡库区生态经济区	**Ecological Economic Zone in ThreeGorges Reservoir Area**	**21.82**	**13.10**	**9.44**	**5.67**	**12.38**	**7.43**	**1301.11**	**516.03**	**39.7**
#一小时经济圈	**One -Hour Economic Circle**	**21.87**	**11.78**	**11.28**	**6.07**	**10.59**	**5.71**	**1804.54**	**1195.36**	**66.2**
渝中区	Yuzhong District	0.36	6.26	0.31	5.50	0.05	0.76	63.9	63.9	100.0
大渡口区	Dadukou District	0.19	8.10	0.09	3.85	0.10	4.25	31.58	29.98	94.9
江北区	Jiangbei District	0.47	8.49	0.26	4.62	0.21	3.87	77.66	72.13	92.9
沙坪坝区	Shapingba District	0.71	8.97	0.36	4.51	0.35	4.46	104.35	95.82	91.8
九龙坡区	Jiulongpo District	0.79	9.52	0.30	3.57	0.49	5.95	111.63	98.65	88.4
南岸区	Nan'an District	0.64	10.36	0.25	3.97	0.39	6.39	78.98	72.47	91.8
北碚区	Beibei District	0.53	8.39	0.39	6.21	0.14	2.18	72.1	54.44	75.5
渝北区	Yubei District	1.20	11.47	0.57	5.45	0.63	6.02	138.64	104.14	75.1
巴南区	Ba'nan District	0.98	11.08	0.46	5.20	0.52	5.88	93.47	69.68	74.6
涪陵区	Fuling District	1.51	12.99	0.66	5.67	0.85	7.32	108.36	62.37	57.6
长寿区	Changshou District	0.91	10.04	0.51	5.64	0.40	4.40	78.29	43.06	55.0
江津区	Jiangjin District	2.19	14.59	1.07	7.12	1.12	7.47	124.93	71.67	57.4
合川区	Hechuan District	1.55	9.96	0.84	5.37	0.71	4.59	131.25	75.51	57.5
永川区	Yongchuan District	1.36	12.06	0.71	6.31	0.65	5.75	104.44	61.2	58.6
南川区	Nanchuan District	1.13	16.75	0.45	6.68	0.68	10.07	53.79	26.59	49.4
綦江区	Qijiang District	1.34	11.08	1.01	8.35	0.33	2.73	107.59	54.25	50.4
大足区	Dazu District	2.58	25.15	0.84	8.15	1.74	17.00	72.97	33.18	45.5
潼南县	Tongnan County	1.27	13.56	0.38	4.06	0.89	9.50	64.25	25.83	40.2
铜梁县	Tongliang County	0.71	8.51	0.71	8.54	0.00	-0.03	60.1	25.89	43.1
荣昌县	Rongchang County	0.98	11.73	0.61	7.29	0.37	4.44	66.69	28.48	42.7
璧山县	Bishan County	0.47	7.38	0.50	7.93	-0.03	-0.55	59.57	26.12	43.9
渝东北翼	**Northeast of Chongqing**	**13.94**	**12.77**	**5.79**	**5.31**	**8.15**	**7.46**	**832.57**	**321.59**	**38.6**
万州区	Wanzhou District	1.82	10.48	0.87	4.98	0.95	5.50	157.22	89.24	56.8
梁平县	Liangping County	1.79	19.55	0.63	6.92	1.16	12.63	68.39	24.54	35.9
城口县	Chengkou County	0.36	14.63	0.13	5.39	0.23	9.24	19.03	5.13	27.0
丰都县	Fengdu County	0.58	6.94	0.44	5.26	0.14	1.68	63.95	23.11	36.1
垫江县	Dianjiang County	0.99	10.26	0.54	5.61	0.45	4.65	70.1	25.15	35.9
忠 县	Zhongxian County	1.19	11.81	0.72	7.21	0.47	4.60	74.82	25.84	34.5
开 县	Kaixian County	2.16	13.17	0.68	4.17	1.48	9.00	116.08	43.54	37.5
云阳县	Yunyang County	1.70	12.72	0.71	5.30	0.99	7.42	91.11	30.78	33.8
奉节县	Fengjie County	1.52	14.35	0.41	3.85	1.11	10.50	81.93	27.77	33.9
巫山县	Wushan County	0.97	15.29	0.25	3.98	0.72	11.31	48.99	15.47	31.6
巫溪县	Wuxi County	0.86	16.05	0.41	7.59	0.45	8.46	40.95	11.02	26.9
渝东南翼	**Southeast of Chongqing**	**5.46**	**14.85**	**2.48**	**6.75**	**2.98**	**8.10**	**281.89**	**89.01**	**31.6**
黔江区	Qianjiang District	0.79	14.72	0.31	5.66	0.48	9.06	44.63	18.21	40.8
武隆县	Wulong County	0.46	11.04	0.28	6.83	0.18	4.21	34.85	12.04	34.6
石柱县	Shizhu County	1.03	18.94	0.35	6.43	0.68	12.51	41.14	13.97	34.0
秀山县	Xiushan County	0.85	13.01	0.47	7.29	0.38	5.72	49.75	15.74	31.6
酉阳县	Youyang County	0.99	11.76	0.49	5.78	0.50	5.98	57.46	14.58	25.4
彭水县	Pengshui County	1.34	19.56	0.58	8.49	0.76	11.07	54.06	14.47	26.8

表20.2 各区县就业（2011年）
EMPLOYMENT BY REGION (2011)

区　县	Region	城镇非私营单位职工人数（万人）Employment of Urban Non-private Units (10 000 persons)	其中 of which #国　有 State-owned	#集　体 Collective -owned	年末失业人员登记数（人）Year-end Registered Unemployment (person)
全　市	**Total**	**292.10**	**116.47**	**9.88**	**129565**
#都市发达经济圈	**Metropolitan Developed Economic Circle**	**144.44**	**48.33**	**2.55**	**50207**
渝西经济走廊	**West Chongqing Economic Corridor**	**58.39**	**24.84**	**2.83**	**32023**
三峡库区生态经济区	**Ecological Economic Zone in Three GorgesReservoir Area**	**86.05**	**41.96**	**4.50**	**47335**
#一小时经济圈	**One -Hour Economic Circle**	**225.17**	**80.54**	**6.50**	**93275**
渝中区	Yuzhong District	29.39	12.94	0.46	7499
大渡口区	Dadukou District	6.19	3.47	0.06	1338
江北区	Jiangbei District	12.83	4.15	0.31	5534
沙坪坝区	Shapingba District	16.04	5.38	0.52	10992
九龙坡区	Jiulongpo District	20.52	5.66	0.73	7985
南岸区	Nan'an District	12.56	3.50	0.08	5462
北碚区	Beibei District	7.85	2.84	0.13	3181
渝北区	Yubei District	25.74	6.86	0.11	5243
巴南区	Ba'nan District	13.32	3.53	0.15	2973
涪陵区	Fuling District	12.91	4.73	0.57	7295
长寿区	Changshou District	9.43	2.65	0.55	3750
江津区	Jiangjin District	9.87	3.39	0.46	4413
合川区	Hechuan District	8.42	3.01	0.50	1876
永川区	Yongchuan District	9.18	3.34	0.29	3113
南川区	Nanchuan District	3.26	1.88	0.19	3269
綦江区	Qijiang District	8.66	4.32	0.55	6784
大足区	Dazu District	5.60	1.91	0.23	2146
潼南县	Tongnan County	2.19	1.79	0.04	1552
铜梁县	Tongliang County	3.28	1.84	0.13	2501
荣昌县	Rongchang County	4.01	1.85	0.11	3443
璧山县	Bishan County	3.92	1.50	0.33	2926
渝东北翼	**Northeast of Chongqing**	**48.66**	**24.63**	**2.96**	**26566**
万州区	Wanzhou District	13.99	4.76	0.45	3224
梁平县	Liangping County	5.39	1.93	0.93	1802
城口县	Chengkou County	1.12	0.81	0.08	543
丰都县	Fengdu County	3.07	1.66	0.21	2484
垫江县	Dianjiang County	6.65	3.69	0.64	2469
忠　县	Zhongxian County	1.86	1.75	0.06	1068
开　县	Kaixian County	5.85	3.30	0.05	2954
云阳县	Yunyang County	3.03	2.07	0.07	3180
奉节县	Fengjie County	3.08	2.07	0.10	4779
巫山县	Wushan County	2.08	1.39	0.12	3153
巫溪县	Wuxi County	2.54	1.21	0.25	910
渝东南翼	**Southeast of Chongqing**	**15.05**	**9.95**	**0.42**	**9724**
黔江区	Qianjiang District	3.34	1.70	0.03	2001
武隆县	Wulong County	2.07	1.18	0.02	1278
石柱县	Shizhu County	2.55	1.93	0.09	1892
秀山县	Xiushan County	2.08	1.81	0.15	1641
酉阳县	Youyang County	2.76	1.81	0.12	1318
彭水县	Pengshui County	2.25	1.50	0.01	1594

表20.3 各区县(自治区）生产总值（2011年）
GROSS DOMESTIC PRODUCT BY REGION (2011)

区　县	Region	地区生产总值（万元） Gross Domestic Product (10000 yuan)	其　中 of which 第一产业 Primary Industry	第二产业 Secondary Industry	其　中 of which #工　业 Industry	第三产业 Tertiary Industry	人均地区生产总值（元） Per Capita GDP(yuan)
全　市	**Total**	**100113700**	**8445200**	**55430400**	**46904600**	**36238100**	**34500**
#都市发达经济圈	**Metropolitan Developed Economic Circle**	**43684900**	**897600**	**22986000**	**19748200**	**19801300**	**57553**
渝西经济走廊	**West Chongqing Economic Corridor**	**25088300**	**3383900**	**14940000**	**12814700**	**6775400**	**29869**
三峡库区生态经济区	**Ecological Economic Zone in ThreeGorges Reservoir Area**	**31329500**	**4163700**	**17504400**	**14341700**	**9661400**	**24054**
#一小时经济圈	**One -Hour Economic Circle**	**77628800**	**4931300**	**43752600**	**37695300**	**28944900**	**43500**
渝中区	Yuzhong District	6652881		372777	146128	6280104	104844
大渡口区	Dadukou District	1498530	16702	835478	713387	646350	48590
江北区	Jiangbei District	5165219	24795	1765314	1473799	3375110	68206
沙坪坝区	Shapingba District	5602527	56952	3204333	2754277	2341242	54833
九龙坡区	Jiulongpo District	6905445	84940	3310029	3004607	3510476	62757
南岸区	Nan'an District	4341578	43871	2751502	2399201	1546205	56042
北碚区	Beibei District	3030133	116073	2016824	1745627	897236	43244
渝北区	Yubei District	7678603	214171	4821354	3928840	2643078	56216
巴南区	Ba'nan District	3950968	340114	2185596	1834159	1425258	42635
涪陵区	Fuling District	5573392	372911	3460927	3107210	1739554	51838
长寿区	Changshou District	3176949	276840	1929025	1570871	971084	40916
江津区	Jiangjin District	3838493	552668	2308613	2058284	977212	30926
合川区	Hechuan District	3063624	468583	1464981	1115937	1130060	23517
永川区	Yongchuan District	3801971	359170	2186478	1803559	1256323	36750
南川区	Nanchuan District	1688527	281243	835468	706124	571816	31496
綦江区	Qijiang District	2644078	366164	1344528	1166289	933386	24796
大足区	Dazu District	2338673	286570	1369091	1184593	683012	32235
潼南县	Tongnan County	1469260	335165	608832	377696	525263	22912
铜梁县	Tongliang County	1956376	263650	1104671	969920	588055	32576
荣昌县	Rongchang County	2075526	321936	1237261	1054900	516329	31253
璧山县	Bishan County	2082959	148705	1360282	1242997	573972	35254
渝东北翼	**Northeast of Chongqing**	**17105100**	**2605300**	**8955700**	**7126600**	**5544100**	**20496**
万州区	Wanzhou District	6225938	423372	3511663	3010118	2290903	39715
梁平县	Liangping County	1314575	242912	645603	535207	426060	19171
城口县	Chengkou County	371646	51831	220724	175272	99091	19392
丰都县	Fengdu County	997720	202264	435422	282210	360034	15484
垫江县	Dianjiang County	1474809	253856	748419	657552	472534	20986
忠　县	Zhongxian County	1368694	254713	592923	460738	521058	18254
开　县	Kaixian County	1997778	375974	900835	630056	720969	17214
云阳县	Yunyang County	1092842	288019	371885	266668	432938	11983
奉节县	Fengjie County	1284533	261639	459477	250891	563417	15536
巫山县	Wushan County	634201	141795	225654	140358	266752	12877
巫溪县	Wuxi County	472891	109000	171776	86588	192115	11484
渝东南翼	**Southeast of Chongqing**	**5379800**	**908600**	**2722100**	**2082700**	**1749100**	**19027**
黔江区	Qianjiang District	1291943	137830	715459	622372	438654	28990
武隆县	Wulong County	865824	134621	317695	165924	413508	24756
石柱县	Shizhu County	801520	164312	345468	255632	291740	19396
秀山县	Xiushan County	934894	137558	498385	437764	298951	18715
酉阳县	Youyang County	769639	173837	334378	209427	261424	13354
彭水县	Pengshui County	764940	160398	306734	207240	297808	14091

表20.3 续表 continued

上年=100 (preceding year=100)

区 县	Region	地区生产总值指数（可比价）Indices of GDP (constant prices)	其 中 of which 第一产业 Primary Industry	第二产业 Secondary Industry	其 中 of which #工 业 Industry	第三产业 Tertiary Industry	人均地区生产总值指数 Indices of Per Capital GDP
全 市	**Total**	**116.4**	**105.1**	**121.8**	**122.2**	**110.8**	**115.1**
#都市发达经济圈	**Metropolitan Developed Economic Circle**	**115.2**	**102.3**	**119.4**	**119.2**	**110.9**	**111.6**
渝西经济走廊	**West Chongqing Economic Corridor**	**116.7**	**105.2**	**122.9**	**123.7**	**109.3**	**115.8**
三峡库区生态经济区	**Ecological Economic Zone in Three GorgesReservoir Area**	**117.8**	**105.7**	**124.4**	**125.5**	**111.7**	**117.8**
#一小时经济圈	**One -Hour Economic Circle**	**116.1**	**104.7**	**121.2**	**121.4**	**110.5**	**113.9**
渝中区	Yuzhong District	115.5		110.1	109.2	115.8	115.1
大渡口区	Dadukou District	116.7	102.2	119.0	118.5	114.3	112.9
江北区	Jiangbei District	117.3	80.2	115.6	114.6	118.8	113.1
沙坪坝区	Shapingba District	124.2	101.8	136.6	140.0	111.8	119.7
九龙坡区	Jiulongpo District	116.7	101.0	117.9	117.6	116.0	114.0
南岸区	Nan'an District	116.1	104.0	118.1	117.6	113.0	112.3
北碚区	Beibei District	117.8	105.3	120.9	120.8	112.9	113.9
渝北区	Yubei District	115.3	98.9	115.9	114.7	115.3	108.9
巴南区	Ba'nan District	116.8	106.0	118.8	118.4	116.3	115.1
涪陵区	Fuling District	120.5	106.0	125.7	126.4	114.7	117.6
长寿区	Changshou District	120.0	105.1	124.6	126.0	115.6	118.8
江津区	Jiangjin District	117.9	105.8	123.3	123.7	112.7	117.4
合川区	Hechuan District	116.2	105.6	122.4	123.1	113.6	115.0
永川区	Yongchuan District	119.8	105.8	124.4	125.3	116.0	117.5
南川区	Nanchuan District	116.2	105.5	120.5	123.6	117.3	117.6
綦江区	Qijiang District	115.6	101.6	121.2	122.0	113.7	115.4
大足区	Dazu District	116.3	105.0	121.2	121.3	111.9	116.3
潼南县	Tongnan County	114.6	106.1	118.3	118.8	116.5	115.2
铜梁县	Tongliang County	116.4	105.8	123.7	124.5	109.2	116.2
荣昌县	Rongchang County	117.3	105.5	122.4	122.6	113.5	116.5
璧山县	Bishan County	124.0	105.5	132.0	132.8	112.6	117.5
渝东北翼	**Northeast of Chongqing**	**117.6**	**105.7**	**124.7**	**125.8**	**112.0**	**118.1**
万州区	Wanzhou District	120.1	106.1	124.4	125.0	115.9	118.9
梁平县	Liangping County	117.0	105.7	124.0	124.6	115.4	117.7
城口县	Chengkou County	119.7	105.4	129.0	130.0	110.1	119.2
丰都县	Fengdu County	118.4	105.9	125.7	128.2	117.7	118.6
垫江县	Dianjiang County	116.6	105.8	123.3	123.3	113.6	118.4
忠 县	Zhongxian County	118.6	105.1	128.8	131.0	116.0	118.2
开 县	Kaixian County	118.3	105.6	126.2	128.1	117.3	118.0
云阳县	Yunyang County	118.4	105.9	136.5	145.0	114.4	119.7
奉节县	Fengjie County	118.3	106.0	124.8	128.1	119.4	120.8
巫山县	Wushan County	118.5	105.4	120.8	121.3	124.2	119.4
巫溪县	Wuxi County	118.1	105.4	122.9	124.4	121.3	122.3
渝东南翼	**Southeast of Chongqing**	**116.0**	**105.4**	**122.3**	**124.1**	**112.2**	**115.8**
黔江区	Qianjiang District	119.5	105.5	124.6	125.1	116.3	118.5
武隆县	Wulong County	118.5	106.0	121.5	128.2	120.7	117.9
石柱县	Shizhu County	118.1	105.2	127.3	129.0	116.0	119.1
秀山县	Xiushan County	116.0	105.5	120.2	120.1	114.2	116.0
酉阳县	Youyang County	116.1	105.5	122.0	127.3	116.4	115.8
彭水县	Pengshui County	115.4	105.0	120.8	124.1	116.0	115.2

表20.4 各区县农业和农村经济（2011年）

AGRICULTURE AND RURAL ECONOMY BY REGION (2011)

区 县	Region	农林牧渔业总产值（万元） Gross Output Value (10 000 yuan)	其 中 of which 农 业 Farming	林 业 Forestry	牧 业 Animal Husbandry	渔 业 Fishery	农林牧渔服务业 Farming, Forestry, Animal Husbandry and Fishery Services	农林牧渔业总产值指数（可比价）（上年=100） Indices of Gross Output (constant prices) (preceding year=100)
全 市	**Total**	**12653319**	**7512247**	**380907**	**4253262**	**349432**	**157471**	**104.8**
#都市发达经济圈	**Metropolitan Developed Economic Circle**	**1330890**	**850862**	**27406**	**354277**	**56911**	**41433**	**102.3**
渝西经济走廊	**West Chongqing Economic Corridor**	**4978363**	**2989989**	**120441**	**1677330**	**148403**	**42200**	**105.1**
三峡库区生态经济区	**Ecological Economic Zone in ThreeGorges Reservoir Area**	**6344066**	**3671396**	**233060**	**2221655**	**144117**	**73839**	**105.5**
#一小时经济圈	**One -Hour Economic Circle**	**7271198**	**4407871**	**172508**	**2338315**	**252966**	**99538**	**104.7**
渝中区	Yuzhong District							
大渡口区	Dadukou District	24686	18034	1750	2730	972	1200	102.0
江北区	Jiangbei District	36833	10280	2059	20926	2479	1089	80.7
沙坪坝区	Shapingba District	79266	52459	841	12064	4154	9748	102.0
九龙坡区	Jiulongpo District	123398	73618	2808	40711	3508	2754	99.9
南岸区	Nan'an District	65932	40928	1139	12511	10456	900	102.5
北碚区	Beibei District	171090	131196	1620	29116	6100	3058	105.3
渝北区	Yubei District	329370	193133	10420	106761	7457	11600	98.8
巴南区	Ba'nan District	500314	331215	6769	129460	21786	11085	106.3
涪陵区	Fuling District	554601	352894	18849	153024	20703	9131	106.1
长寿区	Changshou District	407344	214126	5810	153684	26949	6775	104.9
江津区	Jiangjin District	808003	530174	9719	246561	16463	5086	106.0
合川区	Hechuan District	677499	441895	14232	190049	26075	5248	106.1
永川区	Yongchuan District	532197	260979	11586	230929	22892	5811	104.9
南川区	Nanchuan District	416606	238153	14676	148449	10507	4821	105.3
綦江区	Qijiang District	549447	354579	18915	160629	11364	3960	101.5
大足区	Dazu District	424316	257283	14969	134598	14060	3406	103.4
潼南县	Tongnan County	484688	345977	16120	107170	12880	2541	106.4
铜梁县	Tongliang County	391531	184732	5966	180956	15150	4726	105.8
荣昌县	Rongchang County	464410	270523	11872	166913	10028	5075	105.9
璧山县	Bishan County	229665	105693	2387	111075	8985	1526	105.9
渝东北翼	**Northeast of Chongqing**	**3950466**	**2330753**	**139875**	**1352272**	**83603**	**43962**	**105.6**
万州区	Wanzhou District	623165	410640	20953	165620	20901	5051	106.2
梁平县	Liangping County	364311	212056	11660	127765	8944	3886	105.6
城口县	Chengkou County	82119	35666	6723	38256	1003	470	105.4
丰都县	Fengdu County	297448	148123	12404	126176	7636	3109	105.1
垫江县	Dianjiang County	382985	215080	6991	138573	13951	8391	105.8
忠 县	Zhongxian County	385509	241569	9436	125638	4663	4203	104.8
开 县	Kaixian County	571581	338088	15821	197144	15606	4922	106.0
云阳县	Yunyang County	433923	271108	14440	140362	4295	3718	105.3
奉节县	Fengjie County	412244	271468	5036	125900	4798	5042	106.0
巫山县	Wushan County	225469	107862	19972	93757	749	3130	105.5
巫溪县	Wuxi County	171711	79093	16439	73081	1057	2041	105.5
渝东南翼	**Southeast of Chongqing**	**1431655**	**773622**	**68525**	**562675**	**12862**	**13971**	**105.2**
黔江区	Qianjiang District	216494	90497	12317	109757	1772	2151	104.4
武隆县	Wulong County	211776	137334	6540	63559	3667	676	105.4
石柱县	Shizhu County	252788	132195	7967	107510	3333	1782	105.2
秀山县	Xiushan County	213654	129491	9123	67424	1852	5764	105.7
酉阳县	Youyang County	281368	138578	18992	120473	1747	1578	105.5
彭水县	Pengshui County	255575	145528	13585	93951	491	2019	105.0

表20.4 续表1 continued1

区 县	Region	农业商品产值（万元） Output Value of Agricultural Commodities (10 000 yuan)	农业商品率（%） Commercial Rate (%)	乡村从业人员（万人） Rural Employment (10 000 persons)	农作物播种面积（公顷） Sown Areas of Farm Crops (hectare)	其中 of which #粮 食 Grain	农用化肥施用量（折纯）（吨） Consumption of Chemical Fertilizer (net) (tons)
全 市	**Total**	**7802248**	**62.4**	**1370.0**	**3413088**	**2259413**	**956048**
#都市发达经济圈	**Metropolitan Developed Economic Circle**	**834478**	**64.7**	**117.3**	**222937**	**137424**	**52448**
渝西经济走廊	**West Chongqing Economic Corridor**	**3277182**	**66.4**	**467.7**	**1083704**	**689002**	**322267**
三峡库区生态经济区	**Ecological Economic Zone in ThreeGorges Reservoir Area**	**3690455**	**58.9**	**785.0**	**2106447**	**1432987**	**581333**
#一小时经济圈	**One -Hour Economic Circle**	**4718966**	**65.8**	**680.3**	**1568027**	**993522**	**439605**
渝中区	Yuzhong District						
大渡口区	Dadukou District	22588	91.5	2.1	2529	35	2072
江北区	Jiangbei District	22763	61.8	2.3	4217	2895	1620
沙坪坝区	Shapingba District	56517	71.3	8.7	9315	3941	4659
九龙坡区	Jiulongpo District	108590	88.0	12.9	13730	6328	3064
南岸区	Nan'an District	53339	80.9	6.0	4637	2127	3568
北碚区	Beibei District	104194	60.9	20.9	34280	15495	8477
渝北区	Yubei District	155792	47.3	29.7	58420	42119	13400
巴南区	Ba'nan District	310695	62.1	34.8	95809	64484	15588
涪陵区	Fuling District	358827	64.7	52.8	173630	97931	42240
长寿区	Changshou District	248480	61.0	42.6	87756	69165	22650
江津区	Jiangjin District	584186	72.3	69.5	151206	101418	40845
合川区	Hechuan District	411242	60.7	75.4	163246	120813	30761
永川区	Yongchuan District	363491	68.3	36.7	101662	69026	66492
南川区	Nanchuan District	275793	66.2	35.0	86529	56041	23700
綦江区	Qijiang District	286807	90.6	49.4	124379	80640	38662
大足区	Dazu District	291337	126.8	37.4	102662	64577	24377
潼南县	Tongnan County	359638	74.2	49.2	136325	58962	33297
铜梁县	Tongliang County	273680	69.9	40.0	84655	59722	32402
荣昌县	Rongchang County	266107	57.3	42.0	81731	48412	15378
璧山县	Bishan County	164900	71.8	33.1	51308	29392	16353
渝东北翼	**Northeast of Chongqing**	**2282659**	**58.4**	**493.3**	**1232848**	**882436**	**352905**
万州区	Wanzhou District	375768	60.3	72.8	172000	113487	38785
梁平县	Liangping County	205471	56.4	47.4	97629	73741	46586
城口县	Chengkou County	40320	49.1	11.0	53489	31276	6222
丰都县	Fengdu County	176982	59.5	36.5	109216	75975	24255
垫江县	Dianjiang County	269239	70.3	50.4	83758	64116	52934
忠 县	Zhongxian County	251738	65.3	43.3	106497	80803	30805
开 县	Kaixian County	333803	58.4	78.6	173357	126613	53252
云阳县	Yunyang County	230847	53.2	52.0	128185	100187	24430
奉节县	Fengjie County	231269	56.1	43.9	130139	91602	25756
巫山县	Wushan County	90639	40.2	30.4	90582	62708	20925
巫溪县	Wuxi County	76583	44.6	26.8	87996	61928	28955
渝东南翼	**Southeast of Chongqing**	**800489**	**56.5**	**196.4**	**612214**	**383455**	**163538**
黔江区	Qianjiang District	144835	66.9	28.6	88943	57095	23608
武隆县	Wulong County	102711	48.5	23.2	83160	48241	18576
石柱县	Shizhu County	145606	57.6	27.4	88248	55028	24676
秀山县	Xiushan County	124774	58.4	34.4	102896	53352	27522
酉阳县	Youyang County	152220	54.1	45.3	130658	86900	28132
彭水县	Pengshui County	130343	51.0	37.3	118310	82840	41024

表20.4 续表2 continued2

区 县	Region	农村用电量（万千瓦时） Electricity Consumption in Rural Areas (10 000 kwh)	农药使用量（吨） Consumption of Chemical Pesticides (ton)	粮食产量（吨） Output of Grain (ton)	油料产量（吨） Output of Oil-bearing Crops (ton)	甘蔗产量（吨） Output of Sugarcane (ton)	烟叶产量（吨） Output of Tobacco (ton)	茶叶产量（吨） Output of Tea (ton)
全 市	**Total**	**703706**	**20324**	**11269032**	**465073**	**118048**	**93608**	**27895**
#都市发达经济圈	**Metropolitan Developed Economic Circle**	**231833**	**966**	**690715.6**	**6925.5**	**785.0**	**674.0**	**3662.0**
渝西经济走廊	**West Chongqing Economic Corridor**	**240784**	**7898**	**4131973**	**168582**	**97807**	**4551**	**14952**
三峡库区生态经济区	**Ecological Economic Zone in ThreeGorges Reservoir Area**	**231089**	**11460**	**6446344**	**289565**	**19456**	**88383**	**9281**
#一小时经济圈	**One -Hour Economic Circle**	**517644**	**10414**	**5620110**	**189476**	**99639**	**7129**	**19358**
渝中区	Yuzhong District							
大渡口区	Dadukou District	4700	37	223				
江北区	Jiangbei District	1569	18	8180	62			9
沙坪坝区	Shapingba District	75880	53	14070	35			10
九龙坡区	Jiulongpo District	15775	163	27038	805	190		
南岸区	Nan'an District	8823	21	12690				
北碚区	Beibei District	94670	295	60963	1052	117	32	65
渝北区	Yubei District	7351	121	206972	2880	95	101	16
巴南区	Ba'nan District	23065	258	360580	2092	383	541	3562
涪陵区	Fuling District	30410	988	431541	5349	110	1700	689
长寿区	Changshou District	14617	562	365881	8619	937	204	55
江津区	Jiangjin District	28164	996	647618	10950	70123	758	1468
合川区	Hechuan District	14135	671	711842	17989	839	136	87
永川区	Yongchuan District	19133	2243	487576	15320	5380	5	3790
南川区	Nanchuan District	21315	440	329994	18221		2651	2979
綦江区	Qijiang District	29201	511	342221	7418	216	743	2132
大足区	Dazu District	21605	730	441494	31951	2500	220	565
潼南县	Tongnan County	12409	384	359005	33135	8600	28	204
铜梁县	Tongliang County	10949	491	346410	9412	900	3	155
荣昌县	Rongchang County	13112	701	292860	20881	8793	6	3150
璧山县	Bishan County	70761	731	172953	3305	456	1	422
渝东北翼	**Northeast of Chongqing**	**129105**	**6768**	**4016365**	**175018**	**17913**	**35139**	**2727**
万州区	Wanzhou District	14156	932	520748	15556	845	4500	200
梁平县	Liangping County	10114	986	374961	13157	7418	62	151
城口县	Chengkou County	2912	32	99565	3005		62	331
丰都县	Fengdu County	14037	292	335966	17930	28	5377	12
垫江县	Dianjiang County	9327	1238	380033	15750	2504	472	81
忠 县	Zhongxian County	6559	802	400273	28086	1617	265	16
开 县	Kaixian County	21245	731	590372	23558	4851	901	558
云阳县	Yunyang County	12660	490	427623	15431	650	890	377
奉节县	Fengjie County	24885	757	445199	19216		6178	301
巫山县	Wushan County	8220	153	233926	13696		8709	280
巫溪县	Wuxi County	4990	355	207700	9633		7723	420
渝东南翼	**Southeast of Chongqing**	**56957**	**3142**	**1632557**	**100579**	**496**	**51340**	**5810**
黔江区	Qianjiang District	2792	671	243271	14524		8788	652
武隆县	Wulong County	11753	302	166359	7296		9567	124
石柱县	Shizhu County	8861	619	259649	9896	326	5180	172
秀山县	Xiushan County	18984	782	306928	27462		404	3720
酉阳县	Youyang County	8693	298	356321	23088		11401	944
彭水县	Pengshui County	5874	470	300029	18313	170	16000	198

表20.4 续表3 continued3

区 县	Region	水果产量（吨） Output of Fruit (ton)	蔬菜产量（吨） Output of Vegetable (ton)	肉类总产量（吨） Output of Meat (ton)	其 中 of which #猪 肉 Output of Pork	#牛 肉 Output of Beef	水产品产量（吨） Output of Aquatic Products (ton)
全 市	**Total**	**2611604**	**14079653**	**1962848**	**1485523**	**66515**	**275600**
#都市发达经济圈	**Metropolitan Developed Economic Circle**	**184388**	**1474377**	**117018**	**84006**	**597**	**35340**
渝西经济走廊	**West Chongqing Economic Corridor**	**689816**	**5950553**	**758212**	**533505**	**6071**	**130533**
三峡库区生态经济区	**Ecological Economic Zone in Three GorgesReservoir Area**	**1737400**	**6654722**	**1087618**	**868012**	**59847**	**109727**
#一小时经济圈	**One -Hour Economic Circle**	**1121917**	**9326213**	**1007517**	**721398**	**8938**	**203089**
渝中区	Yuzhong District						
大渡口区	Dadukou District	660	63400	1161	847	7	533
江北区	Jiangbei District	2885	15737	2881	1870	11	468
沙坪坝区	Shapingba District	2592	94756	2390	1904	17	3998
九龙坡区	Jiulongpo District	13138	122925	7600	5038	8	3696
南岸区	Nan'an District	5714	47094	2583	2170	28	3309
北碚区	Beibei District	17711	394104	12062	9444	47	4169
渝北区	Yubei District	100435	229240	37341	22084	230	5415
巴南区	Ba'nan District	41253	507121	51000	40649	249	13752
涪陵区	Fuling District	104800	1639685	68932	56744	1497	16502
长寿区	Changshou District	142913	261597	63355	47143	773	20714
江津区	Jiangjin District	186625	678551	91697	71531	402	13408
合川区	Hechuan District	78026	571795	90599	75284	333	22776
永川区	Yongchuan District	110698	495252	104177	63380	195	24491
南川区	Nanchuan District	50358	323317	63260	47967	1596	7649
綦江区	Qijiang District	31193	636948	67670	56832	2145	6962
大足区	Dazu District	38358	286471	59687	47851	135	11689
潼南县	Tongnan County	51496	1524226	56914	51342	463	10314
铜梁县	Tongliang County	27081	509125	85317	46671	190	14182
荣昌县	Rongchang County	29250	378028	68530	52123	547	8043
璧山县	Bishan County	86731	546841	70361	20524	65	11019
渝东北翼	**Northeast of Chongqing**	**1339500**	**3230890**	**667793**	**531081**	**28327**	**64642**
万州区	Wanzhou District	244795	778592	75056	63495	1784	16769
梁平县	Liangping County	71106	375983	68418	50921	914	7323
城口县	Chengkou County	2051	37944	23431	16287	821	408
丰都县	Fengdu County	47904	271929	58050	34200	13140	5071
垫江县	Dianjiang County	53905	287619	64603	55890	820	10744
忠 县	Zhongxian County	204194	205159	61980	49195	1951	4813
开 县	Kaixian County	309430	341544	96449	74281	1460	12892
云阳县	Yunyang County	119632	346098	73820	59675	3936	2849
奉节县	Fengjie County	226737	228925	59713	52219	2412	2364
巫山县	Wushan County	52815	187077	40816	35800	537	567
巫溪县	Wuxi County	6931	170022	45457	39118	552	842
渝东南翼	**Southeast of Chongqing**	**150187**	**1522549**	**287538**	**233044**	**29250**	**7869**
黔江区	Qianjiang District	30115	154895	63416	57214	4729	1186
武隆县	Wulong County	20554	392239	38446	32663	2907	1775
石柱县	Shizhu County	13007	268592	36952	25183	5974	1805
秀山县	Xiushan County	65336	232110	40264	32212	2666	1719
酉阳县	Youyang County	15781	219542	59861	46645	6465	1083
彭水县	Pengshui County	5394	255171	48599	39127	6509	301

表20.5 各区县工业（2011年）
INDUSTY BY REGION (2011)

区 县	Region	工业总产值（万元） Gross Output Value of Industry (10 000 yuan)	工业总产值指数（上年=100） Index of Gross Output Value of Industry (preceding year=100)	工业企业资产总计（万元） Total Assets of Industrial Enterprises (10 000 yuan)	主营业务收入（万元） Revenue from Principal Business (10 000 yuan)	利润总额（万元） Total Profits (10 000 yuan)
全 市	**Total**	**118470581**	**128.2**	**93210985**	**113823442**	**6603471**
#都市发达经济圈	**Metropolitan Developed Economic Circle**	**60536609**	**123.0**	**45733043**	**58460648**	**2719482**
渝西经济走廊	**West Chongqing Economic Corridor**	**30837045**	**133.3**	**21322040**	**29924797**	**2341777**
三峡库区生态经济区	**Ecological Economic Zone in Three Gorges Reservoir Area**	**27096928**	**134.9**	**26155902**	**25437997**	**1542212**
#一小时经济圈	**One-Hour Economic Circle**	**105220826**	**127.4**	**79800076**	**101306927**	**5778011**
渝中区	Yuzhong District	147558	111.5	268173	155332	6209
大渡口区	Dadukou District	2272804	124.8	2597315	2132254	63444
江北区	Jiangbei District	5515913	116.6	4656651	4667197	297977
沙坪坝区	Shapingba District	9019645	150.1	5668417	8973921	332552
九龙坡区	Jiulongpo District	9925058	121.2	7958731	9676372	342268
南岸区	Nan'an District	7122628	120.8	4526252	6979967	246015
北碚区	Beibei District	5589331	122.4	3915026	5419075	284087
渝北区	Yubei District	15060529	115.7	12294903	14622132	903087
巴南区	Ba'nan District	5883143	121.4	3847575	5834400	243843
涪陵区	Fuling District	7698800	133.7	6067656	6989443	631502
长寿区	Changshou District	6148373	136.7	6677336	5932040	85250
江津区	Jiangjin District	6148814	132.8	5539455	5910044	544887
合川区	Hechuan District	2592414	132.2	2133017	2551821	262597
永川区	Yongchuan District	4347797	133.5	2784799	4073058	450145
南川区	Nanchuan District	915886	127.0	1412452	863542	60301
綦江区	Qijiang District	3143105	131.9	3197468	3085041	118030
大足区	Dazu District	3191229	127.1	1199107	3130188	219525
潼南县	Tongnan County	677205	134.0	525385	656508	43517
铜梁县	Tongliang County	2007391	134.8	948123	1977841	91294
荣昌县	Rongchang County	3714336	132.0	1397309	3633999	332073
璧山县	Bishan County	4098867	143.4	2184926	4042755	219408
渝东北翼	**Northeast of Chongqing**	**10042919**	**134.8**	**8121828**	**9534136**	**639617**
万州区	Wanzhou District	5058529	128.3	3370480	4809385	317714
梁平县	Liangping County	787589	134.6	358395	768521	90019
城口县	Chengkou County	232548	137.1	333646	202555	14748
丰都县	Fengdu County	438542	142.3	735618	382351	20715
垫江县	Dianjiang County	848741	135.5	539218	787648	36231
忠 县	Zhongxian County	595427	140.4	825517	549091	50711
开 县	Kaixian County	1159973	143.2	696541	1133220	64949
云阳县	Yunyang County	387302	183.4	334440	359781	7043
奉节县	Fengjie County	259931	148.9	220783	259031	26441
巫山县	Wushan County	159150	140.1	133614	151318	3262
巫溪县	Wuxi County	115187	134.6	573577	131235	7784
渝东南翼	**Southeast of Chongqing**	**3206835**	**134.9**	**5289081**	**2982379**	**185844**
黔江区	Qianjiang District	1256031	132.2	1062273	1175185	88111
武隆县	Wulong County	244103	140.4	876126	240522	17112
石柱县	Shizhu County	579797	141.6	511370	518012	41086
秀山县	Xiushan County	485974	124.9	843653	445213	3019
酉阳县	Youyang County	301844	150.4	638382	304269	30623
彭水县	Pengshui County	339087	133.4	1357277	299177	5893

注：本表为规模以上工业企业统计数。
Note: The data in this table are the data of industrial enterprises above designated size.

表20.5 续表 continued

区 县	Region	经济效益综合指数 Comprehensive Index of Economic Benefit	总资产贡献率(%) Ratio of Total Assets to Industrial Output Value (%)	资产负债率(%) Asset-Liability Ratio (%)	产品销售率(%) Sales as Percentage of Output (%)	全员劳动生产率(元/人年) Overall Labor Productivity (yuan/person--year)
全 市	**Total**	**244.1**	**13.7**	**60.7**	**97.4**	**213463**
#都市发达经济圈	**Metropolitan Developed Economic Circle**	**239.3**	**12.4**	**60.9**	**97.8**	**198147**
渝西经济走廊	**West Chongqing Economic Corridor**	**243.6**	**16.8**	**58.6**	**97.2**	**126227**
三峡库区生态经济区	**Ecological Economic Zone in Three Gorges Reservoir Area**	**258.1**	**13.3**	**62.1**	**96.5**	**197912**
#一小时经济圈	**One-Hour Economic Circle**	**244.9**	**13.7**	**60.5**	**97.6**	**178778**
渝中区	Yuzhong District	234.9	5.5	59.4	99.9	263064
大渡口区	Dadukou District	134.1	6.8	65.4	97.8	109604
江北区	Jiangbei District	205.1	10.5	58.6	94.4	185082
沙坪坝区	Shapingba District	219.1	13.0	73.5	99.8	220562
九龙坡区	Jiulongpo District	195.9	7.8	52.9	97.0	197745
南岸区	Nan'an District	243.2	14.4	58.4	98.0	244881
北碚区	Beibei District	223.4	13.9	54.6	98.2	203847
渝北区	Yubei District	229.7	15.6	62.4	97.8	208283
巴南区	Ba'nan District	174.1	13.0	63.5	98.6	138315
涪陵区	Fuling District	344.9	22.0	62.7	97.5	356858
长寿区	Changshou District	198.9	4.9	62.2	97.1	218140
江津区	Jiangjin District	246.3	14.3	66.6	96.1	223468
合川区	Hechuan District	214.4	18.4	57.5	97.4	104789
永川区	Yongchuan District	228.9	22.8	51.9	95.7	117967
南川区	Nanchuan District	149.9	7.7	78.0	94.1	96456
綦江区	Qijiang District	172.3	9.2	55.9	97.5	122154
大足区	Dazu District	238.7	26.0	54.2	99.4	109743
潼南县	Tongnan County	193.9	14.3	44.6	96.2	109176
铜梁县	Tongliang County	178.8	17.4	52.6	98.8	68090
荣昌县	Rongchang County	254.1	34.0	41.8	97.8	82794
璧山县	Bishan County	216.4	15.5	58.7	98.2	170360
渝东北翼	**Northeast of Chongqing**	**239.8**	**14.4**	**56.1**	**95.6**	**137024**
万州区	Wanzhou District	255.3	17.1	57.3	96.4	226663
梁平县	Liangping County	253.8	38.5	34.2	97.7	85531
城口县	Chengkou County	168.7	12.9	57.3	88.5	91580
丰都县	Fengdu County	124.7	5.7	64.6	89.0	88437
垫江县	Dianjiang County	226.5	11.9	53.8	96.9	214660
忠 县	Zhongxian County	230.3	8.4	41.5	88.6	177713
开 县	Kaixian County	207.3	18.8	58.9	97.8	104353
云阳县	Yunyang County	147.4	6.7	50.8	92.7	97309
奉节县	Fengjie County	158.0	20.0	68.4	99.8	34946
巫山县	Wushan County	115.2	14.4	69.5	94.5	32452
巫溪县	Wuxi County	100.5	3.0	65.6	96.2	44617
渝东南翼	**Southeast of Chongqing**	**250.5**	**12.5**	**70.5**	**95.9**	**180537**
黔江区	Qianjiang District	426.1	31.7	58.3	96.2	464981
武隆县	Wulong County	206.3	4.6	73.6	98.7	149418
石柱县	Shizhu County	167.4	18.3	70.8	90.4	85037
秀山县	Xiushan County	98.2	4.8	64.0	97.4	82473
酉阳县	Youyang County	182.4	9.2	66.4	97.4	121719
彭水县	Pengshui County	213.7	6.8	83.8	98.4	215487

表20.6 各区县建筑业（2011年）
CONSTRUCTION BY REGION (2011)

区 县	Region	企业数（个） Number of Construction Enterprises (unit)	年末从业人数（万人） Number of Employed Persons at Year-end (10 000 persons)	总产值（万元） Gross Output Value (10 000 yuan)	房屋建筑施工面积（万平方米） Floor Space under Construction (10 000 sq.m)	房屋建筑竣工面积（万平方米） Floor Space Completed (10 000 sq.m)	其中 of which #住宅 Residential Buildings
全 市	**Total**	**2530**	**134.84**	**33288252**	**21976.19**	**8989.56**	**6433.18**
#都市发达经济圈	**Metropolitan Developed Economic Circle**	**1308**	**55.95**	**17691401**	**11535.48**	**3604.26**	**2428.74**
渝西经济走廊	**West Chongqing Economic Corridor**	**600**	**38.37**	**7497184**	**5818.07**	**2840.72**	**2146.66**
三峡库区生态经济区	**Ecological Economic Zone in Three GorgesReservoir Area**	**622**	**40.53**	**8099667**	**4622.64**	**2544.59**	**1857.77**
#一小时经济圈	**One -Hour Economic Circle**	**2017**	**98.65**	**25898680**	**17994.60**	**6771.78**	**4863.03**
渝中区	Yuzhong District	167	5.21	2458184	1644.28	405.12	328.55
大渡口区	Dadukou District	75	1.26	600715	319.32	192.64	80.77
江北区	Jiangbei District	123	2.66	1249670	962.84	211.25	149.45
沙坪坝区	Shapingba District	131	6.64	1770707	1144.15	315.05	185.53
九龙坡区	Jiulongpo District	209	6.37	2972103	2592.73	674.35	335.13
南岸区	Nan'an District	106	4.23	1351688	1108.80	361.26	311.85
北碚区	Beibei District	75	6.19	1061974	905.83	300.49	195.73
渝北区	Yubei District	310	16.05	5047317	1802.36	589.50	410.81
巴南区	Ba'nan District	112	7.33	1179043	1055.16	554.61	430.94
綦江区	Qijiang District	73	2.14	287398	290.43	143.04	120.77
大足区	Dazu District	36	2.19	422696	350.62	183.75	166.84
涪陵区	Fuling District	118	10.60	2229503	1450.85	736.87	561.24
长寿区	Changshou District	44	4.00	704189	728.72	319.89	272.48
江津区	Jiangjin District	91	5.82	783699	1124.47	435.92	355.17
合川区	Hechuan District	74	4.00	706153	559.35	258.50	189.15
永川区	Yongchuan District	72	3.56	868338	473.84	266.92	136.12
南川区	Nanchuan District	40	1.21	319901	79.22	49.28	23.69
潼南县	Tongnan County	33	3.97	862983	412.67	289.31	256.97
铜梁县	Tongliang County	37	2.16	420586	404.57	202.18	160.77
荣昌县	Rongchang County	39	1.72	278594	269.45	135.83	97.03
璧山县	Bishan County	52	1.34	323239	314.93	146.03	94.04
渝东北翼	**Northeast of Chongqing**	**415**	**32.66**	**6617687**	**3581.06**	**2067.60**	**1472.55**
万州区	Wanzhou District	150	13.33	2871166	1464.57	812.82	564.09
梁平县	Liangping County	22	3.35	435992	291.15	208.64	155.00
城口县	Chengkou County	7	0.17	82040	4.59	3.44	3.33
丰都县	Fengdu County	20	0.62	164321	130.44	54.38	36.98
垫江县	Dianjiang County	43	2.80	399769	386.65	237.54	217.59
忠 县	Zhongxian County	33	2.41	389107	319.22	179.79	127.81
开 县	Kaixian County	40	5.49	1020166	468.04	298.12	198.40
云阳县	Yunyang County	35	1.99	340077	268.80	115.59	83.84
奉节县	Fengjie County	40	1.50	682152	158.10	98.08	63.41
巫山县	Wushan County	16	0.26	77850	36.59	13.94	0.07
巫溪县	Wuxi County	9	0.76	155048	52.90	45.24	22.03
渝东南翼	**Southeast of Chongqing**	**98**	**3.54**	**771885**	**400.53**	**150.20**	**97.60**
黔江区	Qianjiang District	32	1.48	300347	197.92	82.08	60.31
武隆县	Wulong County	14	0.26	106006	48.59	42.71	18.44
石柱县	Shizhu County	13	0.29	78302	31.87	13.26	12.85
秀山县	Xiushan County	13	0.86	116415	71.84	4.71	2.86
酉阳县	Youyang County	13	0.42	88356	41.60	2.35	1.12
彭水县	Pengshui County	13	0.23	82460	8.71	5.08	2.03

注：本表数据不包括劳务分包企业。
Note: The data in this table exclude construction enterprises of labor subcontracting.

表20.7 各区县总承包建筑业企业主要经济指标（2011年）

MAIN ECONOMIC INDICATORS ON CONSTRUCTION ENTERPRISES OF GENERAL CONTRACTING BY REGION (2011)

区　县	Region	企业数（个）Number of Enterprises (unit)	年末从业人数（万人）Number of Employed Persons at Year-end (10 000 persons)	总产值（万元）Gross Output Value (10 000 yuan)	利税总额（万元）Total Pre-Tax Profits (10 000 yuan)	按总产值计算的劳动生产率（元/人）Overall Labor Productivity by Gross Output Value (yuan/person)
全　市	**Total**	**1530**	**125.46**	**30361775**	**2455101**	**167934**
#都市发达经济圈	**Metropolitan Developed Economic Circle**	**549**	**48.47**	**15194228**	**866744**	**269173**
渝西经济走廊	**West Chongqing Economic Corridor**	**452**	**37. 23**	**7243390**	**728928**	**1878515**
三峡库区生态经济区	**Ecological Economic Zone in Three GorgesReservoir Area**	**529**	**39. 77**	**7924157**	**859429**	**4421288**
#一小时经济圈	**One -Hour Economic Circle**	**1084**	**89.88**	**23110440**	**1661279**	**199942**
渝中区	Yuzhong District	56	3.80	2099849	100641	334142
大渡口区	Dadukou District	30	0.91	332154	10632	250267
江北区	Jiangbei District	40	1.79	1039308	64493	323409
沙坪坝区	Shapingba District	46	5.99	1470168	75590	271740
九龙坡区	Jiulongpo District	67	5.24	2716452	132273	449885
南岸区	Nan'an District	51	3.63	1085457	65841	243409
北碚区	Beibei District	39	5.91	1017619	58171	186952
渝北区	Yubei District	145	14.18	4314451	295544	246122
巴南区	Ba'nan District	75	7.01	1118770	63559	165938
綦江区	Qijiang District	51	2.04	273789	20031	155051
大足区	Dazu District	32	2.14	399034	45576	189637
涪陵区	Fuling District	88	10.37	2178079	212710	245738
长寿区	Changshou District	37	3.93	696490	37342	186541
江津区	Jiangjin District	58	5.61	741156	52777	143738
合川区	Hechuan District	53	3.87	670871	43729	172270
永川区	Yongchuan District	61	3.33	837270	91435	269444
南川区	Nanchuan District	35	1.18	317351	34065	258135
潼南县	Tongnan County	33	3.97	862983	170889	210058
铜梁县	Tongliang County	28	2.06	384269	36506	17314
荣昌县	Rongchang County	24	1.64	264282	24080	165881
璧山县	Bishan County	35	1.26	290641	25395	209395
渝东北翼	**Northeast of Chongqing**	**361**	**32.20**	**6527808**	**708106**	**105347**
万州区	Wanzhou District	119	13.05	2814089	218808	66021
梁平县	Liangping County	18	3.30	428305	82529	137286
城口县	Chengkou County	7	0.17	82040	20595	491849
丰都县	Fengdu County	18	0.61	164082	7239	224217
垫江县	Dianjiang County	36	2.76	396788	34429	132763
忠　县	Zhongxian County	26	2.36	377963	31180	163748
开　县	Kaixian County	40	5.49	1020166	89675	182940
云阳县	Yunyang County	33	1.94	329325	47931	181516
奉节县	Fengjie County	40	1.50	682152	142555	444341
巫山县	Wushan County	15	0.26	77850	11561	288545
巫溪县	Wuxi County	9	0.76	155048	21604	186918
渝东南翼	**Southeast of Chongqing**	**85**	**3.39**	**723527**	**85716**	**222946**
黔江区	Qianjiang District	27	1.44	290887	37142	199744
武隆县	Wulong County	9	0.23	97341	4186	300434
石柱县	Shizhu County	13	0.29	78302	8521	280651
秀山县	Xiushan County	13	0.86	116415	27476	172569
酉阳县	Youyang County	10	0.35	58123	3165	178290
彭水县	Pengshui County	13	0.23	82460	5227	444769

表20.8 各区县专业承包建筑业企业主要经济指标（2011年）

MAIN ECONOMIC INDICATORS ON CONSTRUCTION ENTERPRISES OF SPECIALIZED CONTRACTING BY REGION (2011)

区 县	Region	企业数（个） Number of Enterprises (unit)	年末从业人数（万人） Number of Employed Persons at Year-end (10 000 persons)	总产值（万元） Gross Output Value (10 000 yuan)	利税总额（万元） Total Pre-Tax Profits (10 000 yuan)	按总产值计算的劳动生产率（元/人） Overall Labor Productivity by Gross Output Value (yuan/person)
全 市	**Total**	**1000**	**9.38**	**2926477**	**265812**	**322882**
#都市发达经济圈	**Metropolitan Developed Economic Circle**	**759**	**7.48**	**2497173**	**209030**	**344328**
渝西经济走廊	**West Chongqing Economic Corridor**	**148**	**1.14**	**253794**	**34254**	**2059192**
三峡库区生态经济区	**Ecological Economic Zone in Three GorgesReservoir Area**	**93**	**0.76**	**175510**	**22528**	**3231136**
#一小时经济圈	**One -Hour Economic Circle**	**933**	**8.77**	**2788239**	**248318**	**329462**
渝中区	Yuzhong District	111	1.41	358335	23548	287243
大渡口区	Dadukou District	45	0.34	268561	23527	838990
江北区	Jiangbei District	83	0.87	210361	34582	257922
沙坪坝区	Shapingba District	85	0.65	300538	15418	593363
九龙坡区	Jiulongpo District	142	1.13	255651	14539	229551
南岸区	Nan'an District	55	0.60	266232	24373	417029
北碚区	Beibei District	36	0.28	44355	5233	139088
渝北区	Yubei District	165	1.87	732866	63450	364701
巴南区	Ba'nan District	37	0.32	60274	4360	213661
綦江区	Qijiang District	22	0.10	13609	2251	186941
大足区	Dazu District	4	0.05	23663	2784	568815
涪陵区	Fuling District	30	0.23	51425	4743	247234
长寿区	Changshou District	7	0.07	7699	335	137242
江津区	Jiangjin District	33	0.21	42543	4713	220203
合川区	Hechuan District	21	0.13	35282	3553	227332
永川区	Yongchuan District	11	0.23	31067	3898	159157
南川区	Nanchuan District	5	0.02	2551	407	153645
潼南县	Tongnan County					
铜梁县	Tongliang County	9	0.10	36316	2770	328357
荣昌县	Rongchang County	15	0.08	14313	3081	173909
璧山县	Bishan County	17	0.07	32598	10755	412114
渝东北翼	**Northeast of Chongqing**	**54**	**0.46**	**89880**	**5929**	**198761**
万州区	Wanzhou District	31	0.28	57077	3225	188623
梁平县	Liangping County	4	0.05	7686	408	155281
城口县	Chengkou County					
丰都县	Fengdu County	2	0.01	239	33	45094
垫江县	Dianjiang County	7	0.03	2982	166	100733
忠 县	Zhongxian County	7	0.04	11143	1896	210247
开 县	Kaixian County					
云阳县	Yunyang County	2	0.05	10752	206	881311
奉节县	Fengjie County					
巫山县	Wushan County	1			-5	
巫溪县	Wuxi County					
渝东南翼	**Southeast of Chongqing**	**13**	**0.15**	**48358**	**11565**	**325864**
黔江区	Qianjiang District	5	0.04	9460	868	233573
武隆县	Wulong County	5	0.04	8665	451	230455
石柱县	Shizhu County					
秀山县	Xiushan County					
酉阳县	Youyang County	3	0.07	30233	10245	430063
彭水县	Pengshui County					

表20.9 各区县公路交通运输业（2011年）
HIGHWAY TRANSPORTATION BY REGION (2011)

区 县	Region	公路里程（公里） Length of Highways (km)	其中 of which #等级公路 Expressway and Class I-IV Highways	其中 of which 高速公路 Expressway	公路客运量（万人） Passenger Traffic by Highways (10 000 persons)	公路货运量（万吨） Freight Traffic by Highways (10 000 tons)
全 市	**Total**	**118562**	**83614**	**1861**	**136142**	**82818**
#都市发达经济圈	**Metropolitan Developed Economic Circle**	**9379**	**7150**	**479**	**33287**	**36004**
渝西经济走廊	**West Chongqing Economic Corridor**	**28448**	**21099**	**465**	**42822**	**28457**
三峡库区生态经济区	**Ecological Economic Zone in Three GorgesReservoir Area**	**80735**	**55365**	**917**	**60033**	**18357**
#一小时经济圈	**One -Hour Economic Circle**	**45377**	**34537**	**1045**	**92201**	**71243**
渝中区	Yuzhong District				3217	2942
大渡口区	Dadukou District	199.02	189.75	4.63	574	3290
江北区	Jiangbei District	443.43	443.43	43.79	4486	4505
沙坪坝区	Shapingba District	1079.35	782.40	63.39	2630	3252
九龙坡区	Jiulongpo District	850.59	768.48	50.65	4233	6240
南岸区	Nan'an District	595.38	538.32	33.31	4370	6527
北碚区	Beibei District	1093.15	845.53	55.43	2145	1811
渝北区	Yubei District	2467.92	1954.08	118.22	4422	4742
巴南区	Ba'nan District	2649.87	1627.84	109.60	7210	2695
涪陵区	Fuling District	4387.97	3305.61	19.60	8910	2414
长寿区	Changshou District	3162.37	2982.10	81.33	7182	4368
江津区	Jiangjin District	4108.71	2769.09	55.94	5325	3233
合川区	Hechuan District	3338.75	2854.63	54.58	5189	2954
永川区	Yongchuan District	2773.49	2178.10	31.41	6249	2910
南川区	Nanchuan District	3036.43	2164.49	56.05	3077	812
綦江区	Qijiang District	4802.14	3731.26	123.05	3930	13710
大足区	Dazu District	2333.75	815.61	6.12	5586	1436
潼南县	Tongnan County	2122.21	1950.51	28.00	2064	867
铜梁县	Tongliang County	2117.49	1822.79	44.45	3104	601
荣昌县	Rongchang County	2266.15	1887.40	29.47	4227	626
璧山县	Bishan County	1549.20	925.15	35.91	4071	1308
渝东北翼	**Northeast of Chongqing**	**55293.26**	**34408.60**	**433.77**	**36243**	**9098**
万州区	Wanzhou District	5833.00	3960.20	94.25	15255	2862
梁平县	Liangping County	3829.09	2095.61	47.11	3978	1582
城口县	Chengkou County	2662.24	2371.91	0.00	262	127
丰都县	Fengdu County	4193.25	2256.31	0.00	2853	237
垫江县	Dianjiang County	2377.40	2053.43	76.41	2184	1148
忠 县	Zhongxian County	3819.82	2532.91	58.20	2729	383
开 县	Kaixian County	8325.09	3754.92	19.26	2381	1057
云阳县	Yunyang County	6895.57	4268.44	71.13	2870	380
奉节县	Fengjie County	9272.99	4087.45	54.48	1714	334
巫山县	Wushan County	4494.85	3791.31	12.93	1391	377
巫溪县	Wuxi County	3589.95	3236.12	0.00	626	611
渝东南翼	**Southeast of Chongqing**	**17891.20**	**14668.72**	**382.33**	**7698**	**2477**
黔江区	Qianjiang District	2393.27	2022.23	66.95	2502	402
武隆县	Wulong County	3723.57	2676.12	65.83	827	303
石柱县	Shizhu County	3149.91	2475.99	65.53	665	890
秀山县	Xiushan County	2159.79	1485.24	48.48	1142	226
酉阳县	Youyang County	2690.47	2251.94	68.99	1089	389
彭水县	Pengshui County	3774.19	3757.22	66.56	1473	267

注：1）2006年起，公路里程包括村道。
2）渝中区公路归为市政道路，不属于本表统计范围。
Note: a) The length of highways has included village roads since 2006.
b) The highways in Yuzhong District are municipal roads, not included in the statistic scope of this table.

表20.10 各区县固定资产投资（2011年）
INVESTMENT IN FIXED ASSETS BY REGION (2011)

区 县	Region	全社会固定资产投资（万元） Total Investment in Fixed Assets (10 000 yuan)	其中 of which #建设与改造投资 Construction and Renovation	其中 of which #工业 Industry	#房地产开发 Real Estate Development	其中 of which #住宅 Residential Building	全社会固定资产投资指数（上年=100） Index of Total Investment in Fixed Assets (preceding year=100)
全 市	**Total**	**76858699**	**56707816**	**25312080**	**20150883**	**14384457**	**131.0**
#都市发达经济圈	**Metropolitan Developed Economic Circle**	**29447844**	**15975947**	**6733431**	**13471897**	**9526474**	**125.3**
渝西经济走廊	**West Chongqing Economic Corridor**	**21390858**	**18065492**	**8705940**	**3325366**	**2340059**	**138.5**
三峡库区生态经济区	**Ecological Economic Zone in Three GorgesReservoir Area**	**26019997**	**22666377**	**9872709**	**3353620**	**2517924**	**131.8**
#一小时经济圈	**One -Hour Economic Circle**	**57121856**	**39194977**	**18736142**	**17926879**	**12692754**	**130.3**
渝中区	Yuzhong District	2003347	846002	56070	1157345	516055	108.2
大渡口区	Dadukou District	1382683	807357	305616	575326	326785	125.6
江北区	Jiangbei District	3691939	1180148	529189	2511791	1734853	120.2
沙坪坝区	Shapingba District	3858859	2094735	809890	1764124	1424222	127.3
九龙坡区	Jiulongpo District	3334387	1705588	792817	1628799	1141584	127.1
南岸区	Nan'an District	3420160	1672864	753975	1747296	1212894	118.2
北碚区	Beibei District	3103902	2338422	1100000	765480	665713	134.9
渝北区	Yubei District	5241843	2975385	1379350	2266458	1623882	132.3
巴南区	Ba'nan District	3410724	2355446	1006524	1055278	880486	127.4
涪陵区	Fuling District	3167000	2705285	1370958	461715	322500	135.8
长寿区	Changshou District	3116154	2448253	1925813	667901	503721	122.5
江津区	Jiangjin District	3003263	2556305	1181367	446958	203993	131.3
合川区	Hechuan District	2514888	2090504	882956	424384	295836	131.3
永川区	Yongchuan District	3311924	2767411	1664844	544513	457725	134.3
南川区	Nanchuan District	1482578	1114589	603791	367989	260955	130.9
綦江区	Qijiang District	2343162	2020886	851079	322276	255063	140.5
大足区	Dazu District	1752743	1509654	632511	243089	176476	135.8
潼南县	Tongnan County	968804	848686	206289	120118	107460	138.5
铜梁县	Tongliang County	2018099	1809015	892891	209084	163247	133.6
荣昌县	Rongchang County	1781842	1507616	757815	274226	169916	146.5
璧山县	Bishan County	2213555	1840826	1032397	372729	249388	176.3
渝东北翼	**Northeast of Chongqing**	**13836275**	**12367501**	**4569449**	**1468774**	**1143129**	**132.2**
万州区	Wanzhou District	3410102	3033075	1665017	377027	283275	121.6
梁平县	Liangping County	1052987	961843	319432	91144	82003	139.1
城口县	Chengkou County	434744	420813	155660	13931	11628	134.1
丰都县	Fengdu County	1632272	1534354	327664	97918	68850	132.5
垫江县	Dianjiang County	940087	835519	278201	104568	66341	142.1
忠 县	Zhongxian County	1127212	944974	242885	182238	150610	136.9
开 县	Kaixian County	1452896	1207293	624402	245603	207772	143.5
云阳县	Yunyang County	1196371	1080776	409603	115595	98876	126.8
奉节县	Fengjie County	1285512	1134129	209707	151383	135402	132.4
巫山县	Wushan County	548311	513885	170647	34426	24322	125.0
巫溪县	Wuxi County	755781	700840	166231	54941	14050	152.8
渝东南翼	**Southeast of Chongqing**	**5900568**	**5145338**	**2006489**	**755230**	**548574**	**134.2**
黔江区	Qianjiang District	1290983	1156057	531565	134926	103421	137.7
武隆县	Wulong County	1058882	853855	399002	205027	182618	147.1
石柱县	Shizhu County	1083095	979613	351039	103482	63901	132.0
秀山县	Xiushan County	690289	609309	222167	80980	46882	129.1
酉阳县	Youyang County	955282	790814	278772	164468	112478	122.4
彭水县	Pengshui County	822037	755690	223944	66347	39274	136.0

表20.10 续表 continued

区 县	Region	商品房竣工面积（平方米） Floor Space Completed of Commercial Buildings (sq.m)	其中 of which #住宅 Residential Buildings	商品房销售面积（平方米） Floor Space Sold of Commercial Buildings (sq.m)	其中 of which #住宅 Residential Buildings	商品房销售额（万元） Sales Revenue of Commercial Buildings (sq.m)	其中 of which #住宅 Residential Buildings
全 市	**Total**	**34243331**	**28267842**	**45335019**	**40634236**	**21460860**	**18254119**
#都市发达经济圈	**Metropolitan Developed Economic Circle**	**17645594**	**14279668**	**20880619**	**18538075**	**12459571**	**10608760**
渝西经济走廊	**West Chongqing Economic Corridor**	**8810550**	**7361279**	**10135837**	**8977135**	**4085101**	**3369704**
三峡库区生态经济区	**Ecological Economic Zone in ThreeGorgesReservoir Area**	**7787187**	**6626895**	**14318563**	**13119026**	**4916188**	**4275655**
#一小时经济圈	**One -Hour Economic Circle**	**28472837**	**23235639**	**34543355**	**30683760**	**17703947**	**14931319**
渝中区	Yuzhong District	750085	570471	955163	699765	869663	524790
大渡口区	Dadukou District	684144	599068	1130477	1069400	475399	434119
江北区	Jiangbei District	2420068	1808524	3306076	2874982	2020329	1689661
沙坪坝区	Shapingba District	2750072	2421444	2636964	2506324	1337545	1237980
九龙坡区	Jiulongpo District	2856019	2426725	3091345	2716053	1583812	1387226
南岸区	Nan'an District	2366260	1630807	2159411	1864453	1408282	1156137
北碚区	Beibei District	1022603	897812	1458885	1151086	684410	525346
渝北区	Yubei District	3575098	2932384	3472210	3121836	2709919	2358465
巴南区	Ba'nan District	1221245	992433	2670088	2534176	1370212	1295036
涪陵区	Fuling District	1002398	700132	1032434	843360	465015	381655
长寿区	Changshou District	1014295	894560	2494465	2325190	694260	571200
江津区	Jiangjin District	1642268	1269654	1544319	1038198	727316	404375
合川区	Hechuan District	932644	820577	1290117	1142833	522653	448884
永川区	Yongchuan District	1460302	1129526	1440347	1323192	589775	520181
南川区	Nanchuan District	200598	184536	485221	479625	195013	191115
綦江区	Qijiang District	893087	801970	1068166	1017666	423078	394625
大足区	Dazu District	604928	538101	723332	680648	252780	227815
潼南县	Tongnan County	448445	393710	639019	544151	243593	174328
铜梁县	Tongliang County	548166	517766	757050	745334	283343	273405
荣昌县	Rongchang County	567575	399010	1236360	1089566	484032	394530
璧山县	Bishan County	1512537	1306429	951906	915922	363518	340446
渝东北翼	**Northeast of Chongqing**	**3930395**	**3536601**	**8652738**	**8013368**	**3024290**	**2683263**
万州区	Wanzhou District	1018027	919338	1929871	1778355	718187	646815
梁平县	Liangping County	210637	202530	681477	667169	244943	238652
城口县	Chengkou County	64536	62536	94586	92586	28471	27871
丰都县	Fengdu County	870642	790595	615728	559916	294198	249691
垫江县	Dianjiang County	287818	257352	275662	260704	89741	80204
忠 县	Zhongxian County	336767	309663	1273935	1216538	379294	363010
开 县	Kaixian County	419101	353513	1384970	1197494	591871	463524
云阳县	Yunyang County	155237	141078	786717	748257	195785	187597
奉节县	Fengjie County	372359	355906	1370031	1334341	386002	373245
巫山县	Wushan County	128332	115488	125418	113235	48690	39552
巫溪县	Wuxi County	66939	28602	114343	44773	47108	13102
渝东南翼	**Southeast of Chongqing**	**1840099**	**1495602**	**2138926**	**1937108**	**732623**	**639537**
黔江区	Qianjiang District	303896	255960	441298	424698	151747	145790
武隆县	Wulong County	646235	548642	415151	383113	187672	173068
石柱县	Shizhu County	309581	249989	309282	276608	101211	87926
秀山县	Xiushan County	303788	226569	433148	325292	109197	61177
酉阳县	Youyang County	168019	109528	261571	250950	85615	75885
彭水县	Pengshui County	108580	104914	278476	276447	97181	95691

表20.11 各区县社会消费品零售总额（2011年）
TOTAL RETAIL SALES OF CONSUMER GOODS BY REGION (2011)

区 县	Region	社会消费品零售总额（万元） Total Retail Sales of Consumer Goods (10 000 yuan)	社会消费品零售总额指数（上年=100） Index of Total Retail Sales of Consumer Goods (preceding year=100)
全 市	**Total**	**34878070**	**118.7**
#都市发达经济圈	**Metropolitan Developed Economic Circle**	**18985340**	**121.1**
渝西经济走廊	**West Chongqing Economic Corridor**	**7402941**	**118.9**
三峡库区生态经济区	**Ecological Economic Zone in Three GorgesReservoir Area**	**8489789**	**118.6**
#一小时经济圈	**One -Hour Economic Circle**	**28191729**	**121.0**
渝中区	Yuzhong District	4142816	120.2
大渡口区	Dadukou District	317690	120.4
江北区	Jiangbei District	2911443	125.8
沙坪坝区	Shapingba District	2469218	123.1
九龙坡区	Jiulongpo District	3181401	124.0
南岸区	Nan'an District	2616981	126.5
北碚区	Beibei District	1032857	124.7
渝北区	Yubei District	2871987	124.7
巴南区	Ba'nan District	1380739	128.6
涪陵区	Fuling District	1303252	123.3
长寿区	Changshou District	684460	123.3
江津区	Jiangjin District	1303735	121.4
合川区	Hechuan District	1250843	122.0
永川区	Yongchuan District	1385275	123.6
南川区	Nanchuan District	595992	122.5
綦江区	Qijiang District	878079	118.7
大足区	Dazu District	598884	119.4
潼南县	Tongnan County	466389	116.3
铜梁县	Tongliang County	558195	119.2
荣昌县	Rongchang County	521575	118.1
璧山县	Bishan County	600357	122.1
渝东北翼	**Northeast of Chongqing**	**4912885**	**118.6**
万州区	Wanzhou District	1603176	123.6
梁平县	Liangping County	446025	120.3
城口县	Chengkou County	77663	118.0
丰都县	Fengdu County	374752	120.8
垫江县	Dianjiang County	463147	118.6
忠 县	Zhongxian County	412574	121.0
开 县	Kaixian County	815012	120.0
云阳县	Yunyang County	483620	120.5
奉节县	Fengjie County	357920	120.9
巫山县	Wushan County	220410	119.0
巫溪县	Wuxi County	160551	119.0
渝东南翼	**Southeast of Chongqing**	**1773456**	**118.6**
黔江区	Qianjiang District	440714	121.6
武隆县	Wulong County	265748	118.5
石柱县	Shizhu County	300898	120.8
秀山县	Xiushan County	320443	120.8
酉阳县	Youyang County	297080	118.1
彭水县	Pengshui County	329774	118.6

注：各区县社会消费品零售总额增速采用年度评审数，未按国家口径调整。
Note: The growth rate of the total retail sales of consumer goods by region is the data from the annual review, not modified according to the national scope.

表20.12 各区县财政收支（2011年）
GOVERNMENT REVENUE AND EXPENDITURES BY REGION (2011)

单位：万元 (10 000 yuan)

区 县	Region	区县级地方财政收入 Revenue of Governments at District (county) Level	其中 of which				
			#一般预算收入 General Budgetary Revenue	其中 of which			
				#增值税 Value-added Tax	#营业税 Business Tax	#企业所得税 Corporate Income Tax	#个人所得税 Individual Income Tax
全 市	**Total**	**29089103**	**14883336**	**817765**	**3439155**	**1151108**	**348983**
#都市发达经济圈	**Metropolitan Developed Economic Circle**	**4627404**	**4518749**	**185403**	**854622**	**297013**	**95186**
渝西经济走廊	**West Chongqing Economic Corridor**	**5400872**	**2097251**	**146073**	**285847**	**108872**	**29278**
三峡库区生态经济区	**Ecological Economic Zone in ThreeGorgesReservoir Area**	**3979413**	**2077366**	**171599**	**380409**	**130156**	**40082**
#一小时经济圈	**One -Hour Economic Circle**	**11285592**	**7172240**	**383513**	**1239627**	**441518**	**134517**
渝中区	Yuzhong District	511858	509169	14804	139360	52030	25081
大渡口区	Dadukou District	114067	113297	9825	22778	6008	2551
江北区	Jiangbei District	700018	604417	22125	136419	49860	13728
沙坪坝区	Shapingba District	407221	405341	16891	88083	21321	7706
九龙坡区	Jiulongpo District	602152	600654	32039	100351	30256	10044
南岸区	Nan'an District	552359	551146	20324	91333	24086	8704
北碚区	Beibei District	301268	299896	10068	29536	7223	3270
渝北区	Yubei District	1137439	1134890	48745	200464	95982	21228
巴南区	Ba'nan District	301022	299939	10582	46298	10247	2874
涪陵区	Fuling District	705637	314161	29687	54565	23937	5347
长寿区	Changshou District	551679	242079	22350	44593	11696	4706
江津区	Jiangjin District	707668	287769	26867	37542	26417	4423
合川区	Hechuan District	762191	257016	12586	45194	14457	5036
永川区	Yongchuan District	752181	291076	24487	43191	11410	4876
南川区	Nanchuan District	341942	120065	6862	19081	6547	1451
綦江区	Qijiang District	780896	249851	26492	35634	10532	3230
大足区	Dazu District	508284	210332	7265	22721	6645	1779
潼南县	Tongnan County	202950	86541	6882	12257	3201	1247
铜梁县	Tongliang County	367223	145776	6307	21664	9018	1443
荣昌县	Rongchang County	362393	198680	11455	24788	8473	2735
璧山县	Bishan County	615144	250145	16870	23775	12172	3058
渝东北翼	**Northeast of Chongqing**	**1887766**	**1041176**	**76902**	**169494**	**69495**	**19881**
万州区	Wanzhou District	630063	345800	26205	60461	31275	7472
梁平县	Liangping County	163600	93544	5315	10494	2800	1288
城口县	Chengkou County	45266	20868	3722	3450	1333	937
丰都县	Fengdu County	123039	64617	3419	12678	3758	1341
垫江县	Dianjiang County	187032	85250	5585	13260	5743	1626
忠 县	Zhongxian County	160273	85025	3403	14792	5933	1192
开 县	Kaixian County	200508	96719	9661	17120	6060	1552
云阳县	Yunyang County	104040	63346	3715	13681	3562	1524
奉节县	Fengjie County	126451	95338	7448	11553	5078	1035
巫山县	Wushan County	86875	50451	5651	6810	2207	1174
巫溪县	Wuxi County	60619	40218	2778	5195	1746	740
渝东南翼	**Southeast of Chongqing**	**834331**	**479950**	**42660**	**111757**	**25028**	**10148**
黔江区	Qianjiang District	228481	126177	15252	25207	7286	2486
武隆县	Wulong County	114128	73306	3206	15409	3607	871
石柱县	Shizhu County	117487	55591	4704	22425	4059	1749
秀山县	Xiushan County	130856	97081	7826	15669	4202	2227
酉阳县	Youyang County	122509	69063	7526	15210	2533	1197
彭水县	Pengshui County	120870	58732	4146	17837	3341	1618

表20.12 续表 continued

单位：万元 (10 000 yuan)

区 县	Region	区县级地方财政支出 Expenditure of Governments at District (county) Level	其 中 of which				
			#一般预算支出 General Budgetary Expenditures	其 中 of which			
				#农林水支出 Expenditure for Agriculture, Forestry and Water Conservancy	#教育支出 Expenditure for Education	#卫生支出 Expenditure of Public Health	#社会保障和就业支出 Expenditure for Social Security and Employment Effort
全 市	**Total**	**39598745**	**25702404**	**1989065**	**3187008**	**1436962**	**3387635**
#都市发达经济圈	**Metropolitan Developed Economic Circle**	**7155961**	**5800387**	**217592**	**731412**	**259976**	**583430**
渝西经济走廊	**West Chongqing Economic Corridor**	**7481065**	**4241011**	**478885**	**739754**	**391811**	**567604**
三峡库区生态经济区	**Ecological Economic Zone in Three GorgesReservoir Area**	**8547428**	**6506089**	**969623**	**1089842**	**587475**	**855376**
#一小时经济圈	**One -Hour Economic Circle**	**16412903**	**11120508**	**814460**	**1622755**	**732999**	**1285319**
渝中区	Yuzhong District	734981	664488	274	75823	22636	88706
大渡口区	Dadukou District	236152	197403	4505	35093	11739	26945
江北区	Jiangbei District	952766	772928	20145	104565	23372	57854
沙坪坝区	Shapingba District	704988	499507	17135	66445	27856	67690
九龙坡区	Jiulongpo District	837923	771404	8954	104655	29491	68179
南岸区	Nan'an District	873575	669692	16348	97972	46907	71830
北碚区	Beibei District	439512	398127	53668	61485	23678	46575
渝北区	Yubei District	1795846	1275776	51987	93936	44739	76675
巴南区	Ba'nan District	580218	551062	44576	91438	29558	78976
涪陵区	Fuling District	1035761	640443	62043	90687	48643	74278
长寿区	Changshou District	740116	438667	55940	60902	32569	60007
江津区	Jiangjin District	1010350	597006	62596	100659	54032	86827
合川区	Hechuan District	952237	461027	48734	77227	58580	104267
永川区	Yongchuan District	982746	532664	49490	111750	49661	63362
南川区	Nanchuan District	527309	312717	46767	47463	25700	35220
綦江区	Qijiang District	1100050	574530	64102	91001	47070	72179
大足区	Dazu District	708172	435448	51751	64924	37587	46057
潼南县	Tongnan County	400996	284453	48064	59977	34195	35116
铜梁县	Tongliang County	497823	277852	35875	54578	34064	43523
荣昌县	Rongchang County	511778	348229	39635	62875	27040	40755
璧山县	Bishan County	789604	417085	31871	69300	23882	40298
渝东北翼	**Northeast of Chongqing**	**4655684**	**3682107**	**545804**	**646443**	**363926**	**532677**
万州区	Wanzhou District	1070583	748890	70270	114191	60065	122944
梁平县	Liangping County	339905	281255	44296	54285	29359	40757
城口县	Chengkou County	174228	147525	32669	17437	10940	16225
丰都县	Fengdu County	333064	256726	45095	36607	24622	38115
垫江县	Dianjiang County	387937	276093	45504	56214	30014	33372
忠 县	Zhongxian County	410045	324436	46727	51127	39491	47709
开 县	Kaixian County	571465	454986	70011	87318	52978	75011
云阳县	Yunyang County	404083	354961	61598	69343	43170	54294
奉节县	Fengjie County	416232	369799	50094	81377	33067	45708
巫山县	Wushan County	297976	244710	42891	41642	21456	34334
巫溪县	Wuxi County	250166	222726	36649	36902	18764	24208
渝东南翼	**Southeast of Chongqing**	**2115867**	**1744872**	**305836**	**291810**	**142337**	**188414**
黔江区	Qianjiang District	473863	367671	60791	57512	24054	34633
武隆县	Wulong County	311217	262625	53084	30822	16680	28898
石柱县	Shizhu County	290734	231094	36070	45651	20803	19768
秀山县	Xiushan County	342969	305494	53727	51997	27690	39427
酉阳县	Youyang County	381601	325698	53487	58733	28317	35830
彭水县	Pengshui County	315483	252290	48677	47095	24793	29858

表20.13 各区县金融机构存贷款、人民生活和社会福利（2011年）

DEPOSIT AND LOAN OF FINANCIAL INSTITUTIONS,PEOPLE'S LIVELIHOOD AND SOCIAL WELFARE BY REGION (2011)

区　县	Region	金融机构人民币存款余额（亿元） Total Deposit Balance of RMB of Financial Institutions (100 million yuan)	其　中 of which #城乡居民储蓄 Saving Deposits of Urban and Rural Residents	金融机构人民币贷款余额（亿元） Total Loan Balance of RMB of Financial Institutions (100 million yuan)	城镇非私营单位职工年平均工资（元） Average Salaries of Employees of Urban Non-private Units (yuan)	城镇居民人均可支配收入（元） Per Capita Disposable Income of Urban Residents (yuan)
全　市	**Total**	**15833**	**7046**	**13001**	**40042**	**20250**
#都市发达经济圈	**Metropolitan Developed Economic Circle**	**10305**	**3307**	**10109**	**44589**	**21955**
渝西经济走廊	**West Chongqing Economic Corridor**	**2248**	**1620**	**1276**	**33882**	
三峡库区生态经济区	**Ecological Economic Zone in Three GorgesReservoir Area**	**3217**	**2111**	**1591**	**36070**	
#一小时经济圈	**One -Hour Economic Circle**	**13217**	**5330**	**11879**	**41445**	
渝中区	Yuzhong District	3411	551	3111	53149	22146
大渡口区	Dadukou District	259	123	262	43550	22146
江北区	Jiangbei District	1727	398	2610	45620	22146
沙坪坝区	Shapingba District	806	426	595	42899	22146
九龙坡区	Jiulongpo District	1121	516	970	43401	22146
南岸区	Nan'an District	706	341	594	45053	22146
北碚区	Beibei District	364	220	255	41615	21954
渝北区	Yubei District	1563	504	1401	42456	21954
巴南区	Ba'nan District	348	228	310	36672	21953
涪陵区	Fuling District	389	217	315	40073	19643
长寿区	Changshou District	275	186	179	37763	19447
江津区	Jiangjin District	352	260	179	30331	19330
合川区	Hechuan District	355	264	185	30384	19265
永川区	Yongchuan District	318	216	184	33758	19685
南川区	Nanchuan District	132	92	115	35785	18900
綦江区	Qijiang District	260	178	165	35123	17107
大足区	Dazu District	149	105	80	36190	19430
潼南县	Tongnan County	127	101	45	37965	17910
铜梁县	Tongliang County	186	146	85	38048	19993
荣昌县	Rongchang County	159	109	94	34648	19295
璧山县	Bishan County	211	149	143	36650	20615
渝东北翼	**Northeast of Chongqing**	**2001**	**1363**	**714**	**34680**	
万州区	Wanzhou District	551	349	269	33512	19329
梁平县	Liangping County	168	132	35	30091	18071
城口县	Chengkou County	44	24	19	34005	14202
丰都县	Fengdu County	144	106	56	33532	15765
垫江县	Dianjiang County	156	112	58	39093	18120
忠　县	Zhongxian County	197	144	51	39935	18005
开　县	Kaixian County	266	191	72	34836	15911
云阳县	Yunyang County	187	127	57	38325	14458
奉节县	Fengjie County	130	80	43	35363	14460
巫山县	Wushan County	88	53	30	35049	15770
巫溪县	Wuxi County	69	45	24	33028	13236
渝东南翼	**Southeast of Chongqing**	**553**	**345**	**383**	**36283**	
黔江区	Qianjiang District	120	63	75	40312	16007
武隆县	Wulong County	82	53	90	38937	18030
石柱县	Shizhu County	98	66	36	33908	16555
秀山县	Xiushan County	78	47	60	36619	16823
酉阳县	Youyang County	94	62	43	31317	13415
彭水县	Pengshui County	81	54	80	36632	14670

表20.13 续表1 continued1

区 县	Region	农村居民人均纯收入（元） Per Capita Net Income of Rural Residents (yuan)	农村居民人均生活消费支出（元） Per Capita Living Consumption of Rural Residents (yuan)	其 中 of which #食品支出 Expenditure for Food	农村居民人均住房面积（平方米） Per Capita Residential Floor Space of Rural Residents (sq.m)	城市居民最低生活保障人数（人） Number of Persons Receiving Minimum Living Allowance in Rural Areas (person)
全 市	**Total**	**6480**	**4502**	**2109**	**41**	**568523**
#都市发达经济圈	**Metropolitan Developed Economic Circle**					**105096**
渝西经济走廊	**West Chongqing Economic Corridor**					**151862**
三峡库区生态经济区	**Ecological Economic Zone in Three GorgesReservoir Area**					**311565**
#一小时经济圈	**One -Hour EconomicCircle**	**8339**	**5433**	**2528**	**41**	**292772**
渝中区	Yuzhong District					17692
大渡口区	Dadukou District	10474	7683	3309	48	4868
江北区	Jiangbei District	10474	7683	3309	45	16674
沙坪坝区	Shapingba District	10474	7683	3309	54	12636
九龙坡区	Jiulongpo District	10474	7683	3309	51	15763
南岸区	Nan'an District	10474	7683	3309	48	15171
北碚区	Beibei District	8826	6622	2876	45	8661
渝北区	Yubei District	8319	5621	2694	46	2674
巴南区	Ba'nan District	8250	5182	2490	43	10957
涪陵区	Fuling District	6858	4506	2079	37	28043
长寿区	Changshou District	7897	4556	2194	39	6363
江津区	Jiangjin District	8694	5271	2530	40	16605
合川区	Hechuan District	8524	5393	2553	41	35828
永川区	Yongchuan District	8717	5024	2320	38	14917
南川区	Nanchuan District	7317	4916	2070	51	3300
綦江区	Qijiang District	7477	5255	2630	42	27763
大足区	Dazu District	8169	5840	2770	37	11551
潼南县	Tongnan County	7285	4213	1969	38	8408
铜梁县	Tongliang County	8697	4607	2221	46	6519
荣昌县	Rongchang County	8356	5449	2486	40	18932
璧山县	Bishan County	8863	6601	2996	50	8039
渝东北翼	**Northeast of Chongqing**	**5978**	**4328**	**2064**	**41**	**227766**
万州区	Wanzhou District	6591	5275	2089	43	74103
梁平县	Liangping County	6882	5386	2447	45	5505
城口县	Chengkou County	4576	3910	2084	33	2223
丰都县	Fengdu County	5991	3611	1837	41	15400
垫江县	Dianjiang County	7044	4921	2323	40	10454
忠 县	Zhongxian County	6767	4141	1963	45	17665
开 县	Kaixian County	6323	4077	2065	47	33426
云阳县	Yunyang County	5553	3358	1740	39	24666
奉节县	Fengjie County	5200	4112	2110	39	20754
巫山县	Wushan County	4867	3987	2030	39	17034
巫溪县	Wuxi County	4526	3928	1977	40	6536
渝东南翼	**Southeast of Chongqing**	**5347**	**4481**	**2186**	**37**	**47985**
黔江区	Qianjiang District	5452	5032	2322	42	11526
武隆县	Wulong County	5792	4852	2298	42	6713
石柱县	Shizhu County	5981	5214	2892	41	8103
秀山县	Xiushan County	5110	3477	1645	34	7400
酉阳县	Youyang County	4539	4078	1928	40	6968
彭水县	Pengshui County	5215	4571	2257	32	7275

表20.13 续表2 continued2

区 县	Region	社会福利收养单位（个）Residential Social Welfare Institutions (unit)	社会福利收养单位床位数（张）Beds in Residential Social Welfare Institutions (bed)	城镇社区服务设施数（个）Number of Urban Welfare Facilities (unit)	城镇便民利民服务网点（个）Number of Service Stations for Urban Residents (unit)
全 市	**Total**	**2241**	**106217**	**2124**	**9880**
#都市发达经济圈	**Metropolitan Developed Economic Circle**	**289**	**27925**	**783**	**4532**
渝西经济走廊	**West Chongqing Economic Corridor**	**770**	**32171**	**557**	**1481**
三峡库区生态经济区	**Ecological Economic Zone in Three GorgesReservoir Area**	**1182**	**46121**	**784**	**3867**
#一小时经济圈	**One -Hour Economic Circle**	**1211**	**65644**	**1418**	**8486**
渝中区	Yuzhong District	13	1147	88	315
大渡口区	Dadukou District	13	734	50	264
江北区	Jiangbei District	10	814	88	450
沙坪坝区	Shapingba District	53	4868	78	
九龙坡区	Jiulongpo District	15	1750	104	400
南岸区	Nan'an District	20	2499	91	1558
北碚区	Beibei District	54	2942	62	1200
渝北区	Yubei District	60	3962	111	344
巴南区	Ba'nan District	43	4126	105	
涪陵区	Fuling District	50	2769	44	2473
长寿区	Changshou District	101	2643	34	
江津区	Jiangjin District	57	5854	65	710
合川区	Hechuan District	54	5217	64	53
永川区	Yongchuan District	122	3461	35	550
南川区	Nanchuan District	91	1895	61	46
綦江区	Qijiang District	42	2814	118	62
大足区	Dazu District	97	2479	60	50
潼南县	Tongnan County	95	2401	34	
铜梁县	Tongliang County	82	2890	47	
荣昌县	Rongchang County	101	3281	33	7
璧山县	Bishan County	29	1879	40	3
渝东北翼	**Northeast of Chongqing**	**734**	**29809**	**517**	**891**
万州区	Wanzhou District	166	7054	101	441
梁平县	Liangping County	32	1187	26	20
城口县	Chengkou County	36	930	15	
丰都县	Fengdu County	29	1657	54	152
垫江县	Dianjiang County	29	1742	32	22
忠 县	Zhongxian County	40	2206	40	92
开 县	Kaixian County	175	4756	65	39
云阳县	Yunyang County	60	3355	76	1
奉节县	Fengjie County	83	3767	27	
巫山县	Wushan County	26	950	32	124
巫溪县	Wuxi County	58	2205	49	
渝东南翼	**Southeast of Chongqing**	**296**	**10764**	**189**	**503**
黔江区	Qianjiang District	76	1737	64	420
武隆县	Wulong County	26	1430	13	1
石柱县	Shizhu County	30	1284	29	39
秀山县	Xiushan County	59	2714	21	12
酉阳县	Youyang County	39	1291	35	5
彭水县	Pengshui County	66	2308	27	26

注：都市发达经济圈和一小时经济圈的社会福利收养单位及床位数包含重庆市本级数据。
Note: The number of residential social welfare institutions and the number of beds in the Metropolitan Developed Economic Circle and the One-Hour Economic Circle include the data of institutions at municipal level.

表20.14 各区县教育和文化（2011年）
EDUCATION AND CULTURE BY REGION (2011)

区 县	Region	学校数（所） Number of Schools (unit)	其中 of which #普通中学 Regular Secondary Schools	#小学 Primary Schools	专任教师数（人） Full-time Teachers (person)	其中 of which #普通中学 Regular Secondary Schools	#小学 Primary Schools
全 市	**Total**	**10884**	**1259**	**5248**	**296927**	**110951**	**115343**
#都市发达经济圈	**Metropolitan Developed Economic Circle**	**1799**	**237**	**452**	**82406**	**24719**	**20869**
渝西经济走廊	**West Chongqing Economic Corridor**	**3388**	**382**	**1275**	**81308**	**32086**	**31547**
三峡库区生态经济区	**Ecological Economic Zone in Three Gorges Reservoir Area**	**5697**	**640**	**3521**	**133213**	**54146**	**62927**
#一小时经济圈	**One -Hour Economic Circle**	**5649**	**702**	**1870**	**181163**	**64102**	**59356**
渝中区	Yuzhong District	118	14	31	7165	2475	2175
大渡口区	Dadukou District	77	7	20	2497	986	881
江北区	Jiangbei District	150	18	41	5839	2272	1785
沙坪坝区	Shapingba District	291	33	54	19204	3624	2585
九龙坡区	Jiulongpo District	280	34	50	10521	4038	2998
南岸区	Nan'an District	176	23	35	9749	2278	1852
北碚区	Beibei District	135	22	58	7960	2363	2034
渝北区	Yubei District	361	47	103	11352	3852	3901
巴南区	Ba'nan District	211	39	60	8119	2831	2658
涪陵区	Fuling District	322	55	107	10705	4155	3974
长寿区	Changshou District	140	28	36	6744	3142	2966
江津区	Jiangjin District	594	49	178	11281	4295	4250
合川区	Hechuan District	413	37	125	11364	4017	3693
永川区	Yongchuan District	380	42	213	11918	3488	3666
南川区	Nanchuan District	193	37	61	5312	2048	2460
綦江区	Qijiang District	253	70	84	9684	4457	4229
大足区	Dazu District	537	31	193	8508	3822	3458
潼南县	Tongnan County	237	34	157	5993	2654	2773
铜梁县	Tongliang County	213	25	64	6169	2845	2361
荣昌县	Rongchang County	392	33	154	6148	2474	2832
璧山县	Bishan County	176	24	46	4931	1986	1825
渝东北翼	**Northeast of Chongqing**	**3841**	**393**	**2459**	**82007**	**33968**	**38148**
万州区	Wanzhou District	446	60	185	14812	5445	4984
梁平县	Liangping County	154	34	61	6070	2708	2817
城口县	Chengkou County	188	8	168	2201	758	1176
丰都县	Fengdu County	271	42	143	6128	2696	2983
垫江县	Dianjiang County	276	31	136	6743	2743	3454
忠 县	Zhongxian County	339	30	224	6471	2912	3049
开 县	Kaixian County	798	60	447	13095	5510	6195
云阳县	Yunyang County	443	55	338	8954	3790	4573
奉节县	Fengjie County	377	34	302	7574	3248	3769
巫山县	Wushan County	294	20	237	5064	2245	2447
巫溪县	Wuxi County	255	19	218	4895	1913	2701
渝东南翼	**Southeast of Chongqing**	**1394**	**164**	**919**	**33757**	**12881**	**17839**
黔江区	Qianjiang District	175	23	123	5828	2502	2662
武隆县	Wulong County	134	12	84	3457	1246	1894
石柱县	Shizhu County	261	21	181	5079	1903	2714
秀山县	Xiushan County	375	28	231	6141	2286	3063
酉阳县	Youyang County	245	39	179	6960	2698	3784
彭水县	Pengshui County	204	41	121	6292	2246	3722

注：本表教育数据统计口径包括普通高校、中职学校、普通中学、小学、幼儿园和特殊教育及工读学校（下表同）。
Note: Data of education in this table include regular institutions of higher education, secondary vocational schools, regular secondary schools, primary schools, kindergartens, schools of special educations and reformatory schools (the same below).

表20.14 续表 continued

区 县	Region	在校学生数（人）Total Enrollment (person)	其中 of which #普通中学 Regular Secondary Schools	#小 学 Primary Schools	广播覆盖率（%）Radio Coverage of Population (%)	电视覆盖率（%）Television Coverage of Population (%)	公共图书馆（个）Number of Public Libraries (unit)	公共图书馆藏书（万册）Number of Books in Public Libraries (10 000 volumes)
全 市	**Total**	**5646189**	**1838917**	**1954818**	**98.0**	**98.6**	**43**	**1148.74**
#都市发达经济圈	**Metropolitan Developed Economic Circle**	**1416199**	**342365**	**338347**			**11**	**709.79**
渝西经济走廊	**West Chongqing Economic Corridor**	**1547825**	**506627**	**532375**			**12**	**168.83**
三峡库区生态经济区	**Ecological Economic Zone in Three Gorges Reservoir Area**	**2682165**	**989925**	**1084096**			**20**	**270**
#一小时经济圈	**One -Hour Economic Circle**	**3271643**	**957243**	**969783**	**99.2**	**99.1**	**26**	**1017.03**
渝中区	Yuzhong District	109227	26185	33106	100.0	100.0	2	115.45
大渡口区	Dadukou District	47682	15612	16754	100.0	100.0	1	14.00
江北区	Jiangbei District	100612	37284	28233	100.0	100.0	1	4.61
沙坪坝区	Shapingba District	331805	45519	45148	100.0	100.0	2	357.04
九龙坡区	Jiulongpo District	178397	52364	52705	100.0	100.0	1	21.63
南岸区	Nan'an District	189154	37250	36701	100.0	100.0	1	25.55
北碚区	Beibei District	131790	34496	25156	100.0	100.0	1	116.60
渝北区	Yubei District	186212	53794	60895	100.0	99.5	1	37.16
巴南区	Ba'nan District	141320	39861	39649	98.6	99.3	1	17.75
涪陵区	Fuling District	196210	64707	56548	99.3	97.2	2	74.51
长寿区	Changshou District	111409	43544	42513	99.9	99.8	1	63.90
江津区	Jiangjin District	218502	65449	74287	99.6	99.8	1	26.50
合川区	Hechuan District	227712	71226	62570	98.7	98.3	1	22.17
永川区	Yongchuan District	240830	49641	65498	98.8	99.4	1	12.08
南川区	Nanchuan District	98865	37088	35633	97.1	96.1	1	7.04
綦江区	Qijiang District	164201	65632	61267	98.4	98.8	2	11.42
大足区	Dazu District	141244	51989	51491	97.2	97.3	2	15.04
潼南县	Tongnan County	130013	47710	62168	98.5	99.2	1	11.80
铜梁县	Tongliang County	118402	47310	37328	100.0	100.0	1	22.30
荣昌县	Rongchang County	116817	38616	48989	100.0	100.0	1	30.00
璧山县	Bishan County	91239	31966	33144	100.0	97.6	1	10.48
渝东北翼	**Northeast of Chongqing**	**1731429**	**640646**	**706437**	**96.9**	**98.2**	**11**	**91.71**
万州区	Wanzhou District	301565	103378	88026	99.5	98.5	1	30.45
梁平县	Liangping County	130517	49456	50049	98.5	95.5	1	2.70
城口县	Chengkou County	38203	12299	18758	91.1	93.2	1	5.00
丰都县	Fengdu County	132651	46037	62829	97.1	97.9	1	4.91
垫江县	Dianjiang County	162335	53771	73339	99.2	100.0	1	3.15
忠 县	Zhongxian County	135311	52436	53375	98.6	98.7	1	4.44
开 县	Kaixian County	269579	100449	118657	98.0	98.4	1	20.53
云阳县	Yunyang County	207980	88558	85151	96.3	99.0	1	4.48
奉节县	Fengjie County	170404	66367	72562	92.0	98.5	1	4.86
巫山县	Wushan County	108229	38305	51273	95.0	97.0	1	7.41
巫溪县	Wuxi County	74655	29590	32418	90.0	98.0	1	3.78
渝东南翼	**Southeast of Chongqing**	**643117**	**241028**	**278598**	**95.4**	**97.2**	**6**	**40.00**
黔江区	Qianjiang District	114178	43204	44520	96.8	97.6	1	10.00
武隆县	Wulong County	64649	23167	25136	98.0	100.0	1	9.63
石柱县	Shizhu County	93712	35205	40822	92.3	92.5	1	5.00
秀山县	Xiushan County	101998	38405	43079	97.9	99.1	1	5.39
酉阳县	Youyang County	144867	54793	66441	97.6	98.7	1	6.46
彭水县	Pengshui County	123713	46254	58600	90.1	95.2	1	3.52

表20.15 各区县卫生（2011年）
PUBLIC HEALTH CARE BY REGION (2011)

区 县	Region	卫生机构数（个） Number of Health Care Institutions (unit)	其中 of which #医院、卫生院 Number of Hospitals and Health Centers	卫生机构床位数（张） Hospital Beds in Health Care Institutions (bed)	卫生技术人员（人） Medical Technical Personnel (person)	其中 of which # 执业（助理）医师 Licensed (Assistant) Doctors	#注册护士 Registered Nurses
全 市	**Total**	**17660**	**1407**	**115627**	**120169**	**49585**	**42767**
#都市发达经济圈	**Metropolitan Developed Economic Circle**	**3590**	**286**	**37765**	**46214**	**18311**	**18680**
渝西经济走廊	**West Chongqing Economic Corridor**	**5065**	**345**	**31140**	**28957**	**11993**	**9536**
三峡库区生态经济区	**Ecological Economic Zone in Three Gorges Reservoir Area**	**9005**	**776**	**46722**	**44998**	**19281**	**14551**
#一小时经济圈	**One -Hour Economic Circle**	**9788**	**732**	**76370**	**82773**	**33494**	**30905**
渝中区	Yuzhong District	352	21	8835	12000	4399	5465
大渡口区	Dadukou District	181	16	1148	1420	634	527
江北区	Jiangbei District	342	27	4436	4503	1704	1703
沙坪坝区	Shapingba District	344	35	4626	5154	2041	2079
九龙坡区	Jiulongpo District	557	52	5374	6667	2790	2683
南岸区	Nan'an District	319	28	2413	3876	1549	1525
北碚区	Beibei District	438	34	3480	4319	1907	1529
渝北区	Yubei District	433	43	3492	4350	1690	1515
巴南区	Ba'nan District	624	30	3961	3925	1597	1654
涪陵区	Fuling District	629	57	4342	4662	2016	1581
长寿区	Changshou District	504	44	3123	2940	1174	1108
江津区	Jiangjin District	624	36	4781	3595	1566	1067
合川区	Hechuan District	546	44	3480	4001	1679	1206
永川区	Yongchuan District	510	27	4559	3822	1522	1495
南川区	Nanchuan District	297	41	2470	2035	765	802
綦江区	Qijiang District	602	55	4447	4548	1534	1803
大足区	Dazu District	409	45	3065	2030	834	508
潼南县	Tongnan County	415	26	1670	1827	871	547
铜梁县	Tongliang County	835	29	2414	2659	1150	811
荣昌县	Rongchang County	437	24	2440	2562	1187	729
璧山县	Bishan County	390	18	1814	1878	885	568
渝东北翼	**Northeast of Chongqing**	**6024**	**459**	**29247**	**28936**	**12721**	**9108**
万州区	Wanzhou District	1217	69	7252	8092	3565	3022
梁平县	Liangping County	573	37	2045	2246	992	743
城口县	Chengkou County	161	26	815	616	235	98
丰都县	Fengdu County	434	35	2235	1828	707	633
垫江县	Dianjiang County	370	29	2546	2461	1049	746
忠 县	Zhongxian County	950	51	2525	2340	1077	699
开 县	Kaixian County	612	39	3952	3889	1842	1219
云阳县	Yunyang County	546	60	3176	2756	1362	701
奉节县	Fengjie County	479	53	2642	2181	947	595
巫山县	Wushan County	376	27	1154	1341	529	391
巫溪县	Wuxi County	306	33	905	1186	416	261
渝东南翼	**Southeast of Chongqing**	**1848**	**216**	**10010**	**8460**	**3370**	**2754**
黔江区	Qianjiang District	235	31	2600	2159	783	895
武隆县	Wulong County	278	32	1292	955	414	245
石柱县	Shizhu County	271	35	1690	1459	680	517
秀山县	Xiushan County	287	35	1239	1370	438	413
酉阳县	Youyang County	341	40	1823	1321	553	320
彭水县	Pengshui County	436	43	1366	1196	502	364

注：卫生机构数含个体诊所。
Note: The number of health care institutions include individual-run clinics.

表20.16 各区县高技术产业（2011年）
HIGH-TECH INDUSTRY BY REGION (2011)

区　县	Region	高技术制造业总产值(万元) Gross Output Valueof High-Tech Manufacturing (10 000 yuan)	高技术制造业主营业务收入（万元） Revenue from Major Business of High-Tech Manufacturing (10 000 yuan)	软件业主营业务收入（万元） Revenue from Major Business of Software Industry (10 000 yuan)
全　市	**Total**	**23177908.9**	**21926854.4**	**1238767.7**
#都市发达经济圈	**Metropolitan Developed Economic Circle**	**15114712.8**	**14349240.1**	**1237764.8**
渝西经济走廊	**West Chongqing Economic Corridor**	**2990886.9**	**2826835.5**	**178.4**
三峡库区生态经济区	**Ecological Economic Zone in Three Gorges Reservoir Area**	**5072309.2**	**4750778.8**	**824.5**
#一小时经济圈	**One -Hour Economic Circle**	**20717797.7**	**19655429.7**	**1238256.5**
渝中区	Yuzhong District	2552.6	2529.1	879246.3
大渡口区	Dadukou District	339342.5	365095.2	
江北区	Jiangbei District	1746532.1	1466360.2	6260.8
沙坪坝区	Shapingba District	5249887.8	4997230.7	15014.6
九龙坡区	Jiulongpo District	1962656.5	1883571.2	170628.8
南岸区	Nan'an District	1772254.3	1657329.0	4515.3
北碚区	Beibei District	1185883.3	1123987.5	493.5
渝北区	Yubei District	2621092.8	2613199.4	161255.5
巴南区	Ba'nan District	234510.9	239937.8	350.0
涪陵区	Fuling District	1510620.7	1354184.2	313.3
长寿区	Changshou District	1101577.3	1125169.9	
江津区	Jiangjin District	987953.5	907604.7	
合川区	Hechuan District	164173.3	158098.6	
永川区	Yongchuan District	328049.4	302516.2	91.2
南川区	Nanchuan District	219839.0	196508.7	
綦江区	Qijiang District	100888.9	85377.1	33.8
大足区	Dazu District	106651.9	105831.4	
潼南县	Tongnan County	15491.9	14881.4	
铜梁县	Tongliang County	179964.9	175051.8	
荣昌县	Rongchang County	438200.3	432689.0	
璧山县	Bishan County	449673.8	448276.6	53.4
渝东北翼	**Northeast of Chongqing**	**2186690.3**	**2009396.2**	
万州区	Wanzhou District	1355125.9	1241138.2	
梁平县	Liangping County	125857.1	119179.4	
城口县	Chengkou County			
丰都县	Fengdu County	75492.8	61261.8	
垫江县	Dianjiang County	338084.1	319937.2	
忠　县	Zhongxian County	57004.3	53769.8	
开　县	Kaixian County	87891.9	82643.7	
云阳县	Yunyang County	136910.8	121544.4	
奉节县	Fengjie County	2143.9	2143.9	
巫山县	Wushan County	3631.6	3500.6	
巫溪县	Wuxi County	4547.9	4277.2	
渝东南翼	**Southeast of Chongqing**	**273420.9**	**262028.5**	**511.2**
黔江区	Qianjiang District	38813.3	34656.6	
武隆县	Wulong County	40151.4	40154.8	
石柱县	Shizhu County	118994.6	117243.6	511.2
秀山县	Xiushan County	12108.1	11041.3	
酉阳县	Youyang County	55108.1	55743.7	
彭水县	Pengshui County	8245.4	3188.5	

注：表中的软件业主营业务收入不含嵌入软件类产品。
Note: The revenue from major business of software industry hereof does not include the data of embedded software products.

表20.17 各区县对外经济贸易（2011年）

FOREIGN ECONOMIC RELATIONS AND TRADE BY REGION (2011)

区　县	Region	进出口总值（万美元） Total Imports and Exports (US$ 10 000)	其　中 of which 出　口 Imports	进　口 Exports	实际利用内资（万元） Domestic Capital Actually Utilized (10 000 yuan)
全　市	**Total**	**2921786**	**1983813**	**937973**	**49198400**
#都市发达经济圈	**Metropolitan Developed Economic Circle**	**2376704**	**1603850**	**772854**	**22374348**
渝西经济走廊	**West Chongqing Economic Corridor**	**273662**	**223822**	**49840**	**12842908**
三峡库区生态经济区	**Ecological Economic Zone in Three GorgesReservoir Area**	**271420**	**156141**	**115279**	**13981144**
#一小时经济圈	**One -Hour Economic Circle**	**2824523**	**1900043**	**924480**	**38545601**
渝中区	Yuzhong District	70577	34355	36222	1562325
大渡口区	Dadukou District	100809	35631	65178	1744113
江北区	Jiangbei District	243484	163549	79936	4155842
沙坪坝区	Shapingba District	909459	606600	302860	2553452
九龙坡区	Jiulongpo District	179127	157117	22010	2406130
南岸区	Nan'an District	115349	104441	10907	2071173
北碚区	Beibei District	64291	61340	2952	2468767
渝北区	Yubei District	448220	228112	220108	3121406
巴南区	Ba'nan District	245386	212705	32681	2291140
涪陵区	Fuling District	141915	55882	86033	1722958
长寿区	Changshou District	32242	16487	15755	1605387
江津区	Jiangjin District	85399	56604	28796	2369154
合川区	Hechuan District	40916	40851	65	2006133
永川区	Yongchuan District	45584	36289	9294	3109001
南川区	Nanchuan District	26489	22440	4049	952650
綦江区	Qijiang District	10107	8597	1510	408238
大足区	Dazu District	7743	7273	469	804023
潼南县	Tongnan County	8052	8035	16	310889
铜梁县	Tongliang County	2794	2538	256	994716
荣昌县	Rongchang County	28387	28296	91	858636
璧山县	Bishan County	18193	12899	5294	1029468
渝东北翼	**Northeast of Chongqing**	**59972**	**47246**	**12726**	**7187646**
万州区	Wanzhou District	37826	26371	11455	1616063
梁平县	Liangping County	1826	1810	16	199049
城口县	Chengkou County	186	186		92200
丰都县	Fengdu County	3250	3233	17	995636
垫江县	Dianjiang County	5857	5857		477768
忠　县	Zhongxian County	5215	5213	2	976866
开　县	Kaixian County	2931	2931		868122
云阳县	Yunyang County	1567	331	1236	986000
奉节县	Fengjie County	156	156		526059
巫山县	Wushan County	105	105		182419
巫溪县	Wuxi County	1053	1053		267464
渝东南翼	**Southeast of Chongqing**	**37291**	**36524**	**767**	**3465153**
黔江区	Qianjiang District	5713	5201	512	868677
武隆县	Wulong County	5733	5705	29	416057
石柱县	Shizhu County	876	870	5	950525
秀山县	Xiushan County	2758	2543	216	500275
酉阳县	Youyang County	21394	21389	5	360942
彭水县	Pengshui County	816	816		368677

注：全市进出口数据来源重庆海关，区县进出口数据来源重庆市外经贸委。
Note: The data of import and export of the municipality are provided by Chongqing Customs while the data of import and export of districts and counties are provided by Chongqing Foreign Trade and Economic Relations Commission.

表20.18 各区县法人、产业活动单位数（2011年）

NUMBER OF CORPORATE UNITS AND ESTABLISHMENTS BY REGION (2011)

区　县	Region	法人单位（个） Number of Corporate Units (unit)	其　中 of which #企　业 Enterprises	产业活动单位（个） Number of Establishments (unit)
全　市	**Total**	**223748**	**176839**	**270882**
#都市发达经济圈	**Metropolitan Developed Economic Circle**	**91698**	**82042**	**105670**
渝西经济走廊	**West Chongqing Economic Corridor**	**53325**	**40553**	**68466**
三峡库区生态经济区	**Ecological Economic Zone in Three GorgesReservoir Area**	**78725**	**54244**	**96746**
#一小时经济圈	**One -Hour Economic Circle**	**160672**	**134619**	**193310**
渝中区	Yuzhong District	13218	12062	15566
大渡口区	Dadukou District	3642	3129	4136
江北区	Jiangbei District	10155	9325	11517
沙坪坝区	Shapingba District	12215	11037	13772
九龙坡区	Jiulongpo District	21357	19796	24507
南岸区	Nan'an District	7903	7158	9461
北碚区	Beibei District	6484	5490	7805
渝北区	Yubei District	9142	7704	10279
巴南区	Ba'nan District	7582	6341	8627
綦江区	Qijiang District	6757	5053	8243
大足区	Dazu District	5738	4245	6919
涪陵区	Fuling District	9200	7103	11620
长寿区	Changshou District	6449	4921	7554
江津区	Jiangjin District	6216	5054	8156
合川区	Hechuan District	6958	5451	9300
永川区	Yongchuan District	7817	6618	10437
南川区	Nanchuan District	3896	2777	4864
潼南县	Tongnan County	3191	1883	3667
铜梁县	Tongliang County	4191	3019	5847
荣昌县	Rongchang County	4045	2997	4920
璧山县	Bishan County	4516	3456	6113
渝东北翼	**Northeast of Chongqing**	**46922**	**31329**	**57172**
万州区	Wanzhou District	10208	8048	12371
梁平县	Liangping County	3311	2093	4423
城口县	Chengkou County	1686	827	2013
丰都县	Fengdu County	3711	2397	4608
垫江县	Dianjiang County	4043	2874	4628
忠　县	Zhongxian County	6027	3688	7779
开　县	Kaixian County	4967	3357	5353
云阳县	Yunyang County	4381	2691	5416
奉节县	Fengjie County	4083	2766	4478
巫山县	Wushan County	2229	1518	2932
巫溪县	Wuxi County	2276	1070	3171
渝东南翼	**Southeast of Chongqing**	**16154**	**10891**	**20400**
黔江区	Qianjiang District	2999	2346	3827
武隆县	Wulong County	2759	1835	3365
石柱县	Shizhu County	1737	1103	2513
秀山县	Xiushan County	2507	1614	3167
酉阳县	Youyang County	3656	2635	4477
彭水县	Pengshui County	2496	1358	3051

注：本表数据未经国家最终认定。
Note: The data hereinabove has not been finally verified by the state .

第21章

三峡工程重庆库区移民情况

RESETTLEMENT OF THE RESIDENTS IN CHONGQING RESERVOIR AREA OF THREE GORGES PROJECT

简要说明 BRIEF INTRODUCTION

本章资料包括三峡工程重庆库区经济和社会发展情况、移民工程投资完成情况，由市统计局综合处根据市移民局资料整理编辑。

库区指库区15区县，包括万州区、涪陵区、渝北区、巴南区、长寿区、江津区、丰都县、武隆县、忠县、开县、云阳县、奉节县、巫山县、巫溪县、石柱县。重点库区指8个重点移民区县，包括万州区、涪陵区、丰都县、忠县、开县、云阳县、奉节县、巫山县。

This chapter includes the economic and social development of the reservoir area of Three Gorges Project in Chongqing, the statistics on the completed investment in Three Gorges Resettlement. The data here are provided by Chongqing Migration Bureau and sorted and compiled by Division of Comprehensive Statistics of Chongqing Municipal Bureau of Statistics.

The Reservoir Area refers to 15 districts and counties, namely Wanzhou, Fuling, Yubei, Ba'nan, Changshou, Jiangjin, Fengdu, Wulong, Zhongxian, Kaixian, Yunyang, Fengjie, Wushan, Wuxi and Shizhu. The Key Reservoir Area refers to 8 key districts and counties of migration, namely Wanzhou, Fuling, Fengdu, Zhongxian, Kaixian, Yunyang, Fengjie and Wushan.

表21.1 三峡工程重庆库区经济和社会发展情况（2010－2011年）
ECONOMIC AND SOCIAL DEVELOPMENT OF THE RESERVOIR AREA OF THREE GORGES PROJECT IN CHONGQING (2010-2011)

指 标	Item	2010		2011	
		库区合计 Total of Reservoir Area	其 中 of which 重点库区 Key Area	库区合计 Total of Reservoir Area	其 中 of which 重点库区 Key Area
人 口	**Population**				
户籍总户数（万户）	Total Number of Households (10 000 households)	537.41	318.18	561.82	355.44
户籍人口（万人）	Total Household Populaion (10 000 persons)	1517.97	939.12	1532.26	944.84
非农业	Non-agriculture	431.79	230.51	511.74	288.27
农 业	Agriculture	1086.18	708.61	1020.52	656.57
男 性	Male	787.17	488.52	793.41	490.90
女 性	Female	730.80	450.60	738.85	453.94
年末常住人口	Year-end Permanent Residents (10 000 persons)	1288.04	743.30	1294.73	742.46
城 镇	Urban	615.90	305.42	643.70	318.12
乡 村	Rural	672.14	437.88	651.03	424.34
城镇化率（%）	Urbanization Rate (%)	47.82	41.09	49.72	42.85
工资和收入	**Wages and Income**				
城镇非私营单位职工人数（万人）	Staff and Workers of Urban Non-private Units (10 000 persons)	96.36	40.4	111.40	45.87
城镇非私营单位职工工资总额（万元）	Total Wages of Staff and Workers of Urban Non-private Unit (10 000 yuan)	3008629	1205771	4156367	1655108
城镇非私营单位在岗职工平均工资（元）	Average Wages of Staff and Workers of Urban Non-private Units (yuan)	32200	30628	37483	36113
农民人均纯收入（元）	Per Capita Net Income of Rural Households (yuan)	5284.68	4872.33	6546.85	6080.47
工资性收入	Income from Wages and Salaries	2351.82	2162.26	2922.66	2685.10
家庭经营收入	Income from Household Business Operation	2381.05	2209.12	2850.18	2653.29
转移收入	Income from Transfer	432.45	427.18	617.86	639.41
财产收入	Income from Property	119.37	73.76	156.15	102.67
农民人均消费支出（元）	Per Capita Expenditure of Rural Households (yuan)	3685.26	3341.59	4531.59	4223.43
食 品	Food	1833.31	1660.89	2183.54	2002.11
衣 着	Clothing	209.42	187.35	300.32	270.92
居 住	Residence	514.47	458.20	535.42	478.78
设备用品	Appliances and Articles	283.18	258.04	346.32	309.43
医 疗	Medical Services	255.97	234.45	358.04	354.31
交通通讯	Transport and Communications	286.21	264.75	414.63	412.85
文教娱乐	Culure, Education and Entertainment	249.88	226.60	319.65	321.28
其 他	Others	52.83	51.30	73.66	73.74
国民经济核算	**National Economic Accounting**				
地区生产总值（亿元）	Gross Domestic Product (100 million yuan)	3097.72	1503.54	4000.11	1911.07
第一产业	Primary Industry	332.80	186.49	411.24	232.07
第二产业	Secondary Industry	1799.80	838.36	2382.39	1076.57
#工 业	Industry	1499.34	700.38	1980.15	893.96
建筑业	Construction	300.46	137.98	402.24	182.61
第三产业	Tertiary Industry	965.12	478.69	1206.48	602.43
公有制经济	Public-owned Economy	1229.79	613.44	1544.04	764.43
非公有制经济	Non-public-owned Economy	1867.93	890.10	2456.07	1146.64
地区生产总值结构（%）	Composition of Gross Domestic Product（%）	100.00	100.00	100.0	100.0
第一产业	Primary Industry	10.7	12.4	10.3	12.1
第二产业	Secondary Industry	58.1	55.8	59.6	56.3
#工 业	Industry	48.4	46.6	49.5	46.8
建筑业	Construction	9.7	9.2	10.1	9.5
第三产业	Tertiary Industry	31.2	31.8	30.1	31.6
公有制经济	Public-owned Economy	39.7	40.8	38.6	40.0
非公有制经济	Non-public-owned Economy	60.3	59.2	61.4	60.0

表21.1 续表1 continued1

指 标	Item	2010		2011	
		库区合计 Total of Reservoir Area	其 中 of which	库区合计 Total of Reservoir Area	其 中 of which
			重点库区 Key Area		重点库区 Key Area
固定资产投资（万元）	**Investment in Fixed Assets (10 000 yuan)**				
全社会固定资产投资总额	Total Investment in Fixed Assets	28607651	12464314	31489418	13819676
#基础设施	Infrastructure	8756224	3585160	8718609	4002374
工业投资	Industry	10167454	4634106	11430209	5020883
城 镇	Urban	26285416	11098698	30981771	13492715
#房地产开发	Real Estate Development	5170360	1260956	6465950	1665905
#住 宅	Residential Bulidings	4108641	937804	4764258	1291607
农 村	Rural	2322235	1365616	2701378	1515274
商品房建设情况	**Construction of Commercialized Buildings**				
房地产施工面积	Floor Space under Construction	6407.85	1891.13	7128.46	2222.55
#住 宅	Residential Bulidings	5456.18	1618.05	5749.57	1854.83
房地产竣工面积	Floor Space Completed	916.98	330.25	1277.85	430.29
#住 宅	Residential Bulidings	767.20	283.86	1060.20	368.57
财 政（万元）	**Government Finance (10 000 yuan)**				
区县级地方财政收入	Local Government Revenue	2939296	1275198	4491862	2136886
#一般预算收入	General Budgetary Revenue	1795646	729424	2615421	1115457
区县级地方财政支出	Local Government Expenditure	6155254	3134494	8468236	4539209
#一般预算支出	General Budgetary Expenditure	4731087	2444054	6375059	3394951
农 业	**Agriculture**				
农林牧渔业总产值（万元）	Gross Output Value of Farming, Forestry, Animal Husbandry and Fishery (10 000 yuan)	4977507	2806135	6185248	3503942
#农 业	Farming	2690626	1441910	3759022	2141752
牧 业	Animal Husbandry	1848543	1083801	2008236	1127621
农林牧渔业增加值（万元）	Value-added of Farming, Forestry, Animal Husbandry and Fishery (10 000 yuan)	3328027	1864932	4112412	2320686
#农 业	Farming	1999819	1050300	2788943	1579830
牧 业	Animal Husbandry	989896	587492	1011410	564685
蔬菜总播种面积（万亩）	Sown Areas of Vegetables (10 000 mu)	414.02	265.43	460.97	279.29
蔬菜总产量（万吨）	Gross Output of Vegestables (10 000 tons)	563.45	372.62	650.64	399.90
肉类总产量（万吨）	Gross Output of Meat (10 000 tons)	88.11	52.01	89.91	53.48
#猪 肉	Pork	70.12	42.01	70.40	42.56
禽 肉	Meat of Poultry	10.20	4.52	10.78	4.87
猪出栏量（万头）	Slaughtered Hogs (10 000 heads)	955.43	572.43	956.78	578.66
禽出栏量（万只）	Slaughtered Poultry (10 000 heads)	6481.03	2869.75	6878.52	3120.56
牛奶产量（万吨）	Output of Milk (10 000 tons)	3.55	1.06	2.94	1.11
禽蛋产量（万吨）	Output of Poultry Eggs (10 000 tons)	19.83	10.44	20.00	10.53
粮食播种面积（万亩）	Sown Areas of Grain (10 000 mu)	1768.79	1109.73	1787.53	1123.96
夏 粮	Grain Crops Harvested in Summer	451.37	297.23	450.92	296.62
秋 粮	Grain Crops Harvested in Aulture	1317.42	812.50	1336.62	827.34
#水 稻	Rice	460.64	272.83	463.97	277.51
玉 米	Corn	369.65	215.94	373.05	218.91
薯 类	Tuber	630.75	419.78	641.77	426.82
粮食总产量（万吨）	Gross Output of Grain (10 000 tons)	565.84	339.90	560.04	338.56
夏 粮	Grain Crops Harvested in Summer	89.83	62.84	90.76	63.47
秋 粮	Grain Crops Harvested in Aulture	476.01	277.10	469.28	275.09
#水 稻	Rice	225.15	125.20	216.46	121.84
玉 米	Corn	130.54	75.00	134.42	77.48
薯 类	Tuber	163.05	108.30	162.83	108.29

表21.1 续表2 continued2

指 标	Item	2010		2011	
		库区合计 Total of Reservoir Area	其 中 of which 重点库区 Key Area	库区合计 Total of Reservoir Area	其 中 of which 重点库区 Key Area
工 业（规模以上）	**Industry (above Desingated Size)**				
企业数(个)	Number of Enterprises (unit)	2298	896	1424	527
工业总产值（万元）	Gross Output Value of Industry (10 000 yuan)	38652771	11365682	49937601	15757654
出口交货值（万元）	Sales of Exported Products (10 000 yuan)	1697245	258608	2028043	278111
资产总计（万元）	Total Assets (10 000 yuan)	36008372	11481655	42704990	12384648
主营业务收入（万元）	Revenue from Principal Business (10 000 yuan)	37097640	10579677	47822004	14633619
利润总额（万元）	Total After-tax Profits (10 000 yuan)	2077344	637679	2965385	1122336
利税总额（万元）	Total Pre-tax Profits (10 000 yuan)	4510153	1349028	5398183	2034012
全部从业人员平均数（万人）	Average Emloyment (10 000 persons)	53.05	19.01	53.27	17.93
经济效益综合指数 (%)	Comprehensive Index of Economic Benefits (%)	241.0	233.9	255.4	287.8
总资产贡献率 (%)	Ratio of Total Assets to Industrial Output Value (%)	13.7	13.3	13.9	18.1
资本保值增值率 (%)	Ratio of Assets Appreciation YOY (%)	127.9	130.6	124.5	129.2
资产负债率 (%)	Asset-Liability Ratio (%)	61.7	57.7	62.6	59.6
流动资产周转率(次)	Turnover Ratio of Circulating Assets(time)	2.3	2.36	2.33	2.62
成本费用利润率 (%)	Ratio of Profits to Cost (%)	5.88	6.26	6.44	8.16
全员劳动生产率（元/人年）	Overall Labor Productivity (yuan/person-year)	212553	197468	232947	255792
产品销售率 (%)	Sales as Percentage of Output (%)	97.7	96.5	97.1	96.5
国内贸易	**Domestic Trade**				
社会消费品零售总额（万元）	Total Retail Sales (10 000 yuan)	9548604	4283220	11141906	4950093
限额以上法人企业数（个）	Number of Corporate Enterprises above Designated Size (unit)	1098	516	1447	715
批发业	Wholesale	398	181	520	254
零售业	Retail	439	203	591	296
住宿业	Hotel	98	44	113	52
餐饮业	Catering	163	88	223	113
实际利用内资（亿元）	Domestic Capital Actually Utilized (100 million yuan)	1012.34	385.85	1889.53	787.41
教 育	**Education**				
学校数（所）	Number of Schools(unit)	5341	3440	5246	3290
#普通高等学校	Regular Institutions of Higher Education	14	6	16	7
普通中学	Regular Secondary Schools	584	361	571	356
小 学	Primary Schools	3014	2067	2843	1983
专任教师数（人）	Number of Full-time Teachers (person)	125901	74817	123730	72803
#普通高等学校	Regular Institutions of Higher Education	6516	3202	6950	3349
普通中学	Regular Secondary Schools	48672	29960	49183	30001
小 学	Primary Schools	53113	32206	53058	31974
在校学生数（人）	Student Enrollment (person)	2565003	1624232	2226176	1521929
#研究生	Postgraduates	840		1008	
普通高等学校	Regular Institutions of Higher Education	104759	52893	119198	57757
普通中学	Regular Secondary Schools	883670	582954	850847	560237
小 学	Primary Schools	933403	616786	904141	588421
卫 生	**Public Health**				
卫生机构数（个）	Number of Health Institutions (unit)	8246	5212	8283	5243
卫生机构床位数（张）	Number of Hospital Beds (bed)	401103	23982	46522	27278
卫生技术人员（人）	Medical Technological Personnel (person)	42369	25150	45499	27089
基本单位	**Basic Units**				
法人单位数（个）	Number of Corporate Units(unit)	62202	33484	80967	44806
产业活动单位数(个)	Number of Establishments (unit)	79097	42942	98222	54557

注：1）因卫生统计口径发生变化，2010年指标卫生机构数、卫生技术人员为调整数。
2）本表教育数据统计口径包括普通高校、中职学校、普通中学、小学、幼儿园和特殊教育及工读学校。

Note: a). Due to the change of the statistic scope, the data of "number of health institutions" and "medical technological personnel" are adjusted data.
b). The statistic scope of education data in this table includes regular institutions of higher education, vocational secondary schools, regular secondary schools,primary schools, kindergartens, special education schools and schools for juvenile delinquents.

表21.2 三峡移民工程移民投资完成情况综合表（2011年底止）

COMPREHENSIVE STATISTICS ON THE COMPLETED INVESTMENT IN THREE GORGES RESETTLEMENT (END OF 2011)

指　标	Item	移民投资累计计划 Cumulative Investment in Resettlement Planned					
		小　计 Total	原概算投资 Originally Estimated Investment	规划调整新增投资 Additional Investment by Adjustment of Plan	政策性新增投资 Additional Investment by Policies	一次性补助投资 Lump-sum Subsidy Investment	派生资金 Derived Funds
项目直接费合计	**Total of Direct Cost**	**7032385**	**4292049**	**1444576**	**792458**	**166253**	**337049**
农村移民安置	Resettlement of Rural Residents	2329364	857670	752829	577680	77231	63954
城市(县城)迁建	Resettlement and Reconstruction of Cities	2247558	1525518	354962	96972	27260	242846
集镇迁建	Resettlement and Reconstruction of Towns	488622	298172	145747	17410	6972	20320
工矿企业迁建	Resettlement and Reconstruction of Industrial and Mineral Enterprises	921562	829966	41856	3268	46384	87
专业项目复建	Reconstruction of Special Establishment	679632	507229	67783	94702	6713	3205
环境保护	Environmental Protection	58273	40890	17383			
勘测设计费	Survey and Design Expense	122795	77967	38521	2426	199	3683
监理费	Supervision Expense	52173	35739	16434			
滑坡治理	Landslide Control	79671	75469	2956		1182	65
其　他	Others	52736	43431	6103		312	2890

注：此表投资统计口径含包干内项目直接费、政策性资金、派生资金以及规划调整新增资金。
Note: The statistics scope of investment in this table includes the direct cost of contracts, policy funds, derived funds and additional investment by adjustment of plan.

表21.2 续表 continued

指　标	Item	移民投资本年计划 Investment in Resettlement Planned in Current Year					
		小　计 Total	原概算投资 Originally Estimated Investment	规划调整新增投资 Additional Investment by Adjustment of Plan	政策性新增投资 Additional Investment by Policies	一次性补助投资 Lump-sum Subsidy Investment	派生资金 Derived Funds
项目直接费合计	**Total of Direct Cost**	**644968**		**220599**	**424249**	**120**	
农村移民安置	Resettlement of Rural Residents	503638		81832	421686	120	
城市(县城)迁建	Resettlement and Reconstruction of Cities	88114		88114			
集镇迁建	Resettlement and Reconstruction of Towns	22253		21365	888		
工矿企业迁建	Resettlement and Reconstruction of Industrial and Mineral Enterprises	13186		13186			
专业项目复建	Reconstruction of Special Establishment	2831		1157	1674		
环境保护	Environmental Protection	11021		11021			
勘测设计费	Survey and Design Expense	169		169			
监理费	Supervision Expense	803		803			
滑坡治理	Landslide Control	2952		2952			
其　他	Others						

单位：万元、% (10 000 yuan, %)

移民资金累计完成 Cumulative Investment in Resettlement Completed											
小 计 Total		原概算投资 Originally Estimated Investment		规划调整新增投资 Additional Investment by Adjustment of Plan		政策性新增投资 Additional Investment by Policies		一次性补助投资 Lump-sum Subsidy Investment		派生资金 Derived Funds	
金 额 Sum	比 例 Proportion	金 额 Sum	比 例 Proportion	金 额 Sum	比 例 Proportion	金 额 Sum	比 例 Proportion	金 额 Sum	比 例 Proportion	金 额 Sum	比 例 Proportion
6697899	**95.2**	**4241817**	**98.8**	**1269076**	**87.9**	**703380**	**88.8**	**159022**	**95.7**	**324605**	**96.3**
2161035	92.8	849881	99.1	689870	91.6	490686	84.9	72303	93.6	58294	91.2
2189915	97.4	1518327	99.5	306984	86.5	96642	99.7	26837	98.4	241125	99.3
444187	90.9	290267	97.3	113216	77.7	17130	98.4	5708	81.9	17866	87.9
909270	98.7	823515	99.2	36652	87.6	3068	93.9	45948	99.1	87	100.0
665322	97.9	502811	99.1	61635	90.9	93603	98.8	6563	97.8	710	22.2
52634	90.3	37554	91.8	15080	86.8						
108085	88.0	76779	98.5	25310	65.7	2251	92.8	178	89.4	3567	96.9
47481	91.0	35272	98.7	12209	74.3						
67622	84.9	64919	86.0	1456	49.3			1182	100.0	65	100.0
52215	99.0	42958	98.9	6063	99.3			304	97.3	2890	100.0

单位：万元、% (10 000 yuan, %)

移民资金本年完成 Investment in Resettlement Completed in Current Year											
小 计 Total		原概算投资 Originally Estimated Investment		规划调整新增投资 Additional Investment by Adjustment of Plan		政策性新增投资 Additional Investment by Policies		一次性补助投资 Lump-sum Subsidy Investment		派生资金 Derived Funds	
金 额 Sum	比 例 Proportion	金 额 Sum	比 例 Proportion	金 额 Sum	比 例 Proportion	金 额 Sum	比 例 Proportion	金 额 Sum	比 例 Proportion	金 额 Sum	比 例 Proportion
534097	**82.8**			**181088**	**82.1**	**352889**	**83.2**	**120**	**100.0**		
416479	82.7			65944	80.6	350414	83.1	120	100.0		
74659	84.7			74659	84.7						
14056	63.2			13256	62.0	800	90.1				
12203	92.5			12203	92.5						
2831	100.0			1157	100.0	1674	100.0				
10079	91.5			10079	91.5						
169	100.0			169	100.0						
803	100.0			803	100.0						
2818	95.5			2818	95.5						

第 22 章

基本单位名录库

STATISTICS ON BASIC UNITS

简要说明

BRIEF INTRODUCTION

本章资料包括按行业分的法人、产业活动单位数，按机构类型和登记注册类型分的法人单位数，按行业分的企业法人单位数以及按登记注册类型分的企业法人单位数，由市统计局普查中心根据基本单位统计年报资料整理编辑。

This chapter includes the number of corporate units and establishments by sector, the number of corporate units by institutional type and status of registration, the number of enterprises as corporate units by sector and the number of enterprises as corporate units by status of registration. The data are prepared and compiled by Census Centre of Chongqing Municipal Bureau of Statistics on the basis of the data of the annual statistic report of the basic units.

表22.1 按行业分的法人、产业活动单位数（2010－2011年）
NUMBER OF CORPORATE UNITS AND ESTABLISHMENTS BY SECTOR (2010-2011)

单位：个 (unit)

指 标	Item	2010		2011	
		法人单位 Corporate Units	产业活动单位 Establishments	法人单位 Corporate Units	产业活动单位 Establishments
总 计	**Total**	**177916**	**223968**	**223748**	**270882**
第一产业	Primary Industry	13101	13877	23935	24876
第二产业	Secondary Industry	43737	46481	50076	52892
工 业	Industry	36800	39002	42141	44364
采矿业	Mining and Quarrying	3101	3414	3035	3394
制造业	Manufacturing	31731	32939	37103	38319
电力、燃气及水的生产和供应业	Production and Supply of Electricity,Gas & Water	1968	2649	2003	2651
建筑业	Construction	6937	7479	7935	8528
第三产业	Tertiary Industry	121078	163610	149737	193114
交通运输、仓储和邮政业	Transport, Storage and Post	4529	7209	5046	7914
信息传输、计算机服务和软件业	Data Transmission, Computer Services and Software	4053	5836	5215	6995
批发和零售业	Wholesale and Retail Trades	37345	49709	53380	66739
住宿和餐饮业	Hotels and Catering Services	4794	6979	7222	9263
金融业	Financial Intermediation	1173	6038	1250	6225
房地产业	Real Estate	7138	8780	8470	10324
租赁和商务服务业	Leasing and Business Services	12981	14473	16729	18517
科学研究、技术服务与地质勘查业	Scientific Research, Technical Services and Geological Prospecting	4026	4580	4486	5079
水利、环境和公共设施管理业	Administration of Water Conservancy, Environment and Public Utilities	1506	1862	1676	2031
居民服务和其他服务业	Household Services and Other Services	3408	3897	5101	5608
教 育	Education	7762	10929	8035	11137
卫生、社会保障和社会福利业	Public Health, Social Security and Social Welfare	5897	11691	5933	11620
文化、体育和娱乐业	Culture, Sports and Entertainment	2128	2669	2394	2930
公共管理和社会组织	Public Administration and Social Organizations	24338	28958	24800	28732

表22.2 按机构类型和登记注册类型分的法人单位数（2010－2011年）

NUMBER OF CORPORATE UNITS BY INSTITUTIONAL TYPE AND STATUS OF REGISTRATION(2010-2011)

单位：个 (unit)

指　标	Item	2010	2011
总　计	**Total**	**177916**	**223748**
按机构类型分组	**By Institutional Type**		
企　业	Enterprises	132548	176839
事业单位	Public Institutions	16764	16909
机　关	Governmental Agencies	4468	4458
社会团体	Social Organizations	4196	4558
其他组织机构	Others	19940	20984
按登记注册类型分组	**By Status of Registration**		
内　资	Domestic-funded Enterprises	176647	222365
国　有	State-owned	23998	24061
集　体	Collective-owned	4551	4519
股份合作	Cooperative Share-holding	1332	1457
联　营	Joint Ownership	359	365
国有联营	State-owned	60	66
集体联营	Collective-owned	125	138
国有与集体联营	Joint State-Collective-owned	40	39
其他联营	Others	134	122
有限责任公司	Limited-liability Corporations	17161	20415
国有独资公司	Soly State-owned	548	642
其他有限责任公司	Other Limited-liability Corporations	16613	19773
股份有限公司	Share-holding Limited Companies	3572	3876
私　营	Private	93769	130400
私营独资	Soly Private-funded Enterprises	37649	61279
私营合伙	Private Partnership Enterprises	7509	8883
私营有限责任公司	Private Limited Liability Corporations	43299	54009
私营股份有限公司	Private Share-holding Limited Companies	5312	6229
其　他	Others	31905	37272
港、澳、台商投资	Enterprises with Funds from Hong Kong, Macao and Tainwan	553	623
合资经营	Joint-venture Enterprises	199	226
合作经营	Cooperative Enterprises	16	14
独资经营	Soly-funded Enterprises	294	333
投资股份有限公司	Share-holding Limited Companies	44	44
外商投资	Foreign-funded Enterprises	716	760
中外合资经营	Joint-venture Enterprises	317	309
中外合作经营	Cooperative Enterprises	27	28
外资企业	Soly-funded Enterprises	329	372
外商投资股份有限公司	Share-holding Limited Companies	43	46

表22.3 按行业分的企业法人单位数（2010－2011年）
NUMBER OF ENTERPRISES AS CORPORATE UNITS BY SECTOR (2010-2011)

单位：个 (unit)

指　标	Item	2010	2011
总　计	**Total**	**132548**	**176839**
第一产业	Primary Industry	10674	20841
第二产业	Secondary Industry	43719	50051
工　业	Industry	36783	42117
采矿业	Mining and Quarrying	3101	3035
制造业	Manufacturing	31730	37103
电力、燃气及水的生产和供应业	Production and Supply of Electricity,Gas & Water	1952	1979
建筑业	Construction	6936	7934
第三产业	Tertiary Industry	78155	105947
交通运输、仓储和邮政业	Transport, Storage and Post	4368	4874
信息传输、计算机服务和软件业	Data Transmission, Computer Services and Software	3834	4963
批发和零售业	Wholesale and Retail Trades	37345	53380
住宿和餐饮业	Hotels and Catering Services	4673	7061
金融业	Financial Intermediation	1090	1152
房地产业	Real Estate	6986	8310
租赁和商务服务业	Leasing and Business Services	11798	15494
科学研究、技术服务和地质勘查业	Scientific Research, Technical Services and Geological Prospecting	2249	2709
水利、环境和公共设施管理业	Administration of Water Conservancy, Environment and Public Utilities	876	1025
居民服务和其他服务业	Household Services and Other Services	2992	4622
教　育	Education	665	786
卫生、社会保障和社会福利业	Public Health, Social Security and Social Welfare	226	267
文化、体育和娱乐业	Culture, Sports and Entertainment	1053	1304
公共管理和社会组织	Public Administration and Social Organizations		

表22.4 按登记注册类型分的企业法人单位数（2010－2011年）

NUMBER OF ENTERPRISES AS CORPORATE UNITS BY STATUS OF REGISTRATION (2010-2011)

单位：个 (unit)

指 标	Item	2010	2011
总 计	**Total**	**132548**	**176839**
内 资	Domestic-funded Enterprises	131305	175482
国 有	State-owned	2974	3022
集 体	Collective-owned	2928	2820
股份合作	Cooperative Share-holding	1258	1373
联 营	Joint Ownership	294	289
国有联营	State-owned	55	61
集体联营	Collective-owned	104	106
国有与集体联营	Joint State-Collective-owned	33	33
其他联营	Others	102	89
有限责任公司	Limited-liability Corporations	16981	20219
国有独资公司	Soly State-owned	543	636
其他有限责任公司	Other Limited-liability Corporations	16438	19583
股份有限公司	Share-holding Limited Companies	3525	3833
私 营	Private	91280	127565
私营独资	Soly Private-funded Enterprises	35972	59322
私营合伙	Private Partnership Enterprises	7106	8462
私营有限责任公司	Private Limited Liability Corporations	42973	53639
私营股份有限公司	Private Share-holding Limited Companies	5229	6142
其 他	Others	12065	16361
港、澳、台商投资	Enterprises with Funds from Hong Kong, Macao and Tainwan	539	609
合资经营	Joint-venture Enterprises	193	219
合作经营	Cooperative Enterprises	16	14
独资经营	Soly-funded Enterprises	288	328
投资股份有限公司	Share-holding Limited Companies	42	42
外商投资	Foreign-funded Enterprises	704	748
中外合资经营	Joint-venture Enterprises	314	306
中外合作经营	Cooperative Enterprises	23	25
外资企业	Soly-funded Enterprises	324	366
外商投资股份有限公司	Share-holding Limited Companies	43	46

附 录

APPENDIX

附录1 重庆市国民经济主要指标占全国的比重（2011年）

APPENDIX I: CHONGQING'S MAIN INDICATORS OF NATIONAL ECONOMY AS PERCENTAGE OF WHOLE NATION (2011)

指 标	Item	全 国 Whole Nation	重 庆 Chongqing	重庆占全国的比重（%） Chongqing as Percentage of Whole Nation (%)
土地面积（万平方公里）	Land Area (10 000 sq. km)	960	8.24	0.86
年末总人口（万人）	Year-end Population (10 000 persons)	134735	2919.00	2.17
年末就业人员数（万人）	Year-end Employment (10 000 persons)	76420	1585.16	2.07
国内（地区）生产总值（亿元）	Gross Domestic Product (100 million yuan)	471564	10011.37	2.12
第一产业	Primary Industry	47712	844.52	1.77
第二产业	Secondary Industry	220592	5543.04	2.51
第三产业	Tertiary Industry	203260	3623.81	1.78
主要农业、工业产品产量(万吨)	Output of Major Agricultural and . Industrial Products (10 000 tons)			
粮 食	Gain	57121	1126.90	1.97
油 料	Oil-bearing Crops	3307	46.51	1.41
肉 类	Meat	7958	196.28	2.47
原 煤(亿吨)	Coal (100 million tons)	35	0.45	1.28
发电量(亿千瓦小时)	Electricity (100 million kwh)	47001	529.57	1.13
货运量（万吨）	Freight Traffic (10 000 tons)	3696961	96779.00	2.62
客运量（万人次）	Passenger Traffic (10 000 person-times)	3526319	141204.00	4.00
邮电业务总量（亿元）	Total Business Volume of Postal and Telecommunication Services (100 million yuan)	13379	242.64	1.81
社会消费品零售总额（亿元）	Retail Sales of Consumer Goods (100 million yuan)	183919	3487.81	1.90
固定资产投资额（亿元）	Investment in Fixed Assets (100 million yuan)	301933	7366.15	2.44
#房地产开发投资	Real Estate Development	61740	2015.1	3.26
财政收入（亿元）	Revenue of Government (100 million yuan)	103740	2908.91	2.80
财政支出（亿元）	Expenditure of Government (100 million yuan)	108930	3959.87	3.64
金融机构人民币各项存款余额（亿元）	Deposit Balance of RMB of Financial Institutions (100 million yuan)	809368	15832.81	1.96
金融机构人民币各项贷款余额（亿元）	Loan Balance of RMB of Financial Institutions (100 million yuan)	547947	13001.39	2.37
货物进出口总额（亿美元）	Total Imports and Exports (USD 100 million)	36421	292.18	0.80
出口额	Exports	18986	198.38	1.04
进口额	Imports	17435	93.80	0.54
外商直接投资（亿美元）	Foreign Direct Investment(USD 100 million)	1160	105.29	
建筑业总产值（亿元）	Gross Output Value of Construction (100 million yuan)	117734	3328.83	2.83
在校学生数（万人）	Student Enrollment (10 000 persons)			
#普通高等学校	Regular Institutions of Higher Education	2309	61.30	2.66
普通中学	Secondary Schools	7519	183.89	2.45
普通小学	Primary Schools	9926	195.48	1.97
图书总印数（亿册(张)）	Printed Copies of Books (100 million copies)	77	1.56	2.03
报纸总印数（亿份）	Printed Copies of Newspaper (100 million copies)	467	6.61	1.42
医疗卫生机构（万个）	Number of Health Care Institutions (10 000 unit)	95	1.77	1.86
执业(助理)医师（万人）	Licensed (Assistant) Doctors (10 000 persons)	247	4.96	2.01
医院、卫生院床位数（万张）	Number of Beds in Hospitals and Health Centers (10 000 units)	516	10.71	2.08

注：1）本表中全国数据摘自2012年《中国统计摘要》，部分数据为初步统计数，正式统计数据以《中国统计年鉴—2012》为准(以下各表同）。
2）工业部分为规模以上工业企业数。
3）外商直接投资，由于国家与重庆所用统计口径不同，无法计算比重。

Note: a) The data of the whole nation in this table are extracted from China Statistical Summary—2012, and some of the data are primary statistics. See China Statistical Yearbook—2012 for the official data (the same applies to the following tables).
b) The data of industry refers to the industrial enterprises above designated size.
c) Due to the difference in the statistic scope between the NBS and Chongqing, the percentage of Foreign Direct Investment cannot be calculated.

附录2 全国国民经济与社会发展速度指标
APPENDIX II: INDICATORS ON THE GROWTH RATE OF NATIONAL ECONOMIC AND SOCIAL DEVELOPMENT

指标	Item	2011年	2011年为下列各年（%） 2011 as Percentage of the Following Years (%)				平均每年增长（%） Average Annual Growth Rate (%)		
			1978年	1990年	2000年	2010年	1979-2011	1991-2011	2001-2011
人口	**Population**								
年末总人口(万人)	Year-end Population (10 000 persons)	134735	140.0	117.8	106.3	100.5	1.0	0.8	0.6
城镇人口	Urban Population	69079	400.6	228.8	150.5	103.1	4.3	4.0	3.8
乡村人口	Rural Population	65656	83.1	78.0	81.2	97.8	-0.6	-1.2	-1.9
就业和失业	**Employment and Unemployment**								
年末就业人员数	Year-end Employment	76420	190.3	118.0	106.0	100.4	2.0	0.8	0.5
城镇登记失业人员	Registered Unemployment in Urban Areas	922	174.0	240.7	155.0	101.5	1.7	4.3	4.1
国民经济核算	**National Accounting**								
国内生产总值(亿元)	Gross Domestic Product (100 million yuan)	471563.7	2249.2	798.4	296.0	109.2	9.9	10.4	10.4
第一产业	Primary Industry	47712.0	437.8	229.6	158.1	104.5	4.6	4.0	4.2
第二产业	Secondary Industry	220591.6	3537.0	1163.1	327.0	110.6	11.4	12.4	11.4
第三产业	Tertiary Industry	203260.1	3013.5	832.2	315.2	108.9	10.9	10.6	11.0
固定资产投资	**Investment in Fixed Assets**								
全社会固定资产投资总额(亿元)	Total Investment in Fixed Assets(100 million yuan)	311021.9		6885.6	944.8	111.8		22.3	22.7
城　镇	Urban	271655.3		8296.3	1036.0	112.5		23.8	24.4
#房地产开发	Real Estate Development	61739.8		24374.2	1238.7	127.9		29.9	25.7
对外贸易和实际利用外资	**Foreign Trade and Foreign Capital Actually Utilized**								
货物进出口总额(亿美元)	Total Imports and Exports (USD 100 million)	36420.6	17645.6	3154.9	767.9	122.5	17.0	17.9	20.4
出口额	Exports	18986.0	19472.8	3057.8	761.9	120.3	17.3	17.7	20.3
进口额	Imports	17434.6	16009.7	3268.0	774.6	124.9	16.6	18.1	20.5
外商直接投资	Foreign Direct Investment	1160.1		3327.0	284.9	109.7		18.2	10.0
外商其他投资	Other Foreign Investment	16.9		629.5	19.5	54.6		9.2	-13.8
财政	**Government Finance**								
国家财政收入(亿元)	Government Finance Revenue (100 million yuan)	103740.0	9162.2	3532.1	774.5	124.8	14.7	18.5	20.5
国家财政支出	Government Finance Expenditures	108929.7	9707.7	3532.6	685.7	121.2	14.9	18.5	19.1

注:1) 本表国内生产总值、邮电业务总量按可比价格计算。
2) 平均每年增长速度除固定资产投资按累计法计算。
3) 2006年起，外商直接投资包括银行、证券、保险部门数据。外商直接投资按可比口径计算。
4) 邮电业务总量指标2000年及以前按1990年不变价格计算，2001年及以后按2000年不变价格计算。
5) 社会消费品零售总额1978年为社会商品零售总额，即包括农业生产资料零售额在内（下表同）。

Note: a) The data of GDP and the business volume of postal and telecommunication services and average wages in value terms in this table are calculated at constant prices.
b) The data of average annual growth rate are calculated by cumulative-sum method except the investment in fixed assets.
c) Since 2006, the foreign direct investment has included the data from banks, securities institutions and insurance companies. It is calculated in comparable scope.
d) The data of total business volume of postal and telecommunication services of 2000 and before are calculated at the constant price of 1990, while the data of 2001 and after are calculated at the constant price of 2000.
e) The retail sales of consumer goods in 1978 refers to the total sales of commodities, which includes the retail sales of agricultural means of production (the same below).

附录2 续表 continued

指 标	Item	1978年	2011年为下列各年（%） 2011 as Percentage of the Following Years (%)				平均每年增长（%） Average Annual Growth Rate (%)		
			1978年	1990年	2000年	2010年	1979-2011	1991-2011	2001-2011
主要产品产量	**Output of Major Products**								
粮 食(万吨)	Gain (10 000 tons)	57120.8	187.4	128.0	123.6	104.5	1.9	1.2	1.9
棉 花(万吨)	Cotton (10 000 tons)	658.9	304.1	146.2	149.2	110.5	3.4	1.8	3.7
油 料(万吨)	Oil-bearing Crops (10 000 tons)	3306.8	633.7	205.0	111.9	102.4	5.8	3.5	1.0
肉 类(万吨)	Meat (10 000 tons)	7957.8			132.3	100.4			2.6
原 煤(万吨)	Coal (10 000 tons)	35.20	569.6	325.9	254.3	108.8	5.4	5.8	8.9
原 油(万吨)	Oil (10 000 tons)	20288	195.0	146.7	124.5	100.2	2.0	1.8	2.0
发电量(亿千瓦小时)	Electricity(100 million kwh)	47001	1831.7	756.6	346.7	111.7	9.2	10.1	12.0
粗 钢(万吨)	Steel (10 000 tons)	68388	2151.9	1030.7	532.2	107.3	9.7	11.7	16.4
水 泥(万吨)	Cement (10 000 tons)	208500	3195.9	994.2	349.2	110.8	11.1	11.6	12.0
建筑业	**Construction**								
建筑业企业从业人员(万人)	Number of Persons Employed (10 000 persons)	4311		426.5	216.2	103.6		7.2	7.3
建筑业总产值(亿元)	Gross Output Value of Construction (100 million yuan)	117734		8753.5	942.1	122.6		23.7	22.6
交 通	**Transportation**								
客运量(万人)	Passenger Traffic(10 000 persons)	3526319	1388.4	456.4	238.5	107.9	8.3	7.5	8.2
货物量(万吨)	Freight Traffic (10 000 tons)	3696961	1485.0	380.9	272.1	114.0	8.5	6.6	9.5
沿海主要港口货物吞吐量(万吨)	Cargo Throughput of Major Sea Ports	616292	3107.3	1275.4	490.7	112.4	11.0	12.9	15.6
邮电通信业	**Telecommunications and Postal Services**(10 000 tons)								
邮电业务总量（亿元）	Total Business Volume (100 million yuan)	13379.2	146883.6	32191.0	1044.7	116.7	24.7	31.6	23.8
年末移动电话用户(万户)	Mobile Telephone Subscribers (10 000 subscribers)	98625.3		5479183	1166.7	114.8		68.1	25.0
年末固定电话年末用户(万户)	Fixed Telephone Subscribers (10 000 subscribers)	28511.5	14807.8	4162.1	196.9	96.9	16.4	19.4	6.4
国内贸易和对外贸易	**Domestic Trade and Foreign Trade**								
社会消费品零售总额(亿元)	Retail Sales of Consumer Goods (100 million yuan)	183919	11800.2	2215.9	470.3	117.1	15.6	15.9	15.1
国际旅游	**International Tourism**								
入境过夜旅游者人数(万人次)	Inbound Tourists Staying Overnight (10 000 person-times)	5758.1	8042.0	549.2	184.4	103.4	14.2	8.4	5.7
国际旅游收入(亿美元)	Foreign Exchange Earnings from International Tourism (USD 100 million)	484.6	18425.9	2184.9	298.8	105.8	17.1	15.8	10.5

附录3 全国各省（自治区、直辖市）国民经济主要指标（2011年）

APPENDIX III: MAIN INDICATORS OF NATIONAL ECONOMY BY PROVINCE, MUNICIPALITY AND AUTONOMOUS REGION (2011)

地 区	Region	年末常住人口（万人） Resident Population at Year-end (10 000 persons)	地区生产总值（亿元） Gross Domestic Product (100 million yuan)	其 中 of which 第一产业 Primary Industry	第二产业 Secondary Industry
东部地区	**Eastern Region**				
北 京	Beijing	2019	16011.4	136.2	3744.4
天 津	Tianjin	1355	11191.0	159.1	5878.0
河 北	Hebei	7241	24228.2	2905.7	13098.1
辽 宁	Liaoning	4383	22025.9	1915.6	12150.7
上 海	Shanghai	2347	19195.7	124.9	7959.7
江 苏	Jiangsu	7899	48604.3	3064.8	25023.8
浙 江	Zhejiang	5463	32000.1	1580.6	16404.2
福 建	Fujian	3720	17410.2	1610.6	9167.5
山 东	Shandong	9637	45429.2	3973.8	24037.4
广 东	Guangdong	10505	52673.6	2659.8	26205.3
海 南	Hainan	877	2515.3	659.2	714.5
中部地区	**Central Region**				
山 西	Shanxi	3593	11100.2	641.4	6577.8
吉 林	Jilin	2749	10530.7	1277.4	5601.2
黑龙江	Heilongjiang	3834	12503.8	1705.6	6317.3
安 徽	Anhui	5968	15110.3	2020.3	8226.4
江 西	Jiangxi	4488	11583.8	1391.1	6592.2
河 南	Henan	9388	27232.0	3512.1	15887.4
湖 北	Hubei	5758	19594.2	2569.3	9818.8
湖 南	Hunan	6596	19635.2	2733.7	9324.7
西部地区	**Western Region**				
重 庆	Chongqing	2919	10011.4	844.5	5543.0
四 川	Sichuan	8050	21026.7	2983.5	11027.9
贵 州	Guizhou	3469	5701.8	726.2	2334.0
云 南	Yunnan	4631	8751.0	1407.8	3991.0
西 藏	Tibet	303	605.8	74.4	209.5
陕 西	Shaanxi	3743	12391.3	1220.9	6836.3
甘 肃	Gansu	2564	5000.5	678.2	2524.3
青 海	Qinghai	568	1634.7	155.4	939.1
宁 夏	Ningxia	639	2060.8	184.1	1076.0
新 疆	Xinjiang	2209	6474.5	1139.0	3289.8
内蒙古	Inner Mongolia	2482	14246.1	1304.9	8092.1
广 西	Guangxi	4645	11714.4	2047.3	5736.8

注：本表绝对数按当年价计算。
Note: The values in this table are calculated at current prices.

其 中 of which		地区生产总值指数（上年=100） Indices of Gross Domestic Product (Preceding Year=100)	人均地区生产总值（元） Per Capita GDP (yuan)	人均地区生产总值指数（上年=100） Indices of Per Capita GDP (Preceding Year=100)
其 中 of which #工 业 Industry	第三产业 Tertiary Industry			
3039.0	12130.9	108.1	80394	
5380.5	5153.9	116.4	84337	110.8
11741.9	8224.3	111.3	33571	109.7
10696.5	7959.6	112.1	50299	111.6
7230.6	11111.1	108.2	82560	105.0
22072.3	20515.7	111.0	61649	109.7
14535.5	14015.4	109.0	58665	107.1
7775.1	6632.1	112.2	46972	111.4
21290.3	17418.0	110.9	47260	109.9
24408.1	23808.5	110.0	50295	108.0
475.0	1141.6	112.0	28797	111.1
5903.9	3880.9	113.0	30974	110.4
4907.7	3652.1	113.7	38321	113.4
5583.2	4481.0	112.2	32615	112.0
6979.6	4863.6	113.5	25340	112.6
5611.9	3600.5	112.5	25884	111.8
14401.7	7832.6	111.6	28981	112.2
8538.0	7206.1	113.8	34131	113.5
8083.2	7576.8	112.8	29828	111.2
4690.5	3623.8	116.4	34500	115.1
9491.0	7015.3	115.0	26133	115.9
1969.7	2641.6	115.0	16413	116.1
3205.9	3352.2	113.7	18957	113.0
48.9	321.9	112.7	20077	112.7
5727.8	4334.1	113.9	33142	113.7
2071.3	1798.0	112.5	19517	112.3
775.7	540.2	113.5	28891	112.3
836.9	800.7	112.0	32392	110.8
2764.1	2045.7	112.0	29496	112.0
7158.9	4849.1	114.3	57515	113.8
4914.4	3930.3	112.3	25315	112.0

附录3 续表1 continued1

地 区	Region	农林牧渔业总产值（亿元） Gross Output Value of Farming, Forestry,Animal Husbandry and Fishery (100 million)	其中 of which #农 业 Farming	#林 业 Forestry	#牧 业 Animal Husbandry	#渔 业 Fishery	农林牧渔业总产值指数（可比价）（上年=100） Indices of Gross OutputValue of Farming, Forestry, Animal Husbandry and Fishery (Preceding Year=100)	粮食产量（万吨） Grain Output (10 000 tons)
东部地区	**Eastern Region**							
北 京	Beijing	363.1	163.4	18.9	162.7	11.5	100.9	121.8
天 津	Tianjin	349.5	179.9	2.5	98.5	58.6	104.2	161.8
河 北	Hebei	4895.9	2775.3	58.8	1674.0	163.6	103.9	3172.6
辽 宁	Liaoning	3633.6	1307.2	107.4	1521.1	560.0	106.0	2035.5
上 海	Shanghai	314.6	165.1	7.6	77.4	54.7	99.4	122.0
江 苏	Jiangsu	5237.4	2640.9	92.8	1190.5	1060.4	104.2	3307.8
浙 江	Zhejiang	2534.9	1152.0	134.1	546.3	655.8	103.1	781.6
福 建	Fujian	2730.9	1136.2	237.7	479.2	782.6	104.1	672.8
山 东	Shandong	7409.7	3843.6	100.0	2171.9	999.1	103.8	4426.3
广 东	Guangdong	4384.4	2042.2	208.7	1146.4	843.0	103.9	1361.0
海 南	Hainan	1002.4	401.0	161.4	207.1	204.6	106.6	188.0
中部地区	**Central Region**							
山 西	Shanxi	1207.6	767.1	73.5	295.7	7.5	105.8	1193.0
吉 林	Jilin	2275.1	1020.4	81.9	1074.5	31.1	105.2	3171.0
黑龙江	Heilongjiang	3223.5	1801.8	110.2	1189.9	58.9	105.5	5570.6
安 徽	Anhui	3459.7	1714.8	182.1	1083.5	346.2	104.0	3135.5
江 西	Jiangxi	2207.3	917.8	206.1	734.3	272.2	104.2	2052.8
河 南	Henan	6218.6	3599.9	127.3	2198.4	72.5	103.8	5542.5
湖 北	Hubei	4252.9	2299.3	86.1	1205.8	508.8	104.4	2388.5
湖 南	Hunan	4508.2	2391.7	239.1	1425.6	255.0	104.3	2939.4
西部地区	**Western Region**							
重 庆	Chongqing	1265.3	751.2	38.1	425.3	34.9	104.8	1126.9
四 川	Sichuan	4932.7	2454.3	130.1	2127.2	147.2	104.6	3291.6
贵 州	Guizhou	1165.5	655.3	46.7	381.9	19.9	101.4	876.9
云 南	Yunnan	2306.5	1124.7	245.7	808.2	55.9	106.1	1673.6
西 藏	Tibet	109.4	49.6	2.4	54.1	0.2	103.6	93.7
陕 西	Shaanxi	2058.6	1360.7	42.3	553.4	10.6	105.6	1194.7
甘 肃	Gansu	1187.8	848.5	17.2	210.6	1.6	105.4	1014.6
青 海	Qinghai	230.8	102.9	4.2	119.3	0.2	104.8	103.4
宁 夏	Ningxia	354.7	223.6	9.3	97.6	10.2	105.1	359.0
新 疆	Xinjiang	1955.4	1437.9	38.1	415.0	14.2	106.9	1224.7
内蒙古	Inner Mongolia	2204.5	1057.8	93.2	998.3	23.5	105.7	2387.5
广 西	Guangxi	3323.4	1602.5	217.4	1096.6	303.1	104.8	1429.9

油料产量（万吨） Output of Oil-bearing Crops (10 000 tons)	棉花产量（万吨） Cotton Output (10 000 tons)	糖料产量（万吨） Sugar Output (10 000 tons)	蔬菜产量（万吨） Vegetable Output (10 000 tons)	水果产量（万吨） Fruit Output (10 000 tons)	肉类产量（万吨） Meat Output (10 000 tons)	其 中 of which #猪 肉 Pork	 #牛 肉 Beef	 #羊 肉 Lamb	奶类产量（万吨） Diary Output (10 000 tons)
1.4			296.9	120.9	44.4	24.2	2.1	1.3	64.0
0.7	7.2		431.3	62.6	42.9	27.6	3.1	1.5	69.4
141.8	65.3	46.5	7384.3	1719.2	418.2	246.6	54.5	28.4	466.9
119.8	0.1	7.8	2832.5	810.7	408.2	225.9	42.0	7.9	132.0
1.9	0.5	1.1	408.2	88.0	27.6	19.1		0.6	29.1
144.1	24.7	9.6	4586.9	757.1	375.9	215.9	3.6	7.3	59.2
39.9	3.2	71.1	1815.6	712.4	176.0	135.8	1.2	1.8	19.9
27.5		56.0	1623.4	687.9	183.0	146.6	2.4	1.9	15.8
341.0	78.5		9180.9	2850.8	711.1	346.9	66.2	32.5	279.0
91.9		1390.0	2851.0	1314.3	434.7	271.0	6.6	0.9	14.5
9.9		387.8	469.1	403.7	71.6	42.2	2.4	1.1	0.2
18.7	6.3	32.4	981.9	617.9	71.3	52.2	4.5	5.6	75.9
69.6	1.2	16.3	971.4	225.7	243.9	122.0	43.4	3.9	46.0
23.3		275.0	789.9	279.9	201.2	116.9	39.3	11.8	550.4
213.8	37.8	21.6	2214.0	846.6	375.5	233.1	17.8	14.2	22.5
113.6	14.3	62.8	1165.7	580.6	295.6	224.1	11.7	1.1	12.3
532.4	38.2	26.7	6709.7	2414.1	641.7	406.4	82.0	24.8	321.1
304.7	52.6	32.5	3358.6	855.2	381.9	290.5	18.2	8.0	34.8
215.3	22.7	72.2	3337.4	868.8	489.5	406.1	16.2	10.2	8.1
46.5		11.8	1408.0	261.2	196.3	148.6	6.7	2.6	8.0
278.4	1.5	88.0	3573.6	776.6	651.2	484.8	28.9	23.9	71.7
78.9	0.1	43.6	1250.1	128.0	180.0	148.3	12.0	3.4	4.9
60.7		1898.8	1340.0	476.4	324.4	243.9	30.7	13.0	56.6
6.4			60.1	1.4	26.1	1.4	14.8	8.6	29.8
59.0	6.7	0.2	1432.5	1587.1	99.6	77.3	7.4	6.7	182.4
63.5	7.6	18.1	1320.6	519.1	83.8	45.8	16.1	15.4	37.7
33.3			144.6	4.4	28.8	9.2	8.7	9.9	28.4
18.4			438.7	237.3	25.2	7.3	7.5	7.9	96.0
66.8	289.8	519.0	1866.2	1036.0	120.0	22.5	33.8	46.4	133.9
133.9	0.2	157.7	1440.2	301.4	237.4	71.3	49.7	87.2	931.4
50.1	0.2	7270.0	2246.4	1223.0	391.1	239.8	14.3	3.2	8.9

附录3 续表2 continued2

地　区	Region	水泥产量（万吨） Cement Output (10 000 tons)	钢材产量（万吨） Steel Output (10 000 tons)	汽车产量（万辆） Motor Vehicle Output (10 000 units)	微型计算机设备（万台） Micro Computers (10 000 units)	发电量（亿千瓦小时） Electricity Production (100 million KWH)	客运量（万人） Passenger Throughput (10 000 persons)	旅客周转量（亿人公里） Passenger Turnover Volume (100 million person·km)
东部地区	**Eastern Region**							
北　京	Beijing	911.5	289.6	150.5	1083.7	263.0	139718	412.3
天　津	Tianjin	765.5	5163.8	75.7	0.6	619.1	24934	285.1
河　北	Hebei	13972.4	19256.4	72.1		2310.2	99458	1306.6
辽　宁	Liaoning	5690.1	5754.1	75.5	0.3	1368.1	98606	955.8
上　海	Shanghai	805.6	2483.6	191.6	10162.5	947.0	10033	170.9
江　苏	Jiangsu	14899.7	10011.6	80.4	9408.2	3755.8	246855	1709.7
浙　江	Zhejiang	12122.3	3141.0	30.6	154.9	2774.2	230769	1296.3
福　建	Fujian	6570.9	1561.0	18.6	898.6	1578.9	79549	534.9
山　东	Shandong	15035.6	7033.7	76.3	22.4	3162.3	251187	1740.4
广　东	Guangdong	12607.0	3189.9	150.3	4417.8	3735.5	510653	2600.2
海　南	Hainan	1508.5	23.2	15.2		172.9	46224	170.9
中部地区	**Central Region**							
山　西	Shanxi	3935.6	3371.2	0.6		2344.0	39208	415.8
吉　林	Jilin	4221.3	1069.0	155.7		709.9	68190	515.8
黑龙江	Heilongjiang	4213.9	598.0	18.2	3.5	828.7	50481	541.6
安　徽	Anhui	9204.7	2746.3	117.0	124.0	1632.8	185575	1627.2
江　西	Jiangxi	6782.2	2250.3	34.4	17.8	729.9	78930	941.4
河　南	Henan	13666.0	3553.6	36.6		2583.2	193285	1989.1
湖　北	Hubei	9342.9	3573.4	131.9	825.2	2077.2	112422	1236.2
湖　南	Hunan	9238.6	1947.8	16.2	11.3	1343.5	171371	1565.4
西部地区	**Western Region**							
重　庆	Chongqing	4935.2	948.2	172.2	2547.8	529.6	141204	536.0
四　川	Sichuan	14501.1	2237.7	12.9	2357.2	1980.7	258845	1198.4
贵　州	Guizhou	5000.2	462.9	1.3		1379.3	72428	552.9
云　南	Yunnan	6457.4	1351.9	9.7		1555.7	44963	522.0
西　藏	Tibet	232.8				27.2	3769	32.9
陕　西	Shaanxi	6430.6	1038.2	55.7		1222.5	107032	868.8
甘　肃	Gansu	2746.8	812.8	2.1		1027.9	60902	629.5
青　海	Qinghai	1043.0	142.0			463.1	11870	105.4
宁　夏	Ningxia	1455.5	76.5			939.3	15104	113.9
新　疆	Xinjiang	2993.6	985.1	0.1		875.2	35130	488.5
内蒙古	Inner Mongolia	6396.5	1417.3	3.7		2972.8	26014	410.4
广　西	Guangxi	8640.1	1766.4	142.4	1.1	1039.0	83100	973.0

注：本表各省、市固定资产投资数据不含跨区投资和农户投资。
Note: The data of investment in fixed assets in this table excludes trans-regional investment and investment of rural households.

货运量（万吨） Cargo Throughput (10 000 tons)	货物周转量（亿吨公里） Cargo Turnover Volume (100 million tons·km)	固定资产投资额（亿元） Investment in Fixed Assets (100 million yuan)	其 中 of which #房地产开发投资 Investment in Real Estate Development	商品房施工面积（万平方米） Housing Floor Space under Construction (10 000 sq. m)	商品房竣工面积（万平方米） Housing Floor Space Completed (10 000 sq. m)	商品房销售面积（万平方米） Housing Floor Space of Sales (10 000 sq. m)
24663	999.6	5519.86	3036.3	12065	2245	1440.04
43601	10337.3	7040.48	1080.0	9075	2105	1643.11
189799	9630.4	15795.22	3069.6	26835	5145	5901.36
184982	10404.6	17431.46	4487.6	34512	6359	7561.39
92962	20309.6	4877.01	2170.3	12983	2241	1771.30
202528	6958.0	26299.40	5552.7	40738	8041	7982.67
186376	8634.9	13651.48	4137.3	30318	4423	3827.08
75191	3396.8	9692.55	2402.6	19213	2615	2696.16
318407	12684.3	25928.45	4108.1	36293	6227	9579.60
224394	6905.0	16688.44	4899.2	36312	5801	7761.34
25115	1368.5	1611.41	663.0	3660	376	888.19
134436	3062.5	6837.41	789.9	9326	2084	1263.19
47451	1452.6	7221.64	1165.4	8963	1656	2364.25
63216	1968.2	7206.33	1219.4	12065	2993	3395.42
268413	8446.4	11986.02	2590.1	20744	3064	4581.55
111851	2985.1	8756.10	852.7	8211	1777	2335.36
241017	8530.8	16932.15	2620.0	25281	5307	6304.41
106913	3798.8	12223.71	2063.2	13924	3084	4190.09
168516	3370.0	11360.51	1896.7	20746	3934	4877.65
96779	2528.7	7366.15	2015.1	20397	3424	4533.50
155310	2016.2	13705.29	2836.7	27315	4309	6664.70
44890	1060.7	3734.08	878.7	10395	1462	1889.95
60170	1024.4	5927.01	1272.7	10598	1451	3107.12
1028	40.0	516.31	5.1	49	22	19.36
120908	2824.7	9123.72	1420.5	12180	1104	3068.63
35269	2037.2	3865.99	362.9	3810	656	815.89
12586	486.4	1365.99	144.8	1659	506	348.20
36864	933.0	1583.46	330.6	4041	943	842.89
53252	1475.2	4444.99	518.3	5423	1253	1736.98
168320	5422.3	10291.69	1650.0	16378	2453	3620.12
136132	3478.2	7563.89	1500.5	14448	2184	2934.05

附录3 续表3 continued3

地区	Region	建筑业总产值（亿元） Total Output Value of Construction (100 million yuan)	社会消费品零售总额（亿元） Total Retail Sales of Consumer Goods (100 million yuan)	进出口总额（按经营单位所在地分）（亿美元） Total Imports and Exports(by location of operation units) (USD 100 million)	其中of which #出口 Export	地方财政一般预算收入（亿元） General Budgetary Revenue of Local Government (100 million yuan)
东部地区	**Eastern Region**					
北京	Beijing	6214.3	6900.3	3894.9	590.3	3006.28
天津	Tianjin	2925.6	3395.1	1033.9	445.0	1455.13
河北	Hebei	3931.1	8035.5	536.0	285.8	1737.77
辽宁	Liaoning	6170.6	8095.3	959.6	510.4	2643.15
上海	Shanghai	4579.4	6814.8	4373.1	2096.9	3429.83
江苏	Jiangsu	15062.2	15988.4	5397.6	3126.2	5148.91
浙江	Zhejiang	14686.4	12028.0	3094.0	2163.6	3150.80
福建	Fujian	3696.5	6276.2	1435.6	928.4	1501.51
山东	Shandong	6501.7	17155.5	2359.9	1257.9	3455.93
广东	Guangdong	5859.1	20297.5	9134.8	5319.4	5514.84
海南	Hainan	254.7	759.5	127.6	25.4	340.12
中部地区	**Central Region**					
山西	Shanxi	2246.5	3903.4	147.6	54.3	1213.43
吉林	Jilin	1615.4	4119.8	220.5	50.0	850.10
黑龙江	Heilongjiang	2133.7	4750.1	385.1	176.7	997.55
安徽	Anhui	3599.4	4955.1	313.4	170.8	1463.56
江西	Jiangxi	2077.6	3485.1	315.6	218.8	1053.43
河南	Henan	5335.0	9453.6	326.4	192.4	1721.76
湖北	Hubei	5617.3	8275.2	335.2	195.3	1526.91
湖南	Hunan	3839.4	6884.7	190.0	99.0	1517.07
西部地区	**Western Region**					
重庆	Chongqing	3328.8	3487.8	292.2	198.4	1488.33
四川	Sichuan	5300.4	8044.6	477.8	290.5	2044.79
贵州	Guizhou	825.8	1751.6	48.8	29.9	773.08
云南	Yunnan	1867.1	3000.1	160.5	94.7	1111.16
西藏	Tibet	123.4	219.0	13.6	11.8	54.76
陕西	Shaanxi	4098.4	3790.0	146.2	70.1	1500.18
甘肃	Gansu	911.7	1648.0	87.4	21.6	450.12
青海	Qinghai	319.9	410.5	9.2	6.6	151.81
宁夏	Ningxia	417.1	477.6	22.9	16.0	219.98
新疆	Xinjiang	1274.5	1616.3	228.2	168.3	720.43
内蒙古	Inner Mongolia	1377.9	3991.7	119.4	46.9	1356.67
广西	Guangxi	1552.2	3908.2	233.5	124.6	947.72

地方财政一般预算支出（亿元） General Budgetary Expenditure of Local Government (100 million yuan)	金融机构本外币存款余额（亿元） Total Deposit Balance of RMB and Foreign Currencics of Financial Institutions (100 million yuan)	金融机构本外币贷款余额（亿元） Total Loan Balance of RMB and Foreign Currencies (100 million yuan)	国际旅游人数（万人次） Number of International Tourists (10 000 person-times)	其 中 of which #外国人 Foreign Tourists	旅游外汇收入（亿美元） Foreign Exchange Earnings from Tourism (USD 100 million)
3245.23	75001.91	39660.51	520.4	447.4	54.16
1796.33	17586.91	15924.71	73.1	63.6	17.56
3537.39	29749.53	18460.60	114.1	98.3	4.48
3905.85	30832.44	22831.70	405.3	339.4	27.13
3914.88	58186.48	37196.79	668.6	555.0	57.51
6221.72	67638.75	50283.52	737.3	537.9	56.53
3842.59	60893.14	53239.34	773.7	515.0	45.42
2198.18	21571.60	18982.82	427.4	140.0	36.34
5002.07	46986.51	37521.93	424.2	312.3	25.51
6712.40	91589.51	58611.22	3331.6	749.3	139.06
778.80	4504.54	3194.59	81.4	56.2	3.76
2363.85	21003.24	11265.56	155.3	98.3	5.67
2201.74	10961.95	8240.92	99.3	85.5	3.85
2794.08	14416.36	8761.12	206.5	197.8	9.18
3302.99	19547.33	14146.39	262.9	151.7	11.79
2534.60	14322.05	9301.95	135.8	44.0	4.15
4248.82	26774.76	17648.91	168.3	104.3	5.49
3214.74	24148.26	16323.49	213.5	160.1	9.40
3520.76	19444.10	13462.50	227.6	119.8	10.14
2570.24	16128.87	13195.16	186.4	132.6	9.68
4674.92	34971.21	22514.23	164.0	113.7	5.94
2249.40	8771.34	6875.65	58.5	23.6	1.35
2929.60	15429.41	12347.54	395.4	281.0	16.09
758.11	1662.50	409.05	27.1	24.9	1.30
2930.81	19348.66	12097.34	270.4	189.9	12.95
1791.24	8460.94	5736.20	9.1	5.5	0.17
967.47	2834.81	2238.99	5.2	4.1	0.27
705.91	2978.40	2907.24	1.9	1.4	0.06
2284.49	10442.81	6603.40	56.4	48.8	4.65
2989.21	12132.48	9813.98	151.5	147.6	6.71
2545.28	13527.97	10646.43	302.8	171.5	10.52

附录3 续表3 continued4

地 区	Region	城镇居民人均可支配收入（元） Per Capita Disposable Income of Urban Residents (yuan)	农村居民人均纯收入（元） Per Capita Net Income of Rural Households (yuan)	居民消费价格指数（上年=100） General Consumer Price Index (preceding year=100)	农产品生产价格指数（上年=100） Producer Price Index of Farm Products (Preceding Year =100)	固定资产投资价格指数（上年=100） Price Index of Investment in Fixed Assets (Preceding Year =100)
东部地区	**Eastern Region**					
北 京	Beijing	32903.0	14735.7	105.6	110.7	105.7
天 津	Tianjin	26920.9	12321.2	104.9	105.0	105.7
河 北	Hebei	18292.2	7119.7	105.7	110.9	105.5
辽 宁	Liaoning	20466.8	8296.5	105.2	114.2	106.6
上 海	Shanghai	36230.5	16053.8	105.2	110.9	106.5
江 苏	Jiangsu	26340.7	10805.0	105.3	112.1	106.8
浙 江	Zhejiang	30970.7	13070.7	105.4	113.6	107.5
福 建	Fujian	24907.4	8778.6	105.3	113.3	106.2
山 东	Shandong	22791.8	8342.1	105.0	109.7	106.8
广 东	Guangdong	26897.5	9371.7	105.3	112.4	105.5
海 南	Hainan	18369.0	6446.0	106.1	115.3	106.4
中部地区	**Central Region**					
山 西	Shanxi	18123.9	5601.4	105.2	111.0	105.5
吉 林	Jilin	17796.6	7510.0	105.2	116.8	105.6
黑龙江	Heilongjiang	15696.2	7590.7	105.8	116.5	107.5
安 徽	Anhui	18606.1	6232.2	105.6	112.8	108.1
江 西	Jiangxi	17494.9	6891.6	105.2	114.3	108.4
河 南	Henan	18194.8	6604.0	105.6	111.5	107.4
湖 北	Hubei	18373.9	6897.9	105.8	111.7	107.3
湖 南	Hunan	18844.1	6567.1	105.5	121.9	107.2
西部地区	**Western Region**					
重 庆	Chongqing	20249.7	6480.4	105.3	120.2	105.9
四 川	Sichuan	17899.1	6128.6	105.3	117.8	105.2
贵 州	Guizhou	16495.0	4145.4	105.1	120.3	105.4
云 南	Yunnan	18575.6	4722.0	104.9	117.9	104.6
西 藏	Tibet	16195.6	4904.3	105.0		
陕 西	Shaanxi	18245.2	5027.9	105.7	113.8	105.9
甘 肃	Gansu	14988.7	3909.4	105.9	111.3	104.7
青 海	Qinghai	15603.3	4608.5	106.1	117.3	106.5
宁 夏	Ningxia	17578.9	5410.0	106.3	111.3	107.5
新 疆	Xinjiang	15513.6	5442.2	105.9	103.7	107.1
内蒙古	Inner Mongolia	20407.6	6641.6	105.6	112.8	106.3
广 西	Guangxi	18854.1	5231.3	105.9	124.5	106.2

中国统计出版社最新图书简目

（仅供参考，以最后出书为准）

统计资料

中国统计年鉴-2012
2012中国发展报告
中国劳动统计年鉴-2012
中国建筑业统计年鉴-2012
中国商品交易市场统计年鉴-2012
中国民政统计年鉴-2012
中国科技统计年鉴-2012
中国高技术产业统计年鉴-2012
全国农产品成本收益资料汇编-2012
大中型批发零售和住宿餐饮企业统计年鉴-2012
中国县（市）社会经济统计年鉴-2012
第二次全国R&D资源清查资料汇编—综合卷
中国民族统计年鉴2011、2012

中国统计摘要-2012
中国第三产业统计年鉴-2012
中国社会统计年鉴-2012
中国人口和就业统计年鉴-2012
中国房地产统计年鉴-2012
中国贸易外经统计年鉴-2012
中国农村统计年鉴-2012
中国教育经费统计年鉴-2010
中国科学技术协会统计年鉴-2012
中国农村住户调查年鉴-2012（中、英文）
第二次全国R&D资源清查资料汇编—工业企业卷
2010年中国第六次人口普查公报

国际统计年鉴-2012
中国区域经济统计年鉴-2012
中国城市统计年鉴-2009
中国工业经济统计年鉴-2012
中国能源统计年鉴-2012
2012中国地区经济监测报告
中国农产品价格调查年鉴-2012
中国农村贫困监测报告-2012
工业企业科技活动资料-2012
中国城市(镇)生活与价格年鉴-2012
中国农村全面建设小康监测报告-2012
中国零售和餐饮连锁企业统计年鉴-2012

2012年省级综合统计年鉴系列

北京 天津 河北 山西 内蒙古
河南 湖北 湖南 广东 广西
新疆 新疆生产建设兵团
辽宁 吉林 黑龙江 上海 江苏
海南 重庆 四川 贵州 云南
浙江 安徽 福建 江西 山东
西藏 陕西 甘肃 青海 宁夏

2012年市(县)级综合统计年鉴系列

天津滨海新区
运城 忻州 临汾 呼和浩特
上海浦东新区
杭州 宁波 绍兴 台州 温州
厦门经济特区 南昌 上饶
十堰 荆州 咸宁 长沙 广州
贵阳 昆明 庆阳 西安
石家庄 唐山 邯郸 太原 大同
包头 沈阳 大连 长春 吉林市
苏州 无锡 常州 徐州 南通
金华 嘉兴 衢州
济南 青岛 潍坊 郑州
东莞 惠州 深圳 桂林 南宁
兰州 银川 乌鲁木齐
长治 阳泉 晋城 朔州 晋中
四平 哈尔滨 黑龙江垦区
盐城 镇江 江阴 丹阳
福州 福州经济技术开发区
洛阳 三门峡 南阳 武汉 宜昌
柳州 来宾 河池 海口 成都 绵阳

2010年人口普查资料系列

中国2010年人口普查资料
浙江 安徽 福建 江西 山东
西藏 陕西 甘肃 青海 宁夏
中国分县2010年人口普查资料
北京 天津 河北 山西 内蒙古
河南 湖北 湖南 广东 广西
新疆 新疆生产建设兵团
中国分乡镇、街道2010年人口普查资料
辽宁 吉林 黑龙江 上海 江苏
海南 重庆 四川 贵州 云南
河南省各市2010年人口普查资料丛书
中国分民族2010年人口普查资料

“十一五”规划教材

非参数统计　医学统计学
多元统计分析　经济计量学教程
统计数据处理概论
企业经营管理统计
统计学:从数据到结论
概率论与数理统计　统计学
应用时间序列分析
质量管理统计方法　社会统计学
市场调查与预测
国民经济核算教程(国民经济统计学)
现代金融投资统计分析
统计指数理论及应用
多元统计分析实验
统计学原理（非统计专业使用）
概率论与数理统计(经济、管理类专业使用)

重点图书

挑大学选专业2012—高考志愿填报指南
挑大学选专业2012—考研择校指南

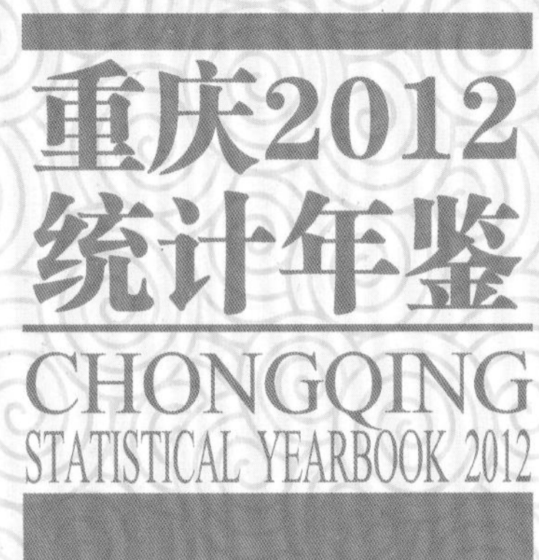

如何使用年鉴浏览

请在阅读光盘前，请选择IE选项/高级/“允许来自CD的活动内容在我的计算机上运行”。

三种浏览方式：为方便用户浏览和使用年鉴，本书提供了超文本（网面格式）、EXCEL电子表格和PDF（电子阅读）三种浏览方式。默认为超文本格式，方便查阅。同时提供安装Acrobat Reader软件，方便阅读PDF文书。

How to use the yearbook to browse

Please choose"contents of CD are permitted on my computer"of IE/senior.

Three modes to browse:In order to browse and use the yearbook easily,three modes-HTML,EXCEL and PDF form are offered.HTML mode is acquiescent,which provides more convenient consultation and temporary calculation.Acrobat Reader is provided to read PDF.

重庆市统计局　国家统计局重庆调查总队 编

CHONGQING MUNICIPAL BUREAU OF STATISTICS
NBS SURVEY OFFICE IN CHONGQING

重庆2012统计年鉴

CHONGQING

STATISTICAL YEARBOOK 2012